Illustrated Guide to the
Game Parks and Nature Reserves
of Southern Africa

Reader's Digest

Illustrated Guide to the Game Parks and Nature Reserves of Southern Africa

Published by the Reader's Digest Association of South Africa (Pty) Limited, Cape Town

Second edition copyright © 1990
Second printing 1991
The Reader's Digest Association
South Africa (Pty) Limited
130 Strand Street, Cape Town 8001

ISBN 0-947008-66-7

Editor: Alan Duggan
Associate Editor: David Rogers
Art Editor: John Meek
Assistant Art Editors: Susan Hart, Alex Dodge
Research Editor: Frances Howard
Researchers: Jane Askew, Anna Baggallay,
Judy Beyer, Sally Graham, Pat Kramer
Project Co-ordinator: Carol Adams
Typesetter: Mary Lacey
Indexer: Ethleen Lastovica
Scientific Consultants: Gideon Louw, M.Sc,
Ph.D, Professor of Zoology, University of Cape
Town; M D Picker, Ph.D, Department of
Zoology, University of Cape Town
Authors: Anthony Hocking, Brian Johnson
Barker, Marilyn Keegan, Paul Tingay, David
Bristow, Jeremy Lawrence

How to use this book

This volume has been designed as a practical guide to the wildlife and floral havens of Southern Africa. It not only covers the game and nature reserves from the Zambezi River in the north to Cape Point in the south, but introduces you to the spectacular diversity of animals and their environments throughout the sub-region.

Where to see our wildlife

To make reference quick and easy, this book has been divided into nine principal geographic regions. These regions are listed on the contents pages overleaf with their appropriate page numbers.

Each region is subdivided into particular zones, each zone featuring a detailed map showing you where the reserves are and what type of accommodation you will find there. The symbol ♠ indicates overnight lodge accommodation is available, while the symbol ♠ indicates there are camping facilities. The parks and reserves are all listed alphabetically, and to help you while you are on the road, we have included detailed information on distances, routes and condition of the roads.

Out in the wild

To help you get the most out of your visits to game parks and nature reserves, we have included 16 special features, covering nature-related pursuits in the wild – from photography and bird-watching, to collecting butterflies and scuba diving. These special features show the variety of ways you can become actively involved with the outdoors.

Identifying wildlife

The final section of this book helps you identify animals and plants in the wild. Because of the huge number of species, however, we have had to be highly selective in preparing these pages, and have therefore included only those animals or plants that you are most likely to see in the various reserves.

Title page: Chacma baboon *(Papio ursinus)*.
Page 4: Malachite kingfisher *(Corythornis cristata)*.
Above: Cheetah *(Acinonyx jubatus)*.
Page 7: Red bishop *(Euplectes orix)*.

CONTENTS

Special features: Out in the wild

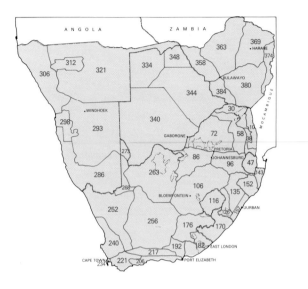

	Game parks, nature reserves and nature areas
☆	Small areas as above and places of interest
	Freeways
	Main roads
	Secondary roads
	Secondary unsurfaced roads
	Minor roads
29	Approximate distances
	Hiking trails
	Railways
	Cities
○	Towns
○	Small towns and villages
♠	Permanent accommodation
	Caravan facilities
▲	Camping facilities
	Rivers, dams and lakes
	Marsh
	International boundaries

Turn to the page number indicated for information on game parks and nature reserves in each area.

LOWVELD

The Lowveld region of the Eastern Transvaal is a slice of raw Africa, a searingly hot land covered with bushwillow, acacia and mopane woodlands that stretch to the horizon. It is also the home of the baobabs — ancient giants which thrust their massive branches heavenwards with a dignity achieved only by trees which may have lived for more than a thousand years.

This land was once infested by tsetse fly and the rinderpest virus: then it began to recover, attracting farmers, adventurers, miners, hunters — and conservationists. Today the Lowveld is rich in many respects, but its richest asset by far is surely the Kruger National Park, one of the great natural sanctuaries of the world and certainly one of the most popular tourist attractions in Southern Africa. The park's 1 948 528 hectares make it larger than Israel.

But Lowveld wildlife is by no means restricted to Kruger Park. Some visitors prefer a stay at one of the exclusive game lodges beyond the park's western fence, from where they track game in open Land-Rovers.

At the northern end of the Escarpment, the Lowveld meets the Soutpansberg and sweeps north to the wild Limpopo. Here the Transvaal Provincial Administration has established several nature reserves to conserve the vegetation and wildlife. Further south, the Lowveld sweeps into the little kingdom of Swaziland, where the authorities have assembled an impressive array of smaller parks and nature reserves on plains as well as on higher ground.

A bushbuck ewe peers from a thick tangle of bush in the Mala Mala Game Reserve, west of the Kruger National Park.

The great spaces washed with sun

Majestic in extent, rich in game, grand in its scenic splendour, the Kruger National Park is South Africa's pride.

This 19 485 km² expanse of savanna and bush country in the north-eastern Transvaal, bounded by the Crocodile River in the south, the Mozambique border in the east, a man-made barrier in the west and the Limpopo 350 km to the north, is a true haven of the wild. Its game population includes 137 species of mammal, more than 450 species of bird, 114 species of reptile, an estimated 40 species of fish, 33 species of amphibian and 227 species of butterfly.

The Kruger Park is big game country. Lion, elephant, buffalo, rhino and tens of thousands of antelope roam the sunlit plains. Leopard stalk the night; shy bushbuck hide in the riverine bush; giraffe browse on the sweet-scented acacias of the south-central region. Vulture glide overhead, alert for kill and carcass.

In no other wildlife sanctuary in the world is so much so readily – and comfortably – accessible to the ordinary holiday-maker. The park has 2 302 km of tarred and gravel roads which take you to prolific waterholes, peaceful picnic spots and grand viewing points. The 17 rest camps

offer a range of accommodation from the rudimentary to the unashamedly luxurious and, together with the caravan sites, shops and restaurants, can cater for the daily needs of more than 3 000 people. For an inexpensive family holiday, the Kruger Park is probably unrivalled.

The Kruger Park has been described as 'Africa's largest hotel', and so it might be because the rest camps are run – and run very well – by a single authority. But it has little of the traditional hotel atmosphere about it. The beautifully thatched clusters of rondavels and bungalows are shady oases in a magnificent wilderness.

Left: A kudu cow in the Kruger National Park. Although females also carry vertical stripes, they are smaller and more slender than the males, and do not have horns. Greater kudu — the only species found in Southern Africa — usually live in family groups of four or five individuals, or in small herds, while lesser kudu (a far smaller species found farther north, frequently in drier country) tend to live in pairs. **Below:** The male horsefly has such large eyes that they occupy the major part of its head. Only the females are blood-suckers: the males use their long proboscises to sip nectar from deep flowers.

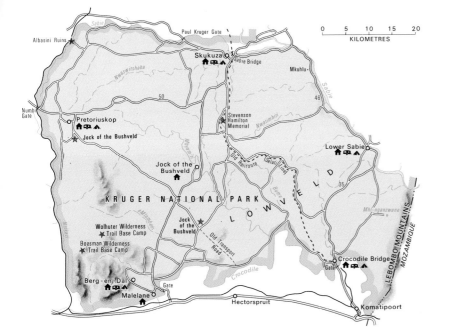

the pot, and punished the boy if he came back empty-handed. Young Kruger was a good hunter, and a brave one. When his thumb was shattered in an accident, he stoically severed the dangling fragments with his knife.

But even as he hunted, Kruger became uncomfortably aware that the once-limitless herds were dwindling. Others were of the same mind: in the 1850s the Transvaal Volksraad drastically curtailed the killing of elephant and forbade hunters to shoot more game than they could consume. In 1870 pit-traps and snares were outlawed, and four years later the Volksraad established closed seasons to allow game to breed. Further restrictions followed during the next two decades, but it was Paul Kruger who, in the 1890s, gave real impetus to the creation of wildlife sanctuaries. The Sabie Game Reserve, between the Crocodile and Sabie rivers, was for-

Although the park is open throughout the year, it is especially popular during the South African school holidays. Generally speaking, the area's climate is subtropical, and the warmth of its days and the cool nights allow easy and pleasant game-viewing for most of the year. In the six-month rainy season which starts around September, though, tall grass will interrupt the view along some of the routes, and a few secondary roads may be closed to traffic for short periods.

Until quite recently the northern areas of South Africa were vast, relatively undisturbed treasure-houses of wildlife. Then, in the late 19th century, came western man. Farmers settled and white hunters brought their formidable fire-power to bear on the herds, taking a devastating toll of buffalo, wildebeest and other species.

It is estimated that over two million hides had been exported to the tanneries of Europe by the end of the 1870s. This is a tragic enough figure, but one which represents just a small fraction of the true extent of the slaughter. For these men hunted for pleasure as well as profit: they killed indiscriminately in game drives that trapped thousands of animals, and left countless carcasses on the plains for scavengers and the bleaching African sun.

Paul Kruger, who at the age of ten travelled north with his family on the Great Trek, was a true child of the veld. His was the time when a Boer gave his son a single cartridge to go shooting for

SOUTHERN KRUGER PARK AT A GLANCE

When to go Game-viewing is easiest in winter but some connoisseurs prefer the lush vegetation of summer. March and April see the dramatic rutting of impala, wildebeest and other species and November and December see the birth of their young. In general, entrance gates and rest camps open at sunrise and close at sunset, and motorists travelling in the park after hours are fined. The park is open year-round, but opening and closing times vary from month to month.

Reservations and information To book accommodation in a rest camp or to apply for a place on the Wolhuter or Bushman Wilderness Trails, write to National Parks Board, P.O. Box 787, Pretoria 0001 (telephone Pretoria 343-1991) or National Parks Board, P.O. Box 7400, Roggebaai 8012 (telephone Cape Town 419-5365) or National Parks Board, P.O. Box 774, George 6530 (telephone George 74-6924/5).

Getting there Enter at one of four gates: Paul Kruger Gate (12 km from Skukuza) and the old Numbi Gate (9 km from Pretoriuskop) are both approached from the west, while Malelane Gate and Crocodile Bridge (both served by their own rest camps) can be approached from the south. There is an airport at Skukuza with daily scheduled flights to and from Johannesburg (Comair). Private pilots must obtain clearance before landing there.

Accommodation There are five rest camps: Skukuza, Pretoriuskop, Lower Sabie, Crocodile Bridge and Berg-en-dal. There are also two small 'private' camps which have to be reserved and occupied as a whole – Malelane (18 beds) near the entrance gate of the same name, and Jock-of-the-Bushveld (12 beds) along the old transport route between Pretoriuskop and Malelane. Accommodation varies, but there is usually a choice of family cottages (two rooms with two beds in each, bathroom, toilet, kitchenette with gas stove, fridge, eating and cooking utensils and gauzed-in veranda); huts with shower and toilet (one room with two or three beds); or ordinary huts (with two, three, four or five beds and a handbasin with cold water close to an ablution block). There are caravan and camping sites at all camps except Malelane and Jock-of-the-Bushveld.

Eating and drinking All camps except Crocodile Bridge, Malelane and Jock-of-the-Bushveld have licensed restaurants which sell snacks, and shops selling fresh meat, groceries, beer, wine and spirits. There are field kitchens and braai facilities close to the accommodation and caravan and camping sites, as well as at the designated picnic places.

Getting around Main roads are tarred and secondary roads are gravelled. Speed limits vary between 40 and 50 km/h. Once outside rest camps, visitors must remain in their cars (except at the picnic spots or designated monuments, where they may alight at their own risk). There are filling stations at all the gates with the exception of Malelane, Jock-of-the-Bushveld and Paul Kruger and at all the rest camps except Malelane. Diesel fuel is available at Lower Sabie, Pretoriuskop and Skukuza. The Automobile Association has an Emergency Service Centre at Skukuza, with a mechanic and breakdown truck in attendance.

Twice a week, on Mondays and Fridays, parties of eight leave Skukuza on the four-day Wolhuter and Bushman Wilderness Trails. Hikers sleep in tented bush camps in the Stolsnek area south of Pretoriuskop. Bedding and food are provided but hikers must take their own drinks.

Special attractions All rest camps except Crocodile Bridge, Malelane and Jock-of-the-Bushveld present a nightly film show (weather permitting).

Special precautions Before entering the park, visitors should take a course of anti-malaria tablets. Because specific drugs are required to combat the various strains of malaria in particular areas, visitors are advised to consult their doctors.

mally proclaimed on 26 March 1898, in the twilight of his presidency of the Transvaal.

In the grim years of the Anglo-Boer War which erupted in 1899, the new sanctuary's status was, understandably, ignored. Both sides hunted to supplement rations. But with peace came renewed awareness of the Transvaal's unique natural heritage. James Stevenson-Hamilton, a former major in the Inniskilling Dragoons who had explored and hunted in Central Africa, was appointed South Africa's first official game warden. Briefed to make himself 'generally disagreeable', he set to work, armed with little more than this vague authority – and a good share of courage and determination. It was enough. Over the years, and with the help of a handful of dedicated men such as 'Gaza' Gray, Cecil de Laporte, Thomas Duke, Major A.A. Fraser and the redoubtable Harry Wolhuter, Stevenson-Hamilton gave shape to what we today know as the Kruger National Park.

Stevenson-Hamilton's African assistants, with good reason, nicknamed him 'Skukuza' ('he who sweeps clean'). Many poachers were caught and convicted – including, on one occasion, a party of senior policemen. The depredations of some species of carnivore, especially lion and wild dog, were brought under control; each year

TIPS FOR VISITORS

● Entry into and travel within the park is confined to daylight hours;

● The speed limits are 50 km/h on tar and 40 km/h on gravel. You can be fined if you exceed these limits and if you feed the animals. Fines for leaving the safety of your car in unprotected areas or disturbing the animal life in any way are especially severe.

● All roads within the park are well signposted, and good maps are available at the gates, camps, and from the Automobile Association at Skukuza. There is a check list of the park's trees and a variety of other publications, including guides to the park's birds, fish, reptiles, small and large mammals and butterflies. Prominent tree specimens, close to the roads, have been numbered to correspond with the listed entries, facilitating easy identification.

● On the forbidden list are pets, open cars and motorcycles. Firearms must be sealed. Boating and fishing are also prohibited. Caravans are allowed only on tarred roads.

● The Kruger Park is low country, on average less than 300 m above sea level – and in summer the sticky, almost suffocating daytime heat is relieved only by sudden rainstorms that roll across the veld. Most people go on their game-viewing drives early in the morning or in the late afternoon, resting during the deep heat of the day (the animals also tend to at this time). However, you should take warm clothing in the winter months.

● Although the larger camps have restaurants, the park is essentially for inexpensive outdoor living – braai facilities are excellent, and visitors can either stock up with provisions before departure or buy their food from the well-provided camp shops.

● During the school holidays you are limited to a maximum of five days' stay at any one camp, and a total of 10 days in the park.

Above: A young roan. This is the third largest antelope (after kudu and eland) and is relatively rare in the Kruger Park. **Left:** A reconstructed Iron Age settlement on an archaeological site near the Kruger Park's Phalaborwa Gate. **Below:** Among the most beautiful of the park's many floral species is the impala lily, with its star-shaped petals. Note the long seed pods.

the veld of the central plains and around Pretoriuskop was burnt to encourage grazing species; new rangers were taken on. And the protected areas grew. By 1903 the Sabie's northern boundary had been extended to the Olifants River. Later, a brand-new reserve, called the Shingwedzi, was established between the Great Letaba and Limpopo rivers.

The game population increased steadily, though by today's standards it remained sparse: in 1912 Stevenson-Hamilton estimated that the two reserves had a combined population of 7 000 impala (now over 130 000); 250 buffalo (now 27 000) and just 25 elephant (now 7 500).

In 1923 the South African Railways included the area in its 'round-in-nine' (days) tour of the Transvaal, and passengers travelled through the Sabie in an afternoon. The keener visitors were taken on a short wilderness trail by a ranger. The tours won many new friends for the sanctuary.

The success of the 'round-in-nine' venture convinced Stevenson-Hamilton that if the reserves were to prosper they would have to earn their keep, and that meant throwing them open to the public. He lobbied for the creation of a publicly owned 'national park' modelled on the highly successful parks established in the United States and Canada, and managed to drum up influential political support.

On 31 May 1926 Parliament passed the National Parks Act. Its first fruit was the consolidation of the Sabie and Shingwedzi reserves with the awkward wedge that separated them. This enormous slice of territory was formally proclaimed a national park and named, appropriately, in honour of Paul Kruger.

There are 17 camps – Pretoriuskop, Malelane, Skukuza, Lower Sabie, Berg-en-dal, Jock-of-the-Bushveld and Crocodile Bridge in the south; Satara, Nwanetsi, Orpen, Olifants, Balule, Letaba and Roodewal in the central region; Shingwedzi, Boulders and Punda Maria in the wilder north. The larger camps have family cottages, many air-conditioned and with kitchenettes, as well as rather less sophisticated accommodation; caravan and camping sites; outdoor living facilities; petrol-filling points and shops. There are restaurants at nine of the camps. Skukuza, Satara and Letaba, from where the Automobile Association operates full services, have motor repair workshops.

The visitor to the Kruger Park has to observe a code of conduct. Ordinary common sense is the basis of regulation: the environment is precious, so do not throw lighted cigarettes into dry bush; drive within the speed limit because you will not see much unless you do and, more important, animals crossing the road could cause a nasty accident. Do not feed the animals. Nature, not man, dictates a creature's diet and baboons, especially, can become dangerously addicted to human hand-outs. Do not get out of your car when in an

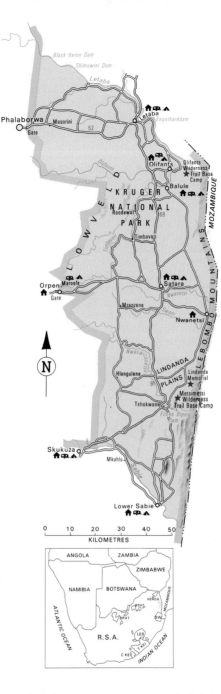

unprotected area, as appearances can be lethally deceptive. Explains a ranger: 'Too many visitors are fooled by what they think is tameness. The lion that strolls quietly by could well pounce, very quickly, if you open the door to get a better picture. Do not drive on closed roads where nobody will find you, in case of a breakdown. Never forget that the Kruger Park is part of Africa, and Africa is wild and cruel.'

The Kruger Park is home to a growing body of scientists and researchers of various disciplines, but to the tourist it is the ranger's job that holds the most glamour. Only a small part of his work, though, brings him into contact with the general public. 'When it's practical I like rangers to spend time with visitors,' says Dr Tol Pienaar,

Chief Director of National Parks. 'But that's not really what they're paid for.'

Rangers are required to spend most of their time in the field. 'I have very little routine work,' explains one. 'What it comes down to is that I have to look after a vast tract of land (40 000 – 60 000 ha) in every way. I'm like a farm manager – only I have to be more versatile. I manage the vegetation and the water supply, and I'm guardian to the animals in my area. My first loyalty is to the wildlife, from the lowliest snail and snake to the mighty elephant.'

One day a ranger may be involved in routine wind-pump maintenance (concrete reservoirs feed the drinking troughs); the next he might team up with rangers from neighbouring sections to burn off a block of veld or, conversely, to fight an unwanted fire sparked by lightning or poachers. Sometimes he will be called out to deal with a sick or wounded animal. Periodically he helps the culling and aerial survey teams.

Each year a research team from Skukuza, 'capital' of the Kruger Park, surveys the park's vegetation and large game from fixed-wing aircraft and a helicopter, gathering information vital to the proper management of the area.

How many white rhino are there, and where are they? Is the number of sable increasing? Where are the kudu, and are the blue wildebeest maintaining their rate of recovery? Some species may be too numerous for their habitat, destroying it both for themselves and for other animals, so the surplus must be removed – culled to restore the balance of nature.

In some African reserves rangers cull on the ground, using rifles. 'But that's messy and unpleasant,' admits Bruce Bryden, Chief Ranger of the park. 'We rather use a helicopter and a dart gun, which is more efficient and less disturbing to the animals. The dart contains a massive dose of a drug that paralyses the animal's muscles. The immobilised animal is then humanely destroyed by means of a bullet through the brain.'

Culling operations dispose of, among other species, several thousand buffalo each year. Between 1969 and 1987 the park removed more than 10 000 elephant as well. In years when fewer animals are born, culling operations are correspondingly decreased or even suspended, until the population again exceeds the acceptable threshold. A separate census by helicopter (specifically for elephant and buffalo) is undertaken in August each year. The census takes 21 days, during which time officials cover more than 13 000 kilometres.

Although safe enough for most of the time, the business of culling does carry a certain amount

Left: A census of the Kruger Park's elephant and buffalo is undertaken by helicopter in August each year. Most elephant occur in the northern part of the park, above the Olifants River. Because the park authorities want to keep their numbers at a specific level, a culling quota is calculated. Although the number of elephants culled may vary according to circumstances, it is usually around 450 a year — roughly equivalent to the annual increase through breeding. Below: Dr Anthony Hall-Martin (second from right) attaches a radio collar to the neck of a drugged subject in the Kruger Park as part of a programme to track the movements and habits of the park's 7 500 elephants. Below left: National Parks Board staff controlling a veld fire. Because the savanna regions of Southern Africa developed under the influence of fire, the park authorities have realised that fire is necessary to maintain its vegetation.

of risk. Veteran ranger Ampie Espag remembers when he and two colleagues were after hippo (rangers use rifles rather than dart guns in this case) at the Orpen Dam, near Tshokwane. 'The plan was to shoot from the shore, and then row out and attach a rope to the hippo's leg,' he says. 'Well, we did this several times, but then the surviving hippo sensed what we were up to. I went out in the boat with two rangers, and one came up underneath us and tipped us into the water. When I surfaced, I saw it coming for me with its mouth wide open. I dived under. That happened a couple of times. The rangers on shore were firing at it, and eventually it went away...'

Balule Rest Camp

More an enclosed caravan park than a camp (there are only five rondavels), Balule is on the Olifants River, in the central Kruger Park – a few kilometres south of Olifants rest camp, to which caravanners go for their shopping, or if they want a restaurant meal.

The Olifants River meanders across the width of the park, from just south of the Phalaborwa gate to the Mozambique border in the east. Its banks are especially lush and rich in game in the Olifants-Balule area.

Balule, tiny and potentially vulnerable, has a high protective fence because animals can (and occasionally do) sneak into the rest camps, especially if they are used to being fed by tourists.

If you feed an animal, you could be signing its death warrant. In 1978 a pair of spotted hyenas took up residence in a storm culvert under the tarred road between Skukuza and Pretoriuskop. They produced cubs which quickly became used to traffic, basking by the roadside while their parents went scavenging. Motorists were thrilled to come across such tame creatures and fed them titbits to entice them even closer. Before long the cubs approached every car that arrived, and the area deteriorated into an eyesore of cans, bottles and litter.

'Animals like that become very dependent,'' says Chief Ranger Bruce Bryden of Skukuza. 'Next thing they'll be raiding the camps.' On one occasion a hyena did enter a camp (Letaba), found a man sleeping on the ground beside his car, and tried to drag him away by the hand.

Hyenas are not the only game misled by tourists. 'Not so long ago there was an elephant at Tshokwane that accepted biscuits,' recalls Bryden. 'One day two old ladies were feeding it, and when it snorted one of them got such a fright she fell down an embankment and broke her leg. It's stupid. One of these days that elephant will get really upset, and he'll trample someone.'

The rangers' biggest headache is the baboon. 'Once he starts taking food he never stops,' says an information officer. 'He'll begin raiding huts in rest camps, and we've had them jumping into the backs of cars. Baboons like that will lead the

rest of the troop into trouble, so we have to remove them from the population.'

Crocodile Bridge Rest Camp

Adjacent to one of the Kruger Park's two southernmost gates is Crocodile Bridge, with its 20 bungalows, small shop and caravan park set charmingly on the banks of the Crocodile River. This is acacia country, and the grass is good, attracting zebra, wildebeest, impala, kudu, waterbuck and large herds of buffalo.

The Crocodile used to be a perennial river, but now it often shrinks to chains of pools during the dry months of winter and in times of drought –

NORTHERN KRUGER PARK AT A GLANCE

When to go In earlier years the northern half of the park was closed in summer, but now it is open year-round. The summer months bring lush vegetation and profuse bird life, and large herds may be seen at waterholes during the dry winter months.

Reservations To book accommodation in a rest camp or apply for a place on the Nyalaland Wilderness Trail, write to National Parks Board, P.O. Box 787, Pretoria 0001 (telephone Pretoria 343-1991) or National Parks Board, P.O. Box 7400, Roggebaai 8012 (telephone Cape Town 419-5365) or National Parks Board, P.O. Box 774, George 6530 (telephone George 74-6924/5).

Getting there To reach Shingwedzi or Boulders from outside the park, enter at the Phalaborwa Gate, or enter by the Punda Maria Gate. To reach Punda Maria or Pafuri, enter by Punda Maria Gate or the Pafuri Gate. The nearest airport is at Phalaborwa and offers daily flights to and from Johannesburg (Comair).

Accommodation Shingwedzi rest camp is in two parts: an old section of rectangular wattle-and-daub huts, each with two or more beds and modernised interiors (shower and toilet), and a modern section in which each hut is equipped with two or more beds, shower and toilet. A large swimming pool is also available. Punda Maria has wattle-and-daub huts with modernised interiors. Both camps have caravan and camping sites.

The 12-bedded Boulders private camp lies between Phalaborwa and Shingwedzi and has to be reserved as a unit. It has 4 two-bedded units and a four-bedded unit, each with bath, shower, toilet and veranda with superb views.

Eating and drinking Both Shingwedzi and Punda Maria have licensed restaurants, and snacks are available. Shops sell fresh meat, groceries, beer, wine and spirits. Both camps have field kitchens and braai places. There are picnic places at Mooiplaas, between Shingwedzi and Letaba; at Babalala, between Shingwedzi and Punda Maria; and at Pafuri on the Luvuvhu River.

Getting around All main roads are tarred and secondary roads are gravelled. The speed limits vary from 40 to 50km/h. There are filling stations at Shingwedzi and Punda Maria (with diesel fuel at Shingwedzi) and there is a garage at Letaba with a breakdown truck. Twice a week, parties of eight leave Punda Maria on the four-day Nyalaland Wilderness Trail. Hikers sleep in huts in a bush camp south of the Luvuvhu River. Bedding and food are provided but hikers must take their own drinks.

Wildlife The northern region is tusker country, famous for the Kruger Park elephant with abnormally large tusks. Antelope, including all the rare species such as eland, roan, tsessebe, sable and nyala, and predators abound, and there are birds everywhere. The Pafuri area of the far north is one of the most picturesque in the park, featuring mammals, birds and insects found nowhere else.

Special precautions Before entering the park, you should take a course of anti-malaria pills (obtainable at entrance gates and rest camps, from family doctors and at any chemist without prescription). Keep to the roads and resist the temptation to explore firebreaks, where nobody will find you in the event of a breakdown.

but it nevertheless manages to support an impressive variety of wildlife.

In fact water is the key to survival, and it is along the banks of the streams and at the pools that visitors can best view the bigger game. Not so obvious are the smaller fauna supported by the park's placid rivers – otter, terrapin, leguaan; colourful waterbirds and the myriad aquatic insects on which they feed. The park is also host to 45 species of freshwater fish and four renegade marine varieties. In 1950 a 1,47m Zambezi shark was found in the shallows of the confluence of the Luvuvhu – Limpopo rivers at Pafuri, nearly 400 km from the sea. About 6 km from Crocodile Bridge camp is a splendid viewing point from where you can watch, among other things, hippo basking on a sandbank. Hippo and crocodile are probably the most spectacular inhabitants of the waterways. The two species (there are over 2 500 of each in the park) share their living space amiably enough for most of the time, each an integral part of nature's delicate balance. But the truce is sometimes broken – crocodile have a taste for baby hippo, and when a cow is about to give birth the big reptiles are chased from the vicinity.

Up to 1 500 kg in mass, with immense jaws and lethal teeth, the hippo is a fearsome enemy, and should be treated with the greatest respect. Peaceful enough in their riverine homes, hippo migrate across the open veld, sometimes over long distances, when water is scarce. They have acute senses of sight, smell and hearing, and they are unpredictable creatures, occasionally attacking without provocation when out of their natural element. Your car and the camp fence, however, are protection enough. Fights between adult males, for dominance of a herd and for territory, are impressive spectacles, almost unequalled among mammals in their intensity. Most of the habits of hippo, though, are rather more endearing, and some a little curious. For instance, they are easily contained. They never attempt to step over an obstruction: a mere metre-high, three-wired fence is enough to turn them away. But water is their element, and they cannot stay on dry land for too long. Their skin, thick (up to 50 mm at the shoulder and back) and tough though it may be, is sensitive to the sun and overexposure can cause injury.

A hippo can stay submerged for anything up to five or six minutes, although on average he surfaces for air every minute or so. While under water he is often party to a curious symbiosis – shoals of a freshwater fish species, *Labeo rubropunctatus*, accompany him, feeding on the algae that grow on his hide.

DEATH OF THE KING

Of all the great tuskers that have wandered over the mopane plains of the Kruger National Park, one in particular will always be remembered – Mafunyane, king of the elephants.

When he died in November 1983, Mafunyane had become the park's best-known elephant, remembered most for his massive tusks – so huge that the ends touched the ground.

Towards the end of his life, Mafunyane's wanderings through the bush were monitored by park officials, who feared poachers might try to lay claim to his tusks – priceless on the illicit ivory market.

Ultimately, though, the legendary tusker eluded everyone and died as he had lived – mysteriously – in the privacy of the bush. His carcass, discovered in a dry riverbed, had already been torn apart by scavengers, the long bones scattered over a wide area. Only a small section of skin remained, and even his radio collar had been partly eaten. From the evidence it appeared that he had died suddenly. His stomach contents revealed that he had been eating normally, and the area around him showed no signs of a struggle. Perhaps he suffered a heart attack, or maybe he simply died of old age. Either way, at 57, Mafunyane 'the irritable' died, leaving a void in the mopane plains of northwestern Kruger Park.

It had always been thought that Mafunyane was a massive tusker, a bull similar to Kenya's Ahmed of Marsabit (declared a national monument when he was alive). However, when Mafunyane was darted and measured in 1978, his tusks were smaller than had been expected. Dr Anthony Hall-Martin recalls: 'Though his tusks rested on the ground they were only 251 cm long but perfectly straight – and I had long estimated them to be about 3 m long.' Extraordinarily this huge amount of ivory was carried by a bull of relatively small size.

Hugo van Niekerk, a helicopter pilot at Kruger Park, refused to be fazed by what the tape measure revealed. 'Mafunyane was huge; he was a giant; he was magnificent. Even in elephant dimensions he was a king.'

The tusks are a fine matching pair, each weighing 51,1 kg, and rightly deserve their place in the Olifants Camp's museum alongside the other great tuskers of the Kruger Park.

The hippo is a vegetarian, daily consuming up to 180 kg of grass (tramping much more under foot) and the young shoots of river reeds. Its main companion the crocodile, however, is a somewhat indiscriminate carnivore. Iron-jawed, living an impressive 100 years and more, it is a dinosaurian oddity – the species has existed virtually unchanged, for about 60 million years.

Crocodiles are essentially fish-eating reptiles but they supplement their diet by taking water tortoises, antelope and other game that come down to the water to drink – sometimes very big game. Their recorded victims include giraffe (two known cases in the Kruger Park), full-grown buffalo, and lion. The great 19th century hunter Frederick Courteney Selous once saw croco-

diles seize, drown and devour a rhinoceros. In fact, it is nearly always by drowning that the crocodile kills its land-based prey, fastening on to muzzle or limb and pulling its victim beneath the surface.

In Africa, crocodiles account for more human deaths than leopards, rhinos, lions, elephants, buffalos and snakes put together. The visitor to

Above: The common joker butterfly (*Byblia ilithyia*), a nymphalid, is distributed throughout the Kruger Park. **Right:** A scrum of hippo in the Luvuvhu River, near the northern boundary of the park. Each adult consumes as much as 180 kg of food a day — mostly grass and the young shoots of reeds. Hippos spend most of their day in water because they cannot endure very high temperatures. In winter, however, they may often be seen sunning themselves on sandbanks. Hippo calves suckle under water, but have to surface at regular intervals (less than a minute) to breathe. They also suckle on land. A hippo bull may attain a weight of 1 500 kg (about 1 300 kg for cows), and a healthy specimen can live for 40 to 50 years. **Left top:** A giant land snail. These snails may often be seen crawling across park roads after rains. **Left below:** Gossamer-like seeds such as these are sometimes carried several kilometres by the wind.

FISH OUT OF WATER

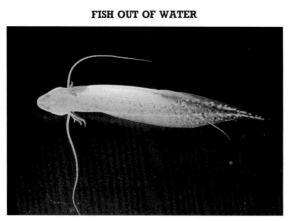

In April 1981 two visiting scientists, in quest of specimens of the rare killifish, collected (for the first time) four specimens of the lungfish in one of Kruger Park's pans along the eastern boundary between the Nwanedzi and Olifants rivers. It was the first of this species to be found within South Africa's borders — a notable discovery, and an ironic one too, for the park's own research and field staff had been looking for this oddity for the past 25 years. Previously it was known to exist, among other localities, in the swampy riverine areas of Zimbabwe, Moçambique and Zaire.

The lungfish is a 'living fossil' — remains of specimens as old as 150 million years have been found in the Karoo. Connected to its throat is an elongated, air-filled sac that serves as a primitive lung. So equipped, the fish can live in — and in fact confines itself to — pans and flood plains which dry up during the winter. The 'lung' enables it to survive while hibernating in the hard clay of the arid ground during the long waterless months.

The lungfish is regarded by zoologists as the immensely ancient link between water- and land-based vertebrates, animate evidence of that far-distant time when creatures with backbones forsook the shrinking lakes and rivers to find a precarious home, and then to thrive and proliferate, on shore.

the Kruger Park is quite safe provided he takes elementary precautions, but the park has not been without incident. One such incident is memorable for the courage and tenacity displayed by the victims.

On a November day in 1976, patrolling rangers Tom Yssel and Louis Olivier accompanied by Hans Kolver, an off-duty helicopter pilot, were crossing a side stream of the Sabie River when a large crocodile erupted from the shallows and seized Yssel by the thigh. It was the start of an epic struggle for survival.

When Yssel fell, the crocodile took a firm grip and began dragging the ranger towards deeper water. Yssel twisted his body and tried to jam his thumbs into the animal's vulnerable eyes, but succeeded only in infuriating it. 'He was shaking me like a rag doll,' he recalls. 'He'd let go, and then he'd bite me again, up my leg and across my belly. I was under the water. I didn't feel pain, but

there was blood everywhere and I thought: "This is it. I'll never get out".'

Quickly grasping the situation, Olivier and Kolver plunged into the water and tackled the 680 kg crocodile. Kolver jumped on its back and lunged for the eyes; Olivier went for its thrashing tail. Kolver was hurled off, climbed back on again, and then found himself submerged as the crocodile turned over.

Olivier moved up to hold Tom Yssel's head above the surface. The crocodile released Yssel and fastened on to Kolver's wrist. Although badly injured, Yssel had no compulsion to escape. Instead, he thought: 'Now there's going to be a real fight. I am going to get him.' But Yssel could not stand up – his leg was broken. He lay helpless while the other two struggled on, Kolver freeing himself briefly only to find his right arm in the vice-like grip.

Finally, Louis Olivier closed in with his hunting knife, plunging its 14 cm blade into the creature's eye. It opened its jaws wide, releasing Kolver, and retreated in defeat to deep water. Olivier was unhurt; Kolver had only slight injuries.

Both men were decorated for bravery. Tom Yssel, though, was less fortunate: he was hospitalised for nine long months. In retrospect, he said he bore the crocodile no grudge, explaining: 'He was only doing his job.'

Letaba Rest Camp

The camp is strategically placed in the central region, nestling comfortably above a sweeping loop of the Great Letaba River. It is also the junction of three main roads: to the west is the Phalaborwa gate; Shingwedzi is to the north; Olifants and Satara are to the south. Visitors enjoy a fine view across evergreen bushes and sycamore figs and the water (stream-linked pools and sandy flats in winter and in drought, wide and grand in flood), which attracts elephant and buffalo, zebra and waterbuck. There are also roan and sable, nyala, tsessebe and cheetah to

be seen in the countryside around Letaba. Neat lawns, the sparkle of flowers and tall shade-trees give the camp its character. Busy little vervet monkeys scramble along the fence – a constant source of amusement and interest.

Letaba is a middle-sized camp, with a restaurant, shop and Automobile Association garage. The adjoining Melville guest cottage can accommodate up to nine people. There are some excellent drives in the vicinity, the best probably the one taking you (for most of the way) south-east along the Great Letaba River to Olifants rest camp. Two nearby look-out points, Engelhard Dam to the east and Mingerhout Dam to the north-west, are well worth visiting.

To the north, about halfway along the tarred road to Shingwedzi, the Mooiplaas picnic and look-out spot is a refreshing place to stop. It has a large, thatched shelter above the Tsende River from which you can watch elephant and buffalo. There are enclosed braai sites stocked with mopane and leadwood.

When driving in the Letaba area, indeed when driving anywhere in the park, you might just see a kill, and that means scavengers: jackal, vulture – and hyena, with their lunatic cackle, something between a giggle and a laugh, that they make when angry or excited.

Of the two types of hyena found in the park, the spotted hyena is larger and much more common than its cousin, the brown hyena. Spotted hyena often hunt in packs but brown hyena tend to be solitary creatures and are generally nocturnal (they sleep heavily during the day). Spotted hyenas gather to follow lion and wild dog on the hunt – then quarrel over the remains of a kill (though they are predators as well as scavengers). With their massive heads, jaws and forequarters, sloping backs and ungainly gait, they are not the most attractive of the park's inhabitants.

More graceful – but only in their natural element, the air – are the Kruger Park's vultures. They can be seen everywhere, soaring high over the dun-and-green veld, eyes missing nothing. Of the six species found in Southern Africa the white-backed vulture is the most common. Cape vultures (similar to but more scarce than the white-backed vulture) tend to nest on rock ledges, while white-backed vultures prefer trees. Then there is the black or 'king' vulture, which is generally so aggressive that it keeps the other birds at bay while it eats its fill of a carcass. Black vultures are less sociable, less gross in their eating habits, and fewer in number.

Opposite page: Yellow-billed storks (also known as wood ibis) paddle in the shallows of the Luvuvhu River in apparent harmony with the crocodiles. The storks feed on frogs, small mammals, fish, crabs and aquatic insects, probing deep or shallow water with their long bills. They nest on cliffs or in trees, producing two or three eggs. **Above:** A nyala ram. There are thought to be between 800 and 1 000 of these large, shaggy antelope in the park. The female is considerably smaller and lacks horns. Nyala are usually seen in small groups, though they have been known to gather in herds of up to 30 individuals. They seldom stray far from water. **Right above:** The striking colours of the carmine bee-eater make it one of the most beautiful birds in the Kruger Park. It is seen only between September and March, spending the rest of the year in the tropics. **Right below:** A tsessebe seeks shelter from the harsh midday sun in the Kruger Park. These medium-sized antelope (they may weigh between 135 kg and 160 kg) live in family groups or small herds which may swell to larger herds during the dry season.

Lower Sabie Rest Camp

Lower Sabie, situated some 35 km from Crocodile Bridge in the south, is a medium-sized camp with pleasant bungalows overlooking the game-rich Sabie River, which affords visitors excellent 'sundowner' viewing. The camp's restaurant is particularly good. There are some rewarding drives in the area, especially one along the tarred road flanking the river's south bank.

If you want to view lion, you are likely to be luckier in the Lower Sabie area than in most others. The 1 400 or so lion of the Kruger Park go where their prey congregates. The Sabie River and the lushness of the countryside attract herds of wildebeest, zebra, kudu, buffalo, giraffe, waterbuck and impala – and predators follow.

The best time to see lion in summer is during the early morning and late afternoon (they tend to rest, in dense bush, during the heat of the day). In winter they appear at the waterholes. When travelling through the Kruger Park in late autumn, winter and early spring, drive especially slowly, because the lion's coat blends almost perfectly with the ochre grass.

Universally known as the 'king of beasts', this large cat certainly looks the part, but its lifestyle is often rather less than regal. Lions are prone to parasite-born diseases and fatal injuries during the hunt. Some are killed by buffalo or by the lethal kick of a giraffe, and a high proportion, particularly old lions, by the humble porcupine, whose needle-sharp quills pierce their throats and tongues and infect them. When the rains are abundant and game is dispersed, many young lions can die of starvation.

It was north of the Sabie River, close to the Lindanda flats, that Harry Wolhuter, armed only with a knife, fought and killed a full-grown lion. It was one night in August 1903 that Wolhuter, on horseback and riding ahead of his assistants, stumbled upon two male lions. His horse bolted and the lions sprang; Wolhuter fell and found his shoulder seized in the great feline jaws. The lion dragged him 50 m into the bush.

The ranger's face was pressed close into the animal's mane, and he heard in its throat that deep, terrifying sound that passes for a purr. Frantically, he searched for his sheath knife, found it, stabbed twice at the heart. The lion, roaring in pain, dropped him but stood its ground, straddling the ranger. Again Wolhuter lunged, drawing spurts of blood from an artery in the throat. The lion made off into the night. It was found later, dead from two knife wounds in the heart and a severed carotid artery.

Wolhuter dragged himself to a tree and managed to climb it. Faint from loss of blood, he tied himself to a branch with his belt. It was just as well he did, for the second lion returned some minutes later and reared up against the tree-trunk. It was eventually distracted by the barking of one of the ranger's dogs.

Later that night, the game guards found Wolhuter, cut him down and carried him to camp, where they dressed his terrible wounds. He was then taken to Barberton, and remained in hospital for many months.

Meanwhile, news of his exploit had made the headlines – and he found himself a celebrity.

The lion's skin and the knife are on display at the Stevenson-Hamilton Memorial Information Centre at Skukuza, and the stump of the tree he climbed can still be seen on the plains of Lindanda.

Malelane Rest Camp

Founded in 1925 as a culling post to control the menace posed to farmers by marauding prides of lion, Malelane is now an attractive little rest camp, close to the park's southernmost gate.

Malelane is a private camp with five huts (18 beds) situated on the Crocodile River. Accommodation is available only on a block-booked basis. The camp is administered by the tourist officer stationed at the entrance gate nearby. If you go north for a short distance along the gravelled road to Skukuza and then turn right for the 53 km stretch to Crocodile Bridge, you are likely to see kudu, buffalo, the familiar impala and perhaps elephant.

Five well-planned circular drives are within easy reach of the camp. This area is a favourite haunt of one of the park's rarer and more fascinating inhabitants, the wild dog.

The wild dog is only distantly related to the dog we know. About the size of an Alsatian, it has a 'tortoise shell' coat, a white tip to its bushy tail, and huge, bat-like ears. It plays an important part in controlling the numbers of its favourite prey – impala and reedbuck. Having eaten its fill, a wild dog rarely returns to the carcass, as it prefers fresh meat.

Observing a pack in the area between Malelane and Skukuza, scientist Allen Reich noted that the dog who had led the hunt had the smallest portion of the carcass. 'All were eating peacefully, save for the subordinate male,' Reich writes.

'He had made the kill; he had trotted back to the others; he had let them taste the blood on his mouth, and he had led them back to the kill. Now he waited for what, to our human minds, was

Left: A white-backed vulture. This species nests mainly in acacia, producing one egg which is incubated by both parents for 56-58 days. **Below:** A nyala ewe. **Right above:** *Euphorbia*, a hardy and well-protected succulent, photographed in the Pafuri area of the Kruger Park. **Right below:** The large and powerful spotted hyena, although ungainly in appearance, is an efficient scavenger and equally good hunter — and quite capable of bringing down prey as large as a zebra. There are about 2 000 spotted hyena in the Kruger Park, and they are a familiar sight wherever there is a carcass. The powerful jaws crunch the bones of its prey with ease.

rightfully his. He eventually managed a few scraps (although not much more). What a remarkable creature!'

This incident illuminates the intricate social order that governs a pack of wild dogs. Each member knows his exact place in the group, who he dominates and to whom he is subservient, with whom he may mate, and his position in the hunt. The order, though, changes from time to time as members pair off, cubs are born, as dominant individuals die, or when their authority is subtly and successfully challenged.

The wild dog's bark is more like that of a baboon than the domestic dog; and its rallying cry, which you can sometimes hear before sunrise or in the early evening, is a plaintive howl, repeated half a dozen or so times.

Nwanetsi Rest Camp

Twenty-five kilometres to the east of Satara, along the central region's Nwanetsi River, is the small

camp of that name. Accommodation is available only on a block-booking basis, and its bungalow and two smaller huts can sleep up to 15 people. Those enjoying this exclusive hideaway check in at Satara, and use Satara's shop and restaurant to stock up and eat out (though the guest-house's kitchen is very well equipped). Close to the rest camp is the attractively sited Nwanetsi picnic site, which offers excellent facilities for the tired tourist and a magnificent viewing spot perched on top

of a cliff and overlooking a waterhole in the Sweni River below.

The 50 km gravel road running south – close to the Mozambique border – takes you to the Lindanda memorial and Nwamuriwa, a hill with a magnificent view across the plains; then, a little farther on, to the Eileen Orpen Dam, where large concentrations of game gather, and finally to Tshokwane, a pretty little resting spot which has a small shop.

THE ORDINARY MEAL OF THE DAY

Rangers estimate that the Kruger Park accommodates over 160 000 impala. They are so common that most tourists simply take them for granted. Yet these graceful antelope deserve more than a passing glance.

Alert and agile, an impala can leap 3 m into the air without any apparent effort — and this in spite of the fact that it is a fairly large animal by antelope standards, weighing up to 65 kilograms. To watch a whole herd move among the thorn bushes, to see them startled by some suddenly discovered danger, and then dashing away in unison, is to witness a natural symphony of co-ordinated movements — a completely fluid motion made up of hundreds of single steps, the kind of action that a ballet troupe might take months to perfect, executed here in the wilderness *sans* choreographer.

The scientist finds an even greater fascination in the impala's behavioural mechanisms. For much of the year impala live in peaceful herds, showing no animosity and little competitiveness, but with the coming of autumn the rut begins and the impala lifestyle changes dramatically. The adult males now become passionately territorial. Researchers have

discovered that the production of male sex hormones increases, the testes grow larger and begin to produce a great amount of sperm cells, and as a result of these changes the males become highly aggressive towards one another. Each discovers an urge to be a proud (and individual) 'landowner', the most assertive among them carving out territories within the most favoured feeding grounds.

Impala have diffuse glandular areas on the forehead, and territorial rams may rub these on bushes — leaving a scent. They have also developed a surprising ability to proclaim their ownership with loud barks and roars — so fearsome that many a tourist visiting the park for the first time in autumn has imagined himself in the company of lions.

Herds of female impala, made up of mothers and daughters, sisters and aunts, wander through these territories that the males have established in the prime feeding grounds, and the females in heat are mounted by the proud males. The males also work hard at keeping their harems within their territory, which means herding them back whenever they approach the boundaries.

Giraffe, zebra and wildebeest abound in the area. And there are elephant too, although most of the herds prefer the mopane country of the park's northern region.

Olifants Rest Camp

Set on rocky cliffs 100 m above the river, visitors can enjoy a grander view from Olifants' terraces and from the windows of its bungalows than at any of the other Kruger camps. Dawn and sunset over the distant hills are spectacular affairs, and wildlife is prolific in the dense riverine greenery below (although you will need binoculars for good game-watching). Next to the camp is a reed-roofed look-out built on a small rock promontory – probably the finest viewing point in the entire park.

Olifants is a modern, well-designed camp. There is a good restaurant, a shop, a conference room (also overlooking the river), a few family cottages for up to six people, rondavels built on terraces, and the luxury C.D. Ellis guest house.

It is a short (35 km) and rewarding drive from Olifants north to Letaba, but travellers should take time to turn left at the junction of the Olifants and main north-south road, and then right, up the hill to the Riverview resting spot. From this high point the breathtaking immensity of river and emerald veld unfolds to the east and south. The alternative route to Letaba winds pleasantly alongside the Olifants and Great Letaba rivers.

On any longish drive in the Kruger Park you are almost bound to see warthog – not the prettiest of the park's animals, but one of the more intriguing.

Early one morning, hikers on one of the park's five wilderness trails (Olifants, Wolhuter, Bushman, Nyalaland and Metsimetsi) gathered around a deserted aardvark burrow as their ranger guide explained how such holes are often taken over by other creatures. Suddenly there was a rumble from below, and the group had to leap for safety as two warthogs exploded from the burrow and raced past, lashing out with their formidable tusks.

'A warthog's burrow is like a loaded cannon,' says Darryl Mason, a member of the park's research team who has made a special study of the species. 'They're tough little animals and can be dangerous. It's only the male, though, that has prominent warts, a pair of 'handlebars' under the eyes and a smaller pair down the snout. The female has only a small pair of warts just below the eyes. The male's handlebars are important when he's fighting – they protect his face rather like an American footballer's mask.'

The elongated snout, too, is unattractive, but again there is a purpose. Explains Mason: 'It serves as a kind of shovel. There's a disc of bone at the tip, and the warthog uses its neck muscles to push it into the soil when it's searching for roots and tubers, and for clearing the earth from its burrow. It scoops the soil with its snout and then flicks it forward. Sometimes you'll see a cloud of earth come shooting out of a hole in the ground – it's the warthog tidying up.'

Other features are no less functional. The lower tusks continually grind against the upper set and so keep razor-sharp, an effective weapon against enemies (one sow was seen treeing a leopard that threatened her young). Its dainty feet carry it at a swift trot. When it senses danger, the tail goes up like a radio antenna, enabling members of a group to keep formation as they run through the long grass.

Orpen Rest Camp

Visitors to Orpen would be wise to travel via Lydenburg and then along the old transport route to Sabie, thence Bushbuckridge and Acornhoek – the eastern Transvaal countryside is especially lovely along this road.

A small gate camp on the western boundary of the park's central district, Orpen is a convenient starting point for whatever part of the park you plan to visit. Halfway along the main tarmac route leading eastward to Satara, travellers can turn right on to the gravel road to reach the big southern camps of Skukuza, Pretoriuskop, Bergen-dal and Lower Sabie; or left to Olifants (via the Timbavati resting spot and the new Roodewal private camp) and the north.

The camp, which has a shop and petrol pump, can accommodate only a couple of dozen people, but nearby, on the banks of the Timbavati River, is the Maroela caravan camp. This is wild country, rich in game. Close by is the Rabelais Dam, notable for the large variety of species that gather to drink.

Among the many species of antelope in the area are waterbuck, distinguished by the white ring around their rumps. They are never far from the streams, and delight in the coolness of reed beds and sand vleis. Only the males are horned, the females looking rather mule-like with their long floppy ears.

The waterbuck is accomplished in self-defence. It will take to water to escape a predator, wading in deep even though crocodiles are present – and it is sometimes caught.

The Kruger Park's other antelope are many and varied. Some, like the few herds of anthrax-prone roan (after kudu and eland the largest of the antelope species) are seldom seen. Wildebeest, on the other hand, are everywhere, but particularly common on the open Lebombo plains of the central and southern districts. There are more than 13 000 of them in the park.

Blue wildebeest, or brindled gnu, are larger and heavier than the black variety (there are

none of the latter in the Kruger Park). They are surprisingly noisy creatures, communicating by means of a nasal-sounding 'kwank'. They have sharp, curved horns. And they can display considerable courage: if lions attack unsuccessfully the herd may follow the retreating cats rather than run, to make quite sure that the lions really have given up.

Pretoriuskop Rest Camp

The 9 km drive from Numbi Gate in the southwest (one of the park's principal entrances, where there's a filling station and first-aid post) to Pretoriuskop rest camp is a traveller's delight, especially in the lushness of summer (it is a high rainfall area), when the tamboekie grass is tall and the sicklebush, marula and kiaat trees are in splendid leaf. On your left looms the grandeur of Shabeni Hill.

The camp itself is the Kruger Park's oldest and third largest, boasting one of only three swimming pools (the others being at Shingwedzi and Berg-en-dal), accommodation (including sizeable family cottages) for more than 400 people, a restaurant, shop, post office and caravan park. The surrounding countryside is enchanting, studded by picturesque granite hills and, in the springtime, by blood-red coral trees, white wild pear trees and the ever-present white and yellow acacias.

Exploring this countryside is a joy. The 47 km eastward drive to Skukuza is worthwhile for both its luxuriant beauty and the game you can see along the way. Better still are the views from the Hippo Pool and Doispane gravelled roads, from where you can look down on the Sabie and its riverine magic. South-eastwards of Pretoriuskop runs the original transport riders' route, now known as the Voortrekker road – Jock of-the-Bushveld country. On the way there are beacons

Above: There are believed to be over 13 000 blue wildebeest in the Kruger Park. They are active throughout the day and night, sometimes migrating in large numbers to areas where food and water is plentiful. During the dry season they may cover up to 50 km in search of water (although they will drink every day if water is available, they can go without water for several days). **Left:** Ground hornbills are more at home on the ground than other species of this genus, and they may often be seen in the park, usually in pairs or small groups. When threatened they will take to the air, but do not fly very far.

Far left: Vervet monkeys are seen throughout the park, where they feed on insects, fruit and birds' eggs. **Left:** Wild dog pups in the Kruger Park. This is a relatively rare predator, and it is believed that competition with other species – lion in particular – could be a reason. Diseases such as distemper are another factor in the limiting of its numbers. **Right:** A leopard crosses a Kruger Park stream in a rainstorm. There are thought to be between 600 and 900 leopard in the park, but few are seen because they are predominantly nocturnal by habit. The leopard's diet is extremely diversified: it eats anything from a mouse to an adult wildebeest. Leopards even attack porcupines – going for the vulnerable muzzle.

to commemorate the life and travels of that most lovable of all South Africa's animal characters.

The region's game is plentiful, especially sable, reedbuck, klipspringer and the lordly giraffe. It is also white rhino country.

Black rhino were once common in the Lowveld but by the 1890s hunters had slaughtered them to the brink of extinction (though spoor were spotted in the southern Kruger Park as late as 1936). The white rhino suffered even more badly: the region's last specimen was spotted in 1873.

But it was the white rhino that was to be the first to make a comeback. In 1961 the Natal Parks Board presented four of the species to the Kruger Park as a pilot project of its 'Operation Rhino'. The pioneering quartet were penned in a 280 ha camp at Pretoriuskop to form a breeding herd. More of the animals were introduced as the years went by, and in 1971 the rhino population received a particularly healthy boost: Natal had built up a large surplus of white rhino, and the Kruger Park agreed to take 200 of them. It was an enormous exercise in capture and translocation, but it succeeded, and the newcomers were all released in the Kruger Park by early 1972. The 'immigrants' flourished in their new habitat, and today the white rhino population exceeds 1 000.

During 1971 the Natal Parks Board also presented the Kruger Park with 20 black rhino. Three were kept in a camp near Skukuza for research purposes and the rest released directly into the bush (those in the camp were set free after five years). In the following year, 14 more rhinos were introduced, 12 from Zimbabwe and two from Hluhluwe. A second phase of introductions commenced in 1980, and since then another 30 animals have been received from Natal and released in the southern and central districts of the park. The park now has a viable and successful breeding population of about 120 animals.

Punda Maria Rest Camp

A small, unpretentious camp of rectangular wattle-and-daub huts set attractively on the slope of a hill, Punda Maria started as a ranger post in 1919 to counter ivory poachers. The place was named by the camp's first ranger, Captain J.J. Coetser, in honour of his wife, Maria, and the Swahili name for a zebra (*Punda miliya*). It is said that zebra were the first animals that Coetser saw on his arrival in the park. It grew in popularity and size as the road network improved, and it now supports a small shop and restaurant.

The region of deep valleys and grand hills north of Punda Maria and around the tropical Luvuvhu River is magnificently wooded – syringa and ebony, ironwood and mahogany (a popular circular drive is the Mahogany Loop, which starts and finishes at the camp), sycamore fig, and always the bright green mopane.

Driving north-east on gravel, you pass Gumbandevu Hill, home of the legendary rainmaker

Left: Pyrrhocorid bugs (seen here in various stages of development) feeding on sap. They are found throughout Southern Africa. **Below left:** Common waterbuck, as their name implies, are usually found near water, which they drink very freely. These large (204 kg), gregarious antelope live in small herds, usually led by a master bull. Adult males are polygamous, with a strong territorial instinct, and will establish and defend areas in which the females graze (mostly on tender shoots). Young bulls generally form their own small herds. They are recognised by a white, crescent-like ring across the rump (it is the only antelope with this marking), white muzzle, long superciliary stripe, white collar beneath the throat and large, broad, black-tipped ears. The coat of the waterbuck exudes an oily secretion with a distinctive musky odour, and the flesh of old males may have the same smell. However this does not deter lions — probably the waterbuck's biggest enemy. **Below right:** *Thylachium africanum*, also known as the cucumber bush, photographed beside the Luvuvhu River in the Kruger Park.

Khama, and then the turn-off to Klopperfontein, a waterhole well worth visiting. Gravel becomes tar after 17 km and the road takes you almost directly north, through baobab and mopane country, to the Luvuvhu River at Pafuri – altogether a 42 km drive from Punda Maria.

East of the road-river junction, towards the picnic spot and police border post of Pafuri, is a forest of ghostly yellow-green fever trees, a

wealth of wildlife, with splendid views of crocodiles and hippos from small loops on the river bank. To the west of the junction is more splendid viewing at Hippo Pool. The riverine forest is the home of the stately and elusive nyala, bushpig, crested guinea fowl and many rare and beautiful species of tropical trees and birds.

The northernmost part of the park is at the crossroads of nine of Africa's major ecosystems.

Here wetland meets the arid bush, forest the open plain, rock the deep sand. The countryside is full of contrasts: there are wide lava flats, high ridges, deep valleys, dramatic river gorges, swathes of woodland – and a prolific wildlife population.

Seldom can you see anything like the Lebombo ironwood, or the primeval baobab forests of the Mashikiri plateau. The Hlamalala plains have been called 'South Africa's own Serengeti'. Seven types of birds (including the long-tailed starling and the yellow-bellied sun bird), Livingstone's suni, the shovel-footed squeaker (a frog), the long-tailed garter snake and many other interesting species are confined to this particular part of the country.

It is here that coking coal – which is essential to South Africa's steel industry – has been discovered. According to the managing director of ISCOR, it is 'coal of outstanding quality'. Says Tol Pienaar, ISCOR's chief director: 'This is biologically the most valuable and undisturbed area of the Kruger National Park.'

Coal-mining means pits and slag-heaps; railway lines, roads, power cables, reservoirs; shops, offices and houses – and people. The northern Kruger Park, its delicate system of rivers, perennial springs and fountains; its plants and animals, will not be able to survive the onslaught. Fortunately, the battle for the retention of this vast wonderland for posterity appears to have been won – for the time being.

Roodewal Rest Camp
Roodewal is a small private rest camp on the banks of the Timbavati River, about 47 km from Satara camp. Accommodation is available only on a block-booking basis: the family cottage and three huts can sleep up to 19 people. Visitors check into the camp at Satara, where they may do last-minute shopping.

To reach Roodewal, drive north on the main tarred road from Satara towards Olifants. About 36 km from Satara (and 4 km short of the Olifants River) turn left on to the northern leg of the Timbavati loop. The camp is situated about 11 km from the turn-off. The Timbavati is one of the most beautiful seasonal rivers in the park and offers outstanding game-viewing.

Satara Rest Camp
Satara, in the park's central region, is a large, modern camp (the second largest in the park) and popular with overseas visitors. The camp has no view to speak of, but its gracious terrace is a delight of dappled shade, flowers and birds. The luminous blue starlings are legion, but there are also yellow- and red-billed hornbills that strut pompously between the tables. Lunchtime at Satara – drinks outside and then an excellent restaurant meal – is an especially pleasant midday break.

Above: An elephant fording a river. Elephant may sometimes be seen completely submerged apart from the trunk, which serves as a snorkel. An elephant needs to spend most of the day eating or drinking to maintain its daily intake, which can be as much as 200 l of water and 250 kg of leaves, grass and bush. Cows weigh around 3 000 kg, while a mature bull may reach 5 500 kg. **Right:** Sharpe's grysbok, a small antelope found mostly in the park's mopane woodlands. They live singly (except in the mating season) and feed on fruit, roots, leaves, young shoots and grass.

The 47 km road west from the camp takes you to the Orpen Gate. But for good game-viewing you should turn right after 7 km (or, preferably, after 18 km) on to the gravel roads that lead to the Timbavati picnic spot. From there the route follows the course of the Timbavati River past the Roodewal turn-off until, after about 25 km, it branches off to join the main Olifants-Satara route.

Along the water pipeline between Satara and the Olifants River there are 13 strategically sited watering places; 20 km from camp is the well-populated Gudzane Dam. Huge herds of buffalo can be seen within easy driving distance of Satara. A gathering of three or four hundred zebra around water is not an unusual sight.

The area has some of the best grazing land in the park, and is famed for giraffe and its predators: visitors stand a good chance of hearing lions roar in the night. On one occasion, guests lined the fence listening to a loud cacophony of lion

grunts, jackal howls and the mad laugh of hyena. From the sound of it, many animals had gathered at a kill. Some of the tourists insisted they could see what was happening and provided a running commentary for their neighbours.

'That was quite amusing, because the whole thing was artificial,' says Ian Whyte of the Kruger Park's research staff. 'The calls were on tape and were coming from two loud-speakers on the roof of a caravan. I was inside, trying to attract a pride of lion to a carcass I'd chained to a tree. That's the way I sometimes carry out lion research. The lions would come to the carcass, some 20 m from the caravan. I then fired darts and drugged them. That way it's safe to measure or mark them or fit radio collars around their necks.'

The park's lion project was launched in response to a drastic decline in the blue wildebeest population. At first it was assumed that lions were the only cause, and it was decided that they should be culled. But the move did not halt the wildebeest slump, so researchers wondered whether the lions had been unjustly accused. 'We began studying their habits,' Whyte explains. 'We looked at their pride structure, where the prides lived, what they ate, how they interacted with other prides.'

The study showed that the lions were only partly to blame. 'A contributory problem was the western boundary fence. Erected as a safeguard against the spread of foot-and-mouth disease, it blocked wildebeest migration to and from areas outside the park. When they came to the fence they couldn't understand what had gone wrong, so they remained in the area next to the fence – which made it easy for lion prides to prey on them. Now the wildebeest have accepted the fence. Another important factor was the tall grass conditions which prevailed throughout this favoured habitat during the 1970s. This again led to above-normal mortality through lion and hyena predation. Their decline has now bottomed out, and the numbers are on the rise again – particularly since the drier habitat conditions and short grazing prevailing in more recent years favour the habitat preferences of this species.'

Shingwedzi Rest Camp

The 73 km road south-east from Punda Maria to the largest of the northern region's three rest camps takes you through flattish savanna country (though there are rocky outcrops) brightened by the perennial green of mopane bush. About halfway along the route is the Babalala resting spot (notable for its splendid fig tree), from where you can continue on tar or, for better game-viewing, turn right on to the 30 km gravelled loop that follows the Shisha and Mphongolo streams.

Shingwedzi is a medium-sized, somewhat old-fashioned (though part of it is modern), friendly camp which has lovely trees, spectacular pink-and-white impala lilies, rectangular bungalows, a shady veranda, a restaurant, a shop and a swimming pool. There are some very rewarding drives from this pleasant spot – south-west along the Shingwedzi River to the Tshange look-out point, from where you can survey the vastness of parkland, or south-east, following the same river to the Kanniedood Dam and Crocodile Pool not far from the Mozambique border. From there you carry on south for 47 km to rejoin the main Shingwedzi-Letaba road, crossing the Tropic of Capricorn and passing the Hlamfu and Shawu dams on the way.

The riverine forest around and north of Shingwedzi is home to some of the Kruger Park's 900 plus leopard. Beautiful, secretive, brave, unsociable, silent, these big cats are seldom seen, resting in tree or rock in the hot hours of the day or stalking the thick riverine reed beds. The smaller antelope – reedbuck, impala, duiker – provide the bulk of their diet but they are more

or less indiscriminate hunters, capable of bringing down something as large as a kudu, but not averse to small fry such as cane rats, fish and porcupines. Monkeys and baboons also feature on the menu, though old male baboons will often fight back, quite effectively, rather than run. Oddly enough, and quite unlike the domestic cat, the leopard takes easily to water. Females feeding cubs have been seen swimming to the islands of the Sabie River, sometimes carrying with them prey as large as impala.

Kruger Park has fewer of the leopard's cousin, the cheetah – possibly no more than three hundred. Smaller, longer legged, these fine hunters are built for speed (one has been clocked at 110 km/h) and thus prefer the open countryside to the dense bush that covers a large part of the park. You are most likely to see cheetah on the open plains around Satara, in the central region and in the Pretoriuskop section, particularly on the burn areas.

A FLASH OF POWDER IN THE NIGHT

Paul Selby was an American mining engineer who managed a Johannesburg gold mine in the 1920s. In 1924 he and his family were introduced to the Sabie Game Reserve, and thereafter he made frequent trips to Pretoriuskop to photograph game. He set up his camera on the back of a truck and went to elaborate lengths to disguise the vehicle with branches. There he would sit, with a large camera fitted with a 500 mm lens (powerful even by today's standards), waiting patiently until giraffe and other animals came into view.

The results, from the beginning, were spectacular. Selby had special success with photographs taken at night. Flashbulbs were not yet on the market, so he had to rely on magnesium powder held aloft on a tray and ignited as he exposed a plate.

When Parliament debated the National Parks Bill in 1926, Selby was asked for prints so that members could see what the reserve was all about. The pictures were enthusiastically received, and played a significant part in helping the House to come to its decision.

Skukuza Rest Camp

Although the old Selati railway line, completed in 1912, has long since been re-routed outside the park, there remains a short stretch over the cantilevered Sabie Bridge, only a stone's throw from Skukuza rest camp. When the Sabie floods its banks, staff from the camp man small rail trolleys to ferry passengers to and from the airport across the river. James Stevenson-Hamilton would feel at home: in the early days he rode such trolleys all the way to Komatipoort, and he must often have seen the Sabie in flood.

Skukuza itself, however, would surprise him: what he knew as a tiny, ramshackle camp has grown into quite a large settlement. Apart from the rest camp that caters for the ever-rolling tide of visitors, there is an attractive staff village with its own church, primary school, (unfenced) golf course, extensive maintenance workshops and even a sophisticated meat-processing factory that disposes of culled game.

Above: White rhino in the Kruger Park. There are more than 1 000 white rhino in the park (341 were introduced between 1961 and 1972) – most of them in the area between the Sabie and Crocodile rivers. This species differs from the black rhino in several respects: the white rhino is a grazer with a big, wide mouth, whereas the black rhino has a pointed mouth with a prehensile upper lip which it uses to strip leaves from branches; the white rhino keeps its head low, while the black rhino generally keeps its head in line with its back; the white rhino is heavier and less aggressive, and prefers open areas while the black rhino likes thickets. Despite the names both species have the same colour. **Left above:** *Ipomoea*, photographed near the Luvuvhu River in the Kruger Park. **Left below:** The fever tree is found in low-lying, swampy areas, and grows in groups. Its characteristic yellow or yellow-green bark is best seen in spring, when the trees are bare of leaves. Because fever trees grow in swampy areas – ideal breeding grounds for mosquitoes – they were once regarded as a cause of malaria. **Right above:** The marabou stork, a large and unlovely bird, is frequently seen with vultures at a carcass. The marabou stork nests in large trees and occasionally on cliff ledges, producing a clutch of two to four eggs. **Right below:** Bushbuck are generally found in thickets in the Kruger Park, and keep to water courses. There are estimated to be over 1 000 bushbuck in the park.

For visitors, the heart of Skukuza is the large thatched complex, on the bank of the Sabie River, which houses a restaurant, shop and offices. There is also a large reception area at the gate to the camp which has a bank, a post office, and a car-hire office. Not far away is the Stevenson-Hamilton Memorial Information Centre, which accommodates a well-stocked library and an impressive exhibition hall. Close to the camp is a nursery where indigenous plants, such as palms, cycads, baobabs and so forth – are cultivated and sold to the public at very modest prices.

There are luxury caravans, family cottages, self-contained huts and camping sites – a total of over 600 beds. As in other camps, visitors of all races are welcome.

During 1896 and 1897, the buffalo as a species was almost exterminated by the epidemic of rinderpest that devastated most of Africa south of the equator. But over the decades the herds recovered, and thousands can now be seen throughout the Kruger Park.

Normally shy, retiring creatures, the buffalo can be savagely vengeful if wounded or molested: it is one of the most dangerous of the big game animals. Adult, healthy buffalo do not often fall victim to lion or other predators: when threatened, they tend to form a defensive ring, reminiscent of a laager.

Rangers tell a charming story of an especially hospitable herd of buffalo. In 1971 five baby elephants who had survived a veterinary experiment were released near a dam south-west of Skukuza. There was an elephant herd nearby, and it was assumed that the five would join it.

Months later, however, a tourist reported spotting a young elephant in the middle of a group of buffalo. Park authorities thought this was the product of an overactive imagination until the aerial census crew came upon the group and took photographs: the elephant already stood half a metre taller than the buffalo.

The growing elephant stayed in close contact with the buffalo, though not necessarily with the same group (buffalo come together at waterholes, and it would have been easy for the elephant to arrive with one herd and leave with another). Dirk Swart, then a ranger at Skukuza, studied the elephant's behaviour, and was amused to see that it was adopting buffalo habits. When approached by a vehicle, buffalo dash away for a short distance, then return to inspect the intruder. The elephant did the same, with his little trunk held high. Park biologists were confident that the elephant would soon forsake the buffalo and join up with its own species, but each year during the aerial census they found he had remained with his friends. Interestingly, he was moving north, and by 1980 he was in the Balule area south of the Olifants River. By that time he was ten years old and of formidable size.

One day a tourist watched amazed as the elephant and 20 or so buffalo teamed up to drive eight lions from a dam. The lions fled, two of them taking refuge up a tree. As the tourist described it afterwards, the buffalo bellowed and the elephant trumpeted, and the noise alone must have terrified the lions. The group encircled the treed cats, who tried to retaliate with roars. Eventually the elephant and buffalo lost interest and went back to the dam for a drink. The lions waited 15 minutes before venturing very cautiously from the safety of their tree.

Since 1980 this curious elephant has spent time in the Satara and Tshokwane areas. Zoologists say he is now sexually mature, and should soon become involved with his own kind, but Ted Whitfield, a ranger, believes he is afraid of other elephants. 'I've seen him drinking with the buffalo when a herd of elephant arrive,' says Whitfield. 'The buffalo made off, and so did he. But just in case he changes his mind, we've marked him in such a manner that we'll be able to recognise him wherever he goes.'

A pleasant halfway resting place on the road north from Skukuza is Tshokwane, where there is a tea-room and picnic spot. The area features a large number of wildlife species and, for the bird-lover, it is an enchanting piece of veld. There are some splendid gravel drives from Tshokwane, especially the route eastwards to the Eileen Orpen Dam – a fine viewing place. But although this region has great scenic appeal, it is probably best known for its unusual lions.

Back in 1927, it is said, a ranger named Crous shot a white lion near Tshokwane. Explains Dr Tol Pienaar: 'In the early days there was a policy of carnivore control – in some areas lion and other predators were destroyed to keep their numbers down. Ranger Crous shot the white lion and kept the skin, but the old boy would never show it to anyone.'

Even so, many people knew about the unusual skin and they supposed the lion to have been an albino. There had already been reports of albino waterbuck and reedbuck in the park, and James Stevenson-Hamilton had once spotted an albino ground hornbill.

Then, in 1959, two rangers patrolling near Tshokwane came upon a pair of white lion cubs. The pair was not seen again and probably perished, but these were not albinos – for there was colour in their eyes.

So far there was only mild interest in the white lion phenomenon, but that changed dramatically in 1976 when a snow-white male was born at Tshokwane – and seemed set to survive. Shortly afterwards three white lions were born in the Timbavati Private Nature Reserve across the Kruger's western fence. Two of the three were later translocated to the National Zoological Gardens in Pretoria (the third disappeared without trace), and in the meantime Tshokwane's white male was seen regularly. Clearly it was flourishing.

Since 1979 at least nine more white cubs have been born near Tshokwane and Timbavati. Bi-

ologists say they are the product of a recessive gene, present in local prides, which determines a lack of melanin pigment in the hair of these animals. In every case the white cubs have had normal brothers, and as a rule other lions seem to accept them without question. Several of the white variety have reached maturity – but, to the frustration of tourists, their coats and particularly the manes of the males have gradually darkened to a light straw colour (or darker).

Walking in the wilderness

Overlooking the spectacular Luvuvhu Gorge is a ruined hilltop citadel built by an eccentric Venda chief, Makahane. When this cruel leader suspected undue interest in the royal wives by one of his warriors, he made the man, and the wives, strip naked and work together in the fields. If the warrior's interest then became obvious, he was hurled to his death from the cliff.

That, anyway, is the story told by rangers on the Nyalaland Wilderness Trail, one of five wilderness trails currently operating in the park. The ruined citadel is a regular stop on this, the northernmost trail, and as the ranger relates his tale, his charge of eight trailists take in the magnificent views of the gorge and its surroundings. Here, black eagles swoop and wheel in their quest for food, and far below, the cry of the crowned eagle on its nest in a baobab resounds through the valley.

Trails in Kruger operate twice a week throughout the year in the southern, central and northern

28

A lioness with her giraffe kill in the Kruger Park. In one recorded case, 19 lions — some of them cubs — fed on a giraffe for over a week.

districts of the park. In addition to the Nyalaland trail are the Wolhuter and Bushman trails in the south and the Olifants and Metsimetsi trails in the central region.

Accommodation on all trails consists of rustic wood and thatched huts, in base camps which are a peaceful retreat from civilisation.

Prior to leaving for these camps, parties assemble at specific rest camps, and are taken to base by vehicles. They arrive in time for a healthy evening meal and, early the following morning, set off on the first day's trail.

Groups are accompanied by two trained rangers, whose task it is to interpret for the party the complexities of natural ecosystems, stopping often to discuss signs of the wild, and the wonders of nature. The rangers know their territory and are glad to share their knowledge.

The pattern is repeated on the following two days, and on the fourth day the party returns to the rest camp. All food is provided, but trailists must supply their own drinks.

The emphasis is on relaxation and enjoying nature, and although game is often encountered, trails are not 'foot safaris to view animals', but rather a total experience of the bush, where all parts of the wilderness – rocks, trees, birds, fish, reptiles and insects – can be discovered.

Kruger offers nearly 20 000 km² of unspoilt bush. Wilderness trails are the ideal way to experience this raw Africa, for the sights, sounds and smells of the bush are that much more real – far more so than when you travel by car.

In story books he is portrayed as the King of the Beasts, a dignified ruler of mane and muscle that few of his subjects would dare to cross.

In reality, however, this large cat is the sleepy-eyed sultan of the savanna, his reign a succession of lazy days spent eating, sleeping and playing with his offspring.

But Africa's largest and most powerful carnivore should not be dismissed as a mere pussycat. He can break a wildebeest's neck with one swipe of a massive paw and he is so powerful that he can carry twice his weight in those terrible jaws. At times he will do his duty by his lusty harem in a snarling display of passion unmatched in the animal world.

Many myths surround these mammals — including the mistaken belief that they cannot climb trees, or are afraid of water. The lion is an accomplished climber. In a chase, he can cover a hundred metres in four seconds.

Another of his talents is the ability to see clearly in what we would regard as darkness. Caught in the glare of a torch or a car's headlights, his large eyes glow like two reflectors — and in fact that is what they are. Like other members of the cat family, the lion's vision is aided by a special tissue, known as the *tapetum lucidum*, lining the retina of each eye.

Any light that passes the rods of the retina is reflected back thereby concentrating the incoming light. This remarkable structure enables the lion to see 50 per cent more light than he would see without it.

Despite the obvious differences in appearance, the lion is a close relative of the Asiatic tiger, and the two species can interbreed, producing baby 'ligers' or 'tigons'. The tiger has stripes which conceal it as it stalks its prey through tall grass and jungle, while the lion has a tawny hide that blends into the dry grass of the African bush country.

But while there are many similarities, there are distinct behavioural differences. While the tiger is strictly a loner, the lion is very much a social animal, living in loosely formed prides of 30 or more members. In fact it is not entirely accurate to look upon the lion as the overlord of the African carnivores: instead it is really the lion pride that ranks top of the hunting hierarchy.

One benefit of living in a pride is that it makes finding a meal far easier. A solitary lion does not have the speed or the stamina to run down a healthy antelope or zebra, and even the stalk-and-pounce technique is only occasionally successful. But a whole pride of hungry lions can and does resort to much surer methods. The male will approach a herd of antelope at a very leisurely rate, while the females circle the herd and conceal themselves on the far side. When they are in position, the male closes in and drives the herd towards the spot where the females lie in wait.

However the males do play a part in defending the pride. Lionesses might be driven from a kill by a particularly bold band of hyenas, but if a male lion suddenly appears on the scene the hyenas promptly retreat. Males will also defend the pride's territory from encroachment by other lions.

Mopane country with a baobab king

Seemingly limitless numbers of mopane trees dominate the northern half of the Kruger National Park and the rest of the northern Transvaal Lowveld that sweeps to the Limpopo and South Africa's boundary with Zimbabwe. Occasional hills and mountains interrupt the spreading plain, but none comes close to matching the mighty Drakensberg and Soutpansberg ranges that buffer the northern Lowveld from the high country to the south-west. Dotting the mopane plains are awesome baobab 'elephant trees' that reach a great age.

The Transvaal Provincial Administration's Directorate of Nature and Environmental Conservation has five sanctuaries in the northern Lowveld: Hans Merensky and Langjan nature reserves, both important for the scarce species they contain; Messina Nature Reserve, which accommodates an interesting concentration of baobabs; Fanie Botha Dam Nature Reserve near Tzaneen; and the tiny Lillie Nature Reserve which conserves a rare cycad. The province's Public Resorts Board runs the Honnet Nature Reserve at Tshipise; the Republic of Venda features Nwanedi National Park, Makuya National Park, Nzhelele Nature Reserve; and the Modjadji Nature Reserve is in Lebowa.

Fanie Botha Dam Nature Reserve

Completed in 1977, the Fanie Botha Dam near Tzaneen is situated in one of the most picturesque yet curiously atypical spots in the Transvaal. Extensive pine plantations on the hills overlooking the water give it the look of Canada or Scandinavia, and to complete the effect there is a large sawmill on the far shore. The dam is well stocked with fish such as barbel, tilapia, black bass and yellowfish and is a popular haunt for anglers and those who like to camp or picnic in idyllic surroundings. The 1200 ha dam and 200 ha of the shore were proclaimed a nature reserve in 1978.

The land area offers a limited game population (bushbuck and duiker), while the dam is ideal for bird-watching. More than 150 species have been identified in the area, including fish eagle, tropical waterfowl and fish-eating birds.

The heart of the recreation area is a 65-stand caravan park within 50 m of the water's edge. Not far away are a number of day picnic sites and launching ramps for motorboats. The reserve is open daily from 5 a.m. to 8 p.m. and is reached from a well-signposted turn-off on the road between Tzaneen and Duiwelskloof. For further information, you can write to The Officer-in-Charge, Fanie Botha Dam Nature Reserve, P.O. Box 1397, Tzaneen 0850 (telephone Tzaneen 5641) or alternatively contact The Regional Representative, Directorate

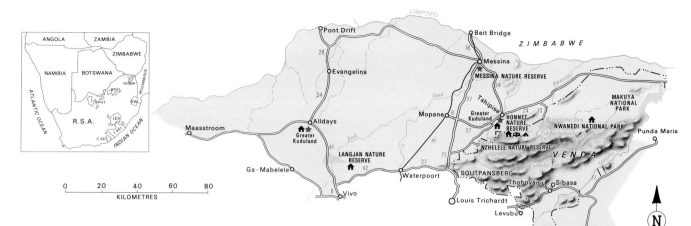

of Nature and Environmental Conservation, P.O. Box 217, Pietersburg 0700 (telephone Pietersburg 7-4948).

Greater Kuduland

Your time's your own in Greater Kuduland's two 10 000 ha privately owned game reserves. Both are situated in the northern Transvaal, one near Tshipise and the other near Alldays.

With a professional game ranger always on hand, visitors are free to set their own schedules, which might include bird-watching, hikes and game-drives. Both areas, incidentally, are regarded as a paradise for bird and animal watchers. And the reason is simple: thanks to their varied vegetation, the reserves play host to more than 50 species of game and more than 200 different kinds of birds.

Sleeping quarters at both main camps are in African-style bungalows with baths and showers (the Tshipise camp has air-conditioned rooms). There is a dining room and an outside lapa for braais. For those wishing to 'rough it', bush camps are also available.

Above left: The Fanie Botha Dam, near Tzaneen, is one of the most beautiful spots in the northern Transvaal Lowveld. **Above right:** A tree frog perches above its foam nest on a branch overhanging water. **Left:** A red-knobbed coot chick. Coots are distributed throughout Southern Africa, and are common wherever there are rivers or expanses of water. **Right:** This newly-moulted earwig can be recognised by the pair of pincers on its tail. Its name is something of a mystery: scientists say they are harmless, and there is no foundation in the belief that they crawl into people's ears.

Greater Kuduland operates a hunting lodge mainly for international clients.

For further information, contact The Director, Greater Kuduland Safaris, P.O. Box 1385, Louis Trichardt 0920 (telephone Louis Trichardt 9663).

Hans Merensky Nature Reserve

About 70 km east of the Fanie Botha Dam is a much larger and more complex provincial sanctuary – the Hans Merensky Nature Reserve, which includes the Eiland Mineral Spa. In 1950 the province acquired the farm Eiland for the sake of its hot springs, and soon afterwards began using it to breed species then scarce in most parts of the Transvaal – notably giraffe and sable. As a result the farm was proclaimed a nature reserve in 1954 and re-named to honour a well-known geologist and agriculturist who had put the region on the map and donated a vital bore-hole.

Both giraffe and sable flourished in the new sanctuary, and in 1962 a number of young giraffe were captured and translocated to the province's Loskop Dam and Langjan nature reserves. Since then more than 200 giraffe have been moved to new homes all over the Transvaal and, in several cases, to Natal. In 1964 the province developed a prestigious spa which is now managed by the Transvaal's Public Resorts Board.

Today, the spa provides accommodation for those visiting the nature reserve, while the reserve offers a diversion for those staying at

31

When to go The reserve and resort are open daily throughout the year but are most popular in winter when temperatures are lower and game is easier to spot. During the winter school holidays the resort is liable to be full to overflowing.

Reservations and information If you would like to book accommodation in the public resort, you should contact The General Manager, Eiland Mineral Baths, Private Bag 527, Letsitele 0885 (telephone Laparisa 667 or 759). For further information on the nature reserve, you should contact The Officer-in-Charge, Hans Merensky Nature Reserve, Private Bag X502, Letsitele 0885 (telephone Laparisa 632/3) or The Regional Representative, Directorate of Nature and Environmental Conservation, P.O. Box 217, Pietersburg 0700 (telephone Pietersburg 7-4948).

Getting there From Tzaneen or Gravelotte, follow the signs to Eiland and turn north-east at Letsitele. After 38 km the road enters the reserve: the Visitor Centre and the public resort are on the right.

Accommodation The Eiland Public Resort offers 100 rondavels in five categories: 'AA' and 'A' rondavels for five people with bath, shower and toilet; 'B' rondavels for four persons with shower and toilet; 'C' rondavels for four persons with shower and toilet; and 'D' rondavels for four persons without shower or toilet but close to an ablution block. All rondavels are fully equipped. There is a caravan and camping site with 425 sites.

Eating and drinking Each rondavel has its own kitchenette, and there is a supermarket, bottle store, licensed restaurant and snack bar.

Getting around Private vehicles are not allowed in the nature reserve. Instead, information officers take visitors on bus trips departing from the Visitor Centre. Book through the reserve office. On request, the information officers lead foot trails to the Black Hills on the reserve's eastern boundary. In addition there are three self-guided trails, each starting from the Visitor Centre: the Letaba Trail to the river, which involves an hour's walk; the Waterbuck Trail, a round trip of 12 km; and the 33 km Giraffe Trail (with an overnight hut). Permits for the walking trails are available from the Officer-in-Charge. During school holidays the public resort organises horseback trails in the course of which riders spend two hours inside the reserve.

Special attractions The Transvaal Provincial Museum Service runs a 'Tsonga Kraal and Open-Air Museum' in the reserve, staffed by Tsonga craftsmen who demonstrate their techniques. Visitors travel to the kraal by minibus. The public resort offers an indoor therapeutic bath, outdoor swimming pools and tennis courts.

Wildlife Hans Merensky has giraffe, sable, zebra, waterbuck, blue wildebeest, bushbuck, kudu, steenbok, Sharpe's grysbok, impala, grey duiker, hippo, crocodile and leopard.

---

the spa. The Directorate of Nature and Environmental Conservation's offices are an easy stroll from the public resort, and two information officers organise bus tours of the reserve. Regular wildlife film shows are held in the directorate's own auditorium. Private cars are not allowed in the reserve, but visitors are welcome to set out on the four hiking trails.

Hans Merensky's northern boundary is the Letaba River. The reserve is 5 185 ha in extent,

but is divided into two camps by the busy public road which runs south of the river. Inside, visitors may spot giraffe, zebra, kudu, blue wildebeest, waterbuck, impala, warthog, duiker, steenbok, Sharpe's grysbok, sable (if they are lucky) and a rich bird life.

At least five leopards have made their homes in the doleritic Black Hills that form the reserve's eastern boundary. They are seldom seen, but one of them provided some excite-

ment for a nature conservation officer while he was patrolling the reserve's boundary fences on a motorcycle. An impala ram was running along the firebreak road towards an anthill when suddenly a leopard emerged from behind the anthill and tripped the impala with his paw. The officer was so fascinated by the incident that he rode straight into the fence, landing in a heap on the ground.

When he picked himself up he saw that the leopard had the impala by the throat – but had turned to watch the spectacle on the road, only 20 m away. The officer departed the scene with some alacrity.

The Giraffe Trail in Hans Merensky Nature Reserve is an easy way to discover the beauty of the Lowveld on foot. The 33 km trail takes three days and begins and ends at the nature reserve offices. No more than 13 km is covered each day which makes it perfect for beginners, leaving plenty of time to relax or to explore the surroundings. The trail's overnight hut overlooks a waterhole where wildlife enthusiasts may see a variety of game. The hike is best undertaken during winter – mosquitoes and high temperatures are a problem during summer.

Honnet Nature Reserve

Eiland's sister spa, Tshipise, is on the farm Honnet, about 87 km north-east of Louis Trichardt. The Tshipise hot spring has been sacred to local Venda for centuries: on the rare occasions when it dried up, a chief arrived to pray for the water to return – and according to legend was never disappointed. Honnet has been government property since 1912, and in 1934 the provincial administration erected the first few rondavels in what is now a flourishing public resort. The rest of the farm forms the 2 200 ha Honnet Nature Reserve.

Like the spa, the reserve is run by the Transvaal's Public Resorts Board, and its chief purpose is to entertain. There is a handsome *lapa* used for large braais and the occasional breakfast; in school holidays there are open-air dances in a sandy riverbed with a local band in attendance, and the spa stables organise guided horse rides (lasting four hours) on which the riders explore the trails and examine the reserve at leisure. If you are a keen hiker, the scenic 26 km (two-day) Baobab Hiking Trail should be an ideal way to see the reserve's abundant wildlife, which includes giraffe, kudu, waterbuck, nyala, sable, blue wildebeest, tsessebe and duiker. Private vehicles are not permitted in the reserve.

Accommodation at Tshipise includes a hotel, 130 rondavels, each with either four or five beds, and 300 caravan and camping sites. The spa has a therapeutic bath, swimming pools, tennis courts and bowling greens. To reach Honnet, take the signposted turn-off on the high-

Left: Mole snakes have been described as the most valuable to man. Found all over Southern Africa, they are highly effective in checking the population of moles, rats and other rodents. In his informative and amusing book *The Reptiles and Amphibians of Southern Africa*, naturalist Walter Rose wrote of a Cape farmer who had for some years protected several mole snakes that lived near his barns and which, like most animals that are not persecuted, had lost their fear of mankind. 'Returning home one day after a few hours' absence, he found some visitors awaiting him with the self-satisfied greeting, "We have been doing you a good turn. We have just killed several big snakes near your ricks." The farmer's reply cannot be recorded in a book intended for general circulation.'

Top: Myriad silken strands surround a spider's nest in the Langjan Nature Reserve. **Left:** A large spotted acraea, newly emerged from its pupa. This butterfly has a wingspan of 6-7 cm. **Above:** An impressive snarl from a baby leopard. There are usually two or three cubs to a litter, and the gestation period is between 93 and 103 days. The upbringing and training of the cubs is undertaken by the mother: the male is essentially a loner, usually abandoning the female after mating.

way between Louis Trichardt and Messina and drive another 28 km to the east. For further information, or to book accommodation, write to The General Manager, Tshipise Mineral Baths, P.O. Box 4, Tshipise 0901 (telephone Tshipise 4).

Langjan Nature Reserve

Gemsbok are more readily associated with the Kalahari than the Lowveld, but a tongue of Kalahari sand creeps into the Transvaal bush at the western end of the Soutpansberg to provide an ideal gemsbok habitat. During the 1920s and

1930s small groups of gemsbok roamed farms in the area, but by the 1950s the only ones left were in a herd protected by the owners of the farm Langjan: these were the last naturally occurring gemsbok in the Transvaal. To protect them, the province's Directorate of Nature and Environmental Conservation bought the farm and proclaimed it as Langjan Nature Reserve.

Disappointingly, from a peak of 34 animals in 1959 the herd's strength dwindled rapidly, and in 1964 only four were left. A rescue operation was launched and new animals were in-

troduced from the Kalahari. Today the reserve holds nearly 200 gemsbok, and each year surplus animals are taken off and distributed to other nature reserves and private individuals. The gemsbok share the reserve with giraffe, kudu, waterbuck, red hartebeest, blue wildebeest, impala, black-backed jackal, caracal, bat-eared fox and other species.

Originally Langjan covered only 1 900 ha, but its growing game population needed more room. So in 1978 the province bought three more farms and increased its area to 4 800 hec-

Left: Ants tend a treehopper (seen here laying eggs) in search of the sweet liquid exuded by the bizarrely-shaped bugs. The horn-like projections on the treehopper's back make it resemble a thorn, and this camouflage protects it from predators. The female lays her eggs in slits cut in trees and shrubs.
Below: The insectivorous hedgehog is found in a variety of habitats ranging from open grassland to bush-clad koppies. The hedgehog has no permanent home in the summer and sleeps in bush, rock crevices, abandoned snake holes, termite mounds and just about any place which provides shelter. It becomes lethargic in the cold winter months, however, and may hibernate.

THE WILD GEESE OF TSHIPISE

Most people would expect international film stars such as Roger Moore and Richard Harris to be spotted at exclusive game lodges rather than at a public spa, but in 1977 both spent several months at Tshipise and the Honnet Nature Reserve. They and 300 others were there for the filming of *The Wild Geese*, the story of 50 mercenaries who entered a central African country to rescue its deposed and imprisoned president.

In their time at Tshipise the film-makers worked from dawn to dusk and tensions ran high. Of course, there were lighter moments. Both Richard Burton and Roger Moore celebrated birthdays at the resort – Burton with a large party in the restaurant, Moore (who turned 50) with a braai in Honnet's *lapa*. As a special bonus, in all their time at Honnet only one day was overcast and shooting was completed two months ahead of schedule.

tares. Its terrain is consistently flat and featureless except where it is crossed by the Brak River, a usually dry watercourse that marks a dramatic division in the vegetation. One side features scrub and grass but few trees; the other is relatively densely wooded.

To reach Langjan, take the road from Pietersburg to Alldays. The reserve is 22 km north of Vivo. Langjan's remote location means that few people visit it, but those who make the trip may stay in a bush camp of carpeted rondavels containing beds and nothing else. Vehicular tours and walking trails are available for visitors, who must make prior arrangements with The Officer-in-Charge, Langjan Nature Reserve, P.O. Box 15, Vivo 0924 (telephone Vivo 1211).

Letaba Ranch
This 45 000 ha reserve attracts trophy hunters from all over the world and is a major source of income for Gazankulu's Division of Nature Conservation. Elephant, buffalo, leopard and antelope are culled here but these removals are strictly controlled by scientific monitoring.

Letaba's woodland, open savannah and animals are much the same as those found in Kruger Park. The ranch's camps and rondavels are served by a dining area that overlooks the Groot Letaba River.

The ranch is well signposted from Phalaborwa and Eiland. Further information can be obtained from Letaba Ranch, P.O. Box 120, Phalaborwa 1390 (telephone Gravelotte 95).

Lillie Nature Reserve
In the 1920s the naturalist and poet, Eugène Marais, discovered a beautiful cycad in the Transvaal's Waterberg range – but details of its locality died with him. Later, when Marais' niece, Dr Inez Verdoorn, helped to rediscover the species she named it *Encephalartos eugene-maraisii* (it has since been renamed *Encephalartos dyerianus*). Apart from its occur-

THE LIFE AND DEATH OF AN ELEPHANT TREE

Like the elephant in the animal kingdom, the massive baobab tree easily eclipses its fellow species both in size and age. A baobab's spread of branches can reach nearly 40m across. The 'baobab forest' south of Messina is one of the wonders of the northern Transvaal and anyone who has seen this gathering of portly giants will not forget it in a hurry.

In earlier times, tribal Africans were much impressed by the baobab's huge proportions, but failed to connect it with the slender saplings that were really young baobabs. Where could the giant trees have come from? The suggestions were ingenious: some said they were the children of an elephant; others deduced that they had dropped from the sky, and explained that the bare branches exposed in winter were its roots clawing at the air.

As the tribesmen discovered, the baobab has its uses. There is always a cavity among the branches that often holds water (even in the driest months), and anyone who clambers up may be able to slake his thirst. The leaves can be boiled and eaten as a vegetable; the seeds can be sucked, or ground and roasted to make a drink like coffee; and the pollen can be used to make an acceptable glue. The fruit pod contains tartaric acid, used to make sherbet, and the spongy wood can be processed into ropes.

Although a baobab lives for centuries, it must eventually perish – perhaps through disease, or on rare occasions because it collapses after absorbing too much water. When that happens the tree's collapse is spectacular. What seems so solid and permanent is really only pulp and water, and the once stately baobab crumbles in on itself in an untidy heap of white flakes. Insects and the elements attack the remains relentlessly, and in little more than a year there is hardly a trace of the massive tree that took so long to grow.

Top: The klipspringer, being adapted to a rocky habitat, rarely strays from its home on rocky hillsides, ridges or koppies. This klipspringer is marking its territory by rubbing its scent gland on a twig. During the daylight hours, one or two males keep watch from a high lookout: when danger threatens they emit a regular cry. Because klipspringers are monogamous, they are usually seen in pairs. **Above:** *Steganotaenia araliacea* (carrot tree or pop-gun tree), which smells strongly of carrots. Children make pop-guns (or blow-pipes) by slipping the bark from a narrow stem. Some people believe the tree can produce abortion in goats, and it is said that sore throats may be relieved by chewing the roots.

rence in the Waterberg, the cycad is found in a 2ha area north of Mica. To protect it the Transvaal's Directorate of Environmental and Nature Conservation has proclaimed a 57ha nature reserve, but keeps its whereabouts secret.

Mabuda-Shango Hiking Trail
This long and scenically spectacular trail begins at the office on the Tate Vondo plantation, in the forestry region of Venda. The first (15,3km) stretch of the four-part trail passes through the Nzhelele-Tshirovha catchment area, offering glimpses of mountains, tea plantations and a variety of indigenous and exotic plants. Hikers spend the night at the Fundudzi rest camp, which nestles in the valley of the Mutale River.

The second leg leads through pine plantations and the Thathe 'holy wood' to the Mahovhohovho waterfall. Hikers spend the night in the open (this leg extends for 16km). The third leg leads from the waterfall to the Tshatshingo potholes and back again (12,2km): hikers also spend the third night at the waterfall.

The fourth and final leg takes them to the head of the Olifants River which offers magnificent views of the countryside. They then follow a meandering path along the slopes of the Soutpansberg, through bubbling streams and shady pine plantations, back to the office at Tate Vondo.

The total length of the trail is presently 53,5km, but there are plans to extend it to the Nwanedi National Park in the east and link up with the Soutpansberg Hiking Trail in the west.

To book for the trail, write to The Secretary, Department of Agriculture and Forestry, Private Bag X2247, Sibasa, Venda (telephone Sibasa 3-1001 ext. 2167).

Above left: The Modjadji cycad (*Encephalartos transvenosus*), one of the largest cycads in the world, exists in natural forests near Duiwelskloof in the north-eastern Transvaal, where they are protected. **Above right:** A termite soldier sinks its formidable jaws into human skin, drawing blood. Like the workers, the soldiers are blind males and females that have not developed fully: they cannot feed themselves, and rely on the workers to keep them alive. Soldiers have swollen heads and huge jaws. Termites live in large colonies that have a highly developed social structure.

TO CATCH A GIRAFFE

Each year the Directorate of Nature and Environmental Conservation's game-capture team spends a few weeks at each provincial nature reserve in pursuit of young giraffe and other game that are to be translocated to other areas. The team arrives with a special transporter vehicle which resembles a furniture removal truck. Large as it is, the vehicle cannot accommodate giraffe more than 4 m high – and the team steers clear of giraffe less than 3 m tall because they are too young to survive the effects of quarantine.

That means the team must look for giraffe between three and four metres tall. 'You'd think it would be easy, but it's very difficult to judge a giraffe's height and weight,' said a nature conservation officer. 'The only sure way to do it is to wait until the giraffe you've selected is browsing on a branch. When he wanders off, you quickly measure the branch's height with a tape measure. The animal's weight is then extrapolated and the correct dosage of tranquilliser prepared for the dart-gun.'

The giraffe is ambushed, and when the dart hits him he takes off at speed with a vehicle in hot pursuit. 'Eventually he'll fall over, and if you don't reach him within several minutes you may lose him,' said the conservation officer. 'He is dehydrated and suffering from shock and exhaustion. You have to give him an antidote and get him back on his feet. Meanwhile you blindfold him and put a harness over him while the team brings in the capture vehicle and digs a trench to ease the loading of the giraffe.'

The team gently tugs on ropes attached to the harness to coax the giraffe up the ramp and into the truck. The men must be careful not to let the giraffe touch the sides of the vehicle, as he may take alarm, rear up, and injure himself or break free from the harness. Once he is inside the doors are closed and he can be transported to his new home.

Makuya National Park

Filling a long narrow strip along the north-western boundary of Kruger National Park is the 18 000 ha Makuya National Park. This unspoilt area, managed by the Venda Nature Conservation Administration, is only accessible on a 53 km hiking trail. On this exciting trail you will be accompanied by an experienced park ranger as large game such as elephant, buffalo, lion, hippo and leopard are common sights.

In the future two camps at the northern and southern ends of the park will cater for hikers wishing to undertake day hikes from a base camp. Further information about The Makuya National Park should be addressed to the Department of Environmental and Water Affairs, Private Bag X2503, Sibasa, Venda (telephone Sibasa 3-1001).

Messina Nature Reserve

This botanists' delight has some 350 species of trees and shrubs, including mopane, corkwood, white seringa, impala lily, and, of course, the park's principal attraction, baobabs. Some 12 000 of these trees are found in this 3 700 ha reserve – one is 25 m tall with a girth of 16 m.

There is also plenty of game including giraffe, kudu, nyala, sable, blue wildebeest, impala, duiker, Sharpe's grysbok and steenbok.

Game-viewing is permitted from private vehicles and the Officer-in-Charge is usually only too pleased to show visitors around. Overnight facilities are available for hikers.

The reserve is reached 3 km south of Messina on the Pietersburg road. The gate is open between 7 a.m. and 5 p.m. For further information, write to The Officer-in-Charge, Messina Nature Reserve, P.O. Box 78, Messina 0900 (telephone Messina 3235) or The Regional Representative, Directorate of Nature and Environmental Conservation, P.O. Box 217, Pietersburg 0700 (telephone Pietersburg 7-4948).

Modjadji Nature Reserve

When H. Rider Haggard's novel *She* was published in 1887 it drew the world's attention to Modjadji, the hereditary 'Rain Queen' who ruled a section of what is now Lebowa.

Modjadji's kraal is set in mountainous country north-east of Duiwelskloof and to this day her subjects stand in awe of her. On the mountain top above the kraal is a 305 ha forest of 'Modjadji palms' – actually the cycad *Encephalartos transvenosus* – which have special significance in Modjadji's rain-making formula and as a result are jealously conserved by the royal family.

The forest, which has been a national monument since 1936, was proclaimed a nature reserve in 1985. It seems set to become Lebowa's principal reserve with a rest camp being planned for the future. A network of trails (about 4 hours duration in total), an information centre and a picnic area with toilet facilities have already been developed and indigenous game, such as impala, blue wildebeest, nyala and kudu, re-introduced.

The 'Modjadji palm', one of the world's largest cycads, grows to heights of three or four metres, with magnificent specimens sometimes reaching eight metres.

The route to the Modjadji Nature Reserve is well signposted from the scenic Pietersburg-Duiwelskloof road. For additional information contact The Secretary, Department of the Chief Minister, Division of Land Affairs and Tourism, Private Bag X27, Chuenespoort 0745, Lebowa (telephone Chuenespoort 3-5516/7/8).

Nzhelele Nature Reserve

In 1954 the Transvaal Division of Nature Conservation established a 25 ha nature reserve on a peninsula in Nzhelele Dam, about 55 km north-east of Louis Trichardt. The reserve became popular with anglers and remains so, though today it is within the Republic of Venda and is managed by Venda's Nature Conservation Administration and covers a much larger area of some 2 000 hectares.

Anglers need a Venda fishing permit, which can be obtained from the Venda Nature Conservation Administration or any Venda magistrate. To reach Nzhelele, take the road from Louis Trichardt to Messina and follow the signs. For further information, write to The Secretary, Department of Environmental and Water Affairs, Private Bag X2503, Sibasa, Venda (telephone Sibasa 3-1001).

Above: The lesser bushbaby's night vision is very good, and it can leap a considerable distance in the dark in perfect safety. **Left:** The barred owl is fairly common in the denser acacia bush of the north-eastern Transvaal – especially along rivers. It eats insects and small vertebrates such as mice and lizards. **Below:** A praying mantis devours a painted lady butterfly (it is perched on a *Euphorbia cooperii*). The mantis' jaws are capable of reducing bees and wasps to a mince. It is also known to feed on its own kind – even after copulation.

Nwanedi National Park

Nzhelele Dam was completed in 1948, and a few years later South Africa's Department of Water Affairs began work on an unusual development some 30 km to the north-east, where the Nwanedi and Luphephe (pronounced *Lu-pe-pe*) rivers emerged from hills and joined forces to flow north to the mighty Limpopo River. Just above the confluence, the department built twin dam walls (one for each river), and in the process created two new lakes. The dams were completed in 1960 and before long became firm favourites with local anglers, picnickers and scores of tourists.

Like Nzhelele, the two dams were included in the area set aside as a 'homeland', eventually becoming part of the territory of the Republic of Venda. In 1979 the Venda Government set aside 12 500 ha as the Nwanedi National Park and a Pietersburg firm began erecting a perimeter game fence.

In 1981 the reserve was proclaimed as Nwanedi National Park. Its game population is small, but visitors are compensated by fine scenery, including the dams and the Tshihovhovhohovho Falls on the Luphephe River.

Visitors may spot kudu, impala, duiker, warthog, nyala, and zebra, blue wildebeest and eland (the park's cheetah and lion are penned in special camps).

NWANEDI AT A GLANCE

When to go The park is open daily from 6 a.m. to 6 p.m. (game viewing is best in winter).

Reservations To make a booking, or for further enquiries write to The Secretary, Central Reservations, Venda Tourism, P.O. Box 9, Sibasa, Venda (telephone Sibasa 4-1577 and for last minute bookings to the Venda Development Corporation (telephone Tshipise 723).

Getting there Follow the provincial road running east of Tshipise and turn right after 24 km; then take the dirt road for 13 km to reach the park gate.

Accommodation The park offers accommodation in a small hotel, luxury rondavels with four beds, kitchenette, bathroom and toilet and ordinary rondavels served by an ablution block.

Getting around There are access roads to angling sites on the dams and also several game-viewing drives. On request the park provides visitors with a guide who takes them to the lion and cheetah camps and the Tshihovhohovho Falls.

Wildlife Apart from lion and cheetah penned in camps, the park features kudu, impala, duiker, warthog, red hartebeest, waterbuck, nyala, eland, blue wildebeest and zebra. A big attraction is the white rhino which have been introduced.

Fishing There is fine fishing in the two dams – bream, yellowfish, barbel and tigerfish. Venda fishing permits are available at the park office.

West of Kruger

West of the Kruger National Park are three private nature reserves that are believed to be the largest such sanctuaries in the world: Klaserie, Sabi Sand and Timbavati. Each reserve consists of a number of independent game properties whose owners elect a joint policy committee and employ a warden and ranging staff. There are no fences between the farms, and game wanders freely from property to property. However, there is a fence around the perimeter and access is restricted to those with special permission.

Most landowners in the three reserves live far from the Lowveld but maintain private camps that they and their guests visit at irregular intervals. To help defray their heavy expenses, a handful of the owners in Sabi Sand and Timbavati operate game lodges or camps for paying guests or allow a tenant to run such a lodge on their property. The lodges generally tend to be exclusive and expensive but they enable those people who can afford the tariffs to enjoy some of the densest game concentrations – animals include lion, elephant, rhino and leopard – in the Lowveld.

The private game lodges in Sabi Sand Private Nature Reserve include Inyati, two at Londolozi and four at Rattray Reserves – Mala Mala, Kirkman's Kamp, Harry's Huts and Trekker Trails. The lodges in Timbavati Private Nature Reserve are Tanda Tula, Ngala and Cheetah Trails. (Just outside the reserve in Umbabat is Motswari M'Bali, but guests tour Timbavati by arrangement). Klaserie has a tented camp which is attached to the privately run Klaserie Lowveld Trail.

West of Timbavati is Thornybush and Matumi, while to the north lies Tshukudu Game Lodge. Tucked between Timbavati and Sabi Sand and adjoining the Kruger Park is Manyeleti Game Reserve. This and Andover Game Reserve are administered by Gazankulu. Near the Kruger Park's southern tip is Mthethomusha Game Reserve, the Lowveld National Botanic Garden and Nelspruit and Komatipoort nature reserves.

Andover Game Reserve

With over 7 000 ha of marula-dotted parkland, Andover Game Reserve provides an ideal setting for wildlife photographers, or gametrackers. An armed guard will always be close at hand as white rhino and elephant are resident in the reserve. Other game to be seen include wildebeest, impala and hippo.

The reserve, which is administered by Gazankulu, lies some 30 km from the western edge of Kruger Park between Orpen Gate and Hoedspruit. Visitors are accommodated in 6 two-bedded rondavels, which are self-catering. A rustic camp is being developed, but no camping is permitted.

The best time for you to visit the reserve is from May to August, to escape the searing summer temperatures. For booking and enquiries write to The Officer-in-Charge, Andover Game Reserve, P.O. Box 70, Klaserie 1381 or c/o Department of Chief Minister and Economic Affairs, Private Bag 573, Giyani 0826 (telephone Giyani 2-3131).

Above left: A wild dog (sometimes known as hunting dog) at Klaserie. They are found in packs or groups of up to 40 animals. The principal prey is medium-sized ungulates such as impala, waterbuck and gazelles (sometimes the young of larger antelope). Healthy adults can live for up to 12 years. **Above right:** A cluster of nests built by lesser masked weaver birds in the eastern Transvaal. This species builds its strong, kidney-shaped nest from leaves or strips of reed, suspending the structure from a tree — sometimes overhanging a river or stream. **Left:** A black monkey orange in the Lowveld Botanic Garden. This tree generally grows to about 6 m in height and occurs in riverine fringes, koppies and open woodland. **Opposite page:** The flap-necked chameleon is found all over the Lowveld. Chameleons can produce an impressive display when angered or threatened: the lungs inflate until the body swells enormously, the throat is distended and the mouth opens wide to expose the red interior.

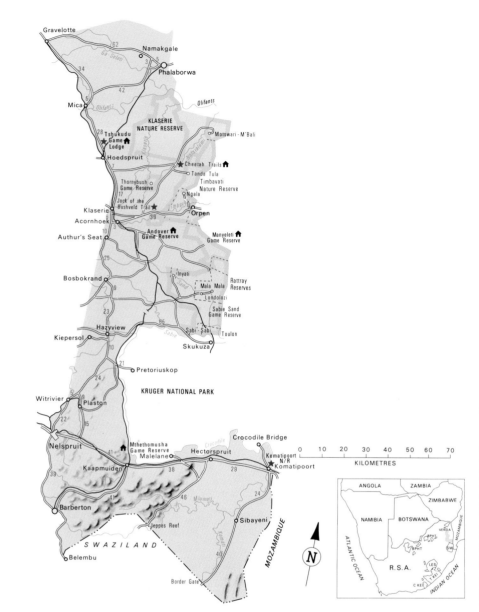

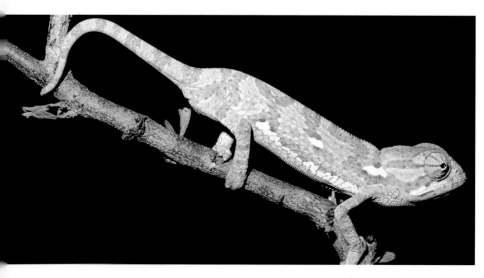

Jock of the Bushveld Trail

Operated by the Wilderness Leadership School, this 5-day trail is run in an area of the Lowveld along the Timbavati River. Hikers see a variety of big game and bird species along the route, which begins at Hoedspruit.

The organisers provide sleeping bags, groundsheets, tents, transport, meals and all necessary utensils. Participants are advised to take anti-malaria precautions before entering the area. To book a place on the trail, you should write to The Wilderness Leadership School, P.O. Box 87230, Houghton 2041 (telephone Johannesburg 453-1462).

Klaserie Private Nature Reserve

The absence of commercial game lodges makes Klaserie the least known of the 'big three' private reserves. Klaserie is 30 km long and 25 km wide and covers about 60 000 ha on either side of the Klaserie River, a tributary of the Olifants. The eastern edge of the sanctuary adjoins Timbavati Reserve.

Recent game counts show that Klaserie contains some 30 000 larger mammals, including 20 000 impala, 6 000 blue wildebeest, 2 300 zebra, more than 1 500 giraffe and more than 100 elephant.

Short of being invited as a guest of a landowner (the reserve is shared by over 100 owners), the only way members of the public may visit Klaserie is by way of the five-day Klaserie Lowveld Trail organised by Educational Wildlife Expeditions (also known as Clive Walker Trails), a non-profit organisation based in Johannesburg. Participants leave a Johannesburg hotel at 6 a.m. on a Thursday and travel by minibus to Klaserie via the scenic Strydom Tunnel. They have time for a late afternoon walk along the banks of the Klaserie River before returning to their 'Elephant' tented camp on the Klaserie River in time for a shower, sundowners and a relaxed supper.

Days two to four are spent mainly on foot in the reserve observing and having the secrets of the bush explained by an experienced field officer. As a bonus, visitors may encounter elephant, rhino, buffalo and lion. Walks are usually confined to the cooler hours of the day. Weather permitting, one night is spent out in the bush away from the tented camp (only sleeping bags and food are taken). This 'night out' is the highlight for many visitors.

On the fifth day the party returns to Johannesburg. Each trail is limited to eight people and is led by an armed field officer. All food and camping equipment is provided and the visitors need only take boots, clothing, binoculars, insect repellent and beverages. For more information, write to Educational Wildlife Expeditions, P.O. Box 645, Bedfordview 2008 (telephone Johannesburg 53-1814).

Komatipoort Nature Reserve

Situated at the confluence of the Crocodile and Komati rivers, this 93 ha reserve offers good fishing and excellent bird-watching. The river banks are covered by thick vegetation and conceal small bushbuck and other woodland species of animals.

You are advised to stay well back from the water's edge as the rivers here are infested with crocodiles. Local tribespeople are frequently taken in this area by these reptilian giants, in which case nature conservation officers invariably are obliged to track down and shoot the animal responsible.

For more information write to The Chief Directorate of Nature and Environmental Conservation, P.O. Box 1232, Nelspruit 1200 (telephone Nelspruit 2-8491).

Lowveld National Botanic Garden

In 1969 the Nelspruit Municipality and a local citrus-producer provided 154 ha of land on the banks of the Crocodile and Nels rivers for a Lowveld garden, a regional garden of the National Botanic Gardens.

The Crocodile River sweeps through this garden from west to east, on the way negotiating the spectacular Nelspruit Cascades, and is joined by the Nels River (from the north) by way of the Nels River Falls. The cascades are most impressive during the summer rainy season, when the rivers are in flood.

Much of the Lowveld garden remains pure wilderness. A granite koppie lying north of the Crocodile River has been left intact, and on the south bank the 1,5 km River Trail meanders along the steep cliff face and through the forest overhanging the Nelspruit Cascades. A plant survey commissioned when the garden opened has shown that at least 500 different species are indigenous to the Nelspruit area. Only 22 ha are in any way developed, and they feature species drawn from all over the Lowveld, and from the slopes of the Drakensberg.

Among the trees to be seen here are kiaat, paperback thorn tree, yellow fever tree and wild pear. Flowers include the impala lily, Barberton daisy and pride-of-De-Kaap, and these are at their best in the summer months when the garden is open daily from 8 a.m. to 6 p.m. During winter the garden is open from 8 a.m. to 5.15 p.m. To reach the garden, follow the signs from the centre of Nelspruit.

Manyeleti Game Reserve

During the early 1960s the South African Government began buying up white-owned farms adjoining the Kruger National Park for the purpose of resettling local families. One owner refused to sell his farm unless the Government undertook to turn it into a nature reserve. The result is Manyeleti.

The terrain and vegetation is much like that of the Kruger Park, as is its population of larger mammals – among them more than 5 000 impala, 350 blue wildebeest, 450 zebra, 150 giraffe and 200 buffalo. The reserve's predators include cheetah, leopard and up to 50 lion, but for most of Manyeleti's visitors these are eclipsed by the massive dignity of the occasional elephant. The only species which have been reintroduced to Manyeleti are white rhino (which have flourished) and sable (rather less successful).

Manyeleti's staff present a variety of video and slide lectures to the schoolchildren who comprise some 60 per cent of Manyeleti's visitors. The children sleep in six special dormitories in the reserve's rest camp. The reserve attracts upwards of 22 000 people a year. The rest camp offers visitors both luxury and standard rondavels, a restaurant, bar, shop, post office, bottle store and filling station.

Two additional camps at Manyeleti provide visitors with back-to-nature wildlife experiences – with the emphasis on walking trails in the company of armed, professional rangers. There are also game drives after dark in 4-wheel-drive vehicles. Khoka Moya Camp can accommodate up to eight people (in four *en suite*

NATURE'S AMAZING DO-IT-YOURSELF PROGRAMME

A lesser masked weaver constructs its nest at the end of a slender branch. The finished product is sturdy and secure from most predators.

For a species to survive, it must breed. But the newly born animal is especially vulnerable to predators, and surviving the first few days of life is the weakest link in almost every animal's life cycle. Birds have a particularly tough time: they are first locked away inside an egg; then must survive for a while longer as a nestling – unable to fly, and clearly not equipped for defence. A host of wild creatures dine on eggs and nestlings – rats, cats, mongooses, snakes and many others.

Even a nest built high in a tree is far from safe: many predators can climb trees. So the weaver bird's answer to the problem is a hanging nest tied securely to the end of a long, slender twig that would pose difficulties even for a snake. The ball-shaped nest is so constructed that it cannot be entered from the twig to which it is attached: the only way to get in is to fly through the air or enter from below while clinging to the supporting twig – a trick that only certain snakes have mastered. In addition to protecting the young from predators,

a nest such as this offers shelter from rain and the merciless heat of the summer sun. But the greater marvel is invisible – the extent to which the entire programme for building such a nest has been encoded into the weaver bird's genetic blueprint.

The nest is mainly the work of the male bird. The energetic little home-builder first selects a suitable site, then begins to twist and knot pieces of grass and leaves around a supporting twig. He flies back and forth with strands of grass in his bill, tucking each new piece into the existing structure, then flying around to the opposite side and pulling the loose end through. Again and again he holds, tucks, twists and pulls, and in this way creates an amazingly sturdy piece of tightly knotted basketwork.

Once the main framework is in place, an inner lining is moulded into a smooth-walled chamber. By the time the building stops, a complete little home has been constructed, conforming exactly to the age old design typical of the particular species.

wooden 'bandas'), Honeyguide up to 12 (in six *en suite*, luxury tents). For more information, you can write to Safariplan/Gametrackers, P.O. Box 4245, Randburg 2125 (telephone Johannesburg 886-1810).

Manyeleti lies 45km east of Acornhoek in Gazankulu and is signposted from the tarred road between Acornhoek and Orpen Gate. For further information, write to The Manager, Manyeleti Game Reserve, P.O. Manyeleti 1362 (telephone Manyeleti 3).

Matumi Game Lodge
Bring a sleeping bag if you want to take up one of the options at Matumi Game Lodge: a night spent in a bush lapa, with your guide and a fire for protection. Should the spine-chilling laughter of hyenas – and other assorted wildlife noises – disturb your sleep, that's part of the bush experience.

Accommodation at the lodge itself comprises 2 six-bed and 12 four-bed chalets situated on the banks of the Klaserie River. The river offers excellent fishing (barbel, bream, yellowfish), and the dense vegetation on its banks provides a haven for bird- and insect-life. Game-viewing trips take place in open Land-Rovers, while for the hiking enthusiast there are bush trails.

A swimming pool and a recreation hall are among the many other facilities at Matumi. For further information you can write to Matumi Game Lodge, P.O. Box 57, Klaserie, 1381 (telephone Hoedspruit 4313).

Motswari-M'Bali
Opened in 1977, Motswari Game Lodge and its sister camp, M'Bali offer visitors luxurious base camps from which they can set out to discover the game and bird species of the internationally-renowned Timbavati and Umbabat private nature reserves.

Motswari accommodates a maximum of 26 guests in luxurious thatched rondavels, which overlook a dam on the Sohebele River. M'Bali, which is reminiscent of Ernest Hemingway's hideaway in Africa, consists of seven tents, raised above the ground to ensure maximum comfort for its guests.

Two game drives are conducted daily in open 4-wheel-drive vehicles under the guidance of professional game rangers who will also take you on walks through the bush. You can also relax in a hide beside a waterhole and observe a variety of mammals and birds coming to drink.

Both camps have swimming pools and are well known for their excellent cuisine (three full meals are served daily).

For further information or bookings, you should write to Motswari Game Lodges, P.O. Box 67865, Bryanston 2021 (telephone Johannesburg 463-1990/1 or 706-3225).

Above: A giraffe and its offspring in the Manyeleti Game Reserve adjoining the Kruger National Park. These huge creatures have only one natural enemy – the lion. Although the giraffe's large hoofs are formidable weapons it usually defends itself by running away (an adult can reach a speed of about 50 km/h). Lion sometimes kill giraffe by surrounding them and tiring them out, and individual lion have been known to clamber up their victim's back and dispatch them with a bite in the neck. **Right above:** A sulphur butterfly, typical of the many beautiful species of butterfly in the Eastern Transvaal Lowveld. **Right below:** Termite workers remove newly laid eggs from the grossly swollen body of the queen. Termites (often referred to incorrectly as 'white ants') have evolved a highly complex social system which regulates the lives of every individual in a colony which may consist of hundreds of thousands. Their fortress-like mounds, a familiar sight in many parts of Southern Africa, are considered by entomologists to be the oldest examples of organised communities in existence.

Mthethomusha Game Reserve

It's hard to believe that the rolling hills of Mthethomusha at the tip of Kruger Park were once exploited as farming land.

Fortunately, it is restored to its original splendour as a wilderness area. Kangwane Parks Board has restocked the reserve with white rhino, giraffe, zebra, antelope and smaller animals. Among the kiaat trees, giant sycamores, marulas and *Erythrina* with their brilliant scarlet blooms, birds of prey such as bateleur and crowned eagle may be seen.

While picnic sites and game-viewing hides are provided for day visitors, overnight guests to Mthethomusha may stay in a luxury privately run game lodge which can comfortably accommodate up to 60 people.

To maintain the wilderness atmosphere at Mthethomusha, private vehicles are not permitted beyond the picnic and parking areas, instead professional guides show visitors around in 4-wheel-drive vehicles.

For more information, write to Kangwane Parks Board, P.O. Box 1990, Nelspruit 1200 (telephone Nelspruit 5-3931/2).

Nelspruit Nature Reserve

A kloof in the hills overlooking Nelspruit from the north-east contains this 50 ha reserve. It is long and narrow, and within it is the Green Heritage Trail, a gentle walk along the bottom of the kloof. To reach the reserve, drive south from the town hall to Van Wyk Street, then into Waterbok Street, right into Impala Street and down to the entrance gate in the kloof.

The reserve is noted for its indigenous Lowveld trees and shrubs, and visitors may spot bushbuck, klipspringer and duiker. It is open all year, from 7a.m. to 5p.m.

Sabi Sand Private Nature Reserve

Although Klaserie has no game lodges at all, and Timbavati's are small and unobtrusive, at Sabi Sand the situation is completely different. There the various private lodges are spread over nearly three-quarters of the beautiful sanctuary's 60 000 ha.

Over the years they have evolved a daily programme that keeps their guests busy from dawn until well after dark. In summer, the visitors are woken at about 5.30a.m. and served tea or coffee and rusks before setting out on an early morning game drive. They might have breakfast in the bush, but whatever happens, they will return to camp before the heat becomes oppressive. They spend the rest of the morning on an escorted walk, in a hide, or just lazing in camp.

Some guests take a nap after lunch while others relax at the swimming pool. After tea there is another game drive which continues until 'sundowner' time and perhaps later, in

which case guests watch for game by spotlight. Dinner is served in an open-air lapa, or boma, a circular meeting-place ringed by tall reeds and open to the stars, with a blazing log fire in the middle and the guests seated at a circle of small tables. After dinner there may be another game drive by spotlight (though many guests will opt for a relatively early night).

In winter the morning drive begins after breakfast and may continue until lunchtime, while the afternoon drive will certainly end after dark. In both winter and summer, a guest's average stay is three days and two nights.

Sabi Sand: Inyati

Situated in north-western Sabi Sand, Inyati comprises nine exclusive, thatched chalets, which are scattered among manicured lawns overlooking the Sand River.

The highlight for most people who visit private game reserves is the game-viewing safaris in open 4-wheel-drive vehicles. Inyati is no exception. Accompanied by a tracker and an armed ranger you will have an excellent chance of spotting rhino, elephant, buffalo, lion and leopard. And if that's not enough excitement for one day you can also arrange night

TALL AS THE TREES

Giraffe gather at a waterhole in the Timbavati Private Nature Reserve.

A fully grown bull giraffe is the tallest creature on earth, soaring to a full six metres on its stilt-like legs. It is also one of the four largest land animals, weighing in at 1,5 tons.

Yet despite its bulk this gentle giant blends almost perfectly with its surroundings, the patchwork hide matching the sun-dappled thorn trees of the African savanna so perfectly that it is possible to walk past an entire herd of giraffe without noticing them.

The giraffe's long neck is a classic example of form being moulded by natural selection: the taller individuals could eat leaves and shoots that were beyond the reach of shorter giraffe, and therefore enjoyed a larger food supply.

Their ability to feed more easily, and their improved chances of survival in the lean seasons, enabled the taller giraffes to breed more successfully – thus concentrating in the ancestral gene pool those particular genes which made them grow tall.

While the advantages of such a long neck are fairly obvious, the biological engineering problems which had to be overcome in its design are perhaps less apparent.

Like any other mammal, including man, the giraffe has only seven vertebrae in its neck,

but these have become enormously elongated, and are attached to one another with ball and socket joints that give the whole structure flexibility. The giraffe also has a unique 'plumbing' system: to pump blood 2,5m uphill to the brain, it has had to develop a large heart, with walls more than 7cm thick.

To make matters more difficult, Nature had to find a way of controlling the flow of this blood; otherwise, every time the giraffe lowered its head, the rush of blood to the brain would knock the animal unconscious. To solve this problem the giraffe maintains an aortic blood pressure twice that found in man.

The jugular vein (which returns blood from the brain to the heart) has a series of one-way valves that prevent the blood from flowing back to the brain when the head is lowered, and the huge carotid artery which carries oxygenated blood from the heart to the brain, divides into a great network of lesser blood vessels before it actually reaches the brain.

This structure is known as a *rete mirabile* (wondrous net) and as it passes through a pool of cool venous blood which has drained from the nasal sinuses, it acts as a heat exchanger, thereby keeping the giraffe's brain cool.

safaris, guided walks and fishing trips (within earshot of harrumphing hippo).

Visitors enjoy sumptuous meals served in a central dining room, while at night braais are served in a boma around a campfire. There is a swimming pool.

Inyati has its own airstrip. Motorists can reach it via a turn-off on the Hazyview-Skukuza road. For booking and further information, write to Inyati Game Lodge, P.O. Box 783365, Sandton 2146 (telephone Johannesburg 883-5458).

Sabi Sand: Londolozi

In the middle of Sabi Sand is Londolozi Game Reserve, the creation of brothers John and Dave Varty. Starting in the early 1970s with four primitive rondavels, they gradually extended and improved the camp as funds allowed. Before long Londolozi became one of the most popular lodges in the Lowveld.

Londolozi is a Zulu word meaning 'protector of living things', and that has been the lodge's aim from the outset. The Vartys have involved themselves in a host of projects ranging from rescuing endangered cheetah (and releasing them in Sabi Sand) to introducing 34 elephant cows in a bid to start a breeding herd. They have publicised some of their projects by enlisting the help of show business celebrities, and Londolozi is as famous for beautiful people as it is for beautiful animals.

The main camp at Londolozi accommodates up to 24 people in tree-shaded chalets and the four original rondavels – greatly improved since the early days. The chalets and the lodge's fine diningroom overlook lush riverine vegetation in the bed of the Sand River. Separate from the main camp but only 1 km upstream is a luxury bush camp with accommodation for eight people. It has its own ranger and a Land-Rover. For the ultimate wildlife experience there is a tree camp, which offers accommodation for eight people.

For further information or bookings, write to Londolozi Game Reserve, 26 Stanley Avenue, Auckland Park 2092 (telephone Johannesburg 726-7360 or Skukuza 6-5653).

Above: A leopard, ever watchful, rests in dry grass at the Londolozi Game Reserve, in the eastern Transvaal. Leopards are rarely seen by the casual visitor to parks and reserves, as they are predominantly nocturnal by nature — and masters of camouflage. **Right:** A long-tailed shrike. This bird is common to thornveld savanna such as that found in the eastern Transvaal, building its nest on a forked branch of a thorn tree. It usually produces four or five eggs. Long-tailed shrikes live on insects and small reptiles such as lizards.

Sabi Sand: Rattray Reserves

Only a few minutes' drive from Londolozi is Mala Mala, the flagship of four camps that comprise Rattray Reserves. Sited within an oxbow in the Sand River, Mala Mala is both the longest established and most expensive of the Lowveld private camps, and is proud of its reputation for luxury and exclusivity. The camp accommodates up to 50 guests, who are easily outnumbered by the staff, among them 10 highly trained rangers whose job it is to anticipate their guests' every need.

At first sight Mala Mala seems much like other lodges, but there are differences. The luxury huts at Mala Mala each have two bathrooms, so enabling couples to prepare at leisure for the early morning game drive. Each ranger is allocated two Land-Rovers – one open vehicle for regular use and the other closed for use in rainy weather.

Rattray Reserves extend over 45 000 ha, so Mala Mala's game drives are not limited by lack of space. Rangers take special pride in showing their guests the big five species that so fascinated the hunters of the 19th century: lion, leopard, elephant, rhino and buffalo. At the end of 1981 Mala Mala launched a 'Big Five Club' with automatic membership and a certificate for guests who scored a 'grand slam' in game-viewing. Within three weeks, the membership stood at more than two hundred.

Mala Mala's high tariffs appear to hold no terrors for overseas guests, but they tend to intimidate South Africans. To attract more local customers, Rattray Reserves offer three other choices, each bearing the stamp of Mala Mala professionalism: the opulent Kirkman's Kamp on the Sand River, a farmhouse and cottages decorated in the style of the 1920s; the medium-priced Harry's Huts, also on the river and a favourite with young people; and Trekker Trails (for the budget conscious), a bush camp offering only foot safaris. The bush camp accommodates six guests at a time (they prepare their own meals). Kirkman's Kamp accommodates 20 guests and Harry's Huts 14 guests: each has its own rangers and own Land-Rovers. For further information on the Rattray Reserves, write to Reservations, P.O. Box 2575, Randburg 2125 (telephone Johannesburg 789-2677/8/9).

Sabi Sand: Sabi Sabi Game Reserve

Visitors to Sabi Sabi have a choice between two luxury lodges from which to explore the animal-filled paradise of Sabi Sand Game Reserve. Each offers a unique wildlife experience. River Lodge overlooks the Sabie River, where hippo and crocodile abound, while Bush Lodge lies 10 km to the north in typical Lowveld thornveld where the lion is king.

The main attraction of both camps is game-viewing drives (day and night) in open 4-wheel-drive vehicles. The reserve's prolific wildlife includes lion, buffalo, leopard, cheetah, giraffe and over 350 species of bird.

Both camps offer luxury two-bedded rondavels, a swimming pool, conference facilities and a 'bundu' shop stocked with African curios. You will be pampered during your stay and enjoy excellent cuisine. South African breakfasts and buffet lunches are served on the safari terrace, while venison and braai dinners are enjoyed in the open air boma.

Both lodges are reached via a signposted turn-off 37 km from Hazyview on the Hazyview-Skukuza road. Accommodation is limited (River Lodge 40; Bush Lodge 50) so booking is essential. For more information write to Sabi Sabi Game Reserve, P.O. Box 52665, Saxonwold 2132 (telephone Johannesburg 88-4840).

Thornybush Game Lodge

Lowveld old-timers will remember the days when the eastern Transvaal was virtually fence-free and the abundance of game could wander wherever it wanted to go. 'Since then the area has been chopped up into little boxes,' says Frank Dyason, who runs Thornybush Game Lodge on what used to be his family's private hunting farm. 'We're supposed to be fenced all round – but elephant have broken through in several places, and my neighbours now agree that we should leave the game to migrate as it likes. We haven't tried to repair the damage.'

Like other Lowveld lodges, Thornybush offers scenic game drives in open Land-Rovers in the early morning and late afternoon. The lodge has traversing rights over neighbouring properties and the more than 4 000 ha is open for game drives.

An additional attraction is an after-dinner visit to Thornybush's 50 ha cheetah enclosure. A Land-Rover carrying meat as 'bait' is driven

through the enclosure. It is a familiar routine for the cheetah, which are clearly illuminated by spotlights as they run alongside. The cheetahs' dinner is then tied to a peg on the ground, providing visitors with a unique opportunity to photograph them as they eat.

But there is a lot more to the cheetah of Thornybush than an entertaining show for the guests. The ruthlessness of these fleet-footed animals was demonstrated in quite dramatic fashion one night in 1981.

Frank Dyason tells how a cheetah, named after him, dominated all the others with the help of two elderly consorts.

'When Frank's supporters died, the balance of power shifted,' said Dyason. 'I put Frank in a separate enclosure for his own protection. But the other cheetahs managed to break in. They then proceeded to kill and eat him. Next morning, only his head and part of his shoulder were left.'

Thornybush's main camp consists of comfortable thatched rondavels, a thatched restaurant, lounge and bar complex (the bar is home to a tame warthog named Miss Piggy) and a picturesque boma.

Above left: A male waterbuck in the Mala Mala Game Reserve, near the western border of the Kruger National Park. The waterbuck seldom moves far from its home territory. When hunted it may seek refuge in water, sometimes hiding in reeds with most of its body submerged. **Above right:** A female waterbuck lacks horns and is generally smaller and lighter than the male. **Left:** Buffalo in the Mala Mala Game Reserve. These large, powerful creatures are frequently a match for lions, which prefer to attack females and their young. Because they have a large daily liquid intake, buffalo seldom stray far from water. **Right above:** A bloom of *Gardenia spatulifolia* in the Mala Mala Game Reserve. This shrub may grow up to 5 m in height. **Right below:** A shield bug. These brightly coloured insects (sometimes known as 'stink bugs' because they produce an unpleasant odour if roughly handled) are common throughout Southern Africa. They can seriously damage fruit crops if left unchecked.

Besides its own attractions, Thornybush offers one-day trips to the Kruger Park or Klaserie Dam (rich in waterfowl), or otherwise a trip to the forests of Mariepskop on the slopes of the Transvaal Drakensberg (visible to the west). Thornybush has its own airstrip, but most guests arriving by air take scheduled flights to Phalaborwa, where they are collected by car.

Motorists trying to find their own way to Thornybush will be frustrated by signless roads and should telephone Hoedspruit 2602 for detailed directions. The lodge's mailing address is P.O. Box 169, Hoedspruit 1380.

Timbavati Private Nature Reserve
The third of the Lowveld's great private sanctuaries dates from the mid 1950s, when a landowner named Peter Mostert urged his neighbours to help create a 'private Kruger Park' for their mutual benefit.

The various Timbavati farms are the property of more than 30 separate landowners, who have made a point of banning professional trophy-hunting on the reserve and pooled resources to reintroduce important species like white rhino and sable, and to give Timbavati's cheetah population a healthy boost.

Among Timbavati's claims to fame are white lion (also found in the Kruger Park) and what is said to be the densest giraffe population in the world (though there is another impressive giraffe population in the Klaserie reserve across the provincial road to the west). The reserve also has 13 000 impala, 4 500 blue wildebeest, 2 500 zebra, 100 buffalo, about 100 elephant (including a few breeding herds), a number of kudu and waterbuck, predators, small mammals, and a bird population that for many visitors is the greatest drawcard.

Timbavati: Cheetah Trails
Game drives at Cheetah Trails – a private game lodge in Timbavati Private Nature Reserve – mean bundu-bashing in sturdy 4-wheel-drive vehicles until you can literally smell the lion, cheetah or hyena. It is an exhilarating experience guaranteed to ruin ordinary game drives forever.

On night drives you will glimpse nocturnal animals like leopard, civet and genet caught in the beam of a powerful spotlight.

The small rustic lodge has comfortable rooms with *en suite* bathrooms, and although there is no electricity, water is heated in the traditional bushveld manner and lights are battery powered. Meals are sumptuous and are served in a boma around a camp fire.

For a wilder experience (although you will be accompanied by a ranger and tracker) visitors may stay at Khankhanka ('cheetah' in Shangaan), an attractive bush camp beside the Nharalumi River.

To make enquiries and bookings write to Cheetah Trails, P.O. Box 721, Riverclub 2149. (telephone Johannesburg 706-2692).

Timbavati: Ngala Game Lodge
Nearly all of the Lowveld's private lodges adopt one or other wildlife emblem to adorn their stationery, their vehicles and their staff members' epaulettes. Sabi Sabi's emblem is an elephant, Mala Mala has a sable and Thornybush a leopard.

A luxurious new game lodge, which was opened in the south of Timbavati in 1981, was named Ngala, the Shangaan word for lion, so the lodge appropriately chose as its emblem the lion's four-toed pug (footprint).

Many treats await visitors to Ngala, but nothing compares to that first, close encounter with an elephant bull, or the heart-stopping thrill of spotting a lion less than 3 m away. Visitors explore in 4-wheel-drive vehicles, on day and night safaris, or on foot, accompanied by an armed ranger, to get an even closer feel of the real Africa. However, if you really want to take it easy, you can even watch game from the comfort of the lodge's relaxing lounge which overlooks a waterhole.

45

The lodge provides luxurious air-conditioned accommodation for a maximum of 32 guests. It has a swimming pool, landing strip and conference centre catering for up to 28 delegates.

To reach Ngala, enter Timbavati from a turn-off (signposted 'Argyle') 6,6 km from Hoedspruit on the Hoedspruit-Acornhoek road. After 31 km along this road, follow signs to Ngala.

For bookings and further information, write to Ngala Central Reservations, Club Africa Pavilion, P.O. Box 4068, Rivonia 2128 (telephone Johannesburg 803-7400). There are two scheduled flights a day to Ngala (contact Comair), and the lodge operates 'fly in safaris'.

Timbavati: Tanda Tula Game Lodge

Tanda Tula is a small and exclusive lodge whose three rangers tailor programmes to their guests' individual requirements.

Its main camp is a complex of thatched chalets (with accommodation for 14 people) set around a swimming pool. The game drives range over 7 000 ha of varied terrain, and a speciality is a daily 'bush breakfast' served during the morning expedition. Occasionally the lodge organises a surprise 'bush supper' to coincide with the full moon. To reach Tanda Tula, enter Timbavati by the main gate on the road to Shlaralumi and follow the signs. For further information, write to Safariplan, P.O. Box 4245, Randburg 2125 (telephone Johannesburg 886-1810) or otherwise telephone the lodge through Hoedspruit 2322.

Tshukudu Game Lodge

Imagine a star-filled African sky; the sizzle of venison steaks in a boma braai; orphaned animals roaming freely about a camp; and mouth-watering 'African home cooking'. These are just some of the memories that visitors to Tshukudu Game Lodge near Hoedspruit, have taken home with them.

No more than 16 visitors are allowed at a time on the 5 000 ha reserve, which allows complete privacy for the guests.

Among the activities offered is a ride with an armed ranger in an open vehicle, through countryside known for its lion, leopard, cheetah, giraffe, kudu, zebra and rhino. The more adventurous can hike along a trail so narrow 'that you can almost feel the animals' presence'. However, those who wish to laze around the camp all day are free to do so, too. At Tshukudu, the guests themselves decide what they want to do.

Accommodation is in a comfortable rondavel with private facilities. A bush camp for the adventurous, a cheaper alternative to the Game Lodge, takes a minimum of four people.

For bookings and details, write to The Director, Tshukudu Game Lodge, P.O. Box 289, Hoedspruit 1380 (telephone Hoedspruit 6313).

Above: A rare white lion cub in the Timbavati Private Nature Reserve. Its brother (background) has conventional colouring. **Right above:** A broad-nosed weevil in the eastern Transvaal bush. If threatened, a weevil will immediately sham death by falling on its side and extending its legs. This is an automatic reflex triggered by the insect's nervous system. Weevils make up the largest of the beetle families – indeed, the largest animal family – in the world. There are more than 2 500 species in Southern Africa alone. The 'snout' or rostrum at the front of the head varies in shape and size among different species – from short and squat, to long and narrow. Weevils enjoy an unenviable reputation for being pests. They are perhaps most notorious for destroying stored grain. Many cultivated plants are at risk. **Right below:** The lucky bean creeper is a familiar sight throughout the eastern Transvaal Lowveld, and its seeds are very poisonous. This specimen was photographed in the Timbavati Private Nature Reserve.

Kingdom of the wild

Swaziland's coat of arms consists of the Swazi royal shield supported by a lion on the left and an elephant on the right. The lion represents Swaziland's king, who traditionally looks after warfare, hunting and other manly pursuits. The elephant represents the queen mother, who by Swazi custom wields nearly as much authority as the king. She operates an appeal court over unpopular judgements given by the king, governs internal relations, and acts as custodian of the ritual rain-making equipment.

While the lion is no longer found in this charming country elephant have been re-introduced after a 100-year absence. Swaziland is also home to other fascinating species of animals, including leopard, cheetah, white rhino, buffalo, giraffe and a wide range of antelope. They can be seen to advantage in the kingdom's variety of game parks and nature reserves.

King Sobhuza II has recognised the importance of protecting the wildlife of Swaziland and some 4 per cent of the country is now protected, administered either privately or through the Swaziland government. Altogether six areas are open to the public.

The Mlilwane Wildlife Sanctuary, south of Mbabane, was established in 1960 and has long been a favourite of both local people and tourists from outside. Hlane Game Sanctuary in the Lowveld to the east, belongs to the king, who holds it in trust for the nation (part of this land is the royal hunting preserve). Mlawula Nature Reserve lies north-east of Hlane on the Swaziland border, while in the north-west the Malolotja Nature Reserve offers some of the most spectacular scenery in Southern Africa. Mkhaya and Phophonyane are two most recent additions to the country's fine line-up of parks.

Hlane Game Sanctuary

One of the highlights of Swaziland's social round is the annual Butimba, a week-long hunt in an area adjacent to the royal game reserve at Hlane. Hundreds of Swazis in traditional dress follow the king into action. The hunters may carry spears, knobkerries and guns, and the game they kill is presented to the king.

Elsewhere, conservationists might view Butimba with dismay – but Swaziland's game rangers believe this ritual hunt is a valuable way of emphasising traditional values and a useful means of culling surplus game.

Hlane came into being during the 1940s when the king acquired a large private ranch on behalf of the Swazi nation. A section of the ranch had no water, but was ideal game country, so it was set aside as a royal reserve. Unfortunately the game soon attracted large numbers of poachers who set snares and other traps. In 1967 the king proclaimed the area a game sanctuary.

At the time, Hlane was a paradise of virgin savanna. The grass was sweet and the bush had not encroached, but there was very little game to be seen in the area – no more than 200 zebra, 200 blue wildebeest and perhaps 600 impala, with small numbers of greater kudu, bushbuck and other antelope.

A team of rangers worked hard to drive out the poachers, and before long the game population started to increase dramatically. Waterbuck found their own way in and 35 white rhino were translocated from the Umfolozi Game Reserve in Natal.

By the late 1970s, Hlane's wildlife population had become too large for its resources: the antelope hungrily devoured the sweet grass and bush invaded the areas which were left bare. To add to Hlane's problems, a road running through the reserve is to be converted into a highway, effectively dividing it into two, and degrading it as a wildlife sanctuary.

Left: Blue wildebeest drinking at a dam in the Hlane Game Sanctuary. There is usually a gathering of harem troops on the remaining pastures at the beginning of the dry season, after which these split up to join large herds. With the appearance of fresh grass after the first rains, the herds once again split up into troops dominated by old males, which establish and protect their territories against incursions by other males. On their massive migrations, the younger, non-territorial males are relegated to the perimeter of the herd, often relying on the timidity of accompanying zebra for an early warning if predators are about. Blue wildebeest are tough and, although normally timid, will fight ferociously when cornered. The young, born in early summer to take advantage of the summer rains, are able to follow the mother within five minutes of birth and are very playful.

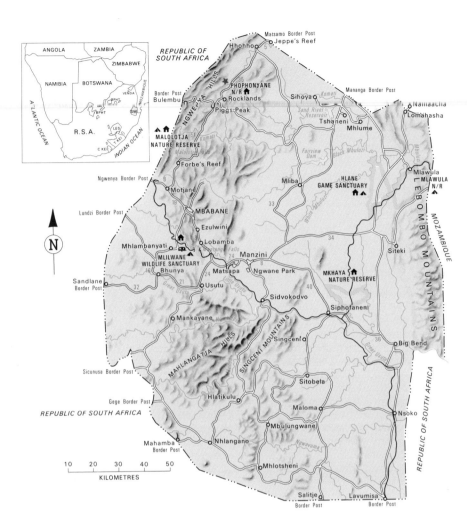

In spite of Hlane's doldrums, there is still much to enjoy in the 14 000 ha reserve. There are more than 10 000 animals including white rhino, young elephant (in an enclosure), giraffe (from the Transvaal), and cheetah re-introduced from Natal and the Transvaal. Other large mammals in the reserve include zebra, kudu, waterbuck, steenbok and grey duiker.

The reserve is watered by the Black Mbuluzi River, which also forms part of the north-western and western boundaries. The banks of this river attract many animals during the dry winter months: during the wet summer months the game moves to the south. The vegetation includes fine knobthorn and ancient leadwood.

An exclusive camp has been built overlooking the Umbuluzana River. Each cottage has a stove, fridge, cutlery, crockery and bedding supplied.

Visitors may also stay at an attractive campsite nearby but must supply their own food, bedding and utensils. Land Rover tours may be arranged. To reach the reserve, take the road between Manzini and the Lomahasha customs post and

watch for the sign. For further information, write to Mlilwane Wildlife Sanctuary, P.O. Box 33, Mbabane, Swaziland (telephone Swaziland 6-1591/2/3/4) or The Hlane Game Sanctuary, P.O. Box 216, Simunye, Swaziland (telephone Swaziland 3-8100).

Malolotja Nature Reserve
One method of reducing Hlane's game population has been to translocate species to the impressive Malolotja Nature Reserve in Swaziland's western highlands. The park is an ambitious venture of Swaziland's National Trust Commission, founded in 1972 to oversee nature conservation and the preservation of Swazi heritage. Ian Grimwood, a conservationist working with the United Nations Food and Agriculture Organisation, was brought to Swaziland to advise on setting up a system of national parks and recommended Malolotja as a top priority.

The 18 000 ha park is named after the 90 m Malolotja Falls, the highest in Swaziland. Other attractions include superb mountain scenery and

the breathtaking Komati Gorge, the sides of which are so steep that hikers wanting to explore it have to take to the river. An attraction of a different sort is the abandoned Ngwenya iron ore mine, an immense pit with terraced sides and deep pools of water at the bottom.

On the north-west side of the pit is a small mine from which red haematite pigment was removed (for colouring purposes) over 40 000 years ago. Middle Stone-Age artefacts have been found in abundance on the north-east side of the pit.

Even without its game Malolotja's scenery is sufficiently impressive to qualify it as one of the leading nature reserves in Southern Africa. The wildlife is a bonus: it includes the indigenous oribi, bushbuck, mountain reedbuck, grey rhebok, baboon, klipspringer, leopard, caracal and serval. Malolotja's grassland is in prime condition and the game is thriving.

This is primarily a walking reserve with trails suitable for almost all degrees of fitness. You will see many of the reserve's 280 bird species, which include two resident colonies of bald ibis and also rare blue swallow. There are two small dams for trout fishing.

To reach Malolotja, take the road between Motjane (north-west of Mbabane) and Piggs Peak and watch for the signs.

Accommodation in the reserve is in self-catering log cabins and at a campsite. Bookings should be made through The Swaziland National Trust Commission, P.O. Box 100, Lobamba, Swaziland (telephone Swaziland 6-1179). En-

Left: *Adenium swazicum* (summer-flowering impala lily) in the Hlane Game Sanctuary. This lily produces its bright pink or reddish-purple flowers in January. **Right:** The distinctively-crested African hoopoe at its nest hole. This bird is distributed all over Southern Africa, where it is usually found in savanna veld (though it sometimes enters towns). It nests in hollow trees, beneath eaves, among stones and even in termite mounds, producing 4-7 eggs which hatch after 17 days. The hoopoe's name is derived from its well-known call in the breeding season – a repeated 'hoop, hoop' sound. **Far left:** Cattle egrets (or 'tickbirds') in the Mlilwane Wildlife Sanctuary. These birds provide an 'early warning' system for game: they take flight at the first sign of danger.

quiries should be directed to the Malolotja Nature Reserve, P.O. Box 1797, Mbabane, Swaziland (telephone Swaziland 4-3060).

Mkhaya Nature Reserve

'If you don't see black rhino at Mkhaya then chances are you never will', claim the owners of what is fast becoming known as Swaziland's 'Rhino Reserve'. Although the small private reserve offers visitors one of the best opportunities for seeing these endangered animals in Africa, it was the re-introduction of elephant here in 1986 that really attracted attention. Mkhaya's small herd features the first elephants to live in the country for over 100 years despite their featuring in Swazi folklore and on the Swazi crest.

The association of Mkhaya, Swaziland's newest reserve, with conservation dates back to 1976 when King Sobhuza II expressed concern that the Nguni – Swaziland's indigenous cattle – were being wiped out as a pure breed. Since then, this colourful, resilient strain has been successfully preserved and bred for export throughout Southern Africa, at Mkhaya.

The 6050 ha wilderness of broadleaf and acacia-dominated savanna, incorporating the once-famous Red Tiger Ranch, teems with game such as elephant, black rhino, white rhino, hippo, crocodile, tsessebe and kudu. Over 100 species of birds are found including hawk, hornbill, francolin, Wahlberg's, booted and crowned eagle and one of the reserve's most prized residents, the bateleur. This rare bird returned to

Mkhaya after a 20-year absence and is one of the amazing success stories of this magnificent sanctuary for endangered animals.

Stone Camp caters for exclusive groups of up to 27 guests, in secluded and comfortable tents. There is a kitchen, an ablution block with solar-heated water and even a honeymoon tent – equipped with a kingsize bed!

Trips in 4-wheel-drive vehicles enable visitors to get close to the bigger game while guests can get nearer to nature by walking through the bush.

Only overnight guests who have booked in advance are permitted to visit the reserve. For bookings write to Mkhaya Nature Reserve, P.O. Box 33, Mbabane, Swaziland (telephone Swaziland 6-1591/2/3/4).

Mlawula Nature Reserve

The Swaziland railway runs east of Hlane Game Sanctuary and divides it from the new Mlawula reserve, another venture of Swaziland's National Trust Commission.

Mlawula's 18 000 ha incorporates the Ndzindza Nature Reserve and lies partly in the Lowveld and partly on the Lebombo mountains bordering Mozambique. From vantage points on the mountaintops you will have spectacular views across the Lowveld and Middleveld beyond, with the even taller peaks of Swaziland's Highveld just visible in the west.

The reserve's surprises include a dark forest of ironwood and other species including the cycad *Encephalartos umbeluziensis* – which

grows nowhere else. Elsewhere there are intriguing examples of termatarium bush clumps – bush-grown termite mounds that look like islands in the surrounding sea of thick grass. In the wide Siphiso Valley and woodland of the west there are some 50 km of game-viewing roads waiting to be explored.

You are likely to see white rhino, zebra, oribi, blue wildebeest, waterbuck, warthog, impala, kudu and if you are lucky leopard, nyala, spotted hyena, honey badger and antbear. There are abundant crocodile in the Mbuluzi and Mlawula rivers.

Birds are everywhere (over 350 species have been recorded), including African finfoot and the spectacular narina trogon. Bird-watchers may also visit the 'raptor restaurant'. From this hide you will see up to five species of vulture, including the endangered Cape vulture, which are lured by carcasses left there by park officials.

Mlawula has two campsites (suitable for caravans), and also offers accommodation in a fully-equipped tented camp. Short hiking trails lead from the campsites (longer trails are currently being developed).

The entrance to the reserve lies just off the Manzini-Lomahasha road, 10 km north of Simunye. For more information write to The Swaziland National Trust Commission, P.O. Box 100, Lobamba, Swaziland (telephone Swaziland 6-1179) or The Officer-in-Charge, Mlawula Nature Reserve, P.O. Box 312, Simunye, Swaziland (telephone Swaziland 3-8239).

Above: A thick-tailed bushbaby at its hole in a tree in the Mlilwane Wildlife Sanctuary. It lives alone or in pairs, sleeping during the day and emerging at night to feed on roosting birds, fruit and seeds. **Above right:** *Dicoma zeyheri* in the Malolotja Nature Reserve. This perennial plant belongs to the daisy family. **Right:** 'Winnie', a female hippo calf imported from England's famous Whipsnade Zoo as a mate for 'Somersault', a popular denizen of the Mlilwane Wildlife Sanctuary. **Far right:** The Mbuluzi River Gorge in the Mlawula Nature Reserve, home for more than 350 different species of birds. **Opposite page:** A bateleur eagle, one of the most familiar birds in any game reserve.

Mlilwane Wildlife Sanctuary

Straddling the escarpment that divides Swaziland's Lowveld from the Highveld is one of the country's top tourist attractions – the Mlilwane Wildlife Sanctuary.

This scenically beautiful reserve is watered by four rivers centred on the Ezulwini valley. To the north the land climbs away to the famous 'She-ba's Breasts' – twin, sharp-peaked koppies that are said to have suggested the scenario for Rider Haggard's classic, *King Solomon's Mines*. These mountains are a natural backdrop to a varied population of animals ranging from small scavengers such as the jackal, through a wide variety of buck, to one of the park's major attractions: white rhino.

Being situated near the country's major tourist hotels, Mlilwane is an obvious destination for motorists. Nearly 100 km of good gravel roads

take the visitor to a number of observation points – including specially constructed hides for the photographer. Bird-lovers are also well catered for, with hides overlooking several dams in the reserve.

Mlilwane is justly famous for its wide variety of bird life. There are about 240 different species in the reserve, including such unusual species as black eagle, plum-coloured starling, blue crane, several species of duck and the brightly flashing and ever-active sunbirds.

Visitors without cars can usually arrange tours at the rest camp (although advance booking is advisable). Bridle trails take pony trekkers through magnificent scenery – providing the added thrill of game-spotting from horseback. Visitors are reassured to learn that the reserve's white rhino are non-aggressive (unlike their black cousins). Most of these huge beasts will

co-operate quite trustingly while being photographed at close range, though visitors are understandably cautious.

Most tours of Mlilwane begin at the rest camp, and this alone is worth lingering over. Tame animals – including the rather sinister-looking warthog – live at the camp, providing a special treat for children. Here, too, visitors are likely to run into the reserve's founding father, Ted Reilly – who gained his early knowledge of the wild as a game ranger in Natal, the Transvaal and Northern Rhodesia (Zambia). When his father died, he inherited the family farm Mlilwane, south of Mbabane, and decided to turn it into a game sanctuary.

There was a lot to do. At the time, the only animals left on Mlilwane were a few grey duiker, steenbok and other small mammals. During 1960 and 1961, Reilly began capturing zebra,

blue wildebeest and impala in other areas of Swaziland (where they were in danger of extermination) and moved them to Mlilwane. Later, he re-introduced several species from South Africa, among them white rhino, hippo and giraffe. The sanctuary was opened to the public in 1964 and aroused considerable interest – and support from King Sobhuza II, whose chief residence was close by.

Since then, Mlilwane has grown to nearly ten times its original size, and now occupies an area of about 4 545 hectares.

One disappointment for the Mlilwane Wildlife Sanctuary is a hydro-electric development that bypasses the Mantenga Falls, undoubtedly the most spectacular cascade in Swaziland. This will reduce water over the falls to a trickle. However the Swaziland National Trust Commission is investigating how the scenic aspect of the falls can be maintained.

Years ago Mlilwane was mined for tin, and a dam has been built to hide the most visually offensive workings (at the same time providing a home for crocodile, hippo and waterfowl). There is also a series of vleis or shallows along one of the two perennial streams flowing through Mlilwane, leading to a deep pool beside the rest camp. The mining scars have been allowed to grass over and indigenous trees have been planted at strategic points throughout the sanctuary.

One of the most startling sights at the reserve is a collection of more than 200 000 poachers' snares – crude wire hoops strung on a cable overhanging a walkway in the rest camp. The snares have been amassed since 1960 as the rangers wage a never-ending war on poachers.

Mlilwane was Swaziland's pioneer reserve, and it remains the front-runner today. Among its visitors are parties of schoolchildren who camp overnight and attend the National Environmental Education Centre, a project funded by the Swaziland National Trust Commission and by United States aid. The establishment of the centre aroused widespread interest. 'Lots of the kids have never seen an impala before, let alone anything rare,' said a worker.

Phophonyane Nature Reserve

Those who have already savoured Swaziland's imposing line-up of tourist attractions will know that a small stretch of paradise lies tucked away in a nature reserve, about 14 km north of the pretty mountain village of Piggs Peak.

The reserve (and lodge) is called Phophonyane – and behind its gates you will find a world where river, mountain, forest and garden reverberate to a non-stop, combined chorus of songbirds and cascading waterfalls.

Although it is situated within walking distance of one of Swaziland's premier tourist routes, one of the hallmarks of Phophonyane is the privacy it is able to guarantee its visitors.

Here, in delightful seclusion, guests can participate in activities that range from footslogging across rugged countryside to drives in luxury minibuses. Several walks and hikes – offering views of the surrounding countryside – are handy for energetic lovers of the outdoors. But worth considering, too, are the trips (in 4-wheel-drive vehicles) to places such as the Mlumati Valley cycad forests, the Nkomati San paintings and the spectacular viewsites along the Sondeza Mountain. Guided tours of parks such as Malolotja, Mlawula and Hlane are also offered.

Phophonyane's attractive accommodation is in the form of two double-storey thatched cottages, a honeymoon suite and an exclusive tented camp. All units are self-contained, fully serviced and an à-la-carte restaurant is available. The maximum number of people that can be accommodated is 18 – so booking is essential.

For further information write to Phophonyane Lodge and Nature Reserve, P.O. Box 199, Piggs Peak, Swaziland (telephone Swaziland 7-1319).

Hiking and backpacking

South Africans have taken to hiking and backpacking (the hiker is usually a short-distance traveller, while backpackers take everything needed for an overnight stay) with such fervour that few of the country's myriad trails are left unexplored. They enjoy nature's unspoilt beauty as they hike along winding paths with their 'homes' on their backs, and revel in what may often be tests of endurance.

Once the preserve of experienced mountaineers, backpacking today attracts fishermen, casual weekenders, fitness fanatics – just about anyone who wants to get away from it all. Among the requirements are common sense, respect for nature, and carefully chosen equipment.

Unless of the right size, weight and quality, hiking boots can ruin your trip. They should be suitable for the terrain and for the length of the hike, and should always be broken in before you start on a long hike: ill-made or ill-fitting boots will raise blisters in a remarkably short time. The boots should fit snugly over woollen socks, but the toes must be able to move freely. There is a trend towards wearing canvas hiking boots or quality running shoes. These are light, dry quickly and can take the punishment of the trails. However, if you are carrying a

A hiking party passes through the hilly beauty of Transkei's Wild Coast. Backpacking is one of the most exciting and rewarding ways of exploring Southern Africa, but novices would be well advised to try short hikes before attempting marathon expeditions. Maintain a steady, rhythmic pace and make rest stops at sensible intervals.

heavy pack, boots will provide far better ankle support.

Ask experienced hikers for their advice on waterproofing and storing boots: they are the most important part of the hiker's equipment.

Backpackers may choose from a wide variety of locally made and imported sleeping bags. The bag is designed to trap some or most of the heat radiated by the body and the ideal sleeping bag is strong, light and easily compressed, with good insulating properties. Duck and goose down sleeping bags fill all these requirements, but are considerably more expensive than the fibre-filled variety, and are not as resistant to water. Bags with synthetic fillings are increasingly popular. They are lighter,

ideal for rough conditions. Both types have sealed tongues. When unlaced, there should be a space of about 3 cm between the boots and the heels. When laced, however, the heel must not slide up and down inside the boot — otherwise blisters will form. **Right:** The correct way to wear a rucksack. The top straps should fit snugly against the shoulder, the hip belt should be placed above the pelvis with the weight taken above the hip-bone, and the pack must lie vertically against the back. Above all, it must be comfortable. Avoid the temptation to pack items 'just in case' you may need them.

The pack illustrated is a sturdy design with two compartments and two large side pockets, with a comfortable padded hip belt. It is made of a fairly waterproof cordura material and has a capacity of 60 litres.

When packing your rucksack, try to pack a layer of clothing between your back and the frame (anyone who has hiked with a frying pan

handle sticking into his back will not forget it in a hurry). Items such as sunburn ointment, maps and toilet paper would logically go into the side pockets.

Left: A sleeping bag with three-quarter down filling. **Top:** A pair of women's boots, ideal for all conditions. **Above:** These 'Vibram'-soled boots are comfortable and

1. A compact benzine stove with its own windshield and a top that doubles as a billy. **2, 2A.** A cheap, lightweight stove which uses solid fuel. Because of its size, this type is best suited to day outings. **3.** This self-priming pressure stove burns benzine. It has several attractions, among them easy starting and efficient operation at high altitudes. It packs neatly into a container which splits into billies.

4, 4A. Packed and 'exploded' views of an ingenious cooker which uses methylated spirits. The kit includes a frying pan and two pots. The stove works well in the wind, but has a disadvantage in that the hiker needs to carry quite a lot of fuel.

5. A Primus stove, one of the most enduring designs, burns paraffin with a clean flame and carries enough fuel in its tank for the average weekend. It will work only if protected from the wind.

warmer and more compact than in the past and have the advantage of being machine washable and quick-drying.

Another consideration is the shape of the bag. The tapered type retains more body heat, but the rectangular bag usually has a zip – a boon if you suffer from mild claustrophobia. Down-filled sleeping bags (some of which have zips) can become uncomfortable on a warm summer's night. Whatever the type used, it is essential to insulate the bag from the ground. A closed-cell (synthetic) foam pad would be ideal. In extremely cold conditions, an aluminium 'space' blanket makes a huge difference.

Manufacturers offer rucksacks for every conceivable situation, and backpackers should determine which design suits them best. Frameless rucksacks are generally used on short hikes, when no overnight gear is required and loads are lighter, whereas longer hikes necessitate a framed rucksack with plenty of room for sleeping bag, clothing, cooking utensils – and perhaps even a tent.

Some hikers prefer the H-framed pack, a strong, rigid design with a lightweight alloy frame, padded shoulder straps and, most important, a hip belt. A newer design with an internal frame is increasingly popular. With this type, careful packing is crucial if the hike is to be comfortable. In general, heavier items should be placed to the front and aligned with the body's centre of gravity (along the spine). The most-used items should, wherever possible, be placed in the outside pockets.

Weather protection is crucial on a hike: take sensible shirts, trousers or shorts, sweaters and 'windcheaters', a hat or cap to protect your head from harsh sunlight and prevent heat loss in cold conditions, and rain gear such as cagoules, ponchos, rain jackets and anoraks.

Backpackers expend a lot of energy on the trail and will have to eat nutritious meals to keep up their strength. Many people buy dehydrated food from specialised camping stores or mix their own meals (canned food is too bulky and heavy for most hikers). Experienced hikers usually plan their meals ahead, packing the ingredients in easy-to-reach containers. Lightweight cooking equipment and miniature gas or spirit stoves are available in a variety of designs.

A backpacker's check list

Wet-weather gear
Sun hat or woollen cap
Water canteen
Mug
Powdered drink
Teaspoon
Trail snacks
Tea/coffee brewing ingredients
Toilet kit
Small towel
Mirror
Make-up (optional)
Shaving gear (optional)
Sleeping bag
Inner sleeping bag
Pillow
Insulating foam pad
Tent
Cooking pan (containing day's food)
Plate
Eating utensils
Anorak
Pullover
Running shoes
Food
Underwear
Socks

'Space' blanket
Handkerchief
T-shirts
Swimming costume
Sleeping gear

Maps
Notebook
Pencil
Permit
Stove
Spare fuel
Windbreak
Tin opener
Cooking pot holder
Matches
Dishcloth
First aid kit
Repair kit for tent
Whistle
Pocket knife
Toilet paper
Cord
Torch and batteries
Candle
Lip salve
Sunglasses
Camera and films
  (optional)

Exploring on foot

Southern Africa is criss-crossed by trails leading through scenery both beautiful and spectacular. Hikers and backpackers may choose from a large number of routes which pass through terrain varying from rugged desert to picture-postcard settings of undulating mountains, tall trees and gentle streams.

New trails are being opened all the time, and many sections of the National Hiking Way – a route which may eventually enable hikers to make a complete circuit of South Africa – have been completed. Trails and a variety of interesting walks (for the less fit) are constantly being developed.

These are strictly controlled by various authorities, including the National Hiking Way Board, the National Parks Board, the various provincial nature conservation departments and the Natal Parks Board. Some hiking trails are on private property . Permission to walk them is invariably required from the affected landowners.

Here are some hints to help you enjoy the trails:

Booking your trail. Advance booking is advisable wherever possible, and although some trails and walks are open to hikers without advance bookings, these usually require permits (parties are likely to be given priority). Some trails have restrictions on age, and novices are advised to try unfamiliar trails with experienced friends or in organised groups. Hikers should plan ahead, studying the official brochures and route maps and following all the instructions.

It is very important to have safety uppermost in your mind when preparing to go on a long hike. Do not attempt a hike if you are not fit, or if your boots have not been 'broken in'. Avoid overloading yourself with unnecessarily heavy equipment and food. Select your provisions with care: your body needs food and water to fuel it during the strenuous hours of hiking, but ill-chosen and heavy supplies could be counter-productive. As a general rule, food should be high in energy and low in bulk. Freeze-dried and dehydrated foods are ideal, since they need only the addition of water to make palatable dishes (with these foods it is essential that you camp near a water supply). Calculate your needs for the duration of the hike, and stick to your plan.

Check weather reports (always be prepared for the sudden onset of cold or wet conditions) and make provision for emergencies. Do not forget your water bottle.

If you are lost, do not blunder off to seek help. While this might be heroic, it could mean that the authorities have to send out two search parties instead of one. Boil your drinking water in areas where there is bilharzia or pollution, and ensure that you are inoculated or otherwise protected in areas which are affected by malaria and other diseases. A hint for novices and experienced hikers alike: do not pretend to know it all. The man on the spot always knows more, and will be glad to advise you.

Left above: A stretch of indigenous forest along the Soutpansberg Hiking Trail. The route takes hikers across the southern slopes of South Africa's most northerly mountain range, leading through an ever-changing vista of grassland, scrub, bushveld, plantation and dense forest. The wild and beautiful area has been described as a storehouse of Venda legend and history. **Left below:** The unspoilt grandeur of the Mdedelelo Wilderness Area attracts many visitors each year. **Opposite page above:** The Mac-Mac hut on the Fanie Botha Hiking Trail. The name recalls the gold rush in the eastern Transvaal in the 19th century, when many Scots joined the search for instant riches. This trail leads through varying terrain, taking hikers into pine plantations and indigenous forest, up mountains and across open grassland. The three-day trail also passes the impressive Mac-Mac Falls before reaching the Graskop hut and God's Window, from where hikers have a spectacular view of the Lowveld. **Opposite page below:** The Bain's Kloof section of the Boland Hiking Trail. This demands a fair degree of physical fitness: hikers should remember that a fairly fit person can carry about one-third of his body weight with ease.

Among the unanticipated hazards faced by hikers are bites and stings from snakes, scorpions, spiders and ticks. However, a little prudence will help you come through unscathed. If you're sleeping outdoors in grassy areas, examine your body, including your head, for ticks every morning and evening.

If cream or petroleum jelly fail to dislodge a tick, carefully remove it with a pair of tweezers. Take care not to leave the head embedded.

When venturing into areas far from food and fresh water supplies, you should make allowance for unforeseen emergencies. The survival ration pack with high-protein biscuits (**above**) and emergency ration pack with protective wax coating are useful. The survival kit (**far left**) contains a selection of high energy foods, coffee, creamer, sugar, soup cubes, sweets, stirrer, solid fuel, matches, water bag, water sterilising tablets, whistle, and instructions on survival and first aid. Drinks are heated in the container, the lid folds to make a burner stand, and the label can be used as a waterproof patch. Even the opener which comes with the kit has a second practical application: it is magnetised, and may be used as a compass.

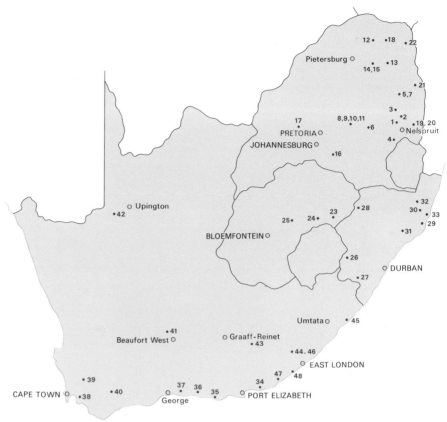

Always carry a snake-bite outfit, memorise the instructions, and make sure the anti-venom has not passed the expiry date printed on the ampoule. Current opinion is that cutting or sucking a snake-bite wound is not recommended, and the use of potassium permanganate is discouraged. A snake-bite victim should be calmed and reassured, and the affected limb immobilised.

Take the victim to a hospital as soon as possible. Try to identify the snake – kill it and take it to the hospital with you.

A victim of a scorpion sting or a bite from a venomous spider should also be taken to hospital as soon as possible.

When parking your car at the starting point of a trail, ensure that it is locked, and that you have removed all valuables. Try to leave the area you visit unspoilt for hikers that follow you. To avoid causing erosion keep to the paths as much as possible and adhere to the National Hiking Way Board's motto: 'Take only photographs, leave only footprints.'

The Hiking Way Board, which is closely associated with the country's major conservation, tourist, educational and recreational bodies, operates under the auspices of the Department of Environment Affairs. Maps of trails administered by the National Hiking Way Board can be obtained by writing to the National Hiking Way Board, Private Bag X447, Pretoria 0001 (telephone Pretoria 310-3911).

Major South African Hiking Trails

Transvaal
1. Fanie Botha
2. Blyderivierspoort
3. Prospector's
4. Gold Nugget
5. Eerste Liefde
6. Elandskrans
7. Op-de-Berg
8. Cycad
9. Suikerbos
10. Baboon
11. Tarentaal
12. Soutpansberg
13. Giraffe
14. Magoebaskloof: Dokolewa
15. Magoebaskloof: Grootbosch
16. Suikerbosrand
17. Rustenburg
18. Mabudashango Wilderness Trails: Kruger National Park
19. Wolhuter
20. Boesman
21. Olifants
22. Nyalaland

Orange Free State
23. Rhebok
24. Brandwater
25. Korannaberg

Natal
26. Drakensberg: Giant's Cup
27. Ngele
28. Holkrans
29. Mziki
30. Dugandhlovu Wilderness Trails
31. Umfolozi
32. Mkuzi
33. St Lucia

Cape Province
34. Alexandria
35. Otter
36. Tsitsikamma
37. Outeniqua
38. Boland: Hottentots Holland
39. Boland: Limietberg
40. Swellendam
41. Springbok
42. Klipspringer
43. Mountain Zebra
44. Kologha
45. Transkei Hiking Trail
46. Amatola
47. The Shipwreck
48. Double Drift

HIGHVELD

Like waves washing against a sea wall, the green hills of the low country roll westwards until they strike the stark escarpment fringing the plateau of the interior. Transvalers know the escarpment as the 'Edge of the Berg' — a reference to the imposing mountain range that the Voortrekkers dubbed the Drakensberg, or 'Dragon's Mountains'. North of the Drakensberg is the east-to-west range known as the Soutpansberg, an equally impressive boundary between the low country and the interior. Both ranges are cloaked in indigenous and exotic forests.

The country to the west and south-west is often loosely described as Bushveld, a land of sweet and sour grazing and low scrub that merges gently with the windswept Highveld of the Southern Transvaal and Orange Free State. To the west are mountain ranges that offer a striking contrast to the spreading plains — the Waterberg and Magaliesberg, overlooking a stretch of Kalahari sand and the Pilanesberg of the Republic of Bophuthatswana.

The Transvaal and Orange Free State have lively nature conservation departments which run networks of provincial nature reserves, among them the Transvaal's Blyde River Canyon and the Free State's Tussen-die-Riviere reserve, in the far south. Bophuthatswana offers the Pilanesberg National Park and the National Parks Board has the Golden Gate Highlands National Park in the Orange Free State. Lesotho's Sehlabathebe National Park is set in an extension of the Drakensberg.

A baby cheetah photographed at the De Wildt Cheetah Breeding Station, west of Pretoria.

Crystal cascades and the river of joy

Seen from the Lowveld, the granite wall of the Drakensberg Escarpment seems grey and forbidding. There is no hint of the natural wonderland at the top – verdant forests and myriad mountain streams that create a hundred crystal clear cascades. The Sabie area features some of the prettiest waterfalls in the whole of Southern Africa, and there are more in the Magoebaskloof area west of Tzaneen and in the Soutpansberg range, running west and east of Louis Trichardt in the north.

Among the escarpment's streams are two named by Hendrik Potgieter's Voortrekkers in 1840. While some of the men descended to the Lowveld to seek a route to the coast, the others (mostly women and children) camped by a watercourse. Weeks went by, and when the men did not return, the women named the stream Treur ('Mourning') River and began to return inland. All was well, however, and the scouting party overtook them at a second stream that they named Blyde ('Joyous') River.

The flow of the Treur and Blyde rivers to the edge of the escarpment is blocked by hard rock that forces them to change course. They meet at right angles with such force that the resulting turbulence has created the famous Bourke's Luck Potholes. Downstream of the potholes, the rushing water has gouged through softer formations to create the Blyde River Canyon – centre-piece of an exquisite provincial nature reserve.

The Blyde River area is a major feature of South Africa's National Hiking Way, a planned sequence of trails that will eventually lead all the way from the northern Transvaal to the Cape Peninsula. Several important sections of the trail system are found on the escarpment, including the Fanie Botha, Blyde River Canyon, Prospector's and Magoebaskloof hiking trails, and two through the Soutpansberg.

Ben Lavin Nature Reserve

One of the most restful hideaways in the northern Transvaal is a 2 500 ha sanctuary that lies

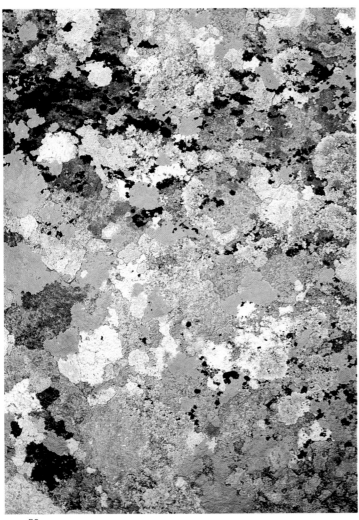

Left: Lichen on a rock in the Blyde River Canyon. **Above:** The awesome beauty of the canyon itself (the cylindrical formations are known as The Three Rondavels). The area is rich in natural treasures, and visitors delight in exploring the hundreds of kilometres of footpaths in and around the reserve. You may see the most northerly remnants of Cape flora such as true yellowwood, protea and heath as well as rain forest reminiscent of equatorial jungle, with orchids, ferns and tree moss. There are seven species of heather, six species of protea and two cycad. The Blyde River Canyon Nature Reserve is considered to be among Southern Africa's most beautiful natural showpieces, occupying a large area of the escarpment between the Lowveld and Highveld.

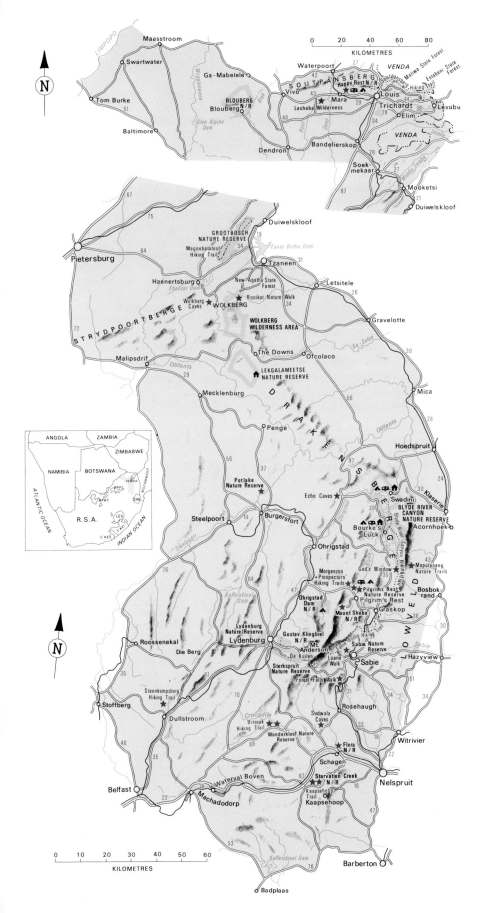

12 km south-east of Louis Trichardt. The sanctuary was originally a farm owned by Ben Lavin and his wife Molly – both keen conservationists. When her husband died in the early 1970s, Molly Lavin asked the Wildlife Society of Southern Africa if it was interested in taking over the farm and running it as a nature reserve. The society was interested, and within a few years the farm's transformation was complete.

Neighbouring farmers say that the Ben Lavin reserve has some of the sweetest veld in the Transvaal – and it shows. The gently rolling terrain features an unobtrusive network of roads and walking trails, but otherwise nature is in control. Giraffe peer over the tree tops, impala swarm in the bushes, and blue wildebeest and zebra run free on the grassy plains. The reserve is also noted for its prolific bird life – ranging from the large Wahlberg's eagle to the tiny lesser double-collared sunbird. Rare game species, such as tsessebe and red hartebeest have also been introduced.

Some visitors like to spend time in the three hides overlooking waterholes – one of them only a stone's throw from the shaded rest camp, which features charming four-bedded thatched cottages, which have electricity and are fully equipped. There are also tents for hire: otherwise visitors sleep in their own caravans or tents. To reach the Ben Lavin reserve, take the road north from Pietersburg and turn right to Fort Edward, 8 km short of Louis Trichardt. The entrance is reached after 5 km along this road.

The reserve is open daily from 6 a.m. to 7 p.m. Prior arrangements can be made to keep the gate open for visitors arriving from far away. For further information, write to The Ben Lavin Nature Reserve, P.O. Box 782, Louis Trichardt 0920 (telephone Louis Trichardt 3834).

Blouberg Nature Reserve
Several sections of land which once formed part of the Transvaal are now incorporated into Lebowa, the self-governing homeland of the Bapedi and other peoples. One of these sections lies west of the Soutpansberg range and contains the Blouberg, an outlying mountain mass (inselberg) that rises from the surrounding bushveld like an island.

It is home to Southern Africa's largest breeding colony of Cape vultures and is rich in other bird species. The area is also known for its indigenous forests of true yellowwood and other large trees and contains impala, gemsbok, waterbuck, ostrich, zebra, kudu, eland, giraffe, hartebeest and smaller antelope.

The reserve, which covers 4 450 ha along the north-western slopes of Blouberg, may soon be enlarged to include additional areas, which are presently administered by the Department of Development Aid.

A selection of game-viewing drives is on offer, picnic sites and ablution facilities have been provided and there are plans in the pipeline to provide accommodation. For more information write to The Secretary, Department of the Chief Minister, Division of Land Affairs and Tourism, Private Bag X27, Chuenespoort 0745 (telephone Chuenespoort 3-5529)

Blyde River Canyon Hiking Trail

God's Window is an important landmark on South Africa's National Hiking Way. It marks the end of the Fanie Botha Trail and the beginning of the trail named after the Blyde River Canyon. Some enthusiasts combine the two as a 9-day marathon. Many hikers go all the way from God's Window to Swadini, five days' distance; but the majority of them stop short at Blydepoort Public Resort.

The trail and the reserve share the same name and for much of its length the trail passes through the reserve. Hikers spend most of

the second and all of the third day of the hike outside the reserve's boundaries and the fourth day's route is only just inside. All the trail's overnight huts are within the reserve and are maintained by its conservation officers.

Fann's Falls, New Chum Falls and Bourke's Luck Potholes are welcome landmarks along the trail route, but most hikers agree that the climax comes with the final leg between Blydepoort and Swadini. The route takes them through magnificent scenery dominated by The Three Rondavels (clearly visible from the resort), down to the Blyde River and across it by a dramatic suspension bridge (built by the reserve staff), then along the shore of the Blydepoort storage dam. Below the dam wall they rejoin the Blyde River for the final walk to the Sybrand van Niekerk Resort at Swadini.

The Blyde River Canyon overnight huts accommodate up to 30 hikers at a time, thus setting limits on the number that may tackle the walk. Bunks, mattresses, cooking utensils and

firewood are supplied but hikers must provide everything else.

Those accepted for the trail are supplied with detailed maps of the route and helpful lists containing practical advice. To apply for places or request further information, write to Officer-in-Charge, Blyde River Canyon Nature Reserve, P.O. Bourke's Luck 1272 (telephone Bourke's Luck 29). The Officer-in-Charge can also provide information on two other trails through the canyon: the 22 km (two-day) Yellowwood Trail and the 40 km (four-day) Protea Trail.

Blyde River Canyon Nature Reserve

Several of South Africa's provincial nature reserves fully deserve national park status, and a prime example is the Transvaal's Blyde River Canyon. Its scenery is unsurpassed, its vegetation is both varied and lush and its rich selection of bird life includes a breeding colony of the rare bald ibis.

The canyon from which the reserve takes its name cuts nearly 20 km through the Escarpment's granite, and in some places is 700 m deep. Just over halfway down, the Blyde River is joined by the Ohrigstad River from the west. Here engineers have built an unobtrusive dam wall in a bottleneck below the confluence. The result is the glorious Blyde Dam.

The Blyde Dam is the heart of the reserve, but its nerve centre is the nature conservation team's headquarters at Bourke's Luck. Close by, a network of pathways and footbridges allows visitors to explore the potholes at the confluence of the Blyde and Treur rivers. Some of them are 6 m deep. Another attraction at Bourke's Luck is the visitor centre, which has numerous interesting displays.

Wildlife in this area varies as much as the habitats. There are mountain reedbuck on the escarpment, dassies on the canyon walls, hippo in the Blyde Dam and impala, kudu, zebra, blue wildebeest and waterbuck on the Lowveld plain near the canyon's mouth.

To most visitors, the 22 667 ha reserve is a two-level affair to be approached from west or east. A public road runs along the long western boundary and there is easy access to beauty spots like The Pinnacle, God's Window with its kloof-framed view of the Lowveld, Bourke's Luck, and a lookout point fronting on The Three Rondavels – unusually shaped hillocks that are also visible from the Blydepoort Public Resort a short distance to the north. Anyone wanting to explore the upper level more carefully should take to the trails from the Blydepoort Public Resort.

The eastern approach, at Lowveld level, is a road that enters the reserve on the flank of the Mariepskop and follows the canyon bottom to the Sybrand van Niekerk Resort at Swadini. This represents a good example of planning:

BLYDE RIVER CANYON AT A GLANCE

When to go The reserve and its two resorts are open throughout the year. The resorts tend to be rather crowded at weekends and in school holidays (there is ready access: their gates are manned 24 hours a day).

Reservations and information For information on the reserve as a whole, write to The Officer-in-Charge, Swadini, Box 75, Hoedspruit 1380.

Addresses for the two resorts are: The General Manager, Blydepoort Public Resort, Private Bag 368, Ohrigstad 1122 (telephone Ohrigstad 881, 901, 924 or 951) and The General Manager, Sybrand van Niekerk Resort, P.O. Box 281, Hoedspruit 1380 (telephone Blyde Dam 1).

Getting there Bourke's Luck, the exact location of the famous potholes and headquarters of the reserve's nature conservation team, is close to the public road running along the reserve's western boundary. The entrance to the Blydepoort Public Resort is 16 km to the north. As the crow flies the Sybrand van Niekerk Resort at Swadini is only a few kilometres away, but the road trip involves a journey of 120 km around the head of the Drakensberg. However, there are alternative routes: visitors may approach from Hoedspruit or Bosbokrant (via Nelspruit) in the Lowveld.

Accommodation The F.H. Odendaal camp at the Blydepoort Public Resort offers fully equipped chalets with up to five beds in two bedrooms, a sitting room, bathroom and kitchen, and also two-bed suites with sitting room and bathroom but no kitchen. There is a caravan and camping site. The Sybrand van Niekerk Resort at Swadini provides family chalets with five beds in two bedrooms, sitting-cum-dining room, bathroom, large kitchen and patio. Again, well equipped caravan and camping sites have also been provided.

Eating and drinking Both the Blydepoort and Sybrand van Niekerk resorts have licensed restaurants, bottle stores, cafeterias and supermarkets selling, among other goods, fresh meat. There are braai facilities at the chalets and at the caravan and camping areas.

Getting around Motoring in the reserve is severely restricted through lack of roads, though the various viewpoints are easy to reach. Lookout points like God's Window and Lowveld View are readily accessible from the public road running along the reserve's western edge. Hikers, however, can move more freely. There are four short nature walks around Blydepoort resort and more around Swadini's visitor centre; more ambitious hikes begin and end at Bourke's Luck visitor centre. Bookings are made by writing to The Officer-in-Charge, P.O. Box Bourke's Luck 1272 (telephone Bourke's Luck 29 during office hours). The reserve also contains sections of the Blyde River Canyon Hiking Trail – part of the National Hiking Way.

Special attractions The Bourke's Luck and Swadini visitor centres offer outstanding introductions to the reserve's vegetation and wildlife. The public resorts offer swimming pools, tennis and other entertainments (Blydepoort resort also features horse and pony rides and mashie golf).

Wildlife The Blyde River Canyon is more famous for scenery than for its wildlife but one of its distinctions is that it can claim to have representatives of all Southern Africa's primates: chacma baboon, vervet and samango monkey, bushbaby – and man. Other species indigenous to the area include bushbuck, bushpig, mountain reedbuck, klipspringer and the occasional leopard. Impala, waterbuck, kudu, zebra and blue wildebeest have been re-introduced to Swadini.

Left: Pinnacle Rock overlooks the sweep of the escarpment and Graskop region of the Lowveld. The Blyde River Canyon Nature Reserve, which lies within this majestic sweep of natural beauty, was established in recognition of its scenic appeal. A road called the Panorama Route leads along the escarpment from Graskop to Quartskop, taking visitors to viewpoints and picnic sites. From Quartskop the route leads away from the escarpment and links up with a tarred road at Bourke's Luck Potholes (this road runs alongside the canyon). **Top:** *Protea rubropilosa*, one of the most beautiful species of protea in the Transvaal. **Above:** *Athanasia acerosa*, a common sight along the Blyde River Canyon Hiking Trail.

the dam-builders stayed in houses which now function as chalets for visitors.

Beyond, the road continues to the nature conservation visitor centre, built on high ground overlooking the Blyde Dam. In effect, the reserve's lower level is quite separate from the upper and offers quite different experiences. The only direct link between them is the final leg of the Blyde River Canyon Hiking Trail, and even that is strictly one-way (the authorities ultimately rejected the idea of a cableway after much careful consideration).

Echo Caves

In 1923 a farmer bought land in the hills north of Ohrigstad, and an old tribesman told him of an underground river that had created a network of caves in the dolomite. Years earlier, Bushmen, Swazis and others had periodically taken refuge in the caves with their cattle. The farmer was able to turn the caves to his advantage. First he excavated large quantities of bat guano (a valuable fertiliser); then he used the caves to dry tobacco; and eventually he developed them as a tourist attraction.

Cave explorers say that the complex stretches a considerable distance, but today only a small portion is open to the public. A tour guide taps stalactites with a rubber hammer and produces the echo effect for which the caves are named. According to legend, they are the tomb of a party of mysterious white-robed strangers. Local people distrusted them and led the newcomers to the caves, where they were immured in a side-passage. Historians have speculated that the strangers were early Arab traders in search of gold.

The remains of skeletons have been found, but they are those of Bushmen or Swazis. These are displayed at a small Museum of Man in a Bushman-painted shelter close to the caves' approach road. Because of their historical importance, the caves have been proclaimed a national monument.

They are open throughout the year from 8 a.m. to 5 p.m. and are reached from a signposted turn-off west of the road between Ohrigstad and Strijdom, 23 km north of Ohrigstad. Visitors may stay in a motel at the caves. For information, write to The Manager, Echo Caves Motel, P.O. Box 36, Ohrigstad 1122 (telephone Ohrigstad 971).

Entabeni Nature Reserve

Among the grandeur of the Soutpansberg about 40 km from Louis Trichardt on the road to the northern Kruger National Park (and well signposted), lies the Entabeni Nature Reserve and its two sister reserves (the three will shortly be consolidated) Ratombo and Matiwa, noted for its spectacular look-out point. The reserves all lie in the Entabeni State Forest.

JOCK OF THE DRAKENSBERG

Illustration of an incident in *Jock of the Bushveld*, by Sir Percy FitzPatrick.

Sir Percy FitzPatrick's *Jock of the Bushveld* is a true account of the adventures of a young ox-wagon driver and his wonderful dog during the eastern Transvaal's gold-mining boom of the 1880s. Most of the book is set in the low country that wagons had to cross on their way between the coast and mining settlements inland, but an entrancing section deals with the steep ascent of the escarpment and the beautiful bergland on top. In this setting the dog hero becomes Jock of the Drakensberg.

Paradise Camp, south of the Blyde River Canyon, was where transport drivers spent their summers — away from the sweltering humidity of the low country and safe from the tsetse fly. There Jock was reunited with his mother Jess, who belonged to another transport driver. On one occasion these fearless terriers, their masters and a servant set off to track a leopard. Later, after discovering its lair, they came upon a troop of baboons.

As FitzPatrick describes, the baboons were responding to the anguished cries of a sentinel. The three men watched as the angry baboons formed an irregular semi-circle and slowly advanced down a steep cliff-face, throwing handfuls of stones and earth ahead of them. At first the onlookers could not understand what was happening, but then they spotted the baboons' target: a leopard, sprawled on a rock ledge with its left paw pinning down a baboon.

'The voices from the mountain boomed louder and nearer,' wrote FitzPatrick, 'as, clattering and scrambling down the face, came more and more baboons; there must have been hundreds of them; the semicircle grew thicker and blacker, more and more threatening, foot by foot closer. The tiger [sic] raised himself a little more and took swift looks from side to side across the advancing front, and then his nerve went, and with one spring he shot from the rock into the bush.'

The baboons rushed forward and swarmed on to the ledge to rescue their comrade. Two grabbed the injured baboon by the arms and helped him climb the hill. The men stared in fascination as the baboons regrouped — then realised the two dogs were missing: they were after the baboons. FitzPatrick and his companions ran down the cliff in hopes of heading them off, but came to a halt at a steep precipice above a stream. There they took their station, ready to fire on any baboon that tried to come to grips with their dogs.

'With guns gripped and breath held hard, watching intently every bush and tree and rock, every spot of light and shade, we sat not daring to move. Then, over the edge of a big rock overlooking the two dogs, appeared something round; and smoothly yet swiftly and with a snake-like movement, the long spotted body followed the head and, flattened against the rock, crept stealthily forward until the leopard looked straight down upon Jess and Jock.

'Three rifles cracked like one, and with a howl of rage and pain the leopard shot out over the dogs' heads, raced along the stony bed, and suddenly plunging its nose into the ground, pitched over — dead!'

Running through this misty forest sanctuary is the Entabeni section of the famed Soutpansberg Hiking Trail, which, in turn, forms part of the National Hiking Way.

Entabeni boasts a number of protected plant species such as the tree fern (*Alsophila dregei*) and various aloe species. True yellowwood, broom, cluster fig, Cape chestnut and Cape blackwood can also be seen in the lofty ever-green forests. There is wildlife, too, some of it found only in the few remaining indigenous forests: crowned and black eagle; bronze-naped pigeon and samango monkey (subject of a special research programme).

No vehicles are permitted. The best months to visit are between March and September. The reserves are open from sunrise to sunset, and a permit is required. Further information may be obtained from The State Forester, Entabeni State Forest, Private Bag X2646, Louis Trichardt 0920 (telephone Levubu 2).

Fanie Botha Hiking Trail

South Africa's National Hiking Way came into being in 1973 upon the launch of its first section, named after a former Minister of Forestry. The full Fanie Botha trail requires five days and takes hikers from the Ceylon Forest Station (close to Sabie), through Tweefontein and Mac-Mac state forests, past the town of Graskop, and finally to God's Window. Those with less time or energy may end or start the trail at Mac-Mac Forest Station, take shorter routes, or opt for one- or two-day routes that both start and end at Ceylon or Mac-Mac.

Hikers regard the Fanie Botha trail as one of the most strenuous segments of the National Hiking Way. Many are exhausted after the second day, which involves much climbing; others are worn out by the 19,4km walk between the overnight huts at Hartebeestvlakte and Mac-Mac. The route passes Mount Anderson. Lone Creek Falls and (if hikers are not tempted to take a short cut) Mac-Mac Falls and the cool Mac-Mac Pools a few kilometres downstream are among several welcome swimming spots along the route.

The Pinnacle, a tower of rock that rises steeply from the bottom of a kloof, is a landmark on the later stages of the walk. Officially the famous Bridal Veil Falls are on the trail too, but they will be seen only by those opting for the two-day route through the Ceylon forest.

Overnight huts on the trail accommodate up to 30 people. Those who embark on the hike must have the necessary permits and must stick to the arrangements they have made: in particular, they must sleep at the right hut, as the others may already be full. A deviation from the original plan may necessitate a search by forestry officials, though this rarely happens.

Starting-points for the Fanie Botha Trail at the Ceylon Forest Station are reached from Sabie (there is a signposted turn-off on the road to Graskop) and Mac-Mac Forest Station (on the road from Sabie to Graskop, 11km from Graskop). The trail may be tackled year-round but the most popular times are school holidays and weekends from spring to autumn. For further information, or to apply for the necessary permits, write to The Regional Director, Eastern Transvaal Forest Region, Private Bag X503, Sabie 1260 (telephone Sabie 196).

Flora Nature Reserve

Situated between Nelspruit and Lydenburg in the lovely eastern Transvaal Drakensberg, this small (47ha) reserve was created for the protection of one cycad species, *Encephalartos humilis*, which is unique to the area.

There is an exquisite little waterfall, part of a stream that (lower down) joins others to form the Houtbosloop River. The reserve is open during daylight hours, and a permit is required. Further information is available from The State Forester, Uitsoek State Forest, Private Bag Schagen 1207 (telephone Schagen 1250).

Forest Falls Walk

Close to the Mac-Mac Forest Station, the Department of Environment Affairs provides a neat picnic place which is the start (and finish) of a short walk to the Forest Falls.

Walkers traverse grassveld, indigenous forest and peaceful plantations of pine trees during a round trip of some 3,5km. Across the road from the picnic site are old miners' graves and a swimming hole.

Grootbosch Nature Reserve

Some of the finest of all South Africa's indigenous forests are in the Magoebaskloof area around Tzaneen. Large parts of this beautiful region, including well-known landmarks like Debengeni Falls, are now protected by the 4625ha Grootbosch Nature Reserve.

Above: Bourke's Luck Potholes, at the confluence of the Treur and Blyde rivers, where the grinding action of sand and pebbles has hollowed out formations in the soft rock. **Right:** A cuckoo wasp about to enter the mud nest of a mud-dauber wasp, where it will parasitise the larvae. The parasite's emerging larva feeds on the host's larva (or on its feed supply). When fully grown, the parasite spins a cocoon inside the cell, emerging as an adult the following season.

Typical evergreens include true yellowwood, broom, cluster fig, bastard stinkwood, wild peach and forest elder. These give shade and shelter to leopard, oribi, the rarer samango monkey and red duiker. The densely wooded mountain slopes are often shrouded in soft mist; summers are humid and winters dry and cold – snow falls about once every ten years.

Wild, beautiful and unspoilt – the area can be explored on the Grootbosch and Dokelwa sections of the Magoebaskloof Trails. In addition, motorists can venture through the forest on the Forest Drive.

More information can be obtained from The Regional Director, Northern Transvaal Forest Region, Private Bag X2413, Louis Trichardt 0920 (telephone Louis Trichardt 5-1159).

Gustav Klingbiel Nature Reserve

During the 1950s the Lydenburg Town Council, at the instigation of a member, Mr Gustav Klingbiel, began introducing game species on municipal land east of the town. There are nearly 500 blesbok and eland, kudu, Burchell's zebra, blue wildebeest and smaller antelope.

Four trails let visitors explore the reserve. One of these has an overnight hut. The reserve also has a museum in the grounds and is open daily. For more information write to The Town Clerk, Lydenburg Municipality, P.O. Box 61, Lydenburg 1120 (telephone Lydenburg 2121).

Happy Rest Nature Reserve

The reserve is situated on the southern slopes of the Soutpansberg, 18 km west of Louis Trichardt, and covers an area of 2 700 hectares. The reserve extends from the base of the mountains to the top of high cliffs and contains magnificent scenery – including a group of rare cycads (*Encephalartos transvenosis*). There are also many indigenous trees such as Outeniqua yellowwood, lemonwood, marula, bushman's tea, baobab and water berry.

Most of South Africa's snakes are found in the reserve, while mammals include kudu, impala, red duiker, bushbuck, bushpig, porcupine, and jackal. Among the birds are black eagle and crested guinea fowl.

One of the Transvaal's Department of Education's 'veld schools' for high school students (participants learn veld craft) is in the reserve.

The reserve, managed by the Directorate of Nature and Environmental Conservation, is not open to the public at this stage. Anyone requiring further information about the veld school may write to The Principal, Schoemansdal Veld School, P.O. Box 737, Louis Trichardt 0920 (telephone Louis Trichardt 4181).

Kaapschehoop Trail

Two disused railway coaches (called 'Barretts') at the Berlin Forest Station are the somewhat

unusual base camp for some magnificent mountain trails near Kaapschehoop. The figure 8 trail-system can be hiked over three or four days and covers some 50 km.

One demanding route takes hikers from the escarpment into the Lowveld – a descent of some 1 000 m that is rewarded by beautiful views of the Ngodwana Dam.

Kaapschehoop's mountain region is the site of one of the country's earliest (and least successful) gold rushes. A thousand dreams for riches must have died among the old stone buildings and mine shafts you will see dotted along the side of the mountain.

Today, these mountains conceal treasure of a different sort; they are the breeding area of the endangered blue swallow.

Accommodation for hikers is in overnight cabins and in campsites. For more information contact The Regional Director, Southern Transvaal Forest Region, Private Bag 11201, Nelspruit 1200 (telephone Nelspruit 5-2169)

Lekgalameetse Nature Reserve

South of the Wolkberg Wilderness Area lies 18 000 ha of mountains, caves, sinkholes and deep forested gorges – a reserve ideal for hikers, bird-watchers and nature-lovers.

A highlight for hikers is the Lekgalameetse Hiking Trail, a circular two- or three-day ad-

venture where wooden chalets provide idyllic overnight accommodation. If you are not a very keen hiker there are also seven luxury log cabins nestled in a kloof. From here you will be able to venture on short day-trips to natural swimming holes in the crystal-clear, mountain water of the Makhutse River.

At Lekgalameetse you will find a mosaic of grassland, woodland and forest. In the cool high-lying valleys moist carpets of epiphytic orchids are found near the giant yellowwood, Natal mahogany, big leaf, protea and matumi.

The reserve is renowned for its rare butterflies, many of which have still to be classified. Other animals which can be seen here are mountain reedbuck, bushbuck, duiker, klipspringer, baboon, vervet monkey and black-backed jackal. At night you will see the glinting eyes of bushbaby, genet and civet.

The reserve includes the Downs Nature Reserve and is administered by the Department of Development Aid for future inclusion into Lebowa. Further information can be requested by writing to The Manager, Lekgalameetse, P.O. Box 186, Trichardtsdal 0890 (telephone Trichardtsdal 1613).

Lesheba Wilderness

Some private game lodges in the far northeastern Transvaal are bigger than Lesheba

Left: Mac-Mac Falls. The story goes that the falls and siding of that name were named after Scottish diggers who worked the goldfields in the Pilgrim's Rest district. **Right above:** A vervet monkey with its young. This is an agile, intelligent monkey found in dense bush and thick forests. It lives in family groups of 6-20 (occasionally as many as 100), spending its day feeding (on fruit, insects, leaves, shoots, birds' eggs and sometimes crops), grooming, and producing the cacophony typical of its kind. Vervet monkeys may be recognised by their black- and yellow-flecked fur (with white patches on the cheeks, forehead, stomach and throat) and black-tipped tail (the male's scrotum is bright blue). Their major enemies are leopards and large birds of prey. **Right below:** Spiny coreid bug (*Pephricus livingstonei*). **Far right:** Dense vegetation in one of the Magoebaskloof forests. In some areas the undergrowth is so thick as to be impenetrable, and visitors might be excused for thinking they were in a South American jungle.

Wilderness. Others have camps that are more luxurious. But few can claim to match the feeling of old-time romance that permeates this 4 250 ha 'naturalist's retreat', situated between the towns of Vivo and Louis Trichardt.

The fact that Lesheba is stocked with an enormous diversity of wild animals, exotic birds, rare plants and giant trees can be attributed to just one thing: its location.

A subtropical setting atop the Soutpansberg means balmy temperatures and an abundant rainfall; good rains mean succulent vegetation – which, in turn, means an influx of different species of birds and animals.

The rare Cape vulture, the black eagle and the purple-crested loerie are some of the birds that have found homes here. Among the animals that can be seen are leopard, antelope, monkey and white rhino.

A bonus for nature-lovers (as well as photographers) is the magnificent scenery provided by the high cliffs, deep gorges and giant, eroded rocks.

Accommodation is at the Duluni and Hamasha camps in two sleeping huts (12 beds each) which have their own washbasin, flush-toilet and a gas-heated shower. Kitchens are equipped with a hot-plate, a refrigerator and a freezer. Braai areas have been set up outside. Visitors are requested to book in advance.

For further information, contact Lesheba Wilderness, P.O. Box 795, Louis Trichardt 0920 (telephone Vivo 3004).

Loerie Walk

The Bridal Veil Falls and the lesser Glynis and Elna falls to the north-east are on the route of the 13,6 km Loerie Walk, organised by the National Hiking Way Board. The walk begins and ends at the Ceylon Forest Station, 6 km from Sabie, or alternatively at the Castle Rock Municipal Caravan Park on the outskirts of Sabie. The walk leads through grassveld, indigenous forest and plantations of pines and bluegums. For further information, write to The Regional Director, Eastern Transvaal Forest Region, Private Bag X503, Sabie 1260 (telephone Sabie 196).

Magoebaskoof Hiking Trails

The Dokelwa and the Grootbosch hiking trails provide two walking adventures in a setting of great beauty. Hikers walk through plantations of exotic pine trees and through Grootbosch, the largest indigenous forest in the Transvaal.

On the Dokelwa section, the easier of the two trails, hikers cover 36 km over two or three days. Groups of up to 20 hikers are permitted and are accommodated in huts along the way. The huts are equipped only with essentials, such as firewood, cooking pots, lamps, bunks, mattresses, toilets and water. Hikers must provide food and sleeping bags.

The 50 km Grootbosch section is Spartan by contrast, with an overnight hut only on the first night. The remaining two nights, hikers sleep in simple overnight shelters, with no facilities provided. Hikers must provide food, lighting, first-aid equipment and sleeping bags. Groups may not exceed 12 people.

Both trails start from the De Hoek Forest Station, in De Hoek State Forest, about 22 km from Tzaneen. The De Hoek hut is reached from the national road between Tzaneen and Pietersburg (take the Debengeni Waterfall turn-off and follow the road to the forest station.)

Book well in advance by writing to The Regional Director, Northern Transvaal Forest Region, Private Bag X2413, Louis Trichardt 0920 (telephone Louis Trichardt 5-1159).

Mapulaneng Nature Walks

Hiking enthusiasts will be pleasantly surprised to discover this wonderland of forests, streams and mountains in Mapulaneng Nature Reserve – only a hop away from the Blyderiviersport Hiking Trail.

A comfortable, fully equipped log cabin is the focal point of the reserve and from here hikers tackle either the Tambourine Trail which runs for some 17 km, or the shorter Trogon Trails covering a distance of 11 kilometres.

Paths lead beneath the humid, dripping forest with its yellowwood, stinkwood and Cape chestnut trees, passing orchid, slippery moss and dripping liana vines. Through the trees you will catch fleeting glimpses of the spectacular Drakensberg and beautiful forest birds such as the Knysna and purple-crested loerie, and spectacular narina trogon. There are also many butterflies and monkeys.

The 6 600 ha nature reserve, administered by the Department of Development is to be included in Lebowa. It is reached by a turn-off 30 km north of Bosbokrand on the road to Hoedspruit. Bookings for the six-bedded cabin should be made to The Secretary, Department of the Chief Minister, Division of Land Affairs and Tourism, Private Bag X27, Chuenespoort 0745 (telephone Chuenespoort 3-5529) or The Director, Department of Development Aid, P.O. Box 384, Pretoria 0001 (telephone Pretoria 312-9303).

Mount Sheba Nature Reserve

Mining and forestry ventures long ago put paid to most of the indigenous forest of the Pilgrim's Rest area, but an impressive remnant survives on a 1 500 ha private nature reserve that hugs the slopes of the towering Mount Sheba. The reserve, founded and established by Ian Crabtree in 1963, was proclaimed in 1967. It took on a fresh lease of life when new owners transformed the rest-camp into a luxury hotel. Exquisite surroundings, dramatic architecture and the charm of the nature reserve make the hotel very appealing.

At least 1 000 plant species have been identified in the Mount Sheba Reserve, among them 100 tree species, 60-odd ferns and a number of terrestrial and tree orchids. They can be seen to advantage in the course of forest walks – some strenuous and others less so. A drive to the top of Mount Sheba provides views over the whole area.

To reach the reserve, drive west from Pilgrim's Rest and follow the signs to Mount Sheba Hotel. For reservations or further information you should write to Mount Sheba Hotel, P.O. Box 100, Pilgrim's Rest 1290 (telephone Pilgrim's Rest 17) or contact Portfolio of Places, P.O. Box 52350, Saxonwold 2132 (telephone Johannesburg 788-1258).

Ohrigstad Dam Nature Reserve

The hilly country west of Mount Sheba features an important water storage dam on the Ohrigstad River. The dam is the centre-piece of a 2 645 ha provincial reserve that stretches both upstream and downstream and consists of grass-grown hills and ridges and densely wooded ravines and kloofs. The reserve is situated near the Lydenburg-Pilgrim's Rest road, about 40 km from Lydenburg. Ohrigstad's wide variety of flora includes several species of orchid and aloe and also the intriguing 'resurrection plant' (*Myrothamnus flabellifolius*), so named because in the dry season it appears dead and brittle. After a shower its branches are revitalised, becoming soft and supple.

Ohrigstad's bird life includes some aquatic species as well as the narina trogon and piet-my-vrou (or red-chested cuckoo). Indigenous game includes eland, klipspringer, mountain reedbuck and duiker, while kudu and Burchell's zebra have been re-introduced. Anglers and boating enthusiasts use the dam (they can camp in the reserve overnight, but only beside

Left: *Impatiens sylvicola*, a small perennial plant which grows on the edges of forests in the northern Transvaal. This specimen was photographed at Magoebaskloof in October. **Right:** A hawk-moth caterpillar displays its highly effective defence — false eyes which it uses to scare off enemies. **Below:** Ohrigstad Dam Nature Reserve, near Lydenburg. Visitors to this attractive reserve are likely to see a variety of buck (summer is the best time to visit).

the dam). Field toilets are the only facilities for visitors. The reserve is open from 6 a.m. to 6 p.m. throughout the year. For further information, write to The Officer-in-Charge, Ohrigstad Dam Nature Reserve, Private Bag X1018, Lydenburg 1120 (telephone Ohrigstad 851).

Pilgrim's Rest Nature Reserve
About 30 km south-west of Bourke's Luck Potholes, the Blyde River passes the old gold-miners' village of Pilgrim's Rest, a national historical monument that has been taken over by the province and turned into a public resort. The river is narrow but fast-flowing and clear, and provides excellent trout fishing.

A 1 800 ha provincial nature reserve stretching 7 km downstream has been proclaimed over the river and its banks. The reserve is regularly restocked with trout and is open for public fishing throughout the year.

Anglers must possess current Transvaal trout-fishing licences, obtainable at the Information Centre opposite the Royal Hotel from 8.30 a.m. to 4.30 p.m. Close to the office is a large caravan and camping site with a cafeteria attached. Visitors may stay in the old Royal Hotel or in one of several restored miners' cottages (there is also a restaurant). To reserve accommodation write to The General Manager, Pilgrim's Rest Gold Mining Village, P.O. Box 59, Pilgrim's Rest 1290 (telephone Pilgrim's Rest 4).

Potlake Nature Reserve
The Lebowa Government is introducing a wide range of species to its 2 768 ha Potlake (pronounced Pot-la-ki) reserve in the mixed bushveld of Sekhukhuneland. Giraffe, kudu, nyala, blue wildebeest, red hartebeest, Burchell's zebra, impala, gemsbok, ostrich and waterbuck have already been introduced to the reserve to boost the existing population of duiker, steenbok, baboon, vervet monkey, klipspringer and various bird species.

At the entrance to the reserve there is an information centre which has a curio shop and lecture hall. Refreshments are sold, and there are braai and picnic facilities nearby.

There are numerous trails and, in the future, roads which will enable game-viewing drives are to be built. For further information, write to The Secretary, Department of the Chief Minister, Division of Land Affairs and Tourism, Private Bag X27, Chuenespoort 0745 (telephone Chuenespoort 3-5529).

Prospector's Hiking Trail
Starting from Mac-Mac Forest Station, hikers on the Prospector's Hiking Trail will follow parts of the Fanie Botha Trail before branching off through historic Pilgrim's Rest, in the direction of Morgenzon State Forest and the trail's end at Bourke's Luck.

PROTEAS OF THE TRANSVAAL

Protea simplex, photographed in the Wolkberg area of the north-eastern Transvaal.

The great Swedish botanist Carl Linnaeus named the genus Protea after a Greek god who was said to be able to change his shape at will. Africa south of the Sahara offers at least 114 species of protea, and 13 of them are found in summer rainfall areas of the Transvaal.

The most famous of the summer rainfall proteas is the Transvaal sugar-bush or suiker-bossie (Protea caffra). Heildelberg's Suiker-bosrand (or Sugar-bush Ridge) is named after the species, as is the provincial nature reserve that has been established there. The sugar-bush is also found in the Magaliesberg and on mountains to the east and south. It blooms in winter and is often confused with Protea gaguedi, which grows in the same areas and flowers during summer.

Protea rubropilosa is the prettiest of the Transvaal proteas, and earns its name through the hairy red-brown covering on its bracts (petals). This shrub blooms in spring, and is found in the Blyde River Canyon and Wolkberg areas. Protea laetans is a newly discovered species growing in the canyon.

Most of the Transvaal's proteas are tree varieties, and they include one of the rarest: the Barberton sugar-bush or Protea comptonii, found only in the mountains around Barberton. The tree grows up to 6 m tall and in winter produces an array of white to pink flowers. As with all the Transvaal species (except the Protea roupelliae) the blooms's petals are shorter than the flowerhead.

The protea is not peculiar to South Africa. Twenty-three species were grown in England's famous Kew Gardens in 1810, and they grow readily in the Scilly Isles, California and Australia. Although these beautiful plants are usually associated with the south-western Cape, the species found in the Transvaal are a rich and colourful constituent of the province's floral heritage.

The 69 km (five-day) trail is easy when compared to other National Hiking Way Trails, but there are also shorter alternatives.

The trail's four overnight huts each accommodate 30 people and provide basic essentials such as firewood, cooking pots, bunks, mattresses, water, toilets and rubbish containers. As in other sections of the National Hiking Way, hikers are advised to book places on trails well in advance (weekends and school holidays are especially popular).

A feature of the trail is that it includes the 1 000th kilometre of the National Hiking Way.

The notable achievement is marked by a plaque that can be seen on the fourth day of the hike.

For bookings and further information, write to The Regional Director, Eastern Transvaal Forest Region, Private Bag X503, Sabie 1260 (telephone Sabie 196).

Provincial Fisheries Institute
Lydenburg's attractions include the 40 ha landscaped grounds of the Transvaal's largest research station, which is concerned with research and field work. The Lydenburg In-

stitute has research laboratories, a large reference library and the F.C. Braun Aquarium, named after a local jeweller who founded a 'trout protection society' in the 1920s. In 25 years the organisation introduced 600 000 trout fingerlings to streams in the Lydenburg district. The aquarium features examples of most of the species found in eastern Transvaal waters, among them indigenous species including tilapia and yellowfish, and exotics such as trout, carp and black bass.

The aquarium is open daily from 8 a.m. to 4 p.m. To find your way to the institute, follow the signs from a turn-off on the road between Lydenburg and Sabie.

Rooikat Nature Walk

An 18 km forest walk named after the caracal or 'rooikat' follows a circular route in the New Agatha State Forest, 18 km from Tzaneen. For much of its length the walk follows the Bobs River, crossing and re-crossing it several times. Attractions along the way include a picnic place at Die Akkers, 6 km from the start and an impressive view from the top of the Letsitele Valley. Older visitors and those with less time or energy may take a short cut and reduce the journey to 15 km (however they will miss the view of the Letsitele Valley).

The walk begins and ends at the New Agatha Forest Station. Free entry permits may be obtained at the Forester's office daily between 6 a.m. and 4 p.m. (but those wanting to walk at weekends or in school holidays should make arrangements in advance). To reach the New Agatha State Forest, take the road out of Tzaneen (it is signposted 'Agatha'). Drive for 10 km, turn left at a T-junction, and follow the road for a further 3 km: the New Agatha signpost is on the right. According to the Forester, the walk makes an ideal day trip, as there are many spots where walkers will want to stop. For further information, write to The State Forester, New Agatha State Forest, Private Bag X4009, Tzaneen 0850 (telephone Tzaneen 2-2347).

Soutpansberg Hiking Trails

The Entabeni and Hanglip sections of the Soutpansberg Hiking Trail provide two separate routes on which you can explore South Africa's northernmost mountain range.

The four-day, Entabeni or Eastern section starts from the Entabeni Forest Station, reached by way of a turn-off on the Louis Trichardt-Thohoyandou road. Hikers walk about 12 km each day. The Hanglip section, which takes two days, starts at Hanglip State Forest, only a few kilometres from the middle of Louis Trichardt (the route is well signposted).

Both trails have huts at the start enabling you to start hiking fresh and early on the first day. The huts cater for parties of up to 30 and sup-

ply bunks, mattresses, cooking utensils and firewood. Hikers must supply the rest. To ensure accommodation in the huts, hikers should book places on the trail well in advance. For further information, write to The Regional Director, Northern Transvaal Forest Region, Private Bag X2413, Louis Trichardt 0920 (telephone Louis Trichardt 5-1152).

Starvation Creek Nature Reserve

Drained by the Elands River, which plunges into this forest reserve in a splendid waterfall, Starvation Creek is a 140 ha (though it is to be enlarged) sanctuary about halfway between Nelspruit and Machadodorp on the escarpment of the eastern Transvaal Drakensberg. The origin of the name is not known for certain, but at the turn of the century the area was temporary home to gold prospectors. They found no gold – only hunger and loneliness. One of the main reasons for its existence – apart from the beauty of the countryside – is the protection of the endangered Kaapschehoop cycad species. In the wooded upper reaches of the valley there are forest bushwillow, real yellowwood and notsung; the lower gallery forest has waterberry, and in the scrub thornveld of the dry northern slopes one can see mitserie trees (*Bridelia micrantha*).

The reserve is reached from a turn-off about 40 km from Nelspruit. It is not signposted, as it is closed to the public (however visitors may enter if in possession of a permit issued by the State Forester). The Kaapschehoop Hiking Trail passes the reserve. For more information write to The Regional Director, Southern Transvaal Forest Region, Private Bag 11201, Nelspruit 1200 (telephone Nelspruit 5-2169)

Steenkampsberg Hiking Trail

Discover a mountain getaway with stunning views, varied bird life and a profusion of colourful wildflowers along the Steenkampsberg Hiking Trail on the outskirts of tiny Dullstroom in the eastern Transvaal.

The trail starts 4 km west of Dullstroom and follows a series of high ridges, vleis, deep ravines and gurgling streams for 32 km over two glorious days.

On the way there are numerous photographic opportunities, particularly among the vleis and streams where impressive landmarks are cut through white quartzite rock.

The best time to book a place on the trail is from October to February. That's when the wildflower (of which there are more than 200 varieties) is king – and the mountainside is covered in a carpet of brilliant colours. An annual rainfall figure of 820 mm means that the area always has plenty of lush, green vegetation – an ideal habitat for birds, including the endangered wattled crane.

There are no huts, hikers stay at campsites where water, firewood and toilet facilities are provided. The trail is especially recommended for reasonably fit and experienced weekend hikers. For further information, write to Mrs C. Eloff, P.O. Box 135, Dullstroom 1110 (telephone Dullstroom 18).

Sterkspruit Nature Reserve

To preserve the purity of the Sterkspruit (strong stream), the province bought the farms De Kuilen and Sterkspruit, which together cover about 1 600 ha. These were proclaimed as the Sterkspruit Nature Reserve. The area was later expanded when neighbouring landowners suggested that their property be included within its bounds, and today it covers about 10 000 ha – most of it consisting of grass-grown hills and valleys. Most of this area is private

Left above: *Amanita muscaria* (or fly agaric) in its juvenile button form. This mushroom, photographed near Lydenburg, is hallucinogenic and highly poisonous. **Left below:** *Moraea spathulata*. The flowers of this plant grow at the tips of long stems, and generally appear in autumn in the Transvaal (in the eastern Cape it flowers in spring). The plant forms a large clump of long green leaves (they grow to over a metre in length) with prominent mid-ribs. **Right above:** A newly-hatched rainbow trout, with the yolk sac still attached to its body (fingerlings subsist initially on the yolk). The rainbow trout, recognised by the iridescent red-mauve stripe on its sides, was imported from America in 1897 and introduced to South African dams and rivers. Hatcheries throughout the country ensure a continuous supply of healthy stocks. The anatomical structure of the trout allows milt or ova to be expressed by hand without injuring the fish. Ova are expressed from the hen fish into a bowl, and the milt from a cock fish is added (together with water). The fertilised ova are washed and placed on trays in hatching troughs through which well-oxygenated water is circulated. When the ova reach the 'eyed' stage, some are packed in damp moss and taken to other hatcheries, while others are retained and hatched for use as breeding stock. **Right below left:** *Tetraselago wilmsii* is found high up in the mountains of the eastern Transvaal. **Right below right:** A tree fern (*Alsophila dregei*) in the Sterkspruit Nature Reserve.

property; only 1600 ha belongs to the Transvaal Provincial Administration.

As yet no game species have been re-introduced to Sterkspruit, but the reserve already features oribi, bushbuck, grey rhebok, mountain reedbuck and other mammals. The resident nature conservation officer is removing alien flora to restore the natural habitat.

The reserve is not yet open to the public.

Sudwala Caves

In the mid-19th century the Swazis occupied much more land than they do today, and one of their strongholds was a series of caverns in the mountains north-west of what is today Nelspruit. The caverns had been bored through dolomite by a long-vanished underground river, though its opening was high on a steep hillside. There was enough room inside for warriors, their families and their cattle, and a flow of fresh air protected the defenders from enemies who tried to smoke them out. The caverns were sufficiently important for the Swazis to post a guard party in the vicinity. They were captained by one Sudwala, who was to give his name to the caves.

But it was only in the 1960s that a road was built up the steep hillside and the cavern opened to visitors. Today, the Sudwala Caves rank among the eastern Transvaal's prime tourist attractions. The present owner (the caves are on his farm) has introduced sophisticated but tasteful lighting schemes.

Young guides lead visitors on an hour-long tour every day. These are held regularly between 8.30 a.m. and 4.30 p.m. Included in the tour is a visit to a massive chamber with a 67 m dome that has near-perfect acoustics: it has even been used as a concert hall. The more comprehensive Crystal Tour (it explores the famous Crystal Chambers) takes 6 hours and is held only on the first Saturday of every month.

Adjoining the caves is a very different attraction – the world's most ambitious dinosaur park, where full-scale models of the giant reptiles are displayed in well planned surroundings. The first of Sudwala's dinosaurs was commissioned to illustrate the age of the caves (upwards of 100 million years). Now there are 36 dinosaurs in the park, some representing species that once lived in Southern Africa, and others drawn from around the world. The Dinosaur Park is open every day from 8.30 a.m. to 5 p.m. Visitors tour on their own, using the leaflet provided.

To reach Sudwala, follow the signs from the main road between Machadodorp and Nelspruit (there is a signposted turn-off 20 km from Nelspruit) or take the road heading south from Sabie. For further information on Sudwala, write to The Director, Sudwala Caves, P.O. Box 30, Schagen 1207 (telephone Schagen 3911).

Uitsoek Hiking Trail

In the depths of Uitsoek State Forest you will find a network of scenically attractive one- and two-day walks that has been carefully laid out by the Roodepoort Hiking Club. The area is liberally dotted with pools and cascading waterfalls, which will provide cooling relief if the going gets hot. There is also an invigorating rock slide.

Crossing the streams and rivers has been made easy by two dozen wooden footbridges that have been sturdily built. Trees have been numbered for easy identification and include the massive Cape holly, forest cabbage, forest bushwillow and saffronwood. The forest is dominated by a mass of sandstone mountains, topped by the 2154 m Skurwerant Peak.

The walks are situated in the Wonderkloof Nature Reserve, near Sudwala Caves. For booking and further information you can write to The Regional Director, Southern Transvaal Forest Region, Private Bag 11201, Nelspruit 1200 (telephone Nelspruit 5-2169).

THE BATS OF SUDWALA CAVES

An insectivorous bat (note how the claws of its 'thumbs' and feet grip the bark).

Sudwala Caves, in the eastern Transvaal, once accommodated many millions of bats, most of them belonging to species of the 'horseshoe' family, so named because of a horseshoe-shaped ridges on the nose. The bats remained until electric lighting was introduced for the benefit of the visitors. 'That was too much for them,' explains the proprietor of the caves, Mr 'Flip' Owen, 'and there was a mass exodus to a cave up the hill that was free of disturbance.' Today no more than 200 bats remain in the main cavern — tiny bundles hanging by their feet from the rock ceiling. Five distinct species of horseshoe bat are found in the eastern Transvaal — Hildebrandt's, Rüppell's, Geoffroy's, Darling's and Lander's.

Like their cousins in other genera, these primitive mammals bear live young and suckle them. The most striking characteristic of a bat is its wings — membranes of thin skin stretch-ed between its enormously long 'fingers' which can be spread like an umbrella's ribs.

The wing membranes stretch down the bat's sides and tail and cover its hind legs up to the toes, which are relatively short and tipped with claws. The bat uses the claws as hooks when hanging upside down. Because its knees point backwards and cannot be straightened, the bat is incapable of walking on all fours. Instead, it moves along the ground by hooking the claws of its thumbs into a protrusion and dragging itself along. The bat also uses its claws to climb a rock-face.

In flight the bat emits a series of high-pitched sounds which 'bounce' off objects and return to its ears, thus providing a natural 'radar' detection system which enables it to avoid obstacles in flight and detect prey. The sounds have a frequency far beyond the auditory range of the human ear.

Vertroosting Nature Reserve

This reserve was proclaimed for the sake of a single plant species – in this case a rare red-hot poker (*Kniphofia splendida*), which grows in only a few places in the Transvaal and Zimbabwe. Despite its common name, this plant actually produces yellow flowers. The reserve covers 27 ha in the mountains south of Sabie but to foil plant poachers the authorities keep its location secret. It is closed to visitors.

Wolkberg Caves

The impressive Wolkberg Caves in the mountains south of Magoebaskloof came to light only in the 1920s, when a hunter tracked his dog (and the wounded mountain reedbuck it was pursuing) to the lip of a deep hole concealed by a wild fig tree. The hole proved to be a vertical shaft 20 m deep, and both animals lay dead at the bottom. The shaft opened into a chamber rich in stalactites and stalagmites. Today the inner chambers remain unspoilt, but the outer chamber has suffered from visitors who broke off stalactites and stalagmites as souvénirs. Further damage was caused by diggers who removed bat guano (for use as fertiliser). To protect the caves, the province's Directorate of Nature and Environment Conservation took control. The caves are not open to visitors.

Wolkberg Wilderness Area

The Wolkberg's high mountains and deep valleys belong partly to the Transvaal Drakensberg and partly to the Strydpoort range. The Department of Environmental Affairs has set aside 17 390 ha of the region, containing several noted peaks and a number of minor rivers, as a wilderness area. Indigenous forests thrive

Opposite page right: Autumn colours create scenic contrasts near Pilgrim's Rest. **Left:** Silvery mists rise above the floor of the Blyde River Canyon, a region of unsurpassed beauty and charm. **Above:** A nesting pair of bald ibises. Although this photograph was taken in the eastern Transvaal, most of these large birds are found in the Natal Drakensberg, where they breed in small, isolated colonies. **Right:** Sudwala Caves, north-west of Nelspruit, are among the Transvaal's top tourist attractions. A 12 m-high corridor leads from the cave entrance to a huge hall with a diameter of 66 metres.

in the valleys and on the southern and south-eastern slopes of the mountains, while grass-land is predominant in most other areas.

The area features mostly mixed sour grass-veld on the high plateaus and savanna-type bushveld on the drier slopes. Trees vary from marula (*Sclerocarya caffra*), kiaat and round-leaved kiaat (*Pterocarpus angolensis* and *Pterocarpus rotundifolius*) in the grassveld and bushveld to evergreen species in the forest. The Thabina Falls, several lesser falls and potholes on the Mohlapitse River are all worth a closer look.

There is rich bird life in the Wolkberg, including lilac-breasted roller, goliath heron, Egyptian goose, black eagle, white-bellied stork, rock kestrel, lesser honey guide, hamer-kop and fork-tailed drongo. Game is relative-ly scarce (the result of an era when dagga growers hid in the ravines and lived on buck).

However visitors may spot leopard, brown hyena, grey rhebok, mountain reedbuck, ver-vet monkey, samango monkey and caracal. The Directorate of Nature and Environment Conservation allows up to 30 day visitors in the area at a time (and up to 30 overnight visitors). Permits are required and visitors must adhere to strict rules. An overnight group is limited to 10 members, and all visitors must enter the area on foot.

Fishing and hunting are banned, and so is the making of fires (visitors may use portable stoves). Nobody may use soap or detergents in the streams (visitors are asked to do their washing in a light plastic bowl). Entrance is by way of Serala Forest Station, reached via a turn-off from the Pietersburg-Tzaneen road. For more information, write to The Officer-in-Charge, Private Bag X102, Haenertsburg 0730 (telephone Haenertsburg 1303).

Wonderkloof Nature Reserve
The most striking feature of this reserve is its fine waterfall, delighting eye and ear as the Houtbosloop River tumbles over the Transvaal Drakensberg escarpment between Nelspruit and Lydenburg (there are signposts 9 km from the Sudwala Caves).

The reserve includes attractive indigenous trees such as Transvaal teak, quinine, water-berry, candelabra, lemonwood, bastard lavender and cabbage trees. The trail is traversed by the Uitsoek Hiking Trail.

Of historical interest are the remains of An-glo-Boer War fortifications and the packed stone walls of Late Stone Age peoples.

Entry is restricted to daylight hours, and pri-or permission is required. A permit and further information may be obtained from The State Forester, Uitsoek State Forest, Private Bag, Schagen 1207 (telephone Schagen 1250).

The heart of the old Transvaal

Most Transvalers can distinguish between the Lowveld and the Highveld, but they are not as familiar with the large stretch of country west of the Drakensberg and north of Johannesburg. This region is bounded by the Soutpansberg to the north, the Drakensberg to the east, the Witwatersrand and Magaliesberg to the south and the Kalahari sandveld to the west. The region features a host of parks and reserves and several minor mountain ranges, among them the Waterberg.

The nature reserves at Doorndraai Dam, near Naboomspruit, and Loskop Dam, north of Middelburg, are the largest of several provincial sanctuaries in the central Transvaal. There is a scattering of conservation areas in and around Pretoria, including the South African National Zoological Gardens, and the city is also the headquarters of South Africa's National Parks Board. But the region's largest and most impressive sanctuary is the Pilanesberg National Park, located in an area that used to be part of the 'Old Transvaal', but now belongs to Bophuthatswana.

Austin Roberts Bird Sanctuary

Nieuw Muckleneuk in Pretoria features a fascinating bird sanctuary, extending for nearly four city blocks (11 ha), named in honour of the great naturalist whose book on South African birds remains the standard work on the subject. Much of the 11 ha sanctuary is hidden in dense vegetation and is closed to the public but there is a dam in the north-west corner with a hide overlooking it. Visitors can watch activity on the dam from outside the fence or from the hide, which is open daily from 7 a.m. to 4 p.m. The Austin Roberts sanctuary attracts both city and country birds, among them aquatic species like duck, cormorant and heron. The most impressive aspect of the sanctuary is the large number of heron and egret that return to roost in the late afternoon. Several small antelope have been introduced to the sanctuary, and some are so tame that they approach visitors standing outside the fence.

The entrance to the hide is in Boshoff Street, Nieuw Muckleneuk, which runs eastwards from Queen Wilhelmina Avenue.

Ben Alberts Nature Reserve

The Iron and Steel Corporation (ISCOR) has established a 2 156 ha game reserve near to its iron ore mine at Thabazimbi, in the north-eastern Transvaal. The spot provides welcome relaxation for employees and their families, and for the public.

The reserve, named after a former manager of the mine, is set in a river valley flanked by steep hillsides. It was originally confined to the

Above: The European bee-eater, a summer migrant, is found all over Southern Africa. It has a beautiful, bubbling call, used to maintain contact between birds in flight. **Left:** Waterside willows camouflage a bird-watching hide at the popular Austin Roberts Bird Sanctuary in Pretoria. With the introduction of several small antelope, the sanctuary has extended its appeal to weekend visitors. **Right:** The Indian seringa is an invasive weed tree which competes with indigenous tree species by attracting Rameron pigeons, the natural seed dispersal agents of many South African forest trees.

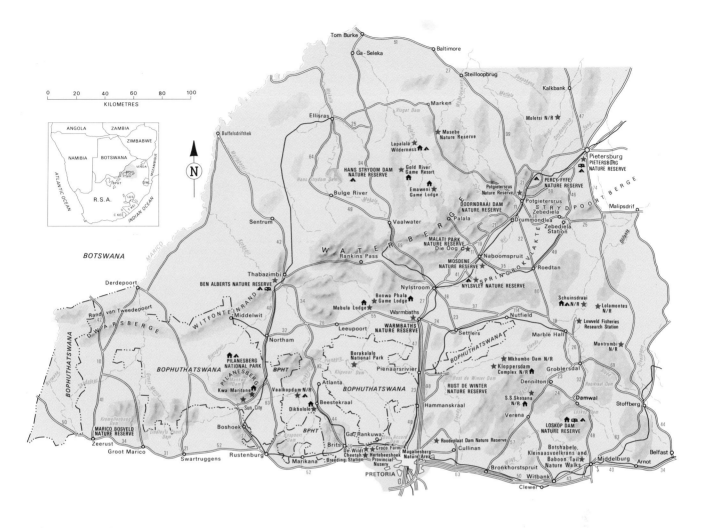

river's north bank, but has since been extended to the south.

The Ben Alberts Nature Reserve, which forms part of Thabazimbi's recreation complex, offers fine scenery and an abundance of game – you should have no trouble seeing white rhino, giraffe, eland, kudu and waterbuck, just a few of the species found there. A network of roads takes visitors to all parts of the reserve, (a detailed map is printed on the reverse side of the entrance ticket). Some of the roads lead to various look-out points, one of them high on a koppie that commands views over the whole area.

There is a small rest camp with caravan and camping sites just outside the gates. The reserve is open daily throughout the year, from 8 a.m. to 6 p.m., and is at its best in the winter months (when the grass is not too long).

To reach the reserve, take the signposted turn-off from the road between Thabazimbi and Northam, about 5 km from Thabazimbi. For further information, write to The Ben Alberts Nature Reserve, P.O. Box 50, Thabazimbi 0380 (telephone Thabazimbi 2-1509).

Bonwa Phala Game Lodge

It's dusk at Bonwa Phala Game Lodge – and as a thin column of smoke from a boma braai fire wafts across a windless Bushveld sky, large herds of game begin their homeward trek across the wide-open plains.

Soon, with the lengthening of shadows, will come the noises of the night: the combined chorus of thousands of crickets; the hoot of an owl; the far-off bark of a jackal.

Although these are the untamed sounds of old Africa, Bonwa Phala, 'the place where the impala drinks', can hardly be described as being off the beaten track. It lies near the R516 only a few kilometres west of the resort town of Warmbaths.

Although a wide range of modern conveniences – from a fully stocked bar to electricity, to hot and cold water – have been laid on, they do not detract from the rustic atmosphere of the camp.

Bonwa Phala's main camp offers comfortably furnished thatched huts (with twin beds) with electricity and en suite bathrooms. Other attractions include the use of a swimming pool, a selection of walking trails, sizzling campfire meals and early-morning and late-night game-drives in 4-wheel-drive vehicles, with an experienced ranger in attendance. Among the animals that can be seen are antelope, rhino, zebra and giraffe.

Only twelve people can be accommodated at the lodge, although rustic bush camps are also available, so booking is essential. For further information write to The Director, Bonwa Phala, P.O. Box 252, Warmbaths 0480 (telephone Warmbaths 4101).

Borakalalo National Park

Ever since a whopping 4 kg kurper caught at Klipvoor Dam broke the all-time South African record, anglers of all ages have flocked to its shores hoping to land 'the big one'.

Today this dam on the Moretele River forms part of Borakalalo, Bophuthatswana's second largest National Park, where fishing is just one of a host of attractions that include hiking, bird-watching and game-viewing.

White rhino, sable, eland, giraffe, zebra and gemsbok are examples of some of the 30 large mammal species that can be seen from some 60 km of gravel road west of the dam. The area to the east of the dam is maintained as a wilderness area with no man-made structures at all.

Self-guided walks through the well-wooded banks of the Moretele River offer bird-watchers the chance to see some of the reserve's 300 birds. Notable among these is the distinctive African fish eagle.

Accommodation is offered in two secluded, tented camps and in a third campsite where visitors supply their own tents. Bookings and enquiries should be addressed to The Officer-in-Charge, Borakalalo National Park, P.O. Box 240, Jericho 0264 (telephone Jericho 2-1102).

The Wilderness Leadership School offers weekend trails through the reserve. More information about the school may be obtained by writing to The Director, Wilderness Leadership School, P.O. Box 87230, Houghton 2041 (telephone Johannesburg 453-1462/53-4873).

Botshabelo, Klein Aasvoëlkrans and Baboon Trail Nature Walks

The Botshabelo Nature Walk is an easy three-hour walk on the escarpment surrounding Botshabelo Mission Station, which has been declared a national monument. On the route you can see a variety of bird life, baboon, vervet monkey and small antelope such as duiker, klipspringer, steenbok, grey rhebok and oribi. You will also pass the historic Fort Merensky, built in 1865.

On the six-hour Klein Aasvoëlkrans and the eight-hour Baboon Trail nature walks (both start from Botshabelo village) you can explore the Klein Olifants River gorge and discover dense stands of cycads and a host of indigenous trees and shrubs. On the way you may also see game such as eland, zebra, hartebeest and black wildebeest. The routes are circular and are clearly marked by white footprints.

Overnight accommodation is available and the kiosk can provide basic supplies. There is bilharzia in the river so swimming is not recommended. Take drinking water. For information, write to The Curator, Botshabelo Municipality, P.O. Box 14, Middelburg 1050 (telephone Middelburg 2-3897 or 2-5331).

De Wildt Cheetah Breeding Station

This remarkable sanctuary, designed for the breeding of cheetah in captivity, was established in 1969 on 50 ha of land offered to the National Zoological Gardens of South Africa by Ann and Godfrey van Dyk. In the late 1960s it was thought that the cheetah would not breed in captivity, but Dr D.J. Brand, Director of the National Zoological Gardens, was determined to accept the challenge.

The Van Dyks fenced off part of their farm at De Wildt and acted as honorary game

ALL THE BIRDS OF SOUTHERN AFRICA

In spite of challenges from younger rivals, the book that bird-lovers know simply as 'Roberts' remains the leading authority in its field. Austin Roberts was on the staff of Pretoria's Transvaal Museum when he produced *Birds of South Africa* in 1940.

Despite its title, the book set out to describe bird life all over the Southern African subcontinent. Each species was given a 'Roberts number', which it still retains, and since Roberts's death in 1948 his book has been revised in the light of new research.

Unfortunately for novices, Southern African bird life can be bewildering. 'Roberts' lists about 870 species, and often the males, females and juveniles of a single species have quite different plumage patterns — making the identification of a bird in the wild a great problem.

However, the Transvaal Museum provides a first-rate training ground where bird-lovers can hone their skills. Its 'Austin Roberts Bird Hall' displays specimens of all the birds that Roberts describes, from the ostrich (number 1) to the Cabanis' yellow bunting (number 875) — not forgetting variations in plumage. This hall is unique in the world, being the only complete display of a country's avifauna.

The bird hall is on two levels. The systematic collection is on a mezzanine floor, arranged in continuous glass cases lining all four walls. The specimens are arranged in family groupings identified by backdrops in special colours. Each species is accompanied by a distribution map, an egg, and wherever possible, a nest. Downstairs are educational displays illustrating the origin of birds, their mode of flight, and their usefulness to man. The museum is directly opposite the Pretoria City Hall and is open every day of the year except Christmas and Good Friday. On weekdays it opens from 9 a.m. to 4 p.m. and on Sundays and Public Holidays from 2 p.m. to 5 p.m.

Above: A king cheetah (right) shares the sun with a more conventional companion at the De Wildt Cheetah Breeding Station in the Transvaal. The king cheetah is distinguished from the normal cheetah by its long, broad stripes, and by the shape and length of its body. Cheetah may live in small parties of up to six, hunting together in the daylight hours and running down their prey. **Right:** The lunate ladybird *(Cheilomenes lunata)* lays her eggs in clusters of 20 or 30 on the undersides of leaves. In two weeks the eggs hatch into small, black larvae which feed on aphids — spearing them with their sharp, sickle-shaped jaws and sucking the juices from their bodies. The adult ladybird protects itself from predators by exuding a yellow, bitter-tasting fluid from between the joints of its legs.

Dikhololo

Where would you be if you woke up and saw a thorn tree in your bedroom or a natural rock wall enclosing your living room? In the luxury game reserve named Dikhololo, probably.

Situated north-east of Brits and about 60 minutes' drive from Pretoria, Dikhololo (Tswana for 'place of the klipspringer') is an exclusive resort offering top-class accommodation and a time-share project.

The development consists of thatched double-storey chalets, clustered around rocky ridges — but built in such a way as to fit comfortably into its bushveld surroundings and to ensure total privacy. Chalets are available with two, three or four bedrooms, two bathrooms, a lounge, a dining room, a kitchen and a braai area.

While game-viewing, either from a 4-wheel-drive vehicle or from horseback, is a major attraction, tennis courts, squash courts, pools, saunas and a waterslide have been built for those with less adventurous interests.

A fully licensed restaurant, specialising in traditional South African gourmet food and home-made bread, baked in an outside oven, are other drawcards.

For further information, write to Dikhololo, P.O. Box 912-1046, Silverton 0127 (telephone Pretoria 86-2041/2/3 or 86-2174/5/6).

Doorndraai Dam Nature Reserve

The escarpment of the Waterberg range provides a spectacular backdrop for the 442 ha Doorndraai irrigation dam on the Sterk River, roughly 50 km north of Naboomspruit. The dam is an angler's dream, containing blue kurper, red-breasted kurper, carp, yellowfish, large-mouth bass and several other species. Power-boats are allowed, but are restricted to the northern half of the dam.

The dam is in the middle of a 7 000 ha provincial nature reserve that specialises in the protection of rare species — particularly the sable and tsessebe. Sour bushveld dominates the vegetation at Doorndraai (Transvaal silver-leaf, boekenhout, wild olive and wild seringa), and the tsessebe have thrived on it and many surplus animals have been distributed to other reserves. Kudu, reedbuck, mountain reedbuck and leopard also live in the reserve, and birds include fish eagle, Wahlberg's eagle, black eagle, martial eagle and a variety of hawk.

The Doorndraai reserve has two gates, one on the road approaching from Naboomspruit and another on the road from Potgietersrus. They are joined by a 14 km road that runs along the dam's eastern shore. Other reserve roads are unsuitable for conventional vehicles.

Doorndraai is open throughout the year (the gates are open between 6 a.m. and 6 p.m.), and visitors may camp on the dam's eastern shore.

rangers. Godfrey died in 1976, but Ann has continued her work on the project. Help came from a veterinarian, Dr Woody Metzer, who in a voluntary capacity attended to the animals and started a research programme. In fifteen years the breeding station has produced over 350 cubs, of which roughly two-thirds have survived.

Many of De Wildt's cubs have been distributed to various game parks, nature reserves and zoos throughout Southern Africa and even farther afield. Some of these have been released into the wild.

'The cubs haven't been taught how to hunt, yet they do it instinctively,' says Ann van Dyk. 'We released three young cheetah in the Timbavati Reserve bordering Kruger Park and they promptly pulled down a young giraffe.' De Wildt cheetah roam the Pilanesberg National Park in Bophuthatswana, and live in a camp at Nwanedi National Park in Venda.

De Wildt's greatest pride is the king (or striped) cheetah, which features an individual variant colour pattern that years ago misled scientists into believing there was a separate species. Like the white lions of Tshokwane and Timbavati, king cheetah result from recessive genes in both parents. These at De Wildt are the only king cheetah ever born in captivity.

Visitors are welcome at De Wildt, provided they make arrangements in advance. Adults are taken on a vehicle tour of the area while school parties may walk along a nature trail. Besides cheetah, they may see wild dog, caracal and brown hyena.

For further information, write to The De Wildt Cheetah Breeding Station, P.O. Box 16, De Wildt 0251 (telephone De Wildt 4-1921).

Above left: A tsessebe pauses to pick up a scent in northern Transvaal savanna. It is believed to be one of the fastest of all African antelope. **Above right:** Ostriches, the largest living birds, can flee predators at speeds of up to 60 km/h. Once threatened with extinction by the ostrich feather boom, they are today protected in many sanctuaries throughout Southern Africa. They are capable of surviving in a very harsh environment. **Left:** The Transvaal Provincial Administration's plant nursery, north-west of Pretoria, features over 200 tree species.
Right: The yellow-billed stork comes to South Africa as a migrant from the northern tropics of Africa and Malagasy. It nests on large trees or cliffs, and forages near or in dams, rivers, streams and estuaries. This bird is comparatively tame and when not feeding, may rest on islands or protected sand banks in the company of herons, spoonbills and other large wading birds. The flight is stork-like, with projecting neck and feet.

Facilities are limited and include braai spots and tables and toilets. There are plans to establish permanent camping facilities, caravan parks, a visitor centre and youth camp. Permits for boating on the dam are available *in situ*. Visitors are warned that bilharzia has been confirmed in this dam. For further information, write to The Officer-in-Charge, Doorndraai Dam Nature Reserve, P.O. Box 983, Potgietersrus 0600 (telephone Sterkrivier 629).

Emaweni Game Lodge

'The only game lodge in the world with its own hydro and health spa,' is the proud boast of the Emaweni Game Lodge. And that's not all...

Situated in the well-known Tafelkop Nature Reserve, about 100 km from Nylstroom, in a section of beautiful countryside, Emaweni appears to have something worth savouring for everyone – including more than 40 species of game, myriads of birds and some fine examples of San rock art.

Accommodation comprises thatched-roof chalets (with *en suite* bathrooms), situated on the slopes of a mountain, overlooking a lake. For further information, write to The Director, Emaweni, P.O. Box 823, Pretoria 0001 (telephone Pretoria 21-1778/325-3601).

Faerie Glen Regional Park

Surrounded by the suburbs of Faerie Glen, Lynnwood Park, Lynnwood Glen and Lynnwood Ridge, this 100 ha nature area has been described as one of the prettiest open spaces in Pretoria.

Several markedly different soil types occur at Faerie Glen and this, coupled with varying micro-climates, has given rise to a fascinating variety of plant communities.

Due to Pretoria's position at the transition from highveld to middleveld, a large variety of birds is found in the city's natural areas, and this is especially true of Faerie Glen.

Gold River Game Resort

Huge herds of giraffe, hartebeest, gemsbok, kudu, zebra and impala have given this private 4 000 ha game resort a reputation as one of the most densely populated game areas in South Africa. It lies about 300 km north of Pretoria and is an ideal retreat for families or groups wishing to get away from it all.

You can swim, trampoline, fish, canoe, or go on game-drives from Main Camp, which consists of 6 six-bedded, 10 eight-bedded chalets, a luxury seven-bedded house and youth group facilities. There are also guided walks to enjoy and highlights include a visit to San paintings and to a look-out in the trees which offers a panoramic view over the reserve.

In addition to Main Camp, Wooden Camp and Fountain Camp accommodate up to 35 hikers each. For more information write to Mr F. Deysel, P.O. Box 425, Vaalwater 0530 (telephone Vaalwater 3212).

Groenkloof National Park

South Africa's National Parks Board has its headquarters on Muckleneuk Ridge in Pretoria's southern suburbs, and the grounds that surround it have been proclaimed a national park in their own right. Groenkloof's 6,8 ha were originally part of the old Fonteindal Game Reserve, proclaimed in the 1890s.

The Parks Board headquarters complex contains administrative offices, the national reservations office and its computers. There is also a bookstore selling National Parks publications, and a visitor centre where maps and photographs of the many parks are on display. Groenkloof National Park adjoins the grounds of UNISA (the University of South Africa) and the National Parks Board is clearly signposted from Railway Street, the southern extension of Paul Kruger Street.

boating, and visitors may camp along the shore in a demarcated campsite (there is an access road). Otherwise there are no navigable roads in the reserve.

On written request, nature conservation officers lead guided tours in the reserve, but self-guided trails are also being developed. To reach the reserve, follow the signs from Ellisras or Nylstroom. For further information, write to The Officer-in-Charge, Hans Strijdom Dam Nature Reserve, P.O. Box 473, Ellisras 0555 (telephone Ellisras 3-3384).

Kloppersdam Complex Nature Reserve
Game-viewing, bird-watching and hunting are all offered to guests at Kloppersdam, situated in Kwandebele. It adjoins Umkhombo Nature Reserve including scenic mountains and typical bushveld flats. Game includes kudu, impala, zebra, wildebeest, hartebeest, tsessebe, rhino, gemsbok, waterbuck, giraffe and eland.

Accommodation is provided for up to 15 people in an old farmhouse. Enquiries should be directed to The Secretary, Department of Agriculture and Environmental Affairs, Private Bag X4017, KwaMhlanga 1022 (telephone KwaMhlanga 2326).

Kwa Maritane
An underground hide, walking trails and bundu-bashing game-drives that bring you breathtakingly close to large game such as rhino and elephant are the heartstopping thrills you will experience at Kwa Maritane – 'the place of the rock'.

The luxury game lodge lies 8 minutes from Sun City in the koppie-sprinkled plains of Pilanesberg National Park, in Bophuthatswana. This massive 55000ha wilderness pulses with the varied sounds of over 500 species of wildlife, including elephant, rhino, buffalo, giraffe, leopard, cheetah, antelope, zebra and hippo. The black eagle and the majestic fish eagle are just two of over 320 bird species which have been recorded in the reserve.

Accommodation at Kwa Maritane is at a hotel (there are also time-share units) which has a swimming pool, tennis courts and sauna. Meals are served at a restaurant overlooking a hide and offers fare such as kudu steaks.

For bookings and enquiries write to Kwa Maritane, P.O. Box 784737, Sandton 2146 (telephone Pilanesberg 2-1820).

Lapalala Wilderness
The Palala and Blocklands rivers are the scenic focal points of the 24400ha Lapalala Wilderness, a privately owned stretch of territory which is situated in the Waterberg Range, north-west of Nylstroom.

Although you could encounter zebra, wildebeest, hippo, giraffe, tsessebe, kudu, gemsbok,

Groenkloof Nature Reserve and Fountains Valley Regional Park
The Fountains Valley, or Groenkloof, is Pretoria's southern gateway and one of the most beautiful areas in the city. As early as 1895 the Transvaal Volksraad proclaimed the valley as Fonteindal Game Reserve. Much of its indigenous vegetation has survived the rapid encroachment of buildings, roads and railways, and blesbok, Burchell's zebra, impala and other mammals already occur in the reserve. There are plans underway to remove the alien vegetation and introduce more game. Meanwhile, Fountains Valley's chief importance is as a recreation area.

Some 60ha of the 500ha reserve is the Fountains Valley Regional Park, with picnic facilities, tennis courts, a swimming pool, a children's playground, a tea-room and a miniature train for children. Close by is a municipal caravan and camping site – one of two in the city. The

regional park is open throughout the year from 6a.m. to 8p.m., but the train is open only on weekends. To reach it, drive to Fountains Circle in Pretoria's southern suburbs and take the turn-off leading to Johannesburg and Verwoerdburg. The entrance to Fountains Valley is to the left, about 1km farther on.

Hans Strijdom Dam Nature Reserve
Roan and Sharpe's grysbok survive naturally in the Waterberg range, and to protect them the Province has created a 4600ha nature reserve around the Hans Strijdom Dam near Ellisras. Visitors may spot these two rare species as well as other antelope typical of the region. The terrain is hilly and in parts mountainous, and the vegetation is mostly mixed bushveld, which makes it relatively difficult to spot game – particularly during the summer months. The dam, which covers 914ha of the reserve, is open for fishing and pleasure-

roan and rhino at Lapalala, the prime objective of this unique wilderness is not simply to seek out the biggest game, but, rather of gaining a broader and more intimate experience of nature, conservation and ecology.

This philosophy has led to the establishment of the Lapalala Wilderness School, which offers comprehensive two- to five-day courses for schoolchildren. Although the courses are largely conservation-orientated, the scholars also have plenty of time for such pursuits as walking, swimming, climbing, canoeing, or simply being alone with nature.

The main camp, Rapula House (36-bedded) is a beautiful stone and thatch building, and there is additional accommodation at Mosetse Camp (22-bedded) and Molope Camp (12-bedded), situated beside the Palala River. Each camp is fully equipped (scholars have to bring their own sleeping bags), and can accommodate one adult. Participants assemble in Johannesburg on a Friday afternoon, drive straight to Lapalala and their camp and then return to Johannesburg on Sunday.

Bookings for the school should be addressed to Lapalala Wilderness School, P.O. Box 577, Bedfordview 2008 (telephone Johannesburg 53-1814 or 53-8411).

In addition to the school, Lapalala offers accommodation at Kolobe Lodge, a 16- to 22-bedded exclusive camp, where you can discover tranquillity while enjoying luxury comforts and excellent food. Other major attractions are bush-drives, adventurous guided and self-guided walks, visits to San paintings, a filtered swimming pool, conference facilities and a discreetly located tennis court.

Less exclusive, but still very comfortable accommodation is provided in Lapalala's seven individual bush camps. The bush camps are called Tambuti (8-bedded); Marula (6-bedded); Lepotedi (6-bedded); Munadu (4-bedded); Umdoni (4-bedded); Mukwa (2-bedded) and Mogonono (four 2-bedded tents), and are all situated on river banks, but are some distance away from one another to ensure privacy. Each has its own walks, trails, fishing spots and swimming holes and offers plenty of opportunity for bird-watching. Visitors to the bush camps have to bring their own provisions, but bedding, cooking equipment, firewood, crockery and cutlery are all provided. There are bomas for fireside meals.

There is a landing strip in the sanctuary, and those arriving by air will be met and driven to their camp. Visitors can also drive to the camp in their own transport.

Bookings for the lodge and bush camps should be addressed to Lapalala Wilderness, P.O. Box 645, Bedfordview 2008 (telephone Johannesburg 53-1814 or 53-8411).

Lolamontes Nature Reserve

Fishermen trying out their luck at the Lolamontes Dam will also delight in the sights and sounds of the surrounding 1 610 ha nature reserve. The mixed bushveld vegetation is dotted with round-bouldered koppies and has been restocked with impala, waterbuck and kudu, that timidly approach the dam at dawn and dusk. Hundreds of bird species inhabit the thick bushveld trees.

The reserve is situated north of Marble Hall, near the Tompi Seleka Agricultural College. All but the last 5 km of road is tarred. Camping facilities are provided. For more information you should write to The Secretary, Department of the Chief Minister, Division of Land Affairs and Tourism, Private Bag X27, Chuenespoort 0745 (telephone Chuenespoort 3-5529).

Loskop Cheetah Sanctuary

Des Varaday is a former hunter who in 1960 established Southern Africa's first cheetah sanctuary near Loskop Dam. He attempted to breed cheetah, but had no success for 15 years. Then he agreed to take a number of goats and calves from a neighbour who was down on his luck. 'That did the trick,' he says. 'The cheetah could see a potential food supply, and felt it was worth their while to produce offspring. Since then we've never looked back.' Altogether some 112 cubs have been bred at Loskop.

The chief function of Loskop is to provide an infirmary for aged and disabled cheetah and it is not generally open to the public. However, the sanctuary welcomes veterinarians and scientists in pursuit of research. It is located 2 km from the Loskop Dam Public Resort, on the road to Middelburg. For further information, write to The Loskop Cheetah Sanctuary, P.O. Box 108, Middelburg 1050 (telephone Groblersdal 4194).

Loskop Dam Nature Reserve

The cheetah sanctuary adjoins one of the largest and most beautiful of the Transvaal's provincial reserves. At its heart is the Loskop irrigation dam on the Olifants River originally completed in 1938 but much enlarged in the late 1970s when the dam wall was raised. The dam's sur-

Left: The cup-shaped *Tritonia lineata* shows its six-petalled face to the sun in the Loskop Dam Nature Reserve. Each flower has delicate, faint stripes of dark brown. **Above left:** The Loskop Dam Nature Reserve is a favourite haunt for biologists, because its vegetation represents a change from the bushland in the south to the grasslands in the north. A variety of animals abound in the reserve, including white rhino, blue wildebeest, buffalo, giraffe, eland and kudu. There are regular guided tours of the 15 000 ha reserve. **Above right:** The reserve is a haven for myriad butterflies, one of the most prolific being the African monarch, also known as the African queen (*Danaus chrysippus*). The photograph shows an African monarch drinking from moist sand.

face area is 2 300 ha – (it stretches for 24 km), while the nature reserve as a whole covers 15 000 ha – most of it on the north shore. Visitors have a fine view of the dam and the bush-covered hills that surround it from the attractive public resort near the dam wall.

For biologists, Loskop's chief attraction is its remarkably varied bushveld vegetation representing an intriguing transition from the lush trees and shrubs typical of the Lowveld to the grasses which tend to dominate the higher altitudes. For some visitors, however, there is more interest in the many animal species that have been reintroduced, among them white rhino, ostrich, giraffe, zebra, buffalo, eland, kudu, waterbuck, sable and blue wildebeest. Visitors are allowed into the reserve in their own vehicles.

There has been a public resort at Loskop Dam for a long time, but it had to be rebuilt on higher ground when the dam was enlarged. Today it offers smart log cabins situated well apart to ensure privacy. The cabins are fully equipped and sleep three or five people. There is also an extensive caravan and camping site. A restaurant complex, launching ramps, swimming and paddling pools and tennis courts complete the picture.

There is a 1,6 km nature trail across the road from the public resort which leads to a look-out point high above the dam. Those wanting a closer look may embark on the resort's 26-seater pleasure craft, which takes visitors on two-hour tours. Tickets are sold on board on a first-come, first-served basis.

There are several routes to Loskop Dam but the most popular approach is from Middelburg, which is 53 km to the south. The resort is between the road and the dam and the turn-off is 1,5 km from the dam wall. Other routes approach from Groblersdal to the north and Bronkhorstspruit to the south-west. The resort operates year-round (the gates are manned 24 hours a day). To make reservations for the resort, write to The General Manager, Loskop Dam Public Resort, Private Bag X1525, Middelburg 1050 (telephone Groblersdal 3075/6/7).

Lowveld Fisheries Research Station
At first sight, Marble Hall and its surroundings are reminiscent of the 'real' Lowveld of the eastern and northern Transvaal. Though there is a marked difference in elevation, the vegetation is similar – and so are the conditions affecting the fish population. This is the home of the Lowveld Fisheries Research Station, an institution run by the Transvaal Provincial Administration's Directorate of Nature and Environmental Conservation.

The station, situated 13 km north-east of Marble Hall, covers 50 ha and contains roughly 100 ponds of many shapes and sizes.

The striking white markings on the head, rump and legs of these blesbok (in the Malati Park Nature Reserve) make them an easy target for camera-toting visitors to this lush, mixed bushveld area. Blesbok are grazers, inhabiting open grassland in herds ranging from six to 30 in number (though occasionally their ranks may swell to hundreds). When disturbed, a herd usually forms a single file and runs upwind.

The station is concerned with research on Transvaal river systems, particularly the investigation and development of recreational fishing, in which larger impoundments are stocked with suitable fish after field data for a catch analysis has been collected and evaluated by staff at the station.

An important element of the project is a model fish farm where researchers test the results of their research. Close by is a garden which features a variety of indigenous plants. Visitors are welcome to visit the station (it is open daily from 8 a.m. to 4 p.m.).

Mabula Game Lodge
An African king named Mabula once reigned over this stretch of north-western Transvaal bushveld. Now his title is shared by this luxury game lodge where visitors seldom miss seeing the 'big six' of the continent's animal kingdom, while on guided Land Rover tours of the reserve.

More than 10 000 ha in extent, Mabula Game Lodge stretches from just off the R516, outside Warmbaths, into the game-rich foothills of the Waterberg where more than 30 species of wildlife, as well as 200 species of birds have been recorded. The reserve is particularly well-known for white rhino, with the largest privately owned herd in South Africa.

Accommodation takes the form of luxury thatched chalets, all with private bathrooms. Time-share units are being sold. Besides excellent bar and restaurant facilities, the reserve also offers three excellently fitted out conference rooms.

The resort is served by a private airstrip and helicopter landing pad. For further information and bookings, write to The Director, Mabula Lodge, Private Bag X16651, Warmbaths 0480 (telephone Rooiberg 616/717).

Malati Park Nature Reserve

The privately owned Malati Park Nature Reserve covers roughly 1 200 ha of rolling terrain and mixed bushveld and is located some 14 km west of Naboomspruit. White rhino, giraffe, eland, kudu and sable are among the species to be seen in the reserve, and there is also an extensive fish hatchery that specialises in carp. Most visitors are drawn from families staying at the various spas and resorts in the area, notably Rondalia's 'Die Oog', which is situated close by.

Malati Park is open daily throughout the year, from 6.30 a.m. until sunset. Visitors drive through in their own cars. There is luxurious overnight accommodation for visitors within the sanctuary. To reach Malati Park, leave Naboomspruit on the road to the north-west and follow signs to Die Oog; then watch for the reserve on the left. To make bookings and enquiries you should contact the owners (telephone Naboomspruit 3-2015).

Masebe Nature Reserve

Sable and tsessebe are among the antelope you are likely to see among the thickly wooded mixed bushveld of this 4 500 ha nature reserve on the Potgietersrus-Marken road, in north-western Transvaal.

Despite its cumbersome shape, the tsessebe is probably the fastest of the South African antelope, capable of speeds of up to 60 km/h for great distances. The sable is graceful by contrast, sporting long, scimitar-like horns. Other game which may be seen are gemsbok, eland, impala, red hartebeest, zebra and bushbuck.

San paintings decorate some of the sheer cliffs which are typical of this scenic reserve. A picnic site caters for day visitors, while nature trails and a rustic bush hut for 24 people will be developed. For more information write to The Secretary, Department of the Chief Minister, Division of Land Affairs and Tourism, Private Bag X27, Chuenespoort 0745 (telephone Chuenespoort 3-5529).

Moletzie Nature Reserve

Imagine sitting in a rustic mountain hide and being virtually guaranteed an aerial display by vulture, eagle and ibis as they swoop and soar, testing their skill on updraughts.

This magnificent bird display is made possible by Lebowa's first 'raptor restaurant', where carcasses are left out for the birds to feed on once a week. The restaurant's primary objective is to provide a regular source of food for

the Cape vulture. These magnificent birds of prey are rare throughout South Africa.

Also attracted to the weekly feast at Moletsi are bald ibis (which are also endangered), black eagle, lanner falcon, lappet-faced vulture, yellow-billed kite, maribou stork and migratory stepped eagle.

A short trail traverses one of the reserve's koppies and enables visitors to observe the interesting flora of the area. An information centre, braai, picnic and ablution facilities are provided.

The 200 ha reserve lies about 35 km northwest of Pietersburg. More information and directions to Moletzie can be obtained by writing to the The Secretary, Department of the Chief Minister, Division of Land Affairs and Tourism, Private Bag X27, Chuenespoort 0745 (telephone Chuenespoort 3-5529).

Moreleta Spruit Nature Trail

Pretoria's Moreleta Spruit winds through a variety of natural landscapes in the city's eastern suburbs. At one point it enters a chain of vleis flanked by reeds; at another it crosses open grassy plains; elsewhere it runs through areas of thick bush. The Pretoria Municipality has established a nature trail along the banks of the spruit, starting at a stone beacon in Menlyn Drive, Constantia Park (near the source of a minor tributary of the Moreleta Spruit) and continuing beyond the Witbank freeway to Hardekool Avenue in Val de Grace, a total distance of about 8 km. A second section has also been opened between Watermeyer Street in Meyerspark and the Pioneers Open-air Museum in Pretoria Street, Silverton. In time the trail will be extended to the Magaliesberg and upstream to its source near the Van Riebeeck Nature Reserve.

The trail can be completed in a day; otherwise hikers may join it or leave at points along the route. There are no braai or toilet facilities along the route. Hikers are advised to take a water bottle. The municipality suggests that hikers use local bus services to reach their starting-point, and for the return trip. That way they avoid the nuisance of having to return to the starting-point to pick up their cars.

Mosdene Private Nature Reserve

For bird-lovers in the Transvaal, one of the most rewarding localities is a 5 241 ha cattle ranch situated some 10 km south-west of Naboomspruit. More than 400 species have been spotted there (compared with just over 450 for the whole of Kruger National Park) and they include both aquatic species (drawn to the Nyl River and the vleis it creates when in flood) and terrestrial birds. The river's floodplains attract species from the west and east, and migrants from north and south.

The Mosdene reserve is privately owned, but the owners welcome bird-lovers and others who are genuinely interested in nature. Visitors to the reserve are accommodated in campsites but must be self-sufficient and remove their own refuse. The owners insist that visits must be arranged in advance (telephone Naboomspruit 3-1933 or 3-1938), and all visitors must report to them on arrival. To reach Mosdene, drive 10 km along the road from Naboomspruit to Roedtan and turn right at the signpost to Boekenhout Station. The entrance is on the left 2 km down this gravel road.

National Zoological Gardens of South Africa

Southern Africa's oldest zoo covers roughly 55 ha in Pretoria's northern suburbs. The Apies River runs through the centre and a steep hillside marks the northern boundary, providing an impressive backdrop for the rest of the zoo. During the depression of the 1930s, an 'army' of unemployed men built massive stone terraces on the hillside, giving it the look of an Inca temple. The terraces are partly landscaped and provide unusual settings for the zoo's lions, tigers and barbary sheep.

All told, the zoo features some 140 species of mammals and 200 bird species, some indigenous to Southern Africa, but the majority from other parts of the world. The zoo is particularly proud of its antelope collection which

Above left: *Triumfetta sonderi*, photographed in the Pilanesberg National Park. **Above right:** The Percy Fyfe Nature Reserve. Breeding of the roan and tsessebe in this sanctuary has assured their survival in the Transvaal. **Left above:** The pygmy hippopotamus from west Africa is a rare and valued possession at the Pretoria Zoo. It is about the size of a wild boar and has pig-like characteristics, with a relatively small head and a massive body. It lives in swampy forests and along creeks and streams. **Left below:** Albino and melanistic springbok at the Pretoria Zoo contrast sharply with the more colourful members of their group. **Right:** Wahlberg's praying mantis *(Pseudocreobotra wahlbergi)*, a spiny creature with purplish-pink markings, changes colour as it gets older. The adult is known to expose distinctive 'eyes' on its wings when confronted by an adversary. Because of its colourful markings, this mantis is often mistaken for part of a flower.

includes several endangered species from other parts of Africa – such as the giant eland, scimitar-horned oryx and addax. In each case the zoo has built up a breeding herd, and is in a position to supply animals to other zoos.

Although the zoo has long been one of Pretoria's premier attractions, the display of animals is not its sole function. Conservation and education are high on its list of priorities. Several staff members are full-time education officers, and while their chief task is to look after school parties, they also provide courses for interested adults: even the casual visitor can learn a great deal. The zoo collection includes caracal, civet, genet and other creatures that are seldom seen in their natural habitat.

Adjoining the main part of the zoo is an impressive aquarium and reptile collection. Among the reptiles are several full-grown crocodiles and a selection of Southern Africa's poisonous snakes. Both sections of the zoo are open daily from 8 a.m. to 5.30 p.m. To reach them from central Pretoria, drive north on Paul Kruger Street and watch for the Aquarium and Reptile Park on the right. The entrance to the main part of the zoo is in Boom Street, which crosses Paul Kruger Street at right angles.

Nylsvley Nature Reserve

The largest natural vlei in the Transvaal lies on the sprawling floodplain of the Nyl River, some 20 km south of Naboomspruit. What used to be the farm Nylsvley is today a 3 100 ha provincial nature reserve. Its chief attraction is its birds: more than 400 species have been sighted, including both aquatic birds drawn to the vlei and the river, and land birds attracted by the savanna woodland that flanks the water. The spring breeding season is probably the best time to watch the woodland birds, but most water birds occur later in the year (from December to April), depending on the extent of flooding in the Nyl River floodplain.

Kudu, impala and smaller antelope occur naturally at Nylsvley, and roan and tsessebe have been reintroduced. The terrain is relatively flat and it is easy to spot game and birds.

To reach the reserve, take the Boekenhout turn-off on the road between Naboomspruit and Nylstroom, 13 km south-west of Naboomspruit. Cross the railway line and watch for the reserve's entrance on the left. The reserve may be explored by car or on foot. There is a small camping spot offering toilets, cold-water showers and communal fireplaces. A trail cuts through the floodplain of the Nyl River. It caters for parties of up to eight people. The reserve is open daily (including weekends) from 6 a.m. to 6 p.m. For further information, write to The Officer-in-Charge, Nylsvley Nature Reserve, P.O. Box 508, Naboomspruit 0560 (telephone Naboomspruit 3-1074).

Percy Fyfe Nature Reserve

This Transvaal sanctuary has been used to breed threatened antelope. The roan and tsessebe, in particular, were bred here so successfully that their survival in the Transvaal is now assured. The reserve is named after the farmer who donated it to the province. A road and a railway line divide the Percy Fyfe Nature Reserve's 3 462 ha into three sections, one large and two somewhat smaller. The large area is used for breeding roan from animals captured on farms in the Waterberg range. The breeding programme has been successful, and surplus animals have been moved to the Doorndraai and Nylsvley reserves. The smaller camps are used to breed sable and tsessebe respectively.

Ironically, Percy Fyfe's chief interest was in a species no longer found on his farm. In 1933 he bought a few head of blesbok in the Orange Free State, and within 20 years there were more than 600 in the herd. In 1954 he gave his sanctuary to the province, and while he was alive it was managed as such – even though blesbok were never naturally recorded off the Highveld and were historically alien to the lower altitudes. After 'Oom Percy' died they were moved to more appropriate habitats, notably the Suikerbosrand Nature Reserve.

At Percy Fyfe's request, part of his farm was developed as a camping area for youth organi-

Above: The Pilanesberg in Bophuthatswana, once the scene of volcanic activity, is now a beautiful sanctuary for a variety of game.
Right: The white rhino, also known as the square-lipped rhino, uses its wide, flat mouth to crop short grasses almost to ground level. In common with other rhino species, the white rhino has a penchant for mud baths. This habit is not simply a cosmetic indulgence: the mud traps ticks, and when this dries and is rubbed off, or falls off, the parasites are shed at the same time.

sations. Groups provide their own tents, bedding and other equipment, and must be fully self-sufficient. Visitors are welcome, but they are asked to make arrangements in advance. The three camps have locked gates and visitors wishing to pass through them must be accompanied by a member of the reserve staff.

The Percy Fyfe reserve is about 35 km northeast of Potgietersrus. To reach it, drive north from Potgietersrus on the road to Pietersburg and take the signposted turn-off to the left. From there the route is well signposted as far as the reserve's main entrance at Lunsklip Station. To arrange a visit or request further information, write to The Officer-in-Charge, Percy Fyfe Nature Reserve, Private Bag X2585, Potgietersrus 0600 (telephone Potgietersrus 5678).

Pietersburg Nature Reserve
A 3 100 ha area of the town commonage south of Pietersburg has been set aside as a game sanctuary – one of the largest municipal nature reserves in the Transvaal. The terrain is mainly flat and the bush cover relatively sparse, allowing fine game-viewing. There are 21 species of game, including white rhino, eland, red hartebeest, blue wildebeest, zebra, impala, springbok, nyala, gemsbok and even

tsessebe. A hiking trail leads through the reserve, providing a glimpse of the game and the wide variety of birds that are found.

The Pietersburg reserve is open year-round from 7 a.m. to 6 p.m. in summer and until 5 p.m. in winter. Just outside the entrance is the municipal caravan and camping site and Pietersburg's Union Park, which features a picnic area and rondavels. At Union Park you can book for the hiking trail and pay entrance fees to drive into the reserve. To reach the reserve follow the signs from the middle of town.

Pilanesberg National Park
The crater of a long-extinct volcano is the setting of the largest sanctuary on the Middleveld, a 55 000 ha national park created by the Republic of Bophuthatswana. The heart of the crater is fringed by three concentric ridges or rings of koppies and the whole formation rises from the surrounding plains like a bubble. Pilanesberg itself (pronounced Pi-larns-berg) is the highest peak, and gives its name to the whole formation. It overlooks the Mankwe Dam, which is right in the middle.

Until the mid-1970s the Pilanesberg area accommodated a large population of farming families. Then the Bophuthatswana Government

Scimitar-horned oryx usually live in small, nomadic herds which may wander great distances in search of grazing. These large, pale-coloured animals, bred in the Potgietersrus Nature Reserve and Game-breeding Park, are the most endangered of all the antelope. They have been hunted by desert tribesmen in northern Africa for centuries, and were once kept by the ancient Egyptians as domestic animals.

decided to create a substantial game reserve (not the least of their intentions was to attract foreign tourists and their money: the Sun City hotel and casino complex is a close neighbour). The resident farmers agreed to move to new farms, a game fence was erected, and the stage was set for 'Operation Genesis', one of the most ambitious game-stocking ventures ever carried out in Southern Africa.

Much of the impetus of Operation Genesis came from the Southern African Nature Foundation, an arm of the World Wildlife Fund. Eland were brought from Namibia; Burchell's zebra from the Transvaal; red hartebeest from Namibia and the northern Cape; white rhino from Natal; waterbuck from the Transvaal; and elephant and buffalo from the Addo National Park, in the eastern Cape. The Natal Parks Board donated 17 black rhino.

Pilanesberg's rangers were drawn from as far afield as the animals, though most came from Natal and Zimbabwe. They planned Pilanesberg's priorities, deciding that utilisation and education were more important than recreation. 'If we'd developed Pilanesberg as a playground for the wealthy it wouldn't survive very long,' explains the park's first director, Jeremy Anderson. 'It's no good expecting the

local people to value wildlife because it looks pretty – the Tswana word for antelope is the same as their word for meat.'

Instead, the park staff encourages local people to think of the park as an important economic asset. 'We will cull surplus animals regularly and sell the meat at low prices,' says Anderson. 'It will help to show them that wildlife can bring them great benefits.'

Many of Pilanesberg's visitors are drawn from its close neighbour, the Sun City hotel and casino complex. Visitors can go on two- to three-hour safaris in open Land-Rovers or open buses. The safaris are in the early morning and late afternoon – the best times for viewing game. Visitors staying in the park can also go on exciting night drives and book for some fascinating nature walks.

Potgietersrus Nature Reserve and Game-breeding Centre

South Africa's National Zoological Gardens has established two animal-breeding centres, one near Lichtenburg in the western Transvaal and the second on the northern outskirts of Potgietersrus, in the Bushveld. The Potgietersrus Game-breeding Centre covers some 800 ha of what used to be farmland and consists partly

of bush-covered koppies (one hillside features an extensive stand of aloes), an extensive grassy plain, and a fair-sized dam surrounded by reeds. As might be expected, the breeding centre specialises in rare species from Southern Africa as well as other parts of the world. Part of the reserve (close to the entrance) features a hotch-potch of llamas from South America, *banteng* wild cattle from southeast Asia and *mouflon* wild sheep from the Mediterranean region.

A railway line divides the exotic from the indigenous African species – the latter having the run of the rest of the reserve. They include pygmy hippo from West Africa, and scimitar-horned oryx and addax from North Africa.

A variety of game may be seen at Potgietersrus, including herds of tsessebe (the original animals came from the Doorndraai reserve), sable, lechwe, nyala, blue wildebeest, Burchell's zebra and Hartmann's zebra. Waterbuck, impala and white rhino frequent the bush areas.

The Potgietersrus Centre is open year-round from 8 a.m. to 6 p.m. in summer and until 5.30 p.m. in winter. To reach it, take the Potgietersrus-Pietersburg road and watch for the sign. Visitors drive through the reserve in their own cars, following a one-way route that takes two hours to complete. There is a picnic site close to the large dam, and across the highway is a municipal caravan and camping site.

Pretoria National Botanical Garden

With the amalgamation of the head offices of the National Botanic Gardens in Kirstenbosch, and the Botanical Research Institute in Pretoria, the 77 ha Pretoria National Botanical Garden has become the joint organisation's eighth National Botanic Garden. The research headquarters of the newly formed body is built on a hill at the centre of the garden.

The garden is divided into a number of specific biomes, or vegetation types, including savanna, Karoo, coastal forest and the dry veld of Namibia. More than half of South Africa's tree species grow in the garden (over 500 species are represented), and besides the plants growing in the open there are many more in hothouses and shade-houses. All told, more than 5000 species are grown here.

The Pretoria National Botanical Garden is open to visitors every day from 6 a.m. to 6 p.m. Entrance is free but a fee may be charged in the future. The nursery can be viewed by appointment only. To reach the garden from central Pretoria, take the road to Silverton and then follow the signs to the CSIR. The garden and the Botanical Research Institute are on the left, and are well signposted. For further information, write to The Director, Pretoria National Botanic Garden, Private Bag X101, Pretoria 0001 (telephone Pretoria 86-1164).

Roodeplaat Dam Nature Reserve

The provincial reserve at Roodeplaat Dam north-east of Pretoria is special for several reasons. One is its position (within 30 km of South Africa's administrative capital), a second is the dam's Olympic-standard rowing and canoeing course (six lanes wide, 2000 m long, and supported by boat-houses and launching-ramps); a third is its Overvaal Resort on the border of the reserve.

Set on the Pienaars River, the Roodeplaat Dam has a surface area of 395 ha (the total area of the reserve is 1695 ha).

The dam has been specially zoned in order to avoid conflicting interests between various rowing, canoeing, power-boating and shore-fishing enthusiasts.

Because some activities disturb birds, the upper reaches of the dam have been cordoned off as a bird sanctuary. More than 275 species have been spotted on and around the dam, among them fish eagle, black eagle, various kingfisher, duck and egret.

Roodeplaat's shore area is also zoned. The western portion is largely recreational with shady picnic, caravan and camping sites. The eastern portion, scenically the most beautiful part of the reserve, has the Overvaal Resort. The south has been left as a natural area and features game such as kudu, sable, waterbuck, Burchell's zebra, impala and smaller species. A camp here for 100 people provides accommodation for nature-orientated groups.

Roodeplaat Dam is open year-round and the gates are open from 6 a.m. to 6 p.m. To reach it from Pretoria, take the Pietersburg highway and drive north through the Magaliesberg range (which overlooks the city), then turn off the highway at the Wonderboom and Cullinan sign. Take the right turn and continue on that road until a four-way stop, then turn left and follow the signs to Roodeplaat.

For further information, write to The Officer-in-Charge, Roodeplaat Dam Nature Reserve, P.O. Box 15163, Lynn East 0039 (telephone Pretoria 808-1164).

Above: An African fish eagle, one of the most plentiful birds of prey in Southern Africa. **Right:** Pretoria's wonderboom has become a major tourist attraction.

LIZARDS OF THE ROCKS

A Transvaal flat rock lizard suns itself on a rock.

Describing an animal as 'cold-blooded' does not mean its blood is permanently cold, but rather that it lacks control mechanisms to keep its body temperature constant whatever its surroundings.

Such a creature relies on the sun to warm its blood and enable it to become active. On cold days a lizard stays inactive and in winter it may hibernate, but on sunny days it alternately basks in the sun and shelters in shadow when it becomes too hot. The warmer the sunshine, the more active it becomes.

Southern Africa contains a great variety of lizards and other cold-blooded animals, among them species of a fascinating genus known as *Platysaurus*, or flat rock lizards. They are brightly coloured, and therefore unusually attractive, and uniquely adapted to live on rock outcrops — in particular large sheets of bedrock. Their body shape is so flat and low-slung that they can easily creep into the narrowest crevices and cracks. *Platysaurus* lizards spend their days foraging and basking on the rocks in their home range, keeping a wary eye for aerial predators. When basking they lie flat, pressed to the rock surface to absorb the sun's warmth. When foraging they make short, sharp rushes over the rock surface in search of their prey. Invertebrates such as ants, beetles and insect larvae make up most of their food, though two species also feed on flower petals, leaves and seeds.

The various species appear to be strongly territorial. A brightly coloured male dominates an area of rock face and within it a group of females, juveniles and immature males. The females have a more drab colouring than the males, which in most species is a green upper body with an orange tail and underparts varying in colour from blue-black or azure to black. A dominant male's colours are even brighter than those of the other males in his family, and he shows it off to special advantage when challenged by a rival.

Rust de Winter Nature Reserve

Some 60 km north of Roodeplaat Dam is another provincial nature reserve that has an irrigation dam as its focal point – this time on the Elands River, near Rust de Winter.

The dam's surface area is 566 ha and the nature reserve as a whole covers some 1200 ha. As yet the reserve is not open for game-viewing, but the dam has long been popular with anglers and a dedicated fraternity of watersport enthusiasts.

Fish include bass, mudfish, kurper, barbel, carp and yellowfish. There are also crocodile in the dam, but this does not appear to deter sailing and skiing enthusiasts. Overnight camping is allowed in the reserve (no booking is necessary), but there are no facilities, and visitors should bring everything they need.

To reach the Rust de Winter Dam, take the Pretoria-Pietersburg highway and then turn off at the Pienaarsrivier-Rust de Winter intersection.

S.S. Skosana Nature Reserve

While S.S. Skosana Nature Reserve's conference facilities and informal lapa provide an ideal business venue, its 1800 ha of unspoilt bush also offer surroundings tailor-made for relaxing.

The thrill of game-tracking and the patient art of bird-watching are some of the highlights on the 19 km Nkonkoni Trail – a highlight of the reserve and an opportunity to see the huge numbers of birds and animals. Game includes kudu, wildebeest, eland, tsessebe, zebra and waterbuck, as well as large predators, such as leopard, brown hyena and lion.

The reserve offers self-catering accommodation for 32 people in two- and three-bedded

to The Officer-in-Charge, Vaalkopdam Nature Reserve, P.O. Box 1846, Rustenburg 0300 (telephone Beestekraal 676/704).

Warmbaths Nature Reserve

A 50ha nature reserve adjoining the public resort at Warmbaths' hot springs contains a few head of red hartebeest, Burchell's zebra, impala and other (smaller) game. Visitors need permission to explore the reserve on foot.

The spa is the busiest in the province's network of public resorts and is generally considered the best in the world after the spa at Baden-Baden. Besides the reserve, it offers fully equipped chalets, a caravan and camping site and the complex of hot-water pools that makes Warmbaths famous. Other attractions include water slides, a wave pool and mini-golf.

The resort is close to the centre of the town. It is open year-round and the gates are manned 24 hours a day. For further information, write to The General Manager, Overvaal Warmbaths, P.O. Box 75, Warmbaths 0480 (telephone Warmbaths 2200).

rondavels. The reserve is reached 95km after turning off the N1 towards Marble Hall. Booking is essential.

For more information write to The Secretary, Department of Agriculture and Environmental Affairs, Private Bag, X4017, KwaMhlanga 1022 (telephone KwaMhlanga 2326).

Schuinsdraai Nature Reserve

Fishing for bream at Arabie Dam is the main drawcard to Schuinsdraai Nature Reserve but other attractions are the many open bushveld areas which are ideal for game-viewing. Animals include herds of impala and zebra, and blue wildebeest, mountain reedbuck, klipspringer, duiker, steenbuck and warthog. If you are lucky you may even hear the distant bark of a brown hyena or catch a fleeting glimpse of a prowling leopard.

Crocodile lurk in the depths of the 1 300ha dam and although they usually feed on the slow-moving barbel, they are opportunists, and fishermen should keep well back from the water's edge.

This 9 037ha reserve, named after a sharp bend in the Olifants River, lies north of Marble Hall and is administered by the Department of Development Aid for future inclusion in Lebowa. Hunting will be allowed in the reserve when game numbers warrant culling.

Accommodation is in a bungalow camp or in a caravan park beside the dam, where a boat launching site is provided. Shops and fuel are available at Marble Hall. For more information contact The Department of Development Aid, P.O. Box 384, Pretoria 0001 (telephone Pretoria 312-9303 or 312-9304).

Umkhombo Nature Reserve

You can hunt, fish, hike and view game at this 11 000ha reserve on the Elands River, near Rust de Winter. Hunting, however, is permitted in certain areas of the reserve, far from the ears of the hikers and fishermen.

Kudu, impala, wildebeest, hartebeest, zebra and warthog are the most common species which require culling, and profits are a vital source of income for conservation authorities running this huge area.

Fishermen should be wary of crocodile in the Elands River and in the dam, which is an excellent fishing spot. Camping is permitted.

For more information write to The Secretary, Department of Agriculture and Environmental Affairs, Private Bag X4017, KwaMhlanga 1022 (telephone KwaMhlanga 2326).

Vaalkop Dam Nature Reserve

While many visitors enjoy the fine fishing and boating opportunities at Vaalkop Dam, this 1 873ha nature reserve is tailor-made for bird-watchers. Over 290 birds, mainly waterfowl have been recorded in the reserve and there is a checklist available which helps to keep track of your tally.

Swimming, waterskiing, boating and canoeing are all possible in the dam, while fishing for carp and large-scale yellowfish is also a very popular pastime.

More than half of the reserve is wetland, but around the edges there are kudu, impala, waterbuck, spotted hyena and antbear to be seen. Picnics and camping are permitted.

The dam lies near Beestekraal, north-east of Rustenburg. For bookings and enquiries write

Wonderboom Nature Reserve

Pretoria's wonderboom or 'wonder-tree' is the sum of many parts. At its heart is the trunk of a wild fig (*Ficus salicifolia*) more than 1 000 years old and some 5,5m in diameter. Branches from this trunk first spread out radially but gradually drooped towards the ground, where they sent out roots from which sprang a circle of new trunks. In time, two of the offspring produced a third generation.

Today the wonderboom has 13 distinct trunks with a 'canopy' spreading across 55m (it reaches a height of 15m). The tree would be able to provide enough shade for more than 1 000 people.

In earlier times the wonderboom's 'umbilical cords' were clearly visible, but they have been broken over the years.

In the 1920s there were rumours that the legendary 'Kruger millions' were buried among the roots of the wonderboom, and fortune hunters dug holes up to 3m deep. Now the tree has been proclaimed a national monument, and the Pretoria Municipality has created a 150ha nature reserve around it. There are many picnic and braai sites located among the trees, and a nature trail leads to an Anglo-Boer War fort on top of a koppie.

To reach the wonderboom from central Pretoria, drive north on Paul Kruger Street, pass through the wonderboom poort in the Magaliesberg Hills (which overlook the city) and follow the signs to Warmbaths. The reserve is on the right, within 1 km of the turn-off beyond the entrance to the poort, on the northern side of the Magaliesberg. The reserve is open daily throughout the year, from sunrise to sunset.

Sandy plains and the mighty Magaliesberg

Flat, sandy grassveld and an overwhelmingly blue sky are the hallmarks of the western Transvaal. The region hints strongly of the great Kalahari thirstland to the north-west: the sand is white rather than red, but the thorn clumps scattered in the sweet and sour grassveld are plainly related to the vegetation of Botswana. The similarity extends to many bird and game species, though the black wildebeest – a creature of the southern Transvaal and Free State Highveld – is a notable exception. Nature reserves near Lichtenburg, Klerksdorp, Bloemhof and Christiana illustrate the consistent flatness of the western Transvaal – valued by those who live there, but unsettling for visitors used to more varied terrain. There is a different feeling at Krugersdorp, on the threshold of the beautiful Magaliesberg range, and this feeling is even more pronounced at Hartbeespoort Dam and at the provincial nature reserve near Rustenburg, which includes the range's highest points.

Abe Bailey Nature Reserve

Early this century, the mining magnate Sir Abe Bailey maintained a stud farm and shooting box on a stretch of land some 5 km north of where Carletonville stands today. Sir Abe was a member of the Transvaal Game Protection Association, forerunner of the Wildlife Society of Southern Africa. In 1977 the Society obtained a lease on his old property and began to create a nature reserve named in his honour. The reserve was later enlarged to its present 3 000 ha and soon afterwards the Society handed all but a small part of it to the Transvaal Provincial Administration's Directorate of Nature and Environmental Conservation.

The reserve's terrain is flat and the vegetation is part grass and part bush. Highveld species such as springbok, black wildebeest and red hartebeest have been re-introduced. The reserve's special pride, however, is its waterfowl. Water pumped from local mines has created vleis with a total area of nearly 400 ha. Many scores of species are regular visitors here, including flamingoes and fish eagles.

The reserve is still being developed, but day visitors may make arrangements through The Officer-in-Charge, Abe Bailey Nature Reserve, P.O. Box 13, Carletonville 2500 (telephone Carletonville 2908). To reach the reserve, leave Carletonville by the Pretoria road and after about 5 km, turn left towards Welverdiend. The reserve is 5 km from the turn-off. The old shooting lodge is still controlled by the Wildlife Society, and is now used as an educational centre.

Above: Night herons at their daytime roost in the Barberspan Nature Reserve. At dusk these nocturnal birds move to rivers and streams, where they spend the night hunting for crabs, frogs and fish. **Left:** Red-knobbed coots at Barberspan. They are aggressive birds, and have often been seen harassing other waterfowl. Nests are of the floating type, built of reeds and weeds. **Right:** A termite soldier and pale worker feeding on white fungus nodules they have grown in their nest.

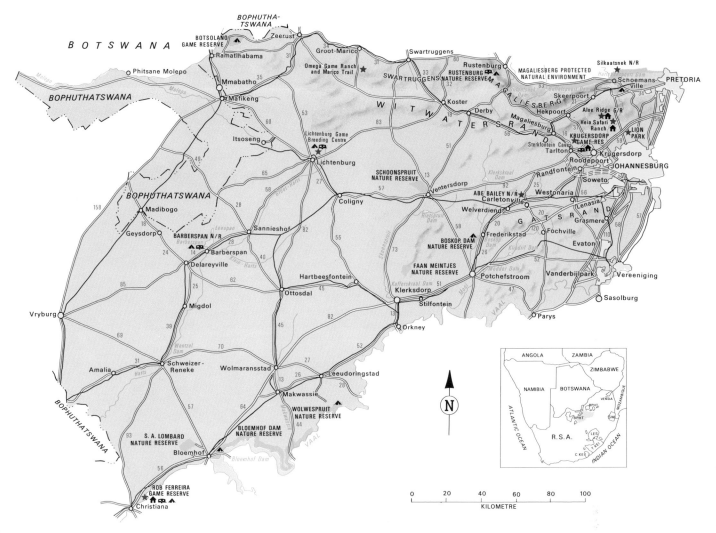

Aloe Ridge Game Reserve

Aloe Ridge's game reserve, hotel and Zulu village are magnificently situated at the foot of the Swartkops Hills, near Muldersdrift.

The reserve offers game-viewing in open Land Rovers, hiking and excellent bird-watching. At Phumangena Umuzi, a Zulu village and handicraft centre, visitors are treated to traditional meals and dances. Overnight accommodation is offered in 'beehive' huts.

The main accommodation is at Aloe Ridge Hotel, which has 72 bedrooms, four suites, a restaurant, indoor heated pool, outdoor pool, tennis and squash courts and excellent conference facilities. To request further details or accommodation write to Aloe Ridge Hotel, P.O. Box 3040, Honeydew 2040 and for reservations telephone Johannesburg 659-0605.

Barberspan Nature Reserve

The Transvaal's largest waterfowl sanctuary is Barberspan, a 1 800 ha body of water located some 16 km north-east of Delareyville. The pan is the focal point of a 3 100 ha provincial nature reserve, and is fed by the Harts River. Over the ages, herds of springbok and other species trampled the bottom of the waterhole, steadily enlarging the area eroded by wind. The spring-bok have disappeared, but bird-watchers have counted more than 350 bird species. Barber-span's terrain is flat and grassy and sometimes seems rather bleak – but the rich bird life pro-vides a beautiful contrast.

The abundant bird life makes Barberspan an ideal study area, and each year research sta-tion staff ring birds to monitor their migration patterns. The results can sometimes be startling: a ruff ringed at Barberspan was found in Siberia only two months later.

The pan's population varies greatly from month to month. For example, between Novem-ber and January Barberspan's ducks leave the pan for breeding grounds in other areas. Waders, herons and egrets take their place, but in autumn the ducks return. Because it is a perennial pan, it provides sanctuary for birds when the other pans are dry.

The south-eastern part of the pan is set aside for anglers, and there is a caravan and camp-ing site with toilets and braai sites. The re-mainder of the reserve has been preserved as a natural area, providing outstanding bird-watching and walking possibilities. The reserve is open daily from 6 a.m. to 6 p.m. To reach it, approach from Delareyville or Sannieshof and take the Deelpan turn-off.

For further information on Barberspan, write to The Officer-in-Charge, Barberspan Nature Reserve, P.O. Barberspan 2765 (telephone Bar-berspan 1202).

Bloemhof Dam Nature Reserve
Eland, red hartebeest, blesbok and springbok used to roam freely on the sandy grassveld of the western Transvaal, and all are represent-ed in a 14 000 ha provincial nature reserve on the north shore of Bloemhof Dam. The dam ex-tends upstream as far as Kommandodrif, while a southern arm of the dam reaches Hoopstad in the Orange Free State. An impressive bar-rage spans the Vaal River at Bloemhof. The na-ture reserve stretches 136 km east from Bloemhof and faces the Free State's Sandveld reserve across the water, on the south shore.

Black wildebeest, zebra and ostrich add var-iety to the Bloemhof reserve's game population (white rhinos are to be introduced), but as yet most of its visitors are anglers and their fam-ilies, who spend most of their time on the shore-line. The 22 802 ha dam is stocked with carp, yellowfish, mudfish, barbel and other spe-cies. Many anglers set up camp close to the reserve's main gate, only a stone's throw from the bridge that crosses the dam on the road be-tween Bloemhof and Hoopstad. The gate is open daily from 8 a.m. to 6 p.m.

Above: A blesbok herd at the gallop in the Bloemhof Dam Nature Reserve. **Below left:** A Cape fur seal in the Hartbeespoort Snake and Animal Park. **Below right:** A leaf-cutter bee lines its hole with a rolled-up leaf. The female uses oval sections of leaves or flower petals to line her nesting cells, in which she lays her eggs. **Right:** The 'Fiestaland' recreational area on the Crocodile River, just below Hartbeespoort Dam.

The Hoopstad bridge provides fine views of both the Bloemhof reserve and the Sandveld reserve on the other side. To the west is the barrage; to the east, the dam and its flat shores stretch to the horizon. Visitors who wish to see game should obtain permission from the Officer-in-Charge and enter the reserve through a gate between Bloemhof and Wol-maransstad (there is a signposted turn-off 6 km east of Bloemhof). For further information, write to The Officer-in-Charge, Bloemhof Dam Nature Reserve, Private Bag X7, Bloemhof 2660 (telephone Bloemhof 1122).

Boskop Dam Nature Reserve
The 373 ha Boskop Dam, situated on the Mooi River about 20 km north-east of Potchefstroom, is the heart of a 3 000 ha provincial nature reserve noted for outdoor recreation. Yachts-men and canoeists ply the dam's surface while fishermen probe beneath it for bass, carp, bar-bel, yellowfish and mudfish. The dam and its surroundings feature a rich bird population in-cluding ducks, crakes, avocets, goliath herons and fish eagles. The reserve's wildlife also in-cludes black wildebeest, eland, springbok, red hartebeest, zebra and blesbok.

Boskop Dam is one of the most-visited reserves in the western Transvaal, but few peo-ple spot one of its rarest species – Lithops les-liei, a succulent that resembles a stone. However the well-known Vaal River lily (Cri-num bulbispermum) and the beautiful coral bush (Erythrina zeyheri), with its characteristic scarlet flowers, are more readily visible.

Overnight camping is allowed at the reserve, and the gate is open daily from 8 a.m. to 6 p.m. To reach it, take the road between Potchef-stroom and Carletonville and follow the sign-posted turn-off.

For further information, prospective visitors may write to The Officer-in-Charge, Boskop Dam Nature Reserve, P.O. Box 24, Boskop 2528 (telephone Potchefstroom 2-2430).

Carlos Rolfes Nature Reserve

This 90 ha wetland near Jan Smuts Airport has been fenced off to protect the breeding ground of various waders and, most curious of all, grey-headed seagulls which breed here in winter. The public is not allowed into the vlei area, but the birds can be viewed through the fence. The reserve is reached off the R21 south of the airport, taking the turn-off to the World Trade Centre. For more information write to The Officer-in-Charge, Carlos Rolfes Nature Reserve, P.O. Box 12137, Daggafontein 1573 (telephone Johannesburg 734-9642).

Faan Meintjes Nature Reserve

One of the loveliest municipal sanctuaries in the Transvaal is Klerksdorp's Faan Meintjes Nature Reserve – 1 300 ha of grassy plains and sandy ridges located some 14 km north of the town. The sweet and sour grassveld supports buck such as eland, gemsbok, red hartebeest, black wildebeest, waterbuck, sable, blesbok and springbok, and visitors may also spot buffalo, giraffe, zebra and white rhino. Some species are so well established that each year the municipality brings in trophy hunters (under strict control) to remove surplus animals.

The Faan Meintjes Reserve, named after a local businessman, has become one of Klerksdorp's most valued tourist assets. Three guest-houses cater for overnight visitors, while a picnic spot at the heart of the reserve is a favourite destination of day visitors, particularly over weekends and public holidays.

A drive over the 40 km road that winds through the reserve takes motorists two hours if they observe the speed limit. Overnight camping is not allowed, but the reserve is open daily throughout the year from 10 a.m. to 6 p.m. in summer and until 5 p.m. in winter.

To reach the reserve, follow the signs from the middle of Klerksdorp or from the road between Klerksdorp and Ventersdorp. The reserve is located west of the road to Goedgevonden, 11 km from a turn-off on Klerksdorp's northern limit.

For more information write to The Town Clerk, Klerksdorp Town Council, P.O. Box 99, Klerksdorp 2570 (telephone Klerksdorp 64-1371).

Hartbeespoort Dam Nature Reserve

The 2 000 ha Hartbeespoort Dam at the foot of the Magaliesberg is one of the Transvaal's favourite playgrounds. Yachtsmen, anglers and water-skiers are among the thousands of regular visitors, and the shores are lined by holiday and retirement homes. The water surface is controlled by the Directorate of Nature and Environmental Conservation, as are five sections of land along the shoreline that form part of the Hartbeespoort Dam Nature Reserve. Together the five sections stretch for 40 km.

Botsalano Game Reserve

At Botsalano, which means 'friendship' in Tswana, visitors can expect not only to be well looked-after but also to be treated to some first-class game-viewing, picnicking and camping facilities.

Despite the fact that in the old days a combination of rinderpest and hunters almost wiped out herds of indigenous game, numbers in the 5 800 ha reserve have started to swell once more. You should be alert for white rhino, giraffe, hartebeest, springbok, eland, gemsbok, zebra and impala, particularly around the reserve's well-marked game-drives and at dams and waterholes. Other species common to the area are kudu, steenbok, duiker, wart-hog and jackal. Birds typical of the dry grassland of the region are bustards and korhaans.

Game can even be seen from Mogobe Camp, which has 4 two-bedded tents beside a shady thicket, on the bank of Mogobe Dam. Visitors can also stay at Botlhaba Camp – an A-frame chalet with four double and two single beds.

At the entrance to the reserve a boma caters for groups and there are also camping and picnic sites with water and toilets provided.

Botsalano is situated some 30 km north of Mmabatho, the capital of Bophuthatswana. For bookings, write to The Manager, Botsalano Game Reserve, Private Bag X2078, Mafikeng 8670 (telephone Mafikeng 2-4114).

Four of the five sections – Schoemansville in the north, Oberon to the west, Meerhof and Ifafi to the south-east – are little more than beaches. All are open to visitors daily (throughout the year). Camping is allowed at Schoemansville, Oberon and Ifafi. Gates are open from 6 a.m. to 6 p.m. Boating is permitted, and anglers may fish from the shore. Schoemansville is not clearly signposted, but Meerhof and Ifafi are easily reached from the road along the dam's eastern shore.

The fifth section is Kommandonek, which is located off the road to Kosmos. This 200 ha section features an attractive recreation and camping area for visitors.

Hartbeespoort Snake and Animal Park

The steep shoreline rising from Hartbeespoort Dam's northern boundary is an entrancing setting for one of South Africa's smaller, yet most-visited zoos. Visitors can see Kalahari lion, leopard, cheetah, tiger, puma and panther as well as chimpanzee and a variety of mongoose. The park also features a fine reptile collection. The zoo contains a large arena in which visitors are given regular snake- and animal-handling demonstrations, and is much in demand with school groups. Other visitors embark on a passenger launch that makes tours of the dam, or ascend to the top of the Magaliesberg by means of a 1,2 km cableway. Nearby is the Hartbeespoort Aquarium, which displays both fresh- and salt-water species and also crocodiles and performing seals. The aquarium is located beside the road that runs along the dam's eastern shore, while the zoo itself is on the main Hartbeespoort Dam-Johannesburg road.

Both the zoo and the aquarium are open daily throughout the year, from 8 a.m. to 5 p.m. in winter and from 9 a.m. to 6 p.m. in summer. For more information you should write to Hartbeespoort Dam Snake and Animal Park, P.O. Box 109, Hartbeespoort 0216 (telephone Hartbeespoort 3-0162).

CORNWALLIS HARRIS

'Hunting the Ostrich' — a lithograph from a book by Cornwallis Harris.

HUNTING THE OSTRICH

A century and a half ago much of the Transvaal was home to an incredible variety of game, a Mecca for sportsmen who came to Africa not just to hunt, but also to record for posterity the many and fascinating wild animals of Southern Africa.

Such a man was Captain Sir William Cornwallis Harris, an Indian Army officer who left behind a superb collection of illustrations of African game and an account of his travels in *Narrative of an Expedition into Southern Africa*, first published in Bombay in 1838.

Harris arrived in Algoa Bay in May 1836 and travelled to the frontier town of Graaff-Reinet where he kitted up for his expedition north. He crossed the Orange River below its junction with the Vaal and moved on to Kuruman and the kraal of the Ndebele king Mzilikazi — then at war with immigrant boers trekking north. Harris entered the Magaliesberg, where he reported seeing up to 300 elephant in one herd, 32 white rhino, large numbers of giraffe and antelope of all kinds.

It was in the Magaliesberg that Harris saw an antelope no European had ever reported. He managed to shoot one bull (he also tried for a cow), and took the complete skin back to civilisation and the taxidermist. For many years this beautiful antelope was referred to widely as the 'Harris buck'. Later it was re-named sable, the name it still bears today.

Harris also crossed the Witwatersrand and travelled down the Mooi, Vaal and Modder rivers before reaching the Orange River near Philippolis.

By January 1838 Harris was back in India, where he published the first account of his travels. He also painted many pictures of the animals he had seen on the expedition, 32 of which were later published as engravings in a single volume — today regarded as a rare collectors' item.

Harris never returned to Southern Africa, although he did lead an expedition to Ethiopia in 1841. He died of 'lingering fever' near Poona, India, in 1848.

Heia Safari Ranch

The Heia Safari Ranch in Muldersdrift's Swartkops Hills caters for conferences and also welcomes private guests. The ranch consists of two-bedded luxury, thatched bungalows and a licensed restaurant complex set in koppies on the bank of the Crocodile River.

Blesbok, zebra and impala wander through the grounds and guests spend their time fishing, riding and generally 'taking it easy'. There is a traditional braai every Sunday, followed by tribal dancing. To reserve accommodation, or to request further details, write to Heia Safari Ranch, P.O. Box 1387, Honeydew 2040 (telephone Johannesburg 659-0605).

Johannesburg Lion Park

Among the more unusual game parks in the Transvaal is a 200 ha lion reserve that features more than 60 lions – and the population is growing. Visitors drive along a (one-way) winding road through the game area, where they may see black wildebeest, gemsbok, impala, blesbok, zebra and ostrich. Thereafter they travel through the lion area. The lion park is open daily between 8 a.m. and 4.30 p.m. but many visitors like to be there between 9 a.m. and 9.30 a.m., when the lions are fed. The park also has an entertainment area which offers a restaurant, an old Ndebele village, swimming pool, picnic spots and other facilities. To reach the park from Johannesburg, drive to Four Ways, north of Bryanston, then follow the signs to the Pretoria-Krugersdorp road and turn left.

Kloofendal Nature Reserve

Roodepoort's Kloofendal Reserve offers indigenous trees, proteas, orchids and other flora, and includes an attractive rocky koppie. A stone amphitheatre on the western edge is used for open-air events, and a walking trail takes visitors past old gold mine shafts and other places of interest. The reserve has a diverse bird population. It is open 1 September to 30 April, from sunrise to sunset.

To reach the 100 ha reserve, drive along Ontdekkers Road from west to east, turn left into Christiaan de Wet Road, then turn left into Wilgerood Road, left into Topaz Avenue and right into Galena Avenue which leads to the entrance. For further information, write to The Chief, Parks and Recreation, City of Roodepoort, Private Bag X30, Roodepoort 1725 (telephone Johannesburg 472-1439).

Krugersdorp Game Reserve

Grassy hills and bush-filled ravines provide a widely varying habitat for animals in this 1400 ha game sanctuary run by the Krugersdorp municipality. Visitors may spot giraffe, white rhino, eland, blue wildebeest, kudu, sable, roan, buffalo, blesbok, impala – and baboon, which

Above: One of the most treasured animals at the game-breeding station in the Lichtenburg Nature Reserve is this giant eland bull from west Africa. The giant eland has a particularly well-developed sense of smell, and has larger ears than the common eland. **Right:** Greater flamingoes wade through a pan in the Lichtenburg Nature Reserve. Like the lesser flamingo, this bird is a filter-feeder, collecting its food by sweeping its beak through shallow water. The greater flamingo, however, feeds almost exclusively on small crustaceans. Both species may travel great distances across Africa.

are liable to attack unwary visitors when seeking food. A special attraction is a 100 ha lion camp at the heart of the reserve.

The Krugersdorp sanctuary is little more than 40 minutes' drive from the centre of Johannesburg, and is one of the most-visited reserves in the Transvaal. There is a tearoom and picnic spot in the middle of the reserve, and visitors may stay in a rest camp offering chalets, rondavels and a caravan park. The chalets have two bedrooms, a bathroom, a combination bedroom/dining-room/kitchen, and an open garage. The rondavels contain a dinette/bedroom, kitchen, shower and toilet. Bedding is provided but visitors should bring their own cooking equipment, crockery and cutlery. Regular half-day educational trails are operated by the Krugersdorp branch of the Wildlife Society. The trails extend for 7-10 km and last up to four-and-a-half hours.

The sanctuary is open daily from 8 a.m. to 5 p.m. To reach it, drive out of Krugersdorp on the road to Magaliesberg, and watch for signposts indicating a turn-off to the reserve on the right. For further information, and to book accommodation, write to The Tourist Officer, Department of Parks, Recreation and Game Reserve, P.O. Box 94, Krugersdorp 1740 (telephone Johannesburg 660-1076).

Lichtenburg Game-Breeding Centre

Pretoria's National Zoological Gardens of South Africa has a lively offspring on the flat grassveld of the Lichtenburg district. The 6 000 ha game sanctuary which is situated north of the town is first and foremost a breeding station that concentrates on valued species of animals (both indigenous and exotic). White rhino and Hartmann's Mountain Zebra share the reserve with scimitar oryx from north Africa and water buffalo from India, while hippo from Southern Africa live beside pygmy hippo (rapidly diminishing in number in the wild) from Ivory Coast, Liberia and adjacent areas of Sierra Leone.

Fences divide the Lichtenburg reserve into three main sections. The largest section covers 4 000 ha and features a comprehensive road network. This is where most of the animals are to be found. Near the entrance are 25 ha of shallow pans that are home to a number of bird species. The second section covers 2 000 ha and is for species that might interbreed with animals in the main enclosure. The third (and smallest) section is a 200 ha cheetah camp.

The flat terrain and stunted vegetation make it easy to spot game in the Lichtenburg reserve, and visitors are advised to pack a set of binoculars along with other essentials. The sanctuary is open daily throughout the year, from 8 a.m. to 6 p.m. in summer and to 5.30 p.m. in winter. To reach the reserve, drive out of Lichtenburg on the Koster road and turn left at the four-way stop. Then drive a further 2 km to reach the entrance gate, which also gives access to the adjoining municipal caravan park and camping site.

A long-horned cricket eats aphids on a *Cotyledon* flower. This cricket, widespread in the Transvaal, is a nocturnal predator, spending the day in a shelter of rolled leaves secured by fine strands of silk.

Magaliesberg Protected Natural Environment

A few hours from Johannesburg's skyscrapers, smog and traffic lies an unspoilt wilderness where you can still get-away-from-it-all and witness such beautiful sights as rare Cape vultures, soaring on strong mountain updraughts. This is the Magaliesberg – a 125 km ribbon of mountain that stretches from Pretoria to Rustenburg.

In 1977, to preserve this wilderness from relentless urban spread, farming and other developments, the 40 000 ha region was placed in the capable hands of The Directorate of Nature and Environmental Conservation.

While much of the Magaliesberg is private land, you can still absorb the mountain atmosphere in selected places such as the Rustenburg Nature Reserve, which offers a two-day hiking trail and the Mountain Sanctuary Park. Both of these give access to the streams and cliffs, which are typical of the area.

Certain climbing areas, such as Castle Gorge, Tonquani and Cedarberg are controlled by the Mountain Club of South Africa, which issues a limited number of permits each week.

Vulnerable Cape vultures are found nesting on south-facing slopes, west of Olifantsnek, while brown hyena, leopard and baboon are found amongst the inaccessible ravines of the area. Duiker, steenbok, jackal and reedbuck are common.

For more information or enquiries write to The Directorate of Nature and Environmental Conservation, Private Bag X209, Pretoria 0001 (telephone Pretoria 323-3403).

Omega Game Farm and Marico Trail

To the majority of people who have read Herman Charles Bosman's books, Groot Marico comes across as a charming little town brimming with colourful characters. Although the real place is a little different, the region still gives you a glimpse of Africa as it was then – a land of game, clear streams, bushveld and sunny days.

One of the best ways to explore this area is on the Marico Trail, which traverses the Omega Game Farm. You will venture on foot along the Marico River for two glorious days, swimming, sunning yourself and admiring the birds, plants and animals.

The base camp and overnight hut have running water, toilets and showers and sleep up to 20 hikers. Comfort-seeking visitors will prefer the accommodation at The Omega Game Farm, which sleeps 22 guests and has electricity and a lapa for potjiekos and braais. From here day walks, of between 30 minutes to two hours, are offered.

Omega Game Farm has 12 types of antelope with herds of gemsbok, springbok and impala. There are over 100 species of birds and diverse vegetation.

For more information write to J. Pienaar, Omega Game Farm, P.O. Box 8, Bührmannsdrif 2867, (telephone Slurry 502).

Rob Ferreira Game Reserve

Overvaal Resorts runs a mineral spa beside the Vaal River, north-east of Christiana. One of its attractions is a well-stocked game reserve between the river and the main road to the north – 2 500 ha of flat, sandy grassveld that is typical of the western Transvaal. Animals include eland, black wildebeest, red hartebeest, zebra, blesbok, gemsbok, springbok, white rhino and impala.

The river runs along the reserve's southern edge and for much of the year provides a natural boundary. In winter, however, it becomes so shallow that buck can easily walk across (in the past they fell easy victim to biltong-hungry farmers).

Today there is a fence on the river bank. Perhaps it is a blessing in disguise, for it provides a rhino-proof corridor along the bank which is part of an 8 km hiking trail. Hikers walk to a nine-bunk overnight hut and return to the spa on the following day.

Walking and riding are banned in the reserve, but the spa has horses for hire. Rhinos are one of the factors which led to the prohibition of riding, while another is jealous zebra: they are liable to challenge the horses. Instead, visitors travel through the reserve in their own cars, or by bus. The reserve is open daily from 7 a.m. to 5 p.m., and the road network takes visitors to all parts of the reserve, including the river bank – which is rich in riverine bush and is the favourite habitat of the rhino and impala.

The Rob Ferreira Resort, named after a former M.E.C. of the Transvaal Provincial Council who took special interest in public spas, is known as one of the most progressive in the province. The complex includes 100 fully equipped chalets, two-person flats, restaurants, a supermarket, a fine auditorium and a caravan and camping site.

There are two swimming pools and a mineral bath. The resort is especially busy during the Christmas and Easter school holidays, though its dry climate makes it popular throughout the year.

To reach it, take the main road from Christiana to the north-east and drive about 4 km (the resort is on the right, well signposted from the road). For further information, and to apply for accommodation, write to The Chief Director, Overvaal Resorts, P.O. Box 3046, Pretoria 0001 (telephone Pretoria 346-2288).

Rustenburg Nature Reserve

The Magaliesberg range is among the most beautiful in the Transvaal, and is within easy reach of the province's larger cities. On top is a plateau, part of which falls within a 2 898 ha provincial nature reserve that extends down the mountains' northern slopes. Steep quartzite cliffs and enormous boulders tower over wood-

Above: *Frithia pulchra,* a species of dwarf vygie indigenous to the Magaliesberg. The flowers of most vygies are open on most sunny days, but some open only at dusk, or even when the sun has set. **Left:** Cabbage trees *(Cussonia paniculata)* in the Rustenburg Nature Reserve, a beautiful sanctuary situated on a plateau in the Magaliesberg. **Right:** Mountain reedbuck. This buck may live in open grassland as well as on hills and mountains. It is fiercely territorial, marking and guarding its home ground against other adult males.

ed ravines where mountain streams plunge over high precipices.

The stream has created a number of crystal-clear rock pools. In 1981, part (1 359 ha) of the farm Baviaanskrans, which adjoins the reserve's eastern boundary, was bought with the intention of incorporating it into the existing sanctuary.

Long ago, the Rustenburg Nature Reserve was a farm that belonged to Paul Kruger. It later became the property of the Rustenburg Municipality, which donated it to the province. More than 140 bird species have been spotted in the area and the game population includes sable, waterbuck, kudu, red hartebeest, mountain reedbuck, springbok and eland.

One of the best ways to explore the Rustenburg Reserve is to set out on its two-day hiking trail. Many hikers like to arrive at the sanctuary in the afternoon or evening and spend the first night in Kudu Hut, near the entrance. On the following day they walk 9 km to Red Hartebeest Hut on the plateau, after which they walk another 12 km to return to their starting-point. Both reed huts accommodate ten hikers, and each consists of two bedrooms and a cook-

ing/dining area. Cooking pots, a grid and firewood are provided. The Peglerae Nature Trail offers day visitors a pleasant hike lasting about three hours.

Those with less energy may choose to drive through the reserve or peruse the wildlife displays on exhibit at the reserve's visitor centre, which is situated in the middle of the sanctuary. Close by is a small caravan and camping site (with ablution block) and picnic area.

Day visitors are admitted to the reserve between 8 a.m. and 4 p.m. (the reserve's gates officially close at 6 p.m.).

To reach the reserve, follow the signs from the centre of Rustenburg. There are two entrances – a northern entrance, suitable for those who have booked places on the hiking trail and for those going to a group camp located in the reserve. The eastern entrance, reached by a circular drive through the Magaliesberg foothills to the summit, is the main route to the reserve office and visitor centre. Those seeking further information should write to The Officer-in-Charge, Rustenburg Nature Reserve, P.O. Box 511, Rustenburg 0300 (telephone Rustenburg 3-1050).

S.A. Lombard Nature Reserve

Named in honour of a former provincial secretary who did much to create an awareness of the need for conservation, this provincial reserve lies in the extreme south-western Transvaal, north-west of Bloemhof.

The reserve covers 3 660 ha of flat grassveld dotted with small clumps of thorn trees. After heavy rains a large pan in the sanctuary fills with water, and is a favourite with large flocks of waterfowl. More than 250 species of birds have been spotted in the district. Typical of these are the black korhaan, white-browed sparrow-weaver, ant-eating chat, shaft-tailed widow-bird and blue crane.

Since its inception, the reserve's priority has been the breeding of Highveld game species. Black wildebeest were introduced as early as 1949 (from the last remaining herd in the Transvaal), and today the reserve has a large herd. Gemsbok were introduced in 1952, and since then have been joined by eland, red hartebeest, blesbok and springbok. These animals are distributed to other reserves.

Capturing the animals without injuring them is a difficult task, but it has been made simpler since the introduction of a new radio-controlled device in 1987. The animals are captured while drinking at a waterhole, and minimal injuries occur.

Research into problem animals (once a function of the reserve) was concentrated on black-backed jackal and caracal, although at one time the reserve bred hounds which were used to hunt jackals. The dogs were replaced by the more humane and efficient 'coyote-getter' imported from the United States. The Problem Animal Control Unit has since been transferred to the central Transvaal, and the facilities are now made available for research.

Day visitors are welcome, but should obtain permission from the Officer-in-Charge. To reach the reserve, leave Bloemhof by the road to Schweizer Reneke and after 5 km turn left at the sign indicating the reserve; then drive another 12 km along a dirt road.

For further information on the reserve, write to The Officer-in-Charge, S.A. Lombard Nature Reserve, P.O. Box 174, Bloemhof 2660 (telephone Bloemhof 4203).

Silkaatsnek Nature Reserve

Giraffe, eland, blue wildebeest and kudu are among the animals to be seen at this 400 ha private nature reserve on the slopes of the Magaliesberg, some 10 km from Hartbeespoort Dam. Zebra, blesbok, springbok, impala, waterbuck, duiker, warthog and ostrich may also be found in the area. There is a picnic area with pools and braai facilities at the foot of the mountains. The reserve is partly hilly and partly flat, and is open to visitors daily (except Mondays) from 7 a.m. to sunset, throughout the year. To reach Silkaatsnek, take the road between Pretoria and Brits and follow the clearly sign-posted route from a turn-off approximately 35 km from Pretoria.

Sterkfontein Caves

The area north of Krugersdorp features a number of impressive cave formations left by dissolution of the dolomite. In the 1890s a prospector blasted his way into one of the caves and began exploiting it for lime – in the process destroying glorious stalactites, stalagmites and pillars of crystal. The miner paid scant heed to deep beds of fossilised animal bones found in the caves, though many were kept as souvenirs by visitors.

That was the position until the 1930s, when an enterprising Krugersdorp man began to promote one of the cave formations as a tourist attraction. He issued a pamphlet which contained an intriguing invitation: 'Come to Sterkfontein and find the missing link' – a reference to a discovery made in 1924 at Taung, where a young anatomist, Professor Raymond A. Dart, identified the skull of an 'ape-child' that he dubbed *Australopithecus africanus*. The skull had come to light in association with the remains of long-extinct baboons and Dart was convinced he had found the 'missing link'.

The invitation could not have been more prophetic. In 1936 two anatomy students discovered fragments of baboon skulls at Sterkfontein and showed them to Dr Robert Broom of the Transvaal Museum in Pretoria.

Broom immediately embarked on excavations at Sterkfontein and soon found the skull of an adult *Australopithecus*. Before long, other remains came to light, both at Sterkfontein and at the Kromdraai caves close by.

When the owner of the land died in the late 1950s, his children presented a handsome part of it to the University of the Witwatersrand as the Isaac Edwin Stegmann Nature Reserve. Later the University bought a neighbouring farm (Swartkrans) which also contains a rich fossil cave deposit. Thus the University owns two sites in the area – Swartkrans Cave to the west and the main Sterkfontein complex, which is open to the public.

Limestone mining and natural cave formation have hollowed out large chambers within Sterkfontein, but it is not difficult to imagine the caves as they used to be. In places there are remnants of the old fossil-laden deposits, the deepest of them over three million years old.

In the underground galleries is a large lake of crystal-clear water extending far into unex-

WHERE VULTURES DINE

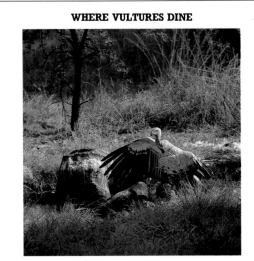

The Magaliesberg range is one of the last strongholds of the Cape vulture, once a familiar sight all over Southern Africa but today threatened by a variety of factors including poisoning, shooting, electrocution (on power lines), possibly a declining food supply – and a shortage of calcium in the diet.

The problem lies with the extermination of the bone-crunching hyena in this region: adult vultures can no longer find the bone fragments so essential to their chicks' diet.

Without this important source of calcium, the chicks develop crippled limbs – and eventually perish. Adult birds find the calcium in the form of bones stripped from carcasses, but modern farming practices leave few such carcasses, and the vulture population has declined dramatically as a result.

To help remedy the situation, the Vulture Study Group have encouraged local farmers and landowners in the Magaliesberg area to create a number of 'vulture restaurants' where carcasses of domestic animals are provided for the birds. The 'restaurants' are open spaces where the carcasses of cattle, horses, pigs and sometimes game are laid out. When the carcasses have been scraped clean, volunteer groups crush the bones, using mallets in order to provide the birds with much-needed bone fragments.

Not everyone finds the vulture appealing, but its less attractive features have a purpose in nature. Its bald head and neck are thrust deep into a carcass, receiving a potentially harmful coating of bacteria – yet there is nowhere for the bacteria to breed, and germs will be killed off by sunshine. The same goes for the vulture's bare legs, which often come into contact with putrid flesh (in nature, vultures prefer fresh meat to putrid carcasses). However, like other scavengers, they are highly resistant to bacterial contamination of their food, and experiments have shown them to be resistant to anthrax and botulism toxin. The massive beak is a highly effective implement designed to tear hide and flesh. Nature's feathered undertaker may not be pretty, but he is certainly efficient. To find out more information write to The Vulture Study Group, P.O. Box 72334, Parkview 2122.

Above: Cosmos blooms transform drab fields into riots of colour in autumn. Although regarded as a weed in South Africa, it is cultivated in gardens. **Below:** Burchell's zebra are generally gregarious by nature, and will even associate with other animals, such as impala and wildebeest. They are also very inquisitive.

plored chambers. In the water are minute blind shrimps no more than 1 cm in length.

The Sterkfontein Caves are open to visitors every day except Mondays, and on all public holidays. Tours are conducted every half-hour from 9 a.m. to 4 p.m. A guide leads visitors into the caves and recorded talks in several languages explain their history. There is a tearoom near the entrance, and beside it the Robert Broom Museum, which contains exhibits illustrating the processes of fossilisation and the area's natural history. To reach the caves, drive out of Krugersdorp on the road to the north-west, pass the Sterkfontein Hospital and watch for the signposted turn-off to the right.

Witwatersrand National Botanic Garden
This scenically beautiful site of 223 ha is within easy reach of Roodepoort and Krugersdorp. Surrounding the 70 m-high Witpoortjie Falls – the focal point of the garden – is dense riverine woodland surrounding the rich bird life. Over 170 species have been recorded, including the only pair of breeding black eagle on the Witwatersrand.

The garden also supports aloes, summer rainfall protea species and other flora. An interpretative centre displays the history, geography, fauna and flora of the garden.

The garden is open to the public from Mondays to Fridays from 7.30 a.m. to 4.30 p.m. and on weekends and public holidays from 8 a.m. to 5 p.m. The Botanic Society of South Africa operates a tea kiosk on Sundays from 10 a.m. to 4.30 p.m. and on Wednesday mornings from 10 a.m. to midday. Indigenous plants are on sale by appointment only.

The gardens are in Malcolm Street in Roodepoort. For more information you should write to The Witwatersrand National Botanic Garden, P.O. Box 2194, Wilropark 1731 (telephone Johannesburg 662-1741).

Wolwespruit Nature Reserve
Originally an isolated section of Bloemhof Dam Nature Reserve, Wolwespruit is now a sanctuary in its own right. The reserve covers 2 500 ha and is situated along the Vaal River upstream of the Bloemhof Dam and is named after a tributary of the Vaal. Impala, duiker, steenbok and zebra are indigenous and introduced game includes blesbok, red hartebeest and black wildebeest. Anglers may camp in the reserve, surrounded by the attractive riverine vegetation. To reach the reserve, drive from Leeudoringstad and follow the signs to Kommandodrif. Take the Klipspruit turn-off and then the Rustkraal turn-off. For further information, write to The Officer-in-Charge, Wolwespruit Nature Reserve, P.O. Box 237, Leeudoringstad 2640 (telephone Leeudoringstad 705).

A region where the bird is king

From its roster of nature reserves, the south-eastern Transvaal appears to be a bird paradise. The region contains five sanctuaries devoted to birds, among them Germiston's Rondebult and Nigel's Marievale, which are among the most important in South Africa. Birds are the prime attraction at several of the provincial reserves created around water storage dams (among them Vaal Dam Nature Reserve) and figure prominently at Johannesburg's Melville Koppies – the city's chief nature sanctuary.

Most of the bird reserves are relatively small and compact and are easily overshadowed in size by the province's Suikerbosrand Nature Reserve near Heidelberg and KaNgwane's Songimvelo Nature Reserve. These two reserves conserve the south-eastern Highveld at its best – rolling terrain, grassveld vegetation and a variety of game, including eland, black wildebeest, red hartebeest, Burchell's zebra, blesbok and springbok.

Badplaas Nature Reserve

The blue-green Hlumo-Hlumo Mountains provide an attractive backdrop for Badplaas, literally 'bath farm', one of the most popular of the Transvaal's hot-water mineral spas. The scenic slopes and foothills, which adjoin the spa (administered by the Overvaal Resorts) cover an area of 1 000 ha, providing plenty of room for the reserve's growing animal population as well as for hiking trails and riding – one of the Badplaas specialities.

The reserve's terrain is hilly and the vegetation is largely grassveld, which means it is easy to spot game. Badplaas features species such as eland, black wildebeest and red hartebeest, springbok, zebra, steenbok, duiker, bushbuck, blesbok and impala.

The reserve is open year-round, from 2 p.m. to 5 p.m. in school holidays and from 9 a.m. to 5 p.m. at other times. There is a fine road network which gives visitors access to all parts of the reserve, and horses may be hired from the resort stable. The resort's accommodation includes rondavels, flatlets, a caravan site (with electric points) and campsite. There is also a restaurant, cafeteria, supermarket, butchery, bank, garage and a hotel with a bottle store. Recreational facilities include three outdoor swimming pools, two pools for toddlers, a hydro spa with four swimming pools and private baths, tennis courts, a bowling green, a miniature golf course and an entertainments hall.

Above: Looper caterpillars (measuring worms) have no feet with which to support the middle part of their bodies, and walk by arching the body to bring the hind legs close to the front legs. Like all caterpillars, their bodies are made up of the head capsule, three thoracic segments and ten abdominal segments. The simple eyes (usually six) are on the head at the base of a pair of very short antennae. **Left:** A distant shower at sunset in the Suikerbosrand Nature Reserve.
Right: The hardy monkey's tail (*Xerophyta retinervis*), manages to survive long periods of drought. Its bristly, stunted trunk sprouts wiry stalks which are tipped with attractive, sweet-scented blooms.

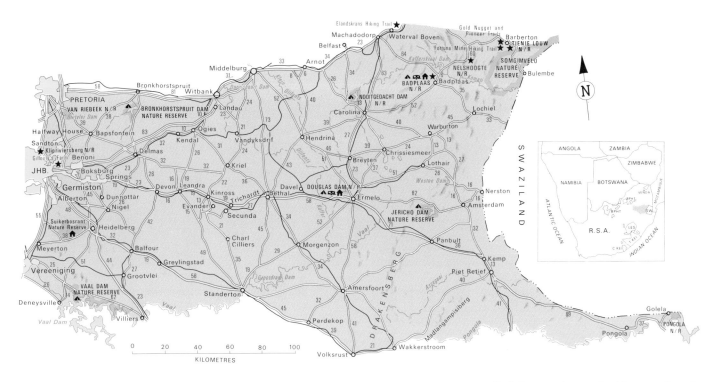

A DAISY FROM THE DIGGINGS

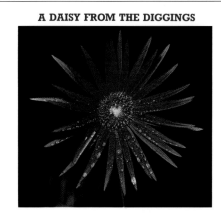

The town of Barberton had its start in a short-lived gold rush of the early 1880s. The boom attracted fortune-hunters from far and wide, among them a Durban jam manufacturer named Robert Jameson, a keen amateur botanist who served on the committee of the Durban Botanical Garden. Jameson spent only a short time on the diggings, but while he was there he grew to admire a 'dandelion' of brilliant scarlet that grew in profusion throughout the region. He uprooted samples of the species and presented them to the curator of the Durban garden.

Jameson's dandelion (or *Gerbera*) is the well-known Barberton daisy, a favourite with gardeners all over the world. Its international 'career' began in 1889, when the curator of the Durban Botanical Garden sent plants to Kew Gardens in London. One of them survived and flowered. At about the same time another amateur botanist on the Barberton fields sent seeds of the same species to a friend living in Cornwall. The friend raised seedlings and presented them to Kew Gardens and to the Cambridge Botanic Garden.

The curator of the Cambridge garden began breeding the new daisy, and in the years that followed steadily improved its quality, developing hybrids of other colours. Commercial growers followed suit, and the Chelsea Flower Show of 1912 featured Barberton daisies with colours ranging from the original scarlet to orange, yellow, buff, salmon pink and rose. The daisies became firm favourites in the Netherlands and other European countries and gained a strong foothold in North America and Australia. The humble Barberton daisy had arrived.

Badplaas can be reached by tarred roads from Carolina, Machadodorp and Barberton, and all routes are well signposted. For further information, or to book accommodation, you should write to The Resort Manager, Overvaal Badplaas, P.O. Box 15, Badplaas 1190 (telephone Badplaas 4-1022/3).

Bronkhorstspruit Dam Nature Reserve

One of the newer provincial reserves in the Transvaal is set around the Bronkhorstspruit Dam, 15 km south of Bronkhorstspruit on the road to Delmas. The 952 ha dam has long been popular with boating enthusiasts and fishermen, many of whom camp at the dam at weekends and during school holidays. The 1800 ha reserve has been fenced, but as yet the only game reintroduced to the area has been black wildebeest, steenbok and blesbok. There is an impressive variety of birds – predominantly waterfowl – in the reserve, which is open from 6 a.m. to 8 p.m. Facilities for campers include braai stands, toilets and drinking water. For further information, you should write to The Officer-in-Charge, Bronkhorstspruit Dam Nature Reserve, P.O. Bronkhorstspruit 1020 (telephone Bronkhorstspruit 2-1621).

Douglas Dam Nature Reserve

A large part of the area around Ermelo's Douglas Dam, about 6 km from Ermelo on the Hendrina road, has been developed as a 540 ha reserve stocked with Highveld game such as eland, zebra, blesbok and springbok. It also features European fallow deer – a decidedly exotic species. Hiking trails have been carefully laid out and the dam offers angling and watersport opportunities.

Visiting hours are from 8 a.m. to 5 p.m. throughout the week. Adjacent to and serving the reserve is Republic Park, which offers visitors caravan and camping sites, ten rondavels, braai facilities and ablution blocks. For bookings and further information on the reserve, write to The Caretaker, Republic Park, P.O. Box 48, Ermelo 2350 (telephone Ermelo 4093). The caretaker will also issue you with a permit to enter the reserve.

Elandskrans Hiking Trail

Waterval-Boven sits atop the Drakensberg Escarpment, a good 200 m higher than its counterpart Waterval-Onder. Each weekend the village council organises a novel hike through a private nature reserve on the slopes of the escarpment. Hikers assemble early on Saturday morning at the Elandskrans Holiday Resort, walk through the day and spend the night in a hut which can accommodate 26 people. Firewood is provided. On Sunday they complete their walk to Waterval-Onder, then catch a train for a 12 km ride that takes them back up the escarpment to their starting-point. Trees along the route are identified and numbered.

To book places on the trail, write to The Village Council, Private Bag X05, Waterval-Boven 1195 (telephone Waterval-Boven 56).

Flora Reserves

The Barberton area has three 'special status' provincial nature reserves, each dedicated to conserving a single rare species. None of the three is open to the public and Transvaal's

Above: *Aloe vryheidensis*, a rare species conserved in the Cythna Letty Nature Reserve, near Barberton. **Left above:** A tree cricket. The male of this genus may often be found wedged in a pear-shaped hole he has gnawed in a leaf. When he stridulates, his wings are extended and pressed against the leaf to seal the hole – thus increasing the resonating surface of his 'sound baffle'. **Left below:** A gorilla in the specially-built gorilla enclosure at the Johannesburg Zoo. The gorilla occurs only in Africa, and the populations are believed to be declining. **Right:** The Florence Bloom Bird Sanctuary – refuge for a variety of waterfowl.

THE OLDEST FOSSILS

Until relatively recently, the world's oldest sedimentary rocks — forming part of the Swaziland System, near Barberton — were believed to contain no trace of life. Then, in 1966, two scientists named Barghoorn and Schopf, using an electron microscope, discovered fossil bacteria in wafer-thin slivers removed from the rocks known as the Pre-Cambrian Fig-Tree Series.

The discovery of these minute fossil bacteria (*Eobacterium isolatum*) in rocks over 3 000 million years old excited world-wide attention, and revolutionised the study of early life on earth. Microscopically small algae and fungi were found in the same rocks, and chemical analyses indicated that these ancient plants had the ability to photosynthesise: they were thus the earliest of the countless small green plants which released oxygen into the thin atmosphere, permitting the evolution of higher forms of plant and animal life — including our own.

Directorate of Nature and Environmental Conservation tries to keep their locations secret in an effort to frustrate would-be plant thieves. The reserves conserve aloes.

The 10 ha Tienie Louw Nature Reserve, named after a well-known economist, protects *Aloe albida* and *Aloe chortolirioides*. The Thorncroft Nature Reserve covers some 16 ha of the mountains near Barberton and safeguards the rare *Aloe thorncroftii*, discovered there by Mr G. Thorncroft in 1914.

The 8 ha Cythna Letty Nature Reserve, which is named after a well-known botanic artist, conserves the rare *Aloe vryheidensis*. For further information on the reserves, you should write to The Regional Representative, Directorate of Environmental and Nature Conservation, P.O. Box 1232, Nelspruit 1200 (telephone Nelspruit 2-8311).

Florence Bloom Bird Sanctuary

Johannesburg Municipality's Delta Park features a large camping ground for youth organisations, the headquarters of the South African

Nature Conservation Centre and the Southern African Wildlife Society, and the 10 ha Florence Bloom Bird Sanctuary — set around two small dams. Visitors may watch the birds from a tall mound or from two hides. Over the past few years 194 species of birds have been sighted. The hides are open to the public daily; there are no time restrictions.

Delta Park itself has a gift shop and information centre including exhibition halls, auditorium, meditation room and aquarium. To reach Delta Park, turn east off Rustenburg Road (the northern extension of Johannesburg's Barry Hertzog Avenue) at Road No. 3, Victory Park.

Fortuna Mine Rotary Nature Trail

This 2 km walk leads through the Barberton Indigenous Tree Park (the trees and shrubs are labelled), across hills and through gorges. The circular route requires about one-and-a-half to two hours to complete.

One of the most interesting sections of the walk is through a 600 m tunnel cut through rock to link the old Fortuna Mine to the Mill (a torch

Harvey Nature Reserve

Owned by the Johannesburg City Council, this 6 ha reserve – situated on Linksfield Ridge – offers visitors varied and interesting vegetation and occasional glimpses of small mammals. A detailed handbook is being prepared on the Dassie Trail, which leads through the reserve.

Jericho Dam Nature Reserve

The 979 ha Jericho Dam area is fast being developed as one of the Highveld's premier nature reserves. Its prolific bird life includes waterfowl, wattled crane, crowned crane and kori bustard. Among the animals are oribi, steenbok and duiker. The dam's clear water and the exotic black bass it supports are renowned among anglers. Camping is permitted and drinking water is available.

To reach the dam, approach by the dirt road from Sheepmoor, Roodewal or Bankkop, or from the roads between Ermelo and Amsterdam or Ermelo and Piet Retief. For further information, write to The Officer-in-Charge, Jericho Dam Nature Reserve, P.O. Box 74, Amsterdam 2375 (telephone Amsterdam 307).

Johannesburg and Sandton's Urban Trails

Witwatersrand means 'ridge of white waters', and the little streams that gave birth to the name are still in existence. Among them is the Braamfontein Spruit, which springs from northern Hillbrow and flows north to join the Jukskei River on the northern boundary of Sandton.

The city councils of Johannesburg, Randburg and Sandton have joined forces to develop various trails along the ribbons of open spaces created by these rivers so that picnickers, hikers and even horseback riders can enjoy themselves within this otherwise developed area.

The first and most successful of the urban trails is Braamfontein Spruit Trail which passes through Johannesburg and Sandton. The 25 km Braamfontein Spruit is divided into various sections, each taking less than 2 hours to complete. The Jukskei Trail, another major urban pathway, is made up of two separate routes. One, the Randlord's Heritage Walk, starts in Parktown and passes Melville Koppies Nature Reserve, Emmarentia Dam and Delta Park (the Southern African Wildlife Society's Headquarters) until it ends at Lone Hill Tor, 100 m south of the Jukskei River. Here a large variety of plants and animals can be found. The second leg begins in Hillbrow and follows Mervyn King Ridge to Bezuidenhout Park.

This park also marks the start of the 12 km Sand Spruit Trail encompassing Bruma Lake Bird Sanctuary, The Wilds and Melrose Bird Sanctuary before the Sand Spruit's confluence with the Braamfontein Spruit at Frankenwald.

Despite being laid out within South Africa's largest metropolitan area, the trails pass

---

is essential for this section). The Barberton Publicity Association will supply visitors with a sketch map and information sheet.

Gillooly's Farm

This 44 ha farm in Bedfordview, on the eastern side of Johannesburg, was once owned by James Gillooly, who sold it to the Town Council in 1944. The farm is being developed by the Johannesburg City Council, which plans to establish picnic sites, walks and a bird sanctuary.

Gold Nugget and Pioneer hiking trails

You can follow in the footsteps of early miners in their quest for gold on two hiking trails that wind through the mountains around historic Barberton. The Gold Nugget Trail offers either a strenuous (two-day) 37 km hike or a very strenuous (three-day) 44 km circular trail. It begins and ends in the parking area opposite Barberton police station.

The 28,5 km Pioneer Trail takes two days to complete, and while less strenuous than the Gold Nugget Trail, participants encounter some steep gradients, such as the ominously named Low Gear Ridge. Pioneer Trail starts and finishes at Dias Base Camp to the west of Barberton.

Hikers spend the night in huts equipped with bunks, mattresses and firewood (they must provide their own food, sleeping bags and cooking utensils). Children under 10 are not allowed, and unfit hikers are discouraged. For information and reservations write to Barberton Publicity Bureau, Box 221, Barberton 1300 (telephone Barberton 2-2121).

through a wide variety of natural vegetation as well as important archaeological sites. Further information can be obtained by writing to the Johannesburg Publicity Association, P.O. Box 4580, Johannesburg 2000 (telephone Johannesburg 29-4961/5) or Sandton Civic Centre, P.O. Box 78095, Sandton 2146. (Telephone Johannesburg 884-1317).

Johannesburg Zoological Gardens

Wildlife from all over Southern Africa is on display in the sprawling 54 ha Johannesburg Zoo, along with scores of other species from around the world. In recent years the zoo has moved away from the traditional 'postage-stamp' approach, in which each species is exhibited in its own cage or compound, and instead accommodates many of them in barless enclosures that come closer to representing their natural environment. Animals and visitors are separated by moats.

In all, the zoo accommodates more than 300 species of mammals, birds and reptiles. Of spe-cial interest are the elephant section, the impressive, newly erected 1000 m² gorilla enclosure and the ever-popular farmyard. The zoo recently became the first in the world to breed white lions. It has existed since 1904, when the 200 ha Hermann Eckstein Park, of which it forms a part, and a collection of animals were given to the municipality. The animal collection was donated by the late Sir Percy Fitz-Patrick, author of *Jock of the Bushveld*.

The zoo is located east of Jan Smuts Avenue in the northern suburb of Parkview (parking is in Upper Park Drive to the south). It is open daily from 9 a.m. to 5 p.m.

Klipriviersberg Nature Reserve

This nature reserve, the property of the Johannesburg City Council, is dotted with the remnants of old kraals, evidence of the presence of Bantu-speaking peoples in the area before the coming of the white man.

The reserve covers 550 ha to the south of Mondeor and is made up of portions of three early Witwatersrand farms: Vierfontein, Rietvlei (of which the farmhouse and *waenhuis* still exist, though in a vandalised state) and Olifantsvlei.

An impressive array of 175 species of bird, and small mammals such as steenbok, grey duiker, black-backed jackal, porcupine, hare and dassie may be seen.

Although certain species of alien vegetation such as the silver wattle, silver poplar and the prickly pear have invaded different parts of the reserve, there is an impressive variety of indigenous vegetation to be seen.

Guided tours of the Klipriviersberg Nature Reserve, which last about three hours, are held at 9 a.m. on the second Sunday of every month. The tours leave from Silent Pool which is at the cul-de-sac of Frandaph Avenue in Mondeor. At other times the public has free access to the reserve. No dogs are permitted. For further information and enquiries you can write to Klipriviersberg Nature Reserve Association, P.O. Box 990140, Kibler Park 2053.

Southern Africa's most common duck is the yellow-billed duck *(Anas undulata)*, easily identified by its bright, black-patched beak. Related to the exotic mallard (the two can inter-breed if brought together), it finds much of its food on land, though it keeps close to inland water and the river estuaries. Unlike its northern hemisphere cousins, who fly long distances between breeding and wintering grounds, the yellowbill is not migratory, but a vagrant. It remains fairly sedentary during the day, making short foraging flights to water towards dusk.

Korsman Bird Sanctuary

Benoni's suburb of Westdene has a novel attraction in the 50 ha Korsman Bird Sanctuary (considered by some to be one of the best in South Africa), which centres on a shallow pan and is encircled by a road. The pan attracts large numbers of migratory waterfowl, including ibis and flamingo, and the surrounding shore is home to ostrich and game such as blesbok, springbok, steenbok and duiker.

The Witwatersrand Bird Club has a hide in the sanctuary and its members have a key to the gate, but otherwise people are not allowed in. However, visitors have a fine view from outside the fence.

The sanctuary is encircled by a road called The Drive, and is situated directly south of and adjacent to the Benoni Lake golf course.

Marievale Bird Sanctuary

A 1 000 ha bird sanctuary is located on a large vlei formed by the Blesbokspruit, a stream flowing close to Nigel's municipal boundary. Three well-organised hides have been built in this provincial sanctuary, and more than 300 species of birds have been spotted there – chiefly waterfowl, including greater and lesser flamingo, African spoonbill, virtually every indigenous species of duck and goose, and some rare wader migrants from the northern hemisphere.

Marievale is open daily from sunrise to sunset. To reach the sanctuary from Nigel follow the signs to Marievale (on some maps marked 'Marieshaft'). At the mine complex, turn right and keep going on the road through the reeds. There is a picnic spot near one of the hides.

Melrose Wild Bird Sanctuary

Like the Braamfontein Spruit, the Sand Spruit flows through Johannesburg's northern suburbs and in the process creates the vlei at the centre of Melrose Wild Bird Sanctuary – only a stone's throw from Johannesburg's M1 freeway. The 10 ha sanctuary contains reed beds and indigenous trees which provide ideal nesting sites for a large number of bird species. There is a hide for bird-watchers. The sanctuary forms part of the Ethel Gray Park and is owned by the Johannesburg Municipality. It is open from sunrise to sunset.

Melville Koppies Nature Reserve

One of Johannesburg's showpiece sanctuaries is the 80 ha Melville Koppies Nature Reserve, which straddles D.F. Malan Drive in the city's north-eastern suburbs. The highway divides a 60 ha fenced section in the east from an unfenced 20 ha section to the west. The reserve's principal attraction is its flora, which includes 80 per cent of the species recorded on the Witwatersrand. In addition, it conserves a valua-

Above: *Clematopsis scabiosifolia*, an attractive wild shrub that graces much of the Transvaal's countryside. **Above right:** *Diospyros lycioides* (*jakkalsbessie*), a tropical tree which grows in woodland bush. The fruits are edible when ripe, and are eaten by a huge variety of birds and animals. **Right:** A brown lacewing larva of the insect family Hemerobiidae eating its favourite food — aphids (a dietary habit that endears it to farmers and gardeners). The adults are frequently attracted to lights, and are characterised by large golden eyes and green-brown, glass-like wings.

ble example of Witwatersrand geology, and an archaeological site occupied by man for an estimated 100 000 years.

Of the area's many hundreds of plant species, more than 30 are edible, 112 are used medicinally, eight are potential poisons, two are valued perfumes and 34 are used as ingredients in ritual magic. Melville Koppies (it has been a nature reserve since 1959 and a Natural and Historic Monument since 1968) is also a magnet for the bird-watcher – ornithologists have recorded more than 150 species, including spotted eagle owl, red-billed hoopoe and red-throated wryneck.

Officially, Melville Koppies is open to the public only on the third Sunday of each month from September to April inclusive (from 3 p.m. to 6 p.m.), when members of the Johannesburg Council for Natural History are on hand to lead conducted tours. Alternatively, visitors may follow a nature trail with the aid of a Melville Koppies pamphlet – obtainable at the reserve. At other times parties wishing to visit the reserve should write (at least one month in advance) to The Secretary, Johannesburg Council for Natur-

al History, Parks and Recreation Department, P.O. Box 2824, Johannesburg 2000 (telephone Johannesburg 407-6111).

Nelshoogte Nature Reserve

The most prominent feature of this 211 ha nature reserve, situated within the Nelshoogte State Forest, some 40 km from Barberton on the Badplaas road (the turn-off is not signposted), is the 'Devil's Knuckles', a strikingly precipitous ridge of hills. Close by the Nelshoogte Nature Reserve is the 25 ha Dr Hamilton Protea Reserve, established exclusively for the protection of the rare *Protea roupelliae* sub-species *hamiltonii*. A picnic spot and dam lie between the two reserves. Visitors may obtain further information and entry permits for both reserves from The State Forester, Nelshoogte State Forest, Private Bag 608, Barberton 1300 (telephone Barberton 2-3691).

Nigel Nature Reserve

Nigel's municipality has set aside an attractive 45 ha nature reserve on the town's outskirts and stocked it with duiker, ostrich and a small herd of springbok (there are a number of ducks and geese on a small dam).

The public may not enter the reserve, but there are good vantage points on a terrace situated just outside the fence. The reserve is situated off the Nigel-Devon road. Entry to the terrace is from Bloekom Avenue, in the suburb of Ferryvale.

Nooitgedacht Dam Nature Reserve

This 3 350 ha provincial reserve, about 7 km north-west of Carolina, is expected to become a popular focus for anglers and watersport enthusiasts. A number of shallow-water areas are to be cordoned off as bird sanctuaries.

Game species which were once indigenous to the area will be reintroduced, joining the grey rhebok, steenbok and grey duiker already in the sanctuary. Facilities are at present confined to temporary toilets for day visitors and campers. Further information can be obtained by writing to The Officer-in-Charge, Nooitgedacht Dam Nature Reserve, P.O. Box 327, Carolina 1185 (telephone Carolina 3-2603).

Peacehaven Nature Reserve

Vereeniging's suburb of Peacehaven has a modest 30 ha nature reserve which contains fallow deer, Indian water-buffalo and other exotic species – but as yet no indigenous species other than the ostrich. It will shortly be developed into a bird sanctuary. The public is not allowed inside, but there are good views from raised areas outside the fence. The reserve is bordered by General Hertzog Road, Dee Drive, Golf Road and Waterkant Street.

Pongola Nature Reserve

On 13 June 1894 President Kruger proclaimed a game reserve of nearly 20 000 ha in the Pongola district, a narrow corridor of land between Swaziland and Natal that rises steeply to the top of a 600 m cliff – forming the spectacular Lebombo escarpment. The corridor followed the course of the Pongola River through countryside thick with trees and rich in game. The sanctuary, the first to be proclaimed in Africa, paved the way for the Sabie Game Reserve (later expanded into the Kruger National Park), but in the early 1900s it was neglected and deproclaimed.

The Pongola district was divided up as farmland. Then, in the 1970s, South Africa's Department of Water Affairs developed the Pongolapoort Dam (originally known as 'J.G. Strijdom Dam', but since renamed) in the valley below the Lebombos.

A 10 000 ha provincial reserve has been re-established on part of this historic ground on the Transvaal shore and is being developed both for recreation (chiefly fishing and boating) and nature conservation.

Wildlife includes southern reedbuck, mountain reedbuck, bushbuck, grey duiker, red duiker, steenbok and suni, and the reintroduced impala and blue wildebeest. There are also a number of rare reptile, bird and plant species.

The reserve is open daily from sunrise to sunset (overnight camping is not yet allowed). To reach it, drive to Golela on the Swaziland border, then take the road towards the mountains. Further information can be obtained by writing to The Officer-in-Charge, P.O. Box 29, Golela 3990 (telephone Golela 5-1012).

Rondebult Bird Sanctuary

The Transvaal's best-organised and most-visited bird sanctuary is Rondebult, which covers 94 ha of vlei and marshland and protects over 150 species of bird. Although it is situated on the outskirts of Germiston in an area dominated by industrial activity, the sanctuary is a haven of tranquillity. Visitors may stroll around the sanctuary or look out on the vlei from five well-constructed observation hides which are roofed, carpeted, cushioned and equipped with colour photographs of many of the species that frequent the sanctuary. Three

---

SUIKERBOSRAND AT A GLANCE

When to go Both the reserve and the Kareekloof resort are open year-round. Although situated within the reserve, the Kareekloof Resort does not form part of it. The gates open daily at 7 a.m. and close at 6 p.m. Winter nights can be cold in this region (warm clothing is essential), and hikers usually visit in spring, summer or autumn.

Reservation and information To reserve a camping site at Kareekloof, write to The Manager, Overvaal Kareekloof, P.O. Box 372, Meyerton 1960 (telephone Henley-on-Klip 5334). For further information about Diepkloof and the reserve, and to book places on the hiking trails (and accommodation in the overnight huts), write to The Officer-in-Charge, Suikerbosrand Nature Reserve, Private Bag H616, Heidelberg 2400 (telephone Heidelberg 2181/2/3).

Getting there To reach the reserve's conservation headquarters at Diepkloof, take the dirt road (this road is in good condition) branching west from the main highway between Heidelberg and Johannesburg and follow the signs to Diepkloof. To reach the Kareekloof Public Resort, take the signposted turn-off north of the main road between Heidelberg and Meyerton, 28 km from Heidelberg. This clearly signposted road leads to the resort.

Accommodation There is no overnight accommodation at Diepkloof. The Kareekloof resort caters for caravanners and campers but has no huts or rondavels. A public resort with huts is being developed by the Board for Public Resorts at Heidelberg Kloof in the east of the reserve. Suikerbosrand's hiking trail network has six overnight huts (advance booking is essential). There are three group camps near Diepkloof, but these are very much in demand, and it is advisable to book well in advance.

Eating and drinking Kareekloof has a licensed restaurant. Braai facilities have been supplied for day visitors and for those occupying the caravan and camping site. Bread, milk and other groceries are on sale in the resort shop. Diepkloof has no restaurant, but does have an attractive and popular picnic area. There are plans to build a kiosk in this area.

Getting around A 60 km circular route leads through the reserve. It may be undertaken daily from Diepkloof or over weekends and public holidays from Kareekloof. No petrol is available in the reserve, the nearest sources are Kliprivier and Heidelberg. Suikerbosrand features a network of hiking trails with a total length of 66 km. Anything from one to six days can be spent on the trail. Hikers must book accommodation in the reserve's overnight huts well in advance. Visitors may choose to take the 4 km Cheetah Trail laid out in a loop northwest of Diepkloof's visitor centre.

Special attractions Diepkloof has an impressive visitor centre with displays representing Suikerbosrand's habitats and species. Close by is a Voortrekker farmhouse, dating from the 1850s, which has been restored and now functions as a farm museum. Kareekloof also has a handsome swimming pool.

Wildlife The acacia country in the south-west attracts eland; the grassveld elsewhere is the haunt of black wildebeest, blesbok and springbok, while red hartebeest, oribi, zebra, mountain reedbuck, grey rhebok, grey duiker, steenbok, kudu and brown hyena are found throughout the reserve. Suikerbosrand is also famous for its cheetah.

of Southern Africa's four ibis species may be seen at Rondebult, and other attractions include spectacular species like the purple gallinule, painted snipe and avocet.

Most of the waterfowl species breeding in Southern Africa have been spotted at this pleasant sanctuary. Visitors watch for the avocet as it 'side-sweeps' the water with its bill upturned, and for the filter-feeding greater flamingo as it sieves the water for its food.

Rondebult's heronry has always been popular, and its population includes black-headed heron, cattle egret, grey heron, night heron and African spoonbill. Information obtained from a check-list compiled by the Witwatersrand Bird Club reveals that more than 150 species of bird have been recorded at the sanctuary.

The reserve is open daily from 8 a.m. to 5 p.m. To arrange a visit at other times you should contact the sanctuary directly (telephone Johannesburg 893-2307). To reach it, take the N3 freeway heading south from Germiston, then turn onto the Heidelberg road (follow the signs to Rondebult Bird Sanctuary).

Songimvelo Nature Reserve

Songimvelo – the pride of KaNgwane – is a vast 49 000 ha reserve, situated south-east of Barberton, which stretches from Swaziland's high peaks to the plains of the Transvaal Lowveld. Besides grassland and savanna, elements of the Cape floral kingdom, shrub forest as well as three types of cycads are found in this splendid wilderness.

Hikers, picnickers and campers can discover mountains, forested ravines, waterfalls and pools, while kayakers can try their skill on the white water of the Komati River. Otter are com-

Above: Black wildebeest on the lush plains of the Suikerbosrand Nature Reserve. **Right:** The elegant greater flamingo, which congregates and migrates in huge flocks, is a familiar sight in and around coastal lagoons and large stretches of water throughout Southern Africa.

Above: Beautiful but deceptive — the wild flower *Striga elegans* (witchweed) is a member of the foxglove family. It is a root parasite, receiving water and food from its host. **Left:** An exotic tamarin monkey, whose natural habitat is the forests of South and Central America. This specimen is a resident of the Transvaal Snake Park near Pretoria. **Opposite page top:** Eland graze in the well-stocked 3 000 ha Van Riebeeck Nature Reserve. **Opposite page right:** The fan-shaped *Boophone disticha*, otherwise known as *gifbol* or red posy. The flowers form a large pink ball. **Opposite page far right:** Water lilies in The Wilds, one of the Transvaal's finest botanical centres.

mon in the river and over 270 birds have been identified, mainly around the thickly wooded river banks.

Herds of blue wildebeest, blesbok, impala, hartebeest and zebra roam the bushveld plains between the Komati and Lomati rivers, while black wildebeest, mountain reedbuck, grey rhebok, eland and leopard are found on the mountain slopes. Other large game is being introduced from throughout Southern Africa.

The game scout centre for the KaNgwane Parks Corporation is located here and a comfortable tented camp, offering horseback safaris, is planned for the future. Anyone wishing to visit the area should write to the KaNgwane Parks Board, Box 1990, Nelspruit 1200 (telephone Nelspruit 5-3931/2).

Suikerbosrand Nature Reserve
Portions of 65 farms are included in the province's Suikerbosrand Nature Reserve near Heidelberg — 13337ha of ridges and dramatic kloofs that typify the Highveld. Blesbok and black wildebeest graze on the plateaus; eland gather in the acacia veld of the south-west; red hartebeest roam everywhere.

Suikerbosrand's chief purpose is to provide a day's recreation for families living in the densely populated cities of the Witwatersrand and areas to the south. Visitors make their way to Diepkloof on the reserve's northern edge — headquarters of the conservation staff. There they may embark on a two-hour circular route that takes them through the reserve on 60km of tarred roads. Information officers present film and slide shows in Diepkloof's visitor centre. In the centre of the reserve is the fenced off Kareekloof Public Resort, another popular spot with visitors.

There are picnic spots at Diepkloof, and visitors can dawdle over the 4km Cheetah Trail that winds over the hillsides north-west of the visitor centre. A trail handbook describes sights along the route. Those with more time and energy will tackle Suikerbosrand's famous network of true hiking trails.

Scattered through the trails' network are six overnight huts, each named after a game species found in the reserve. The huts consist of two bedrooms, each with five concrete bunks and a central living area, with a braai place and a stack of wood just outside.

In planning a route, hikers must book places in a particular overnight hut and should avoid changes *en route*, as the huts are fully booked for most weekends. One rather special place is the 'meditation hut', for those visitors who value solitude and quiet. Only one person is allowed in at a time.

One of the great attractions of Suikerbosrand is the chance to see cheetah in the wild. In 1975 and 1976, five male and three female cheetahs were released in the reserve, and were soon responsible for a small cheetah population explosion. 'They had no natural enemies, so there was no stopping them,' explains Jan du Toit, Suikerbosrand's Officer-in-Charge. 'Normally, half of a cheetah's litter fails to make it. Here, a mother produced six cubs and all six survived.'

Also of much interest (at the Diepkloof visitor centre) is the beautiful diorama (a three-dimensional picture) painted by well-known American artist Timothy Prutzer, depicting a cheetah hunting scene.

The Wilds
A major attraction of the Empire Exhibition held in Johannesburg in 1936 was a display of South

Africa's indigenous flora. The response to the display prompted the development of a park wholly devoted to South African plants, shrubs and trees. The 20 ha park was established on two koppies in Houghton and became known as The Wilds. It featured lawns and a dam as well as paths among the flora.

To reach The Wilds, turn into Houghton Drive from Louis Botha Avenue and proceed to the car park at the bottom of the hill. The park is open at all hours. Visitors are advised to visit the park in groups for their own safety. There is a refreshment kiosk.

Transvaal Snake Park

Halfway House, which is situated between Johannesburg and Pretoria, is the home of the privately owned Transvaal Snake Park, where visitors may see up to 150 species of snake,

other reptiles and amphibians from Southern Africa and farther afield.

Crocodile, alligator and terrapin are in special pools, poisonous snakes of Southern Africa may be seen in a snake-pit (staff herpetologists provide regular lecture-demonstrations), and the more exotic species are in a climate-controlled terraquarium which sets out to re-create their natural environment.

The snake park was the brainchild of Bernie Keyter, who worked on venom extraction at the South African Institute for Medical Research in the 1950s. So many people asked to see the snakes that he decided to sink his savings into a permanent exhibition. The park opened in 1961 with 25 species on display. Today there are over 80 exhibits. However, the emphasis is less on collecting specimens than on developing captive breeding programmes

– especially those relating to endangered species.

To reach the park, follow the clearly signposted road to Halfway House (the park is about 1 km south of the village). It is open from 9 a.m. to 5.30 p.m. on Sundays and from 9 a.m. to 4.30 p.m. on weekdays and Saturdays. There are reptile demonstrations on weekdays at 11 a.m. and 3 p.m., on Saturdays at 11 a.m. 2 p.m., 3 p.m. and 4 p.m., on Sundays and public holidays at 11 a.m. and thereafter every hour until 4.30 p.m. The park is open every day of the year except Christmas Day.

Vaal Dam Nature Reserve

Boating, fishing and picnicking are the chief attractions of the 350 ha Vaal Dam Nature Reserve, located within 3 km of the dam wall and 40 km from Vereeniging. The vegetation is typical of the Highveld, with red grass broken by occasional clumps of Karoo thorn and karee.

The dam is stocked with barbel, carp and yellowfish, and attracts many bird species, including yellow-billed duck, coot, great white egret, Egyptian goose and fish eagle.

There are plans to develop the reserve, but until then it will remain closed to the public. On the drawing board are caravan sites, launching ramps, parking areas and ablution blocks.

Van Riebeeck Nature Reserve

Rietvlei Dam, situated within the Pretoria municipal area and on the boundary of Verwoerdburg, is an important source of water for Pretoria. It is the centre of a 3 100 ha municipal nature reserve, previously called the Rietvlei Reserve for Game and Indigenous Flora and renamed in 1952 to mark the tercentenary of Jan van Riebeeck's arrival in South Africa.

The reserve was once open to the public, but so little interest was displayed that it was closed. The animals remained, however, and now there are plans to re-open the reserve. Visitors are taken on escorted bus tours.

The reserve is some 1 470 to 1 550 m above sea level (considerably higher than Pretoria) and it is the only proclaimed bankenveld nature reserve on a dolomite formation in South Africa. This veld type is valuable agricultural land so it is likely that this city reserve will remain the only one of its kind. It contains impressive herds of blesbok, eland, Burchell's zebra, black wildebeest, steenbok, grey duiker, springbok and red hartebeest, as well as several rare or threatened species of game such as oribi, white rhinoceros and aardwolf, and birds such as martial eagle.

Guided tours leave from Pretoria on a regular basis. For more information contact the Pretoria Information Bureau, P.O. Box 440, Pretoria 0001 (telephone Pretoria 21-2461).

Grassy plains and teeming game

Early in the 19th century, the area now known as the Orange Free State was a hunter's paradise. Its grassy plains were alive with game, and it seemed the supply of game could never dry up. Then settlers, both black and white, entered the area and the great herds were rapidly reduced to a fraction of their former strength. The spreading plains were divided up, fenced in, and turned over to agricultural production. Apart from a few token herds preserved by conservation-minded farmers, the Free State's game population simply faded away.

The 20th century saw the stirring of awareness in the Free State and, indeed, elsewhere in Southern Africa. Encouraged by the success of the handful of small nature reserves that was established in the 1920s and 1930s, the Orange Free State Provincial Administration proclaimed the Willem Pretorius Game Reserve at Allemanskraal Dam. The South African National Parks Board's contribution was

even more impressive – the proclamation of the Golden Gate Highlands National Park in the foothills of the Maluti Mountains. Later these two important sanctuaries were joined by several new reserves and botanic gardens.

Today the most impressive game reserves in the Free State are Willem Pretorius, Tussen-die-Riviere Game Farm on the Orange River in the south and Sandveld Nature Reserve in the vicinity of the Bloemhof Dam in the far north of the province. Soetdoring Nature Reserve near Bloemfontein boasts a large variety of game, as does the Golden Gate park, which is the most attractive reserve from a scenic point of view. The region's flora is conserved at the Orange Free State National Botanic Garden in Bloemfontein.

Bloemfontein Zoological Gardens

Those wanting a closer look at Free State game can do worse than start at Bloemfontein Zoo,

a 13ha retreat of green lawns and shady trees, lying close to the city's heart. The species on view include elephant, white rhino, leopard, cheetah and gemsbok as well as lechwe and nyala (indigenous to Southern Africa but not the Free State), and a variety of primates and ungulates (hooved animals). All told the zoo has more than 100 species of mammals and reptiles and more than 70 species of birds. It is open daily, from 8a.m. to 6p.m. in summer and to 5p.m. in winter.

Caledon Nature Reserve

The 1500ha Welbedacht Dam is on the Caledon River, south of Wepener in the southeastern Free State. About 1200ha of land around the dam is being developed as a provincial reserve. Black wildebeest and several blesbok have been introduced to the sanctuary while a herd of springbok has already found its own way to the reserve.

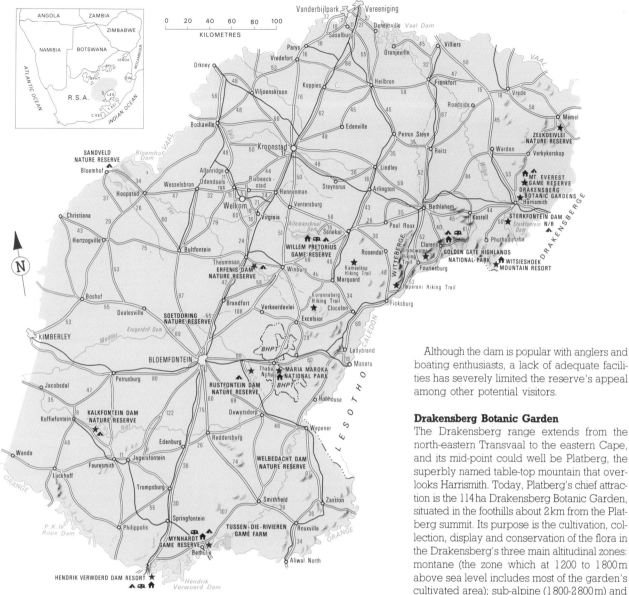

Far left: This strange formation in the Rooiberg mountain range, known as Mushroom Rocks, forms part of the Golden Gate Highlands National Park — a scenically spectacular region of sculpted mountain and green valley.
Left: *Dierama*, a member of the iris family. Some botanists believe there are only a few species in Southern Africa (with many variations), but others recognise more than 20 species in South Africa alone. **Right:** A cetoniid (fruit) beetle burrows in soil preparatory to laying its eggs. The adult beetle bores into ripe fruit to feed on the juice, while its larvae feed on decaying vegetable matter (they may often be found in compost heaps).

Although the dam is popular with anglers and boating enthusiasts, a lack of adequate facilities has severely limited the reserve's appeal among other potential visitors.

Drakensberg Botanic Garden
The Drakensberg range extends from the north-eastern Transvaal to the eastern Cape, and its mid-point could well be Platberg, the superbly named table-top mountain that overlooks Harrismith. Today, Platberg's chief attraction is the 114 ha Drakensberg Botanic Garden, situated in the foothills about 2 km from the Platberg summit. Its purpose is the cultivation, collection, display and conservation of the flora in the Drakensberg's three main altitudinal zones: montane (the zone which at 1 200 to 1 800 m above sea level includes most of the garden's cultivated area); sub-alpine (1 800-2 800 m) and alpine (2 800-3 300 m).

The Drakensberg garden is administered by the Harrismith municipality and is partly developed and partly wilderness. The developed area centres on two dams built by British forces in the Anglo-Boer War. On the slopes behind them a 1 km 'bush trail' winds through dense forest and past massive rock formations. The hillsides are dotted with berg lilies (*Galtonia candicans*), red hot pokers (*Kniphofia*), grass bells (*Dierama*) and the blue flowers of the bloulelie (*Agapanthus*); while the gnarled, crooked branches of the ouhout (*Leucosidea sericea*) form dense clusters on the slopes. The garden is open daily from sunrise to sunset and is well signposted from the middle of Harrismith, about 5 km away.

Erfenis Dam Nature Reserve
Boating, picnicking and fishing are the most popular activities at the 3 308 ha Erfenis Dam,

GOLDEN GATE AT A GLANCE

When to go Golden Gate is open year-round, and weekends and school holidays tend to be busy. A public road runs through the park, so there are no gates in the east or west. Winters are cold: temperatures can plummet to 12 degrees below zero and there is often snow on the mountains (sometimes in the valleys too). Summer nights can also be cool.

Reservations To apply for accommodation, write to the National Parks Board, P.O. Box 787, Pretoria 0001 (telephone Pretoria 343-1991) or National Parks Board, P.O. Box 7400, Roggebaai 8012 (telephone Cape Town 419-5365) or National Parks Board, P.O. Box 774, George 6530 (telephone George 74-6924/5).

Getting there The park is located south-east of Bethlehem and south-west of Harrismith. It is possible to approach from Kestell, but the road is in poor condition and it is better to travel from the west by way of Clarens.

Accommodation Golden Gate has two rest camps. Glen Reenen features rondavels (with or without shower and toilet) and a caravan and camping site. About 1 km to the west is the Brand-

wag Lodge, with luxury double and single rooms and fully equipped family chalets.

Eating and drinking Brandwag has a licensed restaurant and a ladies' cocktail bar. Glen Reenen has a shop which stocks fresh meat and groceries, and there is a bottle store which supplies beer, wine and spirits. There are braai places among the rondavels, in the caravan and camping site, and at an adjoining picnic place.

Getting around A loop in the east of the park takes motorists through the area where most of Golden Gate's game is concentrated. Golden Gate is also famous for its hiking trails. The two-day Rhebuck Trail starts and finishes at Glen Reenen. There is an overnight stop at a mountain hut in the south-west. Shorter trails (starting at Glen Reenen) lead to landmarks such as Wodehouse Kop, Mushroom Rocks, Boskloof, Echo Ravine and the top of Brandwag, which overlooks Brandwag Lodge. A trail leading to Holkrans starts at Brandwag rest camp. Ponies can be hired at stables near the park's western entrance. A favourite ride leads to the mountain hut on the Rhebuck Trail. Glen Reenen has a filling station.

Special attractions Brandwag rest camp is flanked by tennis courts, a nine-hole golf course and a bowling green and is a favourite venue for conferences. There is a natural swimming pool at Glen Reenen.

Wildlife Golden Gate is best known for its scenery, and game viewing is a bonus. Even so, the park accommodates a population of eland, black wildebeest, mountain reedbuck, grey rhebok, blesbok and Burchell's zebra as well as springbok and oribi. Bird life includes the black eagle and an occasional lammergeyer.

Special precautions Be sure to take warm clothing: sudden chills can occur without warning.

Golden Gate Highlands National Park

Some national parks are famous for their wildlife, others for their scenery. The 6 300 ha Golden Gate Highlands National Park belongs in the latter category. Aeons of erosion have carved freak formations, mainly in the sandstone sediments of the Maluti foothills, resulting in a deep valley that runs through the park's heart. The 'Golden Gate' itself consists of two massive bluffs that face one another across the public road that follows the valley. Each stands about 100 m high, with sandstone faces highlighted by gold and purple tints.

The 'Gate' is spectacular, but an even more striking natural formation is the massive Brandwag, a giant sandstone rampart with the shape of an ocean liner's bow that juts from the valley wall and seems about to topple over. Opposite the Brandwag is a luxury rest camp named after it, and around the corner is Glen Reenen, site of the park's original (and more primitive) rest camp. From Glen Reenen, visitors can hike to the crest of the Brandwag to view much of the park, or set out on the circuitous Rhebuck Trail (named for both the grey rhebok and the mountain reedbuck), a two-day 26 km hike.

A high average annual rainfall of 806 mm ensures a rich flora in the area. From spring to autumn the valleys and surrounding mountains appear fresh and green and there is a dazzling variety of wild flowers – watsonias, fire lilies, red hot pokers, arum lilies and many more. In such glorious surroundings wildlife tends to take a back seat, but hikers and those who drive through the park's eastern hills may come upon eland, black wildebeest, blesbok and other Highveld species such as the timid oribi, as well as a variety of birds.

Since 1978, Golden Gate has put considerable effort into environmental education. The park has a large youth hostel, and schoolchildren, not only from the Free State but also from the Transvaal, Cape and Natal, attend courses that last from one to seven days. In the mornings the children are taught various aspects of conservation; in the afternoons there are physical activities such as canoeing, riding, swimming or hiking; and in the evenings there are discussions and slide shows.

Hendrik Verwoerd Dam Nature Reserve

The Free State's largest nature reserve is a combination of the 36 487 ha Hendrik Verwoerd Dam on the Orange River and an 11 237 ha game sanctuary on its northern shore. The dam was officially opened in 1972 and has long been popular with anglers and boating enthusiasts. The game reserve accommodates a larger population of springbok than any other reserve in the province, and also features black wildebeest, red hartebeest and ostrich.

between Winburg and Theunissen in the central Free State. A 343 ha provincial game reserve adjoining it is also worth a visit. The reserve's modest size makes it relatively easy to see species such as black wildebeest, red hartebeest, mountain reedbuck and Burchell's zebra as well as two intriguing Free State specialities: white springbok (a colour variant rather than a subspecies, found with normal springbok) and yellow blesbok.

One of the reserve's charms is its waterfowl, particularly the African shelduck and Egyptian geese that gather here by the thousands in their moulting seasons.

The reserve is open daily from 7 a.m. to 6 p.m., and there are excellent facilities for camping and caravanning (advance booking is unnecessary). To reach the dam, follow the signs from the Winburg-Theunissen road. The turnoff is 14 km from Theunissen.

Franklin Nature Reserve

Naval Hill is one of the landmarks of Bloemfontein, so named because a naval detachment was stationed here during the Anglo-Boer War. On the summit and slopes is the 253 ha Franklin Nature Reserve, established in the 1930s and run by the municipality in conjunction with Bloemfontein Zoo.

A network of roads runs through the reserve and provides visitors with glimpses of game such as eland, blesbok and springbok. The exotic fallow deer and Barbary sheep in the reserve are being removed, while red hartebeest and wildebeest are being added.

The Franklin reserve is open daily and can be reached from the west side of Naval Hill. Within the boundaries of the reserve are an impressive radio communications complex and Bloemfontein's old Lamont-Hussey Observatory, today used as a theatre.

Top: Mating ladybird beetles. Most ladybirds (both adults and larvae) feed on soft-bodied insects such as mealybugs and aphids, but species of vegetarian ladybirds also occur in Southern Africa. These are identified by their orange and black colouring. Predaceous ladybirds have a shiny carapace coloured red and black. The females lay clusters of eggs on the undersides of leaves or in other spots infested by aphids. When the eggs hatch two weeks later, the larvae feed on the aphids, penetrating their soft bodies with sharp, sickle-shaped jaws and drawing out the body juices. **Left:** A fairytale stream meanders through the Golden Gate Highlands National Park. **Above:** A honeycombed sandstone formation on the floor of a cave in the Rooiberg mountains.

Adjoining the reserve, to the west, is a handsome public resort administered by the Free State Provincial Administration. It is located close to the Hendrik Verwoerd Dam wall. The resort's special pride is a number of luxury two- and three-bedroomed rondavels, each with a lounge-cum-dining room, fully equipped kitchen, bathroom and carport. Other facilities include fully furnished holiday houses and single quarters, a restaurant and entertainment area and a caravan park and camping site. To reserve accommodation (or for further information), write to The Manager, Hendrik Verwoerd Dam Resort, Private Bag X10, Hendrik Verwoerddam 9922 (telephone Hendrik Verwoerd 45).

Kalkfontein Dam Nature Reserve

The 5 101 ha Kalkfontein Dam, north of Fauresmith in the south-western Free State, is one of the few angling areas in the province where yellowfish are relatively abundant. Not surprisingly, then, anglers are frequent visitors to the complex. The dam and its adjoining area of 162 ha have been proclaimed a provincial nature reserve, but the land area is too small to support significant quantities of game. Instead the reserve is advertised chiefly as a recreational area catering for anglers, campers, picnickers and boating enthusiasts. The reserve is open daily from 7 a.m. to 6 p.m. and visitors are allowed to camp overnight.

Right: The African honeybee is well adapted to the harsh conditions of its natural environment. Although the long periods of drought, numerous predators and irregular supplies of nectar take a heavy toll of colonies, this species compensates by its ability to migrate to areas where food is more plentiful, by rapid reproduction and by the accelerated development period of queens, drones and workers. **Below left:** Grey rhebok are generally found in hilly or mountainous areas. **Below right:** Eland: these large browsers feed on bushes and fruits.

THE GROUND SQUIRREL

The speedy ground squirrel is a resourceful little animal. Known also as the Cape ground squirrel – it uses its tail as a sunshade while feeding, holding it in a bent position over its back. The squirrel also uses its tail as an alarm signal, moving it up and down in the face a danger.

This little creature confines its activities to the ground (it is a poor climber) and to the daytime. Colonies numbering up to 30 live in a complicated network of interconnecting burrows, often betrayed by a low mound of soil raised by excavations from the warren. Quite often the warren is shared with suricates and yellow mongooses – amicably for the most part, although mongooses have the nasty habit of killing and eating old ground squirrels.

They sunbathe with their bellies to the ground and all four legs stretched out. They 'dustbathe' in the same position, every now and then scratching the sand all over their bodies and then shaking it off.

The social organisation of ground squirrels is a feminist's fantasy: groups consist of females and their offspring, the dominant female defending the territory.

Mynhardt Game Reserve

The attractive old world town Bethulie (the name means 'chosen by God'), in the Free State's deep south is sandwiched between two major provincial reserves: the Hendrik Verwoerd Dam to the west and Tussen-die-Riviere Game Farm to the east. Even closer to home is Bethulie's 160 ha municipal nature reserve at the town dam. Named after a former mayor of the town, the Mynhardt reserve was established in 1937 – which makes it one of the oldest in the province. Its game population includes black wildebeest, blesbok, zebra, gemsbok, impala and springbok.

Signs at the entrances to Bethulie direct visitors to the reserve, which features a small holiday resort (open day and night) of chalets, rondavels and a caravan and camping site. Visitors wanting to stay in the chalets and rondavels must provide their own bedding, cutlery, crockery and cooking equipment. There are ablution facilities (hot and cold water). The resort is useful for those visiting Tussen-die-Riviere Game Farm, which offers overnight accommodation to hunters only.

For further information, write to The Town Clerk, Bethulie Town Council, P.O. Box 7, Bethulie 9992 (telephone Bethulie 2).

Orange Free State Botanic Garden

One of Bloemfontein's treasures is the 45ha botanic garden on the city's north-western fringe. Some 12 ha of the garden has been developed to display and preserve as much of the Free State flora as will grow there – with particular emphasis on species such as *Crinum*, klip-dagga and witgousblom.

The naturally wooded koppies beyond the cultivated garden contain cabbage trees (*Cussonia paniculata*), white stinkwood (*Celtis africana*), false olive (*Buddleia saligna*) and wild olive (*Olea africana*). Allow about two hours to explore the walks that have been laid out here.

The garden is at its best in spring, when most of its flowers bloom, but there is something of interest at all times of the year – even in midwinter, when the blue felicias and red cancer bushes are in full bloom.

The garden has a well stocked nursery where surplus indigenous trees, shrubs, bulbs and succulents are sold. The garden is open daily from 7 a.m. to 6 p.m. and can be reached by way of General Dan Pienaar Drive (the turn-off is clearly marked).

Qwa-Qwa hiking trails

Qwa-Qwa is the homeland of the South Sotho people, occupying what used to be part of the Orange Free State. It offers a choice of three hiking trails, and though they vary in length and in level of difficulty, mountain scenes of great natural beauty are common to all three. The Wetsi Caves Hiking Trail starts 15 km from the Information Centre on the Monontsha Pass road; a walk of 90 minutes brings you to the majestic hollow cliffs and caves.

The Metsi Matsho Hiking Trail starts at the popular Witsieshoek Mountain resort and runs along the Qwa-Qwa/Natal escarpment to end at the Swartwater or Metsi Matsho ('black water') Dam – a distance of about 15 km, taking approximately five hours. You can fish for trout in the dam. If you want to stay overnight there's a 10-bedded hut, about 1 km away.

A steeper challenge is provided by the Brandwag Peak Hiking Trail (Sentinel Hiking Trail). The route includes a chain ladder about a two-hour walk from the parking area where the trail ends. There are ablution blocks and basic facilities but it is necessary to bring all your own camping equipment to stay on the mountain overnight.

For further information about the trails, you may write to The Head of Tourism, Private Bag X814, Witsieshoek 9870, Qwa-Qwa (telephone Phuthaditjhaba 3-0576).

Sandveld Nature Reserve

The 23 035 ha Bloemhof Dam, at the confluence of the Vaal and Vet rivers in the north-western Free State, has created a large peninsula north

DOWN CAME A BLACK BIRD

There are three species of crow in Southern Africa, ungainly birds that have relatively few admirers because their habits can be messy and annoying. Some clutter telegraph poles with their nests (and have been known to short-circuit the wires); others dig newly planted crops from the fields; yet others are said to attack sick and weak sheep. Around settlements they raid rubbish tips, on farms they peck their way into grain bags; on roads they scavenge carcasses run over by vehicles.

The most common of the three species is the pied crow, black all over except for its snow-white breast and shoulders. It is found throughout the subcontinent. The black crow has a similar distribution, but is absent from Tonga-land and Moçambique. The third species is the white-necked or Cape raven (pictured above), also black but with a broad white band behind its neck. Its distribution is from the south-west Cape to Namaqualand, then eastwards to Zimbabwe and beyond.

The raven has a large, hooked beak quite different from the comparatively slender bills of the other species, but otherwise the three crows have much in common. Crows may gather in quite large parties, but generally they attach themselves to a mate and remain constant for life. Each pair builds an untidy platform nest of twigs and other materials — the white-necked raven on a cliff ledge and the pied and black crows in a tree or up a telegraph pole.

A tortoise beetle displays its striking colour and metallic sheen — caused by the reflection of light on different layers of cuticle. The female lays her oval yellow eggs on leaves, each egg encased in a cocoon of transparent liquid that hardens rapidly. The larva appears after 10-12 days. It feeds on leaves, and carries its cast-off moults at the end of its body. The pupa anchors itself to the leaf.

of Hoopstad. The Sandveld reserve encompasses the north-west area of the peninsula and a small area across the dam to the west: its total size is 14 700 ha. The flat terrain and thorny vegetation have much in common with the sandy Kalahari to the north-west, and the province intends to conserve the sandveld vegetation as a unique feature of the Free State.

Sandveld has been under development since the mid-1970s, and today ranks as one of the three main provincial reserves in the Free State, along with the Willem Pretorius Game Reserve and Tussen-die-Riviere Game Farm. The game re-introduced to the area includes giraffe, eland, gemsbok, red hartebeest and springbok.

Smaller game such as duiker and steenbok abound in the Sandveld reserve. Its bird life includes white-backed vulture, kori bustard, yellow-billed hornbill and long-tailed shrike. Yellowbill, spur-winged geese and redbill teal are found at the dam – popular with anglers

and boating enthusiasts – and certain areas of the reserve have been set aside for caravanning, camping, and picnicking. Toilets and electricity are provided. To reach the dam, follow the signs from Hoopstad.

Soetdoring Nature Reserve

Lion, cheetah and brown hyena have long been absent from most of the Free State, but the three species are making a dramatic re-appearance in a sanctuary 40 km north-west of Bloemfontein – the 4 117 ha Soetdoring reserve surrounds the 2 050 ha Krugersdrif Dam on the Modder River. The reserve is too small for lion and cheetah to run wild, so each is being installed in a special camp within the reserve's boundaries. The predators are fed on surplus antelope and zebra culled elsewhere in the provincial reserve network.

Soetdoring also features many other species re-introduced to the area, among them eland, gemsbok, Burchell's zebra, red hartebeest and

FREE STATE TO THE RESCUE

An illustration from the book *A Breath From the Veldt*, by the artist and naturalist John Guille Millais.

The blue wildebeest is a creature of the lowlands but its cousin, the black wildebeest, prefers the high country of the Free State grasslands and the southern Transvaal. Early in the 19th century the species was one of the most numerous in the region, but farming settlers soon changed that: the meat of the black wildebeest fed their labourers, and its hide made fine harness straps and even grain bags. This wildebeest is actually coloured dark brown, and is often referred to as the white-tailed gnu.

In the 1870s, professional hunters hastened the wildebeest's decline by shooting it for its hide, which was shipped to Europe for paltry sums. By the end of the century the only black wildebeest left were on two private farms in the Free State. The great hunter Frederick Selous believed that the species would have become extinct had it not been for the farmers concerned. In the 20th century, other Free State farmers followed their example.

In 1936 the Free State Provincial Administration was persuaded to buy a few black wildebeest from one of the farmers and place them in its Somerville Game Reserve, close to Bultfontein. More animals were added, and by 1945 they numbered 52.

Early in the 1960s the Somerville reserve was closed and its game moved to the new Willem Pretorius Nature Reserve around Allemanskraal Dam. By 1966 there were 370 black wildebeest in the reserve, and their numbers were still growing. The Administration began relocating the surplus in other reserves.

Today there are almost 700 black wildebeest in the Willem Pretorius reserve, more than 370 in Tussen-die-Riviere and lesser numbers in several other Free State reserves. Many private farmers have built up herds of black wildebeest, and the species is no longer endangered. Indeed, it is so numerous that it is once more being hunted.

Above: *Wahlenbergia* (also known as bell flower and wild bluebell) is a large genus (over 140 species in South Africa). **Left above:** The female horse fly exhibits the mouthparts used to pierce her victim's skin (the hollow lancets, used to suck blood, are concealed within). **Left below:** *Geigeria ornativa*. Other species of Geigeria are highly poisonous to sheep, goats and cattle, causing vomiting and paralysis. **Below:** Spur-winged and Egyptian geese. Despite their names and their similarity to geese, these birds are regarded as ducks.

springbok. Although the roads are inadequate, the reserve is open to visitors and anglers are allowed to make use of the dam. Picnicking is permitted. To reach Soetdoring, take the road to Bultfontein and follow the signs.

Theronia Pan

Saline water pumped from the Free State's gold mines has created a number of large, shallow pans around Welkom and Odendaalsrus, in the north-east of the province. These pans attract thousands of waterfowl to the Free State, in particular large numbers of greater and lesser flamingo and, curiously enough, even seagull – though the sea is nearly 650 km away. Bird-watchers converge on the pans from far afield, and the most accessible of them is Theronia Pan (within Welkom's city limits), which has been developed as a municipal park.

Tussen-die-Riviere Game Farm

South Africa's Department of Water Affairs originally planned to build the Hendrik Verwoerd Dam east rather than west of Bethulie, at the confluence of the Orange and Caledon rivers. The dam was expected to flood a large area, so a number of farms were bought and evacuated. But then the plans were changed – and rather than return the farms to the agricultural sector, the department handed them over to the Free State Provincial Administration for a nature reserve. The result is the 21 000 ha Tussen-die-Riviere Game Farm.

The reserve's western tip where the two rivers converge is a flood plain, but otherwise the rivers are separated by high rocky ridges, occasional plateaus and lower-lying grassy plains. The area was proclaimed a nature reserve in 1972, and at the time it contained only a few mountain reedbuck and occasional duiker and steenbok. Before long a massive re-stocking programme was under way, with the result that today Tussen-die-Riviere has more game than any other reserve in the Free State. The species represented here include eland, kudu, gemsbok, Burchell's zebra, black wildebeest, red hartebeest, mountain reedbuck, blesbok, springbok and white rhino.

From 1 September to 30 April Tussen-die-Riviere functions like any other game reserve, opening throughout the week and welcoming visitors from sunrise to sunset. In winter, however, the atmosphere is very different, for then the reserve is open to hunters. 'The fact is, there is too much game,' explains a nature conservation officer. 'One way or another we have to dispose of the surplus. At Willem Pretorius we capture game and sell it. At Tussen-die-Riviere we hunt it, giving sportsmen an opportunity to take part.'

Before the hunting season starts, the reserve's conservation staff makes a count of every spe-

WILLEM PRETORIUS AT A GLANCE

When to go The reserve and the adjoining public resort are open throughout the year. The resort, at the west end of the reserve, is open at all hours, but the reserve is closed between sunset and sunrise (which means there is no way of crossing it from the eastern gate). The resort tends to be full at weekends and during school holidays.

Reservations Applications for accommodation should be addressed to The Resort Manager, P.O. Willem Pretorius Game Reserve, via Ventersburg 9451 (telephone Ventersburg 4229).

Getting there The reserve can be approached from west or east. From the west, watch for the signposted turn-off on the trunk road between Winburg and Ventersburg, 17km from Ventersburg. From the east, watch for the turn-off (also signposted) on the road from Ventersburg to Senekal, 19km from Senekal.

Accommodation The public resort is sited on a koppie and features rondavels, family huts and luxury flats. The flats have one bedroom, a lounge-cum-dining-room, fully equipped kitchen and bathroom. Luxury rondavels have two bedrooms, a lounge-cum-dining-room, a fully equipped kitchen and a bathroom. Semi-luxury rondavels have two beds, a refrigerator, a two-plate stove, and a shower and toilet. Standard rondavels (two beds) and family cottages (up to six beds) have a refrigerator, a two-plate stove, and a shower and toilet. Additional beds are available. There is also a caravan and camping site.

Eating and drinking The resort has a licensed restaurant and a supermarket selling groceries and fresh meat. There are braai facilities among the rondavels, in the caravan and camping site, and in the adjoining picnic area.

Getting around The northern half of the Willem Pretorius reserve has an extensive network of good quality roads. Visitors must remain in their cars. There are speed limits of 50km/h in the reserve and 25km/h in the resort. Petrol and oil are available from a filling station at the entrance to the resort.

Special attractions The public resort organises launch trips on the dam, and other facilities include tennis courts, a bowling green, nine-hole golf course, swimming pool and entertainment complex offering badminton, billiards, snooker and table tennis.

Wildlife Giraffe, white rhino and buffalo are among the larger species to be seen in the game reserve. Visitors are also likely to spot eland, kudu, black wildebeest, red hartebeest, blesbok, springbok and impala. More than 200 bird species have been recorded in the area – many of them close to the dam.

Fishing There are carp, bass and yellowfish just waiting to be hooked from the dam, but anglers must hold a Free State angling licence (obtainable from the resort office). Fishing is allowed only within the area demarcated by red floats.

cies. Ecologists inspect the veld and decide how many animals it can support. The findings of these investigations dictate which species can be hunted during the season. There are two parties of hunters each week and each party contains ten members who go out in two groups of five or five groups of two. Each group is accompanied by a reserve official.

Tussen-die-Riviere's hunting programme has become enormously popular both with Free Staters and outsiders. No more than 300 hunters can be accommodated each season, but there are as many as 6000 applications, and a computer is employed to make a random selection. Hunters usually spend two nights in the reserve and simple accommodation is provided for them (summer visitors are not permitted to camp overnight). To reach the reserve, take the signposted turn-off on the road between Bethulie and Smithfield, about 10km from Bethulie.

Willem Pretorius Game Reserve
The land areas of the Willem Pretorius reserve lie north and south of the Sand River and the Allemanskraal Dam at its western end. To the south the reserve consists of grassy flats, ideal for springbok, black wildebeest and other species that favour open country.

The north is an area of plains, koppies and ridges of the Doringberg range. Its dense bush (some trees have been numbered for easy

Left: Tranquillity radiates from the countryside between Fouriesburg and Clarens. Over the centuries erosion has sculpted a remarkable variety of forms from the sandstone sediments in the area. Some of the most dramatic are in the Golden Gate Highlands National Park. **Right above:** Long legs distinguish the grey duiker from other duikers. This is a widespread species, occurring in dense savanna, high mountains and even at the edge of a desert. It is mainly nocturnal, feeding in the early morning and in the evening. **Right below left:** A wood engraving by G. Baxter from the book *Missionary Labours and Scenes in Southern Africa*. This engraving is entitled 'Stratagem in Hunting Ostriches', and shows a Bushman, bow in hand, stalking his prey in the guise of an ostrich. The author was Robert Moffat, a Scottish-born missionary who came to South Africa in 1817 to carry out work on behalf of the London Missionary Society. **Right below right:** *Agapanthus inapertus.*

identification) is favoured by white rhino, giraffe, buffalo and impala – the last mentioned very much at home in the Free State, though strictly speaking they are not indigenous to the region.

This is the Free State's major provincial reserve, proclaimed in 1962 after a land swop with the old Somerville Game Reserve near Bultfontein (established in 1924). Most of Somerville's game was moved to the new reserve, including a growing herd of black wildebeest.

A public resort was established at the western end of the reserve and soon became a major attraction for Bloemfontein residents and families living on the goldfields.

Facilities include a restaurant, tennis courts, a bowling green, a nine-hole golf course (plus a miniature golf course) and a swimming pool. Accommodation is in rondavels, and there is a caravan and camping site.

The southern part of the reserve is maintained as a wilderness area and there are no roads (but visitors with binoculars can see the game without difficulty). One hilltop, dotted with the remains of 'beehive' huts left by a vanished tribe, offers fine views over the Sand River's upper reaches. At other points, the roads lead visitors close to the dam shore, from where they can view a variety of waterfowl.

Witsieshoek Mountain Resort

This spectacular mountain resort in the South Sotho homeland of Qwa-Qwa nestles against the rim of the Drakensberg, overlooking Royal Natal National Park's famous Amphitheatre rock formation. Facilities at the resort include chalets and luxury rooms, and a licensed restaurant which is open all year.

Besides Royal Natal, Witsieshoek provides accommodation in close proximity to the massive Sentinel and Mount-aux-Sources.

From the resort you will see an exciting display of soaring raptors, including the impressive bearded lammergeyer.

For further information, write to The Manager, Witsieshoek Mountain Resort, Private Bag 828, Witsieshoek 9870, Qwa-Qwa (telephone Ha Mota 5). A map of the area may be obtained at the resort.

Zeekoeivlei Nature Reserve

Swampy vleis in the Klip River at the appropriately named Memel (Prussian for 'surrounded by water'), in the far eastern Free State, are important breeding grounds for thousands of waterfowl. The province's 379 ha Zeekoeivlei reserve protects the flow of the river and thus the breeding grounds.

The reserve is intended only for conservation purposes, so is not open to visitors unless special arrangements are made.

For further information, you should direct enquiries to The Director, Division of Nature Conservation, Provincial Administration of the OFS, P.O. Box 517, Bloemfontein 9300 (telephone Bloemfontein 405-5243).

Where only the sky is the limit

Lesotho is Southern Africa's Kingdom in the Sky, a geologist's wonderland of towering peaks, table-top plateaus and verdant kloofs: in this tiny country, only the sky is the limit. Even the lowest point in Lesotho is more than 1 250 m above sea level. Lesotho also has the highest peak in Southern Africa: Thabana-Ntlenyana, 3 482 m above sea level and the pride of the Maluti range.

Roughly 85 per cent of Lesotho's 30 300 square kilometres are mountainous, offering spectacular scenery that delights hikers and pony trekkers. Among the attractions are Maletsunyane Falls, one of the highest in Africa, Ha Baroana rock paintings (with a nature reserve around them), fossilised footprints like those at Moyeni, a selection of fine tourist lodges such as the New Oxbow Lodge (a cluster of comfortable chalets used as a base by riders and climbers), the Outward Bound adventure school in the Maluti foothills (with courses for all age groups), and the spectacular Sehlabathebe National Park in the east.

Late in the 18th century, a Griqua hunter passed through Lesotho on horseback. Local tribesmen had never seen a horse before, and supposed it was an ox without horns.

But before long, traders introduced Javanese horses that were the progenitors of the famous Basotho pony.

Today's Basotho still travel long distances on horseback, as do visitors who want to take advantage of Lesotho's tourist attractions. Many of the country's hotels and lodges have ponies for hire and supply guides.

More ambitious (and experienced) riders may embark on a four-day cross-country pony safari to Marakabei and the Maletsunyane Falls, beginning either at the Molimo-Nthuse Hotel on the 'Mountain Road' or at Qaba, east of Mafeteng (the latter route takes in other falls along the way). Ideally, a party includes between six and ten riders who assemble in Maseru and are driven to the starting point by bus. A guide and grooms accompany them, and each day they ride up to 20 km, spending five or six hours in the saddle.

The going is rough, and even hardened riders become saddlesore. At night the party camps in huts. Food is supplied by the outfitter but riders must provide their own sleeping bags and warm clothes. At journey's end the party returns to Maseru by air. Although the trip is physically demanding, it offers an opportunity to view spectacular scenery and is an adventure you will never forget. The safaris are organised only when there is a demand for them so prospective riders must book well in advance.

For further information and details on how to book for the trail, write to The Lesotho Tourist Board, P.O. Box 1378, Maseru, Lesotho (telephone Maseru 32-2896).

Above: Water tumbles over the Maletsunyane Falls near the village of Semonkong, south-east of Maseru.
Left: Bright clusters of everlastings (*Helichrysum ecklonis*) brighten the veld in Lesotho's Sehlabathebe National Park. The dried blooms are often used in flower pictures and wreaths, and were once used to stuff mattresses. These hardy plants are widely distributed in Southern Africa.

Fossil Footprints

Several sites in western Lesotho feature remarkable collections of fossil footprints left by reptiles that stalked the region some 200-million years ago. In most cases the footprints were left in mud, covered by drifting sand and possibly lava, compressed in a layer of sandstone, and finally re-exposed through the forces of erosion. The most famous of the sites is Moyeni in the Quthing district of the far south, where palaeontologists have identified more than 500 sets of prints – most of them left by three-toed creatures that are believed to have been dinosaurs.

Another rich site is the mountainside at Morija, between Maseru and Mafeteng, on which may be seen large numbers of fossil footprints, and petrified wood that pokes from the rock. Geological specimens, fossils and Stone-Age tools are displayed in a small museum at Morija. At Tsikoane, near Leribe, there are caves with 'relief' footprints in the roof.

Qalo (near Butha-Buthe in the north), Kolo (west of Morija) and Maphutseng (near Mohale's Hoek in the south) all have interesting fossil collections.

Lesotho draws palaeontologists from around the world. In some cases the scientists can link the footprints to fossil bones found in Lesotho or elsewhere; in others the footprint may be the only relic of the passing of a species.

Ha Baroana

To the visitor Lesotho contains relatively little evidence of abundant wildlife, but centuries ago it was a different story. Lion, leopard, eland, red hartebeest and smaller antelope are featured in rock paintings which were left by artists of a long-dead culture at sites throughout the kingdom. The finest collection is at Ha Baroana, a rock shelter accessible from the 'Mountain Road' branching north from the highway between Maseru and Roma. The shelter is in a small nature reserve and is open daily from 9 a.m. to 5 p.m.

Some of Ha Baroana's paintings are certainly over 1 000 years old. They represent the work of the San who lived in the region until they were absorbed by Bantu-speaking people from the north and west.

Maletsunyane Falls

Lesotho's many waterfalls include one of the highest in Africa, variously known as Lebihan Falls (after a French missionary), Semonkong ('the place of smoke', referring to the spray) and Maletsunyane (after the river that plunges 193 m over a rim of basalt).

Below the falls the river has excavated a deep gorge which can be descended by a steep path (but visitors should beware of stinging nettles near the bottom, and remember the

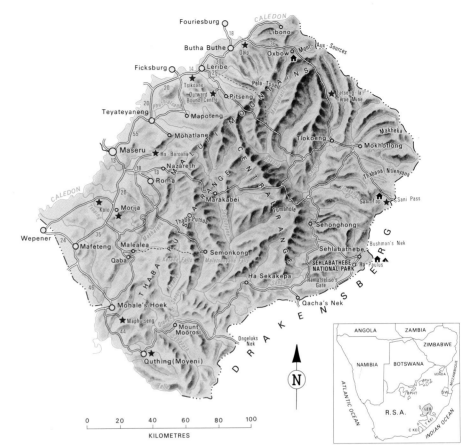

ROLLING HOME THE DINNER

To the ancient Egyptians it was an object of reverence, a symbol of renewed life. Its likeness has been found inscribed on monuments, tombs and ornaments. In Southern Africa the familiar scarab beetle is better known as the dung beetle, from its amusing habit of rolling balls of dung with its back legs.

The dung beetle is a natural scavenger of the veld, carving out for itself a generous portion of dung which it pats into a rough sphere. This is rolled away (the beetle using its back legs), gathering dirt and dust en route. Finally a suitably soft spot is chosen and the ball is buried a few centimetres underground. The

beetle then eats away at the ball.

The female beetle has a further use for the dung ball. She chooses soft and nutritious pieces of dung which are buried in a chamber about the size of a man's fist. She pats these into smooth spheres, leaving an egg on top of each. These eggs eventually hatch into white grubs that live off the dung until they metamorphose into adult beetles.

Competition for good dung is keen — and two or more beetles can often be seen fighting over a particularly appealing ball of droppings. The beetles are also severely at risk from predatory birds while rolling their dung.

arduous return journey; you should be reasonably fit). Lesotho's rare spiral aloe grows on the surrounding hillsides, providing a splash of colour in November.

Maletsunyane can be reached by foot or on horseback from Semonkong, a small village about 4 km away. Ponies may be hired at Semonkong Lodge, which is attached to the local trading post. The lodge makes a good base for exploring the surrounding countryside: bedding, cutlery, crockery and cooking equipment are provided and food is obtainable at the store. To reach Semonkong, visitors may either fly from Maseru, drive from Roma (though not in a vehicle with a low chassis), or join a pony safari from Qaba/Malealea.

The pony safari from Qaba/Malealea takes in two other notable waterfalls: Ribaneng on the Ribaneng River and Ketane on the Ketane River (which requires a special diversion). Guests at Semonkong Lodge may organise an all-day pony expedition to Ketane and back. To reserve accommodation at Semonkong Lodge, write to The Manager, Fraser Lodge System, P.O. Box 5, Maseru, Lesotho (telephone Maseru 31-2601). For further information on bookings and flights to and from Semonkong, you should write to the Lesotho Airways Corporation, P.O. Box 861, Maseru, Lesotho (telephone Maseru 31-2453 or 32-4507).

New Oxbow Lodge

Tourist brochures sometimes describe Lesotho as 'the Switzerland of Africa' – referring to its winter resorts. The most popular is New Oxbow Lodge, a cluster of chalets in the Butha-Buthe district of the north. Snowfall is erratic – in some years there is none until spring, and even after a blizzard the snow usually disappears within a few days – so it has not been worthwhile to invest in a ski-lift.

In summer (and in those winters when there is no snow) the lodge makes a useful base for hikes and rides in the surrounding mountains. There is good fishing in the area around the lodge. To reach Oxbow, take the road between Butha-Buthe and Letseng-la-Terae diamond mine (east of Oxbow the route is not suitable for conventional vehicles, but plans are under way to improve the road as far as Mokhotlong). For further information on the lodge or on ski conditions, write to the Leribe Hotel, P.O. Box 14, Leribe, Lesotho (telephone Leribe 40-0242).

Outward Bound Centre

Canoeing, rock-climbing and map-reading are only a few of the activities at Lesotho's Outward Bound Centre, a wilderness adventure school that sets out to encourage initiative, responsibility, comradeship and concern for the needs of others. The Outward Bound concept originated in Wales in the Second World War,

118

A HEAVYWEIGHT IN EFFORTLESS FLIGHT

More than 240 species of birds have been spotted in Lesotho, but easily the most impressive is the large and powerful lammergeyer, or bearded vulture. The lammergeyer feeds on carrion — often dead sheep and goats — but otherwise it is more eagle than vulture. Their heads and necks are feathered (a vulture's is bare); they live in pairs rather than colonies; and unlike the vulture they can carry prey in their claws. Their 'beards' consist of long bristles under the beak.

In earlier times the lammergeyer had an extended habitat, but today it is rarely seen farther afield than the Drakensberg and Maluti ranges. The species generally nests on a precipice, and the eggs are laid on a jumble of sticks surmounted by softer materials — often wool. The male and female take turns to incubate two eggs while the other goes hunting. When the eggs hatch, the senior offspring kills the junior: a phenomenon common among birds of prey. From an early stage, the survivor is fed meat and bone fragments.

Lammergeyers sometimes fly up with a bone, then drop it on a rock to smash and expose the marrow. The species is noted for its outstanding speed, strength, courage and eyesight — qualities that so appealed to the 19th century Basotho that they expected the same of their military leaders. Praise-poems of the time regularly compared the chiefs with their aerial counterparts.

when young merchant seamen were sent on a course to learn how to survive shipwreck by enemy action. After the war the course was successfully adapted to civilian needs, and today there are more than 30 Outward Bound Centres around the world.

Lesotho's school, established in 1974 and open to all races, is the only one in Southern Africa. Its most popular course lasts two weeks and is designed for young men between 17 and 30 years old. The participants are divided into groups of 10 or 12 and led by professional instructors, who introduce them to something fresh every day – like sailing, orienteering (a kind of cross-country race using map and compass), abseiling (a roped descent of a sheer cliff) and raft-building. To end the course, each student spends two days alone in the wild.

The centre organises a similar course for girls, a less arduous 'senior course' for the older generation, and a 'junior course' for youngsters. No previous experience of the wilds is required for one of Outward Bound's chief aims is to show people that they are more resourceful than they imagined, and can make major advances within a short period. The centre is reached from a signposted turn-off on the road from Leribe to Pitseng. For further information, write to The Director, Outward Bound, P.O. Box 31443, Braamfontein 2017 (telephone Johannesburg 659-0524).

Sani Top

The most dramatic route into Lesotho climbs from Natal by way of the Sani Pass, 2 873 m above sea level. Beyond the South African border post is Sani Top, with an arch of welcome and a mountaineers' chalet containing six bedrooms. Bedding, cutlery, crockery and cooking equipment are provided but visitors must supply their own food. Most types of liquor are available at the bar. The chalet is used by those hiking, climbing and fishing in the surrounding mountains, among them the imposing 3 482 m Thabana-Ntlenyana – the highest point in Southern Africa.

Winter snowfalls attract optimistic skiers to Sani Top, but the snow does not last for long. Only 4-wheel-drive vehicles are allowed to attempt Sani Pass, but Mokhotlong Mountain Transport of Himeville in Natal runs a daily Land-Rover service to Sani Top (provided there are at least four passengers). For further information on transport write to Mokhotlong Moun-

Above: A student at Lesotho's Outward Bound Centre negotiates rapids in the Tsoinyane River as part of his training as a canoeist. The course may sometimes be arduous, but the adventure is unforgettable. **Left:** Black wildebeest graze in the lush hills of the Sehlabathebe National Park. Once faced with extinction, these ungainly grazers — they sometimes go down on their knees to get their moustached faces to the ground — are now off the danger list, and their numbers are increasing in Southern Africa. The early Khoikhoi, always closely tuned in to the ways of the wild, called the black wildebeest 'gnu' because of its cry: *ge-nu*, which it bellows when alarmed.

tain Transport, P.O. Box 12, Himeville 4585 (telephone Himeville 1302). To make bookings for the Sani Top Chalet write to Himeville Hotel, P.O. Himeville 4585 (telephone Himeville 5).

Sehlabathebe National Park

The 6 500 ha Sehlabathebe National Park, in the south-eastern corner of Lesotho, is characterised by mountains and grassveld punctuated by striking outcrops of sandstone. It is intersected by the twisting Tsoelikana River.

To most visitors, Sehlabathebe's chief attractions are its scenery and its solitude. Merely getting there is an adventure. The most comfortable way is to fly from Maseru to the Ha Paulus landing strip, 12 km from the park lodge (guests ride the rest of the way by Land-Rover, or on horseback). More enterprising visitors may drive to the park by way of the trans-Lesotho 'Mountain Road' (which in its eastern stages is suitable only for 4-wheel-drive vehicles) or by the southern road that approaches from Qacha's Nek and Ramatseliso's Gate.

Yet another method is to arrive through the 'back door', walking into the park by way of the South African border post at Bushman's Nek. In this case, visitors leave their cars at Bushman's Nek Hotel, 2 km short of the border. Once inside the park, they either walk to the lodge or cover the 10 km on horseback (provided they have arranged to be met with ponies). Sehlabathebe has little game apart from a resident population of mountain reedbuck and wildebeest (two adult wildebeest were brought in a few years ago, bringing the total to four) and occasional eland and oribi that find their way in from Natal and then leave again when snow arrives. The park also accommodates baboon, black-backed jackal, wild cat, otter and a host of birds and fish. Four dams close to the park lodge are stocked with trout and other species, and there is said to be even better fishing in the south, downstream from a 20 m waterfall that is a favourite destination for hikers and riders. The Tsoelikana River, which runs through the park, harbours the little-known fish *Oreodaimon quathlambae*, a minnow-like species which was once thought to be extinct.

Most of Sehlabathebe's visitors sleep in the park lodge, which has rooms with two or four beds and provides everything except food. The adjoining eight-bunk hostel is designed for youth groups. Hardier visitors may camp out in the park but must be self-sufficient. All visitors should take enough food.

To reserve accommodation or request further information on Sehlabathebe, write to Lesotho National Parks, Ministry of Agriculture, Conservation Division, P.O. Box 24, Maseru, Lesotho (telephone Maseru 32-3600).

Bird-watching for the novice

Birds reflect many of the qualities we admire most in people. Their industry, beauty, variety of habits and general liveliness make ornithology one of the most attractive fields in the study of nature. And birds may be observed through the window of your home or motor car just as effectively as in the veld.

Local branches of the South African Ornithological Society produce cards which will enable you to keep a record of birds you are likely to see in your area.

Record your own data in a field notebook which should fit your pocket or backpack so as to leave your hands free to manipulate binoculars. Books bound with a spiral wire provide a useful place to attach a string tied to a pencil. Decide for yourself the amount of detail to record of each sighting, but the three most important entries are *date*, *time* and *place*.

Naturally, before you can make a valid sighting-report, you must be able to identify the various bird species with a reasonable degree of accuracy.

How to identify a bird There are various reference books on Southern African birds. Choose one which suits your pocket and has the sort of detail that you require.

Learn something about the physical make-up of birds: unlike the animal and insect worlds, birds are comparatively uniform in structure. Their feet and bills, in particular, are adapted to their way of life. For example, wading birds have long legs, and the jacanas have immensely long toes and claws which distribute their weight over a wide area to enable them to run across floating lily leaves.

Birds' bills are usually adapted to their preferred food or method of feeding. The slender, curved bill of the sunbird enables it to reach deep into flowers to draw out the nectar, while the short, strong bills of the sparrow and weaver are ideally suited to cracking seed-pods and seeds.

Use a field guide to familiarise yourself with the standard size-silhouette and always follow a set procedure each time you see an unfamiliar bird.

Many novice bird-watchers attach too much importance to colour – yet there are many birds whose colour is not helpful at all in identification, such as all-brown birds or all-white birds. Instead you should:

1 Note size (compare your subject with a familiar bird).

2 Note size and shape of bill (this gives a clue to feeding behaviour).

3 Note relative size of eye (large or small): birds of prey (such as owls, vultures and eagles) have relatively large eyes, while seed-eaters (such as sparrows, canaries and parrots) have relatively small eyes.

4 Note general proportions of bird and specific characteristics (crests or type of tail feathers).

5 Note whether gregarious or solitary.

6 Note behaviour.

7 Note colour of bill, legs and feet.

8 Note general pattern and colouring (but be careful – a white-chested bird in a leafy tree at dusk can appear yellow-chested, a bar on the chest can be a shadow cast by a twig!).

By the time the observer has noted all other points he or she should have a good idea of

Left: A permanent hide overlooks the water at the Rondebult Bird Sanctuary, near Germiston. **Above:** This portable hide consists of a 'knockdown' metal frame and canvas cover which may be erected wherever the bird-watcher wishes.

Left: A selection of rings used to identify individual birds. Anyone finding a ringed bird should make a note of the relevant details and report it to: Zoo Pretoria, P.O. Box 754, Pretoria 0001 (telephone Pretoria 28-7328). **Below:** The physical features to be noted when identifying a bird. **Opposite page above:** A compact pair of binoculars. **Opposite page below:** A bird-watcher using binoculars. When in the field, they should be worn at chest level for rapid access.

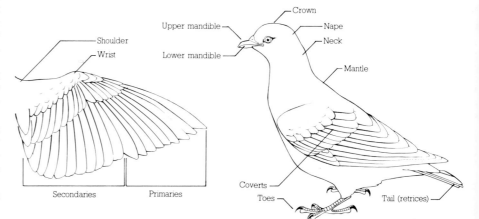

the colour pattern anyway — but the first points noted will give the complete novice a better clue to identity.

When birds are nesting, it is unwise to approach too closely: rather view them through binoculars. Nesting birds are very sensitive to disturbance, especially in the early stages, and may easily abandon the nest. Even when the chicks are being fed regularly, you should never look into the nest while a parent bird is inside — the sudden apparent closing of the nest's only exit is likely to induce panic.

Although many birds and animals can be identified by their songs or calls, visual recognition is probably the most important way to distinguish the precise species. You will find that a suitable pair of binoculars is an invaluable aid to accurate observation.

Remember that the slightest unsteadiness of your hand is exaggerated in proportion to the magnifying power of the binoculars, so that with very powerful glasses it may be difficult to obtain a steady image. A small, steady image is of much more value than a larger, shaking one.

Above: A black-headed oriole, found in well-wooded localities. It builds its nest at the end of a slender branch.
Right: The paradise flycatcher, a common migratory species which is easily recognised by its long tail-feathers and blue wattle.

The prospective buyer should choose his combination of magnification and field in accordance with prime interest. Thus a garden bird-watcher will find a 7 or 8 magnification quite adequate; somebody working in dense vegetation (such as forests) does not need large magnification, but must give attention to 'field' because light is dim in such habitats, and the more that can be admitted the better. But a person who is particularly interested in ducks, sea-birds or hawks and eagles, for example, which may be seen at great distances but are relatively unapproachable, will need larger magnification — a minimum of 10. A good-quality 8X30 instrument with coated lenses is the best general purpose choice for the layman's use in game parks and nature reserves.

Special binoculars may be obtained for use in conjunction with spectacles. They are more expensive, but they impose less eyestrain, and the time saved by not having to remove spectacles may mean that you will not miss an important sighting.

Test binoculars before you buy. Focus on the edge of a white building in bright sunlight, and then move the binoculars so that the edge of the building is close to the edge of the field of view. If the wall appears to bend or blur, or if coloured bands appear on the edge, the lens system is faulty.

Place the binoculars on a table or similar rest, and look through each eyepiece alternately, paying attention to the edges of the fields. The images should be identical. If there is the slightest difference, the binocular's prisms are incorrectly aligned, and this will not only prove annoying in use, but will strain your eyes.

Most binoculars have one eyepiece which can be rotated independently of the main focusing system. This is to compensate for the differences of vision between the eyes of the individual. Focus by looking through only the non-adjustable eyepiece, and then, without changing the main focus, look through the other eyepiece and rotate it until the image comes into sharp focus. This adjustable eyepiece usually has graduation marks to line up with a reference mark on the body of the glasses. Remember the position which suits your eyes — this will save time in the field — and ensure that the image is circular by aligning the eyepieces in the centre of each eye.

Your binoculars should be treated as a delicate instrument. Exposure to sand and dust, dropping or rough handling may affect the optical system even where no obvious damage can be seen. Ensure that the strap is in good condition, and that the stitching is still firm.

When you join a bird-watchers' club, you become at the same time a member of the South African Ornithological Society. This in itself is a contribution towards conservation.

A popular magazine for bird-watchers, *Bokmakierie*, is published by the society.

Useful addresses
● South African Ornithological Society, P.O. Box 87234, Houghton 2041 (telephone Johannesburg 782-1547).
● Cape Bird Club, P.O. Box 5022, Cape Town 8000.
● Eastern Cape Wild Bird Society, P.O. Box 27540, Greenacres, Port Elizabeth 6057.
● Natal Bird Club, P.O. Box 1218, Durban 4000.
● Natal Midlands Bird Club, P.O. Box 2772, Pietermaritzburg 3200.
● Northern Transvaal Ornithological Society, P.O. Box 4158, Pretoria 0001.
● Witwatersrand Bird Club, P.O. Box 72091, Parkview 2122.

Collecting butterflies

A well-mounted butterfly collection not only makes a colourful and attractive display; it also provides a fascinating introduction to natural history. Most of the equipment you need to build up a worthwhile collection can be made easily at home.

The basic tool of every entomologist is the net. Use any strong gauze material through which you can see the butterfly, and which passes easily through the air. Nylon, organdie and tulle are suitable, and the bag of the net should be about the length of your arm. Eight-gauge fencing wire makes an ideal frame and should be bent into a pear shape or circle with a diameter of 40-50 cm. The net must be broad and rounded at the end, and the mouth re-inforced by a length of strong, folded cloth through which the wire is passed.

Aluminium tubing or a wooden pole about 20 mm in diameter and between 50 cm and 100 cm in length can be used for the handle. Drill holes on opposite sides of one end (stagger the holes for extra rigidity) and insert the bent ends of the wire frame. The frame is secured by encircling the ends of the wire with two jubilee clips and clamping them in place (see below).

A well-prepared display of butterflies is as colourful and attractive as a good painting, and will be a tribute to your skill and patience.

Practise using the net. You will soon achieve the smooth swing necessary to trap the swiftest flyer. To seal the net and trap the insect, quickly twist the handle to fold the bag over the rim. Expand the end of the net with one hand and hold it up – trapped insects tend to fly upwards and may then be grasped in a convenient fold. Turn the rest of the bag inside out and slide in the killing bottle to trap the butterfly.

Some collectors kill a butterfly by clasping the abdomen and then carefully but firmly squeezing the thorax between thumb and forefinger. This method prevents damage which may be caused by the butterfly fluttering in the bottle, but requires much practice.

If the butterfly's wings turn down while it is in the bottle, remove it and gently raise the wings above the body. Specimens should remain in the bottle for at least 30 minutes before final removal. Butterflies can be stored safely in paper 'triangles' until you are ready to mount them (see photos below).

Newly-caught butterflies can be pinned and mounted as soon as you choose, but if they are dry or brittle they should first be softened in a 'relaxing box'. Use a plastic box with a tight-fitting lid and line the bottom with cotton wool or plaster of Paris. Moisten this with water and occasionally add a few drops of disinfectant to prevent the growth of mould. Place the butterfly on a saucer or watchglass on top of the cotton wool or plaster (it should not come into direct contact with the water). A butterfly left overnight in a relaxing box will be soft by the next day.

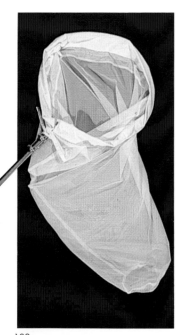

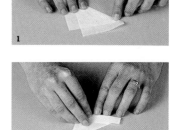

Left A butterfly net made as described in the text.

Right Any wide glass container with a tight-sealing lid will serve as a killing bottle. You will need plaster of Paris and ethyl acetate – available from most chemists. Fill the bottle with sawdust to a depth of about 2 cm and make a thin paste with the plaster of Paris and water. Pour this onto the sawdust to form a layer about 1 cm deep. Before it sets, pierce this layer with a toothpick so that when it has set there will be a tiny hole through to the layer of sawdust. This hole enables the ethyl acetate to be more readily absorbed by the sawdust 'reservoir' after soaking through the plaster of Paris. Wait until the plaster of Paris is completely dry before pouring just enough ethyl acetate to thoroughly moisten the sawdust. Ethyl acetate evaporates very quickly, and the frequency with which you will have to recharge the bottle will depend on how often the bottle is opened and on the tightness of the lid. A small bottle of the chemical should be a part of your field equipment. Do not use ethyl acetate near a flame.

Right A triangle for holding a specimen is easily made from a rectangle of paper about 150 mm by 100 mm. **1** Fold the paper diagonally to leave equal tabs. **2** Bend the tabs over. **3** Open to insert the specimen, refold and label a tab for identification.

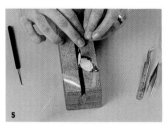

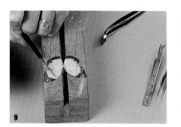
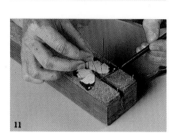
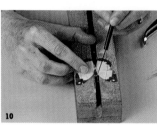

1 To set a butterfly you will need the following: SETTING BOARDS: These are easy to make. They should be 30 cm long and graded in total width and groove width. Convenient widths – total and groove – are 12 cm and 1,0 cm; 10 cm and 1,0 cm; 5 cm and 0,5 cm; 2,5 cm and 0,5 cm. The groove and upper edges must be lined with cork (obtainable at most hardware shops). STRIPS: These may be cut from strong tracing paper or plastic. Each strip should be wide enough to cover a wing of the butterfly you intend to set. PINS: Fine dressmaking pins may be used for holding the wings in position but special entomological pins should be used for actual pinning of the

specimens. Most other pins are too short, and tend to rust. Museums and universities can advise you on how to obtain entomological pins. SETTING NEEDLE: Press a medium-sized darning needle point-first into the end of a soft length of wood about the size of a pencil. About half the length of the needle should protrude, and it should be firmly fixed into the wood.
2 Hold the butterfly and press the entomological pin vertically through the centre of the thorax until only about a quarter of the length of the pin is exposed above the body. **3** Press the pin into the centre of the groove of the setting board so that the base of the wings is level with the top of the board.

Press an ordinary pin into the groove against the left side of the abdomen – this will prevent the butterfly from swivelling in a clockwise direction when the left wings are moved forward. Hold the wings down with the strip of paper or plastic. **4** Gently ease the left forewing forward by holding the setting needle against one of the long veins. **5** Move the left hindwing a short way forward, and then move the forewing again until its inner margin is at right angles to the thorax. Position the hindwing, and after checking that the forewing is still in the correct position, fix pins through the strip immediately in front of and behind the wings to hold them in place. Be careful not to pierce

the wings. **6** Before moving the right wings, transfer the pin against the abdomen to the right side. **7 and 8** The right hindwing is positioned as was the left. Hold it in place, cover with a plastic strip and secure it with pins. **9, 10 and 11** Position the antennae and, if necessary, brace the abdomen with pins. **12** Pin the descriptive label. The specimen can now be left to dry. In dry weather a small butterfly should be dry after about ten days. Larger specimens should be left undisturbed for about three weeks. Use a pin to determine whether the drying process is complete: if the body and wings move when the abdomen is pressed, then the butterfly is ready for mounting.

Ask a carpenter or the local handyman to make a glass-fronted display case. It is essential to put naphthalene flakes into the cases to keep out scavenging insects such as the museum beetle. The naphthalene should be placed in a special trough or linen bag, or it can be scattered along the bottom of the case. It should not be allowed to come into contact with the specimens. Naphthalene is not an insecticide, and if a display case is invaded by scavengers, it may be necessary to use a commercial preparation to get rid of them. A specimen which is being eaten can be dipped in benzine. It will then have to be set again.

Not even the rarest specimen – whether butterfly, gemstone or flower – is of any scientific value unless it is clearly labelled.

Details should be kept with the butterfly at all stages – from notes on the closing-flap of the paper 'triangle' to a neatly-printed card in the display case. The amount of information which is to be recorded is a matter of personal choice, but the minimum is:
1 The place where the specimen was found; and
2 The date.
If it was caught on a mountain, the approximate altitude should be given. Record the general type of vegetation, such as 'pine forest' or 'fynbos'. The time of the catch should be recorded, and whether or not the butterfly was active at that time.
It is useful to take a notebook on field trips. Details of catches can later be amplified or copied into a register opposite numbers

which correspond to the specimen labels.

Out of bounds

Collecting insects is not as strictly controlled by law as, for example, gathering flowers or birds' eggs. Because insects are so abundant, large numbers can usually be collected without in any way endangering a species. A combination of collecting and habitat change has, however, drastically reduced the numbers of some butterflies, and the authorities have been obliged to ban collecting within certain areas. An example is the Table Mountain area and surrounding forest reserves. If you are in any doubt about the legality of collecting in a particular area, check with the nearest magistrate's office, nature conservation or forestry official.

NATAL

This verdant and beautiful region, bordering the east coast of Southern Africa from Port Edward north to the Mozambique boundary, is regarded as South Africa's 'garden province'. Natal's subtropical coastline, its sweeping savanna in the east and the magnificent Drakensberg range in the west, provide a naturally opulent backdrop for its rich wildlife heritage. The lammergeyer soars majestically over its mountain kingdom, the buffalo ranges the plains of Umfolozi, stately palms grace the playgrounds of Durban and Margate.

At the helm of the province's complex of wilderness trails, game parks and nature reserves is the Natal Parks Board, a semi-autonomous body which controls 64 sanctuaries stretching from Sodwana Bay in the north to Umtamvuna Nature Reserve in the south; from the Royal Natal National Park in the west to the eastern seaboard. The Board's conservation activities are aimed at promoting the wise use of natural resources in perpetuity and to prevent degradation of the environment; to this end it operates a wide range of educational programmes, keeping in constant touch with the media.

Natal's parks and reserves offer visitors an opportunity to see wildlife in habitats varying from scrubland to dense forest, from green hills to spray-lashed seashore, ranging in size from the 47753 ha Umfolozi Game Reserve to the modest, 5 ha Doreen Clark Nature Reserve.

KwaZulu has a Bureau of Natural Resources to administer its magnificent reserves in northern Natal – these include Ndumo, Kosi Bay and Lake Sibaya.

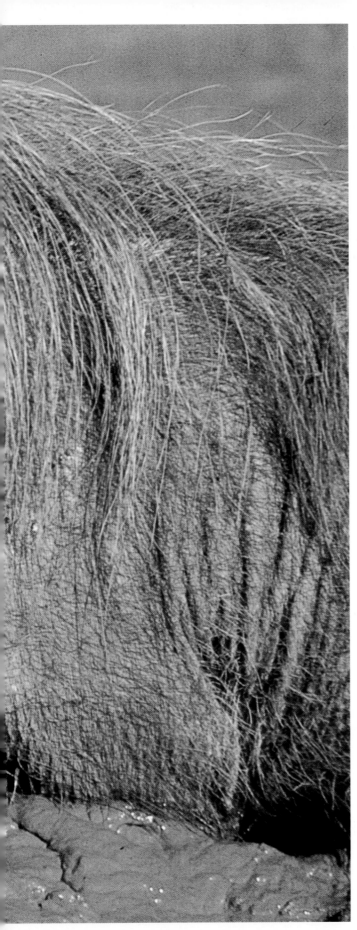

A pensive warthog in a mud wallow. This uncompromisingly ugly animal is found mostly in family parties. It feeds on herbs and short grasses, which it plucks with its incisors, but may also root for bulbs and tubers – much like a pig.

The Dragon's Fangs

The Natal Drakensberg, moss green in summer and icy white to grey in winter, is one of the world's loveliest mountain ranges. Dividing Natal from the high African roof of Lesotho, the mountains run 200 km along Natal's western boundary. Home first to the eland and the little San (Bushmen) who hunted them, they are today the winter playground of South Africa. It is to this ancient wilderness of flower-decked foothills, trout streams and fearsome lava peaks that a stream of visitors is being drawn.

They delight in the rugged splendour of the Giant's Castle Game Reserve – over 34 000 ha of grassy plateaus and deep valleys ranged by a large variety of wildlife. The more intrepid

visitors may even choose to sleep in a cave or mountain hut.

Rivers, waterfalls and a huge backdrop of majestic mountains characterise the Royal Natal National Park, where visitors spend the days exploring the many trails on foot or on horseback, and the nights in comfortable bungalows and cottages. Hiking trails abound in the reserves and wilderness areas of the Drakensberg, and the Department of Environment Affairs has produced helpful maps for visitors.

Coleford Nature Reserve

Underberg is South Africa's premier trout-fishing area – the rainbow trout here are

magnificent. A series of man-made and natural impoundments formed by the Ingwangwane and Ndawana rivers as they meander through a valley form part of the 1 272 ha Coleford reserve. Access is 1 km east of Underberg on the Bulwer road (and then 21 km on gravel).

Accommodation in the reserve is varied: the hutted camp comprises six rest huts, five bungalows, 2 three-bedroomed cottages (with communal lounge and kitchens) and ablution blocks. Visitors provide their own food and drink. Sunnyside Cottage and Rondavel (about 8 km from the main camp) accommodates seven visitors. Blesbok and black wildebeest predominate on the open foothills of the

Top: *Delosperma herbeum* (a vygie) among dolerite rocks in the Kamberg area. **Above:** *Wurmbea krausii*, at an altitude of 3 000 metres, photographed in October. **Right:** The eastern buttress of Devil's Tooth, one of the best-known rock formations in the Drakensberg range. These mountains draw many hundreds of hikers and climbers every year, and the experience is frequently put to good use on expeditions abroad.

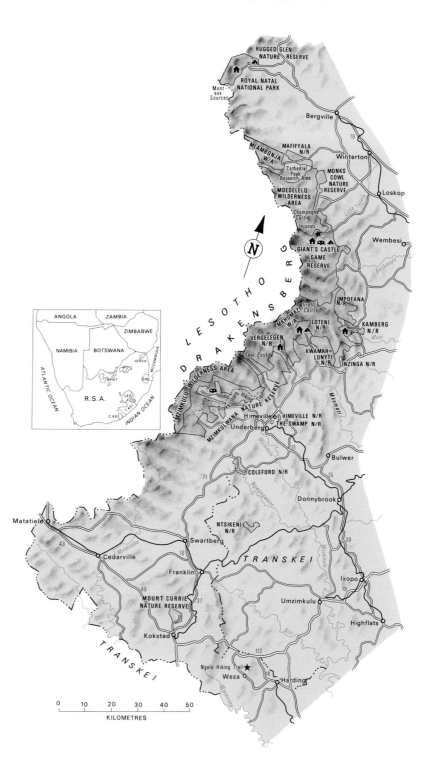

reserve, which offers facilities such as riding, tennis and a provincial library.

Good rainbow-trout fishing is available in the reserve, and both a daily angling permit and a provincial licence are required: these two documents are obtainable from the camp superintendent.

The reserve is open daily from 6 a.m. to 6 p.m., and there are braai and picnic sites in the camp for the use of day visitors. Visitors may also picnic anywhere along the river (though fires are prohibited). To make reservations, write to The Reservations Officer, Natal Parks Board, P.O. Box 662, Pietermaritzburg 3200 (telephone Pietermaritzburg 47-1981).

Drakensberg Hiking Trail: Giant's Cup Section

The Giant's Cup Section of the Drakensberg Hiking Trail passes through one of the most beautiful parts of Southern Africa, winding among the foothills of the Drakensberg and taking the hiker through a rich variety of indigenous flora. The full distance requires five days, starting at the foot of the Sani Pass and ending at the Silver Streams Hut, which lies about 1 km beyond the Lesotho border post at Bushman's Nek.

Hikers are reminded that fires are not allowed at all of the overnight huts, and they should take along billy-cans and portable stoves. Snakebite kits are also recommended.

The route is indicated by white footprints painted on rocks, trees and piles of stones. Yellow footprints indicate connecting or alternative routes, and blue footprints indicate the route to drinking water or a swimming spot.

Anyone wishing to undertake this hike should write to The Reservations Officer, Natal Parks Board, P.O. Box 662, Pietermaritzburg 3200 (telephone Pietermaritzburg 47-1981).

Giant's Castle Game Reserve

In the 19th century, as each new migrating human wave – Zulu, Voortrekker, Briton – swept over Natal, the 25 km long and 3 000 m high wall of the berg now known as Giant's Castle acquired new names. Its English name dates back to 1865.

Until little more than a hundred years ago, and for centuries before that, the berg was home to the San or Bushmen, the 'people of the eland', as the victims of their lightning cattle raids called them. Unlike the black men and the white men, the little hunter-artists who followed the herds of eland were not conquerors. So they were conquered, and vanished. They have left monuments to their passing in their stick-like animal paintings, of which there are 700 in a cave-site museum in the Giant's Castle Game Reserve. Forty per cent of all known rock art in South Africa is in the twilight overhangs of Giant's Castle and in Ndedema Gorge, in the Cathedral Peak area farther north. The ranger-naturalist at Giant's Castle (which was originally proclaimed a reserve to protect the eland) will show visitors a San candle, a hand-stitched eland scrotum water gourd and the Polludada caterpillar cocoon from which deadly hunting poison was squeezed.

There are 800 species of flowering plants, including 63 ground orchids, in the Drakensberg.

Game in the reserve includes 11 species of antelope (some introduced) – eland, mountain reedbuck, common reedbuck, grey rhebok, oribi, klipspringer, bushbuck, blesbok, red hartebeest and grey duiker. Black-backed jackal, baboon, serval and caracal are also found. Trout are found in the Bushman's River. A hide from which visitors may observe the rare lammergeyer and other birds of prey may be reserved. Visitors can also visit the Bushman Site Museum, which is situated not far from the Giant's Castle hutted camp.

A variety of accommodation is available, including cottages, bungalows, a caravan park, three caves and three mountain huts.

Once known as Solitude Mountain Resort, Injasuti is part of Giant's Castle Game Reserve.

Now run by the Natal Parks Board, the area is named after the triple eNjesuthi peaks that form part of the 3 000 m high northern buttress of adjacent Giant's Castle, on its border with the Mdedelelo Wilderness Area. It is through an exceptionally beautiful valley of forests and sandstone cliffs that the Injasuti River flows. Autumn in the Injasuti Valley, when the trees display their browns, reds and golds, is particularly lovely. The reserve is dominated in winter by a looming wall of ice and snow: the 3 207 m Great Injasuti buttress.

There are 17 cabins at Injasuti, each with a stove and fridge; and a campsite.

Himeville Nature Reserve

Himeville reserve – 105 ha, adjacent to the Drakensberg foothills village of Himeville – is a popular trout-fishing spot and camping-caravan site among blue gums. The site overlooks two small dams. Waterfowl of several species are attracted to the dams, as is the occasional antelope. To get there take the Underberg road from Pietermaritzburg. The reserve, which opens from sunrise to sunset, is signposted from Himeville village. Bookings for the ten campsites are made through The Officer-in-Charge, Himeville Nature Reserve P.O. Himeville 4585 (telephone Himeville 36). Provincial fishing licences and daily rod tickets are obtainable from the reserve's office.

Impofana Nature Reserve

'Impofana' is the Zulu name for the Cape eland, the largest antelope species resident in the Drakensberg. The gracefully undulating hills of this nature reserve provide a home for these and many other animals, including grey rhebok, mountain reedbuck and oribi. The only nesting site of wattled crane in the Natal Drakensberg is to be found here; and the area also contains the largest breeding colony of bald ibis – a threatened species – in any protected area of Natal.

Impofana is a large reserve, 7 626 ha, lying mainly on a section of the Highmoor plateau and bordering the Mkhomazi Wilderness Area, for which it is one of the entry points. Apart from Mike's Pass at Cathedral Peak, Impofana is the only place permitting public access by vehicle to the top of the Little Berg. Anyone bold enough to walk to one of the many vantage points will be rewarded with magnificent panoramic views of both the Little Berg and the main Drakensberg escarpment.

Three dams in the nature reserve are annually stocked with trout, which provide trophy fishing for the angler. Present around the dams is a wide variety of water birds, including the white-backed duck and the osprey.

To reach the reserve take the Nottingham Road/Rosetta turn-off from the N3. At Rosetta turn left until, 100 m past the Kamberg turn-off, the road forks. Take the left fork to Highmoor State Forest. Access to Impofana Nature Reserve is by permit only. For further information, write to The Director, Natal Parks Board, P.O. Box 662, Pietermaritzburg 3200 (telephone Pietermaritzburg 47-1961); or to The Officer-in-Charge, Highmoor State Forest, P.O. Box 51, Rosetta 3301 (telephone Mooi River 3-7240).

iNzinga Nature Reserve

At the centre of the iNzinga Nature Reserve is the picturesque iNzinga Valley. To the west lies part of the Mkhomazi Wilderness Area, while to the east are private farms. It is an area largely unknown to most tourists, and indeed the rough gravel roads that provide access prevent many of them from venturing there.

Nor are there any accommodation facilities. Most people who pass through the nature reserve travel on to explore the extensive Mkhomazi Wilderness Area, where they camp in tents or in demarcated caves.

Access to the nature reserve is by permit only. To reach the reserve turn off the N3 to

Above: Giant's Castle from above the Bushman's River. The peak's name was originally applied to a castle-shaped mountain near Underberg, but was later transposed. The reserve abounds in peaks, valleys and tumbling streams. **Right above:** *Aster perfoliatus* at an altitude of 2 500 metres. **Right:** An eland – the largest of the African antelope – in the Giant's Castle Game Reserve.

Nottingham Road where you should follow the signs to Sani Pass/Loteni until Mkhomazi State Forest is reached. For more information write to The Director, Natal Parks Board, P.O. Box 662, Pietermaritzburg 3200 (telephone Pietermaritzburg 47-1961); or to The Officer-in-Charge, Mkhomazi State Forest, P.O. Box 105, Nottingham Road 3280 (telephone Mooi River 3-6444).

Kamberg Nature Reserve
The great white shields carried by warriors of the Zulu Royal Regiments came from the hides of royal cattle that Shaka, founder and fighting chief of the Zulu nation, kept in the Kamberg area of the Drakensberg.

Today, this impressive 2 232 ha reserve, set in the vicinity of the Loteni and Giant's Castle sanctuaries, caters for the less bloodthirsty pursuits of brown trout fishing in the Mooi River and, as always in the Little Berg, mountain walks in a beautiful setting. The trout hatchery here supplies trout for all Natal Parks Board areas in the Drakensberg. Trout-fishing clinics are held at irregular intervals.

Natal Parks Board staff at Kamberg have organised seven walks and climbs, one of which is specifically designed to include the yellow-wood, tree fern (*Cyathea*) and protea of the area. A recent innovation is a nature trail devised for visitors in wheelchairs.

Kamberg is 42 km from Rosena, which is itself 11 km south of Mooi River. Another way to get there is via the village of Nottingham Road. Kamberg offers a delightful hutted camp comprising five rest huts, a comfortable communal lounge, a six-bedded cottage, ablution and kitchen blocks and a rustic cottage where visitors do their own cooking. Visitors provide their own food and drink.

Visitors are likely to see a variety of game including black wildebeest, emblem of Natal, and eight other species of antelope.

Accommodation can be booked through The Reservations Officer, Natal Parks Board, P.O. Box 662, Pietermaritzburg 3200 (telephone Pietermaritzburg 47-1981).

KwaMehlenyati Nature Reserve
This 3 785 ha nature reserve owes its existence to the efforts of Mr V. W. M. Campbell, who sold his properties to the government at a special price so that they could be afforded protection and managed as a reserve in perpetuity. The local Zulu called Mr Campbell 'KwaMehlenyati', meaning 'the eyes of the buffalo'.

Impressive sandstone cliffs form a natural boundary between the reserve and the Mkhomazi Wilderness Area to the north-west. Other features include the Nhlambamasoka River and waterfall. There are several walks and hikes here; most of them serve as routes for the hiker or climber travelling through to the wilderness area.

The reserve lies within the Mkhomazi State Forest and access is by permit only. For information and permits write to The Director, Natal Parks Board, P.O. Box 662, Pietermaritzburg 3200 (telephone Pietermaritzburg 47-1961); or to The Officer-in-Charge, Mkhomazi State Forest, P.O. Box 105, Nottingham Road 3280 (telephone Mooi River 3-6444).

Loteni Nature Reserve
Loteni is wild and lonely, a ravine hideaway in the shadow of the high Drakensberg. It means 'in the ashes', from the burnt appearance of the shale found in this river-flanked valley reserve of 3 984 ha, 76 km from the village of Nottingham Road, about 14 km north-east of the Loteni Store on the direct Nottingham Road-Himeville route. In the early 19th century the

Loteni Valley was a San cattle-raiding route. Later part of it became a sheep farm run by William and Catherine Root. A settlers' museum – exhibiting farm implements, furniture and household utensils – is sited in the reserve.

Brown trout fishing in the shallow-flowing Loteni is a major attraction. The green flanks of the valley provide refuge for mountain reedbuck, eland and grey rhebok while the bird life, which includes eagle, kingfisher and stork, is excellent. There are two cottages, a hutted camp of 12 bungalows for which visitors must bring their own food, a fisherman's rustic cottage and a campsite. The latter may be booked through The Camp Superintendent, Loteni Nature Reserve, P.O. Box 14, Himeville 4584 (telephone Himeville 1540). The reserve is open from sunrise to sunset. Fishing licences and fishing permits are available in the reserve. To book accommodation, write to The Reservations Officer, Natal Parks Board, P.O. Box 662, Pietermaritzburg 3200 (telephone Pietermaritzburg 47-1981).

Mafifiyela Nature Reserve

Numerous footpaths meander through this popular nature reserve whose name, meaning 'the one who squints from under his eyebrows when talking', honours the late Mr Albert van der Riet, first owner of the Cathedral Peak Hotel. It was he who donated the mountainous parts of three properties to be included in the reserve. Some 2200 ha in extent, it borders the Mlambonja Wilderness Area, for which it acts as a buffer zone, and it contains some of the best-preserved areas of valley scrub in the Drakensberg.

Features include the Clarens sandstone cliffs and Baboon and Mushroom Rocks. Excellent trout fishing is available in the picturesque berg rivers, the Mlambonja and Mhlawazini.

The reserve lies within Cathedral Peak State Forest and access is by permit only. For further information and permits write to The Director, Natal Parks Board, P.O. Box 662, Pietermaritzburg 3200 (telephone Pietermaritzburg 47-1961); or to The Officer-in-Charge, Cathedral Peak State Forest, Private Bag X1, Winterton 3340 (telephone Bergville 38-1806).

Mdedelelo Wilderness Area

The little farming town of Winterton, with its cluster of churches, 23 km off the N3, is the jump-off point for innumerable 'berg resorts': Cathkin Park, The Nest, El Mirador, Kelvin Grove, Dragon Peaks, Champagne Castle and Cathedral Peak. Beyond is the Cathedral Peak State Forest, access to which is through the Mlambonja River valley.

The heart of this section of the Drakensberg, bounded on the north by the 3004 m Cathedral Peak and in the south by the even higher Cath-

kin and Champagne Castle mountains, is the Mdedelelo Wilderness Area, extending for 29 000 hectares. In it is the magnificent Ndedema Gorge and 147 rock shelters of San paintings. This was one of the last areas to be penetrated by white men. Black basalt tentacles claw at the sky, giving it a 'badlands' look.

The Drakensberg is a place of fierce and frightening storms. Ndumeni Dome, right in the middle, with the Cathedral to its left, is 'the mountain of thunderstorms', while Ndedema or 'Ndidima' means 'the place of rolling thunder'.

Gentle streams, cascades, deep forests and waterfalls are the other side of Mdedelelo – a true wilderness.

Entry into the wilderness area is by permit only. For further information write to The Director, Natal Parks Board, P.O. Box 662, Pietermaritzburg 3200 (telephone Pietermaritzburg 47-1961); or to The Officer-in-Charge, Cathedral Peak State Forest, Private Bag X1, Winterton 3340 (telephone Bergville 38-1806).

Mkhomazi Wilderness Area

Mkhomazi, or Umkomaas, means the 'place of cow whales', so called because the river estuary not far from Amanzimtoti on the south coast used to be a favourite with these giant mammals. The river is born 150 km away in the

Drakensberg from a meeting of the Mkhomazi, Lotheni, KaNtuba and Mkhomazana rivers; and this region is known as the Mkhomazi Wilderness Area. Giant's Castle is at its northern fringe and the Sani Pass at the southern. The Loteni, Vergelegen, iNzinga and KwaMehlenyati nature reserves are contained within this area, which forms part of the Mkhomazi and Highmoor State forests.

Access to the mountain rim and Mohlesi Pass is along the 34 km Vergelegen road. For permission to explore the Mkhomazi Wilderness Area, and for further information, write to The Director, Natal Parks Board, P.O. Box 662, Pietermaritzburg 3200 (telephone Pietermaritzburg 47-1961); or to The State Forester, Highmoor State Forest, P.O. Box 51, Rosetta 3301 (telephone Mooi River 3-7240). To get to Mkhomazi, take the Merrivale turn-off from the N3 north of Pietermaritzburg and drive for 134 km via Bulwer and Underberg to reach the entrance at the Sani Pass.

Mlambonja Wilderness Area

Mlambonja Wilderness Area boasts some of the Drakensberg's most scenic features, including the towering Cathedral Peak, The Bell, Inner and Outer Horns, Twins, Mount Helga, Cleft Peak and spectacular Rainbow Gorge.

Left above: *Helichrysum squamosum.* **Left below:** The call of the cicada (Christmas beetle) is probably the most familiar of all sounds in the wilds of Southern Africa. It is only the male that produces the shrill cry: the sound-producing organ consists of a cavity on either side of his abdomen in which the timbals (or miniature drums) and folded membranes are lodged. The cicada makes these timbals vibrate, and the membranes amplify the noise. The sound is believed to act as an assembly call, and may also be part of a mating ritual. **Right above:** A San cave museum in the Giant's Castle Game Reserve illustrates the centuries of San occupation from the late Stone Age. This reconstruction portrays a group of these ancient hunter-gatherers in their cave home. **Right below:** San cave paintings in the Drakensberg. Many of these paintings have been destroyed by thoughtless visitors over the years: people scribbled on them, lit fires in the caves and even splashed water and other liquids on the paint in attempts to enhance the colours. **Bottom right:** *Hesperantha schelpeana* high on the slopes of Sentinel Peak, in the Drakensberg.

MOTHERHOOD — THE EASY WAY

A striped cuckoo's greenish-blue egg (far left) is an almost perfect match to the eggs of an arrow-marked babbler. In this species, the chick does not attempt to evict the eggs or young of the host bird.

One of the mysteries of evolution is the enigma of the brood parasites — birds that lay their eggs in the nests of other species and leave the upbringing of their chicks to an unknown mother. The best known of these is the cuckoo.

The cuckoo breeds in summer after migrating south from the African tropics. The female looks out for a suitable host nest before laying a single egg among the 'foreign' clutch. Up to 15 eggs are laid by the cuckoo in different nests — and usually the cuckoo eats one of the host eggs while laying her own.

Hatching takes about two weeks — after which the battle for survival starts in earnest. Although blind and fragile-looking, the young cuckoo has powerful feet, a flat back and strong wing stubs. By lying on its back and using the wing stubs to manoeuvre, the baby bird pushes the egg or nestlings out and over the edge of the nest. This eviction impulse lasts about five days. If any 'host' chicks survive, they and the cuckoo grow up together. The 'foreign' mother then raises the young cuckoo as her own.

Certain honeyguides, whydahs and finches are also brood parasites. A newly hatched honeyguide uses a remarkable hook at the end of each mandible to kill the other occupants of the nest. This bill-hook disappears during the nesting period. The cuckoo finch does not evict its nesting mates, but being smaller and weaker, the host chicks usually die off. Whydahs also leave the host brood alone and several can be raised alongside the host chicks.

A fascinating aspect of this evolutionary contrick is that the eggs of the parasitic birds have come to resemble those of the host bird; nature's way of ensuring that the host mother cannot recognise the menace among her own eggs until it is too late. Nature has come up with yet another marvel: some parasitic birds use more than one host, and apparently produce a suitable egg for each host.

These massive mountains, with undulating grassland in between, provide magnificent opportunities for walking, hiking, camping and rock climbing. There is also superior angling in the tributaries of the Mlambonja River's upper reaches.

A pair of binoculars is useful for keen bird-watchers as the precipitous mountain slopes are the home of a variety of birds, including the bearded and Cape vulture, martial eagle and black and white stork. In all some 190 species of birds and over 300 indigenous species of plants have been identified.

There is a camping and a caravan park or, for those who prefer the trappings of greater comfort, the Cathedral Peak Hotel.

Access is by permit only. To reach the area take the Winterton turn-off from the N3. From Winterton follow signs to Central Berg Resorts and then to Cathedral Peak State Forest. For further information write to The Director, Natal Parks Board, P.O. Box 662, Pietermaritzburg 3200 (telephone Pietermaritzburg 47-1961); or to The Officer-in-Charge, Cathedral Peak State Forest, Private Bag X1, Winterton 3340 (telephone Bergville 38-1806).

Monk's Cowl Nature Reserve

In more than one part of the Natal Drakensberg Reserve, 'buffer' zones have been created between, on the one side, official wilderness areas and, on the other, private properties. The aim is to screen the effects of man and his activities, and as far as possible to keep the wilderness zones in their largely unspoilt state. Monk's Cowl Nature Reserve was proclaimed to act as a buffer zone. It is situated on the eastern border of the Mdedelelo Wilderness Area and is 3 814 ha in size.

To reach the reserve follow the Berg Resorts signboards from Winterton, until Monk's Cowl State Forest is reached. Access to Monk's Cowl Nature Reserve is by permit only. For further information and permits write to The Director, Natal Parks Board, P.O. Box 662, Pietermaritzburg 3200 (telephone Pietermaritzburg 47-1961); or to The Officer-in-Charge, Monk's Cowl State Forest, Private Bag X2, Winterton 3340 (telephone Winterton 2204).

Right: The Tugela gorge, a dramatic cleft in the Drakensberg Mountains sweeping through the majestic Royal Natal National Park. This 8 094 ha wonderland, foremost of the Drakensberg parks, offers enchanting walks such as Fairy Glen, a short walk from the Warden's office, with its *Begonia* and *Streptocarpus*; Gudu Falls (a three-hour walk); Surprise Ridge and Cannibal Caves (five hours); and Buttress Grotto, which is characterised by a profusion a cycads.

ROYAL NATAL AT A GLANCE

When to Go The Christmas and Easter holidays are the favourite visiting times in the mountains, and accommodation is then much in demand. The Tendele Camp and Royal Natal National Park campsite gates are open between sunrise and sunset. Entrance to the Royal Natal National Park Hotel is not restricted.

Reservations and information The 15 Tendele bungalows and cottages are usually booked out months ahead. Tendele Lodge provides luxury accommodation for six people in three *en suite* bedrooms. For reservations, write to The Reservations Officer, Natal Parks Board, P.O. Box 662, Pietermaritzburg 3200 (telephone Pietermaritzburg 47-1981). The campsites at Mahai are booked through The Officer-in-Charge, Royal Natal National Park, P.O. Mont-aux-Sources 3353 (telephone Bergville 38-1803). There is a visitor information centre in the park and a comprehensive brochure is available.

Getting there The park is 42 km (tarred) west of Bergville, or 72 km from Harrismith via the Sterkfontein Dam and Olivieroshoek Pass.

Accommodation Apart from the Tendele bungalows and cottages and the campsites at Mahai, accommodation is also available at the Royal Natal National Park Hotel, P.O. Mont-aux-Sources 3353 (telephone Bergville 38-1051). This is a privately run hotel.

Eating and drinking Limited food supplies can be purchased at the hotel shop.

Getting around The speed limit is 40 km/h and visitors are asked to exercise caution. The horse-riding service is excellent. Hiking and climbing are the main activities.

Special attractions There is a small museum in the visitor centre with exhibits covering the vegetation, history, archaeology, fauna and geology of the park. There are many protea and other wild flowers, none of which may be picked. Yellowwood, stinkwood, wild chestnut, assegai and dog plum grow in the forests.

Wildlife The checklist of birds recorded in the park covers 184 species, including the lammergeyer, Cape vulture and black eagle. Mammals include hare, the agile klipspringer in the high mountains, baboon, bushbuck, mountain reedbuck, black-backed jackal, porcupine, grey rhebok and, in the savanna, grey duiker.

Fishing There is a large dam to fish in. Licences are available from the visitor centre.

Special precautions Visitors intending to climb or walk to the summit of the Drakensberg should always obtain prior permission from the reserve warden. This applies to all the more difficult climbs as well. Rescues are organised from the warden's office (fatal accidents unfortunately continue to occur). There are two basic rules: never walk or climb alone, and if mist comes up, do not move away until it clears.

Mount Currie Nature Reserve

In spring, the protea on this 1 777 ha Natal Parks Board reserve (on the slopes of Mount Currie) are particularly lovely. Visitors may spot mountain reedbuck, grey rhebok, oribi, bushbuck, blesbok and springbok roaming this wild and beautiful area, which overlooks the waters of Crystal Dam.

Bird life at Mount Currie includes blue crane (South Africa's national bird), rock kestrel, jackal buzzard and eagle. Picnic areas and campsites have been provided for visitors. The reserve is situated about 5 km southeast of Kokstad, off the Franklin-Swartberg road. It is open all year, from sunrise to sunset.

A national monument in the Mount Currie reserve commemorates the memory of Adam Kok III, the Griqua leader who sold all his land to the Free State government and led his 2 000 Griqua, their wagons and 20 000 head of stock in an epic trek over the Lesotho mountains to their new home, Nomansland – the capital of which later became Kokstad.

For further information, and to reserve campsites, write to The Officer-in-Charge, Mount Currie Nature Reserve, P.O. Box 378, Kokstad 4700 (telephone Kokstad 3844).

Mzimkulu Wilderness Area

There is a holiday home for children called Restmount beneath Bamboo Mountain in the Drakensberg Garden area, the southernmost foothills of the mountains. This is close to the 28 140 ha Mzimkulu Wilderness Area, named after the 'great home of all rivers' that reaches the sea at Port Shepstone. The Mzimkulu is the largest river of the south coast.

The Drakensberg Garden resort, 34 km from Underberg, has a golf course, stables, light aircraft landing strip and trout fishing. This is perfect picnic country, with dozens of walks and picnic spots alongside any one of the many icy pools of the Mzimkulu tributaries. They have such charming names as Queen's Pool, Mermaids' Pool, Champagne Pool and Paddy's Pool. There is a caravan park at the hotel.

The wilderness area features stately evergreen yellowwood forests, evergreen and seasonal grassland, montane heath scrub and several other major vegetation types, and offers sanctuary to various antelope and bird species, such as the black eagle, martial eagle, bald ibis and Cape vulture.

Further information, and permits to enter the wilderness area, can be obtained from The Director, Natal Parks Board, P.O. Box 662, Pietermaritzburg 3200 (telephone Pietermaritzburg 47-1961); The State Forester, Cobham State Forest, Himeville 4585 (telephone Himeville 1831); and The State Forester, Garden Castle State Forest, P.O. Box 90, Underberg 4590 (telephone Underberg 1722).

Far left: The green mamba is rarely found outside forest or thick bush. This snake is often confused with the similarly coloured boomslang but the boomslang has a larger eye and blunt snout. **Left:** The elegant markings and large size of the wattled crane make it highly visible and easy to distinguish from other cranes. Wattled cranes are common at Ntsikeni in Transkei and other moist parts of Southern Africa, usually occuring in pairs or small groups.

Mzimkulwana Nature Reserve

As in other parts of the Natal Drakensberg area, this 22 751 ha Reserve is rich in flora as well as endangered fauna. Visitors may spot black eagle, martial eagle, jackal buzzard, lammergeyer (or bearded vulture) and Cape vulture. Antelope include eland, duiker, oribi, grey rhebok and mountain reedbuck.

The Giant's Cup Section of the Drakensberg Hiking Trail traverses this nature reserve of rolling green hills, pine-sharp air and lofty peaks stretching from the Sani Pass road to Bushman's Nek, site of a Lesotho border post.

Mzimkulwana, part of the Cobham and Garden Castle State Forests, is in one of South Africa's major catchment areas, and is managed for production of clear, silt-free water. Other management objectives are the protection of flora and fauna – with emphasis on endangered species, the protection of cultural and historical assets such as rock art, and the provision of extensive outdoor recreation.

The reserve is open all year, and the best time to visit is the period September to June. For further information, write to The Regional Director, Natal Forest Region, Private Bag 9029, Pietermaritzburg 3200 (telephone Pietermaritzburg 42-8101); The State Forester, Cobham State Forest, Himeville 4585 (telephone Himeville 1831); or The State Forester, Garden Castle State Forest, P.O. Box 90, Underberg 4590 (telephone Underberg 1722). The reserve is 14 km from Himeville, at the end of the D7 road (clearly signposted 'Cobham').

Ngele Hiking Trail

The Ngele trail, part of the National Hiking Way, is a 'family trail' in the Weza State Forest between Harding and Kokstad, in southern Natal. Weza forest incorporates the largest manmade plantation in South Africa.

Indigenous forest and the grassy slopes of Ngele Mountain feature in two circular trails. One of them is intended as a weekend trail of two days while the other is being extended to make it a three-day trail. White footprints show hikers the way. Rustic huts provide overnight accommodation. There is a large population of bushbuck in the area and the mammalian predators include caracal, black-backed jackal, polecat and serval. The red-chested cuckoo (*Piet-my-vrou*), Knysna loerie, Narina trogon and fork-tailed drongo (or *in-Tengu*) are a few of the many birds to be seen and heard on the trail. The indigenous forest section is alive with wild flowers, including orchid. Many of the indigenous trees *en route* are marked with their National Tree List numbers.

To arrange a hike, apply in writing to The Regional Director, Natal Forest Region, Private Bag 9029, Pietermaritzburg 3200 (telephone Pietermaritzburg 42-8101). Hikers are reminded of a basic rule on trails: take only photographs, and leave only footprints.

Ntsikeni Nature Reserve

The wattled crane, the rarest and largest of this graceful crane family, is found among the vleis, swamps and grassland at Transkei's enclave in the Drakensberg foothills.

In order to protect these beautiful birds, the Transkei Nature Conservation Division has proclaimed some 10 000 ha of wetland at Ntsikeni as a reserve, where they rub shoulders with crowned crane, Stanley's bustard, rail, crake, and shy and retiring flufftail. Common reedbuck inhabit the sedge and marsh areas, while mountain reedbuck graze on the grassland. Although this reserve is not open to the public, future plans include the development of a trail that will allow visitors to explore the area on foot. For further enquiries write to Transkei

Nature Conservation Division, Department of Agriculture and Forestry, Private Bag X5002, Umtata, Transkei (telephone Umtata 2-4322).

Royal Natal National Park

This park is a majestic oval, bounded by green-clad mountains which rise towards the sky like the walls of an Olympian amphitheatre. It is the foremost of the Drakensberg parks, extending for 8 094 hectares. Because of its size and terrain the park is probably best explored on horseback. There are several bridle path trails with horses to hire. Hiking is another way of seeing it, and 31 walks and climbs have been mapped out, ranging from the 3 km Otto's Walk (for the beginner) to the more adventurous 45 km Mont-aux-Sources. You can also try trout fishing or go for a swim in crystal-clear streams, picnic in fairy-tale glens, watch birds, paint or just absorb the beauty of this lovely wilderness.

The Mont-aux-Sources area of the Royal Natal National Park is the backstage plateau of that towering amphitheatre of solid rock that cups the Tendele Valley far below, an awesome panorama of mountain beauty and one of the grandest sights in all of Southern Africa. The Mont-aux-Sources peak itself is a large but rather unprepossessing hump on top of the Drakensberg rim above the snow-bound and boggy plain between Lesotho and Natal.

Natal's largest river and highest waterfall, the Tugela, and eight other rivers, including tributaries of the 2 000 km long and westward-flowing Orange River, start at Mont-aux-Sources. The Elands River is born here, flowing into the Vaal River, which itself becomes part of the Orange.

Visitors can drive along the rim of the 'berg' for 8 km – almost as far as the Sentinel, the northernmost wing of the Amphitheatre. The Sentinel is situated 150 km from the Royal Natal National Park via Oliviershoek Pass.

Top: A beautiful everlasting daisy *Helichrysum adenocarpum* found in the Drakensberg during Spring.
Above: A species of *Hesperentha*.

NATAL PARKS BOARD ACCOMMODATION GLOSSARY

Cottage: A cottage is really a two- or three-bedroomed house with lounge/diningroom, bathroom, toilet, kitchen (equipped with cutlery, crockery, stove and fridge). Linen is provided and a cook is in attendance.

Chalet: A chalet is a self-contained, serviced dwelling with one or more bedrooms, lounge/diningroom, bathroom, toilet and kitchenette (equipped with cutlery, crockery, stove and fridge). Linen is provided. Visitors staying in chalets do their own cooking.

Bungalow: A bungalow is a fully equipped one- or two-bedroomed house with lounge/diningroom, bathroom and toilet. Crockery, cutlery, a fridge and linen are provided. Food is prepared by a cook in a central kitchen.

Bush Camp: Bush camps provide rustic accommodation and are fully equipped with cutlery, linen, crockery and cooking utensils. A small gas fridge and stove are provided, although cooking is usually done over an open fire. Visitors do their own cooking.

Cabin: (Injasuti) A cabin is a fully equipped self-contained serviced dwelling having two bedrooms, a lounge/diningroom, bathroom, toilet and kitchenette. Linen is provided. Visitors do their own cooking.

Log Cabin: (Umlalazi, Cape Vidal and Mapelane) A log cabin is a serviced, two-bedroomed building with beds for 5 people (3 beds as well as one double bunk). It contains a bathroom, toilet and kitchen (equipped with cutlery, crockery, stove and fridge). Linen is provided. Visitors do their own cooking and washing up.

Leisure Home: (Umlalazi) The Leisure Home contains two bedrooms (one with a double bed, the other with a double bunk and single bed): Two additional beds for children can be installed. The home has a gas fridge, stove, bathroom, toilet and lounge. Visitors do their own cooking and washing up.

Lodge: A lodge contains the same facilities as a cottage (see cottage category) but on a more luxurious scale. Reservations for lodges are only accepted two calendar months in advance.

Rondavel: (Albert Falls only) A rondavel comprises 2 beds, bathroom, toilet and kitchenette (equipped with cutlery, crockery, linen, stove and fridge). Visitors do their own cooking and washing up. The rondavels are serviced.

Rest Hut: A rest hut is a fully equipped two- or three-bedded rondavel or squaredavel, provided with cutlery, crockery, fridge and linen. Communal bathrooms are used. Food is prepared by cooks in a central kitchen.

Rustic Cabin: A rustic cabin is a fully equipped four-bedded hut equipped with cutlery, crockery, hot plate and fridge. The units are served by a communal ablution block. Linen is provided. Visitors do their own cooking and washing up. Rustic cabins are serviced.

Rustic Cottage: Rustic cottages are provided with crockery, cutlery, cooking utensils, fridge and stove. Visitors do their own cooking and must provide pillowslips, sheets and towels.

Rustic Hut: Rustic hut accommodation is provided with crockery, cutlery and cooking utensils, but contains no fridge or stove. Meals are prepared by visitors over outside open-hearth fires. No linen or towels are provided.

Trail/Mountain Huts: One large room with a divider. Four double bunk beds and mattresses (two at Meander Hut), a two-plate gas cooker, cold water and toilet only are provided. If booking is heavy, visitors may have to share the accommodation with other hikers.

The 18-hour (45 km) return walk to the Sentinel from the Visitor Centre in the park via Tendele Camp and Mahai Falls finally ascends the amphitheatre by means of two chain ladders of 100 rungs. Climbers should exercise particular care in winter, when the rungs ice up and become extremely slippery.

The top of the Drakensberg can be treacherous in both winter and summer. The beginning of winter is probably the safest time to hike on the massif itself because the weather tends to be predictable: very cold, perhaps a little snow, but usually no rain. In summer the weather is extremely variable.

Rugged Glen Nature Reserve

This 762 ha reserve is adjacent to the Royal Natal National Park. Dominated by the 1 890 m Camel's Hump mountain, the campsite among fir trees is a five-minute drive to the right of the Royal Natal National Park entrance gate. Nature trails and horse rides are available from the Rugged Glen Stables.

The game and mountain bird life are similar to that found in the Royal Natal National Parks,

and the sanctuaries share access roads from Harrismith (gravel) and Bergville (tar).

For further information about the reserve, and to book campsites, you can write to The Officer-in-Charge, Royal Natal National Park, P.O. Mont-aux-Sources 3353 (telephone Bergville 38-1803).

The Swamp Nature Reserve

The focal point of the 220 ha Swamp Nature Reserve is some 60 ha of wetland that attracts a wide range of waterfowl including the rare wattled crane, largest of the indigenous crane species, and the crowned crane. Southern reedbuck occur in the vlei areas.

The best time of year to visit the reserve is summer; the wetland is often frozen over in winter. The reserve is reached by travelling from Himeville 14 km eastwards on the Pevensey Road. There are no facilities.

For further information write to The Officer-in-Charge, Himeville Nature Reserve, P.O. Box 115, Himeville 4585 (telephone Himeville 36).

Vergelegen Nature Reserve

Pine-covered Vergelegen, in the Umkomaas or Mkhomasi Valley, is a beautiful Natal Parks Board reserve in the Drakensberg area. It lies 19 km up the Mohlesi Pass road to Lesotho (there is no through road). Access to the reserve is via Nottingham Road on gravel, or 50 km farther on tar via the small towns of Bulwer, Underberg and Himeville.

At 1 500 m, Vergelegen's 1 100 ha of mountain sourveld, sliced by deep valleys flowing down from the Drakensberg, is particularly secluded. Two self-contained, five-bedded thatched cottages, each with a cook in attendance, provide accommodation. To make a reservation write to The Reservations Officer, Natal Parks Board, P.O. Box 662, Pietermaritzburg 3200 (telephone Pietermaritzburg 47-1981).

Obtain day permits and provincial fishing licences (there are brown trout) in advance. Bring your own food. There are no camping facilities in the reserve, which is open from sunrise to sunset.

'Twixt berg and beach

There is a little of England and much of Africa in the Midlands of Natal, that fascinating mixture of undulating farmland and towns that lie between the snow-topped Drakensberg and the holiday beaches of the coast. This was where Boer and Briton fought 80 years ago, and there is many a lonely cross to remind one of it. The great herds of highveld game that once wintered here are all gone now, but remnants have been preserved in reserves and parks which still perpetuate the original habitat.

Albert Falls Public Resort Nature Reserve

This is one of the most inviting spots in the Natal Midlands and it lies only 23km from the centre of Pietermaritzburg. Sloping grassy banks – ideal for picnicking and bird-watching – surround the 3012ha Albert Falls Dam and surrounding resort.

There is plenty of scope for horseback riding, sailing and canoeing, while fishing and walking are also very popular. One exciting walk takes you along narrow forest paths – via a suspension bridge spanning the Umgeni River – to the old gold-panning falls. The reserve also provides opportunities to see game such as zebra, impala, blesbok, reedbuck, grey duiker, springbok, bushbuck, red hartebeest and oribi in natural surroundings.

Notuli Camp and Bon Accorde are the two separate camps within the reserve. Accommodation includes chalets and rondavels fully equipped with stove, fridge, linen, pots and cutlery: visitors are required to supply only their food and drink. Bon Accorde offers tennis and squash courts, a swimming pool and a soccer field. To make reservations for huts and chalets, write to The Reservations Officer, Natal Parks Board, P.O. Box 662, Pietermaritzburg 3200 (telephone Pietermaritzburg 47-1981).

There are camping facilities at both camps and to book sites, write to The Officer-in-Charge, Albert Falls Public Resort Nature Reserve, P.O. Box 31, Cramond 3420 (telephone Cramond 202/3). To reach the reserve, take the Church Street exit from Pietermaritzburg for Greytown (R33) and drive for 18km before turning left. The resort is signposted. Visitors are admitted throughout the year, and a game guard is on duty at the gate all the time.

Chelmsford Public Resort Nature Reserve

Leokop Mountain dominates the 6015ha Chelmsford public resort, whose waters are rich in Egyptian and spur-winged goose, spoonbill, yellow-billed duck, darter and dabchick. Powerboats ply the waters, and fishermen may take carp, mudfish and bass. The game park section has been stocked with springbok, black wildebeest, zebra, red hartebeest, rhino and blesbok. There are seven chalets (each with four beds), and camping and caravan sites are available for hire. The resort is 20km south of Newcastle, on the Ladysmith road. It is open all year, 24 hours a day.

Above: Egyptian geese (the bird at far left is a knob-billed duck) occur throughout Southern Africa, having adapted remarkably well to the incursion of Man into their territory. It is the only species of duck (in spite of its name, it is really a form of shelduck) that breeds both north and south of the Sahara. **Left:** The famous Howick Falls.

A second resort known as Richgate Park, on the southern bank of the lake, has chalets and camping facilities. Access is via the R205 (then D445), 28 km south of Newcastle on the main road to Ladysmith. To reserve camping and caravan sites, write to The Officer-in-Charge, Chelmsford Public Resort Nature Reserve, P.O. Box 3, Ballengeich 2942 (telephone Newcastle 7715). Chalets may be booked through The Reservations Officer, Natal Parks Board, P.O. Box 662, Pietermaritzburg 3200 (telephone Pietermaritzburg 47-1981).

Craigie Burn Public Resort Nature Reserve

This small (330 ha) resort on the Rietvlei road halfway between Mooi River and Greytown is a cluster of picnic sites on the banks of a dam in which fishing and boating are the major pursuits. Waterfowl congregate on the dam at certain times of the year. It is open 24 hours a day.

Doreen Clark Nature Reserve

Only 5 ha in extent (the smallest of the Natal Parks Board reserves), Doreen Clark is an 'island' of indigenous evergreen forest 12 km from Pietermaritzburg in the Mount Michael/Hilton area, off the Johannesburg highway. It is open throughout the year, and is noted for its pleasant Sunday walks. There is also a small picnic site.

Game Valley Estates

Huge sandstone cliffs tower above the attractive Game Valley Estates, beside the Umkomazi River at Hela Hela. The ranch has been declared a Natural Heritage Site and stocks mammals such as oribi, wildebeest, zebra, nyala and warthog. It is also the breeding ground of one of Southern Africa's most endangered bird species, the blue swallow.

The ranch offers hiking, hunting and photographic safaris, but also caters for casual visitors. A trail camp, camping area and lodge offer year-round accommodation.

The main entrance to the ranch is 25 km from Richmond, reached 2 km from the bridge over the Umkomazi River. For bookings and enquiries contact Game Valley Estates, P.O. Box 70, Richmond 3780 (telephone Richmond 3171).

Green Belt Trails

A network of pleasant trails has been laid out on the escarpment north-east of Pietermaritzburg, and riders and walkers follow logos on white-painted stones. There are plans to enlarge the 20 km network and link it to urban walks, thus providing recreation of both scenic and historical interest.

For more information and detailed maps of the Green Belt Trails, you should write to The Pietermaritzburg Publicity Association P.O. Box 25, Pietermaritzburg 3200 (telephone Pietermaritzburg 5-1348/9).

Left: The jumping spider is common to most parts of Southern Africa. These small, strongly-built spiders circle their prey and capture it with an impressive leap. Their enormous eyes, situated at the front of their heads like headlamps, make them the most long-sighted of all spiders. **Right:** *Sandersonia aurantiaca* ('Christmas bells'), photographed in a sheltered glade beside a stream. This beautiful plant – a climbing member of the lily family – is threatened in many parts of Natal by indiscriminate picking. It flowers in the final months of the year, and remains dormant during the winter. **Below:** Sailing on Midmar Dam. Powerboating and waterskiing are also permitted, but are restricted to the top end of the dam.

Holkrans and Berg-waters Trails

Two private trails have been developed in the Drakensberg foothills near Newcastle by landowners who wish to share their own mountain heritage with the public.

One of the highlights of Holkrans Trail – 'Hole in the rock' – is its tunnel, through which hikers can walk upright for several metres! The trail offers a 17,5 km (two-day) stroll through indigenous forest and grassland where bushbuck, grey duiker, mountain reedbuck and common reedbuck can be seen at close quarters, as well as shy forest birds. Trees in the forest are numbered for identification. Elderly people are catered for by the Holkrans Senior Trail which covers 3-8 km over three leisurely days. Holkrans has a base camp and a 'Zulu kraal' with traditional, beehive-shaped huts.

San paintings, streams, waterfalls and panoramic views are the 'hall-marks' of the Berg-waters Trail. At one point on this 26 km (two-day) trail you will be able to look out over the Orange Free State and the Transvaal while standing in Natal.

Both trails have base camps as well as overnight huts and accommodate up to 60 people. Bookings can be made by writing to Mr and Mrs D van Niekerk, P.O. Box 2734, Newcastle 2940 (telephone Normandien 600).

Howick Falls

Named after Viscount Howick (later Earl Grey), Secretary of State for the Colonies from 1846 to 1852, the picturesque borough of Howick and its famous waterfall lie 22 km from Pietermaritzburg, off the Johannesburg freeway.

The 111 m high falls are only a minute's drive from the centre of town. A small caravan park has been established beside the falls, and near-by are the Howick Falls Hotel (established in 1872) and the Fall Inn tea-room. From the viewing platform, the Umgeni River hurtles down into a deep pool to continue on its way through a twisting forest gorge. A steep, winding path leads precariously down to the foot of the falls, where a cairn commemorates the death of the son of the first hotel-keeper in Howick: he was washed over in a flood.

Itala Game Reserve

One of the few signs of civilisation in the rugged 30 000 ha Itala Nature Reserve, near Louwsburg in northern Natal, is the row of telephone poles – and these are regularly flattened by rhino using them as rubbing posts. Part of the old Pongola Game Reserve, the first to be proclaimed in Africa, this green, knuckle-ridged wilderness through which six rivers flow to join the Pongola River boundary – is home to Natal's only herds of tsessebe.

It contains the province's largest concentration of klipspringer, crocodile, leopard, cheetah, blue wildebeest, red hartebeest, giraffe, white and black rhino, warthog and a variety of raptors in the jagged dolerite cliffs.

Among the birds of prey which may be seen are martial eagle, black eagle, Wahlberg's eagle, fish eagle, black-breasted snake-eagle and the rare southern banded snake-eagle. There is also a breeding colony of the threatened bald ibis or *umXwagele*, as it is known locally.

Ntshondwe hutted camp accommodates 150 people and provides its guests with a confer-

Left: *Aloe marlothii* grows in almost any terrain in Natal. This is among the most attractive aloes, producing orange-yellow flowers through most of the winter. The dried leaves are used by some tribesmen to make snuff. **Right:** Fire-lilies are so named because some species appear in profusion after veld fires. This species, *Cyrtanthus contractus*, was photographed among dolerite boulders in the grassland of Natal. **Below:** An oribi doe in the foothills of the Drakensberg near Estcourt. These rare antelope are usually found in short grass, near water.

ence centre, restaurant, take-away food outlet and a swimming pool. If you prefer a more untamed environment then there is the eight-bedded Mbizo bush camp and the four-bedded Thalu bush camp, which may be hired. Bookings are made through The Reservations Officer, Natal Parks Board, P.O. Box 662, Pietermaritzburg 3200 (telephone Pietermaritzburg 47-1981).

The Natal Parks Board organises day and weekend wilderness trails in Itala Game Reserve. There are two picnic sites and a rustic campsite.

Visitors should direct their enquiries regarding campsites to The Officer-in-Charge, Itala Nature Reserve, P.O. Box 42, Louwsburg 3150 (telephone Louwsburg 1413).

Entrance to the reserve is through Louwsburg. It is open to day-visitors all year, between sunrise and sunset. Anti-malaria precautions are recommended in this area.

Karkloof Falls
Twenty kilometres from Howick are the Karkloof Falls, considered by some to be even more beautiful than the Howick Falls: the drop is an impressive 88 metres. There are picnic and braai spots for visitors.

138

Karkloof Nature Reserve
Bushbuck, bushpig, blue duiker and possibly even leopard roam in the 936 ha Karkloof Nature Reserve, 20 km north of Howick in the rugged Karkloof Mountain range. Although it is not yet open to the public, group visits can be arranged: these groups are always accompanied by a game ranger.

Crowned and martial eagle breed in the mainly indigenous yellowwood and rare black stinkwood forest. To arrange a visit, write to The Reservations Officer, Natal Parks Board, P.O. Box 662, Pietermaritzburg 3200 (telephone Pietermaritzburg 47-1981).

Malandeni
A 1,5 km long vlei on the eastern side of Ladysmith, about 3 km from town, is a Wildlife Society sanctuary with about 130 species of birds having been recorded. The shallow lake adjacent to the Klip River is unusual in that it borders on a sewerage farm, and its waters are re-cycled effluent which promotes algal and insect growth, thus providing an ideal food source for bird life. The sanctuary is open all year, from sunrise to sunset. The area is kept locked and keys must be obtained for entry.

For further information you should contact Mr A. Clarkson (telephone Ladysmith 2-2185 or 2-2457) or Mr K. Gordon (telephone Ladysmith 2-6819 or 2-3780).

Mhlopeni Nature Reserve
The 814 ha Mhlopeni Nature Reserve between Greytown and Muden in the Natal Midlands supports a rich variety of birds and animals which include impala, blesbok, bushbuck, duiker, zebra, oribi and reedbuck.

Accommodation consists of three attractive campsites tucked away under the shade of beautiful indigenous trees. Rondavel and rustic hutted accommodation is available for groups of up to 12. To book accommodation and for further information write to Mhlopeni Nature Reserve, P.O. Box 386, Greytown 3500 (telephone Greytown 722).

Midmar Public Resort Nature Reserve
The 2 844 ha resort is situated 24 km from Pietermaritzburg on the N3 highway, and is surrounded by the Inhluzana hills. In keeping with the elegant setting, the lawns are manicured, yachts bob in the water of the Midmar Dam, and tea is served in the restaurant.

Right: The scenic Valley of a Thousand Hills is believed to have taken its present form during the Pleistocene geological period when the ocean receded to about 100 m below the present sea level. That was when rivers, such as the Mgeni which meanders through the valley for over 60 km, gouged a path deep into the earth, and were subsequently refilled when the sea rose again.

This pleasant resort is open 24 hours a day, throughout the year. From Parks Board vehicles or boats one can view black wildebeest, blue wildebeest, springbok, impala and waterfowl. The resort has much for sporting visitors, including tennis, bowls and squash. There is a swimming pool, a children's playground and camping and caravan facilities. Fishermen are also catered for: bass and carp are found in the Umgeni River.

Adjacent to the resort is Midmar Historical Village and its associated displays that together recall Natal's pioneering past. Among the authentic displays are a blacksmith shop, a traditional Zulu homestead with beehive huts, two steam locomotives, a fire engine and numerous agricultural implements. One of the highlights of the village is the original York Public Library which was dismantled and meticulously rebuilt here, brick by brick. The Village Hall has also been created in keeping with tradition, but its interior is equipped for film shows, lectures and audio-visual programmes. There are further plans to extend the village in the relatively near future.

Reservations for chalet accommodation should be addressed to The Reservations Officer, Natal Parks Board, P.O. Box 662, Pietermaritzburg 3200 (telephone Pietermaritzburg 47-1981).

Camping and other enquiries should be addressed to The Officer-in-Charge, Midmar Public Resort Nature Reserve, Private Bag Howick 3290 (telephone Howick 2067).

Moor Park Nature Reserve

Moor Park is named after the family who originally donated the land. Sir Frederick Moor was Natal's last Prime Minister. The reserve's high, brooding bluffs – thick with trees and mist – overlook the waters of the Bushman's River and Wagendrift Dam.

The wildlife at Moor Park includes black wildebeest, mountain reedbuck, grey duiker,

A COLOURFUL SUPERBUG

The beautiful dragonfly does not possess a sting, and is harmless to humans.

Is it a bird? Is it a plane? No, it's the superbug of the insect world . . . the dragonfly. This remarkable creature is deserving of many superlatives; it is one of the largest insects on earth and, at speeds in excess of 60 km/h, is probably the fastest.

Dragonflies (there are about 120 species in Southern Africa) generally live near water, and a fisherman is the most likely person to see the flash of colour and hear the whirr of wings that signals the approach of a male insect patrolling his territory.

The male stakes out a territory for hunting prey and for mating, and will vigorously defend this area against invaders: mid-air battles can result in mutilated wings and legs. After mating, the female dragonfly lays her eggs in, or close to, water — usually depositing them on underwater plants or forcing them into moist sand at a river's edge. Occasionally the female skims the water, her eggs dropping just under the surface from the tip of her abdomen: the eggs then drift to the bottom.

The eggs hatch into gill-breathing nymphs hidden in the mud or among aquatic plants. They live on other insect larvae, tadpoles and small fish until ready to transform into adults. They then crawl above the water surface and cling to a support — such as a plant — while shedding their nymphal skins for the last time. The life cycle from egg to adult dragonfly can take up to three years, depending on the species.

The dragonfly remains a predator at all stages of its life. The flying dragonfly captures insects in mid-air by forming its six legs into a 'basket' which scoops up the victim. This has earned it the sobriquet 'mosquito hawk'.

bushbuck, blesbok, zebra and impala. Adjacent to the reserve is Greystone Adventure Centre which offers young men and women a chance to test their endurance in such activities as hiking, canoeing or rock climbing on the dolerite krantzes.

The self-guided 'Old Furrow Trail', which lies within the reserve, follows the course of an old irrigation furrow. Interpretative displays are placed along the route.

To reach Moor Park, take the Ntabamhlope route from Estcourt and follow the signposted road. Information on Greystone Adventure Centre is obtainable from P.O. Box 78, Estcourt 3310 (telephone Estcourt 3-2739).

Natal National Botanic Garden

The 110-year-old Natal National Botanic Garden, off Mayor's Walk in Pietermaritzburg, consists of two sections, one featuring exotic trees and the other flowers and plants indigenous to Natal. The 49 ha garden offers lily ponds, show gardens, a 200 m avenue of plane trees, Muscovy ducks on the lake, a tea-room, a demonstration garden, a fever tree vlei, forest walks and a rich variety of birds.

To reach the garden, take a Prestbury or Linwood Drive bus from behind the City Hall. The garden is open daily from 7.30 a.m. to 5.30 p.m. There is a restaurant.

Natal Lion Park

This privately owned park, 16 km from Pietermaritzburg off the Durban freeway, is a sure way of seeing the lion and other animals you missed at Umfolozi and Hluhluwe. The park is situated 72 km from Durban and is open from 7.30 a.m. to 4.30 p.m. Opposite the Lion Park are the Natal Zoological Gardens, featuring smaller game and a large variety of birds. Other animals include monkey, cheetah, jackal and an exotic orang-outang.

New Formosa Nature Reserve

A variety of buck and small game may be seen in the 250 ha reserve, situated about 2 km from Estcourt. The reserve is open all day throughout the year. There are no camping facilities, and vehicles are prohibited, but there is a caravan park about 1 km away. Permission to enter the reserve should be obtained from The Town Clerk, Borough of Estcourt, P.O. Box 15, Estcourt 3310 (telephone Estcourt 2-3000).

Queen Elizabeth Park Nature Reserve

Headquarters of the Natal Parks Board and home of the sophisticated Douglas Mitchell research, education, film, theatre and library centre, this scenic reserve is situated 8 km west of Pietermaritzburg. One of the major functions performed at the modern Douglas Mitchell

Centre is the processing of thousands of requests for accommodation in the Natal Parks Board's reserves. This is a massive task — with over 2 000 beds in total — and incoming calls have to be channelled through nine separate telephone lines.

On the 93 ha of wooded slopes, which surround the centre, there are white rhino, zebra, impala, blesbok and grey duiker to be seen, while forest footpaths lead to pleasant picnic sites and river cascades.

The reserve is constantly being improved by the planting of indigenous vegetation and there are hundreds of species of aloe, cycad and protea which add to its beauty. A helpful question-and-answer worksheet has been prepared for school children visiting the reserve. There is a curio shop.

To reach the reserve, take the Montrose exit from the Johannesburg freeway or the Howick road from town. If approaching from the direction of Durban, drive through the centre of Pietermaritzburg. The reserve is open throughout the year, from sunrise to sunset.

Pietermaritzburg Bird Sanctuary

The 100-year-old Pietermaritzburg Bird Sanctuary is situated opposite the brickworks off Chatterton Road, near the Hyslop intersection. Snow-white cattle egrets, with their yellow bills and harsh 'kraak-kraak' call are there by the thousand in the trees around the lake. Visitors

---

MUTUAL CO-OPERATION IN THE WILD

A honeyguide chick emerges from its foster parents' nest.

One of Southern Africa's most remarkable birds is the honeyguide, a small, rather drab creature which employs an unorthodox method of obtaining its favourite foods — beeswax, bee grubs and honey. When a honeyguide finds a nest of wild bees, he quickly seeks out a honey badger or even a human to help. This he accomplishes by 'displaying' and making a chattering noise to attract attention: once this has been achieved, he leads the way to the nest.

The honeyguide perches nearby while the nest is torn open and robbed of its honey — and then it is his turn. His helper was interested only in the honey, but the honeyguide seeks out the beeswax and grubs. A special enzyme in his digestive tract enables him to break down the wax into substances of nutritional value — something no other bird is able to do.

Men and honey badgers are not the only helpers exploited by this bird. Like the cuckoo, it lays its eggs in another bird's nest, delegating the upbringing of its young to foster parents.

Above: A fruit beetle. **Left:** Morning glory (an exotic) is represented by many species in Southern Africa, and in some areas exotic species have become troublesome weeds, choking existing vegetation and blocking off sunlight. One genus, *Cuscuta*, is parasitic (because it cannot create chlorophyll, it is totally dependent on its host). **Right:** A lithograph by the artist William Cornwallis Harris, illustrating a somewhat corpulent eland, from his book *Portraits of the Game and Wild Animals of Southern Africa.*

are also likely to see a variety of smaller birds. The sanctuary's lake was formed from the clay pit excavated in 1860 to make the bricks needed to re-build Pietermaritzburg's town hall, which had been destroyed in a fire. The sanctuary is open all year, from sunrise to sunset.

Pongola Bush Nature Reserve

Natal's largest dam is the Jozini Dam on the Pongola River. There are three game and nature reserves on this river: Ndumo, Itala and Pongola Bush. The latter, 858 ha in extent, includes a stretch of indigenous evergreen forest – home to bushbuck, duiker, baboon and samango monkey. Pongola Bush is situated between Vryheid and Piet Retief, about 20 km north-west of Paulpietersburg (on the Transvaal border).

Visitors should make arrangements with the Officer-in-Charge (telephone Vryheid 2492), before their arrival.

Qunu Falls

The 80 m high Qunu or 'thunder' falls are on a tributary of the Umkomazi River in the 283 ha Qunu forest reserve, off the Hela Hela road between Richmond and Eastwolds. To reach the

falls, turn left after 38 km and drive for a further 2 kilometres. This road links up 9 km farther on with the tarred Ixopo-Underberg road. Guides take you through the forest.

Soada Forest Nature Reserve

This 498 ha forest slopes down to the deep Umkomazi River valley, just beyond the Hela Hela bridge and about 24 km from Richmond on the Eastwolds road. It is rich in giant yellowwoods and cycads, and visitors may see bushbuck, vervet monkey, grey duiker and red duiker. Also in the reserve is an impressive two-stage waterfall, with a drop of 90 metres. Although controlled by Natal Parks Board, the only access to Soada Forest is through a privately owned farm – and this may account for the fact that there are few visitors. For further information, write to The Director, Natal Parks Board, P.O. Box 662, Pietermaritzburg 3200 (telephone Pietermaritzburg 47-1961).

Spioenkop Public Resort Nature Reserve

All day long on Wednesday, 24 January 1900, ❯ the noise of battle rolled across the summit of Spioenkop, the rugged mountain that dominates

the Natal Midlands. Boer and Briton fought for control of the high ground just north of Tugela and access to the besieged town of Ladysmith.

Standing on the summit today, visitors look across a grand sweep of Drakensberg peaks, sun-bleached sky and lush green plain – a vista unequalled anywhere in Southern Africa. The Tugela has now been dammed, and its muddy waters attract yachtsmen, weekend fishermen and water-skiing enthusiasts. The 5 979 ha resort, 13 km from Winterton and 35 km from Ladysmith, offers fully equipped chalets and camping and caravan sites. There is also a 'laager area' for groups of up to 120 campers and a tented bush camp sleeping eight people (facilities include a toilet, hot and cold shower and fully equipped kitchen. Sleeping bags and stretchers are provided).

The resort remains open 24 hours a day, throughout the year.

The chalet village offers tennis courts, a swimming pool, open-air chess, a badminton hall, table tennis, children's playground, curio shop, wildlife film shows, horseback riding, boat rides, guided tours of the battlefields, self-guided trails and walks in the adjacent 400 ha game park (stocked with white rhino, wildebeest, eland, kudu, and mountain reedbuck). A highlight is the Anglo Boer War museum. Chalet bookings should be made through The Reservations Officer, Natal Parks Board, P.O. Box 662, Pietermaritzburg 3200 (telephone Pietermaritzburg 47-1981) and campsite bookings through The Officer-in-Charge, Spioenkop Public Resort Nature Reserve, P.O. Box 140, Winterton 3340, (telephone Winterton 78).

Umgeni Valley Nature Reserve

Winding 10 km along the Umgeni valley below the famed Howick Falls, this lush nature reserve contains a wide variety of animal and plant life (it has five different, major veld types). Owned and managed by the Wildlife Society of Southern Africa, the reserve specialises in environmental education: about 15 000 schoolchildren attend its courses each year. These begin at the resource centre (which has lecture facilities and impressive wildlife exhibits), and then progress to the bush camps in the Umgeni Valley. From the camps – home to the youngsters for most of their stay – the society's staff guide their charges on field trips geared to a prepared syllabus.

The facilities are open to the general public when not used for educational purposes. In addition, a cottage is available to visitors throughout the year.

The entrance gates of the reserve are about 1 km from Howick on the Karkloof road. For further information, write to The Secretary, Umgeni Valley Nature Reserve, P.O. Box 394, Howick 3290 (telephone Howick 30-3931).

Umvoti Vlei Nature Reserve

Vleis are vital to many types of wildlife – especially waterfowl. But vleis (reed-fringed pans) take many years to develop, and once destroyed are almost irreplaceable. The Umvoti reserve's 267 ha of vleis in the catchment area of the Umvoti River lie on a turn-off 11 km south of Greytown, on the Pietermaritzburg road. This mist-belt area of reed swamp and open water is an important wildfowl sanctuary. It is controlled by the Natal Parks Board. As the reserve is not yet open to the public, intending visitors should check first by telephoning the Natal Parks Board Information Officer at Pietermaritzburg 47-1961, or by writing to P.O. Box 662, Pietermaritzburg 3200.

Valley of a Thousand Hills

The most spectacular view of this 50 km panorama of rolling hills is from *emKhambathini* – Natal's Table Mountain. But the normal view sites are between Botha's Hill and Drummond, off the Durban-Pietermaritzburg N3 highway. Take the Hillcrest exit 29 km from Durban if driving from the coast (it is 52 km from Pietermaritzburg). Within the valley are hotels, restaurants and a good selection of curio shops. Both the Durban (telephone 32-6421) and Pietermaritzburg (telephone 47-1961) visitor information centres can provide more information.

Vryheid Mountain Game and Nature Park

Vryheid is one of northern Natal's coal towns. It is situated in the lee of a wooded hill that has been converted into an attractive little game reserve containing, among other species, blesbok, eland, wildebeest, kudu, zebra, rhebok, duiker and, most intriguing, a very rare hybrid of kudu and eland.

The reserve, about 1 km from town (follow the signs), is open from 8 a.m. to 5.30 p.m. throughout the year. There are no camping facilities, but there are plans for sites and ablution blocks. For further information, write to The Town Clerk, Borough of Vryheid, P.O. Box 57, Vryheid 3100 (telephone Vryheid 2133).

Wagendrift Public Resort Nature Reserve

The Ntabamhlope road heads east from Estcourt towards Giant's Castle in the Drakensberg. An 8 km drive brings you to the Natal Parks Board's 75 ha Wagendrift Dam resort, situated on Bushman's River and surrounded by hills. The reserve has camping and caravan

Right: A western Natal green snake (*Philothamnus natalensis occidentalis*) glides effortlessly over a moss-covered rock in the foothills of the Natal Drakensberg. These snakes are distinguished by their large eyes and slender body.

facilities. There are ablution facilities (hot and cold water), and the resort is open 24 hours a day, throughout the year. There is also a youth centre, with dormitories and a dining hall for schools during term time.

Fishing, sailing and boating are popular on the dam, and picnic sites have been laid out. The Officer-in-Charge, Wagendrift Public Resort Nature Reserve, P.O. Box 316, Estcourt 3310 (telephone Estcourt 2550) will assist with enquiries and campsite bookings.

Weenen Nature Reserve

The 4 300 ha Natal Parks Board reserve lies just off the road to Weenen, about 20 km east of Colenso. The game comprises some 20 species, including aardwolf, mountain reedbuck, Cape clawless otter, black-backed jackal, white rhino, red hartebeest, kudu, eland and giraffe (re-introduced). Black rhino are to be stocked. Over 100 bird species have been recorded. The caravan site and curio shop are near the entrance gate and a bush camp has been planned.

Prepared walks include the three hour Amanzimyama Trail and a 'Reclamation Trail' – illustrating erosion control techniques used

in the reserve. A railway line linking Estcourt and Weenen runs through the reserve. There are picnic sites (with braai facilities) and there is fishing – tilapia (bream) and bass – for which permits are required. Access is also possible from a 28 km gravel road north-east of Estcourt. The reserve is open all year, from sunrise to sunset. To reserve camping and caravan sites, write to The Officer-in-Charge, Weenen Nature Reserve, P.O. Box 122, Weenen 3325 (telephone Weenen 809).

World's View

The view from the 305 m mountain above Pietermaritzburg is a grand experience. Access is via the Commercial Road/old Howick road exit or via the freeway west of the town, at the Hilton village turn-off. Ask for directions at the first garage and follow the National Monument signs. Originally called Boesmansrand, the old Howick road down to Pietermaritzburg from World's View was the wagon route of the 1837 Voortrekkers. Walking and (unofficial) pony trails link at World's View. For further details and trail map, write to the Publicity Association, Publicity House, Pietermaritzburg 3201 (telephone Pietermaritzburg 5-1348).

Palms, pelicans and dunes of gold

Land of lakes and fires, of golden dunes and swamps. This is Maputaland, that northern slice of Natal named after the lower reaches of the Usutu: the Maputo River which reaches the Indian Ocean at the old Lourenço Marques. Bounded by Mozambique, Swaziland and the Indian Ocean, this 9 000 square kilometre wilderness has had many names. Seeing the slash-and-burn fires, Portuguese explorer Manuel de Mesquita Perestrello, sailing past, called it Terra dos Fumos. Waxing even more poetic, he referred to the northern coast, from Kosi Bay to Ouro Point, today's Mozambique border lighthouse, as Rio de Medaos do Ouro – 'river of the dunes of gold'.

This fragile land of diversity, of palms, pelicans and hippos, is really one enormous nature reserve. It is the transition zone between the tropics and subtropical Natal, and has 21 different ecosystems, including three huge lakes (St Lucia is the best known); the last Natal elephants in the wild in the Tembe Elephant Park; Fomothini Pan; swamps; two magnificent game reserves at Ndumo and Mkuzi; the wide Pongola flood-plain, dotted with one waterfowl-crowded pan after another; turtles, those large and curiously dignified denizens of the great

coral reefs, and the beautiful St Lucia Complex. Evenings vibrate with the mating calls of countless reed frogs.

Maputaland deserves to be classed with the big ones: Kruger, Okavango, Kariba and the Central Kalahari Game Reserve.

Bonamanzi Game Park and Bushlands Game Lodge

At two private reserves in northern Natal you can sleep in splendid isolation, some 5m above the ground – in tree-houses. Situated near the town of Hluhluwe, these camps are close to Zululand's game reserves of Mkuzi, Hluhluwe, Umfolozi as well as Lake St Lucia. The camps, which are run separately, provide different experiences.

Bonamanzi (meaning 'good water') offers two-bedded tree-houses and an eight-bedded tree-lodge. If you prefer sleeping nearer the ground, you can stay in a cluster of 10 thatched huts at Lalapanzi. There is a swimming pool and a network of trails to explore.

Over 300 species of birds have been recorded at Bonamanzi and there are numerous nyala, red duiker, impala and reedbuck to be seen. Also found here are the rare and shy

suni. Bookings should be directed to Bonamanzi Game Park, P.O. Box 48, Hluhluwe 3960 (telephone Hluhluwe 3530).

Bushlands Game Lodge is another 'tree-house' camp, unique in that even the dining room and lounge are raised above the ground.

At this luxury resort you can expect to be pampered by a staff complement which outnumbers guests by two to one. Succulent venison meals are served in a traditional boma and are a Bushlands speciality. Guests also have the use of a swimming pool and bar. The lodge accommodates 16 guests only so booking is essential. For more information contact Bushlands Game Lodge, P.O. Box 79, Hluhluwe 3960 (telephone Hluhluwe 144).

Kosi Bay Nature Reserve

Kosi Bay is a misnomer. Royal Navy Captain W.F.W. Owen, surveying the coast of Maputaland in 1822-3, mistook the series of four shore-hugging and interlinked freshwater lakes for the estuary of the Mkuze River, which he spelt Kosi; and so it has been ever since.

Kosi has long fascinated scientists with its strange temperature variations – the water has a minimum temperature of 18°C but is as high

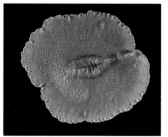

Above: A marine flat worm on the Natal north coast. Scientists have performed a remarkable experiment in which flatworms were taught a specific response to a stimulus, and then cut up and fed to another group of 'naive' flatworms: the second group inherited the memory. The flatworm's digestive processes are equally fascinating: it has a branched gut which distributes food throughout the body. If starved for too long, however, it begins to digest its own tissues, and may be reduced to a fraction of its former size. **Left:** Tropical vegetation on the shores of Lake St Lucia. **Right:** An impala ram in the Mkuzi Game Reserve.

as 30°C in the shallows, and the bottom of the lakes is often warmer than the top. The lakes near the estuary are exceptionally clear, becoming brown further south, due to the peaty water of the Sihadla River. Apart from Lake Amanzimnyama, all have a touch of salt water. Sometimes tremendous cyclones roar in from the ocean which raises the level of the lakes and their salinity.

Under KwaZulu authority, the Natal Parks Board's original 20ha reserve has been expanded to its present size of 11000ha. There are three lodges and 15 campsites on the banks of the largest lake, Nhlange.

Fishing is very popular. Among the resident estuarine and freshwater species to be caught are queenfish, grunter and barracuda which occasionally enter the lakes from the sea. Swimming in the lakes is not recommended because bilharzia, crocodile and hippo are present. However there are three boats as well as canoes for hire.

The three-day Sihadla Hiking Trail takes in the mangroves, marshes, swamp forests and raphia palms which surround the Kosi lakes. There are also water lilies and reeds and, to the west, undulating grassland dotted with wild date and ilala palms. Shorter walks can be arranged to Lake Amanzimnyama as well as Kosi Bay Estuary. It is well worth bringing binoculars as flufftail, palm-nut vulture, fish eagle, white-backed night heron and crab plover are among 247 species of birds found in the area.

At Kosi Bay Estuary a small, densely populated reef provides visitors with excellent snorkeling opportunities. The area is reached only by 4-wheel-drive vehicles, of which five are issued permits each day.

The narrowest part of the coast separating the lakes from the Indian Ocean is Bhanga Nek. A ferry-ride from the camp and a hop over the dunes brings you to this magnificent stretch of unspoilt coastline where the Natal Parks Board's Turtle Survey Team is based. In President Kruger's day, when a gateway to the ocean was vital to the young Transvaal Republic, a harbour at Bhanga Nek (with a channel through to the lakes) was proposed. The idea was dropped – to the relief of the Royal Navy.

To reach Kosi Bay, you must turn off the N2 towards Jozini and follow the tarred Sihangwe-Kwangwanase road. For the last 13km from Kwangwanase to the camp you will travel along a hard dirt road. Reservations and enquiries should be addressed to Central Reservations, KwaZulu Bureau of Natural Resources, 367 Loop Street, Pietermaritzburg 3201 (telephone Pietermaritzburg 94-6698).

There is petrol at Kwangwanase and there are country trading stores *en route*. Bring your own food and drinks. Remember to take anti-malaria precautions before entering the area.

A warthog and its offspring enjoy a mud bath in the Mkuzi Game Reserve. Although essentially grazers, warthogs also live on berries and wild fruits, and dig for roots and tubers with their tusks and cartilaginous snouts. Their hearing and sense of smell are acute.

Lake Sibaya

Lake Sibaya, with an area of 77 km², is the largest freshwater lake to be found in South Africa: its average depth is 13 m with depths of up to 40 m having been recorded in places. It is clear, blue and beautiful.

Baya Camp blends into the setting magnificently. Its wooden bungalows are joined to the communal eating lodge, sundeck and ablution facilities by a network of interconnecting boardwalks. The camp, is situated 150 m from the shore to accommodate the estimated 50-year high-water-mark. Private launches are not permitted but boats can be hired for fishing and sightseeing trips. A multitude of fish may be caught, including Mozambique tilapia. These are small – usually less than 1,5 kg due to a low nutrition content in the water – but large catfish are also caught. There are approximately 120 hippo, many Nile crocodile and bilharzia is present so swimming is limited to a small pool at the camp.

White-tailed mongoose and reedbuck may be seen (if you are lucky!) during a 3 km guided trail which also passes two excellent bird-viewing hides. There are 279 bird species, including pied kingfisher and fish eagle, found in the vicinity of the lake. The sea is only a short hop from Sibaya and permits for picnics at '9 Mile' are available to camp residents.

One of the first references to this lake was in the year 1554, when the Portuguese ship *Sao Bento* was wrecked off Transkei, and the survivors walked some 800 km along the beach in a bid to reach the Portuguese settlement at Delagoa Bay (Maputo).

Then with only 150 km to go, they were killed by local inhabitants, apparently because they had resorted to cannibalism.

Sibaya used to be linked to the sea 5 000 years ago, possibly by a Pongola River with different habits. Today, the lake is cut off by dunes and is topped up by rainwater and a small underground stream. Nevertheless, 10 species of marine fish remain in the lake, having adapted to fresh water.

Sibaya lies (as the crow flies) 20 km north of Sodwana Bay, in coastal forest and grassland. Access is via Mbazwana, 60 km north of the Mhlosinga turn-off on the N2, or via Mseleni on the Jozini-Tshongwe-Kosi Bay road. Access is via sandy roads and 4-wheel-drive vehicles are recommended, although not essential.

Enquiries should be directed to Central Reservations, KwaZulu Bureau of Natural Resources, 367 Loop Street, Pietermaritzburg 3201 (telephone Pietermaritzburg 94-6698).

Malachite Camp

Deep in the northern Zululand bush, near the tiny village of Mkuze, lies a beautiful 6 000 ha private game reserve that offers its guests a

---

MKUZI AT A GLANCE

When to go The reserve is open daily throughout the year. Visitors should report to the Camp Superintendent's office on arrival (open daily from 8 a.m. to 12 p.m., and 2 p.m. to 5 p.m.)

Reservations and information Camping and caravan site bookings should be made through The Camp Superintendent, Mkuzi Game Reserve, P.O. Mkuze 3965 (telephone Mkuzi Reserve Call Office). Reservations for the rustic and main camps should be addressed to The Reservations Officer, Natal Parks Board, P.O. Box 662, Pietermaritzburg 3200 (telephone Pietermaritzburg 47-1981). Reservations for trails and hutted camps and requests for further information should be directed to the same address.

Getting there Visitors arriving from the south should take the signposted turn-off to the reserve along the main north coast road (about 35 km north of Hluhluwe village). Follow the gravel road for 15 km and take the signposted turn-off through the Lebombo mountains: the hutted camp is 15 km from this point. Visitors from the north should travel to Mkuze village, which is 18 km from the reserve's entrance gate and 28 km from Mantuma Camp. The road is well signposted.

Accommodation The hutted camp comprises six rest huts with separate kitchen and ablution blocks, 5 four-bedded bungalows and two 'Duplex' bungalows. Visitors may also stay in 2 seven-bedded cottages. There are four rustic huts with an ablution block (hot and cold water), and a camping and caravan site is situated at the entrance gate.

Eating and drinking In the main camp, meals are prepared by cooks in the communal kitchens and served in the huts. In the rustic camp, visitors do their own cooking (cooking utensils and cutlery are supplied). In the main hutted camp, everything is supplied for visitors except food and drink (there is no shop in the reserve, and provisions should be purchased in Mkuze village).

Getting around Petrol is sold at the entrance gate. An 80 km network of roads leads through a variety of bushveld country, offering excellent game viewing. Day walks are conducted by a game guard (make arrangements a day in advance with the Camp Superintendent). More adventurous visitors may choose to walk the twice-monthly Bushveld Trails, which last three days (these operate between April and October).

Wildlife The reserve has a large herd of impala, and other mammals include black rhino, white rhino, giraffe, nyala, blue wildebeest, warthog, kudu and smaller antelope. Lucky visitors may spot cheetah, hyena and leopard. There is also an extensive bird population, including a variety of waterfowl in the Nsumu Pan.

Special attractions There are three 'hides' for visitors (at the Bube, Malibali and Msinga pans) from which animals may be photographed as they come to drink. There are picnic spots for day visitors at various spots in the reserve.

---

delightful combination of outdoor adventure and five-star comfort.

Boasting four thatched double rondavels on an expanse of emerald green lawns and knobthorn acacia trees, Malachite Camp is an impressive sight from the outside. And the inside takes some beating, too: each rondavel boasts air-conditioning, insect screens on its windows and *en suite* bathroom or shower.

Among the attractions laid on for guests are trips in an open Land Rover with an experienced ranger to view animals such as giraffe, white rhino, nyala, ostrich, wildebeest, zebra and kudu. Walking safaris (with a tracker in attendance) can also be arranged.

Jozini Dam – South Africa's third-largest reservoir (and the one that is said to contain the greatest variety of freshwater fish) – is only a 20-minute drive from the camp. On payment of a fee for a fishing licence, guests may catch as many tilapia, bream or tigerfish as they wish.

Dinner, which could be anything from potjiekos to the fish caught at Jozini, is usually prepared in a boma around a fire.

With the camp being able to take eight guests only, booking in advance is essential. For further information you should write to Rattray Reserves, P.O. Box 2575, Randburg 2125 (telephone Johannesburg 789-2677).

Maputaland Coastal Forest and Marine Reserve

This proclaimed reserve, stretching from Kosi Bay to a beacon 11 km north of Sodwana Bay, can only be described as magnificent. Here you will find isolated white beaches, coral reefs and deep aquamarine pools, unblemished by man. The only developments are 10 (two-bedded) luxury tree-lodges at Rocktail Bay and 10 secluded campsites at Mabibi. Both camps have been designed to blend into the depths of the lush coastal forest.

There are hundreds of varieties of cowries as well as excellent rock-fishing in the vicinity. Goggles are essential equipment as visibility in the warm, clear, reef-water reaches 50 m, with colourful residents such as clownfish and Moorish idols. No vehicles are allowed on the beach – and there are sturdy poles at Mabibi designed to keep it that way.

This is undoubtedly one of Southern Africa's last unspoilt subtropical shores and is recognised as being a coastline of international importance. Many species of turtles, including the endangered leatherbacks, breed along the coast, and are monitored by a research station at Bhanga Nek. Numbered poles dotted at regular 400 m intervals, are part of an ongoing turtle census. From Bhanga Neck to the Mozambique border the marine reserve is only accessible from Kosi Bay.

Bookings and enquiries should be addressed to Central Reservations, KwaZulu Bureau of Natural Resources, 367 Loop Street, Pietermaritzburg 3201 (telephone Pietermaritzburg 94-6698)

The reserve is reached via Mbazwana on the road to Sodwana Bay. Mbazwana, is about 70 km from the N2, and the last stop for petrol and provisions. From here, signs direct the last 20 km to Manzengwenya where you should report to the Officer-in-Charge before driving the final 16 km to Rocktail Bay or 10 km to Mabibi. A 4-wheel-drive vehicle is necessary in order to reach both camps and you would be well-advised to book in advance.

Mkuzi Game Reserve

Mkuzi is the only one of Natal's large game reserves (with an area of 34 644 ha) which has camping and caravanning facilities. It is also a perfect introduction to Maputaland. Nhlonhlela, on the Mkuze River, is a gem – dawn mists, ghostly fever trees and fossil hills showing when the Indian Ocean lapped the Lebombos.

With an informative brochure and a guard to guide you from the Mantuma hutted camp, you can walk its length on the three-hour Nhlonhlela Trail. There are also three-day bushveld trails which operate twice a month, from April to October.

There are also 80 km of roads in the reserve (the speed limit is 40 km/h). One of these passes the Bube and Msinga hides to reach the Nsumu picnic site overlooking Nsumu Pan, a king-size bird-bath 5 km long at the confluence of the Mkuze and Umsunduzi rivers.

The Mkuzi reserve has the Lebombo mountains at its back, the Mkuze riverine forest in front, and a wilderness of tall tree savanna in-between. The list of bird species in the area is impressively long, and fauna in Mkuzi includes impala, nyala, blue wildebeest, zebra, rhino, giraffe, leopard, African python, tortoise

146

and a host of small mammals which would be missed by the casual observer.

South of Nsumu Pan, with its great flocks of wild geese and duck, and stretching as far as the Msunduzi River, is Nxwala, which forms a natural extension of the 25 091 ha Mkuzi reserve, and is administered as part of the reserve.

Mkuzi's vegetation changes quickly from dense thicket to sand forest to savanna, but the most impressive features are its massive sycamore fig forest trees.

Ndumo Game Reserve

Ndumo, the pocket-sized Okavango, is special. Situated in Maputaland (northern Natal) on the Mozambique border, 470 km from Durban, Ndumo's 10 000 ha flood-plain comprises a delicate latticework of lakes and the fish, birds, insects, and other animals that live off them. Nyamithi Pan is 4 km long, and Banzi Pan, with its colourful water lilies is 6 km long. They are breeding grounds for a tremendous variety of aquatic birds. It is here that hunter F.C. Selous came to collect nyala for the London Zoo.

The impressive Lebombo mountains are on the left as you drive to Ndumo. Caution is advised if making detours, which can be muddy experiences – parts of Ndumo are flooded during the rains. Bring a pair of binoculars as there are birds, water terrapin, crocodile, and the fish eagle who mock-dive the goliath heron. There is a hutted camp among giant marula trees and visitors are offered sun-canopied Land-Rover tours of the reserve.

Ndumo is administered by the KwaZulu Bureau of Natural Resources but was originally established in 1924 by the Natal Parks Board to protect hippo. The population of these large mammals has now reached 300, which is considered capacity for this reserve.

Ndumo is possibly one of the most attractive of all the KwaZulu reserves. It may at some time in the future be expanded to include the Tembe Elephant Park, home of Natal's only remaining wild elephant population, and the Kosi Lake system – a future consolidated reserve, which is about 90 km long, stretching from Swaziland to the Indian Ocean.

Above: The Chinese lantern or sickle-bush *(Dichrostachys cinerea)* is characterised by these bicoloured flower spikes. This specimen was photographed in the Ingwavuma region of Zululand. **Right:** A bluebottle fly is attracted by the smell emanating from the newly hatched egg of a crocodile. The mortality rate among hatchlings is very high, and few of a particular brood attain adulthood.

St Lucia Complex

This scenic stretch of country on the central Zululand coast is made up of four separate reserves: the St Lucia Game Reserve, which is the water area and islands of the lake; St Lucia Park, the 1 km strip of land around most of the lake (including Mapelane); False Bay Park, on the north-western shoreline; and the Eastern Shores Nature Reserve, the land between the lake and the sea. This reserve is jointly controlled by the Natal Parks Board and the Department of Environment Affairs.

St Lucia is a mecca for fishermen and campers, a huge complex of shallow lakes, dunes and beautiful beaches stretching from Mtubatuba and Mapelane northwards for 60 km to the Mkuze River swamps. The wildlife found here includes crocodile, hippo, pelican and flamingo.

The wettest months in this region are in summer (November to February). The grunter run at the estuary is usually in October; the prawns and game fish return to the sea in autumn (March to May). Winter (June to August) is the breeding season for birds. Due to the presence of crocodile, no bathing or paddling is allowed in the lake (the hippo can also be dangerous: boats should not venture too close). Remember that anti-malaria precautions should be taken before entering the area.

All reservations for huts and log cabins in the St Lucia Complex should be addressed to The Reservations Officer, Natal Parks Board, P.O. Box 662, Pietermaritzburg 3200 (telephone Pietermaritzburg 47-1981). For camping and caravan accommodation, write to the individual reserve, resort or park. The Public Relations Officer of the Natal Parks Board (telephone Pietermaritzburg 47-1961) will assist with further information.

Campers and those visitors staying in the fully equipped huts and log cabins should bring

TURTLES SAVED FROM THE SOUP

Newly hatched loggerhead turtles head for the sea on Natal's north coast. Very few of the young reach maturity.

For many centuries, Southern Africa's great sea turtles — the 2 m leatherbacks and smaller, loggerheads — came to Natal's Tongaland coast to breed. But they had more than their natural enemies to contend with: the depredations of man reduced their number almost to extinction. Prized for their meat, oil, bones and eggs; in demand as talismans; slow-moving, clumsy and utterly helpless during the nesting season, they were natural and easy prey for poachers.

In 1963 the Natal Parks Board launched an intensive rescue operation, mounting shore patrols and seeking (with gratifying results) the understanding and co-operation of the Tonga villagers. During the ensuing years, the board's staff, helped by the KwaZulu Division of Nature Conservation, released over 120 000 tagged hatchlings.

The results were dramatic: in the 1966-67 breeding season only five female leatherbacks were sighted, and ten years later this figure climbed to 65 sightings. Over 5 000 hatchlings were tagged and returned to the sea in the 1981-82 season. Scientists found that 30-50 per cent of the tagged adults came back to nest at least once (some as many as six times), and the overall turtle population has climbed sharply.

The Natal Parks Board is optimistic that the two still-rare species will survive and flourish to a point where they can once more (though on a controlled basis) become a valuable source of food.

their own food and drink. The St Lucia village resort has a variety of shops where provisions can be purchased.

St Lucia Complex: Eastern Shores Nature Reserve

Cheetah have been re-introduced into the Eastern Shores Nature Reserve – a narrow, 13 873 ha strip of land between Lake St Lucia and the Indian Ocean. The reason: to assist in the reduction of the burgeoning population of more than 5 000 southern reedbuck, the largest concentration in Southern Africa.

When faced with danger, reedbuck run away with a characteristic rocking-horse motion, emitting a shrill alarm whistle and often a 'plop' sound like a cork being removed from a wine bottle. It was found that the little reedbuck were far too well protected, and as a result were overpopulating their habitat. An intriguing outcome was that many more young males than usual were being killed in fights – a symptom of overcrowding.

Cape Vidal is part of the Cape Vidal State Forest and lies 35 km north of St Lucia Estuary. Turn left at the T-junction at the entrance to St Lucia village, and follow the road past the Crocodile Centre to Cape Vidal. The entrance gate near the Crocodile Centre is closed between 9 p.m. and 6 a.m. in winter and between 9 p.m. and 5 a.m. in summer. It is a secluded little camping area within the Eastern Shores Nature Reserve (petrol and firewood are available). The campsites are under the canopy of thick dune forest. This coastal camping area has ablution facilities (hot and cold water). Visitors intending to occupy camping or caravan sites must report to the Natal Parks Board office.

The trees on the western side of the dunes (where they are protected from the salt spray) grow to an enormous size. This is home to red duiker, bushbuck, bushpig, vervet and samango monkey and a bewildering array of birds.

The game fishing is superb; South Ledges and Bishops Rock promise fine surf angling (bring your own ski-boat if you intend to go deep-sea fishing). Skin-diving is permitted, and there is a safe bathing area which is sheltered from the sea by a reef.

The St Lucia Wilderness tented trails start at the reception office at Cape Vidal. Participants should arrive not later than 2 p.m. on the Friday and be prepared for some soggy wading in pans (anti-malaria precautions are recommended). The three-day Mount Tabor or Mziki Trail, part of the system planned to link St Lucia Estuary with Cape Vidal, is 22 km long. You carry what you need on your back, leaving your car at Mission Rocks (14 km from St Lucia village). Book through The Reservations Officer, Natal Parks Board, P.O. Box 662, Pietermaritz-

Left: The blue-raft shell is kept afloat by a frothy 'raft' of bubbles (this specimen was photographed on Natal's north coast). Sea creatures have produced an ingenious array of buoyancy-regulating methods: bluebottles are suspended by their distinctively coloured, gas-filled floats; the nudibranch *Glaucus atlanticus* actually gulps air, and fishes employ swim bladders — small 'balloons' located in the gut cavity, behind the backbone. The bladder's gas content is so regulated that the fish has neutral buoyancy, remaining suspended at a certain depth. The secretion of lactic acid into the blood supplying the bladder results in the reduction of solubility of oxygen in the blood. Gas bubbles form, and these are pumped into the bladder. When the acid additive is removed, the oxygen is re-dissolved, and the fish's buoyancy decreases.

burg 3200 (telephone Pietermaritzburg 47-1981). Hikers sleep in a hut on the biblically named Mount Tabor, where one is asked to bear in mind that 'the litterbug is an unprotected species'. The huts are equipped with bunks, mattresses, gas cooker and lamps. To reserve Cape Vidal campsites, write to The Officer-in-Charge, Cape Vidal, Private Bag, St Lucia Estuary 3936 (telephone St Lucia 1104).

St Lucia Complex: False Bay Park

False Bay Park is the most northerly of the St Lucia reserves, and forms the western cutting edge of this battleaxe-shaped lake. The park's 2 247 ha offer open campsites along the shores, delightful picnic spots, and two bushveld nature trails. There are 45 large, shady camping and caravan sites dotted along its shoreline (overlooking the lake). The sites are served by water points and two ablution blocks.

Visitors who have booked sites should report to the Officer-in-Charge on arrival (the office is open daily from 8 a.m. to 1 p.m. and 2 p.m. to 5 p.m.). The park gates open at sunrise and close at sunset. The overnight (rustic camp) Dugandlovu Trail starts at the Natal Parks Board office, about 16 km east of Hluhluwe Village. The trail lasts for one or two nights (optional) and hikers stay in four-bedded huts, situated about 8,5 km from the entrance gates. A gas cooker, crockery, cutlery and cooking utensils are supplied. The self-guided 'Mpopomeni Trail' (a three-hour walk with picnic spots along the way) provides an interesting day outing for visitors.

From December through to April one of the False Bay game guards does nothing but watch over the only pink-backed pelican-breeding colony in Southern Africa. The birds sit in the trees by the hundred on the banks of the Hluhluwe River and its marshlands, which drain into the lake. Migrating flamingoes, in great flocks of up to 20 000 birds, have been seen on the lake.

The coastal bushland of False Bay Park is particularly rich in game, including nyala, suni, porcupine, reedbuck, bushpig, warthog, grey duiker, red vervet monkey and spotted hyena. Take a launch tour, if only to see the huge mullet jumping out of the water in your wake: you can almost reach out and catch them (the mullet 'perform' only in winter). This tour is restricted to visitors booked into the False Bay Park camping and caravan sites and the Dugandlovu Rustic Camp. Departures are subject to good weather. Bait is available. To reach the park, take the turn-off for Hluhluwe Village from the N2 and follow the road (through the village for 13 km). The nearest petrol source is Hluhluwe Village, 19 km distant.

For further information and bookings for campsites, write to The Officer-in-Charge, False Bay Park, P.O. Hluhluwe 3960 (telephone Hluhluwe 2911). Bookings and enquiries for the Dugandlovu Rustic Camp are made through The Reservations Officer, Natal Parks Board, P.O. Box 662, Pietermaritzburg 3200 (telephone Pietermaritzburg 47-1981).

St Lucia Complex: St Lucia Game Reserve

St Lucia Game Reserve consists of the large lake and its islands. It is connected to the sea by a narrow channel (21 km long) that is rich in hippo, crocodile, goliath heron and other fish-hunting birds. The lake is reed-covered and marshy in the east and, where the Natal Parks

148

Above left: A plate entitled 'New and remarkable species of lepidoptera from Natal and the Zulu country', from a book by the 19th century artist, zoologist and traveller George French Angas. The plate is from *The Kafirs Illustrated*, a volume much prized by collectors of Africana. **Above right:** A female bushbuck at Charters Creek, in the Lake St Lucia complex. Bushbuck vary greatly in size and coloration: one form (there are thought to be over 40) is dark brown with virtually no other markings, while another is coloured bright chestnut, with conspicuous spots and white stripes. **Right:** A painted reed frog calling in the St Lucia estuary. At night these frogs may be heard calling in great numbers, their piercing whistles intensified by the resonant balloon-like vocal sac.

St Lucia Complex: St Lucia Marine Reserve

Coral, cowries and colourful tropical fish predominate in the St Lucia Marine Reserve, stretching from 1 km south of Cape Vidal to 11 km north of Jessop Point, or Sodwana Bay, and 3 km out to sea (the beach is accessible – by 4-wheel-drive vehicles – from both directions). This is an underwater wonderland containing some of the southernmost coral reefs in the world. It is a breeding ground for many of the fish that currents distribute along the Southern African coast, and the natural habitat of turtle, two of which (the loggerhead and leatherback) breed on the beaches.

Rod and line angling, ski-boat fishing, and spearing for game fish are permitted, but bottom fishing is strictly forbidden, as is the collection of bait and any marine specimens.

Part of the reserve – the 25 km between Leven Point and Rooiwal – is a sanctuary area in which no fishing, or even swimming, is allowed. Camping is also taboo along the beach.

St Lucia Complex: St Lucia Park

The park, proclaimed in 1939, consists of land around the estuary and a strip of approximately 1 km around most of the lake shore. Within this area of 12 545 ha are the hutted camp at Charters Creek, the hutted camp and campsites at Fanies Island, the camping and caravanning area at Mapelane, and the St Lucia Resort.

At Charters Creek there are 15 huts perched on the high bank overlooking Lake St Lucia and the distant eastern shore. There are 14 three-bedded huts, another with two beds, a seven-bedded cottage, a community lounge, two centrally situated kitchen blocks and ablution buildings. A small fridge has been installed in each unit, and the deep freezers in the kitchen may be used on request. The shoreline in front of the camp is a grand place to stroll.

There are self-guided walking trails (including the two-hour Isikova Trail, for which a descriptive booklet is available), and you may see a variety of mammals such as Zulu golden mole, vervet monkey, black-backed jackal, duiker, reedbuck, bushpig and spotted hyena.

Bait can be bought and boats (without outboard motors) hired; petrol is available and there is table tennis, a curio shop, library and swimming pool. The turn-off to the camp is 30 km north of Mtubatuba or 20 km south of Hluhluwe Village on the main N2 highway. The entrance gates are 13 km farther on this road (the route is well signposted). In winter, the gates open at sunrise and close at 7 p.m. (they close at 8 p.m. in summer). Visitors arriving to take up accommodation should report to the office by 4.30 p.m. The office is open daily from 8 a.m. to 1 p.m. and 2 p.m. to 5 p.m.

Despite its name, Fanies Island is not an island, but a rather secluded, hutted camp on

Board hutted camps of Fanies Island and Charters Creek are sited in the west, steep-banked and well-treed.

Pelican and flamingo cluster in hundreds and sometimes thousands in the shallows. The pelican, which swoop through the air like flights of bombers, cruise over the water, then 'herd' the fish in an ever-tightening circle before dipping their beaks for the kill. There are rays with a 2 m wingspan, 4 m sawfish, and Cape kabeljou weighing up to 50 kilograms.

The hippo (600 in all) and the crocodiles are everywhere, the former harrumphing and blowing, the latter sliding stealthily off the banks.

Hippo wander at night in search of sweet grazing, and notices in the hutted camps advise you to be careful. Penaeid prawns, spawned at sea, mature in the lake, making the St Lucia lake system the most important prawn habitat in South Africa.

Four rivers feed Lake St Lucia, including the Mkuze and Hluhluwe, and maintain the delicate balance between the inflow of sea water and evaporation. But they are slowly losing the battle: within 200 years, it is predicted, St Lucia will be no more. Roads lead directly to the lake shore at False Bay Park, Fanies Island, Charters Creek and St Lucia Resort.

AN AIRBORNE DESALINISATION PLANT

The giant petrel takes anything up to three months to make the 7 000 km journey from the harshness of the Antarctic wastes to Southern Africa's pleasant shores. It is open sea all the way, a vast expanse of ocean unrelieved by islands or any other source of fresh water. Yet, even though these seabirds have the same body fluids as any other animal, and cannot cope with an excess of salt, they manage to survive this epic flight.

This ability puzzled zoologists for decades, until the secret was revealed during a casual study of the albatross. These huge birds, clothed in seafaring superstition and legend, were much in demand by zoos and other institutions — but until fairly recently, none lived for long in captivity. They were given plenty of water, but died after a few weeks for no apparent reason.

Then an observer noticed a small, steady drip of clear liquid oozing from the beak of one specimen which, on examination, proved to be pure brine. The albatross's diet was changed to include salt; it recovered its health, and was soon thriving.

The conclusions: seabirds have evolved a special mechanism that extracts the salt from seawater, a mechanism essential to the proper function of their bodies and one that cannot be by-passed by the simple ingestion of fresh water. It is a process that man has yet to reproduce and exploit economically. The seabird is, in effect, a highly efficient airborne desalinisation plant.

---

the western shore of Lake St Lucia, 11 km north of Charters Creek. To get there, take the road to Charters Creek and turn left after 12 km; the camp is 13 km from here. The hutted camp consists of 12 two-bedded huts (with small fridges), a kitchen and ablution block and a seven-bedded cottage. Fanies Island also has a camping and caravan area with 20 sites served by two ablution blocks (hot and cold water).

Overnight visitors should report to the office on arrival. The office is open daily from 8 a.m. to 1 p.m. and 2 p.m. to 5 p.m.

The self-guided trail introduces you at shore level to the many species of bird and the smaller mammals of the shoreline. A pair of binoculars will enhance your enjoyment. Bait can be purchased, boats can be hired, and petrol is available. To reserve a campsite, write to the Camp Superintendent, who will also provide further information. The address is The Camp Superintendent, Fanies Island, P.O. Box 201, Mtubatuba 3935 (telephone Mtubatuba 1431).

Mapelane is difficult to get to, but it is worth every one of the 48 pot-holed kilometres from the Kwambonambi N2 turn-off. The last few kilometres are dark tunnels through a tangled primeval forest of red milkwood, wild fig, black mangrove and lianas. The huge forested dune,

Mjakaja Hill, rises steep and pristine from the beach. At its base lies a small complex of nine self-sufficient log cabins that form the Natal Parks Board camp. The beaches, with well-deserved names such as Crayfish Point and Mussel Drop, provide visitors with many hours of enjoyment. But there is titanium in the dunes and tiny (900 ha) Mapelane, with her 9 km long unique forest, is fighting off the encroaching tentacles of the various mining consortia.

Visitors should note that there is no shop, telephone or petrol pump (though bait is available), but there are 170 species of birds, a rickety crocodile hide overlooking the Umfolozi River mouth, excellent ski-boat fishing, forest and beach walks and 44 campsites (there are ablution facilities with hot and cold water). These are booked direct with The Officer-in-Charge, Mapelane, Private Bag, St Lucia Estuary 3936 (telephone St Lucia 20).

The Nile crocodile (*Crocodylus niloticus*) can grow to over 4 m in length. It plays an important part as a consumer in maintaining the ecological balance. Crocodile used to be distributed as far south as Plettenberg Bay; now their southernmost limit is the Tugela River.

The Nile crocodile is probably better looked after in Natal than anywhere else in the world.

The Natal Parks Board's crocodile research station, pool and museum at St Lucia Estuary Village are well worth a visit (the centre is regarded as the best of its kind in the world). To reach it, turn left after crossing the St Lucia Estuary bridge and drive 2 km along the Cape Vidal road. The centre has excellent interpretative displays of the whole St Lucia Park, of the seashore, the coastal grassland, the bird life, the hippos in the reeds, and the ocean. There is also a curio shop. The crocodiles are fed on Sundays at 3 p.m.

There are three campsites at St Lucia village. Two face the St Lucia Estuary; the other is near the crocodile centre (there is a swimming pool). The showers and baths in the ablution block have hot and cold water, and the sites have water points. St Lucia Estuary, 29 km east of Mtubatuba, provides access to Cape Vidal and the Mount Tabor 'Mziki' Trail, and is a good starting point for the Umfolozi, Hluhluwe and Mkuzi game reserves.

Launch tours leave twice a day (except Tuesdays) and are an ideal way to explore the lake shore and see its hippo, crocodile, and many birds. If you are lucky and the ranger is able to rock his water-jet propelled boat across the 15 cm deep water, you may pass great flocks of pelican and flamingo in 'the shallows' at the southern end of the lake.

Visitors may hire boats (without motors). There are hotels and comfortable guest houses in this attractive holiday village, and petrol is available. Campsites and launch tours are booked through The Officer-in-Charge, St Lucia Resort, Private Bag, St Lucia Estuary 3936 (telephone St Lucia 20).

Sodwana Bay National Park

Sodwana means 'little one on its own', a plaintive cry unheard by the 4 000 caravanners who invade the 413 ha forested dunes of this Indian Ocean resort during school holidays. This is 4-wheel-drive territory, but if you are clever and self-sufficient, you will probably make it in a conventional vehicle.

Ski-boats with twin 80 hp engines come screaming through the gap in the reef with their catches of kingfish, tuna, king mackerel, dorado, wahoo, blue marlin, black marlin and the most beautiful of them all, the majestic sailfish. Bravura gamefish competitions are held here on a regular basis, and the catches are almost always magnificent.

The little bay is protected by a reef and the jutting Jessop Point, and is the outlet for the pretty little lakelets of Mgobeseleni and Shazibe. In days of yore a base for ivory hunters and gun-runners, the protected hinterland forest hides suni, steenbok, reedbuck, aardwolf, banded mongoose, thick-tailed bushbaby, bushpig, East African egg-eater, the highly venomous Gaboon adder, and in the swamp forest, huge fig trees.

There is a supermarket, and petrol is on sale. The campsites are noisy and crowded and interspersed with fish-weighing points. Bait, firewood and ice are on sale, and there are some 48 fishfreezer drawers for hire. There is a community centre that can be hired for approved functions, and the range of land-sports includes the popular jukskei. The entrance gate is open daily from 6 a.m. to 6 p.m.

The park is 80 bumpy kilometres from the Mhlosinga N2 turn-off. Groups of Zulu boys perform traditional dances for you on the approach road, and their mothers sell basketwork and bananas at the beach entrance. Pets are strictly prohibited. For information and reservations, write to The Officer-in-Charge, Sodwana Bay National Park, Private Bag 310, Mbazwana 3974 (telephone Jozini 1102).

Tamboti Bush Camp
At Tamboti you will always need to have your camera ready for that priceless moment – such as when you look your first rhino straight in the eye!

Situated on the 4 000 ha Panata Game Ranch, near the town of Hluhluwe and bordering on the Mkuzi Game Reserve, Tamboti Bush Camp has long been noted for the superb game-viewing and bird-watching opportunities it offers its guests. The animal population in the vicinity of the camp varies – from the massive white rhino and giraffe to the smaller warthog;

from species such as wildebeest, nyala, suni, impala, duiker, blesbok and reedbuck to the occasional sighting of a leopard on an unforgettable night drive.

Tamboti can accommodate twelve people in five thatched bungalows. A separate thatched building houses the kitchen and lounge-cum-dining room, used mainly in wet weather! A swimming pool also forms part of the complex. Evening meals (prepared by an experienced cook) are taken outdoors, either under the shade of the Tamboti trees or inside the reed-enclosed boma around a roaring log fire.

Walks may be taken from the camp, accompanied by an experienced game scout. Game-viewing excursions in an open 4-wheel-drive are organised at pre-arranged times, including special late night drives.

For further information, write to Tamboti Bush Camp, 11 Surrey Lane, Kloof (telephone Durban 764-0137).

Tembe Elephant Park
This 29 878 ha reserve was proclaimed in 1983 in an effort to save Natal's last free-ranging elephant herds. In the past the traditional migration route of these elephant took them through Mozambique, where they were frequently poached for their tusks and meat.

Scarred old bulls and others lucky enough to survive are now protected behind the new electric fence surrounding the entire reserve. There are presently 80 resident elephant, but numbers are growing steadily.

The reserve, which is predominantly dry-sand forest, is stocked with suni, leopard, white rhino, zebra, giraffe, kudu, impala and hyena. Three-day expeditions for groups of eight people in an open 4-wheel-drive vehicle are available. Guests stay in a very comfortable tented base camp. There are no facilities for day visitors as roads in the park are still to be developed in the near future. Information and accommodation enquiries should be addressed to Central Reservations, KwaZulu Bureau of Natural Resources, 367 Loop Street, Pietermaritzburg 3201 (telephone Pietermaritzburg 94-6698).

To reach the reserve, take the N2 turn-off to Jozini and travel north 108 km until reaching Sihangwane and the entrance to the reserve. The road is tarred until the reserve gates.

White Rhino Trail and Lake Trail
The Wilderness Leadership School operates two fascinating trails through the Umfolozi and Lake St Lucia areas, and hikers are treated to spectacular views of a variety of game and a myriad water birds.

Adult courses last either four or five days and scholars' courses run for five days. Participants assemble in Durban, from where they are transported to the starting point. The organisers will provide sleeping bags, groundsheets, tents, rucksacks, canoes, meals and utensils. For details write to The Wilderness Leadership School, P.O. Box 53058, Yellowwood Park 4001 (telephone Durban 42-8642/3).

Right: White pelicans at Lake St Lucia. These huge birds have a three-metre wingspan. **Below:** A Gaboon adder – deadly inhabitant of northern Natal's forests.

The peaceful legacy

The pride of Natal is the splendid wilderness of Umfolozi Game Reserve, 270 km north of Durban – where careful conservation rescued the white rhino from the brink of extinction. Nearby, and as rich in wildlife, is Hluhluwe. Despite the encroachment of the cane fields, Zululand has much to offer. Its deep green forest sanctuaries, misty mountain peaks, coastal lagoons, carefully run private game ranches and the refreshing upland reserves around Eshowe offer quietness, beauty and peace in a land which, not so long ago, was torn by bloody territorial battles.

Dlinza Forest Nature Reserve

A 'place of tomb-like meditation' is the meaning of Dlinza (or Hlinza), the 200 ha forest reserve in Eshowe, off Kangella Street. The tracks through it were cut by British troops stationed in the town after the 1879 Anglo-Zulu war, and the clearing known as Bishop's Seat, where nativity plays are held, was made by Bishop Carter, in the best Victorian tradition, for his annual children's picnic. Red and yellow-marked nature trails enable one to stroll through the cool forest. Open from 7.30 a.m. to 5 p.m., the reserve has bushbuck, blue duiker and red duiker, bushpig and vervet monkey. There are picnic and braai spots.

Dukuduku State Forest and Mihobi Nature Reserve

Dukuduku – the 'place of hiding', is so called because it was a sanctuary for both men and cattle during the Zulu succession struggle following Cetshwayo's death. The Mihobi Nature Reserve, which falls inside the State Forest, is an area of 162 ha (to be enlarged). A picnic spot is signposted at the 15 km peg on the road between Mtubatuba and St Lucia.

This nature reserve preserves a characteristic stand of tropical coastal forest, of which very little is still to be found in Natal. Wildlife includes a variety of endangered water and forest birds and several endangered raptors (birds of prey). There are many rare butterflies in the reserve, and the extremely poisonous Gaboon adder (very rare in South Africa) also occurs here.

Entry is during daylight hours only, and visitors explore the area on foot. For further information and permission to explore these forests, write to The Regional Director, Zululand Forest Region, Private Bag X506, Eshowe 3815 (telephone Eshowe 4-2087).

Enseleni Nature Reserve

A swamp trail of 5 km twists through the reserve and along the Enseleni River, a haven for aquatic birds, monitor lizards and lagoon hibiscus. Starting with giant umdoni, or water myrtle trees (*Syzygium cordatum*) at the picnic site, the trail passes on a boardwalk over papyrus swamp, through ilala palms (*Hyphaene natalensis*), 10 m high freshwater mangrove trees and wild figs. The forest canopy is so dense that little light reaches the ground.

There is a 143 ha game park in the reserve, with blue wildebeest, waterbuck, impala, nyala, bushbuck and reedbuck. The reserve is open throughout the year, while the game park

opens on Saturdays, Sundays and public holidays from 8 a.m. to 5 p.m. (extended hours can be arranged).

This 293 ha sanctuary, 16 km north of the timber-and-cane town of Empangeni, is a foretaste of the great Zululand reserves. It is situated 190 km along the N2 from Durban: travelling south, take a left turn 1 km after the Richards Bay turn-off.

Entumeni Nature Reserve

Fields of sugar cane dominate the undulating hills of Natal's north coast, exiling most indigenous vegetation. But here and there the birds have found a sanctuary. The little 393 ha

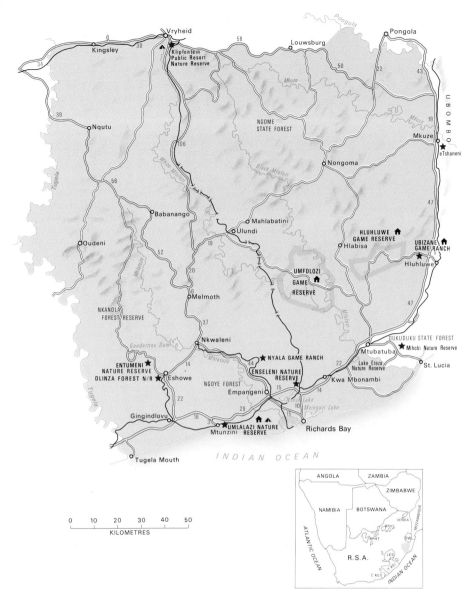

mist-belt reserve of Entumeni, 16km from Eshowe on the Nkandla road, is one of these. Only birds and butterflies seem to move in the gloom of this deceptively still forest, but high in the bastard umzimbeet (*Millettia sutherlandii*), among the ferns and orchids, and on the damp compost of the forest floor, less visible creatures abound. The reserve can be explored only on foot (there is a picnic site).

eTshaneni: the 'Ghost Mountain'

Macbeth would have felt at home in much of Zululand. It is an almost supernatural world of waterfalls, dark pools and misty mountains. Here is the 529m high eTshaneni, 'the place of the small stone', rising above the thornveld and mist of the Mkuze River in the Lebombo Mountains, a range that stretches in a 600km swathe north to the Limpopo valley.

Known to nearby white farmers as Ghost Mountain, eTshaneni is the burial ground of the Gaza chiefs, including Soshangane, whose body was carried at dead of night 1000km from Zimbabwe, where his people had fled in 1819 before an avenging Shaka. Dingaan is also buried in the Lebombo Mountains, but much farther to the north, in the Hlatikulu forest. The body of another great chief, Cetshwayo, rests on the fringe of the Nkandla Mountain Forest near Eshowe.

The Lebombo Mountains, together with the Drakensberg, are the last of the basalt laval sheet that completely covered Natal 150 million years ago. Since then, erosion has whittled away considerable portions of both of these ranges. However, you will still find seashells on the slopes of the Lebombo Mountains – evidence that suggests the Indian Ocean once came this far inland.

Hluhluwe Game Reserve

Hluhluwe has been a game sanctuary since 1897, and before that a hunting preserve of the Zulu kings. Saved by the presence of tsetse fly and the malarial mosquito, which kept man at bay, Hluhluwe is named after the thorny monkey rope, umHluhluwe (*Dalbergia armata*), that flourishes along the banks of the Hluhluwe River. Zulu herdboys use the rope to muzzle calves, weaning them from their mothers and thus leaving the milk for human consumption.

Hluhluwe is not big, but it has plenty of big game. Thirty kilometres across, its 23 000 ha of bush trails, hills and river valleys offer a huge variety of game, including black rhino, white rhino, lion, herds of buffalo and a clan of elephant. There are kudu, impala, nyala, hippo, giraffe, leopard and crocodile.

The bird life in the reserve includes the bateleur eagle, the ground hornbill (resembling a large black turkey) and the white-backed vulture that thrusts its whole head into the belly

Left: A female marico sunbird feeds on *Schotia brachypetala* (or weeping boer-bean) in the Hluhluwe Game Reserve. This sunbird is found mainly in dry (acacia thorn) savanna, and lives on spiders, insects, butterfly larvae and the nectar of certain flowers. The female builds the nest of down and feathers (bark and seeds may be added to the outside of the nest), and suspends it from the branches of acacias and other trees. **Right:** The Dlinza Forest Nature Reserve at Eshowe. Although some visitors come only for braais and picnics, many prefer to spend their day exploring the complex of nature trails leading through the forest. The indigenous vegetation includes trees such as yellowwoods, stinkwoods, figs and forest umdonis.

of a carcass. A resident ranger naturalist at the hutted camp tells visitors about the walking trail into the Mbhombe forest, and the 40km (self-guided) drive.

Hluhluwe has a camp of 20 (two-bedded) rest huts and four (six-bedded) cottages. All you have to do is bring your own drink and food – which is prepared for you by attendants. The reserve is open throughout the year (the gates open at sunrise and close at sunset). The best time to visit is during the cooler months (May to September), when the cover is not as dense as in summer. Water supplies are limited during this period, and game tends to concentrate.

There are facilities for day visitors (including braai sites) at Maphumulo, Hilltop Camp and Gunganeni Gate.

There are two routes to Hluhluwe: follow the main road to Hluhluwe Village, turn left at the sign reading 'Hluhluwe Game Reserve' and follow the tarred road to the reserve entrance. Alternatively, visitors should turn left at a point 3,4km past the Mtubatuba road junction at a sign reading 'Nongoma/Umfolozi Game Reserve'. About 17km further on (at a signpost), turn north onto a gravel road which leads to the reserve. Reservations are made through The Reservations Officer, Natal Parks Board, P.O. Box 662, Pietermaritzburg 3200 (telephone Pietermaritzburg 47-1981).

Klipfontein Public Resort Nature Reserve
Fishing, boating and bird-watching are the main attractions at the Natal Parks Board's 4562ha resort at Klipfontein Dam, near Vryheid. Although not officially proclaimed a nature reserve, Klipfontein Public Resort remains very popular with visitors throughout the year.

Day visitors make use of picnic sites along the banks of the dam, while 10 campsites are available for overnight guests.

The tranquil dam offers a pleasant retreat for bird-watchers too, who will have a feast spotting the waterfowl found in this area.

The turn-off to the dam is 6km south of the town on the Vryheid-Melmoth road. For more information and campsite bookings, write to The Officer-in-Charge, Klipfontein Public Resort Nature Reserve, P.O. Box 1774, Vryheid 3100 (telephone Vryheid 4383). Boats must be registered with the Board before being launched.

Lake Eteza Nature Reserve
Lake Eteza is a shimmering 350ha papyrus pan off the N2 highway 46km north of Empangeni. Waterfowl and a variety of other swamp life seem miraculously to have survived the sugar cane encirclement.

There are no facilities. Check with the Natal Parks Board in Pietermaritzburg beforehand, as the reserve is not yet open to the public (telephone Pietermaritzburg 47-1981).

154

Ngome State Forest and Ntendeka Wilderness Area
Twenty-seven kilometres east of Vryheid on the road to Louwsburg is a turn-off to the Zulu trading village of Nongoma, the 'place of the diviner' (witchdoctor). This mainly gravel road twists its way around the hills for 60km to the village of Ngome, passing the indigenous mountain forest of the same name. In the 1820s this tropical forest once hid a Khumalo ally of Mzilikazi, founder of Zimbabwe's Ndebele nation, and 50 years later provided refuge to Cetshwayo after his capital uluNdi (Ulundi) was put to the torch by the conquering British army.

The list of trees and plants in this majestic expanse of land includes 19 of South Africa's 42 species of epiphytic, or tree orchid. Other rarities include the olive woodpecker, the red bush squirrel and the Ngome lily (Crinum moorei). Wildlife abounds in the forest: there are leopard, baboon, duiker, caracal, samango monkey, a variety of snakes and innumerable birds, butterflies and moths.

Within the State forest is the Ntendeka Wilderness Area, a large (5500ha) stretch of grassland and evergreen forest in which visitors may see remnants of early Zulu occupation, an historic rock shelter, the Ntendeka cliffs and a host of fascinating trees and plants. The vegetation conceals a variety of game such as bushbuck, blue and grey duiker, baboon, samango monkey, caracal and vervet monkey.

Birds include bald ibis and long-crested eagle (both threatened species), purple-crested loerie, Narina trogon and black-headed oriole.

Visitors are admitted during the day only. There are picnic and camping sites at the edge of the wilderness area, and footpaths cross it. Visitors may obtain permits from The State Forester, Ngome State Forest, Private Bag X9306, Vryheid 3100 (telephone Hlobane 883).

Ngoye Forest
There are more than 100 indigenous forests in KwaZulu. Much of the flora and fauna of the 3904ha Ngoye Mountain Forest south of Empangeni, and not far from the University of KwaZulu, is unique to the area. One of the rarest plants in the world, Encephalartos woodii (a cycad), came from Ngoye.

In 1916, a clump of half a dozen male plants of the species were the only ones still surviving. These were removed: one was sent to Pretoria, one to Kew Gardens in London and four were planted in Durban's Botanic Gardens, where they still flourish. No female plants have ever been found.

The red bush squirrel, the forest green butterfly, the green barbet, Delegorgue's (bronze-naped) pigeon, and the Ngoye centipede are all common here but extremely rare elsewhere in Southern Africa.

Write to The Director, Bureau of Natural Resources, Private Bag X23, Ulundi 3838 (telephone Ulundi 20-2717) for further information, directions and permission to explore the forest.

Nkandla Forest Reserve
Nkandla is magnificent – a huge indigenous mountain forest, beautiful and unspoilt.

Left above: A hiker pauses for a rest along a footpath in the Ntendeka Wilderness Area – part of the Ngome State Forest. **Left below:** A green reed frog (Hyperolius tuberlinguis). This small amphibian can change its colour to different shades of green and even yellow. It deposits its eggs in a mass attached to a leaf, reed or stem of grass a few centimetres above the surface of the water. **Right above:** A white rhino in the Hluhluwe Game Reserve. This is the second largest land mammal (after the elephant), the male weighing 3,5 tons. In spite of their intimidating size these rhino are not aggressive: although they may charge when alarmed, they rarely follow it through with an actual attack. **Right below:** Mole crickets use their powerful front legs as digging implements, burying themselves in a remarkably short time. These crickets are familiar throughout Natal. **Far right:** Nyala in the Hluhluwe Game Reserve.

Its 1 620 ha lie astride a mountain pass, 50 km northwest of Eshowe on a good gravel road that, another 50 km further on, joins the main Empangeni-Dundee route. The moisture of perpetually drifting mists maintains the tree ferns, yellow-flowered creepers, cycads, orchids and lianas on the flanks of these brooding mountains. There is a waterfall in the Mome Gorge, the refuge and final stand in 1906 of Bambatha, last of the Zulus to challenge the new order by force of arms.

A signposted turn-off some distance before Nkandla leads 25 rigorous kilometres around to the forest's western fringe, high over the valley of the Tugela River. Here, at journey's end, in a quiet grove of trees, is the grave of Cetshwayo, who died on 23 April 1884. A tombstone of black marble erected by a descendant proudly recalls the part Cetshwayo played in his people's turbulent history.

Leopard, duiker, bushbuck, vervet monkey and baboon inhabit the almost impenetrable forest. Further details and permission to enter the reserve are available from the The Director, Bureau of Natural Resources, Private Bag X23, Ulundi 3838 (telephone Ulundi 20-2717).

Nyala Game Ranch

This privately-owned ranch at Empangeni, in KwaZulu, is a 500 ha sanctuary offering large game species, many and varied birds and a selection of courses and educational trails (which operate by night and day).

There are lectures for organised groups and courses for school children offer subjects such as ecology, game-ranching and conservation (including field work), together with practical activities such as hiking. The Mbondwe Safari Camp features rondavels, electric power, large tents, toilets, a large communal lounge, hot and cold showers and a resident cook; the Hlati Safari Camp provides similar facilities (but lacks the lounge and electricity); the more primitive Umvumvu Bush Camp has tents, mattresses, rustic huts, cooking utensils and cold showers.

Gates open at sunrise and close at sunset (for day visitors). The best time to visit is from April to September, though the period October to March is considered the most suitable for seeing nesting birds and young animals. Visitors may see porcupine, bushbaby, caracal, aardwolf and other small mammals. To make a booking, write to Nyala Game Ranch, P.O. Box 647, Empangeni 3880.

Ocean View Game Park

After the hot, humid coast, the cool 'sighing winds' of Eshowe 30 km inland and 500 m above sea level are a welcome change.

Historical heart of British 'Zoolah-land', Eshowe has a 25 ha municipal game reserve (leased by the Natal Parks Board) called Ocean View Game Park at the southern entrance to the town.

Visiting hours are from 8 a.m. to 5 p.m. A game guard accompanies visitors around its easy slopes, where zebra, impala, bushpig, blesbok, blue duiker and blue wildebeest have been re-introduced. There is also a wealth of bird life. For more information contact The Officer-in-Charge, Ocean View Game Park, P.O. Box 249, Eshowe 3815.

Ubizane Game Ranch

Game-viewing safaris on foot and in 4-wheel-drive vehicles are offered to guests at Ubizane, a private game ranch 8 km from Hluhluwe Village on the Hluhluwe Game Reserve road.

The exhilarating game-viewing drives give you an excellent opportunity to see white rhino (bred on the ranch), giraffe, nyala, impala, blue wildebeest, kudu, blesbok, reedbuck and waterbuck, while night safaris allow views of nocturnal animals such as aardvark, hyena, white-tailed mongoose and jackal.

Visitors stay in luxury at Forest Camp which has three *en suite* timber bungalows. A rustic

155

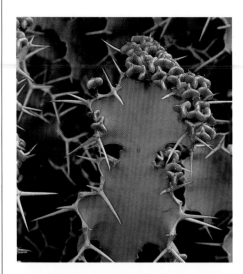

Top: *Euphorbia grandicornis*. This plant's sap can cause skin irritation, while the vapour from a 'bleeding' plant can create a burning sensation in the throat. **Above:** A steenbok at Umfolozi.

naturalist. Sontuli's 'dusty' drive and Nselweni's splendid bush camp, on a bend of the river, come alive under his tutelage as he points out a rhino midden, the umThombothi tree, the guttural 'aahrr' of the great white heron or the sudden flash of cheetah in the sunlight.

To reach the waterhole hide at Umfolozi, visitors make their way quietly along a reed-walled tunnel.

Umfolozi – Hluhluwe Corridor

Natal's two best-known game reserves, Umfolozi and Hluhluwe, are connected by an 8 km wide and 21 000 ha strip. The complex constitutes a massive conservation area of some 100 000 ha. Because there have been no developments in the corridor it possibly contains larger concentrations of game than either of its neighbours.

The corridor may be developed in the future to cater for visitors. For more information you should contact The Director, Natal Parks Board, P.O. Box 662 , Pietermaritzburg 3200 (telephone Pietermaritzburg 47-1961).

Umlalazi Nature Reserve

The fish eagle is the symbol of the 1 028 ha Natal Parks Board reserve of Umlalazi ('the place of the grinding stone'), 1,5 km east of Mtunzini. Forested coastal dunes, mangroves, several small lakes and the Umlalazi River Lagoon, adjacent to the shimmering waters of the Indian Ocean, are the dominant features of this appealing sanctuary.

Silent crocodile still occasionally surprise fishermen in the Umlalazi Nature Reserve, but the main fauna to be found here are bushpig, bushbuck, duiker and reedbuck. On the other side of the dunes, in the sea, huge skates and sandsharks move inshore to breed during the summer months.

Two nature trails, one through the mangroves, the other in the dune forests, have been prepared by Natal Parks Board staff. Trees in the reserve include red milkwood, strangler fig, gwarri and white milkwood.

There are 13 log cabins and a camping site in the reserve. Water is available and showers are provided. Umlalazi is open year-round, and the gates are open 24 hours a day. There is no shop, but the neighbouring town of Mtunzini stocks all requirements. The Mtunzini Lagoon Resort (telephone Mtunzini 19), near the sanctuary, hires out boats and sells bait. The reserve is 128 km from Durban along the main north coast road.

The log cabins are reserved through The Reservations Officer, P.O. Box 662, Pietermaritzburg 3200 (telephone Pietermaritzburg 47-1981), and campsites through The Officer-in-Charge, Umlalazi Nature Reserve, P.O. Mtunzini 3867 (telephone Mtunzini 136).

timber bar-cum-lounge overlooks a forest of yellow fever trees and a reeded boma where the evening braais are held.

For further information write to Ubizane Game Ranch, P.O. Box 102, Hluhluwe 3960 (telephone Hluhluwe 3602).

Umfolozi Game Reserve

Burnt orange and blue – this is sunset at Umfolozi. The 47 753 ha sanctuary is named after the 'zigzag' *Mfolozi Emnyana* (black) and *Mfolozi Emhlope* (white) rivers that meander and marry in this untouched wilderness. It is home to the world's largest concentration of white rhino (*Ceratothenum simum*): some 900 in all. In 'Operation Rhino', 20 years ago, the revolutionary technique of drug-darting these massive

beasts was initiated, enabling surplus animals to be captured without injury and sent to sanctuaries throughout the world: a pair of rhinos even went to Moscow, the Russian capital.

Among the 50 animal species at Umfolozi are 900 buffalo, 1 300 blue wildebeest, 650 zebra, giraffe, lion, leopard, cheetah, mountain reedbuck, kudu, warthog and 300 species of birds.

A primitive 24 000 ha area in the reserve may only be visited by hikers on organised wilderness trails, a scheme launched by the Natal Parks Board. Parties are guided on fairly demanding but fascinating three-day hikes, camping at night in the bush.

There are wildlife scientists on the park's staff, and Dumisani Ngobese, with some 14 years' experience at Umfolozi, is the resident ranger-

Forest, gorge and bountiful sea

Contrary to the expectations of many visitors, the Natal coast is distinguished not only by its bikinis and long stretches of white beach. For the nature lover, it has a great deal else to offer: each of its (mainly forest gorge) reserves is well worth visiting. The finest of these reserves are probably Vernon Crookes, Krantzkloof, Oribi Gorge and, in Durban itself, the popular Kenneth Stainbank Nature Reserve.

The bird life is prolific and fascinating throughout this coastal region, the myriad sea creatures of its shores even more so. There are no elephant left, but most of the reserves have re-introduced antelope and other game.

There is a luxurious tropical ambience about the countryside around Durban: forests and flowers, ilala palms, monkeys and wild bananas are everywhere. But the focus of attention is without doubt the ever-changing seashore – its lagoons, river estuaries and tidal pools.

Amanzimtoti Bird Sanctuary

A haven for exotic and indigenous birds lies some 27 km south of Durban in Amanzimtoti. The focus of the sanctuary is its lake-like stretch of calm water that is framed by ilala palms and forms an ideal habitat for a wide variety of waterbirds.

You can cross the lake, which lies on a tributary of the Amanzimtoti River, by a rustic wooden bridge to reach two well-positioned bird hides. There are also many park benches dotted strategically throughout the sanctuary where you can relax among strutting peacock and enjoy the pleasant surroundings.

The sanctuary lies off Umdoni Road and is open daily from 6 a.m. to 6 p.m. On weekend afternoons you may purchase teas served by voluntary workers.

For more information contact the Publicity Assistant, Borough of Amanzimtoti, P.O. Box 26, Amanzimtoti 4125 (telephone Durban 903-2121).

Beachwood Mangroves Nature Reserve

Howick Falls, Midmar Dam Public Resort, Albert Falls Public Resort and the Umgeni Valley Game Ranch, all on the Umgeni River, are proof of the bounty and beauty of 'the river of the acacia trees', which reaches the Indian Ocean near the Blue Lagoon Amusement Park in Durban. The 76 ha Beachwood sanctuary, access to which is via the Durban North turn-off into Fairview Road (and then turn sharp right), is on the north bank of the Umgeni River.

Mangroves – dense thickets of tropical evergreen trees and shrubs – throw out a profusion of prop roots that trap silt, plants and debris in a thick interlacing mesh that makes them natural 'land' builders, and host to nesting birds, mudskippers (amphibious fish) and fiddler crabs. You need permission from the Durban Office of the Natal Parks Board (telephone Durban 25-1271) to explore the Beachwood mangroves, although there is ready access to the popular beach fishing area.

Bluff Nature Reserve

One of six Natal Parks Board nature reserves within 30 km of Durban, Bluff is a reed-fringed freshwater pan in the saddle between the two great sand dunes that are among Durban's familiar landmarks. To reach the reserve, take the Jacobs-Mobeni exit off the southern freeway, following Quality Street to the corner of Tara Road. Hemmed in by suburbs, this small

Above: Detail of mangrove branches, showing seeds. These mangroves, photographed in the Beachwood Mangroves Nature Reserve, produce strangely shaped roots which protrude from the water and act as 'breathing roots'. Such roots have evolved in response to the low oxygen content of the soil in which the trees grow. **Left:** A spoonbill at its nest in the Bluff Nature Reserve. The spatulate tip of this bird's bill is adapted to its unique method of feeding: it wades into the shallows with its slightly-opened bill sweeping from side to side, feeling for and catching waterborne organisms (including small fishes) with the sensitive inner surface. It also feeds by probing in the mud. **Above right:** A fiddler crab beside its hole in the Beachwood Mangroves Nature Reserve. This crab feeds by scooping up mud with its larger nipper, rolling it into balls, and extracting what food it can before discarding the mud balls.

45 ha reserve of coastal forest and grassland, with its thatched bird-watching hide, is an important centre for nature conservation education. It is open daily from sunrise to sunset.

Burman Bush Nature Reserve

Burman Bush, one of 30 Durban city parks, lies along both sides of Burman Drive and Salisbury Road, off Umgeni Road in the northern suburb of Morningside. It has picnic sites, toilets and nature walks through the 45 ha of indigenous bush. This area is rich in plant and animal life, which is readily visible once one leaves the main road and wanders along the trails that have been cleared through the bush.

However, the animal most often associated with Burman Bush is the vervet monkey (*Cercopithecus aethiops*). There are about 150 of these monkeys in the area, and the well-meaning public spends much time feeding and watching the antics of the various troops. Birds often seen are the hadeda and the African goshawk. Large specimens of forest olive (*Olea woodiana*) and bronze paper commiphera (*Commiphora harveyi*) are found along the bush trails. The reserve is open at all hours.

Clive Cheesman Nature Reserve

This 3,5 ha stretch of land running over the Kloof escarpment was donated to the Wildlife Society by Mrs Cheesman, in memory of her husband. Although it is not yet open to the public, the Society has had several 'bundu-bashing' meetings in the untouched forest that contributes so much to the reserve's appeal.

There are plans in progress to make this one of the many Natal reserves to be linked by a network of walking trails. For further information, you can write to the Natal Branch of the Wildlife Society, P.O. Box 2985, Durban 4000 (telephone Durban 21-3126).

Durban Botanic Gardens

In Queen Victoria's age of exploration and empire, aspidistras, palms and botanic gardens were the rage. Durban's 14,5 ha Botanic Gardens, established in 1849 as a tropical crops experimental site, is a proud example of 19th century enterprise and enthusiasm.

Created on the eastern slope of the Berea Ridge (so named by Captain Allan Gardiner) the gardens were administered by the Natal Agricultural and Horticultural Society.

The Durban Botanic Gardens are world-famous for the original specimens of *Encephalartos woodii*, a cycad that is still acknowledged as being the rarest plant in the world, together with a comprehensive collection of other South African cycad species.

The orchid display house is named after Ernest Thorp (the previous curator), who built it up to its position of world fame as the first 'naturalistic' display house. It is at its best during the spring months, when the orchids transform it into a riot of colour. It is open to the public from 9.30 a.m. to 12.30 p.m., and 2 p.m. to 5 p.m. throughout the year.

The car park is situated in Sydenham Road, and the gardens are easily accessible from the centre of town (a Mynah bus leaves from the Pine Street Terminus for the Botanic Gardens). The charity tea garden, which is staffed by voluntary workers, offers teas and light refreshments from 9.30 a.m. to 4.15 p.m. The Durban

Left: A colourful example of the rich and diverse flora for which the Durban Botanic Gardens has become world-renowned. **Right:** A view of the scenically spectacular gorge forming part of the Krantzkloof Nature Reserve, near Durban. **Far right:** The cycad *Encephalartos ferox*, photographed in the Durban Botanic Gardens. The seed cones of these trees may weigh as much as 34 kilograms. The kernels in most species of *Encephalartos* (and sometimes the fleshy outer parts) contain a substance which is poisonous to humans.

Botanic Gardens are open daily from 7.30 a.m. to 5.15 p.m. (16 April – 15 September) and from 7.30 to 5.45 p.m. (16 September – 15 April).

The Botanical Research Unit, incorporating the Natal Herbarium, is located at the corner of St Thomas Road and Botanic Gardens Road. Operating under the control of the Department of Agriculture, the major aims of the unit are the provision of an information service to the public (regarding identification of the indigenous flora of Natal), and continuing research into the local flora (with the aim of compiling an authoritative study of the flora of South Africa).

The Natal Herbarium contains an impressive collection of more than 80 000 specimens of dried, pressed and catalogued plants – most of which originate from Natal.

FitzSimons Snake Park
Frederick FitzSimons started the Port Elizabeth snake park and wrote the classic *Snakes of South Africa*. His son Vivian wrote the modern successor to the book, called *Snakes of Southern Africa*, while another son, Desmond, launched the FitzSimons Snake Park in 1939. Python, mamba, adder, cobra, boomslang, rattlesnake, crocodile and iguana are among over 100 indigenous and exotic species which are represented. The park's thermostatically controlled glass cabinets provide the ideal conditions for exotic snakes. There are snake demonstrations in the morning and afternoon at weekends, and also on weekdays during the holiday season. Lectures about snakes and their dangers are given in English, Afrikaans and Zulu. There is also a curio shop.

The park is on the No 1 Marine Parade bus route, diagonally opposite the Maharani Hotel. It is open from 9 a.m. to 4.30 p.m.

Harold Johnson Nature Reserve
The Tugela, or Thukela, River – the name means 'something that startles' – rises in the Mont-aux-Sources area of the Drakensberg as a 2 000 m waterfall (the highest in South Africa) and snakes its way down through the Natal Midlands, reaching the sea at Newark, 24 km north of Stanger.

The Harold Johnson Nature Reserve is sited on a grassy hill just off the highway, 24 km north of Stanger – and overlooking the sandy banks of the river mouth and Indian Ocean.

Limited camping facilities are available (there are ablution blocks with toilets and hot and cold showers) in this 104 ha coastal bush and dune reserve, one of a chain that protects some of Natal's unique floral habitats. Beautiful tree orchids proliferate, and bushpig, bushbuck and grey duiker are indigenous to the area. There is an interesting self-guided trail, and short educational trails can be arranged. For campsite reservations and further information, write to The Officer-in-Charge, Harold Johnson Nature Reserve, P.O. Box 148, Darnall 4480 (telephone Stanger 6-1574).

The reserve is open from sunrise to sunset, throughout the year. To reach it, take the turn-off 5 km south of the John Ross Bridge over the Tugela River.

Hawaan Forest
Situated on the south bank of the Umhlanga River, this 60 ha forest contains a variety of rare tree species, some interesting forest birds, and a modest population of small mammals. It is privately owned, and not open to casual visitors, but the Natal Branch of the Wildlife Society operates guided trails on request. For further information, write to The Wildlife Society, P.O. Box 2985, Durban 4000 (telephone Durban 21-3126).

Hazelmere Public Resort Nature Reserve
Although Hazelmere Dam is well known as an international waterski venue and playground for powerboats, the Natal Parks Board has managed to utilise the 304 ha area to cater for everyone's tastes. And it's possible to find a quiet corner of the dam to sail, swim or fish for the large variety of fresh-water species that have been introduced.

Waterbirds are everywhere – and a good way to see them is the 1,7 km Forest Hill Trail. This 45 minute ramble starts on the far side of Hazelmere Dam and leads through coastal lowland forest. Walkers must report to the office before embarking on the trail. Toilets are provided.

Enquiries should be addressed to The Officer-in-Charge, Hazelmere Public Resort Nature Reserve, P.O. Box 1013, Verulam 4340 (telephone Verulam 33-2315).

To reach the Dam, take the N2 north from Durban for some 14 km until you reach the Mount Edgecombe/Umhlanga turn-off. Turn left here towards Mount Edgecombe and follow this road until the Hazelmere Dam signpost, which you will spot clearly on your left after passing under a large arched bridge. The dam is 10 km from here.

Ilanda Wilds Nature Reserve

Ilanda is a lovely forested nature reserve in Amanzimtoti, about 1 km up the Amanzimtoti River. Its total area is approximately 14 hectares. One section of the northern bank is sheer rock face, and is covered with aloes, euphorbia and other indigenous rock-face flora. There are over a hundred different species of trees and shrubs in the reserve, many of which are labelled. Over 300 species of birds have been identified within its boundaries and there are plans to erect hides in the area.

A number of walking trails have been marked out through the wilds and two bridges have been built to provide safe access over the river. There is an information brochure about the reserve and the trails that it offers.

Picnicking is permitted in Ilanda Wilds, but fires are strictly prohibited.

Kenneth Stainbank Nature Reserve

Situated on a spot once known as Ndabenkulu, the Kenneth Stainbank Reserve was a gift to Natal from Kenneth Lyne Stainbank, a man of Natal pioneer stock. The Stainbank family still live in the 214 ha reserve sited along the kloofs and gorge of the Little Umhlatuzana River, 14 km from Durban City centre in Yellowwood Park (off Coedmore Road).

A unique feature of the reserve is the Kenneth Stainbank Special Trail, which has been specifically designed to let handicapped people experience the thrills of a visit to a nature reserve. Included on the trail (for which a booklet is available) is a herb garden where you can enjoy a variety of aromas, and a 'touch box' filled with a carpet of leaves and plants.

The reserve contains Durban's largest remaining coastal forest and is the only sanctuary in the city area with a viable population of the threatened red duiker. Blue duiker and bushbuck are also to be seen. Trees and shrubs include Outeniqua yellowwood, flat-crown tree, and the wild date palm (*Phoenix reclinata*), from which Durban's pioneer settlers wove hats.

Birds recorded in the reserve include purple-crested loerie, hadeda, sacred ibis, fish eagle, African jacana, spotted eagle-owl, giant kingfisher, Natal robin, fork-tailed drongo, pied wagtail, white-breasted sunbird, yellow-billed hornbill and cardinal woodpecker – some 160 species in all. Animals such as impala, giraffe, nyala and zebra have been introduced. There are two attractive picnic sites, and well signposted nature trails. There is a dam in the grassland at the top of the reserve.

The reserve contains the headquarters of the Wilderness Leadership School, whose address is P.O. Box 15036 Bellair 4006 (telephone Durban 42-8642/3). The school runs conservation education courses for groups of people, many

160

Above: A Mauritian sambar deer (stag) and its young, photographed in a small wildlife sanctuary forming part of Durban's Mitchell Park Aviary. **Right:** A yellow-billed hornbill eyes a potential meal. In the dry season it likes to eat ants and termites. Its fare also includes centipedes and scorpions. **Far right:** Camel Rock makes a fine vantage point over the Oribi Gorge Nature Reserve west of Port Shepstone.

of them youngsters (it is open to anyone over the age of 15). The courses include field trips to Timbavati in the Transvaal and to the Umfolozi Game Reserve and the Lake St Lucia region of Natal.

The reserve opens its gates at 6 a.m. and closes them at 6 p.m.

Krantzkloof Nature Reserve

Six kilometres of forest gorge along the eMolweni, or 'greetings', River, and the two-step (90 m high) Kloof Falls, comprise the exceptionally pretty Krantzkloof Nature Reserve, 24 km from Durban. Turn off the N3 at Kloof and follow the Kloof Falls road through a suburb which, while overlooking distant Durban and the Indian Ocean, resembles pure English 'county'. Visitors may eat sandwiches beside rippling streams, visit the tiny nature museum, watch a high-soaring crowned eagle on the krantz or, on the advice of the game guard, choose a nature trail through the dense gorge 'jungle'. There you may see water leguaan, grey duiker, bushbuck, otter, vervet monkey, baboon, bushpig and banded mongoose. There are also rare Natal trees, cycads, many of the 160 species of birds, and the delightful falls. The reserve is open between sunrise and sunset, throughout the year.

Madwala Nature Reserve

This small (7 ha) reserve offers visitors a look at various indigenous tree species and an extensive bird population. Because it contains the

source of the Umhlatuzana River, the reserve is generally swampy.

In the north of the reserve, beside a little stream there is a picnic site and the start of a short trail along the river. Along the trail you will see a weir, a waterfall and the large granite knuckles, or Mudwala, from which the reserve takes its name.

To reach Assagay from Durban, follow the Pietermaritzburg freeway and take the Assagay turn-off (about 30 km from Durban). Follow the road for 5 km to the junction with the old main road and turn left. Drive through Botha's Hill until you reach Heidi's Farm Stall (a local landmark) and turn left into Clement Stott Road. After about 1 km, just before you reach a stream under the road, you will see the picnic spot on the left.

The Madwala Nature Reserve is unfenced, and may be visited at any time. For further details, telephone the Assagay Health Committee at Durban 75-2997 (weekday mornings only).

Mariannwood Nature Reserve

This 14 ha area of grassland, coastal forest and clumps of bush harbours indigenous antelope and other small mammals as well as a variety of birds. Among its features are a bird enclosure and a display centre exhibiting material of educational and conservation interest.

To reach the reserve, travel southwards from Pinetown on Mariannhill Road, pass the Pinetown Licensing Bureau and turn left into Mariannhill Park. Turn left again into Holzner Road,

right into James Herbert Road and continue past Brown's School to the entrance.

It is open daily from 7a.m. to 5p.m. Facilities include a picnic and braai site and toilets.

Mitchell Park Aviary

You will find a colourful population of indigenous and exotic birds and an interesting selection of animals in the Mitchell Park Aviary. It is situated in one of Durban's oldest parks and lies adjacent to the Roberton Jameson Rose Park, in Morningside.

Among the displays are parrot, crocodile, lemur, monkey and a number of giant Seychelles tortoise which are always a delight for children.

To get to the aviary, which is open between 8a.m. and 5p.m., take a Berea Beach bus (Nos. 22 or 22A) or a Mynah bus from Musgrave Road or the Pine Street terminus. To drive there, take the western freeway out of town, bear left at Berea and turn right into Musgrave Road (follow this road to Mitchell Park).

Mpenjati Public Resort Nature Reserve

At popular Palm Beach, near Port Edward, the Natal Parks Board has established a small 23ha resort at Mpenjati River Mouth. Picnic sites and ablution facilities have been laid out on both banks and there is a children's playground on the more popular and shady north bank.

Tern and spotted thrush are found along the tranquil lagoon mouth where recreation activities include fishing and windsurfing, while wild-

life enthusiasts can enjoy a short walk along the north bank. The Natal Parks Board plan further developments at this coastal resort in the future, including a trail on the south bank. Enquiries should be addressed to The Officer-in-Charge, P.O. Box 388, Port Edward 4295 (telephone Margate 3-0447).

New Germany Commonage

A 40ha portion of the New Germany Commonage has been set aside as a reserve for the protection of the indigenous coastal grassland and patches of forest.

An educational brochure adds to the enjoyment of the reserve's beautiful self-guided trail systems. The reserve is open to the public from Wednesday to Sundays and picnic and braai sites are available. For further information write to the Borough Engineer, P.O. Box 2, New Germany, 3620, or contact the ranger (telephone Durban 72-9391).

The Natal branch of the Wildlife Society operates trails in the reserve: write to P.O. Box 2985, Durban 4000 (telephone Durban 21-3126).

North Park Nature Reserve

This 52ha reserve, in Durban's suburb of North-dene, is an attractive refuge. It lies 20km from the city centre at the end of Anderson Road, off Sarnia Road, and consists of a slice of coastal lowland forest as yet unclaimed by sugarcane or concrete. The area is rich in bird life. Paths

have been laid out, and picnic sites and braai facilities are available. It is open during daylight hours (throughout the year).

Oribi Gorge Nature Reserve

There are 73 river estuaries in Natal. From the Tugela north of Durban down to Port Edward on the Transkei border 250km to the south, the coast is sliced through by 20 major watercourses and innumerable streams. In the coastal hinterland the rivers have, over millennia, cut rugged gorges through krantz and kloof in their rush to the sea. It is in these precipitous gorges that Natal's once widespread forests have found their last refuge. The largest and most spectacular of these is the 24km long, 5km wide, 400m deep Oribi Gorge.

The 1837ha reserve along the Umzimkulwana River lies 21km west of Port Shepstone on the Harding road. The forests and sandstone cliffs hide bushbuck, vervet and samango monkey, grey duiker, blue duiker, leopard, water leguaan and innumerable birds.

The turn-off to the Oribi Gorge Hotel is 12km from Port Shepstone and is the start of a 29km scenic drive which offers dramatic views of the converging Umzimkulu and Umzimkulwana gorges. Ending at the nature reserve's hutted camp, the landmarks include the striking rock formations of Baboon's Castle and the Pulpit. Visitors may undertake a variety of pleasant walks and climbs, and self-guided trails.

ORIBI GORGE AT A GLANCE

When to go Oribi is worth a visit at any time of the year (because it is traversed by a public road, the normal opening and closing times are not enforced). To take up your reserved accommodation, you should arrive before 4.30 p.m.

Reservations To book huts write to The Reservations Officer, Natal Parks Board, P.O. Box 662, Pietermaritzburg 3200 (telephone 47-1981).

Getting there Be sure to follow the route marked 'Nature Reserve'. It is 21km along the Harding road from Port Shepstone, which is 128km from Durban.

Accommodation The Natal Parks Board 'Hutted Camp' consists of six three-bedded fully equipped

and serviced huts, an ablution block and a seven-bedded cottage. There are no camping facilities in the reserve.

Eating and drinking Bring your own food and drink to the hutted camp; Natal Parks Board attendants will prepare it for you. There is a braai site at the camp for those who wish to prepare their own food and a picnic site with ablution and braai facilities has been established in the gorge.

Getting around You can drive right down into the Oribi Gorge and up again a distance of 8km from the huts. The 29km circular drive through and around the gorge is worthwhile. Nature walks have been mapped out, and you can stop at a farm for excellent views of the Oribi Heads, Horseshoe Bend and the Overhanging Rock.

Wildlife There are forest creatures such as bushbuck, blue duiker and grey duiker (occasionally leopard). The nearly 200 species of birds include seven eagle and five kingfisher species.

Special precautions There is bilharzia in the river and visitors picnicking on the river bank are advised not to swim or paddle in the water. Fire in a forest gorge like Oribi can be devastating; visitors should be careful with cigarettes.

Left: Brightly coloured anenomes and coralline form a lustrous underwater garden on the Natal coast. **Above:** A family of dwarf mongooses reclines on a perch in the open. These gregarious little animals live in colonies which can number up to 30 members. Like other types of mongoose, the dwarf species includes snakes in its diet, the snake being attacked and killed in a communal effort. **Right:** A zebra crosses a track in the Vernon Crookes Nature Reserve.

Palmiet Nature Reserve

This 50 ha municipal nature reserve is situated in the rugged Palmiet River valley. Its wooded krantzes, riverine forest and open grassland feature over 140 different indigenous trees and about 150 bird species. The name Palmiet is derived from the river plant *Prionium serratum*, which has largely disappeared in this valley through human disturbance. Mammal life is not well represented, but visitors are occasionally rewarded with glimpses of animals such as vervet monkey, duiker and water mongoose.

There are 7 km of hiking trails in the reserve. It is planned to link these trails to the proposed Durban Metropolitan Hiking Trails network, which will join many of the nature reserves between Durban and Pietermaritzburg. Approximately 10 000 people (including many drawn from schools and other educational institutions) visit the reserve each year. A three-hour nature trail is conducted on the first Sunday of the month (leaving at 9 a.m. from People's Chemist in Jan Hofmeyr Road, Westville). In the winter the popular Sunset Trails include a braai at the Cascade Indaba site on the Palmiet River, and a return walk in the dark.

The reserve is open daily (to all races) between sunrise and sunset. To reach it, take the western freeway (N3) to Pietermaritzburg as far
162

as the Westville interchange. Follow St James Avenue for 1 km, turn right into Jan Hofmeyr Road at Hofmeyr Heights Shopping Centre (opposite Westville Hotel) and turn left into David McLean Drive: the reserve entrance is signposted at the end of this road.

Palmiet Nature Reserve is a Borough of Westville nature reserve, and is managed by a committee of the Wildlife Society.

Paradise Valley Nature Reserve

One of Durban's many pleasant picnic spots, the 28 ha Paradise Valley reserve is at the New Germany turn-off, 18 km along the main Durban to Johannesburg (N3) highway. A coastal, evergreen forested valley, Paradise Valley offers forest walks, abundant bird life and a waterfall on the Umbilo River. Wildlife includes bushbuck, grey duiker, blue duiker, vervet monkey and dassie.

Of historical interest in the reserve is an old water works which used to supply water to Durban. As always in Natal, visitors should be careful of bilharzia. The reserve is open from sunrise to sunset, throughout the year.

Pigeon Valley Park

A small reserve next to the Durban campus of Natal University, Pigeon Valley preserves one

of the last remaining stretches of indigenous coastal forest (Stella bush vegetation) in the Durban area. Of the 75 species of trees here, the most valuable are the rare Natal elm (*Celtis mildbraedii*) and the fluted milkwood (*Chrysophyllum vindifolium*). Wildlife includes vervet monkey, slender mongoose and a vast and colourful array of birds, more notable of which are the Natal robin, purple-crested loerie, black flycatcher and spotted thrush.

There are picnic sites. The reserve is open on weekdays only from 7.10 a.m. to 4.30 p.m. To get there from Durban city, take the western freeway and then turn left along South Ridge Road for about 2,5 kilometres.

Sea World, Durban

The aquarium and dolphinarium complex, situated at the point where West Street meets the 'Golden Mile' of the beachfront, is a major attraction for local and overseas visitors.

Sea World offers a close encounter with thousands of intriguing and exquisite creatures gathered mainly from the coastline of Natal. Twice a day (at 11 a.m. and 3 p.m.) the scuba diver feeds the fish in the 800 000ℓ main fish tank. The shark tank, originally built for research purposes, houses one of the world's finest displays of large sharks.

In the dolphinarium a spectacular dolphin, seal and penguin show is presented several times a day, while behind the scenes many stranded and injured mammals are rehabilitated annually.

Sea World is an important part of the South African Association for Marine Biological Research, a non-profit organisation committed to the preservation and wise use of our marine resources. Entrance fees pay for research, undertaken by the Oceanographic Research Institute, into sharks, angling fish, prawns, crayfish, mussels and other vital resources.

Sea World is open daily from 9 a.m. to 9 p.m. (telephone Durban 37-4079).

If sharks interest you, visit the Natal Anti-Shark Measures Board, Umhlanga Rocks Drive, Umhlanga on a Wednesday at 2.30 p.m. for a free lecture and film.

Springside Nature Reserve

A variety of small mammals (including vervet monkey and duiker) and nearly 60 bird species may be seen in this 21 ha reserve, which is controlled by the Hillcrest Town Board. The vegetation is a blend of coastal bush and temperate forest.

There are no facilities in the reserve, and visitors may enter at any time.

Trafalgar Marine Reserve

The 51 km of palm and banana-fringed coast running from south of Port Shepstone to the Transkei border offers a string of 19 holiday resorts whose names would delight Britannia: Margate, Ramsgate, Southbroom, Portobello Beach, Port Edward, Trafalgar.

The last, from the north bank of the Mpenjati River to the south side of Centre Rocks at Marina Beach and stretching 500 m out to sea, is a Natal Parks Board marine reserve – the second, after St Lucia, to be declared along the Natal coast. Swimming and rod and line angling are still permitted but bait collecting is prohibited and the shellfish may not be touched.

Treasure Beach Environmental Centre

This Wildlife Society Education Centre lies at the southern end of Durban's Bluff amid 16 ha of protected coastal grassland and rocky shore. The area is indeed a treasure-house. Pools teem with fish while inland, coastal and dune forest wait to be explored.

Coastal grassland found at Treasure Beach is one of the last examples in Natal. While industry and housing have made severe inroads on natural vegetation along the coast elsewhere, Treasure Beach boasts an unspoilt 'climax' community. This is the ultimate state of equilibrium that can be reached by a mature, vegetation community.

Visitors are welcome to wander through the grassland (at its best between August and September), but visits to the centre must be arranged in advance. Courses are held on environmental education and conducted tours may be arranged.

Details can by obtained from the Treasure Beach Project, 835 Marine Drive, Bluff 4052. (telephone Durban 47-8507/8).

Treasure Beach is part of a proposed reserve which one day will include the Happy Valley Bird Sanctuary and Reunion Rocks area, while a thin strip of coastal forest will connect it to the mangroves at Isipingo Estuary. The proposed reserve will adjoin the Bluff Nature Reserve.

Umhlanga Lagoon Nature Reserve

Umhlanga lagoon is one of Natal's river estuaries that has escaped the depredations of man, and an attractive (26 ha) nature reserve embraces the lagoon area to the east of the national road. It is situated east of the highway about 17 km from Durban.

Effective land management in the Umhlanga catchment area has enabled a rich bird habitat to survive. A historically important shell midden lies within this area. Contact the Umhlanga Branch of the Wildlife Society for details on the short Tegwaan Trail and the 16 km Umhlanga Trail. The reserve is open from sunrise to sunset.

Umtamvuna Nature Reserve

There is a nesting colony of up to 75 Cape vulture in the high precipices of this reserve, situated along the Natal-Transkei border. It is an apt habitat for the large carrion birds whose droppings streak the cliff faces.

This 3 257 ha Natal Parks Board's reserve is home to black-backed jackal, large spotted genet, baboon, reedbuck, bushbuck, blue duiker, grey duiker, serval, oribi, samango monkey, leopard and 80 species of birds. It also offers a kaleidoscope of wild mountain flowers, ferns and lichens. There are several walking trails. To reach the reserve, turn inland at the Port Edward intersection and follow the signs to the entrance (8 km distant). From 1 April to 31 August, the gates open at 7 a.m. and close at 5 p.m. During the rest of the year, they open at 6 a.m. and close at 6 p.m.

Uvongo River Nature Reserve

Natal's rivers tend to be muddy, but there is one, the Uvongo, that runs through cleansing sandstone, fresh and pure, to the sea. The river actually reaches the ocean in a final plunge over a 23 m high waterfall right into a beach side lagoon. Jagged cliffs flank part of the kilometre-long section of the river that forms this community-sponsored reserve at Uvongo village on the south coast, 12 km south of Port Shepstone.

Songbirds accompany visitors as they walk along the cool river-bank forest track, and wildflowers such as the fire lily (*Cyrtanthus*) and September bells (*Rothmannia globosa*) delight the eye. There are also pleasant picnic sites. The two entrances are Edward Avenue for the south bank and Marine Drive for the north. It is open from sunrise to sunset. A booklet on the reserve is available from local chemists.

Vernon Crookes Nature Reserve

The Vernon Crookes reserve lies 8 km north of Umzinto, which in turn is 8 km west of the N2 highway along the Ixopo road. Cane fields and blue gum plantations surround the reserve and tantalisingly separate its 2 198 ha upland grassland and three wooded valleys from equally lush but privately owned indigenous forest on the slopes of nearby hills. The plentiful game includes porcupine, blue wildebeest, eland, nyala, impala, bushbuck, zebra, four species of mongoose and the black-backed jackal.

The bird life in this reserve is a delight and, in September and October, the reserve's blaze of wild flowers almost rivals the displays in Namaqualand. A variety of pleasant drives and picnic sites are available, and conducted walking tours may be arranged with The Officer-in-Charge (telephone Umzinto 4-4222 between 5 p.m. and 7 p.m.). The reserve is open from sunrise to sunset.

Pitons and potholes

Discovering Southern Africa's mountains can be an exciting and fulfilling experience. The majestic peaks of the Drakensberg, the sheer crags of Table Mountain, the daunting Spitzkoppe of Namibia – all these and many more mountains offer the climber an unforgettable adventure.

Your choice of mountain is dictated by several factors, including experience, the type of rock face, equipment available, weather conditions, and your state of fitness. Experienced climbers never relax their rules on safety: they are inviolate and based on sound principles that have saved many lives.

Some of the more important rules are listed below:

● Never climb alone. You will usually find someone willing to accompany you.

● Let someone know where you will be climbing, and what time you expect to return. This will aid rescuers should you get into difficulties.

● Become fit before you start climbing. This is a strenuous activity, and if your strength gives way in a difficult situation it could be disastrous.

● Do not be too ambitious when you start. Build experience by tackling relatively easy climbs, and wherever possible be guided by someone who has done it before. Never be afraid to ask for advice.

● Practise your climbing technique on easier rocks before attempting a sheer face. Your body should be more or less upright and you should move only one leg or hand at a time, thus keeping yourself anchored at three points throughout the climb. Test holds before trusting your weight to them, and remember to watch where you are putting your feet. Experts recommend a rhythmic movement up the rock face, with your boot heels pointed down to provide a better grip.

● Plan your climb. Examine the entire route and decide whether it falls within your capabilities. On a pitch, work out three or four moves in advance.

● Do not expose yourself to risk (and expend all your energy too soon) by climbing too fast. Stay in balance where possible, keep your hands low and allow your legs to do most of the hard work.

Climbers should take care not to dislodge rocks and stones on a mountain – they could kill or injure a climber below. If, however, you do dislodge a rock, shout *Below! Rocks!* to warn others in the vicinity. Another danger faced by the novice is complacency: do not allow your

On Table Mountain. Experienced rock climbers never take chances: all mountains are potentially dangerous. Good climbing technique and the use of ropes and other equipment can greatly reduce the danger, however, as will your choice of climb: avoid a rock face that clearly calls for more experience.

high spirits following a successful climb to affect your concentration when making the descent.

It is always important to find out whether you need a permit before you enter a wilderness or climbing area. It would be a good idea to approach the Mountain Club of South Africa, which has sections in most major centres (including Windhoek).

These organisations have a wealth of experience at their disposal, and would be glad to offer advice and practical help.

Before purchasing any equipment, you should be taken up several times by experienced cragsmen, and you should be sure that rock climbing is for you. Your initial kit should consist of helmet, Kernmantel rope (45 m x 11 mm), climbing harness, four long tape slings, six karabiners (including two of the screwgate type) and rock-climbing boots. If necessary, you could make do without the boots and climbing harness, and use soled 'tackies' and a waist loop.

The realm of the troglodyte

Although caving is a relatively little-known pastime in Southern Africa, there is a growing body of enthusiasts who can think of nothing more enjoyable than spending a weekend underground. Caves are nature's time capsules, harbouring creatures that may not have been seen on the earth's surface for many thousands, possibly millions of years. They also contain some of the world's most spectacular scenery.

Although large cave systems such as the Cango Caves near Oudtshoorn and the Sterkfontein Caves near Krugersdorp are familiar to many thousands of visitors, there are also dozens of smaller grottos and potholes dotted about the country which are known only to those people who explore caves for sport.

Caving requires relatively little special equipment, but you should never attempt to explore a cave or pothole without some basic essentials. Experienced cavers choose their gear with care and take the safety rules very seriously.

The conservation aspect of caving is also very important.

You should treat every cave as the natural treasure that it is, taking care not to disturb formations, and leaving no trace of your passage. The latter rule is all-important: there is nothing more infuriating for a caver than the discovery of debris such as old batteries or empty food cans in what he believed was an unspoilt (and hopefully unexplored) cavern.

Never break off stalactites, stalagmites or other fragile formations to take out as souvenirs, and *never ever* scrawl your initials on a cave wall, no matter how strong your desire for recognition.

Do not pollute cave water in any way or interfere with signs of early human or animal population.

Remember, too, that all land is owned by someone (either an individual, local authority

The correct equipment is crucial for safe and successful rock climbing, and helmet, boots and karabiners (**above left**) should be chosen with care. While beginners working on modest outcrops can make do with lightweight rubber-soled boots, the more serious climber should buy a pair of close-fitting, rigid boots specially designed for this purpose. Karabiners (D-shaped metal snaplinks) should be of a good make,

and capable of withstanding a load of at least 2 000 kg (take care to avoid three-way loading). Kernmantel rope (**above right**), while more expensive than other types, is a tough rope and because of its flexibility and other advantages, is considered suitable for the more advanced rock climber. The climbing harness (illustrated above) is used by some climbers to attach themselves to the main rope.

or government), so it is almost always necessary to obtain permission before you set out on a caving expedition.

How to survive underground

Caving can be dangerous, and you should always take the advice of experienced cavers when exploring unfamiliar caverns. Sudden storms can quickly flood some caves so you should avoid venturing underground if there is any threat of bad weather.

However, if you are determined to explore a cave and you are not sure of the weather, always leave one person 'on guard' at the entrance to warn of rain.

These simple rules will help you to explore caves in safety:

● You should have at least two companions when venturing underground.

● Make sure that someone on the surface knows which cave you are exploring, and when you expect to return.

● Take enough drinking water, and drink every two hours whether you feel thirsty or not. You may also drink underground water – but make sure it is not polluted.

● Have a good breakfast before setting out. You will be working hard, and you will need all the energy you can build up. Choose your day's food carefully to ensure that you get enough protein, fat, carbohydrates and essential vitamins and minerals. Clubs often recommend that a group carries an additional emergency food pack containing such items as glucose tablets, oatmeal, chocolate and similar 'quick-energy' foods.

● If you become lost or trapped in a cave, do not panic. Use your whistle to call your companions or rescuers – you will be able to blow it for longer than you can shout. Keep warm and avoid unnecessary movement (this is particularly important where there is a limited supply of oxygen).

● If you are exploring an unusually complicated cave system, it would be a good idea to mark your route with shiny strips of adhesive tape as you go. These must be removed as you leave the cave.

Useful addresses and where to go

There are several speleological groups and societies in Southern Africa, and you will find them willing to supply information and practical help. Contact the South African Speleological Association at P.O. Box 4812, Cape Town 8000 or P.O. Box 6166, Johannesburg 2000.

Left: A large chamber in the Wolkberg Caves, in the northern Transvaal. Although there are many such chambers in Southern Africa's cave systems, cavers spend much of their time in more cramped circumstances. **Right:** A caver emerges from a water-filled tunnel in a sandstone cave. Personal caving equipment includes a helmet, electric or carbide lamp, small shock-proof torch, overalls, woollen socks, sturdy boots with steel toe-caps, elbow and knee pads, waistband or shoulder/chest harness, strong belt, whistle, wristwatch with luminous or illuminated face, knife, small first-aid kit, equipment bag, and food and water. Group equipment includes safety ropes, karabiners, wire ladders and a first-aid kit.

Seeking a billion-year bounty

A lone figure bends down, picks up a dust-covered rock and taps it gingerly with a sharp-pointed hammer. The rock splits in two – and the happy 'rockhound' gazes upon an array of crystals exposed to the air for the first time in thousands of millions of years.

Southern Africa is a veritable treasure-house of rocks and minerals, attracting amateur rock collectors (or 'rockhounds') from all over the world. The seemingly endless wastes of the Namib, the scrubby plains of the Karoo and northern Cape, the slopes of the Drakensberg, the river beds of the Cape – there are surprises everywhere, and enthusiasts venture into caves, quarries and even abandoned mines in their search for specimens.

What is the difference between a mineral and a rock? A mineral is not typical of the chemistry of living things – it is inorganic – and it occurs naturally. Each type of mineral has a unique composition and is homogeneous – one part is exactly the same as another. With the exception of mercury, or 'quicksilver', all minerals are solid.

A rock is a solid material made up of mineral grains. It may consist of a single mineral (such as limestone, which is composed entirely of calcium carbonate), or of several minerals (such as granite, which usually contains quartz, mica and feldspar). The proportion of the different mineral grains varies between one rock sample and another. Thus there are endless varieties of rock composition – the most common are given names and classified by geologists into three main groups, igneous, sedimentary and metamorphic, according to the way in which they were formed.

Collecting and displaying your specimens can be a rewarding exercise, and once bitten, you are likely to be a collector for life.

A good quality hammer – the geologist's type is ideal – is an essential item, and the rest of the 'rockhound's' equipment is simple and inexpensive. If you are collecting at a quarry or mine dump, where material has already been broken, you will need only a pile of old newspapers for wrapping your specimens, a notebook and pencil, labels, and a strong bag.

Other basic equipment should include a chisel and a magnifying glass. It may be advisable to buy a pair of thick gloves, and goggles to protect your eyes from flying rock-chips. Some collectors also carry a reference book.

Select your specimens carefully. From several that seem suitable keep only one or two.

Members of the South African Archaeological Society explore a cave in the Cape Point Nature Reserve. Caves are often a rich source of information on prehistoric man as well as rocks and minerals — but it should be remembered that it is illegal to remove or damage any archaeological material. Finds should be reported to the nearest museum.

Remember that the rock or mineral specimen you remove will never be replaced. Fist-sized or smaller specimens are ideal. If necessary, and if it will not spoil a natural symmetry, use your hammer to trim the specimen – a few light blows, placed correctly, are usually all that is required.

Wrap each specimen tightly in newspaper, with a numbered label that corresponds with an entry in your notebook. Exposed crystal surfaces should be covered with cotton wool or crumpled newspaper before being wrapped. A delicate mineral specimen should be embedded in cotton wool and placed in a cardboard box.

Classifying and labelling your specimens
Ensure that each label remains with its specimen, and that you have recorded precise details about the site you have been working. *Even the rarest specimen loses its value if the locality from which it came is not known.*

Skill in identifying rocks and minerals comes only with experience. A good field guide will help: take it with you on hikes and holidays. It would also be useful to visit your local museum to familiarise yourself with the minerals and rocks you could expect to find.

A good system of labelling is to put a small spot of quick-drying white paint on an inconspicuous part of the specimen. When the paint is dry, add the number with black indian ink. The number can then be referred to in your list-book or index cards when full details are required.

Classification goes a step beyond mere identification. It involves reference to a standard chemical system showing the relationship between the various species, or families, of rocks and minerals. If you are in doubt about a particular specimen, a more experienced collector may be able to help. Otherwise you could enquire at the geology department of the nearest museum or university.

If you are intending to study the subject in greater detail, it would be a good idea to join a society. There are small but enthusiastic groups in several cities whose members go on organised field trips collecting specimens and learning about geological formations and their mineral content. Some people are interested in scientific collections, and may concentrate on fine crystals. Others may collect material which can be faceted or polished, and go on to learn silversmithing – enabling them to design and set their own jewellery.

The activities of the various clubs in South Africa are co-ordinated by the Federation of South African Gem and Mineral Societies. Each year, members from affiliated societies meet to talk about their hobby and swop specimens. The federation also publishes an official journal, the *South African Lapidary Magazine*.

For further information. write to the federation's Satour Liaison Officer, Mr Horst Windisch, at 30 Van Wouw Street, Groenkloof, Pretoria 0181.

Newly acquired specimens, or those not kept in a closed display-case, may need to be dusted and cleaned. Soap, water and a brush are suitable for the coarser types. More delicate

1 Amethyst, a crystalline quartz, is one of Southern Africa's most popular gemstones. It occurs in granite.
2 Blue tiger's eye is a crystallised quartz derived mostly from an asbestos mineral called crocidolite.
3 Jasper, a variety of chalcedony, is usually coloured red. In its brecciated form (above) it is sometimes called zylite. 4 Sodalite, a mineral related to feldspar, is typically coloured blue, interlaced with a colourless streak. 5 Rose quartz receives its characteristic colouring from traces of titanium.
6 Amazonite is massive microline feldspar, ideally a green gemstone with scattered white flecks. 7 Picture jasper, another popular gemstone. 8 Blue lace agate. 9 Verdite is a soft, brilliantly-coloured stone occurring in the Barberton and Jamestown districts. 10 Yellow tiger's eye. This mineral is unique to South Africa. 11 Smoky quartz, one of the many varieties of this crystal. 12 Sogdianite, a very valuable gemstone found only recently in South Africa.

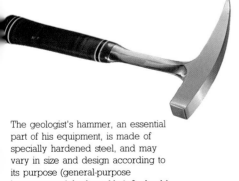

The geologist's hammer, an essential part of his equipment, is made of specially hardened steel, and may vary in size and design according to its purpose (general-purpose hammers weigh about 1 kg). It should be used sparingly to avoid damage to delicate rock features, to avoid an accumulation of sharp debris, which may be harmful to animals, and because there is a danger of injury from chips of rock safety glasses or goggles are recommended.

specimens can be carefully rinsed in luke-warm water. Minerals such as halite (rock salt) will dissolve in water, and should be washed in benzine. Gypsum crystals – such as the 'desert rose' – react with soap and may become covered with a whitish film that will ruin their appearance. Never dry your specimens by artificial heat or in direct sunlight.

Very small crystals can be stored in glass tubes. Use paint and indian ink to label the tubes in the same way as the larger specimens. Small specimens which are readily soluble in water can also be stored in tubes, but collectors should remember to exclude the air by sealing the stoppers with wax. Most chemists should be able to provide you with tubes and stoppers of various diameters. However you decide to display your rocks and minerals, they will represent small but fascinating clues to the secrets of the earth's crust – a billion-year-old bounty.

Because their explorations occasionally take rockhounds into remote areas, construction and excavation sites, and other potentially dangerous situations, certain safety rules should always be observed.
1 Never climb alone or enter a deep cave without a companion.
2 Always tell someone where you are going, and when you expect to return.
3 Equip yourself with a hat (a hard hat is obligatory on construction sites), strong shoes, and a first-aid kit.
4 In remote areas, do not forget your map and compass. Do not trespass.
5 Familiarise yourself with the laws which relate to collecting: some caves are totally protected, as are meteorites (if you discover one, report it to the nearest museum). It is illegal to be in possession of uncut diamonds, and you must report any finds to the police – who will inform the claim-holder.

TRANSKEI AND EASTERN CAPE

A land of rolling hills, summer thunderstorms on the mountains, seemingly endless sweeps of grassland, rocky coves and bleached sea-sand – the eastern Cape is all this and more. Like many parts of Southern Africa, it is a place of contrast: the once-threatened mountain zebra grazes among stunted Karoo shrubs; samango monkeys inhabit the extensive forests; seabirds wheel over the 250km of high cliffs, long beaches and pounding seas of Transkei's Wild Coast.

There is much for the visitor in this, the land of the Xhosa. In the Auckland Nature Reserve, part of the Hogsback State Forest, you may spot a crowned eagle or jackal buzzard. You can learn about snakes at the Port Elizabeth Snake Park, and marvel at the antics of dolphins in the city's famous oceanarium. A visit to the Addo Elephant National Park, between the Zuurberg and the Sundays River Valley, will give you a glimpse of rhinoceros, red hartebeest, buffalo and, of course, elephant.

The eastern Cape has scores of game parks, nature reserves and modest but well-run sanctuaries spread over a wide area. For those who prefer to explore with backpacks, there are hiking trails leading through spectacularly beautiful countryside; for those seeking creature comforts on safari, a choice of accommodation in huts, bungalows and chalets. Variety is the essence of this region: the eastern Cape has something of everything.

A giant mud crab (*Scylla serrata*) waves its nippers in a threatening posture among the aerial roots of a mangrove on Transkei's rugged and beautiful Wild Coast.

Across the Kei

Lying between the Great Kei and Umtamvuna rivers, Transkei is traversed by the N2 highway, which runs roughly parallel to the coast at an average distance of some 60 km from the sea. Most of the conservation areas and scenic attractions are to be found only after venturing down some of the many secondary roads which link the N2 to the beautiful Wild Coast, washed by the warm waters of the Indian Ocean.

The peak visiting periods in Transkei are the Easter holidays, and the months June to July, and December to January. Nature reserves are controlled by the Transkei Department of Agriculture and Forestry, and reservations should be made at least 12 months in advance.

Cwebe Nature Reserve

This reserve lies between the Bashee and Suku river mouths in the Elliotdale district. It is now under development and closed to the public, but when completed will have bungalows and campsites. The Haven Hotel is situated inside the reserve. This area is transitional between the temperate and subtropical forest types, and is rich in indigenous flora and small fauna. There are plans to re-introduce animals which previously occurred in the area.

Dwesa Nature Reserve

This reserve lies on one of the most beautiful and unspoilt stretches of coastline in Africa with the rest camp blending so well into the forest that you could pass close by and not see it.

Dwesa was Transkei's first nature reserve and dates back to 1893. It lies in the Willowvale district and is reached from Idutywa by a 90 km gravel road. The road is usually in good condition, except just after heavy rains.

There are five bungalows with single bedrooms, to accommodate four or five people each, and three bungalows have double bedrooms. The bungalows are fully equipped with gas lighting, stove and refrigerator, as well as crockery, cutlery and bedding. Hot and cold water are laid on. You are not permitted to collect bait or crayfish in the reserve.

There are magnificent views from all of the bungalows, some of which are on stilts, with verandahs jutting out to within reach of the forest canopy. The rest camp is only about 40 m from the beach which forms the southern boundary of this 5 700 ha reserve (the sweep of the Bashee River forms the northern boundary). The terrain includes beaches, open grassland and indigenous forests of yellowwood, Cape ebony and white stinkwood, all garlanded by creepers.

Fishing is allowed in the areas indicated by the official in charge. Fish also flourish in the many rivulets which rise in the forests and form beautiful, unpolluted estuaries. There is no limit to the number of fish which may be caught in the sea with rod and line, but anglers are requested not to catch more than they can carry and use. Spearfishing is prohibited in inland and tidal waters.

There are no roads through the reserve area, but many paths lead through the forest from the camp. Game may be seen even on the beach, and includes blesbok, eland, red hartebeest, buffalo, white rhino, bushbuck, duiker and warthog. A small number of crocodile has been re-introduced, and the narina trogon or bosloerie, and rare mangrove kingfisher are among the many bird species. There is no shop in the reserve, and supplies should be obtained in advance. The reserve is open from 6 a.m. to 6 p.m.

Above: A hand-coloured lithograph by the 19th-century soldier and amateur naturalist Henry Butler, entitled 'The eland blown. Tsitse River'. Soon after shooting the eland, Butler was caught by a severe storm, and was forced to take shelter beneath the antelope's skin — where he passed the night, cold and miserable. In the preface to a volume of lithographs published in 1841, Butler said one of his objects in producing the book was to 'relieve the dreariness of two years' residence upon a barbarian frontier'.
Left: A lonely stretch of beach on the Wild Coast, a magnificent and unspoilt part of Transkei. Clusters of wild banana trees (Strelitzia nicolai) can be seen in the background.
Right: A tricolour tiger moth (Dionychopus amasis).

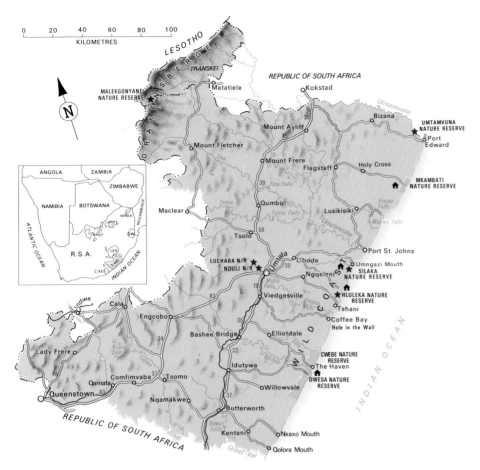

To make a reservation, you should write to the Transkei Nature Conservation Division, Department of Agriculture and Forestry, Private Bag X5002, Umtata, Transkei (telephone Umtata 2-4322 or 24-9309).

Hluleka Nature Reserve

Like Dwesa, Hluleka Nature Reserve includes stretches of unspoilt beach in its area of some 772 hectares. It is 90 km from Umtata, and is reached by taking the tarred road east for some 28 km to Libode. The remainder of the route is along good gravel roads, and is quite well signposted. The reserve has 12 comfortable wooden chalets which can accommodate up to six people each. The chalets are fully furnished and equipped, but the nearest shop lies outside the reserve and can supply only bread, milk and a limited range of non-perishable foods. The chalets blend well into the picturesque surroundings and are only about 20 m from the beach.

Firewood is available from the Nature Conservation Officer and cooking-fires may be made only in allocated places. Fishing is allowed in the reserve. (Transkei's coast is renowned for its angling, providing enthusiasts with good sport as well as good eating.) You are not permitted to collect your own bait or crayfish.

The reserve is open throughout the year from 6 a.m. to 6 p.m. Day visitors need not book in advance. Well-laid and maintained paths lead through most parts of this picturesque reserve, and among the animals to be seen are blue wildebeest, eland, zebra and impala. During spring and summer, the air is bright with butterflies, and bird life is prolific throughout the year.

For more information and bookings write to the Transkei Nature Conservation Division, Department of Agriculture and Forestry, Private Bag X5002, Umtata, Transkei (telephone Umtata 2-4322 or 24-9309).

Luchaba Nature Reserve

Situated at the southern tip of Umtata Dam, this 400 ha reserve and adjoining recreation area provides a fascinating wildlife experience despite being only a few kilometres from Transkei's principal city.

Tall grassland and marsh area in the reserve provide breeding sites for crowned crane, marsh owl, marsh harrier and rare Stanley's bustard. Standing 1 m high, these bustard are an impressive sight, particularly males during courtship, which will try to impress the female, and thwart male competition, by puffing their chest feathers into a huge ball.

The reserve has been stocked with Burchell's zebra, blesbok and red hartebeest, which can often be seen grazing near the dam.

The recreational area, adjoining the reserve, is open daily for watersport and fishing. There is no overnight accommodation. For further en-

Far left: The Natal black snake is usually confined to damp localities in Transkei. Although its bite can produce unpleasant reactions, fatalities have not been recorded. In his informative and often amusing book, *The Reptiles and Amphibians of Southern Africa*, Dr Walter Rose explains the snake's remarkable flexibility: 'The extreme litheness of a snake is due to the structure of the vertebral column, which consists of a great number, from 150 to 500, of small bones beautifully fitted together on the ball socket principle, so as to give a maximum of flexibility and strength.' **Left above:** 'Waterfall Bluff' on the Transkei Wild Coast, where a river tumbles into the Indian Ocean from a high cliff. **Left below:** The tree hibiscus (*Hibiscus tiliaceus*), which bears these large yellow flowers (deepening to orange as they mature), is found at river mouths along the Transkei coast (and in Natal). **Right:** Grassy hills sweep down to the sea at Dwesa Nature Reserve, one of the most scenic parts of the Southern African coastline. Indigenous forests of yellowwood, Cape ebony and white stinkwood flourish here.

HLULEKA AT A GLANCE

When to go You can visit the reserve throughout the year from 6 a.m. to 6 p.m. Day visitors need not book in advance.

Reservations and information For information and bookings write to the Transkei Nature Conservation Division, Department of Agriculture and Forestry, Private Bag X5002, Umtata, Transkei (telephone Umtata 2-4322 or 24-9309).

Getting there The reserve is 90 km from Umtata, and you can reach it by taking the tarred road east for some 28 km to Libode.

Accommodation Lying about 20 m from the beach are 12 comfortable wooden chalets which can accommodate up to six people each. The chalets are fully furnished and equipped.

Eating and drinking There are no restaurant facilities at Hluleka. The nearest shop lies outside the reserve and can supply only bread, milk and a limited range of foods, so take your own provisions.

Getting around Hluleka is a hiker's paradise. Neat paths lead through most parts of the reserve.

Wildlife You can see blue wildebeest, eland, zebra and impala. Bird life is prolific throughout the year.

Fishing Apart from various sharks you can catch kob, grunter and elf at Hluleka.

quiries write to the Transkei Nature Conservation Division, Department of Agriculture and Forestry, Private Bag X5002, Umtata, Transkei (telephone Umtata 2-4322 or 24-9309).

Malekgonyane Nature Reserve

Near the tail-end of the Drakensberg range, on Lesotho's southern border, lies Malekgonyane reserve (formerly called Ongeluksnek), a 10 000 ha delight of montane grassland, streams and imposing cliffs. In spring the slopes of this mountain reserve are transformed from their golden-brown winter hues into a luxurious carpet of green covered by gladiolus, pelargonium, red-hot pokers and flame-red fire-lilies.

Bird life is spectacular and black eagle, jackal buzzard, lanner falcon, Cape vulture, and bearded vulture (lammergeyer) glide overhead. Wherever bearded vulture are found look for 'bone-breaking sites' or ossuaries. The vultures fly to a great height and drop bones, with considerable accuracy, onto the rocks until the bone fragments are small enough to swallow. Unfortunately, as with many raptors, bearded vultures have suffered over the years as lack of carcasses have inevitably driven them to prey on the remains of domestic animals. Many farmers reacted – thinking the birds were a threat to their

livestock – by poisoning these carcasses. Over the years this practice severely decimated the numbers of Cape and bearded vulture. Both species are now protected.

Malekgonyane Nature Reserve will be opened to the public when developments are completed. A rest camp is planned, which will give access to mountain walks, clear streams, quiet pools and tumbling waterfalls. Grey rhebok, klipspringer and baboon are common, and oribi and eland will be introduced.

For enquiries write to the Transkei Nature Conservation Division, Department of Agriculture and Forestry, Private Bag X5002, Umtata, Transkei (telephone Umtata 2-4322 or 24-9309).

Mkambati Game Reserve

The highlights of Mkambati, one of Transkei's finest natural treasures, are isolated beaches, gurgling waterfalls, wide river mouths and deeply incised, forested ravines. The reserve's rocky coastline extends 10 km between the Msikaba and Mtentu rivers, including parts of Pondoland's most scenic and secret coast. Its unique swamp forest, open grassland and ravines hide a variety of fascinating life-forms, including the Mkambati palm (*Jubaeopsis caffra*) which grows only beside the valleys of these two great rivers.

The wide and wooded Msikaba River reaches depths of 33 m in places, making it by far the largest river in the reserve. Its sandy mouth, frequented by busy-looking tern is ideal for walking, looking for shells or simply being alone and collecting your thoughts. Adventurous visitors may also canoe upstream for 2 km. Along the way you will be able to see the feathery-leaved Mkambati palms, growing close to the water line of the shady south bank. There are also various species of erica and protea. The forest canopy and steep-sided cliffs of this beautiful river conceal a number of birds of prey, including the endangered Cape vulture, fish eagle and crowned eagle.

Horses can be hired (with a guide) to provide game-viewing drives with a difference. Animals found in the grassland include gemsbok, red hartebeest, wildebeest, blesbok and eland. There are a variety of walks, including one to the dramatic Horseshoe Falls where clear, fresh water tumbles over spectacular rapids before cascading into the sea below.

Nduli Nature Reserve

This 180 ha reserve is only some 3 km from the centre of Umtata, on the western outskirts, adjoining a hotel complex and ministers' residences.

Nduli is the nucleus for Transkei reserve game animals, which are kept here before being distributed to other areas. It is open daily from 7 a.m. to 5 p.m. for day visits only. Camping and the lighting of fires are not permitted, but there are picnic sites laid out in attractive garden areas where drinking water is available. A circular drive (with a speed limit of 20 km/h) enables visitors to see most of the animals, which usually include Burchell's zebra, black wildebeest, blue wildebeest, eland, red hartebeest, impala, mountain reedbuck, springbok and nyala. There is also a herd of fallow deer. Bird life is rich, and this is a nesting area of the crowned crane. The crane may often be seen 'dancing' with wings outspread, appearing to bounce as though on springs. Its Xhosa name of *Mahem* is derived from its soft, trumpeting call.

Silaka Nature Reserve

Just to the south of Port St Johns, between Second Beach and Sugarloaf Rock lies the small, but beautiful Silaka Nature Reserve amid evergreen forest, grassland and rocky shore.

Set between the dense forest and a sandy beach at Gxwaleni River mouth are 14 thatched cottages and a picnic site, providing a base from where visitors can go for walks into the forest or

along the pebble beaches of this rocky coastline. The rock pools are fascinating, providing a microcosm of marine life, while offshore a colony of white-breasted cormorant and other seabirds inhabit Bird Island. The island is really a rocky outcrop and can be reached at low tide. Cape clawless otter are occasionally seen on the beach.

Exploring the forest is also exciting. Giant trees and water lilies line the fertile banks of the Gxwaleni River where exotic forest birds include cinnamon dove, grey cuckoo shrike and Knysna loerie. You are also likely to see kingfisher along fast-flowing sections of the river. In the forest fringes and on the grassy slopes of Silaka Reserve are Burchell's zebra, wildebeest and blesbok, which have been introduced to complement indigenous duiker and bushbuck.

For bookings and enquiries you should write to the Transkei Nature Conservation Division, Department of Agriculture and Forestry, Private Bag X5002, Umtata, Transkei (telephone Umtata 2-4322 or 24-9309).

The Wild Coast

From the mouth of the Kei River to the Umtamvuna – a distance of some 250 km – stretches the rugged and unspoilt grandeur of Transkei's Wild Coast, a green belt of thick indigenous forest, hilly grassland, and sheer cliffs that fall to white, unspoilt beaches.

The main national road runs (on average) about 60 km from the coast, but a series of secondary roads connects the seaside resorts. The condition of these gravel roads varies greatly and they are generally not suitable for caravans, so choose your routes carefully.

The first resort in the south is Qolora Mouth, close to the Kei River, which you reach by turning off to the coast at Butterworth. There are two attractive hotels at Qolora. Camping outside the resort area – as in all cases throughout the Transkei – is allowed only if a permit has been obtained from the Department of Forestry and Agriculture at Private Bag X5002, Umtata (telephone Umtata 2-4322 or 24-9309). There are no facilities at most campsites. Msikaba (Lusikisiki) and Coffee Bay (Mqanduli) do, however, have ablution facilities.

At Nxaxo, reached via Cebe, hundreds of crowned cranes sometimes roost on an island in the river mouth, and their calls can be heard throughout the night. Superstition has protected them, as they are believed to bring rain. There are no facilities at Nxaxo Mouth, but there is a licensed hotel at the nearby resort of Wavecrest.

The turn-off to the Bashee River mouth is some 17 km past the spot where the N2 road crosses the Bashee River Bridge. The Bashee has cut an impressive and convoluted course to the sea, and at one point returns to within 1 km of its own course 67 km upstream. Near the viewpoint known as Collywobbles is a breeding-site of the Cape vulture. There is a hotel close to the Bashee River mouth known as The Haven, but there are no camping facilities.

Hole in the Wall is reached after 75 km of gravel road from the turn-off at Viedgesville. Here the spectacle of the great cliff-like island rising from the sea – one of Southern Africa's most interesting natural formations – is unforgettable as water roars through the tunnel which has been eroded in its base.

Coffee Bay is a major resort on the south side of the lagoon at the Umtata River mouth, where lush vegetation grows right down to the shore. There are two hotels and a caravan park with an ablution block.

Umngazi River mouth is reached by turning off along the Umtata-Port St Johns road, and has a long lagoon set among green hills. There is a hotel here, but no camping facilities.

The Wild Coast Hiking Trail

Informality and adventure are hallmarks of the Wild Coast Trail – a dramatic route which follows the craggy cliffs and open, white beaches of Transkei's spectacular coastline.

The trail which leads from north to south is usually divided up into five sections: Umtamvuna-Msikaba (3 days); Msikaba-Agate Terrace (7 days); Silaka-Coffee Bay (6 days); Coffee Bay-Mbashe (5 days); Nqabara-Kei River (6 days). The trail is not for the faint-hearted –

Left: Hole in the Wall, known by the Xhosa as *esiKhaleni* (the place of sound), is one of nature's real wonders. **Above:** The magnificent Cape vulture has a breeding site near the Collywobbles viewpoint. **Right:** The crowned crane is easily one of the most striking of Southern Africa's birds.

some of the highlights involve crossing river mouths, where tides, currents and sharks pose particular hazards. You should be cautious at all times and, where necessary, rather cross further upstream.

Each stopover on the trail has two six-bedded huts and a third which serves as a communal dining room. For bookings and enquiries you should write to the Transkei Nature Conservation Division, Department of Agriculture and Forestry, Private Bag X5002, Umtata, Transkei (telephone Umtata 2-4322 or 24-9309).

Umtamvuna Nature Reserve

The Umtamvuna River – the natural boundary between Natal and Transkei – is an area rich in plants and animals. Although separate reserves have been established on opposite banks of the steep-sided ravine they share the same name. The ravine is a treasure-chest of plants, and includes previously unclassified species as well as more common Natal strelitzias (*Strelitzia nicolai*). Umdoni (*Syzygium*) and eastern Cape cycad (*Encephalartos altensteinii*) also occur. Animals found are bushbuck, grey duiker, blue duiker, chacma baboon and porcupine, while rare Cape vulture inhabit the cliffs on both sides of the river.

Unlike the Natal reserve, which is open to visitors, the steep ravines and misty grassland which comprise Transkei's side of the river are undeveloped. There are plans to open the reserve in the future. For further enquiries write to the Transkei Nature Conservation Division, Department of Agriculture and Forestry, Private Bag X5002, Umtata, Transkei (telephone Umtata 2-4322 or 24-9309) or The Director, Natal Parks Board, P.O. Box 667, Pietermaritzburg 3200 (telephone Pietermaritzburg 47-1961).

An ever-changing landscape

The ominously named Stormberg and Winterberg mountain ranges dominate a region of Karoo scrub and grassland, and their deep ravines gave shelter to primitive San and wild animals for centuries. Only rock paintings – in the silence of remote caves or close to the throb of a modern highway – are left to remind us of the San, but nature reserves and a national park re-create the natural wonder of this rugged area.

Here is the home of one of the world's rarest large mammals, the true mountain zebra – so rare that there was once a time when the Mountain Zebra National Park held not a single female of the species it had been created to preserve. This is a land of contrast, providing varying habitats for a large variety of birds and animals. There is the Karringmelkspruit Vulture Reserve of the Witteberg, a sanctuary for hundreds of Cape vultures; the stretch of acacia and savanna veld near Queenstown, where

hikers can explore the interesting Reedbuck, Aloe and Wildebeest trails (all in the Lawrence de Lange Nature Reserve); and the isolated Black Eagle Nature Reserve, where underprivileged children are introduced to the great outdoors on weekend hikes.

In landscapes bare of water, succulent plants manage to flourish. On the higher ground, snowfalls are common during winter – especially in June and September. But throughout the changing seasons there is the constancy of quiet spaciousness, the challenge of a climb or hike, great expanses of water, and the nearness of nature. Few holidaymakers visit this region only once.

Adelaide Nature Conservation Station

Only a few springbok, Namaqua sheep and wildebeest are kept in this 50 ha reserve, where the main activity is the breeding and training of hounds used to control problem animals. The

hounds are taught to ignore all game species and domestic stock when pursuing problem animals, which include jackal, baboon and others which maim or kill stock, or damage crops. Sheepdogs are trained here for the hunting of bushpig, since it has been found that jackal hounds tend to attack fearlessly and without stealth, resulting in a high proportion of injuries and deaths to the hounds. The station is 3 km from Adelaide. Although it is not generally open to the public, visits to the reserve may be arranged by telephoning The Senior Nature Conservation Officer at Adelaide 56.

Black Eagle Nature Reserve

This mountainous reserve, which covers most of the isolated Andriesbergen range, lies on the farm Carnarvon Estates, 22 km east of Sterkstroom in the eastern Cape.

Since 1977 wilderness trails emphasising environmental education have been run for youth

Above: The beautiful and extremely agile caracal, photographed in the Mountain Zebra National Park. This cat's agility enables it to catch birds on the wing with a sudden jump, and it is sufficiently fast to kill poisonous snakes without danger to itself. **Left:** A mountain zebra in the 6 536 ha Mountain Zebra National Park, near Cradock. This species is seldom found more than 150 km inland. Because of its declining numbers, it has been strictly protected since 1950. **Right above:** *Acacia karroo.* The brightly-coloured plant entwined about the thorns is a parasite. **Right below:** Black-footed (or small-spotted) cat.

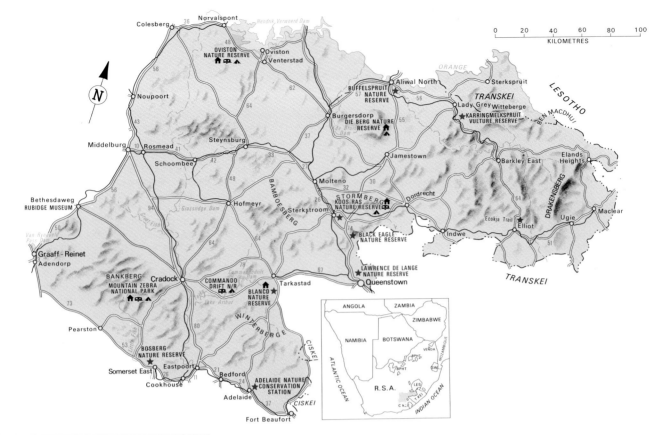

groups in the reserve. In addition, organised hikes cater for backpackers and outdoor adventure groups.

A feature of the reserve is that all profits from these paying trails are used to sponsor an equal number of trails for under-privileged youth.

The basic trail programme starts at 2 p.m. on Friday to 12 noon on Sunday giving participants two full days to share in the unspoilt wilderness.

A permanent base has been established, consisting of a base hut with a lecture-cum-dining room, kitchen and bedroom sleeping four adults. There is also a storage rondavel which doubles as a two-bedded room. Most hikers sleep in two big tents. There is a small electric generator for lighting and two gas stoves. Most cooking, however, is done over open fires.

The reserve itself is remote and only accessible on foot or horseback. The weather from May to August can be very cold, and a certain amount of snow is normally experienced during these months. The reserve contains a large population of fallow deer, mountain reedbuck and grey rhebok, while herds of eland, black wildebeest and blesbok are on the increase. Bird life includes the greywing francolin, Cape vulture and black eagle.

Trails are conducted throughout the year by guides from the Black Eagle and Stagger Inn Game Lodges. The minimum number of children is 15 (plus one teacher), and in the case of hikers, ten adults.

For further information, write to Mr S. Bryan, Stagger Inn and Black Eagle Game Lodges, P.O. Box 9, Sterkstroom 5245 (telephone Sterkstroom 3311/3320).

Bosberg Nature Reserve and Hiking Trail

At this 2050 ha reserve, on the southern slopes of the Bosberg ('Forest Mountain') there are hiking trails offering spectacular views, various species of animals and birds, as well as fascinating plants for the visitor to discover. At the entrance to the reserve you will find exotic and indigenous plants displayed at the botanic interpretation centre. The centre is also the start of the 15 km Bosberg Hiking Trail.

The circular trail traverses glorious fynbos vegetation and patches of relic, indigenous forest, where yellowwood, stinkwood and wild olive trees may be seen. If you are on the trail, keep a look out for shy bushbuck, steenbok, baboon, monkey and rock rabbit along the way.

A highlight of the trail is the flat-topped mountain where you can look out over Somerset East, Bestershoek Valley and a sea of flat-topped koppies. A large dam on the mountain attracts a large variety of birds, including jackal buzzard and booted and crowned eagle.

The reserve also has a fenced game camp which is home to mountain zebra, mountain reedbuck, bushbuck and kudu. A bird-watching hide is planned for the future.

Accommodation on the trail is provided in an overnight hut 5 km from the start. In addition there is a municipal camping and picnic site in the scenic Bestershoek Valley. From here there is an 11 km mountain drive and walks to beautiful spots in the ravines and forest.

The reserve is reached 2,5 km north-west of Somerset East. Bookings and enquiries should be made by writing to The Information Officer, Bosberg Nature Reserve, P.O. Box 27, Somerset East, 5850 (telephone Somerset East 3-2681).

Buffelspruit Nature Reserve

This reserve, which falls under the Aliwal North Municipality, is on the banks of the Kraai River, a tributary of the Orange River. From Somerset Street, turn at the traffic lights into Barkly Street and follow the road for about 1,2 km, continuing straight when the road forks left. The entrance is a large stone structure with a thatched roof. Nearby is a blockhouse and a cemetery dating from the Anglo-Boer War.

The reserve is stocked with springbok, blesbok, gemsbok, red hartebeest, black wildebeest, eland and impala. Waterfowl gather at a reed-fringed vlei.

This reserve covers some 900 ha, of which 260 ha are accessible to visitors. It is open from 10 a.m. to 6 p.m. from October to April; and from 11 a.m. to 4.30 p.m. from May to September.

There is a speed limit of 30 km/h, and visitors are only allowed to leave their cars at the view site, where there are fireplaces. No firewood may be gathered in the reserve. Overnight camping is not allowed, but new facilties and a trail are being planned. For more information contact The Head, Tourism and Recreational Parks, Aliwal North Municipality, Private Bag X1011, Aliwal North 5530 (telephone Aliwal North 2441/2951).

Commando Drift Nature Reserve

Surrounding a large dam, and with views of the Winterberg and Mostertshoek mountains in the distance, Commando Drift is a remote beautiful, wilderness reserve which attracts a great variety of bird life.

The land area of the reserve – some 5 983 ha – is being allowed to recover from farming and overgrazing as indigenous animals are reintroduced in small numbers. The Commando Drift Dam is fed by the Elands, Tarka, Palingkloof and Vlekpoort rivers and lies entirely within the reserve.

The entrance to the reserve is just off the gravel road between Tarkastad and Cradock. From Tarkastad, turn right after 30 km on to a smaller gravel road signposted 'Fourie Schoeman/Commando Drift'. The gateway to the reserve is reached after five kilometres.

From Cradock, take the tarred road to Tarkastad, turn right on to gravel at the signpost reading 'Palingkloof/Lake Arthur' and turn left into the reserve immediately after crossing the first cattle grid.

The Cradock-Tarkastad gravel road may be in poor condition with marked corrugations – particularly after periods of prolonged drought – and should be negotiated with care.

The reserve is open at all hours throughout the year, and visitors are not required to check in. There are caravan and camping sites with toilets and showers, and drinking water is available from one point only. The shower water is not suitable for drinking. All requirements should be taken with you – firewood may not be collected within the reserve.

Hiking trails have not yet been laid out, but the ranger may accompany parties of five or more people (a minimum of 10 is preferred) if this is requested at least a week in advance. To arrange this, telephone The Officer-in-Charge at Cradock 3925. Unaccompanied hiking is also permitted.

Boating is a major attraction, with no restrictions on the types of boat allowed. Angling is permitted south of the spillway, provided you have a Cape Provincial freshwater angling licence. There are no facilities for launching or retrieving boats – so take care when driving vehicles close to the water's edge as cars or trailers may become bogged down.

The reserve holds small herds of blesbok, black wildebeest, springbok, steenbok, duiker and mountain reedbuck. There are three species of mongoose, as well as the Cape clawless otter and the white-naped weasel.

Die Berg Nature Reserve

The historic town of Burgersdorp in the northeastern Cape is overlooked by a short spur of the Stormberg Mountain, known locally as *Die Dorpsberg* (The Town's Mountain), on which a nature reserve is being laid out. An area of 425 ha has been stocked with a variety of game.

A nature trail across fairly rugged terrain is being constructed from the reserve to the J L de Bruin Dam, where there are facilities for boating, camping and angling. There are also ablution blocks and caravan sites and electricity is available.

Ecowa Trail

Starting from Gatberg – a sandstone peak with a hole seemingly bored through its centre – the Ecowa Trail leads through the spectacular sandstone peaks and rolling, green foothills of the Drakensberg to Barkly Pass, a distance of some 40 km.

The delicate-looking pinnacles, buttresses and peaks are often reminiscent of the Natal Drakensberg, and one spectacular formation

---

A FINAL TUMBLE

Under an overhang of shale at the northern end of the Commando Drift Dam are some fading Bushman paintings. In black and ochre, they show men carrying sticks, as well as cattle and an animal that may represent a hyena. Now that the Bushmen have gone, and visitors rarely arrive to disturb the soft, powdery soil, ant lions have populated this sheltered spot with their neat, funnel-shaped lairs.

The adult ant lion resembles a dragon-fly, but can be distinguished by much longer, clubbed feelers, like those of a butterfly. Unlike the dragon-fly, the ant lion is not active during the day, unless disturbed, and it has yellowish wings with brown or black markings.

The ant lion's conical pit — about 2-3 cm in diameter and depth — is excavated by the insect moving about under the surface in ever-decreasing circles, throwing the sand out with a jerk of its head. It waits for unwary ants and other small insects to tumble in. Once over the edge, they slip even further down the steep, crumbling sides (the ant lion flicks sand at its prey to ensure that it does not climb out) until they are within reach of the sharp, curving jaws. The ant lion larva has no mouth, and narrow channels run through each jaw, so that the victims are not eaten, but sucked dry, the empty skins being discarded. If the site of its trap proves to be a poor hunting-ground, the ant lion simply moves off — usually at night — and digs another pit.

Above: The Cape clawless otter, a large species which lacks webs on its feet, is found near water in a variety of habitats south of the Sahara. It lives on fish, crabs, frogs, reptiles, waterfowl and even crocodiles' eggs. It is partly diurnal, and may be seen sunning itself on rocks or sandbars. **Left above:** The scrub hare is generally found on bush-clad stony hills. It is similar to the Cape hare, with long ears and a relatively long tail, and its fur may vary in colour according to the climate. **Left below:** A coloured aquatint by the artist and traveller Samuel Daniell, entitled 'Cascade on Sneuwberg' (from *African Scenery and Animals*).

even has the same name as a similar formation in Natal – 'Giant's Castle'.

Although the mountain landscape is rugged and most suitable for experienced hikers, the unmistakable charm of its mountain streams, crashing waterfalls and conical-shaped Xhosa huts will be difficult to forget. The trail takes its name from the mushrooms (ecowa) which mingle with a myriad wild flowers after spring thunderstorms.

Because the trail crosses private land, groups must nominate a leader who is responsible for the group and ensures that no-one picks flowers, lights fires or defaces San paintings.

There are no huts along the way, but hikers will find shelter in an empty farmhouse and in a cave. Although usually a three-day trail, one- and two-day routes are also available. Bookings and enquiries can be made by writing to the Town Clerk, Elliot Municipality, P.O. Box 21, Elliot 5460 (telephone Elliot 11/238).

Karringmelkspruit Vulture Reserve
This 70 ha reserve lies in the Witteberg, approximately 12 km from Lady Grey on the Barkly East road, and consists mainly of a sheer-sided ravine rising from sandy veld. The vulture are protected largely by the isolation of their breeding sites – although they sometimes pick up meat from poisoned carcasses as they range as far as 160 km in their search for food. The 500 Cape vultures which live and breed here will, in future, be fed in the reserve. Although the area is open to the public, visitors are not encouraged.

Koos Ras Nature Reserve
To reach the reserve from Sterkstroom, take the Dordrecht road and turn right just before you get to the railway line. The gate is 3 km down a good gravel road. The reserve's gate is open only on Saturdays and Sundays, from 8 a.m. to 5.30 p.m.

On weekdays the key can be collected from the municipality. Drinking water is available at the rest camp, which has two family rondavels with gas lighting and stoves, and laid-out sites for 20 caravans and 20 tents.

Fireplaces for cooking, and a large table are provided. Visitors should bring their own firewood, although wood may be gathered in the rest camp area. Pets are allowed in the rest camp, but not in the game area. Smoking is not permitted in the game area.

A speed limit of 30 km/h operates on all roads in the 150 ha reserve. Visitors may spot eland, springbok, blesbok, zebra, impala, gemsbok and kudu.

You are allowed out of your vehicle only once you have reached the rest camp. Hiking trails are being planned. To make a reservation, write to The Town Clerk, Sterkstroom Municipality, P.O. Box 25, Sterkstroom 5425 (telephone Sterkstroom 8).

Above: A long-horn beetle in the Mountain Zebra National Park. The larvae of this species are cannibalistic: on hatching, they immediately begin to eat each other and the carnage ends only when they are too widely scattered to continue the fight. **Left:** The Cape fox is widely distributed in Southern Africa. It digs or 'adopts' a hole in the ground, from where it ventures forth at night in search of prey. It feeds on small mammals, lizards, ground-nesting birds, fruit and berries. **Right:** Blue tulips (*Moraea polystachya*).

Lawrence de Lange Nature Reserve

Acacia and savanna veld dominate this reserve (formerly known as Madeira Nature Reserve) on the slopes overlooking Queenstown. From the robot at the Royal Hotel follow the signs into Kingsway, then turn into Hangklip Road. This leads to the gates of the reserve, which are open throughout the year from 8 a.m. to 5 p.m. Motorcycles and pets are not admitted.

There are three hiking trails within the 818 ha reserve, the longest (the Reedbuck Trail) taking about a day and a half to complete. Hiking parties on this trail will be accompanied by the ranger, provided prior arrangements have been made with the Conservation Officer, Queenstown Municipality, Private Bag X7111, Queenstown 5320 (telephone Queenstown 3131). There are no shops in the reserve – so take everything you need. The hike usually starts at 3 p.m. with an overnight stop in the open. No other overnight camping is allowed in the reserve. School parties must be accompanied by a teacher. The Aloe Trail, which takes about eight hours, leads along the foothills of Madeira Mountain. The Wildebeest Trail is an easy halfday walk on level ground.

Motorists should observe the speed limit of 30 km/h, and visitors are not allowed out of their cars – except when on a hiking trail or with the special permission of the ranger. The reserve might be closed for short periods while grazing areas are rotated.

With the exception of the shy kudu, visitors are likely to see most resident species including grey duiker, springbok, blesbok, mountain reedbuck, red hartebeest, black wildebeest, impala, gemsbok, steenbok, eland and Burchell's zebra.

In the Longhill area, fires are allowed only at picnic sites, and visitors (except those spending the night on the Reedbuck Trail) must bring their own firewood. Fresh water is available.

Visitors may see Cape vulture, black eagle, martial eagle, Egyptian and spur-winged goose, red-breasted wryneck, red-billed hoopoe, hadeda and pied and black crow.

Mountain Zebra National Park

One of the world's rarest large mammals is the Cape mountain zebra (a subspecies) – and today some 200 live in the appropriately named Mountain Zebra National Park near Cradock. Back in 1937, when the farm Babylons Toren was bought as the nucleus of the reserve, there were few of the rare *Equus zebra* left alive. A cabinet minister of the day mockingly described the creatures as 'a lot of donkeys in football jerseys'.

The Cape mountain zebra roam the 6 536 ha of the Mountain Zebra National Park on the northern slopes of the Bankberg, about 27 km west of Cradock. To ensure their survival, a number of Cape mountain zebra have been translocated to other reserves throughout the Cape Midlands – to colonise their former ranges once more.

This is high Karoo country – the highest point in the park is a peak known as Spitskop (1 957 m above sea level), while the average altitude of the park is some 300 m higher than that of the surrounding country, with winter snowfalls on the higher ridges. In summer the weather ranges from mild to very hot.

You will find about 37 km of good gravel roads traversing a combination of arid succulent veld (of the Great Karoo type) and the wetter eastern grassland.

Game-viewing is rewarding throughout the year; particularly on the Rooiplaat plateau, which attracts a large number of grazers – particularly during summer. In addition to mountain zebra, there are eland, springbok, black wildebeest, red hartebeest, blesbok, mountain reedbuck, klipspringer, duiker and steenbok.

The largest carnivore in the area is the caracal, which is rarely seen as it prowls the wooded kloofs. Among 206 bird species recorded in the park is the rare booted eagle.

There are four species of mongoose in the park. One of them, the nocturnal water mongoose, is seldom seen. The Cape grey mongoose is a solitary thicket-dweller, active by day as it searches for a diet of small rodents, insects, birds and fruit. Appearing dark grey from a distance, it is actually pale grey when seen close up. The red mongoose is often seen in open areas, where it lives in large colonies, usually in old spring-hare burrows (although it is itself an efficient burrower). Hunting in pairs – mainly for insects – they are sometimes seen in the company of guinea fowl.

The fourth species is the suricate, which is often confused with the ground squirrel, as both are gregarious and have the habit of standing upright to survey their surroundings.

The Mountain Zebra Hiking Trail starts and finishes at the office at the rest camp, from where a number of shorter, half-day trails may also be followed. The trail covers 31 km with two overnight stops in huts at Olienhut and Kareehut. The first day's hike of 11 km takes five to six hours with climbs and descents through gorges formed by the Fonteinkloof and Grootkloof streams. The second day begins with a back-track to the summit of the Bankberg, with views of the distant Kompasberg (Compass Mountain) and reaches the second hut after 12 km (seven to eight hours). The third day is an easy 8 km walk, covered in two or three hours. Much of the trail is criss-crossed with game tracks.

Oviston Nature Reserve

This reserve, which lies on the Cape side of the Hendrik Verwoerd Dam, is used to breed animals for other conservation areas, support-

ing large herds of springbok, black wildebeest, mountain reedbuck, grey rhebok, red hartebeest, blesbok, steenbok, Burchell's zebra, kudu and eland.

The reserve is open at weekends and on public holidays from 6 a.m. to 6 p.m. The entrance is on the old Venterstad-Norval's Pont road. There are no facilities within the reserve, but an adjacent construction township has been converted into a holiday and residential resort. There is a caravan park, and facilities include hot and cold water, a laundry and connections for lights and appliances.

There is a thatched recreation area, swimming pool, and tennis and badminton courts. Enquiries concerning the holiday resort, which is administered separately from the nature reserve, should be addressed to The Town Clerk, Venterstad Municipality, P.O. Box 24, Venterstad 5990 (telephone Venterstad 4-0224/5).

The reserve has 25 km of fair gravel road, as well as a stretch of tarred road. Pets are not allowed in the reserve, and fires are prohibited. A permit must be obtained at the gate.

Fishing is allowed in demarcated areas along the shore, but anglers require a Cape Provincial freshwater angling licence. If you intend to fish from a boat, make sure that the boat is registered with the Orange Free State Provincial Administration at Oranjekrag. You should also possess a Free State freshwater angling licence.

Boating is a major attraction, but sudden winds make the surface of the dam treacherous, and it is essential to take full safety precautions. People unfamiliar with the area should seek the advice of more experienced boatmen before setting off. The water area, which actually falls outside the reserve, attracts over 100 species of birds.

Van Riebeeck Karoo Garden

The hardy indigenous succulents of the Van Riebeeck Karoo Garden at Cradock, flourishing even when the surrounding countryside withers in the grip of drought, are one of the wonders of the Karoo. The garden also features a number of exotic plant species.

A region of tall coastal dunes, tumbling rivers, dense scrub, forests and abundant wildlife – this is the eastern Cape between the Kei River mouth in the north and Algoa Bay in the south. It is an area of beautiful contradictions, offering a host of nature reserves, state forests, hiking trails and resorts in widely varying terrain.

For those who are prepared to spend a little effort in their appreciation of nature, there are many walking trails – some signposted and others mere depressions in the soil – leading through some of the most attractive countryside in Southern Africa.

MOUNTAIN ZEBRA NATIONAL PARK AT A GLANCE

When to go Visitors are admitted from 7 a.m. to 6 p.m. between 1 October and 30 April, and from 8 a.m to 6 p.m. between 1 May and 30 September.

Reservations and information Applications to reserve accommodation and places on the Mountain Zebra Hiking Trail should be addressed to the National Parks Board, P.O. Box 787, Pretoria 0001 (telephone Pretoria 343-1991) or the National Parks Board, P.O. Box 7400, Roggebaai 8012 (telephone Cape Town 419-5365) or the National Parks Board, P.O. Box 774, George 6530 (telephone George 74-6924/5). If accommodation is required within five days of an intended visit, telephone The Tourist Officer at Cradock 2427.

Getting there Take the Cradock-Middelburg road and turn (west) on to the Graaff-Reinet road about 6 km from Cradock. Drive for about 5 km, then turn left (towards the mountains) and follow the signs.

Accommodation The rest camp has 20 fully equipped chalets, each featuring two bedrooms, double insulation and double glazing, and fireplaces. There are 20 caravan and camping sites, with ablution blocks and laundry facilities. There are also huts for the use of hikers on the Mountain Zebra Hiking Trail. The overnight huts are provided with hot and cold water, beds and fuel. You should bring your own food and sleeping bag, and it is advisable to carry water.

Eating and drinking Meals (à la carte) are available from the restaurant, and a shop supplies milk, bread and basic, non-perishable foodstuffs.

Getting around The park is served by 37 km of gravel roads in good condition (petrol is available at the rest camp during normal selling hours). Visitors may go on one of several short hikes, or join a party on the more ambitious (31 km) Mountain Zebra Hiking Trail, which starts at the rest camp. There is a speed limit of 40 km/h and some roads are signposted for one way traffic only.

Wildlife Among the park's species are the rare Cape mountain zebra, eland, black wildebeest, red hartebeest, springbok, suricate and caracal. There are over 200 bird species.

Eastern Cape wonderland

A region of tall coastal dunes, tumbling rivers, dense scrub, forests and abundant wildlife – this is the eastern Cape between the Kei River mouth in the north and Algoa Bay in the south. It is an area of beautiful contradictions, offering a host of nature reserves, forests, hiking trails and resorts in widely varying terrain.

For those who are prepared to spend a little effort in their appreciation of nature, there are many walking trails – some signposted and others mere depressions in the soil – leading through some of the most attractive countryside in Southern Africa.

Alexandria Forest Nature Reserve

This reserve fringes most of the coastline between the Sundays River mouth and Bushmans River mouth. Footpaths through the forest offer visitors hikes of varying duration, and the wildlife includes bushbuck, wild pig, duiker, small predators and a variety of birds.

A lovely 2-hour beach walk, or short 4-wheel-drive journey, from the resort at Boknesstrand will bring you to the Dias Cross monument, which commands beautiful views and is well worth a visit.

Permits and information about walking in the reserve can be obtained during office hours from The Forester, Alexandria State Forest, P.O. Box 50, Alexandria 6185 (telephone Alexandria 1103).

If you want to explore the region further, the two-day Alexandria Trail is a flat route and is ideal for beginners. The 32km circular trail leads through the Alexandria State Forest, Langevlakte Valley and Woody Cape nature reserves, where an overnight hut provides accommodation for 12 hikers.

Bookings for the trail should be addressed to The Senior Regional Officer, Directorate of Nature and Environmental Conservation, Private Bag X1126, Port Elizabeth 6000 (telephone Port Elizabeth 55-7380).

Amalinda Fisheries Station and Nature Reserve

With its main entrance in Etheridge Road, this 134ha reserve, centred on the old Amalinda reservoir, is entirely surrounded by the industrial area of East London. The fisheries station, being in a frost-free area, was originally established for the propagation of warm-water pond or dam fish and now breeds fish for stocking public dams.

The various habitats within the small reserve, ranging from open water to swampy, papyrus areas, attract a rich variety of bird life – particularly waterfowl (in addition to the main reservoir, there are some 73 ponds).

The reserve area around the dam is open to the public every day throughout the year from sunrise to sunset. Toilets, picnic sites and fireplaces are provided and boating and angling are permitted. Anglers must have a Cape Provincial freshwater angling licence and a permit issued by the Officer-in-Charge at Amalinda. The dam is well stocked, and fish include large-mouth bass, barbel, blue bream, carp, mullet and eel. Among its mammals is the only viable breeding herd of southern reedbuck in the province.

Anyone wishing to visit the research and breeding section of the station should write to The Officer-in-Charge, Amalinda Fisheries Station, P.O. Box 12043, Amalinda 5252 (telephone East London 41-2212).

Amatola Hiking Trail

The tumble of mountains and forests that span the eastern Cape between King William's Town and Katberg are linked by the 105km (six-day) Amatola Hiking Trail. The trail, which starts at Maden Dam in the Pirie Forest and ends at the Tyume River basin, near picturesque Hogs-

Above: A tinted lithograph by T.W. Bowler from his book *The Kaffir Wars and the British settlers in South Africa*. It is entitled 'Keiskamma near Fort Cox, Amatola in the Distance'.
Left: *Pachypodium succulentum*. These plants have very large tubers which enable them to store quantities of food and water (for this reason, they were much prized by the Hottentots). **Right:** Springbok in the Andries Vosloo Kudu Reserve, which features a variety of buck and bigger game.

back, is fairly difficult and should not be attempted by unfit or inexperienced hikers. However, numerous shorter routes of between one and five days allow visitors to experience selected parts of this magnificent hiking trail. These include the one-day Pirie Nature Walk and the two-day Evelyn Valley Loop.

Further information, brochures and bookings should be addressed to The Director-General, Ciskei Department of Tourism, Private Bag X0026, Bisho, Ciskei (telephone Bisho 9-2171).

Andries Vosloo Kudu Reserve and Sam Knott Nature Reserve

The Andries Vosloo Kudu Reserve (6493ha) and the Sam Knott Nature Reserve link up to form this combined conservation area of some 23 000ha. The landscape is harsh, yet dramatic. Among the numerous kloofs which divide the landscape is 58km of the Great Fish River and 16km of the Kat River.

Launched initially as a refuge for kudu in the eastern Cape, the reserve also supports herds of buffalo, eland, red hartebeest and springbok. Warthog, grey duiker, ostrich, black-backed jackal and bushbuck are also present, while brown hyena and leopard also occur. Black rhino and the African rock python have both been successfully reintroduced.

There are no hiking trails in the reserve although interested parties are welcome to make arrangements with the Officer-in-Charge. There are two camping and picnic sites with basic facilities.

The two entrance gates to the reserve can both be reached via the Grahamstown-Fort Beaufort road. The Kamadolo gate lies 29km from Grahamstown and the Dangwe gate which has an information centre 16km further on. Entry permits are available at both gates.

For more information contact The Officer-in-Charge, Andries Vosloo Kudu Reserve, Private Bag 1006, Grahamstown 6140 (telephone Grahamstown 2-7909).

Auckland Nature Reserve

The 218ha Auckland Forest Reserve (its trees include some especially fine yellowwood specimens) is part of the Hogsback State Forest and is situated about 35km from Alice, on the southern slopes of the Amatole Mountains. It is a high rainfall area (summer months are the wettest) and, though cool and refreshing during summer, probably the best time to visit the reserve is between June and September.

Among the more common animals in the reserve are bushbuck, duiker, bushpig, porcupine, vervet monkey and the samango monkey. Visitors may also spot the rare tree dassie, or even a genet.

Auckland is also noted for its rich bird population, which includes raptors, songsters and a variety of gloriously coloured species such as the African golden oriole, the red-billed hornbill and the rare Knysna parrot.

The Madonna-and-Child, the Kettle Spout and several other scenic waterfalls are the pick among a variety of other tourist attractions. The Hogsback Section of the Amatola Hiking Trail passes through the nature reserve.

Visitors may enter the reserve any time during daylight hours provided they have a permit. Numerous well-signposted day trails have been established through the reserve and surrounding state forests. Brochures on these walks are available at local hotels.

For the permit and further information, write to The State Forester, Hogsback State Forest, Hogsback 5312 (telephone Hogsback 55).

Blanco Private Nature Reserve

This 1 060 ha reserve of transitional Karoo grassveld is located between the peaks known as Loskop and Kranskop at the foot of the Winterberg range, 14 km from Tarkastad on the road to Bedford.

Accommodation consists of detached cottages, all with bathroom and toilet. A central dining room serves three meals daily, and although the premises are not licensed there is a bar area in which lockers are available for storing liquor and soft drinks. A vehicle travels to Tarkastad on most days, and goods can be bought there on behalf of visitors.

There are facilities for tennis, golf, swimming, squash, bowls and horse riding. Visitors should bring their own sporting equipment, but rods may be hired for trout- and bass-angling.

No vehicles are allowed in the game reserve area, which features springbok, blesbok, black wildebeest, grey rhebok, mountain reedbuck, waterbuck, impala, red hartebeest, eland and zebra. Visitors may view game on foot or on horseback. Bird life, too, is prolific in the vicinity of the reserve's three dams, where large numbers of waterfowl can be seen.

The reserve does not cater for day visitors. It is closed for six winter weeks (mid-July to early September) and for the two weeks following the end of the December-January Cape school holidays. For enquiries write to Blanco Private Nature Reserve, P.O. Box 50, Tarkastad 5370 (telephone Tarkastad 265).

Bloukrans Nature Reserve

Local schools often visit this 200 ha reserve on the banks of the Blaaukranz River. Here the children are taught about the reserve's birds, animals, conservation education, indigenous vegetation and about the wealth of small aquatic life forms in the little river and its small pools. If you are lucky you will see a rare fish species, the east Cape Rocky (*Sandelia bainsii*), which is protected in the reserve.

184

Bloukrans boasts several low cliffs, highly recommended for rock-climbing. Visitors must obtain permission to visit the reserve, which lies beside the Grahamstown-Bathurst road. For more information write to Algoa Regional Services Council, P.O. Box 318, Port Elizabeth 6000 (telephone Port Elizabeth 52-1616).

Bosbokstrand Private Nature Reserve

The 205 ha Bosbokstrand reserve overlooks the sea just west of Haga-Haga. At Mooiplaas, which lies about 60 km from East London on the main road to Umtata, turn south onto a good gravel road and follow the signs towards Haga-Haga. The turn-off is well signposted and is reached after another 30 km – about 10 km before Haga-Haga. Accommodation consists of 11 fully equipped A-frame chalets for six people, as well as a large caravan park with toilets, hot and cold water, and laundry facilities. Picnic sites are available for day visitors.

A shop in the reserve sells general supplies. Fishing from the beach and rocks is excellent, and bait may be collected, or bought from the shop or at Haga-Haga. Walking trails through the game area are clearly marked by arrows fixed to trees, and visitors may spot eland, blesbok, zebra, bushbuck and impala.

For further information, you should write to The Manager, Bosbokstrand Private Nature Reserve, P.O. Haga-Haga (telephone Mooiplaas and ask for 4512), or contact the owner directly by writing to Bosbokstrand Private Nature Reserve, P.O. Box 302, Randfontein 1760 (telephone Johannesburg 696-1442).

Bridle Drift Dam Nature Reserve

The dam, in a nature reserve of 580 ha, lies on the Buffalo River some 25 km from East London. Sections of the dam have been allocated by the East London Municipality to power-boats and sailing clubs, and fishing permits may be obtained from the municipality's Cleansing Branch office in Beaconsfield Road during office hours. The reserve's gate is attended from 7 a.m. to 5 p.m. and facilities include picnic sites with fireplaces, toilets and fresh water.

The wildlife here consists mainly of bushbuck and the shy duiker while bird life in the dam area is prolific. A herd of donkeys can often be seen in the open areas.

Hiking trails lead to vantage points overlooking the dam, including the spillway, and through along the shoreline past indigenous bush to neighbouring Fort Pato Nature Reserve.

To reach the reserve from East London, take the Mount Coke road to King William's Town and follow the signs from Buffalo Pass.

For permits write to The Director, Directorate of Cultural and Environmental Services, P.O. Box 984, East London 5200 (telephone East London 34-9111).

Cape Henderson Nature Reserve

The reserve lies 60 km north-east of East London. The coastal fringe of this 255 ha area consists of patches of forest where wild banana, milkwood and candlewood trees flourish. There are also steep cliffs broken up by rocky inlets.

Because the climate here is essentially subtropical, the reserve offers an interesting vari-

Above: The crane flower (*Strelitzia reginae*) grows wild in the eastern Cape, and is common in the area of Port Elizabeth. Its orange sepals and brilliant blue petals create a beautiful display. **Left:** The common river frog (*Rana angolensis*) is found throughout South Africa – usually near dams and other permanent bodies of water. **Right:** The ruff is named after the ornate head and neck plumes seen on the males in their Palaearctic breeding grounds.

ety of plant life. The trees are strongly reminiscent of the subtropical flora further east: the Natal wild banana (*Strelitzia nicolai*) is typical, and visitors will also find sweet thorn (*Acacia karroo*), candlewood (*Pterocelastrus tricuspidatus*), milkwood (*Sideroxylon inerme*), coastal milkwood (*Mimusops caffra*) and coast silverleaf (*Brachylaena discolor*).

Wildlife in the reserve includes bushbuck, blue duiker, bushpig, caracal, vervet monkey and smaller mammals; birds include Knysna loerie, black-headed oriole, emerald-spotted wood dove and many seabirds.

The reserve is virtually inaccessible except by foot, though a small area on the western side may be reached by special beach vehicles. A footpath (extending for 5 km) is used by anglers to reach fishing spots along the coast.

For further information, write to The State Forester, East London Coast State Forest, P.O. Box 5185, Greenfields 5208 (telephone East London 46-3532).

Cycad Nature Reserve

The 208 ha area of fynbos and valley bushveld on the south bank of the Kariega River, 30 km south of Grahamstown, includes the largest known colony of the endangered cycad *Encephalartos caffer*. Cycads are strange, palm-like trees belonging to a very ancient species of plants and are one of the world's oldest existing forms of plant life. Although accessible, the reserve is not officially open to the public.

For further information, write to The Officer-in-Charge, Thomas Baines Nature Reserve, Private Bag 1006, Grahamstown 6140 (telephone Grahamstown 2-8262).

East London Aquarium

Indoor tanks at the East London Aquarium provide you with a close-up look at a wide variety of marine life, including a rare pineapple fish, which is usually found only at great depths and therefore rarely captured. The collection also includes invertebrates, and prized angling sea fish such as leervis, kob, white steenbras and musselcracker. The aquarium is famed for its sea horses, coral fish and penguin.

A visit to the aquarium is never complete without seeing the trained seals going through their paces. Shows are held twice daily, at 11.30 a.m. and 3.30 p.m. The aquarium itself is situated on the beachfront esplanade, and is open from 9 a.m. to 5 p.m.

Ecca Nature Reserve

You can follow two well-marked nature trails through the 104 ha Ecca Nature Reserve to discover more information about its fascinating plants, geology and history.

The entrance to the reserve is 15 km from Grahamstown on the Grahamstown-Fort

---

PLANTS FROM THE PAST

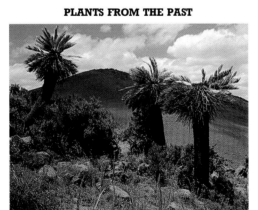

The fascinating white-haired cycad (*Encephalartos friderici-guilielmi*) is found only in a small area of the eastern Cape.

Cycads — which the great naturalist Charles Darwin called 'living fossils' — are the most primitive of all the world's seed-bearing plants. Most of the great cycad forests of the aeons-ago Carboniferous Period have long since turned to coal, and only a few small patches survive, in remote areas and most prominently in South Africa's eastern Cape region.

Carl Thunberg, the Swedish botanist, was the first to describe the Cape cycads — though he mistakenly classed them as a species of palm.

For centuries witchdoctors used the cycad in their concoctions (and almost exterminated it); Hottentots made a type of bread from its pith (hence the term 'bread tree'); and one clump in the Soutpansberg is said to have helped the legendary Rain Queen Modjadji and her successors in their predictions.

It was only when they detected subtle changes in the foliage, and other small cycad signs, that they would order the traditional rain-making ceremonies to begin.

Beaufort road, at Ecca Pass. A plaque at the gate commemorates A. G. Bain who constructed Queens Road. This historic wagon route runs along the reserve's western boundary. Dated about 1845, it was one of the first major engineered roads in the eastern Cape and predates Bain's Kloof by almost 10 years. Bain was not only an engineer, he was one of our pioneer geologists too. During construction he collected many fossils and rocks from which he made important palaeontological inroads into the history of the area. Among the finds credited to this area is the world-famous Mesosaurus – a reptilian fossil.

This reserve was established by the Algoa Regional Services Council and developed jointly by the Wildlife Society of Grahamstown as an environmental project. There is no entrance fee and no permit is required.

For more information on the reserve contact the Algoa Regional Services Council, P.O. Box 318, Port Elizabeth 6000 (telephone Port Elizabeth 52-1616).

1820 Settlers Wild Flower Garden

The garden covers 61 ha of the Gunfire Hill area surrounding Grahamstown's 1820 Settlers Monument, and displays the indigenous flora of the areas where the immigrants settled. It came into being as the first botanical garden to be established by the British in the Cape Colony. Although development was hampered by the frontier wars in the 1850s, the garden gradually took shape until it became one of the town's most popular public gathering places: military bands played on Saturday afternoons and citizens found the avenues of flowers a pleasant haven.

When it was decided to create a living monument to the 1820 Settlers and their descendants, work began on the clearing of exotic trees, shrubs and noxious weeds from the steep terrain. Countless Port Jackson willow trees were removed, and workers fought long and hard to dig out the vast root systems of huge gum trees. Their efforts paid off, and the Gunfire Hill area was transformed.

The Botanical Garden section has a fascinating collection of exotic plants, including a reconstruction of an old English garden, complete with daffodils, rosemary, forget-me-nots, lavender and English roses.

The large protea collection includes the giant protea (*Protea cynaroides*), and makes a colourful display throughout the year. Other indigenous plants include the Cape tree fern, cycads and aloes. There is a restaurant in the 1820 Settlers Monument building.

There are two entrances: the Grey Street entrance is situated on the main Grahamstown-Port Elizabeth road, and the Lucas Avenue gates are between the Albany Museum and the 1820 Settlers Memorial Museum. The garden is open at all times.

Fort Pato Nature Reserve

Fort Pato is a 691 ha forest nature reserve some 25 km from East London along the old King William's Town road. It's *raison d 'etre* is similar to that of the nearby Umtiza Nature Reserve – the protection of a number of indigenous tree species, and of the endangered blue duiker. The rare tree dassie (*Dendrohyrax arboreus*) may be seen in the reserve.

Fort Pato is open to the public only during daylight hours. An 8 km day hike leads through the woodland.

Permits and further information are available from The State Forester, East London Coast State Forest, P.O. Box 5185, Greenfields 5208 (telephone East London 46-3532).

Gonubie Nature Reserve

The seaside town of Gonubie, some 19 km northeast of East London, has a small (8 ha) reserve incorporating two vleis rich in bird life. The reserve is open to the public on Monday afternoons, but may be opened at other times to bird-watchers, photographers or other interested parties by arrangement with the municipal offices. Call at the offices, or write to P.O. Box 20, Gonubie 5256 (telephone Gonubie 40-4000).

The observation stands and hides overlook the vleis and make ideal bases for watching or photography. Waterfowl are the major attraction of Gonubie and a bird check-list as well as information on trees and plants are avail-

Above: The leervis (*Lichia amia*) is one of Southern Africa's best-known game fishes. This fish (the specimen above is a juvenile) may weigh 30 kilograms. **Left:** An endangered cycad, *Encephalartos caffer*, growing in the Cycad Nature Reserve, south of Grahamstown (indigenous peoples made a crude bread from *Encephalartos*). Cycads are protected in South Africa and Zimbabwe.

able in the information centre at the entrance to the reserve. Among some 130 species are crowned cranes, which return annually to breed and raise their chicks.

The reserve has a collection of indigenous plants, including *Protea simplex*. Of interest is the 'Herbalists' Garden', in which indigenous medicinal plants, used by tribal herbalists, are cultivated.

The reserve is signposted at the intersection of the town's Main Road and Seventh Street.

Gxulu Nature Reserve

Situated about 20 km from East London, between the Gxulu and Igoda rivers, this 250 ha reserve consists of shifting coastal dunes separated by wide valleys. The highest dune in the reserve soars to 270 m above sea level. Visitors may observe several transition stages in the growth of dune plants ranging from indigenous coastal scrub and grass to high climatic forest. The climate is subtropical, with an annual (mainly summer) rainfall of more than 800 mm.

Among the flora are such species as sweet thorn (*Acacia karroo*), milkwood (*Sideroxylon inerme*), thorn pear (*Scolopia zeyheri*), septee (*Cordia caffra*), bush-tick berry (*Chrysanthemoides monilifera*) and bastard taaibos (*Allophylus decipiens*).

Mammals in the reserve include vervet monkey, caracal, tree dassie and bushbuck. There is also a variety of birds to be seen, including Knysna loerie, emerald-spotted wood dove and many sea birds.

The reserve may be reached only on foot, and visitors leave from the parking spots at the Gxulu and Igoda river mouths. There are no facilities. Permits may be obtained during office hours from The State Forester, East London Coast State Forest, P.O. Box 5185, Greenfields 5208 (telephone East London 46-3532).

Hogsback and Katberg

These are two holiday resorts on the slopes of the Amatole Mountains, in a region dominated by the ridge said to resemble the bristles on a hog's back, and overlooking the rivers and luxuriant plains of the Tyume Valley.

Among the early settlers was a Mr Summerton, a gardener by occupation, and his attempts to recreate the English countryside can still be seen in apple orchards, avenues lined with hazelnut, berry fruits and the flowering plants which have spread throughout the area.

There are also large tracts of indigenous forest, where bird life includes parrots and loeries. Visitors will be fascinated by the rivers which tumble to the plain, creating a number of small but spectacular waterfalls such as Swallowtail Falls and Kettlespout Falls – where the water flows through a natural spout in the

Poplars (exotic trees) in winter in the Hogsback region. The Hogsback is a region of great natural beauty, with cool and bracing days in summer and sunny days in winter. The rainfall is 1 000 mm a year.

rocks and, in windy conditions, arches up in a feathery plume some 9 m high.

There are a number of hotels, caravan parks and campsites at which facilities are provided for tennis, swimming and bowls. There are two short golf-courses, and horses can be hired. The area is also noted for its angling: some of the rivers are stocked with trout.

Hogsback is 30 km from Alice, which in turn is 22 km from Fort Beaufort. To get to Katberg from Fort Beaufort, take the turn-off to Blinkwater. Katberg Pass is 23 km from Blinkwater.

Joan Muirhead Nature Reserve

Serenely situated beside the seaside town of Kenton-on-Sea, the small 20 ha Joan Muirhead Nature Reserve extends along the coastline in a narrow strip – proclaimed to stabilise the massive dunes which line the coast.

It's well worth walking along the 1 km stretch of coast from Kariega River Mouth to Bushmans River Mouth. Here among high dunes, pristine coastal forest, calcrete cliffs and rocky coves you will find plenty of opportunity for exploring. Three parking lots and a boat launching site are provided for visitors. Additional facilities are at Kenton-on-Sea. For further enquiries write to the Town Clerk, Kenton-on-Sea Municipality, P.O. Box 5, Kenton-on-Sea 6191 (telephone Kenton-on-Sea, 8-1304).

Kap River Nature Reserve

It's easy to become captivated by this delightful little river banked by large trees, colourful flowers and berry-sprinkled shrubs. From the dense foliage comes a chorus of birds, insects and small forest creatures. Wildlife includes many bird species such as heron, martial eagle, hornbill, crowned eagle, oriole and fish eagle as well as numerous small mammals. When developers proposed damming the Kap River, thereby flooding these fertile banks, all this life was nearly lost. Fortunately, Algoa Regional Services Council now owns a 307 ha reserve on the river's eastern bank, which has secured the survival of this charming valley.

If you obtain a permit you are welcome to explore the reserve, although it has no overnight accommodation.

Further south, at the Great Fish River Wetland Reserve, a campsite has been proclaimed at the mouth of the Great Fish River. Enquiries about both reserves may be made by writing to the Algoa Regional Services Council, P.O. Box 318, Port Elizabeth 6000 (telephone Port Elizabeth 52-1616).

King William's Town Nature Reserve

The reserve adjoins the town's northern residential suburbs and comprises some 59 ha of valley bushveld which is maintained as a 'natural' area by the eradication of exotic species. There are two systems of flora – the western Cape fynbos and subtropical evergreen and broadleaf scrub of the eastern maritime slopes. There is no 'artificial' garden, but exploration of the relatively dense and thorny vegetation is made easy by notice boards at the entrances and route signs along the well laid-out trails. The reserve is open from sunrise to sunset. To get there from town follow the signs from the main thoroughfare.

Left above: The Pirie Trout Hatchery, near King William's Town. **Left below:** The dwarf tree *(Oldenburgia arbuscula)*, a member of the daisy family, growing in a quartzite outcrop in the Thomas Baines Nature Reserve, near Grahamstown. **Right:** The Cape centipede-eater *(Aparallactus capensis)* is a small, slender snake (it averages 25-30 cm in length) which is found mostly in open savanna, where it lives beneath shrubs, among grass roots and sometimes in termite mounds — where it eats termite eggs and larvae. Its favourite prey is centipedes, which it swallows head first. There may be a long struggle when it encounters large centipedes (which can attain half the length of the snake), but the snake is usually successful. It appears immune to the centipede's poison, which may be as powerful as a bee's venom. The Cape centipede-eater (also known as the black-headed snake) is found in Zimbabwe, parts of the Transvaal, Free State, Natal and the eastern Cape as far west as East London.

Kologha Forest

At the north-eastern end of the Amatole Mountains near the old frontier settlement of Stutterheim is the Kologha State Forest, the centre of an area rich in indigenous flora.

The forest lies to the north of the gravel road between Stutterheim and Dimbaza, and is a favourite weekend haven for the residents of Stutterheim.

Tall yellowwoods mingle with white stinkwood and broom cluster fig trees. Animal life is mainly of the rodent family, but visitors should watch out for the occasional black-backed jackal. Bats live in the high branches. The occasional troop of baboons may be spotted in more open stretches of the forest. Entry permits are available from The State Forester, Kubusie State Forest, Private Bag X31, Stutterheim 4930 (telephone Stutterheim 3-1546) and can also be obtained at all hours from the Eagle's Ridge Forest Resort (telephone Stutterheim 3-1200).

If you wish to explore the area over two days you can follow the 34 km Kologha Hiking Trail from Isidene Forest Station to the Kologha Forest Station. Highlights include the overnight hut which is scenically situated beside the Gubu Dam and the huge Die Fin Oak Tree. Bookings for the hike should be made (mornings only) through The Regional Director, Eastern Cape Forest Region, Private Bag X7432, King William's Town 5600 (telephone King William's Town 2-3475).

188

Kwelera Nature Reserve

Most of the reserve, which lies between the mouths of the Kwelera and Gonubie rivers, consists of dunes parallel to the coast, with wide valleys in between. The highest dune is about 253 m above sea level. Wildlife includes bushbuck, caracal, vervet monkey and smaller mammals, while birds include emerald-spotted wood dove and Knysna loerie. Indigenous trees include sweet thorn, cherrywood, white milkwood, septee and wild silver oak.

The reserve offers opportunities for recreational activities such as surfing, fishing and swimming, and a small area has been set aside for picnicking. Unlike the nearby Gxulu and Cape Henderson reserves, it is accessible by car. From East London take the Transkei road and turn-off at the 'East Coast Resorts' sign about 10 km from the city.

L.L. Sebe Game Reserve

Named after Lennox Sebe, Ciskei's first president, this 20 800 ha reserve spans the Great Fish and the Keiskamma rivers near Peddie. Despite being located in an area steeped in the blood of many frontier wars, today this reserve is a quiet retreat from city life with freshwater angling, game-viewing, limited hunting and exceptional hiking trails on offer.

Double Drift Trail, named after the British fort located beside the Great Fish River, is a 30 km (two-day) hike along the winding course of the

famous river. Hikers stay at Double Drift Lodge. Other guests of the reserve are accommodated at the colonial-style Mbabala Lodge. Both lodges are 10-bedded and fully serviced (visitors supply food and drink only).

The vegetation consists of succulent valley bushveld and supports animals such as Burchell's zebra, blue wildebeest, kudu, blesbok, impala, bushbuck, warthog and nyala.

In the future this reserve will be linked to Andries Vosloo Kudu Nature Reserve across the Great Fish River. Plans are in the pipeline to turn this proposed 42 000 ha reserve into a sanctuary for black rhino and buffalo.

L.L. Sebe Game Reserve lies 28 km south of Alice on the main King William's Town-Fort Beaufort road.

Bookings and enquiries may be made through The Manager, L.L. Sebe Game Reserve, P.O. Box 408, Alice 5700. (telephone Alice and ask for 1403) or The Director-General, Ciskei Department of Wildlife Resources, P.O. Box 186, Bisho, Ciskei (telephone Bisho 95-2115).

Mpofu Game Reserve

Mpofu offers varied outdoor activities to its guests. You can view game, walk in the high peaks of the dramatic Katberg range, test your angling skills or, if you want to, try your hand at the ancient art of bow-hunting.

The reserve lies in the northern Ciskei, north of Fort Beaufort, between the Katberg range

Above left: White rhinos in the Thomas Baines Nature Reserve.
Above right: A grey rhebok. This buck favours hills, plateaus and grassy valleys, and is sometimes found among low bush and scattered trees on mountainsides. In the breeding season, males frequently thrill visitors to game parks by staging fierce mock battles, pursuing each other and uttering sharp clicking noises. These 'fights' usually end without harm to the combatants.
Right: The rufous-naped lark is a familiar sight in Southern Africa, and may often be seen perched on termite mounds or fence posts. Its nest is covered with a thin canopy.

and the Katberg River in an area of dense yellowwood forest, rolling grassland and bush-covered ravines.

The countryside here teems with animals such as grysbok, black wildebeest, blesbok, bushbuck, bushpig, blue duiker, springbok, Cape fox and red hartebeest. There are also numerous bird species to be seen.

This reserve, near Balfour, is in Ciskei's Stockenström district which was named after Sir Andries Stockenström – controversial lieutenant-governor of the eastern Cape Region – who was fired from office in 1839 after returning the so-called 'buffer zone', between the Kei and the Keiskamma rivers, to its original owners, the Xhosa-speaking people.

Accommodation comprises one 8-bedded lodge, which is self-contained and includes the services of a chef. Two 10-bedded cabins suitable for hikers are to be built in the near future.

Bookings and enquiries should be directed to The Director-General, Ciskei Department of Wildlife Resources, P.O. Box 186, Bisho, Ciskei (telephone Bisho 95-2115) or, to The Manager, Mpofu Game Reserve, P.O. Box 647, Fort Beaufort 5720 (telephone Balfour 11).

Mpongo Game Reserve

At Mpongo, which lies only a stone's throw from East London in the Umpongo River Valley, nature-lovers can see over 40 species of large animals and hundreds of species of birds.

You can explore the reserve in the comfort of your own vehicle (on a 25 km circular road) or venture down narrow trails on horseback or on foot. There is a choice of guided trails which range from 5 km rambles to full-day 20 km hikes. There are also exciting night safaris with an experienced ranger who is always ready to share his knowledge with hikers. A minimum of eight people is required for guided trails.

After all this exercise you may be ready for good food at the Huberta Restaurant, which is scenically located above a hippo pool.

The reserve has a caravan and camping site for overnight guests, although day visitors are also welcome and may use braai and picnic sites. Other features of the reserve are a curio shop and the W. J. Burchell Natural History Museum. For more information write to The Officer-in-Charge, Mpongo Game Reserve, P.O. Box 3300, Cambridge. (telephone Macleantown 669).

Pirie Forest

A turn-off from the main King William's Town-Stutterheim road, about 12 km north of King William's Town, leads to the Pirie Forest.

The best way to see the forest is on the circular Pirie Nature Walk, a delightful path that starts at a kiosk at the southern end of the Maden Dam – also the start of the much longer Amatola Hiking Trail – and winds past a disused sawmill and logging railway into the upper reaches of two streams that drain the forest.

The path then turns north before swinging back to the south-east to follow the course of the Evelyn Stream back to the Maden Dam.

Most of the area is covered by forest, with tall yellowwood (*Podocarpus falcatus* and *Podocarpus latifolius*) dominating white stinkwood and white ironwood.

Bird-watchers will find plenty to see, from the soaring African goshawk to the small chorister robin and the red-billed hoopoe. Water birds include grey heron, dabchick and reed cormorant, while mammals are restricted mainly to rodents and the occasional monkey.

Pirie Trout Hatchery

Established in 1890 by the King William's Town Naturalist Society to acclimatise trout to the eastern Cape, this hatchery, the oldest in Southern Africa, continues to thrive. It is situated off the King William's Town-Stutterheim road and is open to the public during weekdays. Arrangements to visit should be made in advance by writing to The Officer-in-Charge, P.O. Box 35, King William's Town 5600 (telephone King William's Town 2-1001).

Pirie is the principal trout production station in the Cape and provides rainbow trout fingerlings for stocking rivers and dams in the eastern Cape. The hatchery is on the edge of the Pirie Forest, near the source of the Buffalo River in the Amatole Mountains.

Potter's Pass Wildflower Reserve

This 10 ha reserve of unspoilt natural vegetation is located in the built-up area of East London, where some 70 species of flowering plants may be seen. The reserve is always open, but be careful of vagrants in this area.

This reserve, and much of historical East London, may be visited by walking on one of four routes offered on The Urban Trail, for which a brochure is available. Write to The Town Clerk, East London Municipality, P.O. Box 984, East London 5200 (telephone East London 34-9111).

Queen's Park and Zoo

This compact and well laid-out zoo, with its entrance from East London's Beaconsfield Street, is situated in a 34 ha garden of indigenous trees and shrubs on gently sloping ground between the city centre and the Buffalo River.

Left: A female oribi in eastern Cape grassland. There are more than 400 oribi on farms in the Bathurst-Kleinmond area. **Above:** This leaf beetle is just one of 30000 different beetle species represented in Southern Africa. **Opposite page above:** Terrapins move between terra firma and fresh water at will. They are strong swimmers, fond of eating frogs, tadpoles, crabs and fish. **Opposite page right:** A giant kingfisher on the lookout for a meal. This bird's bill equips it well to deal with its favourite food of crabs, which it catches by diving into the water. **Opposite page left:** A vervet monkey on the ground. Found in rural parts of the eastern Cape, these small creatures are regarded as pests by many citrus farmers.

The zoo features 60 mammal species, 120 species of bird and 26 species of reptile. The park and zoo are open to visitors between 9 a.m. and 5 p.m. all year round.

Roundhill Oribi Reserve
When alarmed, the little oribi will whistle loudly and gallop from danger at great speed. As it runs it gives an occasional 'stot' – a delightful, stiff-legged jump – which allows it a view from above the long grass. On first sight it seems nature provided perfect preservation mechanisms for the oribi – but not quite: the little antelope's inquisitive nature usually takes over after about 100m, prompting it to stop – sometimes even to walk back to the source of danger. Many hunters have taken advantage of the habits of these springbok-sized antelope and today their numbers are very low.

190

There are now 12 oribi on the 'Roundhill' (proclaimed in 1985) between Bathurst and Kleinmond, while a further 400 animals have been recorded on farms in the area. The purpose of the 325 ha reserve is to monitor and hopefully breed the endangered oribi. Due to the animals' sensitivity visitors are not permitted to enter the reserve. For more information contact the Algoa Regional Services Council, P.O. Box 318, Port Elizabeth 6000 (telephone Port Elizabeth 52-1616).

Shipwreck Trail and Strandloper Trail
Whether you choose to explore the east coast as a daring shipwrecked sailor, or as a resourceful strandloper (beach walker), your reward will be warm water, unspoilt beaches and only the crashing of waves and the cry of terns, gulls and cormorants to intrude on your

isolation. You will also have the chance for rock- and surf-angling, snorkeling, spear fishing and the ultimate in beach hiking – river-crossing.

Crossing estuaries is fun, but it can also be dangerous. There are rules to remember. Never cross on an outgoing tide (carry a tide-table) and beware of sharks in murky water. If you're in any doubt walk upstream until you find a safer crossing point.

On the Shipwreck Trail you can experience all 64 km of Ciskei's beautiful coast over four days, or spend just one night on any isolated stretch of coast you choose. If camping on the beach doesn't suit you, there are also hotels on the way. Fresh water is available at organised camping spots only. The Gqutywa and Mtana rivers are in a military area and must be crossed between the high and low tidal marks during daytime. Bookings for the Shipwreck

Day and night trails have been laid out, and guests are accompanied by a game ranger. There are also tours in a 4-wheel-drive vehicle.

Fascinating exotic animals introduced at Tsolwana include Barbary sheep, Corsican mouflon, the Himalayan tahr, Indian black buck and fallow deer. Animals indigenous to the area include giraffe, white rhino, eland, Cape mountain zebra, black wildebeest, red hartebeest, springbok, blesbok, grey rhebok, steenbok and klipspringer. Limited hunting is permitted, but only under supervision.

To reach the park, take the Whittlesea road from Queenstown and after 19 km the 'Upper Swart Kei' road. From here a gravel road leads to the entrance which is clearly signposted on the left, some 38 km further on.

The park is open throughout the year (though day visitors enter and leave between 8 a.m. and 6 p.m.). For bookings write to The Manager, Tsolwana Game Reserve, P.O. Box 1424, Queenstown 5320 (telephone Tsolwana 1).

Umtiza Nature Reserve
A pleasant reserve set in the rolling hills of the eastern Cape coastal zone, about 13 km from East London on the Buffalo Pass road, Umtiza's 560 ha of valley bushveld vegetation offers sanctuary to tenderwood trees, cycads and Cape box.

Animals include tree dassie, bushbuck, the endangered blue duiker and Umtiza's samango monkey. Also in the Umtiza Reserve is the umtiza tree, (*Umtiza listerana*), found nowhere else in the world other than here and along a section of the Buffalo River.

There are numerous pleasant day walks through the reserve. Entry is confined to daylight hours and is by permit, obtainable from The State Forester, East London Coast State Forest, P.O. Box 5185, Greenfields 5208 (telephone East London 46-3532).

Waters Meeting Nature Reserve
A unique horseshoe-shaped canyon, through which the Kowie River flows, is a notable feature of the charmingly named Waters Meeting Nature Reserve, an extensive (986 ha, to be enlarged to 4 247 ha) sanctuary near Bathurst (follow the signs reading 'Forestry Department Waters Meeting Nature Reserve').

Various nature trails wind through the area, and there are a number of pleasant picnic spots. Fish eagle, oribi and the blue duiker – all endangered species – are among its wildlife population, though Waters Meeting is primarily a forest reserve: there are dense indigenous woodlands along the river banks.

Entry is during daylight hours only, and a permit is required. This may be obtained from The State Forester, Bathurst State Forest, P.O. Box 116, Bathurst 6166 (telephone Bathurst 3876).

Trail may be made through The Director-General, Ciskei Department of Tourism, Private Bag X0026, Bisho, Ciskei (telephone Bisho 9-2171). A brochure is available.

The complete 94 km (six-day) Strandloper Trail, between East London and the Kei River is a hiking marathon, but it can also be split into smaller sections if you choose. This is an informal hike, and no facilities are provided. Hikers stay in campsites or hotels along the way and may not camp on the beach. It is not necessary to book or obtain a permit.

Thomas Baines Nature Reserve
Situated off the Port Elizabeth road, some 15 km from Grahamstown, this pleasant provincial reserve is open daily from 6 a.m. to 6 p.m.

There are 15 km of road within the 975 ha reserve (speed limit: 30 km/h). The vegetation

consists mainly of valley bushveld with fynbos. Typical species in this region include wild olive, euphorbia and white ironwood.

Among the larger mammals found here are eland, mountain reedbuck, buffalo, bontebok, impala, black wildebeest and white rhino. Prominent among the reserve's prolific bird species are a variety of kingfishers and the red-billed hoopoe. There are toilets in the recreation area at Settlers Dam, but no other facilities.

Tsolwana Game Park
This region of semi-arid plain, rolling grassland and scrub-covered slopes is popular with hikers, sightseers, game-viewers and hunters. Accommodation is in three lodges (8-bedded, 10-bedded and 12-bedded) and in a trail camp. All the huts are fully equipped and staffed (visitors must provide food and drinks).

The last of the Cape herds

Port Elizabeth, capital of the Eastern Province, is a convenient base for exploring the region's many and varied reserves – and the stretches of shimmering coastline, the river gorges thickly blanketed by indigenous trees, and the rolling bush country which is the home of the Addo elephant. Two of the major attractions of the area – the Snake Park and the Oceanarium – are actually within the city, and Port Elizabeth's public parks and gardens are themselves colourful havens of nature in the midst of the commercial bustle.

Addo Elephant National Park

'If ever there was a hunter's hell here it was – a hundred square miles or so of all you would think bad in Central Africa, lifted up as by some Titan and planked [sic] down in the Cape Province.' The words of Major P.J. Pretorius in his book, *Jungle Man*. This was the Addo Bush, where, in 1919, he was employed to eliminate the elephants and to resolve, for all time, the contest between agriculturists and game animals. Pretorius, last of the legendary great hunters, killed 120 elephants before the survivors – about 11 animals – fled to the impenetrable area known as the Harvey Bush.

The 'hunter's hell', between the Zuurberg and the Sundays River Valley, is now a 8590 ha refuge, of which some 7900 ha are available to the elephant at present – an area which, proportionately, supports three times the number of elephants found in any other part of the African continent.

At present, there are 165 elephant in the park. Other animals which have been reintroduced to their ancestral homeland are the black rhino, eland, buffalo and red hartebeest. The largely nocturnal animals found in the park (visitors will probably see only their spoor) include porcupine, jackal, bushpig, aardvark, mongoose and caracal.

Approximately 185 bird species make their home in the sanctuary's valley-bushveld vegetation where the usual forest canopy grows to a height of 3,6 m with taller trees on the slopes and in the ravines. The spekboom (*Portulacaria afra*) predominates in the area and is a favourite food of the elephant.

Among other plant species are the tree fuchsia, sneezewood, guarri, succulents and many types of shrub. There is no naturally occurring surface water within the park, and the authorities have had to sink boreholes, which supply earth dams.

Until recently, tours by motor bus were the only means of viewing within the elephant enclosure, but now visitors are allowed to enter in their own vehicles.

The Addo Elephant National Park (proclaimed in 1931) is 72 km north of Port Elizabeth and is open throughout the year. Tourist accommodation consists of six rondavels, three guest cottages and 24 three-bedded chalets. There is a camping area with sites for 20 tents or caravans.

Above: The num-num shrub (*Carissa bispinosa*) in the Addo National Park carries succulent edible berries. The shrub is easily recognised by its stout green, forked spines. Certain other species of the num-num family are poisonous. **Left:** A bull elephant takes a mud bath in the park. The 165 elephants at Addo are the last remnants of the great herds which roamed the southern Cape over 100 years ago. **Right:** A canopy of green shelters about 185 bird species in the park. Spekboom – the elephant's favourite food – covers a large area of the park.

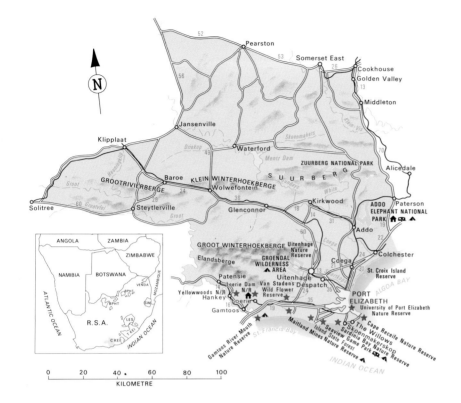

An early problem in the park was the effort involved in keeping the elephants within their boundaries and away from the property of vengeful farmers. Having been hunted almost to extinction, the Addo elephants had the reputation of being the most dangerous in the world. An electrified fence failed to contain them. Farmers and others living near the outskirts of the park suffered damage and claimed large sums in compensation. There were fatal encounters, too, and among the victims were farmers, hunters, a ranger and a woman who blundered into a herd of elephant while making her way home at night.

There is also the story of a farmer who was riding a wagon load of oats into Port Elizabeth when he found that he was being followed by a herd of elephant. Becoming desperate as they gained on him, he threw a bale of oats on to the roadway. This delayed them only a short while, and soon they were on his trail again. Another bale tumbled onto the road. There was little of the farmer's oats crop left when he passed beyond the limits of elephant territory, but the bales had bought him his life.

The park's first warden, Harold Trollope, started putting out hay, pumpkins, pineapples and oranges in an attempt to keep the elephants within the park's boundary. The plan worked, and soon the elephants learnt to expect a regular evening feed. With the completion of an elephant-proof fence in 1954, they were safe from the farmers' guns, but by this time the feeding ritual had become so popular that the practice was continued.

Each day a truckful of oranges was driven to a point close to a viewing ramp. The driver steered in tight circles, pursued by elephants as oranges rolled off in all directions.

The intention was good but the outcome of this feeding ritual was almost disastrous: the elephants became addicted to the citrus: and, during the winter feeding season, they dared not move away from the rest camp area in case they missed the next feed. The result: a very small area of vegetation had to support some 75 per cent of the herd. Plant densities were soon drastically reduced by over-grazing. In addition to the stress on vegetation the behaviour of the elephants was affected: signs of stress and aggression increased as they competed for oranges, which, in 1976, were being fed to them at the rate of about 30 tons a month.

Animals were being injured, and at least one calf was killed, in the scramble for food, so the show was stopped in 1978. Today visitors may not bring any citrus fruits into the park, whether or not for their own consumption.

In 1982 there were 118 elephants in the park, some 30 more than its ideal carrying capacity. These, together with the three elephants believed to live in the depths of the Knysna forests,

are the last remnants of the great herds which roamed the southern Cape as recently as the latter half of the 19th century.

The Addo herd is not a separate subspecies, as was once believed. The Knysna elephants, too, are of the same general type, although each group differs in some ways from the herds found in the Kruger National Park and farther north. Of the Addo elephants, only the bulls have tusks, and these are usually fairly short. Extremely well nourished and secure in the bush, the Addo elephant has a thicker layer of fat than any other elephant in Africa.

One of the Addo elephants is an elderly cow known as Afslurpie – 'cut off trunk'. She has successfully overcome the loss of that extremely sensitive organ, the tip of her trunk. The trunk, an extension of the nose and upper lip, is manipulated by about 50 000 muscles and is the elephant's most important single organ for the purposes of day-to-day survival. With its trunk it feeds and drinks (daily intake is up to 200 kg of vegetation and 90 litres of water), dusts itself, trumpets, touches and smells things – and uses it as a shower. The water-holding capacity of the trunk is about 17 litres.

The low ratio between an elephant's body surface area and body mass means that it has no difficulty in keeping warm – but, by the same token, it may have trouble keeping cool. Where water is available, they wallow, bathe and spray themselves.

An elephant's great ears are not only acute sensory organs; they also act as fans. As the temperature increases, the ears are flapped more frequently. This directs air currents over the body, and also exposes the inner side of the ear, where large veins pass close to the surface. It is estimated that blood flowing through an elephant's ear is cooled by as much as 6°C.

Elephants are highly sociable animals, and the remarkable way they look after their own kind has always evoked a sense of wonder. Hunters found that a herd was often reluctant to desert a wounded companion, and would sometimes range themselves on either side to support it on its feet.

A cow has been seen endangering herself by rescuing her calf from a flooded river; another was seen carrying her dead calf on her tusks (she eventually buried it). Elephants often bury dead animals, occasionally even those of other species. However, the reasons for this, and for their apparent selflessness, remain something of a mystery.

Bushbuck Walk

The walk follows an easy 16 km trail through indigenous forest that was once inhabited by elephant, buffalo and other large mammal species, and now provides the home for over 50 bird species, as well as the vervet monkey, bushpig and small antelope, including the rare blue duiker.

This walk passes through The Island State Forest (495 ha), some 25 km from Port Elizabeth, and offers fine views of the sweep of St. Francis Bay and Jeffrey's Bay.

Among the 40 tree species, ranging from Outeniqua yellowwood to the sweet thorn (*Acacia karoo*), is the curiously named perdepis (*Clausena anisata*). The name derives from the unpleasant smell which is given off when the leaves are crushed, but an infusion of these leaves was once regarded as a very effective

---

ADDO AT A GLANCE

When to go The park is open throughout the year from 15 minutes before sunrise to 15 minutes after sunset. Access to the fenced game area, however, varies with the season. From 1 March to 30 April the gates are open from 6.30 a.m. to 6 p.m.; 1 May to 31 August from 7 a.m. to 5.30 p.m.; 1 September to 28 February from 6 a.m. to 7 p.m. On entry into the park, visitors who have booked accommodation must produce proof that their reservations have been confirmed. December and January are the busiest months. You are more likely to see the elephants during the mornings of warm days than at any other time.

Reservations and information Accommodation may be reserved up to 12 months in advance by writing to National Parks Board, P.O. Box 787, Pretoria 0001 (telephone Pretoria 343-1991) or National Parks Board, P.O. Box 7400, Roggebaai 8012 (telephone Cape Town 419-5365) or National Parks Board, P.O. Box 774, George 6530 (telephone George 74-6924/5). Requests for information may be directed to The Park Warden, Addo Elephant National Park, P.O. Box 52, Addo 6105 (telephone Addo 40-0556).

Getting there When travelling from Port Elizabeth to Grahamstown, take a left turn to Addo some 10 km outside Port Elizabeth. The right-hand turn into the park is some 15 km beyond Addo, just past Coerney Station, and is well signposted. When travelling from East London, take the Grahamstown-Port Elizabeth road as far as the junction with the Cookhouse-Ncanaha road. Turn right and drive as far as Paterson then turn left to the Addo-Ann's Villa junction and left again at Coerney and then after about 3 km turn left again to the park.

Accommodation Addo has six rondavels, 24 three-bedded chalets and three guest cottages for visitors. All are self-contained and include electricity and refrigerators. (A communal kitchen, with crockery and cutlery provides cooking facilities for the six rondavels). The 20 caravan and campsites have fireplaces, and there are ablution blocks with toilets, hot and cold showers, and laundry facilities. For day visitors, there are pleasant picnic sites.

Eating and drinking The camp restaurant serves à la carte meals. Bread and milk, as well as beer and wines, can be bought at the camp. Cooking is done out of doors over open fires, and firewood is sold at the camp shop.

Getting around Visitors are provided with a map showing the park's 43 km of roads and the numbered orientation points. No motorcycles, caravans or open cars are allowed in the park. Petrol is available during the normal selling hours, but not diesel fuel or bottled gas.

Wildlife Elephant are the main attraction of the Addo Park, but there are also a number of buffalo, black rhinoceros, eland, kudu, red hartebeest and various smaller antelope, jackal, caracal and mongoose. The bird population – some 185 different bird species have been recorded – is also a major drawcard at Addo. There is an observation point for bird-watchers at a dam near the restaurant.

Special precautions No citrus fruits of any kind may be taken into the park. Firearms must be sealed at the office, and no pets are allowed.

Left above: A female Cape rock thrush. This species (*Monticola rupestris*) is one of the more common of 37 species of thrushes and chats in Southern Africa, and its song is heard throughout the Addo Park. **Left below:** The male Cape rock thrush is recognised by its slate-grey head, neck, chin and throat, and tawny plumage (the female is spotted and barred, with mottled brown head and neck).
Above: *Schotia* trees in the Addo National Park. These trees, also known as 'boerboon' or 'farmer's bean', have shiny foliage and small, brilliant-red flowers. In bloom, these nectar-rich flowers are a great attraction for birds and insects.

THE BUCK WITH THE CRUMPLED HORN

A bent horn gives a disreputable look to one of two red hartebeest in the Addo Elephant National Park.

When standing still, the red (or Cape) hartebeest is not usually ranked among the most attractive of Southern Africa's antelope. Its shoulders are higher than its white rump, which gives it a sloping back; the blackish patches on its head and legs look like stains on its otherwise chestnut coat; its long and thin face is surmounted by horns that first curve up and outwards, then turn back on themselves to point inwards and backwards.

In motion, however, the hartebeest is more impressive. Its awkward-looking body is designed for speed (its cousin, the tsessebe or 'bastard hartebeest', is probably the fastest of all antelope).

The head and body are streamlined, and the long nose serves as a radiator that cools blood flowing to the brain. The horns come into their own in fights, both in duelling with a rival and battling a predator.

The hartebeest is a social animal and is com- monly seen in harem herds of between five and 30 breeding cows and their calves. One harem may associate with a mature bull and his territory for a considerable period. A mature bull lives in a territory he has marked off, usually by scraping his horns on the ground in various places, depositing excrement, or simply standing in the area to show it is occupied. Such an individual must be especially watchful during the rutting season, when he may have to fight fiercely to keep competitors at bay.

Immature bulls and those too old to participate in the rut frequently join bachelor herds. In spite of their often considerable strength, such herds are excluded from the best grazing areas by the territorial bulls, which allow only the harem to join them.

Red hartebeest were once reduced to near extinction by over-shooting. Today, however, they are plentiful in parks and reserves.

---

medicine, particularly during the devastating influenza epidemic of 1918.

At the starting point of the walk is a picnic clearing with fireplaces (this is the only part of the area in which fires are allowed). Firewood is sold on site.

To reach The Island State Forest from Port Elizabeth, take the Seaview turn-off from the Humansdorp road, some 35 km outside the city. The turn-off to the forest is well signposted.

Permits should be obtained from the Forester-in-Charge (telephone Port Elizabeth 74-1634).

Cape Recife Nature Reserve
This 336 ha municipal reserve, surrounding the Cape Recife lighthouse, is restricted (entrance is by permit only) to allow it to recover from over-exploitation. Anglers have stripped the rocks of shellfish in their search for bait, and off road vehicles have disturbed nesting birds. By damaging vegetation, vehicles have also increased the threat of wind erosion.

Gamtoos River Mouth Nature Reserve
A rich lagoon wetland in the middle of the wide sweep of St Francis Bay is the focus of the 1 000 ha Gamtoos River Mouth Nature Reserve.

Besides being a well-established fishing spot (white steenbras and kabeljou are caught) you will find a huge variety of water birds, including red-billed teal, yellow-billed duck, purple heron, red-knobbed coot and plenty of white egret and osprey.

The osprey, a migratory fish eagle, is usually seen near the water's edge or soaring over the estuary. It is recognised by distinctive white and brown plumage.

A picnic site and caravan park are situated here and a second caravan park is located further upstream. The reserve lies east of Jeffrey's Bay, some 10 km off the N2. For bookings and enquiries contact the Chief Directorate of Nature and Environmental Conservation, Private Bag, X1126, Port Elizabeth 6000 (telephone Port Elizabeth 390-9111).

Groendal Wilderness Area
The whole of this large (25 047 ha) tract of wilderness lies in very broken terrain – rolling mountains, deep river ravines and stretches of very dense valley bushveld. It is situated on the Great Winterhoek mountain range, about 10 km from Uitenhage, and is drained by the Swartkops River. The Groendal Dam is within the area.

Trails have been laid out in the sanctuary, and visitors are warned that it is both difficult and dangerous to hike on routes other than the prepared ones. There is a large variety of flora (60 tree species have been noted) and wildlife includes bushbuck, duiker, grey rhebok, mountain reedbuck, grysbok, bushpig, vervet monkey, chacma baboon and leopard. Visitors may also see many forest birds as well as francolin and pheasant. Permits for hiking and overnight camping are available at the Groendal office, at the entrance to the wilderness area. To get there, drive along Caledon Road (in a

Above: The Cape clawless otter (this one was photographed at the Port Elizabeth Oceanarium) spends less time in water than the spotted-necked otter, and passes most of its time sunbathing on rocks or sandbars. **Right:** A jackass penguin on St Croix Island in Algoa Bay.

northerly direction), turn left into Gibson Road and right into Groendal Road.

For further information, write to The Forester, Groendal Wilderness Area, P.O. Box 445, Uitenhage 6230 (telephone Uitenhage 2-5418).

Loerie Dam Nature Reserve
You can sample some of the magic of the Baviaanskloof Mountains by discovering Loerie Dam Nature Reserve and its spectacular slopes, valleys and streams. It lies north of the town of Loerie, terminus of the famous Apple Express Railway. This old steam train puffs its way through apple orchards in the fertile Longkloof region on one of the last remaining narrow-gauge railways in South Africa. There cannot be a more exciting way to visit the area if you are coming from Port Elizabeth.

The 1 000 ha reserve is used mainly for conservation and environmental education and provides groups of up to 35 accommodation in a converted farmhouse. There is also an 18-bedded timber hut, which is ideal for smaller groups as well as hikers. Some spectacular hiking opportunities are provided by the 7 km Wild Goose Trail, which leads through deep, forested valleys offering walkers a chance to discover the diverse range of fynbos, birds and animals.

For more information, write to Algoa Regional Services Council, P.O. Box 318, Port Elizabeth 6000 (telephone Port Elizabeth 52-1616).

For more information on the Apple Express write to The Curator, Humerail Museum, P.O. Box 1139, Port Elizabeth 6000 (telephone Port Elizabeth 520-2313).

196

Maitland Mines Nature Reserve
The main feature of the secluded 127 ha Maitland Mines reserve, some 30 km from Port Elizabeth near the mouth of the Maitland River, is the large area of indigenous forest which clothes the steep slope of the river terrace. The reserve takes its name from the lead mines which were worked there in the 19th century.

The area has been left undisturbed for many years, and as a result the bird life is prolific. It is sustained by an abundance of food – during one month (October) as many as 35 plant species flower or fruit.

No fires may be made in the reserve, and no accommodation is available (however the reserve adjoins the camping area at Maitland River Mouth). Two short hiking trails have been laid out. To reach the reserve, take any of the roads from Port Elizabeth to Seaview and follow the coastal road to Maitland Mouth. No permits are required to enter the reserve which is open to visitors at all times. For more information contact The Algoa Regional Services Council, P.O. Box 318, Port Elizabeth 6000 (telephone Port Elizabeth 52-1616).

Port Elizabeth Oceanarium
The Oceanarium, part of the museum complex on the beachfront at Humewood, is famous for the performances of its bottle-nosed dolphins.

It is open throughout the year, from 9 a.m. to 1 p.m. and 2 p.m. to 5 p.m. Performances are held daily at 11 a.m. and 3 p.m., and the dolphins can be viewed through the windows of an underwater observatory as they swim about their 6 million litre pool.

Other exhibits at the oceanarium include Cape fur seals and jackass penguins – named for their call, which is remarkably similar to that of a braying donkey. There is also a large fish tank (under cover) containing local fish species, shark and turtle, and a smaller invertebrate tank which houses a colourful collection of corals, sponges, anemones and other sea creatures.

The oceanarium is situated on the beachfront, south of the city centre, and is distinguished by a dolphin mounted on the top of the building.

Port Elizabeth Snake Park
The original snake park consisted of a large outdoor enclosure built in the spacious grounds of the Bird Street Museum. When the museum was moved to its present locality in Humewood, a new snake park was built (opening in 1959). The park maintains the traditional open pit for exhibiting local snakes.

Other snakes may be seen in glass-fronted cases, and indigenous and exotic constrictors can be seen in the new Python House. Other reptiles – including lizard, alligator, leguaan and crocodile – are housed in large open pits, and their feeding is a spectacular show.

In the fascinating Tropical House, which adjoins the snake park, visitors can walk along a path leading through dense and luxuriant vegetation, past waterfalls and around an artificial mountain where large numbers of birds and waterfowl can be seen. The 'Night House', which is well worth a visit, features nocturnal animals which, in conditions of simulated moonlight, are active during visiting times.

The snake park and Tropical House are open from 9 a.m. to 1 p.m. and from 2 p.m. to 5 p.m. Videos on snakes are held daily.

St Croix Island Reserve

The three rocky islands which make up this 12 ha reserve – St Croix, Brenton and Jahleel – are situated just off the mouth of the Coega River in Algoa Bay. The reserve, which may not be visited by the public, was established as a breeding sanctuary for the endangered jackass penguin. When disturbed, this bird tends to leave its nest and so exposes its chicks or eggs to the depredations of gulls.

Sardinia Bay and Sylvic Nature Reserves

These reserves are on a stretch of coast between Schoenmakerskop and Seaview, and are in effect two reserves in one. The 'Sardinia Bay Sea Reserve' was established first (by the Dias Divisional Council). When it was found impractical to administer an area from the high water mark to a point 1 km out to sea, the adjacent land was proclaimed the Sylvic Nature Reserve.

The marine reserve is not only a sanctuary for sea organisms, but also serves as a reference area against which is assessed the impact of civilisation elsewhere on the coast. An area of dune and sand-flats, it is easily subject to human-induced deterioration, a situation which threatened the very existence of Port Elizabeth a century ago.

The balance between dune stabilisation by vegetation, and dune instability resulting from the action of wind and sea, is very delicate. Too much human activity on the dunes will kill vegetation and cause instability of the dunes, so all developments which might lead to high human densities – car parks, toilets and launching ramps, for example – are carefully controlled by the authorities. No vehicles are allowed in the Sylvic Nature Reserve.

Both reserves are open throughout the year. Fishing is prohibited, and nothing may be removed from the area. They can be reached via the Schoenmakerskop, Lovemore Park and Sardinia Bay roads. The control point at Sardinia Bay is 20 km from the Port Elizabeth City Hall.

For more information about the reserves write to The Algoa Regional Services Council, P.O. Box 318, Port Elizabeth 6000 (telephone Port Elizabeth 52-1616).

Seaview Game Park

The Seaview Game Park and Animal Shelter is situated some 25 km west of Port Elizabeth. To reach the game park turn off the N2 national road at the sign 'Seaview/Greenbushes'. After travelling approximately 7,5 km turn left onto a gravel road marked 'Lion Park'. The

WILLIAM BURCHELL: BOTANIST SUPREME

With a specially equipped wagon, two spans of oxen and six Hottentots, a young Englishman, William Burchell, left Cape Town in June 1811 on an expedition that was to last nearly four years. Returning to England, he spent another ten years writing up the results of his observations: his *Catalogus Geographicus Plantarum* records 8 700 South African plants in 14 volumes of neat manuscript which may still be seen in the library at Kew, London. It was a remarkable feat of systematic scientific exploration, and of patient endurance.

Burchell is probably the most renowned of Southern Africa's pioneer naturalists.

His explorations near Prieska enabled him to describe, for the first time, the 'stone plant'

or lithops: almost a century was to pass before botanists noted any of the other fifty-odd species of lithops. He also discovered the world's second-largest land mammal — the white rhinoceros. As a painstaking and meticulous scientist, Burchell did not believe in short cuts. He was not satisfied until he had accumulated data from ten animals.

Some of his reports were received with scepticism in Europe ('There can be no such animal', it was once declared of Burchell's zebra), but Burchell was almost always proved correct. The name of this thorough and adventurous naturalist survives in the scientific names of many South African species, as well as in the plant genus *Burchellia*.

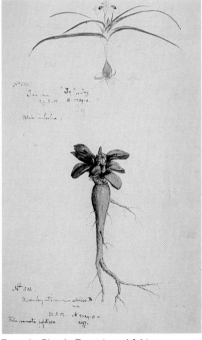

Above and right: Pencil and watercolour illustrations by William Burchell, painted from specimens collected at Kosi

Fountain, Pintado Fountain and Jabiru Fountain (the latter two located in the Kuruman district) in 1812.

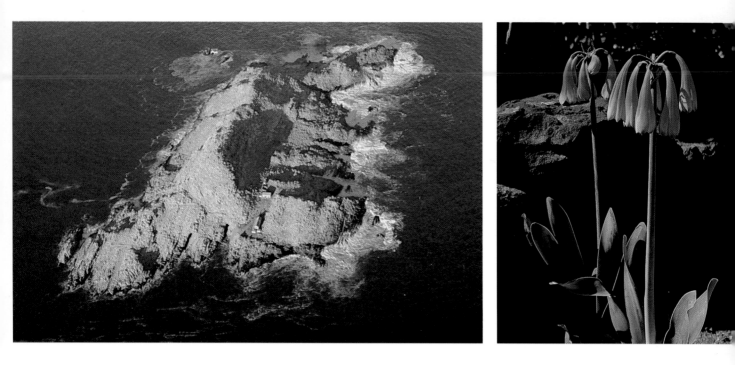

entrance to the game park is reached after approximately 0,7 kilometres.

A variety of game is readily visible from your car, and includes giraffe, lion, zebra, nyala, impala, wildebeest, kudu and blesbok. Baboon, raptors, duiker, caracal, lynx, owl and cheetah may be seen on foot in the animal shelter. Visitors may watch the lion being fed at noon on Sundays; the cheetah at 4 p.m. every Tuesday, Thursday, Saturday and Sunday.

If you feel like walking through the bush the Nyala Trail takes about 45 minutes.

A tea-room serves light meals and refreshments. There are also braai facilities at the campsite which caters for tents and caravans. There are toilet facilities and cold showers. Campers must bring their own firewood and provisions.

The game park is open daily throughout the year between 8 a.m. and 5 p.m. For additional information, write to The Seaview Game Park, P.O. Box Greenbushes 6390 (telephone Port Elizabeth 74-1702).

Settlers' Park Nature Reserve

The four floral regions which converge in the vicinity of Port Elizabeth are represented in this 54 ha reserve close to the city's central business area. The Baakens River, which flows through the reserve, has sculpted cliffs and ravines, and pools and running water sparkle amid wide lawns and a colourful variety of trees and flowers.

Plants characteristic of the western Cape fynbos, such as ericas, proteas, leucospermums

198

and leucadendrons, as well as daisies (belonging to the family *Compositae*) and Cape thatching reed (*Restionaceae*) are to be found in the reserve. The temperate to subtropical coastal flora is represented by both deciduous and evergreen trees including yellowwood and coral tree (*Erythrina*), with climbing plants, forest lilies, ferns and water plants. Grassland flora includes many grass types, herbs and bulbous plants, while Karoo flora and valley bushveld provide spekboom, *Euphorbia*, *Aloe*, *Mesembryanthemum* and other succulents.

Small buck and other mammals live in the reserve but are rarely seen by day. Among resident water birds are Egyptian and spur-winged goose, yellow-billed duck, and moorhen. Other birds include the greater and lesser double-collared sunbird, paradise flycatcher, Knysna loerie, white-browed coucal, doves, thrush, robin, canary and weaver.

There are paths and roads across the reserve between the car parks, and stepping-stones with handrails enable visitors to cross the river at seven places.

Climbing on the cliffs is dangerous. Dogs are not allowed in the reserve, which is open during daylight hours. The main parking area is reached from Park Drive/How Avenue or Hallack Road. There are also entrances off Targetkloof, Fordyce Road in Walmer, and off Brickmakerskloof.

Uitenhage Nature Reserve

Established around the Uitenhage Springs Holiday Resort, the 908 ha sanctuary contains a net-

work of easy paths that lead through typical valley-bushveld to several outstanding viewpoints. To reach it, take the signposted turn-off from the Graaff-Reinet road, about 6 km north of Uitenhage.

The reserve is open from 7.30 a.m. to 7 p.m. from October to March, and from 8 a.m. to 5.30 p.m. during the rest of the year. Permits must be obtained in advance from the Supervisor of the Springs Resort.

The vegetation includes many species of aloe among the area's 300 plant types. Trails have been prepared. Kleinkop Walk is the shortest, taking about 30 minutes to complete, and leads up a koppie where the valley bush thins and is replaced by fynbos. An hour can be added to the walking time by taking the path north from Kleinkop to Grootkop.

A route branching to the left before the summit of Grootkop leads to Bayview, so named for its fine views of Algoa Bay. There is a lookout tower which visitors may use at their own risk. On top of the elevation known as 'The Tongue', reached after a short climb, is a great variety of flowering plants, including *Crassula*, *Pelargonium*, *Mesembryanthemum*, *Haworthia* and *Aloe*.

The reserve has plenty of bird life, and among the mammals are porcupine, duiker, bushbuck, grysbok, steenbok, vervet monkey, bushpig, mongoose and meerkat.

Facilities at the resort include single rondavels, double rondavels and chalets. Visitors staying in rondavels must provide their own linen, crockery and cutlery. There are also caravan

Above: A bushbuck in the Seaview Game Park. This chestnut-coloured, nocturnal browser feeds on leaves, roots and shoots. **Far left:** St Croix Island Reserve, near the mouth of the Coega River, is a breeding sanctuary for the jackass penguin. **Near left:** The attractive soldier lily *(Cyrtanthus obliquus)* grows wild in the eastern Cape.

Yellowwoods Nature Reserve

You can picnic beside a small river under the shade of a canopy of ancient, spreading yellowwood trees in this small 50 ha municipal nature reserve outside Hankey.

At this tranquil spot you can also swim in the stream, run on the grass, or head for the local golf course, which lies next to the reserve. Even if you don't get a 'birdie' during your nine holes you can expect to see kingfisher, francolin and sunbird in this beautiful little reserve.

For the energetic there is nothing to beat a walk up Dassieskraal Mountain – the summit of which provides panoramic views of the whole town, the nature reserve as well as the carefully mown fairways running up and down the golf course.

The reserve and golf course are sign-posted on the road leading to Patensie. There is a camping and caravan site with toilets, showers and electricity in the reserve.

For more information and bookings write to The Town Clerk, Hankey Municipality, P.O. Box 3, Hankey 6350 (telephone Hankey 302).

Zuurberg National Park

Three areas in the Winterhoek Mountains have been added together to create the enormous 20 777 ha Zuurberg National Park – an expanse of undulating hills and deep ravines where unique and fascinating plants are to be found. Some of them, such as the Zuurberg cushion bush *(Oldenburgia arbuscula)* and the Zuurberg Cycad *(Encephalartos longifolius)*, occur nowhere else outside this area.

In this fascinating, undulating landscape – over 600 m separates the highest peaks from the deepest ravines – there are three quite different veld types: false fynbos; spekboomveld and evergreen forest.

The most common of these veld types is false fynbos, or macchia, which includes low-lying shrubs such as sugar bush, heath, 'tolbos' mountain cedars and buchu. In the deep, shady ravines which bisect the rolling hills ironwood, yellowwood, assegaai and white stinkwood trees provide shelter for a host of forest birds, including the exceptional Knysna loerie, black saw-wing swallow and black and crowned eagle.

Large game which used to occur in the area is being introduced, and there is already a large resident population of grey rhebok, mountain reedbuck, bushbuck, grey duiker, bushpig, baboon, caracal and jackal. The park is also a sanctuary for blue duiker – an endangered species. Kudu sometimes migrate in and out of the area.

While there are no tourist facilities in Zuurberg, at present, day visitors are permitted into the park and comfortable accommodation is provided at a nearby hotel.

sites. To make a reservation, write to The Manager, Springs Holiday Resort, P.O. Box 45, Uitenhage 6230 (telephone Uitenhage 6-1161).

University of Port Elizabeth Nature Reserve

Besides being one of South Africa's leading academic institutions, the University of Port Elizabeth has an added distinction – the whole campus has been proclaimed a nature reserve. Students on their way to and from lectures pass grysbok, springbok and on occasion, duiker and bushbuck.

Most of the vegetation in the 716 ha nature reserve has been invaded by the Australian species of acacia, including Port Jackson and rooikrans, but attempts are now being made to re-establish naturally occurring indigenous species back into the area.

This is a private nature reserve. If you would like to have further information, write to The University of Port Elizabeth, Zoology Department, P.O. Box 1600, Port Elizabeth (telephone Port Elizabeth 531-1341).

Van Staden's Wild Flower Reserve and Bird Sanctuary

Situated in east Cape fynbos, with indigenous Alexandria forest in the south, the reserve is some 40 km from the Port Elizabeth city centre,

on the eastern side of Van Staden's Pass. It is open throughout the year. There are picnic sites, and a hiking trail leads down to the Van Staden's River. Walking is encouraged in the reserve, and there are few restricted areas.

Permits to enter the reserve are required only in the case of groups of 20 or more people, and should be requested from The Chief Executive Officer, Algoa Regional Services Council, P.O. Box 318, Port Elizabeth 6000 (telephone Port Elizabeth 52-1616).

The reserve is especially renowned for its wealth of protea, as well as for the beauty of its tree and ground orchids. The crane-flower, *Strelitzia reginae*, is native to these easterly parts of the 'Cape Floral Kingdom'.

An important endemic plant is the fire lily *(Cyrtanthus stadensis)*, and rare tree species include the Cape star-chestnut *(Sterculia alexandri)*, the buig-my-nie *(Smelophyllum capense)* and the Cape wing-nut *(Atalaya capensis)*.

There is a wealth of bird life in the reserve, and among the mammals is the little blue duiker. The dominant trees of the forest are the real, or 'true', ironwood and bastard saffron-wood *(Cassine peragua)*, while the wild pomegranate *(Burchellia bubalina)* is fairly common. There are braai spots at the old bridge over the Van Staden's River, but no other facilities.

199

On the beach

Hikers explore Transkei's Wild Coast. The thousands of kilometres of Southern African coastline offer beach hikers some of the most beautiful scenery in the world.

A knapsack, a pair of water-resistant hiking shoes and a tide table could be sufficient to launch you on an unforgettable hike. The thousands of kilometres of Southern African coastline offer the hiker some of the most beautiful beaches in the world.

Consult a tide table before setting out (coastal radio stations also broadcast tide information) to ensure that you take full advantage of the hours between low and high tide. At low tide you may find the going very easy on the broad 'freeway' of firm sand, but at high tide the same stretch of shoreline could present quite a different prospect: a band of soft, energy-sapping sand into which your feet sink at every step.

Take along your own tide table on longer hikes. Low tide will occur approximately an hour later each day (so, of course, will high tide). If your table records the tide at Cape Point, for example, you would establish the tides for the part of the coast in which you are interested by adding or subtracting the number of minutes listed in the table.

Protect yourself from the sun by wearing a broad-rimmed hat and applying lotion to exposed parts of the body. Avoid hiking in the midday sun without a shirt or some form of covering for the shoulders (your nose and neck are particularly vulnerable). A pair of good sunglasses is recommended for the glare.

You may have to travel long distances between freshwater supply points, so you should carry as much as you can comfortably manage. The water at a river mouth is likely to be salty, and you may have to hike a considerable distance inland to find drinkable water.

You may encounter problems in crossing larger rivers where they meet the sea. Experienced beach hikers recommend taking along a small inflatable dinghy or lilo for transporting your rucksack (the hiker swims alongside). A plastic garbage bag is handy for sealing your rucksack.

Never try to cross a river in flood, and never cross at a river mouth when the tide is going out — the current may sweep you out to sea.

Ensure that the area in which you intend to hike is open to the public. If it is on private land, you may be able to get permission from the owner. Remember, however, that some coastal areas are strictly out of bounds to visitors.

The Southern African coast is a huge storehouse of culinary delights. Such is the wealth and variety of edible marine life in the inter-tidal (between the high and low water

200

marks) and sub-tidal (below the surface) zones that a 20th century Crusoe armed with a knife, a box of matches and a few pieces of driftwood would not only survive — he would flourish!

But there is a snag: the law. Certain limits are imposed on the gathering of shellfish, and there are heavy penalties for breaking the rules — which even specify the width of the blade you use to pry shellfish from the rocks.

Sea Urchin

Location Found all along the coast – mostly in rock pools.
How caught They are simply picked off the rocks. Ensure that they are under water, and use gloves to protect your hands.
Preparation Sea urchins must be fresh: do not refrigerate them or leave them in the sun. Cut around the shell; discard the top. The edible (red) part should be seasoned with lemon juice and cayenne pepper and eaten raw.
The law The limit is 20 per person per day in the Cape, and 25 in Natal.

Periwinkle

Location Found in rock pools all along the Southern African coast.
How caught Picked from the rocks.
Preparation Soak in fresh water for 30 minutes, rinse and drain. Boil in salted water for five

Contravention of any of these regulations is punishable by a fine of up to R7 000 and confiscation of any motor vehicle, diving equipment, boat and other accessories used in contravening the regulations.

You should also make sure that the area you are in is not a reserve. And a word of warning: do not eat shellfish which may have been contaminated by a poisonous 'red tide'.

minutes. Drain, cool and remove periwinkles from shells. Remove stomach and protective disc and serve with French dressing or butter.
The law The maximum is 50 periwinkles per person per day (they are protected in Natal).

Perlemoen

Location Perlemoen (also called abalone) are found mainly between Cape Agulhas and Saldanha Bay.
How caught They are usually available only to divers. Perlemoen should be approached swiftly and prised loose before they sense danger and clamp their suction pads to the rock surface.
Preparation Remove the meat from the shell with a sharp knife, slice out the head and entrails, remove the slime with a hard brush or scourer, trim off the 'skirt' and slice into thin steaks. Tenderise these with a mallet and fry in a batter for a minute. Some people prefer to boil the perlemoen in salted water for 20 minutes, then mince it or eat it in the form of steaks.
The law You may remove five perlemoen (minimum shell breadth of 11,43 cm) per person per day. The maximum blade width is 3,8 cm. Perlemoen are protected in Natal.

Alikreukel

Location These large sea snails are found in rocky pools, gulleys, inlets and bays.
How caught They are simply prised off rocks.
Preparation Cook in (salted) boiling water, in their shells. When the 'trap door' can be removed – usually after about 20 minutes they are ready. Remove the stomach and 'trap door' before serving with lemon and pepper.
The law You may remove 10 alikreukel per person per day. Their shells should measure at least 6,35 cm across.

Oyster

Location Concentrated in rocky pools and on reefs along the south and east coasts of South Africa.
How caught Prised from rocks with a knife.
Preparation Prise open and serve raw with lemon, salt and pepper (or tabasco sauce), bread and butter. Bake or grill in their shells.
The law In the Cape the limit is 25 oysters per person per day, and the shells must have a minimum breadth of 3,8 cm. In Natal you need a licence, (the daily bag limit is eight dozen) and the shells must have a minimum breadth of 4,0 cm. The closed season elsewhere is 1 December to 28 February.

Crab

Location Found in different shapes and sizes between Walvis Bay on the west coast and Kosi Bay on the east coast. Estuarine crabs make their home in mud holes on the banks of rivers or estuaries.
How caught Use baited fishing line, or dive for crabs among rocks on sea bed. Remove estuarine crabs with a long gaff: do not use your hands.
Preparation Immerse the crab in fresh water for a few hours, then plunge it into boiling water (heavily salted) or seawater. Bring back to the boil and simmer for about 10 minutes. Remove from water, drain and cool. Remove abdomen flap and upper shell to extract flesh (discard intestines and gills). Serve with lemon juice and pepper, or in a salad.
The law In the Cape there is a limit of 15 sea crabs per person per day, and there is no size limit. However you may remove only two Knysna crabs per person per day, and their shells should have a minimum breadth of 11,43 cm. In Natal and Namibia the regulations vary according to the species. Consult the relevant authorities. You may not remove a crab in berry.

Octopus

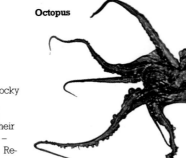

Location Found all along the Southern African coast, usually hiding beneath rocks.
How caught Use a gaff to remove the octopus from its lair.
Preparation Pound the octopus against a rock to kill and tenderise it, and rub off excess slime. Remove the mouth, turn the head inside out and wash. It may then be skinned with a sharp knife. The tentacles should be beaten with a mallet. Steam in its own juices or boil for 20 minutes until it turns red and becomes tender, or cut up and fry in oil or butter. Serve with lemon or a sauce.
The law The limit is two per person per day. The law does not specify a minimum size. The maximum gaff or hook size is 50 mm. A licence is required in Natal.

Limpet

Location Found on rocks in the inter-tidal and sub-tidal zones all along the coast of Southern Africa.
How caught Prised from the rocks with a knife.
Preparation Steam out of their shells, remove radula and serve with garlic butter or French dressing. They may also be brushed with butter and grilled in their shells, or eaten raw.
The law In the Cape, you are allowed 15 per person per day (25 in Natal). Crayfish or general bait licences are required in Natal.

Black mussel

Location Beds of black mussels are found all along the coastline, notably on rocks in and around the inter-tidal zone.
How caught They are plucked from the rocks without difficulty. You may not use an instrument with a blade exceeding 3,8 cm in width.
Preparation Scrape shells and leave mussels in cold water for about 30 minutes. This allows them to eject sand which may have collected inside the shell. Cover bottom of a pot with a little water and steam mussels until the shells open. Discard un-opened mussels. Remove the 'beards' and serve with bread, lemon juice and pepper.
The law In the Cape, you are restricted to 25 mussels per person per day. In Natal the bag limit is 50 a day and a licence is required.

White mussel

Location Found in inter-tidal sands at many spots along the coast between Namibia and the coast of the Eastern Cape.
How caught Dig into the sand with your bare hands (instruments such as spoons and spades are prohibited) or wade into the surf and feel for the mussels with your feet. You may find them by digging where you see small holes in the wet sand.
Preparation As for black mussels.
The law The limit is 50 per person per day. As with black mussels there is no closed season. The minimum size is 3,5 cm (across the breadth of the shell). White mussels are protected in Natal.

Crayfish

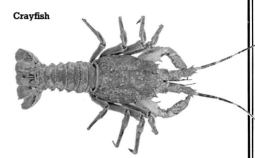

Location Crayfish are found all around the Southern African coast, in both shallow and deep water.
How caught They may be caught in a variety of ways – with ring nets (fish heads are used as bait), traps of various designs, and by diving.
Preparation Immerse live crayfish in salted boiling water and cook until it turns bright red. This usually requires about six minutes per 500 grams. Remove the alimentary canal before eating.
The law The quota is four crayfish per person per day (eight in Natal). You may remove them only during the season (15 November to 15 April in the Cape and Namibia, and 1 March to 31 October in Natal) and then only in areas which have not been declared sanctuaries.

You may not take out a crayfish which has a carapace length of less than 8,89 cm (6,5 cm in Namibia and Natal). The minimum size for the East Coast species is 6,5 cm. It is an offence to take out under-size crayfish, crayfish that are in berry (carrying eggs), or soft-shelled crayfish.

Fishing for crayfish with the aid of aqualungs is forbidden, and no more than 16 crayfish may be transported in a private vehicle at any one time. There are other rules relating to Natal: consult the Natal Parks Board.

Beneath the waves

The rugged, beautiful coastline of Southern Africa, bounded by the Atlantic and Indian oceans, is a popular playground for an increasing number of divers.

Thousands of enthusiasts are taking to the water from Kosi Bay to the Orange River mouth in search of coral reefs, wrecks, and the myriad species of life which inhabit the sea.

Because a diver's life depends on it, his equipment is vitally important and must be carefully chosen and scrupulously maintained. Standard gear for skin-divers in temperate waters consists of a mask, snorkel, flippers, a knife and gloves. Divers who want to join the ranks of the 'spearos' – or spearfishermen – will need a reliable speargun. The spear is attached either directly to the gun or to a reel beneath the shaft by means of a heavy nylon cord, and is propelled by a spring or tough rubber – in the style of a catapult.

Spearguns are illegal for scuba divers (both sporting and governmental authorities regard scuba equipment as an 'unfair' advantage). In the colder waters of Southern Africa, extending more or less from Cape Agulhas to Cape Point on the eastern seaboard, and to Namibia and northwards on the Atlantic coast, a wet-suit is a necessary addition to any diver's wardrobe.

The suit allows a thin layer of water to seep between the nylon lining and the diver's body. This film of water does not circulate, and quickly warms to body temperature. In particularly cold water, the three-piece wet-suit is the most effective combination: a vest (with hood attached) is worn under a zip-up jacket.

The buoyancy of the suit is counteracted by a weight-belt – usually made of nylon or plastic (experts recommend the type with a quick-release buckle).

The word 'scuba' is an abbreviation of 'self-contained underwater breathing apparatus', and it is this apparatus, consisting generally of compressed-air cylinders and demand valve, that allows the scuba diver a more leisurely probe into the ocean's depths.

The flow of compressed air from a diver's cylinder or cylinders to his mouthpiece is controlled by the demand valve, or regulator, so that he can inhale comfortably. This is where diving becomes more sophisticated, and training becomes an essential. Diving clubs in Cape Town, Durban, East London, Port Elizabeth and the Witwatersrand and commercial diving schools hold instruction courses – a must for anyone seriously interested in diving.

Divers enter the sea with aqualungs. There are several basic rules to observe when entering and leaving the water: avoid choppy seas, which may indicate a current; where there is no protection from the surf, find a spot where you can come ashore behind a wave; do not swim in the mouth of a lagoon.

Most reefs, whether natural or man-made, attract an abundance of fish and other marine life. Sodwana Bay, in Zululand, is a mecca for skin-divers in spite of the dangers – its notorious Rock Cod Reef has been the scene of at least two attacks on divers by great white sharks (there have been shark attacks at several other spots along the coast over the years).

Ideal places in the western Cape include Buffels Bay, near Cape Point, where depths reach 20 m and visibility is generally good, and Chapman's Peak to Olifantsbosch – a good summer spot for skin-divers.

Up the west coast from Melkbosstrand to Saldanha Bay, 'spearos' will find large hottentot. The diving is also excellent at Donkergat. Of the many east coast spots, perhaps the most popular are Plettenberg Bay and Cape Infanta while Tsitsikamma National Park features an Underwater Trail – an enjoyable and informative introduction to this stretch of coastline.

The warm waters of the Agulhas Bank around

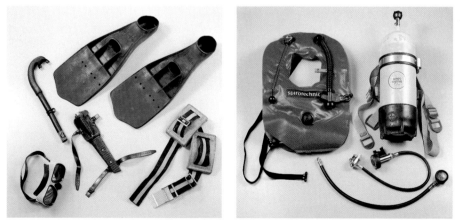

Above left: Basic equipment for the diver (the weight-belt is used only with a wet-suit). When buying a mask, ensure that it is comfortable, and test for leaks before buying. Beginners are advised to use a snorkel with a wide bore until they have mastered the correct breathing techniques. Flippers are available in many designs, but novices are likely to find the closed-heel, medium-length type the most suitable. **Above right:** A lifejacket and aqualung with demand valve and submersible pressure gauge. **Opposite page:** A combination wet-suit (suitable for cold water) consisting of zip-up jacket, pants and vest with attached hood. The boots and gloves are recommended accessories.

Port Elizabeth are teeming with fish and there are several very suitable reefs for skin-divers between the 'Friendly City' and Jeffreys Bay. Sponges, crabs, lobsters and shells of many shapes and colours make reef diving an unforgettable experience.

Artificial 'reefs' have been created by the intentional sinking of derelict ships in popular diving areas, by shipwrecks, and by the assembly of structures that will attract marine life.

The wrecks of the *Rockeater*, the *Good Hope* and the *Transvaal*, sunk in Smitswinkel Bay, near Cape Point, in the 1970s, are popular diving spots. So too is the artificial reef at Glencairn off the Cape Peninsula, which consists of hundreds of car tyres roped together in about 20m of water.

Over 1 000 ships are believed to have gone down off the Southern African coast over the past five hundred years. Most of those discovered so far lie between Cape Agulhas and St Helena Bay. Many more wrecks lie along the notorious Namibia coast (aptly named Skeleton Coast). Some, however, are in prohibited areas controlled by diamond mining companies or the military.

Other celebrated wrecks are the *Het Huis te Kraaiestein*, lying in about 9m of water at

Above left: The sharp spines of the sea urchin can provide a painful surprise for the unwary diver. **Above right:** A brightly-coloured sea slug makes its laborious way across an underwater obstacle on the Tsitsikamma coast. It is thought that their unpleasant taste helps to protect these creatures from predators. **Left:** A pompano fish off the Natal south coast. This species occurs between Knysna and Delagoa Bay.

Oudekraal, near Cape Town; *Merestein*, the Dutch East Indiaman lost in the approaches to Saldanha Bay in 1702; the *Birkenhead*, near Danger Point (a favourite venue for divers), and the 5 000-ton British steamship *Maori*, which went down off Llandudno in 1909.

Legislation concerning wrecks has been tightened up recently, so make sure that you know the law and have the relevant permits before you remove anything from an abandoned wreck. For example, a salvage licence from the Commissioner of Customs and Excise is needed if you intend to remove anything from a wreck: in addition all wrecks over 50 years old are specially protected, so you will also need a permit from the National Monuments Council before you may remove anything. Contravention of the National Monuments Act could mean a (maximum) fine of R10 000 and imprisonment for up to 24 months. The reason for this is that if artefacts are removed from wrecks we face the risk of losing valuable clues to our history.

How to dive – and stay alive

Diving can be dangerous unless you follow certain basic rules.

● Do not dive alone. If you get into trouble, a companion may well be able to rescue you.

● If you get tired or too cold, leave the water immediately. Exhaustion in the water is a small step away from drowning.

● If you are too exhausted to swim, or you feel that you are starting to go under, release your weight-belt. The buoyancy of your wet-suit will keep you afloat.

● If you feel dizzy or faint after surfacing, tell your diving companion and get out of the water.

● Do not hyperventilate. Hyperventilation – or

breathing in and out deeply a number of times before a dive – may extend the time you can remain submerged, but it can also lead to unexpected loss of consciousness and drowning.

● If you develop an arm or leg cramp in the water, do not bend the affected limb. Straighten it out and start swimming gently for the shore.

● Be extremely cautious when entering rough seas or unfamiliar diving spots and carefully observe the run of the swell before deciding whether or not to dive.

● When surfacing, do so in a spiral to give yourself a 360-degree view of possible obstacles. Do not forget to look up as well.

● When using scuba gear, if you surface too fast – particularly from deep water – the expanding nitrogen bubbles in the bloodstream could lead to 'the bends', an acutely painful condition, which may in severe cases affect the nervous system, resulting in paralysis, unconsciousness and even death. Many divers in Southern Africa have been crippled by 'the bends'. Expanding air in the lungs (as the diver surfaces) can also lead to rupture of the lung tissue, and scuba divers must always remember to breathe out as they swim to the surface.

A novice should never dive before receiving training: a careless attitude could lead to his death. The South African Underwater Union, to which virtually all clubs in South Africa are affiliated, has a programme which conforms to international standards. Their address is P.O. Box 201, Rondebosch 7700.

Clubs undertake this training and on the attainment of proficiency the diver receives a certificate which is accepted throughout the world.

THE CAPE

The southernmost edge of the African continent is a glorious mixture of blue mountains, sweeping forests and fynbos, tumbling rivers and seemingly endless coastline that more than justifies its accolade as 'the fairest Cape'.

This is the home of Kirstenbosch – one of the world's most famous reservoirs of indigenous flora – and of Table Mountain, that much-loved, ever-familiar sentinel looming over South Africa's oldest city.

The cheeky chacma baboon wanders through the Cape of Good Hope Nature Reserve, sharing its territory with buck, zebra, porcupine, ostrich and a host of other creatures. Bushpig and caracal roam the Tsitsikamma Forest; vultures wheel over the Potberg.

Much of this natural variety in the western and southern Cape is accessible to the public. Hiking trails meander through ancient forests and across mountains, taking adventurers into country of unforgettable beauty; and there is an increasing number of individuals and organisations dedicated to the recognition, appreciation and protection of the region's natural wealth.

In few other parts of Southern Africa is the public as aware of its natural heritage: the concern for the preservation of indigenous flora and fauna is readily apparent wherever one goes, and local authorities need little urging to create sanctuaries for plants, animals and birds. Private nature reserves abound, and wild flower gardens are around every corner.

Jackass penguins on the Cape's west coast. These penguins are found breeding on islands off the south-western coast of South Africa, and are often seen swimming in small groups – sometimes as far as 130km out to sea.

A stretch of earthly paradise

Entranced by the profusion of flowers near the Great Brak River, the 18th century French naturalist Francois de Vaillant wrote lyrically of 'enamelled meads, and the most beautiful pastures' as two of 'the charms of this terrestrial paradise'.

The region has a rich bounty of sanctuaries, mainly forest and coastal. Among these is the Bontebok National Park, home to several species of buck and a large and varied population of birds. The ruggedly beautiful Tsitsikamma and Knysna forests spasmodically criss-crossed by a number of trails and walks, is another appealing sanctuary: a visit to this unspoilt wilderness of moody forests and myriad hills promises to be an unforgettable experience.

The authorities have laid out a number of walks ranging greatly in degrees of difficulty in the Tsitsikamma Forest and other indigenous forests, allowing visitors to explore huge tracts of countryside along the aptly named Garden Route. There are also many nature reserves featuring a wealth of animal and bird life. Highly recommended to visitors is The Lakes Road, which winds through green countryside between the Wilderness National Park and the Knysna National Lakes Area.

Attakwaskloof Nature Reserve

Spring transforms the valleys and ridges of this 9 800 ha reserve into a carpet of red and pink ericas. This veritable store house of mountain fynbos also conceals pincushions, leucadendrons and the occasional outcrop of rare and beautiful, black disa (*Disa bodkinii*).

The reserve lies in the Attakwaskloof Mountains, west of Robinson's Pass. This scenic road has provided the most direct route between Oudtshoorn and Mossel Bay since being built by master road-builder Thomas Bain in 1869.

Trails lead west from the summit of the pass along the mountain's central ridge. For more information contact The Senior Regional Officer, Southern Cape Region, Department of Environmental and Nature Conservation, Private Bag X6546, George 6530 (telephone George 74-1567/8/9) or The Officer-in-Charge, Outeniqua Conservancy, Private Bag X6517, George 6530 (telephone George 74-2671).

Just outside the reserve, on the southern side of the Attakwaskloof Mountains, is the Eight Bells Mountain Inn – the start of the 9,3 km (three-hour) Ruitersbos Forest Walk. Shorter routes are also available. Information and permits for the Ruitersbos Forest Walk are

readily available from the Eight Bells Mountain Inn, P.O. Box 436, Mossel Bay (telephone Mossel Bay 95-1544).

Bontebok National Park

The traditional home of the bontebok was originally the 56 km wide coastal plain of the southwestern Cape, between Bot River in the west and Mossel Bay in the east. Large herds of shimmering-coated bluebuck once grazed here, but, sadly, by 1800 they had been hunted to extinction, and within 30 years the numbers of bontebok, too, had dwindled to just a few dozen. Remembering the lost bluebuck, perhaps, a few farmers from the Bredasdorp district banded together to ensure the survival of the bontebok.

In 1931 the first Bontebok National Park was proclaimed on an area of strandveld and coastal fynbos south of Bredasdorp, with a breeding nucleus of just 17 animals. However, problems of poor grazing and internal parasites eventually prompted the move to the present site near Swellendam, where the second Bontebok National Park of 2 786 ha was opened in 1961 in the foothills of the Langeberg. Since then the herd has grown from 60 to more than

Left: A large bontebok ram keeps a watch over young lambs in the Bontebok National Park near Swellendam. The conspicuous white patch from the base of the bontebok's horns to its nose makes it easy to spot in its favourite habitat — open grassland. This antelope is a grazer and roams in herds numbering between six and thirty. **Far right:** These chincherinchees (*Ornithogalum*), from the Prince Alfred's Pass, grow abundantly in the southern Cape. They are also known as Stars of Bethlehem, or chinks. The name is said to have been invented in imitation of the sound made by the shiny flower stalks rubbing together. This elegant species, a member of the lily family, is a favourite export flower and is shipped abroad in dry packages, remaining fresh for weeks. **Near right:** An orange-red fungus (*Pycnoporus sanguineus*) grows on a fallen tree in the southern Cape's Tsitsikamma Forest.

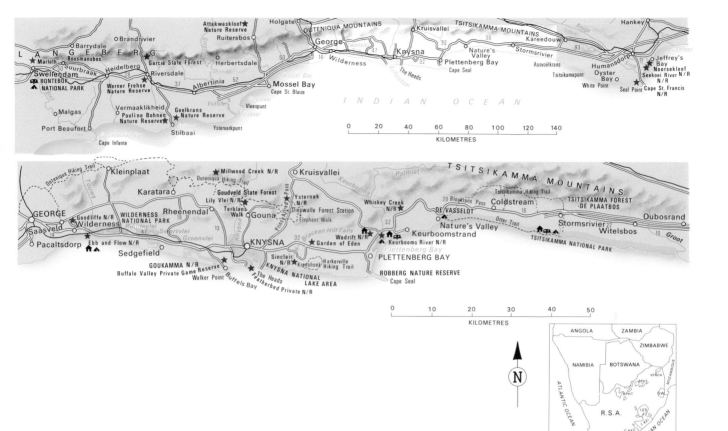

KILOMETRES

lin and even a couple of spur-winged geese which remain in the park throughout the year. Jackal and fox prowl the renosterveld which dominates the low shrub and grassland vegetation of this transitional fynbos region.

The Breede River flows through a part of the park. Carp and large-mouth bass have been introduced. A large 10 kg carp was taken recently and among other fish is the prettily named Kaapse nooientjie (Cape lady) or Cape moonfish (*Mondactylus falciformis*). Remember to obtain a provincial freshwater angling licence (available from any magistrate's office in the Cape) as well as permission from the park warden.

A good gravel road, some 6 km long, leads from the N2 to the park.

Swimming is allowed in the river below the campsite, but boating is prohibited.

A favourite spot for viewing bontebok is at Lang Elsieskraal, site of the camp of an 18th century Khoikhoi chieftainess. Bontebok are born during September, October and November, when many of the park's plants are beginning to flower.

Bontebok National Park is situated within one of the richest floristic kingdoms of the world, more than 470 plant species, including 52 species of grass have been identified.

Boosmansbos Wilderness Area

Rising rivers tumble through precipitous gorges in this rugged 14 200 ha wilderness region in the Langeberg Mountains between Heidelberg and Swellendam. An excellent combination of evergreen trees in the valleys, a large indigenous forest (stinkwood, yellowwood and red alder are prominent) on the southern slopes and the fynbos of the 'Cape Floral Kingdom' help to make this an especially attractive area for hikers. Wildlife includes klipspringer, grysbok, grey rhebok, leopard, honey badger and a splendid variety of birds.

Up to 12 visitors at a time are allowed into the wilderness area. The trails are self-guided; there is no overnight accommodation, and hikers should bring their own camp stoves (open fires are forbidden). The spring-autumn period (September to April) is considered the best time to visit.

Boosmansbos is open throughout the year (the forest station is open from sunrise to sunset), and entry is by permit only (bookings have to be made at least two weeks in advance during the holiday season). Visitors are admitted only on foot (they may sleep in the open or in their own tents). For further information (and to obtain a permit), write to The State Forester, Grootvadersbosch State Forest, P.O. Box 109, Heidelberg 6760 (telephone Heidelberg 1812).

Bracken Hill Falls

A turn-off from the main Knysna-Port Elizabeth road, about 11 km from Knysna, leads through a State forest of gum and pine trees to the Bracken Hill Falls, a series of cascades in the Noetzie River ravine. There are pleasant picnic sites under the trees.

Buffalo Valley Private Game Reserve

The Thesen family is closely associated with the promotion of the beautiful coastal area around Knysna and, true to this tradition, H.P. Thesen has established a charming private game reserve in a virtually unspoilt fynbos area in the Goukamma River Valley.

You can explore the reserve on two trails of three and five hours, together with a guide who will point out interesting features about plants and animals. Look out for Burchell's zebra, bontebok, black wildebeest, bushbuck, grey rhebok and Cape grysbok. Many birds may be seen, including orange-breasted sunbirds, Knysna warblers and Cape francolins.

Booking is essential and may be made by telephoning the Knysna Publicity Association

300 animals, with over 1 000 found throughout South Africa.

Among other antelope which the visitor may see are grey rhebok, Cape grysbok, steenbok and grey duiker. Bird life is prolific and includes the stately secretary bird, Stanley's bustard, several species of sunbird, fish eagle, Cape whydah, guinea fowl, hamerkop, franco-

Above: Nineteenth-century elephant hunts were mainly responsible for the rapid decline in the numbers of the great herds in the southern Cape. Encounters with the few survivors are rare, but they are seen occasionally along the Elephant Walk, near the Diepwalle Forest Station, 32 km from Knysna.
Left: The base of a giant Outeniqua yellowwood tree in the Tsitsikamma Forest. Some yellowwoods in the park are about 800 years old, and reach heights of 60 metres. The crown of the tree is often festooned with 'old man's beard' lichen.

Opposite left: The burrowing rain frog, or blaasop (*Breviceps*), is a stocky, pugnacious looking inhabitant of the Tsitsikamma Forest. These secretive frogs are active on the surface of the ground in rainy weather – hence their name. The rain frog gorges itself on flying ants, earthworms and termites, and spends nine months of the year in suspended animation underground. When the frog is irritated or alarmed, it blows itself up into a round ball. **Opposite right:** Grey rhebok in the Bontebok National Park.

directly (Knysna 2-1610). Alternatively you can make contact with the tour guide after hours (telephone Knysna 4788).

Cape St Francis Nature Reserve
The promontory of Cape St Francis juts into the Indian Ocean some 30 km south of Humansdorp, and the 36 ha provincial nature reserve protects a coastal habitat of sand dune and fynbos rich in bird life. To get there, drive to the village of Cape St Francis and proceed from there on foot, or drive to Sea Vista and walk from there to the reserve (the road from Sea Vista to the point has been washed away, and only 4-wheel-drive vehicles can get through). It is open at all times.

Elephant Nature Walk
The last survivors of the great southern Cape elephant herds are still seen occasionally near the Diepwalle Forest Station, the starting and finishing point of the 18,2 km Elephant Walk, an easy trail through indigenous forest.

From the national road, take the Uniondale turn-off 6 km east of Knysna and drive another 15 km to Diepwalle. Permits are not required. Hikers have to register at Diepwalle Forest Station, where maps are available.

No pets are allowed. Drinking water is available at several places on the route, which is open between 6 a.m. and 6 p.m. and takes some six and a half hours to complete. The trail is marked by elephant silhouettes. Hikers may, however, choose the two alternative routes, which cover shorter distances of 8,9 km and 14,3 km respectively.

No fewer than eight 'Big Trees' – Outeniqua yellowwood – can be seen along the trail and the largest is generally known as the 'King Edward VII Tree'.

Featherbed Private Nature Reserve
The twin headlands that guard the entrance to the Knysna Lagoon are among the most popular attractions in Knysna, but few people realise that the westernmost headland is also a nature reserve that can be reached by a short ferry ride across the lagoon.

At Featherbed, a trailer will whisk you to a viewing platform high up on the headland overlooking town, lagoon and sea. Catering is sumptuous. Oysters, champagne and fish braais are offered, and provide visitors with plenty of kilojoules for an easy-going, hour-long walk through the bush, which teems with an abundance of birds and small animals.

Featherbed is a natural heritage site and has South Africa's largest breeding herd of blue duiker – a species which is, unfortunately, fast becoming endangered.

For more information, you should contact the Knysna Publicity Association (telephone Knysna 2-1610).

Garcia State Forest
This 12 000 ha forest, located in the high Langeberg range near Riversdale, offers indigenous trees and a variety of fynbos in settings varying from moist mountain slope to drier areas reminiscent of the Karoo.

No overnight facilities are provided although day visitors are free to explore along a network of trails in the forest. To obtain the necessary permits, write to The Forester, Grootvadersbosch State Forest, P.O. Box 109, Heidelberg 6760 (telephone Heidelberg 1812).

Garden of Eden
This unspoilt area of indigenous (State-controlled) forest lies to the north of the N2 national road about halfway between Knysna and Plettenberg Bay. It is well signposted and there is a lay-by where cars may be parked near to the main entrance. The area is unfenced and

open at all times (no permits are required). Pets are not allowed. The walk, of just over 1 km, is over level country, with streams crossed by rustic bridges. There are also picnic sites and toilet facilities.

The forest mammals are usually secretive and unseen, but tracks may include those of elephant, bushbuck, blue duiker, honey badger, porcupine, caracal, two species of genet, mongoose, bushpig, baboon and vervet monkey. There are some 40 species of typical forest birds – most of which have loud and penetrating calls (in bird communication and defence of territory, it has been observed that sound is often more important than sight).

Geelkrans Nature Reserve

The 166 ha Geelkrans sanctuary, open to hikers all year round from sunrise to sunset, comprises reclaimed drift sand and is situated about 5 km from Stilbaai East. The best time to visit is between October and March. The reserve is noted for its variety of endangered plant species and visitors may also spot small antelope, other mammals such as shrews, and members of the cat family. Permits are available from The Government Forester, Grootvadersbosch State Forest, P.O. Box 109, Heidelberg 6760 (telephone Heidelberg 1812) or The Regional Director, Western Cape Forest Region, Private Bag X9005, Cape Town 8000.

Goodliffe Nature Reserve

The trail to this wooded sanctuary leads uphill from the Wilderness Hotel, and past the little Anglican church and the 19th century stone building known as 'Kloof Cottage'. Its chief attraction is the profusion of bird species, including the Knysna loerie and narina trogon. The reserve is open at all times.

Goudveld State Forest

Stretching along the upper plateau and across the foothills of the Outeniqua range, the Goudveld State Forest is some 8500 ha in size, of which 3 900 ha are indigenous forest. There are extensive pine and eucalyptus plantations, as well as areas of natural fynbos.

Goudveld's name is derived from the historical Millwood gold fields, the site of a minor gold rush in the 1880s.

Today Millwood is being developed as a tourist attraction, with an information centre housed in the old mining town's last remaining building. A walk through the mining area and to the processing plant of the Bendigo mine (in the process of restoration) is offered. There are also a number of picnic sites and attractively laid-out walks through the indigenous forest.

No permits are required. Visitors must register in the visitors' book at the information kiosk at the entrance to the State Forest. Entrance is permitted between 6 a.m. and 6 p.m. Information leaflets are available.

To reach the reserve from Knysna, cross the national road bridge over the Knysna River, drive 3 km towards George and then turn right onto the Rheenendal road, which joins the historic 'Passes Road' between George and Knysna. The reserve is situated some 25 km from Knysna and is well signposted.

Goukamma Nature Reserve

The Goukamma sanctuary is situated south of the N2 and lies between Sedgefield and the coastal resort of Buffalo Bay. Included in its area of 2 230 ha are the Goukamma River estuary, 11 km of coastline, and Groenvlei, the Garden Route's only freshwater lake. The reserve is open throughout the year and is reached by taking the tarred road to Buffalo Bay. There are toilets at the picnic site on the river bank, and the western section of the reserve has several walking trails. It is open daily from 8 a.m. to 5 p.m.

Among the 150 recorded bird species are fish eagle, jackal buzzard, marsh harrier and a number of hawks. Mammals include grysbok, blue duiker, bushbuck and bontebok.

Groeneweide Nature Walk

The 10 km tarred road to the Saasveld Forestry College leaves the N2 at the eastern approach to George. Hikers must register in the

---

THE MASTER WEAVER AT WORK

The distinctive nest of the ground spider in the Tsitsikamma Forest. This spider can be distinguished from other spiders by its large jaws.

Southern Africa's many spider species are immensely varied in form, colouring and behavioural pattern — and in the ways they spin and use their silken threads.

Gossamer — those fine strands of silk you see floating free in the breeze — is one of the better known types of thread, and it has a unique function: it serves as the baby spider's transport to survival.

When the spiderlings leave the cocoon they go 'ballooning', a fascinating feat which author Jean George describes in *The Amazing World of Nature*. She observed one grass spiderling make its way up a dried stalk, where 'it circled until it faced the wind. Then it threw up its hind feet and stood on its head like an acrobat. In this position it spun out two or three feet of ballooning thread, a dry and wide strand. Then it let go of the stalk, grabbed the silk with its front legs, and in the best circus tradition went flying through the air.

'Aided by the wind, it guided itself by pulling in on the streamer and then letting it out. As it billowed away, it struck the edge of the house and was stopped. There the spiderling reeled in its slender balloon and hurried to the porch roof to take off again. In this splendid manner it sailed out of sight'.

There are also trapping threads, which come in many shapes and sizes, ranging from the conventional and sometimes very beautiful orb of the garden spider to the cent-shaped webs of tiny cave-dwelling species. Examine a trapping thread under a microscope and you will see something resembling a string of pearls. Each 'pearl' is a globule of sticky gum. An insect which touches one adheres to it, and in struggling to free itself contacts more globules — thereby becoming securely enmeshed. The rhythm of the struggling movements alerts the spider to the presence of its prey (spiders detect their prey through the vibrations of the thread). It rushes in, gives a poisonous bite to its victim, and binds it tightly in a swathing band — another kind of thread. Some threads are used for receiving and sending warning or courting signals, for instance — and, in the case of the bolus spider, for 'fishing'. This nocturnal species spins out a single thread weighted at the end by a sticky ball, which it swings to and fro from a tree branch on the off-chance that it will connect with a passing insect.

The intricate silk threads and webs of a spider are therefore its eyes and ears, its voice, its livelihood and its chief weapon in the armoury of survival.

Above: A solitary boat lies anchored in the Keurbooms River Lagoon on a summer's day. **Right:** Abundant foliage forms a protective canopy for birds and insects in the Goudveld Forest Reserve, 25 km from Knysna. **Below:** A Cape grysbok in the Tsitsikamma Forest. This small antelope is mainly nocturnal.

A pleasure boat, called 'The Loerie' operates weekly (more frequently during high season) to take visitors up the river to enjoy the magnificent views. The water and surrounding forests attract a wide variety of birds and small mammals including bushbuck, vervet monkey, baboon and dassie. Bushpig and porcupine often root in the gardens at night.

The resort is on the west bank of the river and is signposted on the N2 from Plettenberg Bay. For reservations, write to The Manager, Keurbooms River Public Resort, Private Bag X1000, Plettenberg Bay 6600 (telephone Plettenberg Bay 9309).

Knysna Indigenous Forests

Famed for its small and endangered herd of Knysna elephant, the wide strip of dense timberland is located on the southern slopes of the Outeniqua Mountains between George and Knysna. Other animal species include leopard, bushpig, bushbuck, mongoose and caracal. But it is for their trees, and the bird life they support, that the forests are most noteworthy. Species include stinkwood, red alder, white alder, yellowwood, forest alder, assegai and the pink-flowered Cape chestnut. The colourful Knysna loerie and the narina trogon are among the birds that live in the high forest canopy. The mountain buzzard, Cape eagle owl, crowned eagle, Knysna scrub warbler and protea seedeater can also be seen in the forests and surrounding mountains.

Hiking trails, nature walks, a youth group centre, viewpoints and picnic spots have been established on State Forest land in the region. Horseback riding is also allowed under certain circumstances.

One of the best ways to discover Knysna Forest's 'big trees', picnic sites and nature walks is via a 48 km scenic drive starting and finishing at Knysna. It takes you along the Uniondale road (Prince Alfred's Pass) towards Diepwalle Forest Station. About 1 km after the sign to 'Elephant Walk' turn left into Kom-se-Pad, a dirt road, which will take you to Gouna.

Enquiries and bookings for hiking trails and the youth group centre at Harkerville Forest Station can be made by writing to The Regional Director, Southern Cape Forest Region, Private Bag X12, Knysna 6570 (telephone Knysna 2-3037). No bookings need be made for nature walks although visitors have to register in visitors' books at certain points.

Knysna National Lake Area

The Knysna Lagoon, dominated by the rocky bastions of the picturesque Knysna Heads is an area of unsurpassed beauty and character. Tales of shipwrecks, gold, elephant and unlimited timber supplies lured many people to this peaceful stretch of water in the early days.

visitors' book at the starting point of the hike, which is at the college. Maps can be obtained from the reception office at the college during office hours, or from the George Publicity Office. No dogs are allowed.

Most of the 15 km main route, and the shorter (11 km) trail is through indigenous forest, with some pine plantation. The walk is open from 6 a.m. to 6 p.m.

Heidelberg Municipal Nature Reserve

The Duivenhoks River bounds this pleasant, unfenced 4 ha reserve of indigenous trees and fynbos. There are no facilities.

Keurbooms River Nature Reserve

For the most part, the reserve is inaccessible to the general public. Its plant life is fragile and the terrain so rugged as to be risky for casual visitors.

However, within the boundaries of the 760 ha reserve, situated around the Keurbooms River estuary 8 km east of Plettenberg Bay, is a pleasant public resort of some 20 fully equipped chalets, space for 70 caravans and 16 camping sites. The river has become a popular venue for anglers, water-skiers and boating enthusiasts.

Guided tours are being planned, and the authorities are presently laying out a circular hiking trail which will eventually extend for 20 km through the reserve.

A comfortable, 12-bedded hut has been constructed to provide overnight accommodation on what is likely to become one of the reserve's most popular attractions.

Today, the lagoon area still lures people – but now they come to enjoy watersports, such as sailing, cruising, boardsailing and angling. This 15 000 ha playground is the country's second national lake area and through sound management, such as zoning ecologically sensitive areas for specific uses, the National Parks Board aims to maintain a healthy balance between conservation and utilisation.

The lakes, which are characterised by sand banks, salt marshes and reed beds, teem with life, providing food for myriad organisms often overlooked by man, but, nevertheless, a critical aspect of the continued survival of all biological life forms. One of the most peculiar and interesting creatures to be found here is the endangered Knysna sea horse (*Hippocampus capensis*).

Although no National Parks tourism facilities exist, the village and surrounding area provide ample accommodation. Further information may be obtained from the National Parks Board office at the end of Thesen's Jetty. For more information write to The Park Warden, Knysna National Lake Area, P.O. Box 314, Knysna 6570 (telephone Knysna 2-2095).

Kranshoek Coastal Nature Walk
This fairly strenuous trail of some 9 km leads through indigenous coastal forest, fynbos and plantations clothing the heights above the Indian Ocean, about halfway between Knysna and Plettenberg Bay. The walk has interpretive signboards along the way.

The walk is reached via the Knysna-Plettenberg Bay road. Take the Harkerville turn-off 17 km outside Knysna and follow the signs to 'Kranshoek'. The starting point, picnic sites and a splendid viewpoint, are reached after about 5 km of winding gravel road through the beautiful Harkerville indigenous forest.

No permits are required, but visitors are required to register in the visitors' book at the start. The walk is open from 6 a.m. to 6 p.m. Intending hikers should be reasonably fit. No pets are allowed. Maps are available from the Forestry Office in Knysna.

Lily Vlei Nature Reserve
The spoor of the last four Knysna elephant, a 'special discovery' among rare and protected species, are occasionally found in the vicinity of Lily Vlei Nature Reserve.

The 1 071 ha reserve, remotely situated in the Outeniqua foothills north of Knysna, has escaped the destructive effects of development. About 50 ha are still virgin forest, dominated by fern, yellowwood and botanically interesting species such as *Faurea macnaughtonii* and *Psychotria capensis*. Beneath this thick forest canopy are bushbuck, blue duiker, bushpig, leopard, caracal, honey badger, vervet monkey, baboon and many birds, including the Knysna loerie, narina trogon and the fish and crowned eagle.

A short section of the Outeniqua Trail passes through the northern part of this reserve. Casual visitors are not allowed in the reserve,

but for more information about forest walks in the area you can contact The Regional Director, Forestry Branch, Department of Environmental Affairs, Private Bag X12, Knysna 6570 (telephone Knysna 2-3037).

Marloth Nature Reserve
Dramatic mountain scenery, evergreen forests, deep cool valleys and a significant stretch of the Swellendam Hiking Trail are the main features of the 11 300 ha Marloth Reserve, set among the slopes of the Langeberg range overlooking Swellendam.

Part of the 'Cape Floral Kingdom', the vegetation comprises a wide variety of proteas, heaths and leucadendrons, and flowering trees such as wild gardenia and wild almond grow among the bigger stinkwood and yellowwood. Wildlife includes leopard, baboon and various antelope. There is also rich bird life, including raptors such as eagles and falcons. The reserve has a large variety of reptiles and amphibians, among which is the rare ghost frog.

There is one large picnic site 'The Hermitage' (charmingly situated) and huts for overnight hikers but no other facilities. To get there follow the 'State Forest' signposts from Swellendam's Andrew Whyte Street. October to March is the best time to visit the reserve. Entry (during daylight hours) is by permit, and these are available from The State Forester, Swellendam State Forest, P.O. Box 28, Swellendam 6740 (telephone Swellendam 4-1410).

Millwood Creek Nature Reserve
Magnificent Knysna Forest trees, including yellowwood and stinkwood, are found at this 6 000 ha reserve on the southern slopes of the Outeniqua Mountains, north-west of Knysna. Millwood is inaccessible to casual visitors, although hikers pass through it on the Outeniqua Hiking Trail.

The vegetation is diverse, with patches of mountain fynbos such as gladiolus, erica and leucospermum mingling with fern on the forest floor. There are also aliens such as hakea and cluster pine, which have to be killed by ringbarking, so they remain upright without damaging the surrounding trees as they fall.

Ivory hunters long ago eliminated the numerous elephant that once occurred here, and today the reserve's wildlife is limited to grey rhebok, klipspringer, duiker, bushbuck and the occasional leopard.

For more information, contact The Senior Regional Officer, Department of Nature and Environmental Conservation, Private Bag X6546, George 6530 (telephone George 74-1567/8/9).

Noorsekloof Nature Reserve
Neatly dividing Jeffreys Bay in two, Noorsekloof Nature Reserve was proclaimed in June

Above: Sea anemones at low tide in the Tsitsikamma Coastal National Park. **Left:** Streams, waterfalls and freshwater pools provide welcome relief to sun-parched hikers along the 48 km course of the Otter Trail. The trail links up at Nature's Valley with the equally impressive Tsitsikamma Trail. Some hikers choose to walk both trails in succession.

1983. The focus of the reserve, a small stream with fern-fringed pools and distinctive slabs of shale, can be followed all the way from the sea on a scenic 3km path up the valley.

About 60 species of indigenous trees may be found in the reserve, including the giant river euphorbia (*Euphorbia triangularis*). Invaders such as Port Jackson and alien acacia have been successfully eliminated.

Wildlife sheltering in the Noorsekloof includes bushbuck, Cape grysbok, the common duiker, the little blue duiker, dassie and vervet monkey. It is also a haven for birds from bulbul, shrike and brilliantly plumed sunbird to African goshawk, gymnogene and raucous-voiced hadedas.

The 28ha reserve is easily accessible from the town centre via Koedoe Street. For further information write to the Jeffreys Bay Publicity Association, P.O. Box 460, Jeffreys Bay 6330 (telephone Jeffreys Bay 93-2588).

Otter Trail

This five-day trail traverses 48km of the Tsitsikamma Coastal National Park, crossing ravines and rivers and winding up to the coastal plateau where only sheer cliffs force it away from the shoreline. It is a trail for the fitter and more experienced hiker – and for those who are not afraid of heights. The rest camp at Storms River Mouth is the starting point.

On the fourth day the trail climbs to the coastal plateau, then drops for the last time to reach the finishing point at Nature's Valley. The energetic hiker can now tackle the Tsitsikamma Trail, which has its start in Nature's Valley and finishes at Storms River Forest Station – in all, a grand, virtually circular tour. To reserve a place on the trail, write to National Parks Board, P.O. Box 787, Pretoria 0001 (telephone Pretoria 343-1991) or National Parks Board, P.O. Box 7400, Roggebaai 8012 (telephone Cape Town 419-5365) or National Parks Board, P.O. Box 774, George 6530 (telephone George 74-6924/5).

A maximum of 12 people per day may start the trail, though hikers are allowed to proceed singly. Participants are required to obtain a permit at the reception area of the Storms River Mouth rest camp before starting. Firewood is usually available at the overnight huts, but a camp stove should be taken. A water bottle is essential. The shop at Storms River Mouth sells bread, fresh meat, 'long-life' milk, tinned foods, soft drinks and liquor. The licensed restaurant serves both *à la carte* and take-away meals.

Outeniqua Hiking Trail

The full trail from George to Diepwalle in the Knysna forest is an eight-day adventure along 142km of mountain track, through fynbos, forest and plantations. Hikers enjoy breathtaking

AN EQUINE ODDITY

The Knysna sea-horse changes colour according to its surroundings.

With its uncannily horse-like head and heraldic posture it looks like a tiny creature of mythology, something dreamt up by the story-telling ancients. But in fact the sea-horse is very real, and a true fish. It has gills, and a mouth which, although more of a tubular snout, is basically a fish's mouth. Through it, the sea-horse sucks in the tiny marine organisms that make up its diet.

Timid and vulnerable to predators, the tiny sea-horse (it is rarely over 12 cm long) rarely swims free, but is nearly always to be found hiding among the plant life of the Cape's tidal reaches, usually erect. It uses its prehensile tail as an anchor, and its head as a kind of hook to pull itself up and around the clusters of seaweed. Like a chameleon, it can change colour to blend with its surroundings, and its eyes also resemble those of a chameleon — they work independently of each other, and provide all-round vision.

One of nature's curiosities, the sea-horse's oddest feature is the pouch on the abdomen of the male, into which the female places her eggs. After this, she takes no more part in the breeding process — the eggs (as many as 600) are fertilised and develop in the pouch, hatch in 30-60 days, and the young are released by their father in a series of exhausting contortions that appear very much like birth pangs.

The five Southern African species are found east of Mossel Bay. All are rare or endangered. The Knysna sea-horse (*Hippocampus capensis*) is threatened by residential development and by human exploitation: highly prized as an attractive aquarium oddity, sedentary and defenceless, it is a sad and declining victim of the skin-diving collector.

views over the Garden Route and Indian Ocean. Shorter trails, lasting two or more days, are also available.

Hikers should book for the trail by writing to The Regional Director, Southern Cape Forest Region, Private Bag X12, Knysna 6570 (telephone Knysna 2-3037).

Pauline Bohnen Nature Reserve

Among the ravines and plains of this 150ha reserve you will find a large outcrop of limestone fynbos – shrubs and plants unique to the calcium-rich, calcrete soils near Still Bay. The reserve is named after Pauline Bohnen, an authority on southern Cape plants, who researched and compiled month-by-month lists of the flowering plants found within the reserve.

During springtime the display of flowers is particularly spectacular and the strong fragrance of pelargonium, blue daisy, painted lady and small granny bonnet attracts sunbirds and sugarbirds to the fynbos nectar. Large trees grow in the ravines and include the endangered bitter bush (*Euryops muirii*) and protected white milkwood (*Sideroxylon inerme*).

Grysbok, bushbuck, puff-adder, mongoose, tortoise and rodent are common in the area.

For further enquiries contact the Still Bay Municipality, P.O. Box 2, Still Bay 6785 (telephone Still Bay 4-1577).

Plettenberg Bay Country Club Private Nature Reserve

Some 67ha of land around the club's golf course in the Piesang Valley about 2km from Plettenberg Bay has been set aside as a reserve. It features small areas of indigenous forest which give sanctuary to buck, monkeys and other small animals. There are also numerous bird species. To reach the reserve turn off the main road from Knysna at the Piesang Valley signpost. Another sign indicates the route to the country club, where visitors should seek permission to walk through the golf course. The reserve is open between sunset and sunrise (throughout the year).

Robberg Nature Reserve

Centuries ago, the 4km-long peninsula of Robberg – 'Mountain of the Seal' – was home to beachcombing Strandlopers, whose caves and middens can still be seen in this impressive 175 ha provincial reserve off the N2 at Plettenberg Bay. The round trip from the car park to The Point takes about three hours by the shortest route. No pets or vehicles are allowed beyond the car park, and fires may be lit only in demarcated areas. Visitors may fish, hike and picnic within the reserve, which is open during daylight hours throughout the year.

Seekoei River Nature Reserve
To reach this 66 ha provincial reserve, take the Jeffrey's Bay turn-off from the N2, and then follow the Aston Bay road. The distance from Port Elizabeth is about 82 km. The reserve, which includes the estuary of the combined Seekoei and Swart rivers, was originally proclaimed as a sanctuary for waterfowl. In the areas of indigenous bush, you will be likely to spot many of the smaller buck species including blue duiker, grey duiker and bushbuck.

The reserve is open on weekdays from 7 a.m. to 5 p.m. Visitors are also admitted at weekends, but most of the game is on the island in the estuary, and the ferry to the island operates only during the week.

Sinclair Nature Reserve
Situated east of Knysna in the Kruisfontein State Forest, this appealing reserve extends over 1 828 ha through some of the southern Cape's most beautiful countryside. An impressive variety of indigenous shrubs and trees flourish among the plateau's hillocks and ravines, among them Outeniqua yellowwood, red alder, witels, Cape redwood, real yellowwood, cherrywood and kamassi. Although there has not yet been a detailed study of the area's wildlife population, the reserve is known to accommodate such animals as honey badger, leopard, grysbok, porcupine and more elusive species such as bats, mice, moles, shrews and mongooses. There is a large variety of birds, such as the Knysna loerie, fish eagle, crowned eagle and Knysna scrub warbler.

Although the reserve itself is not open to the public, hikers can get a feel of it on the Harkerville Coast Hiking Trail. This two-day circular trail starts from Harkerville Forest Station and leads through indigenous forest to the breathtaking Harkerville coastline.

Much of the trail involves clambering over rocks, and participants should be satisfied that they are fit enough before attempting it. Over-

night huts cater for parties of 12 hikers. Bookings are made via The Regional Director, Southern Cape Forest Region, Private Bag X12, Knysna 6570 (telephone Knysna 2-3037). The Harkerville Forestry Station is reached via a turn-off midway between the Plettenberg Bay-Knysna road.

Swellendam Hiking Trail
Part of the National Hiking Way network, this challenging 76 km, five- to six-day trail starts at Koloniesbos, situated 4 km from the Swellendam Forest Station (beyond the waterworks).

There are six 16-bed huts along the route, including the one at Koloniesbos, but four of these are without fireplaces, so visitors should take their own camp stoves.

The terrain along the trail, which winds through both the southern and northern slopes of the Langeberg, is broken and mountainous, and a fair degree of physical fitness is needed, even on the shorter routes. For safety reasons, hikers must travel in parties of three or more. The trail, for which a permit is required, is open throughout the year. For reservations and further information, write to The Regional Director, Western Cape Forest Region, Private Bag X2, Roggebaai 8012 (telephone Cape Town 402-3043).

Terblans Nature Walk
On this walk you can follow bushpig markers for 2 hours through the beautiful Gouna Forest – the domain of the last remaining Knysna elephants. The route is open from 6 a.m. to 6 p.m. No pets are allowed.

While permits are not needed, hikers must register in the visitors' book at the start.

The walk begins and ends at Grootdraai Picnic site, situated 16 km north of Knysna on the Gouna Road (Kom-se-Pad). For maps and more information write to The Regional Director, Southern Cape Forest Region, Private Bag X12, Knysna 6570 (telephone Knysna 2-3037).

The Lakes Nature Conservation Station
The laboratories, an important centre for the study of estuarine and freshwater life, are situated just off The Lakes Road in a 430 ha reserve between Rondevlei and Swartvlei.

Bird-watchers may visit a bird hide, where some 80 species have been recorded. The area around Rondevlei (open on weekdays from 8 a.m. to 4.30 p.m.) consists of coastal duneveld covered with renosterbos and patches of milkwood forest. Mammals include bushbuck, grysbok, porcupine and vervet monkey. Bontebok have been introduced.

To reach the reserve, take the turn-off from the national road, about 10 km west of Sedgefield, and follow the signs.

A 3-hour trail is to be developed in the future.

TSITSIKAMMA NATIONAL PARK AT A GLANCE

When to go Rainfall is perennial but the driest months are generally in mid-winter – June and July. The parks are open daily from 5.30 a.m. to 9.30 p.m.

Reservations and information Enquiries and applications for accommodation (including camping and caravan sites and places on the Otter Trail) should be addressed to the National Parks Board, P.O. Box 787, Pretoria 0001 (telephone Pretoria 343-1991). Alternatively, you can write to the National Parks Board either at P.O. Box 7400, Roggebaai 8012 (telephone Cape Town 419-5365) or P.O. Box 774, George 6530 (telephone George 74-6924/5). The National Parks Board publishes comprehensive guides to the trees, fishes and seaweeds of the parks.

Getting there The turn-off to the park is about halfway between Knysna and Humansdorp on the N2, 9 km west of the Paul Sauer Bridge over the Storms River.

Accommodation At Storms River Mouth there are fully equipped two-bedroom beach cottages, a number of self-contained one-bedroom (four beds) cottages with kitchenette and bathroom and one- and two-bedroomed oceanettes (beach apartments). There are camping and caravan sites. Washing and ironing facilities are provided and there is a swimming pool.

The De Vasselot section has camping and caravan sites and the Otter Trail has overnight huts.

Eating and drinking There is a restaurant and a shop, which sells groceries, perishables and liquor (no liquor sales on Sundays or religious holidays).

Getting around Several trails radiate from Storms River Mouth rest camp, the longest and most dramatic being the well-known Otter Trail, which leads 48 km west, over and around steep cliffs to Nature's Valley. Shorter trails include the Mouth, the Loerie and the Blue Duiker. Swimmers, divers and underwater photographers can view the wonders of the sea on the Scuba Trail. There is also a snorkeling trail.

Fishing Anglers are restricted to a small area of the marine sanctuary. Bait-collecting and spearfishing are forbidden.

Special precautions There are strict regulations governing the lighting of fires. The Otter Trail demands forethought in equipping yourself, stamina (paths rise steeply to circumvent cliffs) and a head for heights.

Tsitsikamma Forest – De Plaatbos

This 478 ha park was proclaimed to preserve the splendour of the evergreen indigenous forests of the southern Cape, and lies just off the main Cape Town-Port Elizabeth road, 100 km east of Knysna and 85 km to the west of Humansdorp.

Largest of the trees is the Outeniqua yellowwood (some in the park exceed 50 m in height). Slightly smaller, but no less impressive, are the stinkwoods, their dull-white boles encrusted with lichens. Even more liberally garlanded with mosses and lichens is the white alder. The 'Big Tree', a gigantic Outeniqua yellowwood, is estimated to be more than 800 years old and is taller than a 10-storey building.

Insects, birds and mammals have adapted to the various layers of the forest. The insects feed on the flowers and aid pollination, becoming part of the food cycle that includes chameleons, arum lily frogs, bats and birds, all of which may fall prey to carnivorous birds, cats, snakes or mongooses. Bushbuck, blue duiker, leopard, caracal, baboon and bushpig frequent the forest.

There are three walking trails within the park. Along the 15 minute Big Tree Trail visitors will see a number of fine examples of stinkwood, ironwood and many species of tree fern. Tree ferns and white alders can be seen in abundance along the one-hour Tree Fern Trail. The Bushpig Trail passes through a fynbos area particularly notable for its protea.

The complex at Storms River Bridge has a restaurant that serves light meals until 7 p.m., a tea-garden overlooking the gorge, a curio shop and a biltong bar, all of which are open seven days a week. The petrol station and takeaway shop are open 24 hours a day.

Tsitsikamma Hiking Trail

The trail can be started and completed at various points, but the full 64 km (five-day) trip starts at Kalander, near Nature's Valley and ends at the Storms River Bridge.

Starting and finishing points at the forestry stations of Bloukrans, Lottering and Kleinbos, at the Boskor Saw Mill, make it possible to use parts of the trail for weekend excursions.

The route takes in a wide range of trees, wild flowers, mountain streams and magnificent views. Stinkwood and yellowwood are among the 48 species of trees which grow here.

Large game animals which once roamed the forests have unfortunately been exterminated, but surviving mammals include bushpig, vervet monkey, caracal, honey badger and otter. Approximately 70 bird species are commonly seen in the area. Overnight huts can accommodate up to 30 people – the maximum number of hikers that may start the trail on any one day. Enquiries should be directed to The

Marooned by the tides, this sea snake lies dying on the Tsitsikamma coast. The meeting of the warm Agulhas and cold Benguela currents along the coastline has resulted in a unique, colourful blending of tropical and cold water species of marine flora and fauna.

Regional Director, Tsitsikamma Forest Region, Private Bag X537, Humansdorp 6300 (telephone Humansdorp 5-1180).

Tsitsikamma Indigenous Forests

Comprising some 700 km² of woodland on the southern slopes of the Tsitsikamma Mountains between the Garden Route town of Knysna and Storms River, the forests are very popular among South African hikers. Passing through them is a self-guided, hutted trail leading on to the Tsitsikamma Hiking Trail. Southwards, winding along the coast, is the famed Otter Trail. There are other forest walks and picnic spots in the area, and there is a campsite at Groot River.

Dominant tree species in the wet uplands are the red alder, the white alder and candlewood. Yellowwood proliferates on the lower slopes and the plateau. Animal and bird life are varied and include leopard, bushbuck, bushpig, chacma baboon, Cape grysbok, fish eagle, mountain buzzard, Cape eagle, owl and hamerkop. For permits and further information write to The Regional Director, Tsitsikamma Forest Region, Private Bag X537, Humansdorp (telephone Humansdorp 656).

Tsitsikamma National Park

From the placid lagoon at Nature's Valley, a rugged and unspoilt shoreline stretches eastward for some 80 km to the mouth of the Groot River, crossed by streams where steep ravines are a wonderland of ferns, trees and flowers.

This is the Tsitsikamma National Park, a narrow coastal plain bounded by cliffs and beaches, and extending 5 km into the sea.

This latter fact implies that the major portion of the park lies hidden beneath the surface of the sea. And in a sense, this is true: Tsitsikamma was the first marine national park in Africa, and below the heaving swells of the Indian Ocean, is a wonderland of marine life equal in all respects to the verdant ravines and valleys of the landward segment.

The De Vasselot section, adjoining Nature's Valley, offers a unique insight into the forest domain of the region, including a number of interesting day trails, and a beautiful camping and caravan site.

Storms River Rest Camp, close to the mouth of the river, offers a wide range of tourist accommodation, from fully equipped log chalets and beach cottages, to oceanettes (beach apartments), all close to the booming breakers of the ocean. A picturesque and well-equipped camping area is also available.

Angling is only permitted along a 2,8 km stretch of shore between Goudgate and the Waterfall. Spearfishing and the removal of bait organisms is strictly prohibited (bait is available from the shop). Indoor and outdoor exhibitions portray the biological diversity of the park, and several Strandloper middens (refuse heaps containing shellfish and other remains) are visible evidence of these early people who inhabited the caves along this shore.

Over and above the famous Otter Hiking

A boat plies a path up the Touw River. The Wilderness Rest Camp, offering chalets, caravan and camping sites, lies on the banks of the river.

Four kingfisher species are found, including the giant kingfisher, which is commonly seen skilfully skimming low across the water in search of its daily prey.

The Kingfisher Trail is a pleasant day excursion through the area. A highlight of the trail is the unique 'boardwalk' – a walkway through the unspoilt inter-tidal zone of the Touw River, and its reed-enshrouded fringe areas.

The Wilderness Rest Camp, located on the bank of the Touw River, offers chalets, caravan and camping sites. There is also a reception office and a shop offering basic commodities. The Ebb-and-Flow Rest Camp which provides more rustic accommodation further upstream, is connected to the Wilderness Rest Camp by a bridge over the Serpentine. Canoes may be hired for an unforgettable few hours' paddling on the lakes.

For bookings and further information write to the National Parks Board, P.O. Box 787, Pretoria 0001 (telephone Pretoria 343-1991) or National Parks Board, P.O. Box 7400, Roggebaai 8012 (telephone Cape Town 419-5365) or National Parks Board, P.O. Box 774, George 6530 (telephone George 74-6924/5).

Ysternek Nature Reserve

About 25 km north of Knysna on the road to Avontuur, the 1212 ha Ysternek reserve offers much to those who enjoy exploring the fynbos and evergreen indigenous forests of the southern Cape countryside. However, the Knysna-Uniondale road (all signposts indicate Uniondale) is unfortunately not suitable for caravans and trailers.

Ysternek was created to conserve mountain fynbos and indigenous forest, part of which includes an area of typical wet mountain forest containing dense stands of tree ferns. Inside this forest is a beautiful picnic spot known as the 'Dal van Varings' (Valley of Ferns). From this vantage point visitors can drive or walk up a steep, narrow road to a viewing site: to the south are the Knysna Forests and Plettenberg Bay; to the north the Buffelsnek State Forest reaches out to the deep and desolate ravines of the Outeniqua Mountains. To the east the eye can follow the Tsitsikamma Mountains almost as far as Humansdorp on a clear day, while to the west you will see forest containing dense tree ferns.

There is also a short walk from the picnic spot through the tree ferns. Bird life is prolific; the mammal population includes leopard, bushbuck and bushpig. Yellowwood and stinkwood are among the tree species.

The best time to visit is from October to May. For further information you are advised to write to The State Forester, Diepwalle State Forest, Private Bag Knysna 6570 (telephone Plettenberg Bay 9301/9780).

Trail, a number of shorter trails exist. Walkers have a choice between the hour-long Mouth Trail (with spectacular views of sea and coast), the Loerie Trail and leading off it, the four-hour Blue Duiker Trail, which leads through coastal forests to join the Otter Trail.

More unusual are the underwater trails which have been marked out here for diving enthusiasts. The snorkeling trail near the start of the Otter Trail, is as popular as the Scuba trail, which starts from the boathouse below the reception centre. It should be noted that only divers who possess a valid SAUU (South African Underwater Union) certificate or recognised equivalent will be permitted to undertake the Scuba trail. The marine life is magnificent on both trails, and is typical of this section of the southern Cape coast.

Van Kervel Nature Reserve

This 9 ha reserve in George is situated near the railway level crossing in Caledon Street. It is open from sunrise to sunset and features a delightful selection of indigenous trees and shrubs. A number of flower species, including the George lily, are also cultivated.

Wadrift Nature Reserve

This privately run reserve on the slopes of the Tsitsikamma Mountains offers nature walks, hiking trails and conveniently central accommodation from which to explore the lakes and dramatic coastline of the 'Garden Route'. It lies in the rural Bitou area, about a 10-minute drive from Plettenberg Bay. The peaceful surroundings include a swimming pool, children's playpark and a farm stall.

Walks vary from a short 1,5 km stroll to an 18 km trail, and offer views of fynbos forest, small antelope and many birds.

For bookings contact The Manager, Wadrift Nature Reserve, P.O. Box 72, Plettenberg Bay 6620 (telephone Plettenberg Bay 9425).

Whiskey Creek Nature Reserve

Exotically named, Whiskey Creek is a far more serene place than its name suggests, although it is more valued by botanists than the average day visitor. (There are no facilities). No fewer than six soil moisture types – ranging from very wet to very dry – have produced varied vegetation, including Karoo scrub, fynbos and forest. There are many keurboom or blossom trees (Virgilia oroboides) that produce a sweet-smelling mauve blossom in summer.

For further enquiries contact The Senior Regional Officer, Department of Nature and Environmental Conservation, Private Bag X6546, George 6530 (telephone George 74-1567/8).

Wilderness National Park

Originally proclaimed in 1983 as South Africa's first National Lake Area, this unique wetland system creates an inter-connected web of vlei, river and fen that stretches from the picturesque village of Wilderness up the coast to as far as the Goukamma Nature Reserve. This area is the heart of the 'Garden Route' and includes the Touw River, Serpentine Channel, Eilandvlei (Island Lake), Bo-Langvlei and Swartvlei – the largest of six lakes in the area, as well as long stretches of rocky coastline.

Certain sections of the lake area have been upgraded to the status of National Park, where zoning principles are applied to ensure that conservation and recreation mix happily. Watersports are a feature of the region and range from angling and sedate canoe-trips to the exhilarating speed of water-skiing and boardsailing.

The wetlands are also an ornithologist's paradise, with waterbirds present in their thousands.

Lure of the Little Karoo

The Little Karoo has been called the 'poor man's desert'. It is a dry and arid valley, 300 km long and 100 km wide, with few obvious redeeming features. Yet nature has endowed this strange region of ochre and khaki with several blessings.

The valley is drained by the Olifants River, so named because when white men first set eyes on the 'Klein Karoo' (in 1689, Simon van der Stel led a party into the area) it teemed with elephant, lion, hippo, quagga, kudu, rhino and buffalo. Not a trace remains of these large mammals – except for leopard, which sun themselves in remote places, and baboon.

The ostrich is another survivor – a primitive running bird which has earned fortunes for the farmers of this region (particularly at the turn of the century, when ostrich feathers were in great demand in Europe). Overnight, the Oudtshoorn farmers became 'feather million-aires', and their ornate and expensive mansions – 'feather palaces' – still bear testimony to the boom years.

The rugged Swartberg, with its strange red hues, has its own treasures. In its foothills are the world-famous Cango Caves – a series of caverns discovered in 1780 and later deve-loped as a major tourist attraction.

Baviaanskloof Wilderness Area

Between Willowmore in the west and Patensie in the east runs one of the most scenically beau-tiful drives in the eastern Cape – through the steeply wooded valleys, mountain streams and tinkling waterfalls of the Baviaanskloof.

This is not yet a declared wilderness area (though it shortly will be). Comprising the three State forests of Baviaanskloof (68 532 ha), Cocks-comb (52 740 ha) and Formosa (50 900 ha), it is a place of steep ravines and the bare peaks of the Baviaanskloof and Kouga mountain ranges – long a favourite haunt of the hardier breed of climbers and hikers.

Visitors may see animals such as chacma baboon, bushpig, klipspringer, rhebok, moun-tain zebra and the occasional leopard. But it is for the many species of birds that the area is particularly well known.

The access road winds through the kloof, several times crossing the Baviaanskloof River in the west and the Witrivier and Grootrivier farther east so that, after heavy rains, the region is inaccessible to vehicles. For permits, you should write to The Senior Regional Officer, Department of Nature and Environmental Con-servation, Private Bag X1126, Port Elizabeth 6000 (telephone Port Elizabeth 55-7380).

Cango Caves

In the southern foothills of the Groot Swartberg, about 28 km north-east of Oudtshoorn, lies one of nature's most enchanting creations – the Cango Caves.

The process of creation began countless cen-turies ago when limestone deposits shattered along a zone up to 90 m wide. Later, this fissure was sealed by calcite, and underground water spilled through the limestone bed to create the vast caverns.

The Cango Caves proper were found by a Khoikhoi herder who had been sent by his em-ployer, a farmer named Van Zyl, to look for missing cattle. The youngster stumbled across a gaping hole covered with brushwood in the mountainside. Curious to know what lay within, he persuaded a man named Oppel (believed to be an itinerant sailor who was working his way to Durban after jumping ship in Cape Town) to visit the spot: Oppel was so impressed that he called Van Zyl and eight helpers to plumb the hole's depths.

In time, the other chambers – leading west-wards for nearly 2 km – were also explored. In 1972 two professional guides working at the cave broke through into what became known as the Wonder Cave. Further extensions to the

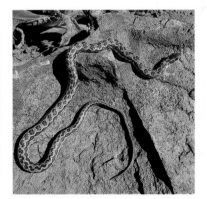

Above left: Mating 'whites' (pierid) butterflies. **Above right:** The rhombic skaapsteker is among the most beautiful of Southern Africa's snakes. It is a curiously gentle snake, and will not bite humans – even given the strongest provocation. Growing to a length of about 90 cm, it lives on small animals such as mice, frogs and lizards. **Left:** A flock of young ostriches on a farm near Calitzdorp.

The ostrich can attain a weight of 156 kilograms. It has several features which distinguish it from other birds, including its long, powerful legs (capable of carrying it at speeds of up to 70 km/h), its oil-less feathers (which soak up water when it rains) and two-toed feet. Two or three females sometimes accompany a single male – and the females may lay their eggs in the same nest.

Right: The world-famous Cango Caves, near Oudtshoorn. **Left:** A crocodile at the Cango Crocodile Ranch, which serves as home to more than 300 of these reptiles.

Short demonstrations are held by guides who actually stand in amongst the cheetah. The catwalk also takes you through a monkey walk, water cascade and bird park.

There is a curio shop and refreshments are served at the 'Hot-Croc-Cafe'.

The ranch is open daily from 8 a.m. to 5 p.m. in season and 8 a.m. to 4.15 p.m. out of season. It overlooks the Swartberg range and is well signposted from the Oudtshoorn-Cango Caves road. For more information write to The Manager, Cango Crocodile Ranch and Cheetahland, P.O. Box 559, Oudtshoorn 6620 (telephone Oudtshoorn 9-2983).

De Hoek Nature Walk

This seven-hour trail is part of the longer Swartberg Trail, and takes hikers through the southern foothills of the Swartberg, near the Cango Caves. The 11,6 km route passes through some rugged territory, and hikers should be reasonably fit.

Proteas, heaths, everlasting and a host of other fynbos species may be seen along the way, and the peaks and cliffs of the mountains provide an unforgettable scenic treat. Further information is available from The State Forester, Directorate of Forestry, P.O. Box 350, Oudtshoorn 6620 (telephone Oudtshoorn 9-1739).

Gamka Mountain Reserve

The dwindling numbers of the rare Cape mountain zebra (*Equus zebra*) have found a sanctuary in this 9400 ha reserve situated (except for a small extension in the north) in the Gamka mountains, south-west of Oudtshoorn.

Visitors are drawn here by the beautiful scenery, and there are particularly good views from Bakenskop (1099 m), the highest point. Four of the major 70 veld types of Southern Africa occur in this reserve: succulent Karoo, false macchia, succulent mountain scrub (spekboomveld) and renosterbosveld. The flowering plants of this arid reserve are also of interest. Roaming freely with the zebra are klipspringer, grey rhebok, grysbok, duiker, caracal, steenbok, dassie and baboon (leopard are occasionally sighted). About 80 species of birds have been identified, including black eagles.

Spring – when wild flowers are in bloom – is the best time to visit the reserve.

The ideal way to sample the delights of this reserve is on foot. The highlight of a two-day conducted trail through the reserve leads past outcrops of *Mimetes chrysanthus*, a newly dis-

Cango Caves have been found, but all (including the Wonder Cave) are closed to the public to prevent damage to the formations.

The caves have become a mecca for tourists: in 1988 there were 203 600 visitors. Facilities include a licensed restaurant, a curio shop, toilets, showers, a large car park, a museum featuring plants, animals and rock formations from the caves; a pets' room, and a crèche. The caves (they were proclaimed a National Monument in 1938) are administered by the Oudtshoorn Municipality.

They are clearly signposted from Oudtshoorn and all along the winding tarred road through Schoemanspoort. Visitors may not enter the caves without a guide.

Tours are conducted every day (every hour on the hour from 8 a.m. to 5 p.m. in December, January, February and April and for the rest of the year every two hours from 9 a.m. to 3 p.m. For further information, write to The Publicity Officer, Oudtshoorn Municipality, P.O. Box 255, Oudtshoorn 6620 (telephone Oudtshoorn 2221).

Cango Crocodile Ranch and Cheetahland

Crocodile, cheetah, jaguar and lion are among the fearsome stars of Cango Crocodile Ranch

and Cheetahland – a ranch outside Oudtshoorn which can offer something to the whole family.

On guided tours (conducted every 30 minutes), you will see more than 300 crocodile and the largest alligator population in South Africa. The crocs range from 50 cm 'babies' to the 4 m-long 'Zindago' – a massive specimen, responsible for killing and eating at least two people in Zimbabwe!

The ranch comes alive thanks to the efforts of professional guides, one of whom reputedly sports the world's only set of dentures made from crocodile teeth!

Once your tour of the croc enclosure is over it is well worth exploring the ranch's well-stocked snake park and crocodilian museum, while children will discover tame and interesting animals to dote on. These include miniature horses, dwarf goat, wallaby, warthog, otter, camel and a rhea, South America's version of an ostrich.

Cheetahland, which was completed in 1988, is a novel concept for visitors. Its natural enclosures which house cheetah, jaguar and lion are connected by an elevated catwalk, which lets you take once-in-a-lifetime photographs.

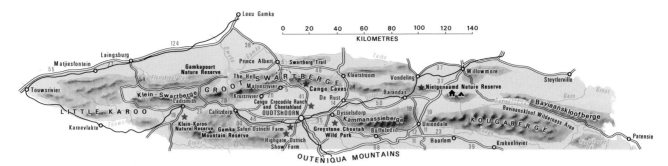

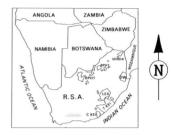

covered plant species, while short day walks are also available. The reserve has a few gravel roads, which can be negotiated only by a 4-wheel-drive vehicle. Among the facilities available to visitors are a picnic site with braai facilities and a pool in which weary hikers can cool off.

To get there, take the Calitzdorp road from Oudtshoorn. After 10 km, turn left onto the old concrete road to Calitzdorp: this will bring you to another sign reading 'Uitvlugt'. Take this route to the reserve gate.

The Calitzdorp Spa, situated approximately 10 km farther along the gravel road which passes the reserve gate, has a restaurant, chalets, a caravan park and a swimming pool. Permits are obtainable from The Officer-in-Charge, Gamka Mountain Reserve, Private Bag X21, Oudtshoorn 6620 (telephone Langverwag 3002).

Gamkapoort Nature Reserve

This reserve, encircling the Gamkapoort Dam is situated 38 km west of Prince Albert, at the confluence of the Dwyka and Gamka Rivers and extends into the northern foothills of the Swartberg range. It is one of the few Cape reserves featuring succulent Karoo veld, and has the most northerly distribution of false macchia veld. Other vegetation types include succulent mountain scrub, spekboomveld and karroid broken veld.

The reserve, which extends for over 8 000 ha, has more than 100 bird species and numerous mammals. These include, klipspringer, springbok, grey rhebok, kudu, bat-eared fox, caracal and black-backed jackal. A picnic site is being developed for day visitors. For permits, and directions to the reserve, write to The Senior Regional Officer, Department of Nature and Environmental Conservation, Private Bag X6546, George 6530 (telephone George 74-1567).

Above: Ostrich chicks and unhatched eggs on a farm in the Oudtshoorn district. An ostrich egg weighs about 1,5 kg and equals 24 chicken eggs in volume. The chicks can run within three days of hatching. **Right:** Gamkapoort Dam, west of Prince Albert.

Highgate Ostrich Show Farm

Owned by the Hooper family, whose forebears came to South Africa from the London suburb of Highgate in 1850, this farm attracts a staggering 80 000 tourists a year. Visitors are met by multilingual guides who take them on a two-hour tour around the farm. One of the highlights of the tour is ostrich riding. Highgate is open from 7.30 a.m. to 5 p.m. (including Sundays and public holidays). Refreshments (such as home-made biscuits and ostrich biltong) are served on the porch of the impressive homestead, and are included in the tour price. The farm is clearly signposted on the road from Oudtshoorn to Mossel Bay, and is situated 10 km from the centre of Oudtshoorn. The farm has a large curio shop which offers ostrich eggs, leather goods and feather boas.

Ladismith/Klein Karoo Nature Reserve

Although still to be fully developed, this reserve (near Ladismith) offers serious plant lovers an opportunity to browse among a wide variety of indigenous vegetation in this 3 300 ha stretch of unspoilt Karoo veld.

The countryside here is quite hilly, and the principal feature is the 760 m Ladismith Hill.

The gates of Ladismith/Klein Karoo Nature Reserve are locked, and prospective visitors must make prior arrangements to collect the keys from the Ladismith Municipality (between 8 a.m. and 5 p.m.).

220

Eland and springbok have been introduced to the area, and there are also duiker and steenbok in the sanctuary. The reserve is 8 km south of the town, on the road to Barrydale. Several gravel roads lead through it, affording visitors a broad picture of the terrain.

Nietgenaamd Nature Reserve

After good rains, at least 26 waterfalls plunge down the Barnardsberg, (named after the farmer who once owned the land) into this exquisite reserve near Uniondale.

Three hundred years ago, the land teemed with elephant, buffalo, hippo, quagga and lion, but today only baboon and a few species of buck remain in the 1 577 ha reserve.

If you take one of the walking trails around the reserve you may be able to spot klipspringer, duiker, grysbok, steenbok, rhebok, baboon and the occasional kudu (there is also good bird-viewing at the dam).

The hot mineral springs are a great attraction at Nietgenaamd (the farm was once called 'Warmbad'). During the feather boom, about 33 families lived near the springs, believing that it would cure their ailments.

Today the springs have been channelled into concrete sitting baths – one for men, one for women and one for children. There are 5 three-bedded rooms, one with a kitchen; 1 six-bedded room with a kitchen, and 1 six-bedded cottage with a kitchen and bathroom. Cutlery, bedding and firewood are provided but visi-

tors must take their own food.

There are several campsites under an attractive grove of oaks, with ablution facilities. The Klein-Karoo Regional Services Council, which administers the nature reserve, plans to create more public amenities.

Succulents (including aloes) and Karoo shrubs dot the landscape, and higher up there is a profusion of fynbos vegetation.

To book a room at the reserve, telephone Uniondale 1912 or write to The Chief Executive Officer, Klein-Karoo Regional Services Council, P.O. Box 127, Oudtshoorn 6620 (telephone Oudtshoorn 2241/2/3/4).

Safari Ostrich Show Farm

Ostrich farms in the Oudtshoorn district draw thousands of tourists from all over the world. Most of the farms offer comprehensive tours which give visitors a good idea of the habits of this huge bird (*Struthio camelus*).

Among these is the Safari Ostrich Farm, about 5 km from the town centre on the road to Mossel Bay. It is clearly signposted on the left of the road.

Tours of the farm last between one-and-a-half to two hours and leave every half hour. Light refreshments are available from a kiosk but full meals are provided only for booked tours. The farm has its own 'feather palace' – a National Monument – with Burmese teak woodwork and Belgian roof tiles. It is open from 7.30 a.m. to 5 p.m.

Rocky shores and green valleys

From the eastern curve of False Bay to the most southerly tip of Africa – Cape Agulhas – and beyond, there is a rugged, beautiful and largely uninhabited coastline. It is guarded by mountain ranges that plunge into plains aglow with wild flowers.

Behind these stark coastal peaks are wide, lush valleys clothed in spring tapestries of wild flowers. The treacherous peaks of the Hottentots-Holland Mountains are the doorway to a wonderland of forested slopes that spill into clear trout streams; where herds of buck graze quietly, undisturbed by man.

Much of the land is protected in State or private reserves. There is a good reason: the western Cape is one of the six floral kingdoms of the world, and parts of it harbour the greatest density and variety of flowers on earth. Great spaces have been exploited for industrial or farming purposes, but nature-lovers are working tirelessly in selected areas to restore the natural beauty that once existed. By the looks of it, they are succeeding.

Assegaaibosch Nature Reserve

Encircled by mountains and bisected by the Eerste River is the picturesque Jonkershoek Valley, named after an early settler, Jan de Jonker. It is here that the Chief Directorate of Nature and Environmental Conservation has established a nature reserve on the northern slopes of the Stellenboschberg.

Principally a fynbos sanctuary, the scenic 168ha area rises steeply up the mountain slopes. About 5ha of the reserve are developed as a wild flower garden with predominant species of protea, erica and indigenous trees like wild olive (*Olea africana*).

A circular trail of 2,5km up the mountain slopes is a particularly pleasant walk in summer as the route follows two mountain streams with plenty of riverine shade. The reserve is always worth a visit, but particularly from September to November when spring flowers add extra colour.

The only facilities provided are picnic sites and a car park about 50m from the entrance.

The reserve is open from 8.30a.m. to 4.00p.m. during the week and from 9a.m. to 6p.m. at weekends. Permits to enter the reserve can be arranged during office hours by contacting The Officer-in-Charge, Assegaaibosch Nature Reserve, Private Bag 5014, Stellenbosch 7600 (telephone Stellenbosch 7-0130). To get there, take Jonkershoekweg from Stellenbosch and follow the road until you see the large green sign on the right indicating the reserve.

Boesmanskloof Trail

Situated in the picturesque Riviersonderend Mountains, this 15,8km trail offers rugged mountain scenery, a variety of fynbos and many large rock pools and waterfalls. The four- to five-hour hike is based on an old track leading through the only gap in the mountain range, and highlights include the Greyton and McGregor valleys, Cape wild flowers and steep gorges.

A fair degree of physical fitness is most certainly required as the trail rises and falls con-

Above: The bluebuck (*Hippotragus leucophaeus*) once inhabited the south-western Cape, but was wiped out by early settlers: the last known specimen was shot around 1800. A near relative of the roan, it was a bluish grey colour, with a brown forehead, short mane on the neck and shoulders, and shorter horns than the roan (though they also had the scimitar shape). Its former limited range in the Karoo is believed to be one of the major contributory factors to its demise. There is evidence that the bluebuck's last stronghold was the Soete Melk Valley near Swellendam. Mounted specimens are exhibited at museums in Vienna, Paris, Stockholm and Leyden. A pair of horns on display in Grahamstown's Albany Museum is widely considered to be those of a bluebuck, and if so are the only remains known to exist in South Africa. **Left:** The Assegaaibosch Nature Reserve near Stellenbosch.

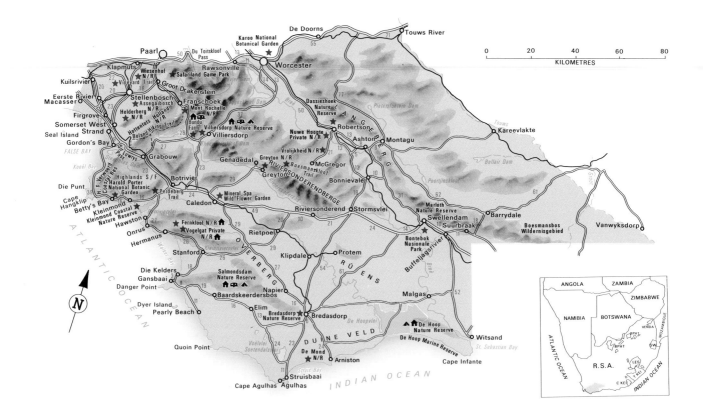

Above: A carpet of flowers transforms the Caledon Wild Flower Garden each spring. Visitors arrive in droves from Cape Town and farther afield to view the display. Although the spectacular garden covers only 20 ha, the remaining 214 ha comprises indigenous fynbos and stunning mountain scenery which is traversed by a network of trails. **Right:** A cetoniid beetle feeding on a protea. Cetoniids can be extremely destructive, some species feeding on rose bushes and others on a variety of fruit.

tinuously with the contours of the Boesmanskloof slopes. Although the trail may later become part of the National Hiking Way System, there are as yet no overnight facilities. To obtain a permit, write to The State Forester, Sonderend State Forest, P.O. Box 128, Robertson 6705 (telephone Robertson 3079).

Boland Hiking Trail: Hottentots-Holland Section

Cutting across the spine of the Hottentots-Holland and Franschhoek mountains, this 54 km trail, established by the National Hiking Way Board in 1975, takes visitors through one of the wealthiest floral kingdoms in the world. There are about 1 500 species of indigenous plants to be seen along the route, and many of these are listed on the back of a comprehensive map available to prospective hikers: this will prove invaluable on the trail.

There are two clearly signposted starting points to the trail. One is at the summit of Sir Lowry's Pass (on the left coming from Cape Town) and can be seen from the road. The other is situated at the Grabouw forestry station, which is signposted from the main road of the nearby town. Both starting points have ample parking space for cars. The full three-day trail (hikers make three overnight stops at huts

Above: *Wachendorfia paniculata* in the Fernkloof Nature Reserve, which overlooks Hermanus.

A GRAIN OF POLLEN

Lobostemon fruticosus is found throughout the coastal districts of the western Cape and extends to Namaqualand. The corolla may be pink or blue.

The origin of the natural vegetation of the western Cape, commonly known as fynbos ('macchia' to the botanist) has been the subject of scientific debate for decades. How old is it, and what vegetation preceded it millions of years ago?

Clues to the answers were to be provided by the discovery of an exceptionally rich fossil bed at a phosphate mine near Saldanha Bay in 1958. In contrast to the immense age of the reptile and plant fossils of the Karoo (about 250 million years old), this fossil graveyard was only four to five million years old.

Few plant fossils were found, and botanists were obliged to speculate on the nature of the vegetation until a major clue was provided by the specialised study of pollen, known as palynology. The evidence was derived from core samples taken from ancient peat bogs discovered on the Cape Flats. The pollen in the various levels of the peat gave an almost unbroken record of the Cape vegetation from the present right back into the mists of time.

Palynologists have deduced that from about 35 million years ago the region experienced fluctuations in temperature, which in turn caused corresponding changes in the vegetation — from sub-tropical palm forests to cooler forests dominated by ancestral yellowwood trees. The Cape, it appeared, enjoyed a summer rainfall and, despite the temperature fluctuations, the climate was warmer and wetter than it is today. However, about 12 million years ago the southern oceans began to cool. The increasing strength of the cold Benguela current off the west coast of Southern Africa introduced a more arid and colder climate, with winter rains.

The arid summers that followed caused the extinction of the remaining palm forests, and the yellowwoods took refuge in the sheltering kloofs of the mountains. Eventually, about 3,5 million years ago, the Cape macchia became the dominant flora of the Cape — hardy and able to withstand the rigours of wind, drought and periodic fire damage.

---

en route; the first at Landdroskop, the second at Boesmanskloof and the third at Eikenhof) begins at Sir Lowry's Pass and ends at the Franschhoek Pass.

Shorter or circular routes can be taken from Grabouw, and full details of these are available from the National Hiking Way Board. There are several day walks which loop through the Grabouw and Nuweberg forests. Permits are required for all walks and trails.

Overnight accommodation at Landdroskop (for 40 people), Shamrock Lodge (for 30), Eikenhof (for 30), Boesmanskloof and Aloe Ridge (30 people each) is fairly primitive. There are bunks with thin mattresses, and water. Visitors provide food, bedding and cooking utensils.

The route from Landdroskop to Jonkershoek Forestry Station is periodically closed and the Boegoekloof route is closed from April to September, so it is important to plan your trail well in advance. Advance booking is essential (although bookings will not be accepted more than 12 months in advance) – particularly at weekends and during school holidays.

The weather in the Hottentots-Holland Mountains is unpredictable, and people have died

from exposure. It is essential to follow the Board's instructions on protective clothing and other precautions. One has to be relatively fit to complete the full trail. For further information, or to make a booking, you should write to The Regional Director, Western Cape Forest Region, Private Bag 9005, Cape Town 8000 (telephone Cape Town 402-3043).

Bredasdorp Nature Reserve
An area of 800 ha has been set aside within the Bredasdorp municipal boundary for the preservation of local fynbos, with its dominant protea and erica families. Small mammals and birds may also be found. Footpaths up the slopes of the 368 m hill in the reserve offer panoramic views of the town and surroundings. The reserve is open all year, but the best time to visit is from the middle of September to the middle of October, when spring flowers are in abundance. With the exception of a thatched roof rondavel there are no facilities, and there is no accommodation. However, a caravan park in the town has 30 sites and seven well-equipped bungalows. To get there from the Napier side, take Independent Road from the

main road (turn right) and then right again into Van Riebeeck Road. The gates of the Bredasdorp Nature Reserve are at the end of this road and are well signposted.

For further information, you can write to The Town Clerk, Bredasdorp Municipality, P.O. Box 51, Bredasdorp 7280 (telephone Bredasdorp 4-1135).

Bundu Farm
This 160 ha area at the foot of the Villiersdorp Mountains is the base for Camp S.O.S. and School in the Wilds. It offers outdoor education classes for youth groups, schoolchildren and trainee teachers.

Situated near the Theewaterskloof Dam, Bundu Farm features rich fynbos and is home to such animals as porcupine, dassie, baboon, klipspringer, Cape grey mongoose and grysbok. The farm can be hired by private groups at weekends and on public holidays, but these groups must organise their own activities. The many facilities include bungalows, large halls, kitchens, hot and cold showers and a swimming pool. The farm is reached from a turn-off on the Villiersdorp-Grabouw road.

Above left: *Helichrysum chlorochrysum* in the De Hoop Nature Reserve near Bredasdorp. **Above right:** The *Peripatus* has long fascinated biologists. It is regarded as a link between worms and arthropods (a phylum which includes spiders, insects and crustaceans). The body is soft and contractile, like that of a worm, but the legs are tipped with claws, an insectan feature. Its only defensive weapon consists of slime papilla on either side of the mouth; these discharge a sticky substance which forms a tangled net of threads (it is also used in prey capture). Most of the African species are found at the southern tip of the continent (a blind species lives in caves on Table Mountain). **Left:** Cape mountain zebra in the De Hoop Nature Reserve. **Right:** The colourful *Leucospermum truncatum* (a pincushion).

For information, write to School in the Wilds, P.O. Box 153, Villiersdorp 7170 (telephone Villiersdorp 3-1138).

Caledon Wild Flower Garden

Every spring, thousands of visitors make a pilgrimage to the Caledon Wild Flower Garden to admire the staggering displays of Namaqualand daisies, gazanias, *Arctotis*, *Lampranthus* and *Dorotheanthus*.

Established in 1927 by a group of nature enthusiasts and now administered by the Caledon Municipality, the garden is well signposted from the national road. It is open all year, and during the peak spring season (from September to October) you can enjoy refreshments at the tea-room.

The 20 ha cultivated section, which is also the venue for the annual Caledon Flower Show, takes up a small section of the sanctuary, which rises up the slopes of a hill and covers an area of 214 hectares.

Early mornings and late evenings (the garden is open from 7 a.m. to 5 p.m.) are good times to spot duiker and other small mammals that inhabit the sanctuary. At the top of the hill is 'Window Rock', from where visitors can get a panoramic view of the surroundings. A 10 km hiking trail covers the more scenic parks of the garden and Swartberg Nature Reserve. The only facilities provided are picnic sites and toilets, but there are two hotels in town and a new resort and hotel is to be constructed at the site of the Caledon hot mineral springs. Enquiries should be addressed to The Town Clerk, Caledon Municipality, P.O. Box 24, Caledon 7230 (telephone Caledon 2-1090/1/2).
224

Centenary Nature Reserve

Situated off Van Riebeeck Avenue in the southern part of the charming village of Montagu, this wild flower garden of 10 ha was established specifically to preserve the indigenous vegetation. There are several footpaths leading through the reserve. Tea and cakes are served by the Horticultural Society every Tuesday morning from mid-June to the end of October. It is open from sunrise to 5 p.m.

Dassieshoek Nature Reserve

Dassieshoek, about 8 km north of the town of Robertson, is a sanctuary for fynbos – primarily members of the protea family. A pleasant feature is its picnic site near a dam, which attracts large numbers of birds. Several footpaths crisscross the reserve, offering occasional glimpses of tortoise and bushbuck, and there are several waterfalls. While there is no accommodation in the reserve (it is open only from sunrise to sunset), the Robertson Municipality, which controls the reserve, has a large resort (Silverstrand) with caravan and camping sites on the Breede River.

Silverstrand and the reserve are linked by the 23 km (two-day) Dassieshoek Hiking Trail, which provides overnight accommodation in a hut situated near the entrance to the reserve.

Permits are required to enter the reserve, and are available at the gate. Large groups should apply for a permit two weeks in advance as the reserve is open only to 100 people at a time. Brochures are provided and there are toilet and braai facilities.

To get there, take Voortrekker Road from Robertson (heading north) and look for the sign-

posts. For further information, write to The Town Clerk, Robertson Municipality, P.O. Box 52, Robertson 6705 (telephone Robertson 3112).

De Hoop Nature Reserve

Despite the proclamation of the Overberg Test Range near De Hoop, this reserve has expanded considerably since it was originally established by the provincial authorities in 1956. Today it includes a 40 000 ha nature reserve between Cape Infanta and Koppie Allen and a 23 000 ha marine reserve which extends three nautical miles out to sea.

De Hoop is unique in that it has a variety of habitats, supporting a tremendous variety of plants, within its boundaries.

The vegetation is classified as coastal fynbos with some 1 400 different plant species – of which about 25 are regarded as rare or endangered. Since the reserve was established, officers stationed there have recorded 63 species of mammal (50 terrestrial and 13 marine), 40 species of reptile and 14 species of amphibian. The major game species present are bontebok, Cape Mountain Zebra, eland, grey duiker, steenbok, rhebok, grysbok and klipspringer.

Some of the tiniest inhabitants of this reserve are also interesting. These include *Peripatus*, which belong to an archaic remnant form bridging the evolutionary gap between worms and insects. The vlei attracts a considerable number of bird species (211 types have been recorded at De Hoop).

Interesting features of the reserve are the vulture-breeding colony in the Potberg – the southernmost vulture-breeding area in Africa

– and the Windhoek Cave, probably the most important bat cave in the Cape.

Environmental education is emphasised at De Hoop, and the Potberg Environmental Education Centre has been established to serve schoolchildren and youth groups. Educational programmes are readily available for adults on request.

Scenic drives along 20 km of gravel roads link points of interest in the reserve, and there are day walks which can be undertaken at Potberg and along the De Hoop Vlei. Guided coastal walks (40 km) can be booked through the reserve office.

Limited tent and caravan facilities are provided, but these will be extended in the future.

De Hoop is signposted 6 km from Bredasdorp on the Swellendam-Bredasdorp road. This road leads to the main entrance of the reserve, which is about 37 km further on. Permits are issued at the gate and the reserve is open from 8 a.m. to 4.30 p.m. The vulture-breeding area is closed to the public.

For further information, write to Chief Directorate of Nature and Environmental Conservation, Private Bag 9086, Cape Town 8000 (telephone Cape Town 203-3911). Enquiries can be made by writing to The Officer-in-Charge, De Hoop Nature Reserve, Private Bag X16, Bredasdorp 7280 (telephone Napkei 782).

De Mond Nature Reserve

The three major goals for this 900 ha reserve are the reclamation of drift-sand areas and prevention of drift-sand formation, the conservation of rare communities of flora and fauna and the provision of outdoor recreation.

CAPE MOUNTAIN SPECTACULAR

One of Southern Africa's richest and most beautiful natural kingdoms is that of the Cape mountains, a majestic and irregular sweep of peak and precipice stretching northwards from the Cederberg, then south to the Cape Peninsula and up to Port Elizabeth and the eastern Cape.

The mountains are supreme recreational areas, and most are accessible by extensive but discreet footpaths. They are a paradise for rock-climbers and backpackers: the astounding combination of magnificent peaks, cool sparkling streams in the well-wooded valleys and the floristic wealth is unsurpassed on earth.

This is the home of the 'Cape Floral Kingdom', or Fynbos Biome. The world is divided by botanists into six botanical kingdoms, of which the Cape fynbos (also called *Capensis*) is one. Although it covers only 0,04 per cent of the area of the earth (compared to the Paleotropic Kingdom, which encompasses 35 per cent and includes the rest of Africa south of the Sahara), it is, in botanical terms, the richest area on the planet.

More than 8 500 plant species are found in the fynbos, of which 6 000 are endemic to specific areas. In a relatively small area of 100 m² in the Hottentots-Holland Mountains you may find as many as 121 different species. To put this into perspective: a nature reserve such as the Hottentots-Holland Nature Reserve (24 569 ha) contains more plant species than the whole of the British Isles.

Fynbos in its typical form has three distinctive elements – the proteoids (proteas, pincushions, mimetes and similar plants), ericoids (heaths and false heather), and restioids (reed-like sedges with beautiful brown flower heads). Many of our familiar garden plants, such as *Sparaxis*, *Ixia*, *Agapanthus*, *Watsonia*, blushing bride, heather, red-hot poker and others, grow naturally in the Cape mountains.

Outcrops of fynbos species are found as far north as Nieuwoudtville and become more common as you move south.

To the south of the Cederberg lie the Kouebokkeveldberge – mostly privately owned, though 98 035 ha have been declared a mountain catchment area. The Citrusdal protea (*Protea Mopina*) and the Bokkeveld ground protea (*Protea scabriuscula*) occur here. Immediately south-west of this area are the Groot Winterhoek Mountains, where a 19 270 ha wilderness area has been proclaimed.

South of the town of Tulbagh, the Elandskloof, Limiet and Slanghoek mountains reach towards Wellington, where they become the Hawequas Mountains. This is the home of three lovely proteas: the mountain rose, a small protea with drooping flower-heads; the very rare Kasteelskloof protea and the krantz protea. The historic Bain's Kloof Pass separates this range from the Du Toitskloof range, which stretches out towards Worcester and becomes Klein Drakenstein, Wemmershoek, Stettyns and eventually Hex River as it reaches De Doorns. Heaths, sedges, disas and many other flowers grow here in profusion.

The mountains of Drakenstein, Franschhoek, Jonkershoek, Simonsberg and Stellenbosch are equally beautiful. In these valleys are the wine routes and the stately Cape Dutch homes.

Farther south, the Hottentots-Holland range reaches towards Sir Lowry's Pass, on the other side of which is the Kogelberg. This is the richest of all the Cape mountains in terms of flora, with its very rare marsh rose, silver mimetes, Stokoe's protea and many other endemic species.

From Betty's Bay to Bot River, the Palmiet Mountain towers above the sea. Various trails can be followed here in the Highlands State Forest – home of a famous export protea – the Bot River protea (*Protea compacta*).

Probably the most famous of all the South African mountains is Table Mountain, with its attendants, Lion's Head, Devil's Peak, Twelve Apostles and Constantiaberg. This area offers a host of rewarding walks and climbs which vary in gradient and intensity to suit hikers of all fitness levels. The Riviersonderend range between Genadendal and the town of Riviersonderend, also offers a variety of tracks and footpaths (maintained by the local nature conservator).

The Langeberg range extends from Worcester eastwards towards the Gourits River: the Little Karoo lies at its northern slopes and the Overberg to the south, presenting the hiker with an ever-changing vista of farmlands. Historic villages such as Swellendam, Montagu, Barrydale, Riversdale and Albertinia nestle at its feet.

Farther to the north rise the austere krantzes of the Anysberg (Aniseed Mountain), Towerkop (Magic Peak) and Swartberg – home of the Towerkop snow protea (*Protea prumosa*). The nature conservator in this area controls large tracts of State land and privately owned catchment areas. It is a place of rare beauty – Gamkaskloof ('The Hell'), Seweweekspoort, Swartberg Pass, Meiringspoort and Huisrivier Pass are all well-known landmarks.

Even drier and more rugged, but equally beautiful are the Baviaanskloof, Kouga and Cockscomb mountains. The State land alone covers an area of over 170 000 ha, South Africa's largest wilderness area. It is a vast undulating expanse of land, with beautiful valleys, rugged peaks and countless twisting footpaths.

To the south is the Langkloof range. The southern valley wall is formed by the lush evergreen peaks of the Outeniqua and Tsitsikamma mountains – thousands of hectares of State land protected by foresters. George Peak and Formosa Peak are well-known landmarks, as are the historic Montagu Pass, Prince Alfred's Pass, Bloukrans and Grootrivier. The forests on the southern slopes are famous for their yellowwood and stinkwood.

Most Cape mountains are managed as nature reserves, wilderness areas or mountain catchment areas by the Chief Directorate of Nature and Environmental Conservation of the Cape Provincial Administration.

Situated on an estuary about 23 km from Bredasdorp (190 km east of Cape Town), the reserve offers visitors a variety of interesting and endangered plants such as *Phylica*, *Erica*, *Watsonia* and *Aspalathus*. There are also sea birds (such as the Caspian tern) and a wealth of aquatic life.

The best time to visit De Mond is between October and March. The reserve is open at all times to those in possession of a permit, issued by The Foreman-in-Charge, De Mond, P.O. Box 277, Bredasdorp 7280.

Dog Trail

A short distance from where the Sir Lowry's Pass village road crosses the railway line is the start of a 'dog trail' established by the Regional Director of Forestry in the Western Cape. It runs through 85 ha of fynbos along a row of flowering gums, offering superb views of the Hottentots-Holland Mountains, the Helderberg and False Bay. For further information, write to The Regional Director, Western Cape Forest Region, Private Bag X2, Roggebaai 8012, Cape Town 8000 (telephone Cape Town 402-3043).

Elandspad River Kloofing Trip

This occasionally strenuous scramble through the Elandspad River Gorge is only for the fit and agile. The starting point is at the parking area near the control point for heavy vehicles at the Du Toitskloof Pass, from where you follow the river upstream.

The trip takes you past sandbanks, a variety of riverine vegetation and dramatic rock formations, and there is also a waterfall which tumbles into a dark pool. If you have never tried kloofing, ask for advice on the correct footwear and how to waterproof your rucksack. Never explore the gorge in rainy or threatening weather – floodwaters could quickly turn it into a death trap.

For day permits, write to The Forester, Hawequas State Forest, Private Bag X14, Huguenot 7645 (telephone Paarl 62-3172).

Fernkloof Nature Reserve

Conservationists at the Fernkloof Nature Reserve wage a continuous battle against alien vegetation which encroaches on indigenous plants. The reserve features a conglomerate of montane coastal fynbos with several species of protea and at least 48 species of erica – an outstanding total for an area of only 1 446 hectares. The wide and interesting diversity of species in the reserve is partly attributed to the elevation range (63 m – 842 m).

This fynbos has no dormant season, so the reserve is interesting throughout the year. At the visitors' centre there is a display of prominent plants which you are likely to see on your walks. Free walking sticks are provided and
226

maps are available for a small fee. The centre is about 500 m from the entrance, which is well signposted from the main road between Hermanus and Voëlklip.

Radiating from the visitors' centre is a network of 40 km of carefully maintained paths that traverse most of the reserve. Three different gently sloping walks are marked, varying from 20 minutes to two hours. A seven-hour Erica Trail is being planned. All paths offer spectacular views of Hermanus and the coastline.

Because the area has been protected for so long, there has been a remarkable resurgence of animals and birds. Over 100 bird species have been sighted, including two black eagles that nest in the Kleinrivier mountain range. Visitors may also spot baboon, genet, mongoose, buck, dassie and porcupine.

In the moist ravines of the reserve small areas of indigenous forest occur. Among the species which may be seen are Cape beech (*Rapanea melanophloeos*), wild olive (*Olea africana*), assegaai (*Curtisia dentata*), hard pear (*Olinia ventosa*) and rooi-els (*Cunonia capensis*).

Also of interest is the botanical centre (for film and flower shows and lectures), with its Hermanus Herbarium, containing over 1 500 species, of which nearly 1 000 occur in Fernkloof.

The reserve is accessible at all times and there is no entrance fee. Picnic sites and toilets are available. A small mountain hut (for four people) may be reserved through the curator. For further information, write to The Curator, Fernkloof Nature Reserve, Hermanus Municipality, P.O. Box 20, Hermanus 7200 (telephone Hermanus 2-2985 – office, or 2-2700 – home).

Greyton Nature Reserve

This 2 220 ha reserve, run by the Greyton Municipality, has been set aside for the preservation of fynbos and buck. The reserve, which is still to be developed, is to the north-east of the town, near the Sonderend Mountains, and is well signposted from the main road.

The best way to explore the area is on the 15,8 km Boesmanskloof Trail which starts at the entrance and leads through half of the reserve. There are also several footpaths but no other facilities are available. The reserve is open at all times, but the best time to visit is from September to November.

H.F. Verwoerd Coastal Reserve

This reserve, situated off the road between Gordon's Bay and Kleinmond, is demarcated by two concrete beacons – one on Stoney Point and the other at 'Jock-se-Baai', to the east of Dawidsbaai.

Swimming, diving, spearfishing and angling are permitted within the reserve along this beautiful stretch of coastline, but the catching or collection of perlemoen, alikreukel, crayfish, black mussel, polychaete worm, crab, octopus, red bait, limpets or any other marine organisms is strictly prohibited.

Harold Porter National Botanic Garden

This garden is situated in the centre of the 'Cape Floral Kingdom', an area with the greatest density of plant species found anywhere in the world. This regional garden of the National Botanic Gardens specialises in the flora of a winter rainfall region.

Above: The Cape dormouse, the largest dormouse in Southern Africa, has thick, silvery grey fur with distinctive white and black patches on the face. This dormouse is usually found in the vicinity of rocks (its head is somewhat flattened, allowing it to squeeze into crevices), while other species live in abandoned birds' nests, bushes and even thatched roofs of houses. **Left:** *Phaenocoma prolifera* in the Fernkloof Nature Reserve.

The 189 ha garden is famous for its ericas, proteas and bulbous plants such as gladioli and watsonias. Only 5 ha of the garden are cultivated, while the rest is made up of coastal fynbos or macchia, the characteristic coastal vegetation of the western Cape. The high peak of the Platberg (917 m) dominates the area and two clear mountain streams run through the garden.

The flowering season extends from October to February and during this time a number of birds are attracted to the area, among them Cape thrush, various sunbird species, sugarbird, ground woodpecker and fiscal shrike. There are several species of buck as well as porcupine, mongoose, baboon (most of them too timid to come near visitors) and a few rarely seen leopard on the plateau.

The garden is open every day of the year from 8 a.m. to 6 p.m. It is situated off the main coastal road, just beyond Betty's Bay, and is clearly signposted. Apart from a few picnic sites in the car park, there are no other facilities. Dogs are allowed if kept on a leash.

Helderberg Nature Reserve

The town of Somerset West is dwarfed by the brooding Helderberg Mountain. On its lower south-eastern slopes and extending halfway up its craggy rockface is the Helderberg Nature Reserve. Proclaimed in 1960, the reserve (245 ha) is a sanctuary for the indigenous flora of the Hottentots-Holland area.

There are seven well-marked gravel paths of varying distances that criss-cross the reserve. The shorter trails (which take anything from 35 minutes to three hours to walk) radiate from the entrance gate in concentric circles and loop back through the densely packed erica and protea bushes to lengthen or shorten the walk as one wishes. One path leads up to the Helderberg Dome, the highest point on the mountain, but this route is recommended for experienced hikers only. Many hikers have lost their lives on the slippery cliffs and treacherous gullies of the Helderberg.

Disa Gorge, part of the reserve's water catchment area controlled by forestry, is fascinating and beautiful. From January to March, *Disa uniflora* is found growing on the higher vertical rock faces of the gorge; lower down is the enchanting *Nerine sarniensis*, which blooms in masses at the same time.

There is a waterfall in the Disa Gorge and a stretch of indigenous forest with the protected stinkwood (*Ocotea bullata*) as well as ironwood (*Olea capensis*) and yellowwood.

Helderberg boasts one of the greatest varieties of pelargoniums and bulbous plants in the Cape. But perhaps its outstanding feature is the bird life – it was awarded first prize by the Ornithological Society as the most bird-orientated (non-Parks Board) nature reserve. Near the en-

Above: A mountain stream in the Harold Porter Botanic Garden near Betty's Bay. **Left:** A Cape dwarf chameleon. The chameleon family is represented in Southern Africa by two genera. *Bradypodion*, or dwarf chameleon (distributed over the central, southern and eastern parts) and *Chamaeleo* — represented by the common or East African chameleon and the Namaqua chameleon. **Below left:** *Erica perspicua* (Prince of Wales heath). Its common name is derived from the similarity of its plumes to the feathers in the Prince of Wales crest. **Below right:** *Dilatris pillansii* in the Fernkloof Nature Reserve.

trance of the reserve, adjoining a large picnic site under oak trees, is the Bertie Kotze Bird Sanctuary – carefully positioned around the town's reservoir. Unfortunately this is out of bounds to the public, but the birds found here are well represented in the reserve. So far, 119 species have been recorded. They include black eagle, rock kestrel, yellow-billed kite, mountain buzzard, African goshawk, the rare Cape eagle owl, Victorin's scrub warbler and many others.

The only facilities are picnic sites and a tea kiosk, which is open only at weekends. In the picnic area is the Basil Maskew Miller Herbarium, which has weekly displays of fresh cut flowers. The reserve is open from 9.30 a.m. to 6 p.m. throughout the year.

From the Cape Town side, entering Somerset West, look for the green signs indicating the reserve (at the first robot). Thereafter the road to the reserve leads through several suburbs

– but is always well marked. The signs will take you to the entrance.

Hortus Botanicus

The Department of Botany at the University of Stellenbosch has a botanical garden (primarily for student research and study) in the centre of the town, on the corner of Van Riebeeck and Neethling streets. The garden confines one of the greatest concentrations of plant species from all over the world within the space of only 1,8 hectares. There is a magnificent arboretum with examples of indigenous trees as well as exotics like Canadian redwood and Chinese maidenhair.

Of special interest is the succulent house, where *Welwitschia mirabilis* (some are over 50 years old) of the Namib Desert has been cultivated from seed to seed.

There is a tropical house, filled with insectivorous plants, orchids, economically important

plants like coffee, tea, ginger and vanilla, gigantic Brazilian ferns and eerie creepers from all over the world, and an outstanding collection of bonsai and aquatic plants. The collection includes the sacred lotus flower of the east (*Nelumbo nucifera*), which has magnificent metre-high blooms that open early in the morning. The noise the blooms make when they open at dawn can easily be recorded on tape. There is also an experimental herb garden where scientists are studying the medicinal, culinary and economic use of the plants.

Hortus Botanicus is open on weekdays from 9 a.m. to 5 p.m. and on Saturdays from 9 a.m. to 10.30 a.m. Groups from schools, clubs and various societies are admitted by appointment only. For further information, write to The Senior Curator, Hortus Botanicus, University of Stellenbosch, Stellenbosch 7600 (telephone Stellenbosch 77-0354).

Hottentots-Holland Nature Reserve

The only way to see this nature reserve is to hike through it on the Boland Hiking Trail – one of the National Hiking Way Board's trails. Access is otherwise completely restricted.

The Directorate of Forestry set aside this 24 570 ha reserve to conserve the great concentration of indigenous fynbos and remnant forest.

The large and impressive reserve stretches from the Jonkershoek Forestry Station in the north to the Grabouw State Forest in the south and from Sir Lowry's Pass in the west to the Franschhoek Pass in the east.

Permits are required to enter the two starting points of the hiking trail at Sir Lowry's Pass and the Grabouw Forestry Station.

The Hottentots-Holland Mountains harbour one of the richest and most diverse floral populations in the world. Although no comprehensive studies have been undertaken of the flora in the reserve, at least 37 threatened plant species are known to occur within its boundaries.

Most of the indigenous forests that once covered the slopes have disappeared, but small remnants remain in the higher kloofs. The dominant vegetation, however, is fynbos, so called for the great number of fine-leaved shrubs such as heaths.

Leopard, caracal and jackal are seen occasionally, and other carnivores such as genet, grey mongoose and clawless otter, although present, are rather elusive. Grysbok, grey rhebok and klipspringer exist in small numbers and birds in the reserve include sugarbird, sunbird and Victorin's scrub warbler.

Jan Marais Nature Reserve

This botanical sanctuary of some 23 ha is almost in the centre of Stellenbosch, and is bounded by Marais Street and Cluver Road on the western side, Merriman Avenue on the north-

---

THE SILENT LANGUAGE OF SCENT

A steenbok rubs its preorbital scent gland on grass stalks to mark its territory. This buck has the curious habit of seeking refuge underground when threatened — particularly in abandoned aardvark burrows.

All around us the air is filled with secret signals, subtle and often undetectable scents that communicate a variety of messages. Scientists are discovering in them a silent language, possibly one that is an older form of communication than even sight and sound. These odours, or pheromones, are common to virtually every creature, and can act as a 'command' delivered to other animals of the same species, or even trigger off the sort of bodily changes that hormones can. By releasing these pheromones into the air or onto a surface, animals can attract a mate, induce fear in competitors, guide allies to a food source, or trigger a mating cycle in members of the same group or colony.

Perhaps the simplest form of 'command' conveyed by a pheromone is the trail left by scout ants leading others to food. These commands can also be carried over considerable distances; the female pine moth can attract a male from over a kilometre away. The eye gland of

several species of antelope carries a pheromone which acts as a territory marker. In warthogs a pheromone triggers aggression in the boars and receptivity to mating in the sows.

Perhaps the most complex and varied use of pheromones occurs in the common honey bee. The worker bee, standing guard at a hive entrance, will warn off bees from other colonies by releasing a pheromone from glands above its jaws. Near the tip of its tail is another gland which secretes a sweet scent even humans can smell, and which the bee uses during swarming and other occasions to say, in human terms, 'Follow me'. The sting gland contains, apart from its venom, a pheromone which, in a variety of concentrations and situations, can convey the commands 'Action stations!' or 'Attack'. Any intruder that has been labelled as a potential enemy with the pheromone from a single sting will be in danger of further attack should he stay in the immediate vicinity of the hive entrance.

Right: *Aloe striata* and brightly-coloured *Dorotheanthus bellidiformis* (Bokbaai vygie) in the Karoo Botanic Garden at Worcester. The daisy-like flowers provide a brilliant display in many parts of the south-western Cape. The plant received its botanical name from Professor Gustav Schwantes, who named it after his mother, Dorothea. **Below left:** A Cape gloxinia *(Charadrophila capensis)* in the Jonkershoek valley, near Stellenbosch. This small herbaceous plant is extremely rare. **Below right:** An Egyptian goose. These birds will nest in a variety of places, ranging from ground level to the tops of tall trees. One enterprising individual built its nest in the belfry of the Grahamstown Cathedral. When the young hatched, they fell into the street (30 m below) with no apparent injury.

ern side, Jannasch Street on the eastern side and the rear boundaries of Jonkershoekweg university residences on the southern side. The main entrance is east of the junction of Marais and Victoria streets, and Cluver Road. The reserve features over 1 000 species of the rich fynbos which covered the area before the founding of the town. It is open every day (from 7.30 a.m. to 6 p.m. between 1 April and 30 September, and from 7.30 a.m. to 5.30 p.m. between 1 October and 31 March). Admission is reserved by the Stellenbosch Municipality, which controls the reserve. There are footpaths leading through the reserve, and benches and toilet facilities have been provided. For further information, write to The Town Clerk, Stellen-bosch Municipality, P.O. Box 17, Stellenbosch 7600 (telephone Stellenbosch 2111 and ask for the Department of Forestry).

Jonkershoek Fish Hatchery

Established in 1893, the Jonkershoek Fish Hatchery, in the attractive Jonkershoek Valley, is one of the oldest fish stations of the Department of Nature and Environmental Conservation in the Cape.

Literature is available from the reception desk at the station, and conducted tours can be arranged for groups of visitors. At the entrance is an information centre and aquarium featuring typical freshwater fish such as indigenous yellowfish, Cape kurper, banded and blue bream, barbel; and exotic carp, blue-gill sunfish, large-mouth bass and trout.

The hatchery is just 9 km from Stellenbosch and is clearly signposted from Jonkershoek-weg. It is open from 8.30 a.m. to 4.00 p.m. from Mondays to Fridays. For further information, write to The Jonkershoek Fish Hatchery, Private Bag 5014, Stellenbosch 7600 (telephone Stellenbosch 7-0130).

Karoo National Botanic Garden

The largest collection of succulents in South Africa is to be found in this regional garden of the National Botanic Gardens. It was established in Matjiesfontein in 1921 but transferred to Worcester in 1946 to make it more accessible. It consists of a cultivated garden, which draws hundreds of visitors in spring, when brilliantly coloured vygies and daisies are in bloom, and a natural veld reserve with low Karoo-type bushes and succulents covering an area of 154 hectares. Common species in the reserve include the Karoo bush (*Pteronia paniculata*) and the Namibian wild grape (*Cyphostemma juttae*).

There are interesting collections of *Lithops*, *Conophytum*, *Drosanthemum*, *Lampranthus*, *Stapelia*, *Crassula*, *Haworthia* and *Aloe*. About 400 species of flowering plant have been recorded in the natural reserve. There is a rich bird life in the area, and the reserve is used extensively by the local bird club and by the Wildlife Society of Southern Africa.

A series of well-maintained trails link the developed garden with the reserve and present a spectacular view of the Breede River Valley. A wide selection of indigenous plants of the Karoo region is available for sale on weekdays.

The garden is situated on low hills about 3 km north of Worcester, and is well signposted from the N1 national road. The garden is open throughout the year, from 8 a.m. to 5 p.m.

Kleinmond Coastal Nature Reserve

A wonderful mixture of river, kloof and seashore, this reserve was established to protect the area's fragile blend of coastal and mountain fynbos. There are between 1 200 and 1 500 species here, including large stands of the rare *Mimetes hirta* and *Erica patersonia*. A feature of the coastal area is the milkwood scrub forest, while indigenous forest remnants occur on the banks of the Palmiet River (the whole estuary of this river lies in the western part of the reserve) and in the kloofs near Fairy Glen. More than 40 indigenous tree species have been recorded in the reserve. There is a variety of buck and small predators, and visitors can examine marine life in the rock pools and inlets along the spectacular 8 km coastal walk which links up with hiking trails throughout the 400 ha reserve.

There is no accommodation here, but there is a large caravan and camping site in the nearby town. Both the nature reserve and the coastal walk are open throughout the year from sunrise to sunset. Moderate winters afford pleasant conditions for hikes and walks, but the period November to April is the best time to visit. If you want to stay in the vicinity overnight you should book well in advance, as this is a high density summer resort.

For more information contact The Town Clerk, Kleinmond Municipality, Private Bag X3, Kleinmond 7195 (telephone Kleinmond 4010).

Maanschynkop Nature Reserve

The marsh rose (*Orothamnus zeyheri*) is an endangered species, but has been successfully cultivated in this 850 ha reserve, established in 1969 and situated in the Klein River Mountains overlooking Hermanus.

There have been setbacks, like fungal infection and deterioration of mature plants, but the project has generally been successful. The Chief Directorate of Nature and Environmental Conservation controls the reserve. Because of the dangers posed by vandalism and indiscriminate picking, Maanschynkop is not open to the public.

Mont Rochelle Nature Reserve

High above Franschhoek on the slopes of Franschhoek Mountain lies the Mont Rochelle Nature Reserve, 1 759 ha of unspoilt mountain fynbos, beautiful walks and spectacular views of the folded Boland mountains. It is particularly rich in fynbos — the smallest yet most varied of the world's six floral kingdoms. The Boland mountains alone contain more than 2 000 different species.

The heart of the reserve lies some 5 km out of Franschhoek on the Franschhoek Pass. On the second hairpin bend of this twisting road look out for a road turning off to the left up to a gate, which is the start of numerous trails and walks. North-bound walks are very popular and lead to viewsites overlooking spectacular Wemmershoek Dam and Tygerkloof Ravine and, if the weather is clear, a vista of distant Table Mountain.

For permits and more information contact The Town Clerk, Franschhoek Municipality, P.O. Box 18, Franschhoek 7690 (telephone Franschhoek 2055) during office hours.

Montagu Hot Springs and Mountain Nature Reserve

This enchanting area near Montagu was entirely destroyed by the floods of January 1981, but has been completely renewed and now comprises a hotel and self-catering cottages.

Two magnificent hiking trails have been built with overnight cabins. Bookings and enquiries

230

Above: The Ocellated gecko, one of South Africa's smallest. **Left:** The evergreen shrub known as the marsh rose is an extremely rare protea which grows only in a small area in the Hottentots Holland mountains. Each translucent, waxy flower has petal-like bracts which are folded over each other — much like a rose.

should be addressed to The Information Officer, Montagu Municipality, P.O. Box 24, Montagu 6720 (telephone Montagu 4-1112/3).

Nuwe Hoogte Private Nature Reserve

About 9 km south of Robertson is an assortment of private reserves – most of them closed to the public. Nuwe Hoogte, however, has limited access by arrangement with the owners. The reserve offers breathtaking vistas of spring flowers, but is probably better known for its gemsbok, black wildebeest and a herd of very tame springbok. For further information, write to The Owner, Nuwe Hoogte Private Nature Reserve, P.O. Box 512, Robertson 6705 (telephone Robertson 4165).

Perdeberg Trail and Three Sisters Walk

The Perdeberg Trail is a rewarding one-day hike within the Nuweberg State Forest near Kleinmond, offering 15 km of easy walking, superb scenery and encounters with the rarer species of western Cape fynbos.

It begins about 8 km from the office of the Highlands Forestry Station, along a dirt road which is clearly signposted. There is ample parking at the starting point. This trail offers good views of the Palmiet River Valley and the Kogelberg State Forest.

The shorter (10 km) Three Sisters Walk starts behind Kleinmond, ascends a steep ridge and leads across streams and a rich growth of proteas before returning to the town.

Permits for the trails can be obtained any time from The Government Forester, Nuweberg State Forest, Private Bag X27, Elgin 7180 (telephone Villiersdorp 4301).

Safariland Game Park

Giraffe, eland, wildebeest, springbok, Burchell's zebra, warthog, ostrich, and several species of exotic animals, including camel, water buffalo and deer, roam freely over this 200 ha piece of privately owned land near the town of Paarl. There are also elephant, but they are kept in enclosures.

Safariland Game Park, with its 10 km of good game-viewing gravel road, is a popular tourist attraction. It has 12 bungalows equipped with everything the visitor could require, including fridges, stoves, kitchen- and table-ware and linen (all you need to take is your food). There are also braai spots, a swimming pool and a curio shop. The park is open daily throughout the year from 8 a.m. to 5.30 p.m.

To get there from Cape Town, take the N1 to Paarl, turn off at the Wemmershoek turn-off (exit 18), turn right at the stop street on to the R303 and follow the road for 8 km, from which point the park is signposted.

Reservations and further information can readily be obtained by writing to Safariland Game Park, P.O. Box 595, Suider-Paarl 7624 (telephone Paarl 64-0064).

Salmonsdam Nature Reserve

The main attraction of this 834 ha reserve between Caledon and Stanford is the spectacular mountain fynbos, which bursts into flower in spring. There are also remnants of indigenous bush in the ravines.

You can explore a short tourist road up Ravenshill, the highest point in the reserve, from where there are good views of the surrounding landscape. There are also three hik-

Above left: A male South African pochard. **Above right:** The angulate tortoise (*Chersina angulata*) is the commonest tortoise of the southern Cape. This specimen was photographed in the Salmonsdam Nature Reserve. The angulate tortoise is recognised by its single gular shield (all other African tortoises have paired shields), which extends quite far beneath the neck, and the elongate carapace, which slopes steeply on the sides. The gular shield is used as an offensive weapon during the mating season, when the males butt each other and attempt to flip their adversaries onto their backs. **Right:** The Palmiet River meanders through the Kleinmond Coastal Nature Reserve.

ing trails of between three and five kilometres to discover. You will see many birds and, if you are lucky, small mammals such as steenbok, klipspringer and bontebok.

The reserve is open daily between 7 a.m. and 6 p.m. There is a self-help permit system for day visitors who may use picnic and braai facilities. There are three bungalows offering primitive accommodation (it is necessary to take all provisions and cooking utensils) and caravan and camping facilities. To book accommodation or request further information on Salmonsdam, write to The Officer-in-Charge, Salmonsdam Nature Reserve, P.O. Box 5, Stanford 7210 (telephone Stanford 789).

Steenbras Dam

Cupped between the Hottentots-Holland Mountains and the stark Kogelberg range is the large sheet of water known as Steenbras Dam. The dam is basically a reservoir of water for the metropolitan area of Cape Town – but its setting is far from basic. It could be a postcard scene from Scandinavia, with crisp-edged islands, pine forests that rise like dominoes from the water, and white, sandy banks that catch metre-high waves in windy conditions.

The Steenbras catchment area is 19 000 ha in extent, of which 1 000 ha is under pine plantation cultivation. Much of this area is out of bounds to the public, but there is a large recreation area near the dam wall. It is well stocked with trout (brown and rainbow). Fishing is the only recreational activity allowed (it must be done from the banks; no wading is permitted).

There are 21 bungalows in the recreation section, each sleeping four people. This accom-modation is strictly functional, and visitors must supply their own bedding, crockery, cutlery, cooking and cooling appliances. Lighting is provided. No camping or caravanning is allowed, but there are several picnic sites.

Among the great attractions of Steenbras, which is administered by the Cape Town City Council, are the magnificent gardens in the recreation area. Below the dam wall, for example, above the deep gulley which stretches down to the Indian Ocean, is a particularly beautiful terraced garden with sandstone footpaths.

The main conservation thrust at Steenbras is the preservation of fynbos endemic to the area.

Day permits are required to enter the area, and these are available from the Cape Town City Council as well as several outlying municipal offices. Reservation forms and permits for use of the bungalows are available only from the Civic Centre in Cape Town.

Steenbras is open every day from 8 a.m. to 5 p.m. in winter and from 8 a.m. to 7 p.m. in summer. Areas accessible to the public are served by tarred roads that wind around the dam, and are pleasantly shaded by flowering gums. The dam is worth a visit throughout the year but the fishing is particularly good in September and October.

The dam attracts a wide selection of birds such as giant kingfisher, Egyptian goose and the occasional fish eagle. Several species of buck have been sighted (most of them in restricted areas) and officials stationed in the pine forests have spotted leopard spoor. Baboon inhabit the rocky promontories near the picnic site (visitors are warned not to feed them).

Steenbras Dam is reached by taking the N2 highway from Cape Town to Caledon. One can use the northern entrance, which is clearly signposted at Sir Lowry's Pass, or the coastal road through Gordon's Bay, where signs on the left of the road guide you to the dam.

For further information, permits and reservations, write to The Civic Amenities Branch, City Administrator's Department, Civic Centre, Hertzog Boulevard, Cape Town 8001 (telephone Cape Town 210-2507).

Villiersdorp Nature Reserve

A small wild flower garden of about 36 ha lies at the foot of a mountain just outside the village of Villiersdorp and adjacent to the 500 ha Villiersdorp Nature Reserve. The garden is interesting all year, but is best seen between August and October, when wild flowers are blooming. Towards the end of this season a wildflower display is held.

About 60 species of protea grow here, including one with the biggest flowers of all proteas – the giant king protea (*Protea cynaroides*), with a diameter of 30 centimetres. Another protea known as the mountain rose (*Protea acumina-*

Far left above: A colour lithograph by George French Angas, entitled 'Baviaans Kloof The 'Glen of Baboons' near Genadendal', from the book *The Kafirs Illustrated*. **Left above:** A white mussel with its inhalant and exhalant siphons extended. These mussels dig into the sand beneath the surf extending their siphons into the water. The inhalant siphon admits organic particles (phytoplankton) on which the mussel feeds, using a fleshy lobe as a 'sieve'. The water is then expelled through the other siphon. The small sand mussel *Donax sordidus* emerges from the sand periodically to allow itself to be moved by the tides. **Far left below:** The king protea (*Protea cynaroides*) is the largest of the proteas, with flowers that may measure 25 cm across (and more) when fully open. Its botanical name is derived from its resemblance to the artichoke. **Left below:** A malachite sunbird. This bird lives on nectar (it may often be seen hovering beside flowers much like a hummingbird), spiders, small moths and other insects. **Right:** Steenbras Dam, a large and beautiful body of water.

STINGING NETTLE OF THE SEA

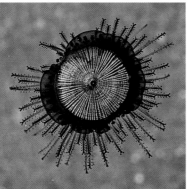

This raft-hydroid (*Porpita pacifica*) has a round, flat float which supports the dangling stinging tentacles.

One of the most amazing creatures in the sea consists of little more than a bag of water. This is the jellyfish, a floating carnivore closely related to the familiar anemone.

Jellyfish occur in a large variety of shapes and sizes, ranging from specimens only a few centimetres across to giants measuring 4 m in diameter — with tentacles that dangle 30 m beneath the surface of the sea. Some are harmless to humans, but others — such as the highly venomous sea wasp — can kill. The sting of the jellyfish is delivered by the nematocysts (stinging cells) that line its tentacles. Some species produce a poison which raises a weal on the skin of the victim, while others inject a neurotoxin that leaves him writhing in agony.

A typical jellyfish is umbrella-shaped (globular or cone-shaped), with tentacles dangling around the margin. The mouth, leading to the digestive cavity, is beneath the umbrella: it is equipped with four 'lips'. The feeding pattern differs widely: one jellyfish may sting and paralyse shrimps and fish before carrying them to the mouth; some trap planktonic animals with sticky mucus on the tentacles; a third type feeds like a sponge, sucking in its microscopic prey through thousands of 'mouths' on the elongated lips.

ta) is indigenous to the area and the garden features a good display of watsonias and ericas.

There is a network of footpaths through the garden with thatched summer houses for resting and picnicking. For the more energetic the mountains are ideal hiking terrain. A camping, caravan and picnic area next to the reserve features five huts, squash and tennis courts, bowling greens and a swimming pool. The reserve is open daily from 8 a.m. to 5 p.m.

From the Grabouw side, entering Villiersdorp, take the fourth turn to the left (look out for the signs) and follow this road directly to the reserve. For further information, you should write to The Town Clerk, Villiersdorp Municipality, P.O. Box 23, Villiersdorp 7170 (telephone Villiersdorp 3-1130).

Vineyard Trail

Set among the beautiful vineyards west of Stellenbosch, this 24 km trail offers a pleasant and reasonably easy way of exploring the countryside. Hiking is permitted daily, but the scenic Boland trail is closed during the grape-harvesting season.

The route leads through privately owned estates and takes in a variety of terrain. You start at the cemetery in Stellenbosch and finish at a tarred road leading to Kuils River (from this point you return to Stellenbosch by train – remember to consult a timetable).

Access to all parts of Vogelgat is provided by 26 km of conveniently graded paths, some of which link up with paths of the adjoining Fernkloof Nature Reserve.

Accommodation consists of three small huts high up in the mountains, and is available only to permit holders. Enquiries from interested people should be addressed to The Warden, Vogelgat Nature Reserve, P.O. Box 115, Voël-klip 7203 (telephone Hermanus 2-4500).

Vrolijkheid Research Station and Nature Reserve

The best time to see Vrolijkheid is in spring, when the mesembryanthemums (vygies) are in flower. There are some 10 km of gravel roads which give visitors access to the various koppies in this 1800 ha reserve, but walking will certainly provide a better opportunity to see the abundance of animals.

There are 40 species of mammals here, including the endangered honey badger and the antbear. More common are the klipspringer, grey rhebok, duiker and the shy steenbok. There is also a small herd of springbok which may be seen in the plains.

A fascinating variety of some 150 birds species are found in the Vrolijkheid Reserve area and include ostrich, black eagle and hadeda, while fish eagle can sometimes be heard near the river.

In the proximity of the river itself lives one of the reserve's prize residents – the endangered Burchell's redfin minnow.

There is no overnight accommodation at present, but there are picnic sites near the offices. The reserve is open daily from sunrise to sunset. Permits to visit the reserve may be obtained by writing to The Officer-in-Charge, Vrolijkheid Nature Reserve, Private Bag X614, Robertson 6705 (telephone McGregor 621). It is situated about 15 km from Robertson on the way to McGregor, and is signposted.

Wiesenhof Private Nature Reserve

One of the most spectacular views of False Bay, Cape Town and the Boland mountain ranges can be obtained from a lookout tower on a hill in the Wiesenhof Reserve, about 40 minutes' drive from Cape Town. The animals – including buffalo, wildebeest, cheetah and blesbok – range freely in the 300 ha reserve.

There is a restaurant, a 10 ha picnic ground, a lake for small canoes, swimming pools and a roller-skating rink. The reserve is open to the public daily (except Mondays) from 9.30 a.m. to 6 p.m., and the animals are fed daily between 11 a.m. and noon.

To get there, take the N1 to Paarl, turn off at the Klapmuts exit, drive under the highway and straight on after the stop street for about 3 km until you see the signposts.

The Stellenbosch Publicity Association issues sketch maps of the route and also supplies the requisite permits.

Vogelgat Private Nature Reserve

A true wilderness area in the Klein River Mountains near Hermanus, Vogelgat is accessible only to a limited number of permit holders (there is a waiting list) whose subscriptions are used to help pay the costs of running the reserve. Visitors are not encouraged, but may be admitted if they are accompanied by a permit-holder.

Vogelgat covers 600 ha of steep mountain slopes which rise 800 m above sea-level. Almost all the invading plants have been eliminated by the dedicated efforts of Dr I. Williams, who bought Vogelgat in 1969 and has preserved it as one of the finest fynbos reserves in the country. It is an area of great scenic beauty, with carefully preserved coastal montane fynbos where over 600 species of plant life have been identified.

The vegetation conceals many small birds and animals. More than 50 species of birds have been recorded, and mammals which may be seen include small populations of klip-springer and grysbok. The resident baboon are shy and elusive although their distinctive bark may often be heard in the vicinity.

Nature's showpiece

From the blunt summit of Table Mountain to the stormy tip of Cape Point the land rises and falls from a curving spine of mountains. And in-between are the dark green forests and fynbos that cling tenaciously to the mountainside.

The Peninsula, however, is densely populated, and ever since the white man arrived three centuries ago, he has cut down the forests, killed the fauna, ripped up the vegetation and built factories. But far-sighted conservationists have devised a plan to save the natural heritage. In 1978, Dr Douglas Hey's one-man commission recommended that the entire range of Peninsula mountains above a certain contour should be declared a natural area. The recommendations are still being considered.

Much of the land on the Peninsula is protected; in the north by the proclamation of the Table Mountain Nature Reserve, in the middle by the Silvermine reserve and at the tip, the Cape Point reserve. There is also Kirstenbosch – the world-famous botanic garden.

While most of the reserves are open to the public, a few of them bar entry – sometimes for good reasons. The few islands surrounding the Peninsula, including Duiker Island and Seal Island in False Bay, are rich in bird life and seals but can be visited only by scientists with a permit from the Directorate of Sea Fisheries. For the rest, it is open house to explore one of the floral kingdoms of the world and its dramatic backdrop.

Cape Flats Private Nature Reserve

A great effort is being made by the University of the Western Cape to preserve the indigenous vegetation of the Cape Flats. The university has established a 21 ha reserve in which the indigenous flora and fauna are protected and studied. Rare and endangered plant species of related veld types are conserved by cultivation. The reserve is not generally open to the public but interested people can arrange a visit by contacting The Curator, University of the Western Cape, Private Bag X17, Bellville 7535 (telephone Cape Town 959-2498).

Cape of Good Hope Nature Reserve

At the tip of the Peninsula is the Cape of Good Hope Nature Reserve. The reserve takes in 40 km of coastline from Smitswinkel Bay in the east to Schuster's Bay in the west. At first glance it appears a bleak and barren place, but in this 7 750 ha area grows more than half of all the floral species found on the Peninsula, and as many plant varieties as there are in the whole of the British Isles. Commonly known as fynbos, with the protea and erica (heath) dominant, this vegetation includes 30 endangered or rare species; 10 of them unique to Cape Point. Unfortunately, exotic vegetation has invaded the reserve and rangers are kept busy throughout the year weeding it out.

Eland, small numbers of bontebok (emblem of the Cape Province), grey rhebok, grysbok and hartebeest are found here, and there are

Above: Bontebok in the Cape of Good Hope Nature Reserve. This buck was once threatened with extinction by indiscriminate hunting, and was saved only by the foresight of a few private farmers. **Left:** A ground orchid (*Disa cornuta*), near Cape Point. In many orchids, the pollen is packed into two large sacs joined by a harness. Insects transport these 'pollinia' from one flower to another. **Right:** The baboons in the Cape of Good Hope Nature Reserve are still — despite repeated pleas — fed by unthinking visitors.

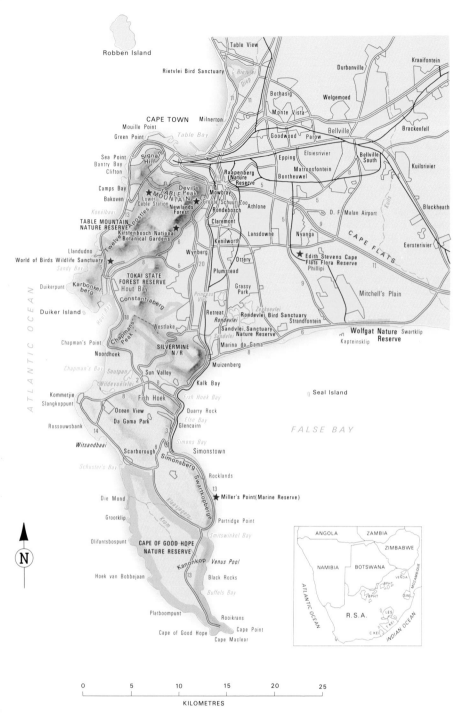

Robben Island

Table View

Rietvlei Bird Sanctuary

Durbanville

Kraaifontein

CAPE TOWN
Milnerton

Bothasig

Welgemoed

Mouille Point
Green Point

Monte Vista

Bellville

Brackenfell

Sea Point
Bantry Bay
Clifton

Signal Hill

Goodwood

Parow

Bellville
South

Kuilsrivier

Raapenberg
Nature
Reserve

Epping

Elsiesrivier

Camps Bay
Bakoven

Devil's
Peak
Lower
Cable Station
Newlands
Forest

Mowbray

Matroosfontein
Bontheuwel

TABLE
MOUNTAIN

Groote Schuur Zoo
Rondebosch

D. F. Malan Airport

Blackheath

TABLE MOUNTAIN
NATURE RESERVE

Twelve Apostles

Claremont

Athlone

Eersterivier

Kirstenbosch National
Botanical Gardens

Kenilworth

Lansdowne

Nyanga

CAPE FLATS

Llandudno

World of Birds Wildlife Sanctuary

Wynberg

Ottery

Edith Stevens Cape
Flats Flora Reserve
Phillipi

Sandy Bay

Plumstead

Duikerpunt

Karbonkel-
berg

TOKAI STATE
FOREST RESERVE
Hout Bay

Grassy
Park

Mitchell's Plain

Duiker Island

Constantiaberg

Retreat

Rondevlei Bird Sanctuary
Strandfontein

Chapman's Point

Westlake

Sandvlei Sanctuary
Nature Reserve

Wolfgat Nature
Reserve

Swartklip

Noordhoek

Chapmans
Peak

SILVERMINE
N/R

Marina da Gama

Kapteinsklip

Sun Valley

Muizenberg

Soutpan

Wildevoelvlei

Kalk Bay

Kommetjie
Slangkoppunt

Fish Hoek

Fish Hoek Bay

Seal Island

FALSE BAY

Rossouwsbank

Ocean View
Da Gama Park

Quarry Rock
Else Bay
Glencairn

Witsandbaai

Scarborough

Simons Bay
Simonstown

Schuster's Bay

Simonsberg

Rocklands

Die Mond

Swartkopberge

Miller's Point (Marine Reserve)

Grootklip

Partridge Point

Olifantsbospunt

Krom

Smitswinkel Bay

CAPE OF GOOD HOPE
NATURE RESERVE

Vleiberge

Kanonkop

Venus Pool

Hoek van Bobbejaan

Black Rocks

Buffels Bay

Platboompunt

Rooikrans

Cape of Good Hope

Cape Point
Cape Maclear

ATLANTIC OCEAN

N

0   5   10   15   20   25
KILOMETRES

ANGOLA   ZAMBIA

ZIMBABWE

NAMIBIA   BOTSWANA

ATLANTIC OCEAN

R.S.A.

INDIAN OCEAN

many signposted fishing spots in the reserve, such as Cape Maclear (popular with divers and crayfish catchers), Platboom, Olifantsbos and Rooikrans (reserved for rock anglers). Anyone wishing to fish in the reserve must first obtain a permit at the entrance gate. Visitors may walk anywhere except in the sanctuary for black oystercatchers on the Atlantic side (Blaauwbergvlei is also closed to visitors). In the future trails will be developed.

Many bird species can be seen, including fish eagle, black-shouldered kite, crowned plover and gannet. Marine life is abundant and visitors may spot shoals of tunny and snoek as well as the occasional whale, seal, porpoise and shark from several view points on the shore. There is a food kiosk at Cape Point and a restaurant midway between the entrance gate and the Point. Near the restaurant is an information centre.

The reserve is open from 8 a.m. to 6 p.m. in winter, from 7 a.m. to 7 p.m. in autumn and spring, and 6 a.m. to 8 p.m. in summer. There is no overnight accommodation, and camping is forbidden. The reserve is served by tarred roads (speed limit: 40 km/h). Boats may be taken in and Buffels Bay has a launching ramp. No pets are allowed (there is a kennel for them at the entrance) and fires can be made only in authorised places at Bordjiesrif and Buffels Bay. While swimming in the sea is not forbidden, visitors are warned that it is dangerous.

To reach the reserve from the city, take the M3 to Muizenberg. At the Westlake intersection, turn left and then right (it is signposted) to get to Muizenberg's main road. From there, follow the M4 Cape Point route.

Duiker Island

Just west of the Sentinel at Hout Bay is Duiker Island, a small, rocky isle of about 1500 m² which is a reserve for seals and seabirds (mostly cormorants). The island is closed to the public (open only to marine scientists with permits) but visitors can get a close look from a motor launch, the *Circe*, which leaves Hout Bay harbour every day at 10.30 a.m. between October and April and every weekend during the rest of the year. In high season *Circe* and her sister launch *R9* leave for the island every hour from 11.00 a.m. to 4.00 p.m.

The seals on Duiker Island come and go throughout the year, so there is never a static population. In summer as many as 4 000 seals have been seen there. To book a trip to the island, telephone Cape Town 790-1040.

Durbanville Nature Reserve

Agriculture has killed off much of Durbanville's indigenous plant life. In this 6 ha sanctuary several species of protea, leucadendron, erica and the dominant aristea (of the family

troops of chacma baboon (despite prominent signs warning people not to feed or interfere with the baboons, they still do so), porcupine, ostrich (often spotted ambling on the beach), and mountain zebra.

Perhaps the most popular spot in the reserve is the Point itself, with its dramatic sea cliffs (the highest in the world) pounded by the restless ocean. You can walk to the viewpoint (a steep climb on concrete paving) or take the 'Flying Dutchman', a bus that stops at a vehicle turning point. The view from the top is stunning and

on clear days visitors are able to see far across False Bay to beyond Hermanus.

There are several recreation areas in the reserve. Bordjiesrif has a large picnic area with braai places, a tidal pool and a large car park. North of this is 'Black Rocks', with its limestone cliffs and historic lime kiln; 'Booiseskerm' (one of the few segments of indigenous forest left); and Venus Pool, a popular fishing spot.

South of Bordjiesrif, also on the False Bay side, is the Buffels Bay recreation area, with facilities similar to those of Bordjiesrif. There are

Iridaceae) are preserved. The best time to visit the reserve is from the beginning of April to the end of October.

A car park, tables and benches, and public toilets are the only facilities that have been provided. Picnics are permitted (no fires). The reserve is open from 9 a.m. to 4.30 p.m. daily.

To reach the reserve, turn off at the Durbanville exit from the N1 to Paarl, and proceed along Durbanville Avenue up to Tindale Road, turn left into Tindale Road and drive up to its junction with Race Course Road. Turn right into Race Course Road. From here the reserve is clearly signposted. Guided tours are available on request. For more information write to The Town Clerk, Durbanville Municipality, P.O. Box 100, Durbanville 7550 (telephone Durbanville 93-6020).

Edith Stephens Cape Flats Flora Reserve

The reserve, which contains a rare marsh plant, *Isoetes capensis*, was donated by the late Edith Stephens to the National Botanic Gardens of South Africa in 1957. The 3,6 ha reserve is situated on the Cape Flats at Philippi and preserves the unique flora of the sandy flats which, outside the sanctuary, is under constant threat from building operators and alien vegetation. The gates are locked and the key is kept by the Head of Kirstenbosch National Botanic Garden. Further details are available from The Head, Kirstenbosch National Botanic Garden, Private Bag X7, Claremont 7735 (telephone Cape Town 762-1166).

Kirstenbosch National Botanic Garden

There is a granite Celtic Cross in Kirstenbosch marking the grave of its first director, Professor Harold Pearson, and it bears the inscription: 'If ye seek his monument, look around.' It is an apt and moving injunction – the grave is surrounded by one of the world's most famous reservoirs of indigenous flora.

Founded in 1913, Kirstenbosch lies on the eastern slopes of Table Mountain. Its landscaped gardens, watered by the Liesbeek River, give way to natural forest that straggles up the mountainside.

Kirstenbosch covers an area of 828 ha, 60 ha of which are cultivated; the rest is a natural flora reserve. It is a living (and quite beautiful) display cabinet featuring 4 700 of the estimated 20 000 species of indigenous South African flora and 40,7 per cent of all the Cape Peninsula's wealth of floral species.

In the cultivated area, related plants are grouped together and radiate from the central lawns like the spokes of a wheel. There are several interesting sections here: the Cycad Amphitheatre, which hosts most species of these 'living fossils' found in Southern Africa; the famed Protea Garden on the higher slopes, with its profuse growth of silver trees (*Leucadendron argenteum*); the J.W. Mathews Rock Garden (named after the first curator) containing succulents of the genera *Crassula*, *Aloe*, *Lampranthus* and *Euphorbia*; the *Erica* Garden, and the *Pelargonium* Koppie. Two streams cut through Kirstenbosch, both laced with besembos, red alder and hard fern.

Of historical interest is an avenue of camphor and fig trees planted by Cecil Rhodes in 1898, and a small section of bitter almond (*Brabejum stellatifolium*) hedge planted by Dutch commander Jan van Riebeeck in 1660.

Within the grounds of Kirstenbosch are the headquarters of the National Botanical Institute, that administer the national network of gardens and associated research institutes. One of these, the Compton Herbarium, is situated at the top of Camphor Avenue in Kirstenbosch itself.

Named after a former director, the Compton Herbarium is dedicated to research, particularly of the Cape Flora. It houses over 250 000 specimens, which includes its own collection and that of the South African Museum dating from 1825. As a data bank, the herbarium is of great historical interest internationally; its records include many rare plants and some which are now extinct.

All paths in the main section of Kirstenbosch garden are paved, but there are two gravel routes to the higher parts of the reserve. The Skeleton, or Smuts' Track (used by the late General J.C. Smuts) leads through the mixed forest of indigenous trees up Skeleton Gorge to the summit of Table Mountain. The other route, the Forest Walk, leads through leafy palaces of ironwood, yellowwood and red alder. There are two special routes along level, paved paths for wheel chairs, prams or the less agile. Known as the Weaver Bird Walk and the Silver Tree Stroll, both are clearly signposted with the wheel-chair sign.

The Braille Trail, for the blind, is a 470 m path which passes through natural Table Mountain forest and fynbos. The plants are clearly labelled with braille and large print labels. The fragrance garden, situated nearby, boasts a fine collection of indigenous aromatic plants (also labelled in braille and large print) set out in a number of raised beds.

TABLE MOUNTAIN'S GIFT OF SILVER

'The Silver-tree', an engraving by William Burchell, from *Travels in the Interior of Southern Africa*.

Perhaps the loveliest of all Southern Africa's indigenous trees grows naturally in just one secluded corner of the sub-continent — on the eastern slopes of Table Mountain and the Vlakkenberg. The flowers of the silver tree (*Leucadendron argenteum*) are attractive enough, but it is the leaves — lance-like, shimmering brightly in the wind — that give it its special beauty.

The leaves are covered with silky silver hairs, which protect the tree in the often harsh Cape climate, and especially from transpiration (loss of moisture) in the dry, blustery months of the year. In summer the hairs press down tightly against the leaves to keep the moisture in; in the moist winter the hairs are raised to allow air to circulate.

The silver tree looks fragile, but it is in fact a hardy species, able to withstand the buffeting of gale-force winds and survive the devastating passage of mountain fires.

The wind plays an important part in the reproductive cycle of the silver tree. The female silver tree develops a cone (bearing a superficial resemblance to those of pines and firs) which contains the seeds. Unlike pines and firs, however, the cones remain upright; waiting for a strong wind in April and May to scatter the seeds on to surrounding mountain slopes.

The tree was first recorded in 1620 by Augustin de Beaulieu, who found 'a great many trees . . . their trunks were straight, in shape like pear trees, the leaves small and whitish, the bark about 50 mm thick and reddish in colour . . .'

The silver tree — in the words of the botanist Linnaeus . . . 'the most shining and splendid of all plants'.

Kirstenbosch is best visited in spring and summer when the gardens blaze with Namaqualand daisies and other annuals, but winter is the best time to see proteas and ericas. The Kirstenbosch information kiosk is open from 8.00 a.m. to 7.00 p.m. in summer and to 6.00 p.m. in winter. Visitors may purchase selected indigenous plants from the Plant Sales Nursery from 9.00 a.m. to 5.00 p.m. daily.

To get to Kirstenbosch take the M3 to Muizenberg. At the Newlands Avenue intersection is a clear AA sign. Turn right into Rhodes Avenue and keep on this road until you see the sign directing you to the gates of the gardens. Picnics and fires are strictly prohibited. Dogs are allowed if kept on a leash.

Miller's Point Marine Reserve

The sanctuary, on the western side of False Bay, can only be reached by walking down the steep slopes of the cliffs that fall away from the M4 to Cape Point. The area is demarcated by two concrete beacons at the side of the road, and notice boards warn that no fishing or spear fishing is allowed in the reserve. Swimming and diving are permitted, and there are picnic sites at nearby Partridge Point.

Raapenberg Nature Reserve

Despite being situated along the edge of the Black River Parkway, one of Cape Town's busiest freeways, this small 10 ha wetland reserve provides a haven for a variety of freshwater and marine birds. Over 55 species have been recorded here, including kingfisher, stilt, heron, purple gallinule and yellow-billed duck. The reserve is popular with bird-watchers and photographers.

While the southern section of the Raapenberg reserve is open, the northern part is fenced in and permits are needed to gain access to this ecologically sensitive area. Access is from Observatory Road, off Liesbeek Parkway or from Black River Parkway.

For further information write to The Director, Parks and Forests Branch, City Engineer's Department, P.O. Box 1694, Cape Town 8000 (telephone Cape Town 210-2269).

Rietvlei Bird Sanctuary

Situated at Milnerton, north of Cape Town, the Rietvlei wetland is the largest breeding area for waterfowl in the Cape. There are over 146 species, including flamingo, pelican, black-backed gull, fish eagle, Egyptian goose and migratory birds such as the Arctic tern.

The vlei, which is reached from Otto du Plessis Drive and Pentz Drive in Milnerton, is privately owned (except for a portion owned by Transnet), and is at present unproclaimed. However, there are plans in hand to proclaim the area from the sea to the Blaauwberg road

Above: Silver trees (*Leucadendron argenteum*) in the famous Kirstenbosch National Botanic Garden, on the eastern slopes of Table Mountain. **Right:** White pelicans in the Rondevlei Bird Sanctuary. These birds sometimes feed in groups, driving schools of fish into shallow water, where they can be seen and caught more easily. The pelican's plumage is tinged with pink in the breeding season. When in breeding condition, the female develops a longer crest, and the bald patch between the bill and the eyes becomes more swollen than in non-breeding birds.

bridge a conservation and recreation area. Fed by the Diep River, the vlei dries up in summer – except for the deep water area dredged for the Table Bay Harbour development, which is now used for recreation purposes. The vlei is linked to the sea by a large tidal lagoon which is popular with canoeists and boardsailing enthusiasts.

Rondevlei Bird Sanctuary

When Rondevlei, a wilderness of reeds, marshland and indigenous vegetation, was established in 1952 by the Divisional Council of the Cape (now Western Cape Regional Services Council), it was a quiet rural area, a natural site to conserve and protect waterfowl. But today the sanctuary's horizon is blotted by suburban sprawl. It still maintains its original function,

however, and provides one of the best bird-watching areas in the Peninsula. So far, 222 species including migratory birds from Europe, have been sighted in the 120 ha sanctuary.

A narrow path, with benches and look-out towers placed at strategic intervals, cuts through the reeds at the vlei's edge and from it visitors have a general view of the bird life. For photographers and bird-watchers there are discreet and well-constructed hides. The best time to visit Rondevlei is between January and March, although there is plenty to see throughout the year.

In recent years the sanctuary has developed into an important environmental education centre with a 50 seat lecture theatre. Audiovisual programmes about the reserve are available for schools and other organised groups.

The Leonard Gill Museum in the sanctuary has a comprehensive display of mounted birds, reptiles and mammals that occur at Rondevlei. Other inhabitants of the sanctuary include small numbers of steenbok, grysbok, mongoose, porcupine and hippopotamus.

There is a small picnic area near the entrance gates as well as an ornamental pond in which a variety of waterfowl can be viewed and photographed. The sanctuary is open every day of the year (except Christmas Day) from 8 a.m to 5 p.m. Binoculars and a bird identification book are more or less essential aids. To reach Rondevlei, turn off Prince George Drive at the Grassy Park sign into Victoria Road, and follow the signposts.

Seal Island

About 5 km off Strandfontein in False Bay is a bald piece of land, about 2 ha in extent, named Seal Island. The island has a population of about 50 000 seals, and also accommodates bank cormorant, penguin and seagull.

Seal culling is allowed on the island during winter months and is carried out in terms of a five year government contract. Visitors are not allowed to land on the island, but boats from Kalk Bay and Gordon's Bay harbours make special trips around the island by arrangement.

The best time to see the seals is in the summer months. Details of boat trips to the island can be obtained from the Harbourmaster at Kalk Bay (telephone Cape Town 88-8313) and the Harbourmaster at Gordon's Bay (telephone Gordon's Bay 56-1482).

Silvermine Nature Reserve

Some of the most attractive mountain scenery and indigenous plants of the Cape Peninsula can be seen in this 2 158 ha reserve, which extends from the Muizenberg and Kalk Bay range of mountains in the east to Noordhoek Peak in the west. A feature of the reserve is the Silvermine River, which flows through a forested gorge and joins up with a tributary flowing over a picturesque waterfall.

Several walks through valleys and up peaks provide breath-taking views of False Bay, Fish Hoek, Noordhoek and Simonstown. Rhebok, grysbok, caracal, porcupine and genet are sometimes sighted on these walks. The reserve contains fine specimens of protea, leucadendron and erica, which attract sugar bird, sunbird and Cape robin.

Many picnic sites are accessible by car, except for those at the Silvermine Reservoir, which is a few minutes' walk from the car park. Braai fires may be made only in the designated spots, and visitors should bring their own firewood. Swimming in the reservoir is prohibited. The reserve is open (throughout the year) during daylight hours. The best time to visit is

238

Above: Sundew plants at the summit of Table Mountain. The leaves of this insectivorous plant are covered with sticky glands on stalks, which close over the trapped insect prey. **Below left:** *Pelargonium cucullatum* in the Silvermine Nature Reserve. **Below right:** A cattle egret, photographed at the popular World of Birds Wildlife Sanctuary in Hout Bay. **Opposite page:** This view of the Fairest Cape from the summit of Table Mountain reveals a panorama of mountains merging with the se...

between October and December and during March and April.

To get there, take the M3 to Muizenberg and turn right at the Westlake intersection and onto Die Ou Kaapseweg. Once on the plateau, signs mark the two entry points (one in the north, the other in the south) to the reserve. An entry fee is payable at the points, where maps and pamphlets are available.

Table Mountain Nature Reserve

Few if any of the world's cities have such a dramatic backdrop as Cape Town. Table Mountain broods immensely over town and bay, its face changing constantly and often suddenly with weather and season.

The mountain, a national monument (and parts of it a proclaimed nature reserve), is both unique and vulnerable. It has been used and abused by man for three centuries and much of the original fauna has been wiped out, though

the flora is – surprisingly – in a reasonable state. Conservationists have planned a strategy to preserve the mountain's character and the authorities wage constant war against vagrants, vandals, alien vegetation and fires.

The reserve covers an area of 2 904 ha, embracing Signal Hill, the right and left face of the mountain, Van Riebeeck Park, portions of Devil's Peak, the top and lower table including Orange Kloof Valley (a totally restricted area where indigenous forest has regenerated) and Newlands Forest. It is open during daylight hours.

The mountain summit is accessible by more than 500 routes, but the easiest and quickest method of getting there is by cablecar. The lower cable station is situated on Tafelberg Road, which winds around the mountain at the 400 m mark.

There are several picnic spots in the area and well-marked walks (the contour path is one

of the most popular) and climbs (a favourite is up the Platteklip Gorge) from the road. Another route from Kloof Nek, turning sharp right, is Signal Hill Road, which takes you to the tip of this small, rounded hill. Views – particularly at night – are spectacular.

At the summit of Table Mountain is a kiosk, and a restaurant that serves lunches and teas. Apart from this, there are few organised facilities (fishing and overnight camping are prohibited, and braai fires are allowed only in designated places in Newlands Forest). Fauna in the reserve includes caracal, genet, dassie, mongoose, baboon and the odd grysbok. Velvet worms, an unusual and rare group of animals sharing both worm and insect characteristics, are found on the slopes. But the reserve is best known for its indigenous flora.

In the 1940s, the Cape Town City Council planted several species of pine on the eastern slopes of Table Mountain for their commercial value, but Newlands Forest is now used purely as a recreational area. It covers about 200 ha between Kirstenbosch and Devil's Peak.

The forest is a favourite walking area among Capetonians, and offers a stunning view of the suburbs and the distant Hottentots-Holland range from many vantage points. It is open all year and no permits are needed. Take the M3 to Muizenberg from the city and at the Union Avenue intersection watch for the Newlands Forestry Station sign on the right.

Tokai State Forest and Walk
Most of the higher parts of the 2 572 ha Tokai State Forest, which includes the Constantiaberg and western table of the Karbonkelberg, are devoted to the preservation of fynbos, indigenous forest and what is left of the area's once abundant wildlife.

The lowest-lying section of the forest is a picnic area (catering for up to 1 000 people). Further up is the entrance to the actual reserve where permits are issued during daylight hours. Here is a magnificent arboretum (the first planted in South Africa) of various trees, and a river, the Prinskasteel. Some of these trees have anodised identification labels.

The start of the Tokai Walk is signposted, the two-hour route leading you up the mountainside, through the forests, to the spectacular Elephant's Eye cave. The trail route is indicated by white 'elephant' markers painted on rocks and tree trunks.

Although the Tokai Walk is the most popular, several other paths criss-cross on the Constantiaberg from Constantia Nek to the border of the Silvermine Reserve. The reserve is always worth a visit, but much depends on the weather, as it must be explored on foot.

To get there, take the M3 to Muizenberg and turn-off at the Tokai/Retreat sign, and right into Tokai Road, which leads directly to the reserve.

Wolfgat Nature Reserve
This stretch of coastline between Mnandi and Monwabisi beaches, with its rugged, limestone cliffs and dramatic views of beautiful False Bay, was proclaimed a nature reserve in 1986. It is the site of the largest mainland breeding-colony of black-backed gulls in Southern Africa (the only one in the south-western Cape).

Fences have been erected around the breeding area, to protect the birds, but the rest of the 268 ha reserve is open to the public.

Small animals found among the dunes include grysbok, steenbok, Cape hare and tortoise. Vegetation includes large areas of strandveld interspersed with pockets of coastal fynbos. Although the stout bushes of these types of vegetation appear hardy they have almost been wiped out in many parts of the Cape Flats by alien species of acacia and increasing urban development.

Signposts direct the way to the reserve from Baden-Powell Drive. No entrance fee is charged and there are no facilities. For further information write to The Director, Parks and Forests Branch, City Engineer's Department, P.O. Box 1694, Cape Town 8000 (telephone Cape Town 210-2269).

World of Birds Wildlife Sanctuary
Nestling in the Hout Bay Valley is a bird sanctuary – the largest in Africa – where visitors are offered a rare opportunity to explore 100 large walk-through aviaries for a truly rich, unforgettable experience.

There are more than 3 000 birds of 450 different species – both exotic and indigenous – and some, like the jackass penguin, white pelican, Cape vulture, bald ibis, and brown-necked parrot are on the endangered list, together with small animals such as tortoises, meerkats, monkeys, dassies and bushbabies.

The World of Birds is South Africa's foremost bird-breeding centre. Of special interest is a variety of ponds where swans, egrets, ibises, herons and cormorants live and breed under a fringe of willow trees.

The park is a photographer's paradise: the birds can be snapped close-up (most of them are tame) with little difficulty and excellent natural results can be achieved.

Walter Mangold, who established the park in the 1970s, plans to expand it by building a tea-room and education and information centre where children and adults can learn more about the bird life around them.

The sanctuary is open every day from 9 a.m. to 6 p.m. It can be reached from Hout Bay's main road, where a sign at the circle directs you to Valley Road.

Sandvlei Sanctuary Nature Reserve
The Sandvlei bird sanctuary covers about 20 ha of typical coastal marshland and is dotted with islands. A network of paths and bridges enables good viewing of pelican, wader, Cape teal and coot, and there are also small hides facing the vlei.

The gates are kept locked but permits are available from the City Council's Parks and Forests Officer (telephone Cape Town 75-3040/1/2/3).

Adjoining the sanctuary is a large recreation area with picnic spots, braai grids and a children's playground – an ideal spot for boardsailors and boating enthusiasts (there are launching ramps). The recreation area is open from sunrise to sunset. It can be reached from Muizenberg's main road (there are signs), but the sanctuary part of Sandvlei is reached by turning left into Military Road at the T-junction (signs to Muizenberg on the right) and then right at the Steenberg railway station. For further information, write to The Director, Parks and Forests Branch, City Engineer's Department, P.O. Box 1694, Cape Town 8000 (telephone Cape Town 210-2269).

Coastal wetlands and floral delights

For most of the year the west coast road from Cape Town to Saldanha Bay runs through a flat and seemingly uninspiring part of the country. The only relief from dull and scrubby bush, so typical of the area, is the occasional glimpse of the icy Atlantic rollers between sand dunes. But in spring the landscape – particularly in the Darling area – is transformed into a blaze of colour when the indigenous flowers carpet the ground.

The west coast buckles into large pans of water which attract thousands of migratory and wading birds. Langebaan Lagoon, for example, is recognised by ornithologists as one of the great wetlands of the world. A string of islands dot the coast. They are inhabited by large breeding populations of seabirds, seals and other forms of marine life, but they are strictly controlled sanctuaries to which the general public has no access.

Farther inland is yet another visual treat – the Cederberg, a land of sculpted sandstone, cedars, waterfalls and gentle slopes that blush with the riotous colours of spring flowers. But the great attraction of this mountain range is its weird rock formations. These grotesque sculptures, fashioned by erosion, are unforgettable.

In the untouched part of the Cederberg, the so-called Wilderness Area, animals once frightened by encroaching civilisation are coming back. It will take time, but conservationists believe the Cederberg will eventually return to its former state of beauty. The area around the Cederberg, particularly the Clanwilliam district, is famous for its spring wild flowers.

Bain's Kloof

The 1840s were the golden years of road building in the western Cape, and the pass, built in Bain's Kloof (above Wellington) and named after engineer Andrew Geddes Bain, takes in a spectacular scenic drive.

Cutting through the Limietberg range, the pass – opened in September 1853 – leads to Ceres and the Breede River Valley, the narrow road winding sharply and steeply for 16 km. It was constructed in such a manner that damage to special trees and rock formations was avoided. Travellers are treated to an ever-changing roadside spectacle – including glimpses of the Wit River, which runs parallel to the road. Like many other mountain streams of the western Cape, this river is refreshingly clear (it offers good fishing).

From the summit of the pass, travellers have spectacular views of the patchwork countryside. A gravel track (chained and out of bounds to those without a permit, issued by Hawequas Forestry Station officials) leads from this point to the upper Wit River Valley.

Above: *Dorotheanthus bellidiformis, Senecio elegans* (mauve) and *Dimorphotheca pluvialis* (white) near the town of Darling. **Left:** Colonies of Cape cormorants and Cape gannets on Bird Island, off Lambert's Bay. The bird populations on the west coast islands have dwindled in recent years due to construction of the harbour, heavy fishing of pilchard shoals in the area (the staple diet of many seabirds), and guano collecting. Today only two islands, Malgas and Jutten, are scraped by a firm contracted to the government. Most of the islands are frequented by European rabbits – the descendants of those introduced to provide food for shipwrecked sailors. **Right:** A bat-eared fox rests on the ground.

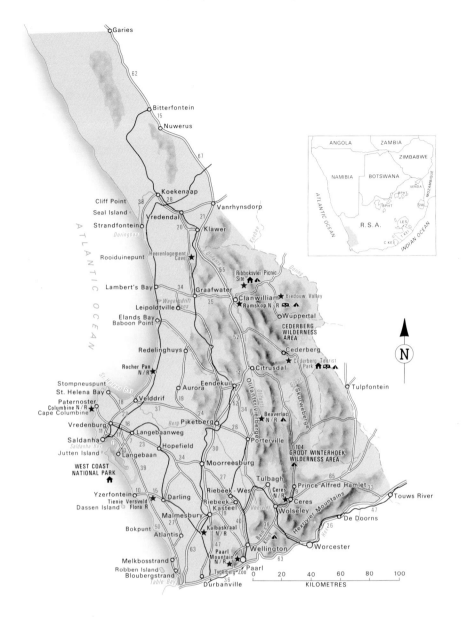

bok, steenbok and duiker. Leopard are sometimes seen and a nearby area has been declared a leopard reserve. There are pleasant scenic walks along the mountainside, and there is good bass fishing especially in the Olifants River. Yellowfish are also found, but they are rare and are protected.

A visitors' permit – effective for a year – is available on application to the owners: write to Beaverlac, Grootfontein, P.O. Box 142, Porterville 6810 (telephone Porterville 2953/2945). There are no facilities other than two ablution blocks: campers should take everything they need. To get to Beaverlac, follow the road north of Porterville for 3 km until you reach the sign 'Cardouw', turn right and drive for 10 km until you reach the sign marking Dasklip Pass. Turn right again, then first left at the pine trees.

Biedouw Valley

Another area worth exploring is the valley which guards the entrance to Namaqualand. To get there, take the road that leads eastwards from Clanwilliam over the Pakhuis Pass. About 40 km from Clanwilliam there is a turn-off to the right marked Wuppertal. Take this road, and after about 15 km you will arrive at the Biedouw Valley. The valley is particularly beautiful in spring, and is a popular spot for viewing wild flowers in August and September.

Boland Trail: Limietberg Section

As you follow the footsteps of pioneer road-builder Andrew Geddes Bain over the rock-strewn Wit River, try to imagine his elation when he at last discovered a passage through the Limietberg (Limit Range) that linked the road from Cape Town to the interior.

Today a 36 km (two-day) trail leads through the Bain's Kloof Pass – named after the Scots-born engineer who built it nearly 150 years ago. A weekend is all you need for an adventure in the beautiful Boland mountains. The trail is of average difficulty and the opportunity to swim in the clear, clean water of several pools along the route more than makes up for the lack of shade. A pool is also situated beside the overnight hut, which has four rooms and sleeps 24 people.

In spring brightly-coloured orchids bloom in the cool recesses near sparkling streams. Small klipspringer, grysbok, grey duiker and leopard live in the mountains, but being shy, they are rarely seen.

The trail starts at Hawequas Forest station near Du Toit's Kloof and ends at Tweede Tol campsite on Bain's Kloof Pass. It's not a circular route, so a car must be left at both ends.

Bookings and enquiries may be made by writing to The Forestry Branch, Department of Environment Affairs, Private Bag X2, Cape Town 8000 (telephone Cape Town 402-3911).

In spring, the valley (known as 'Paradise Valley' or 'Happy Valley') is decked with flowers, and the river is punctuated by a series of pools in which visitors delight. The mountains surrounding the valley offer a number of interesting routes for hikers.

Just beyond the turn-off to Paradise Valley (at the summit), set in a thicket of wattle trees, is a 50-site picnic area with water and toilet facilities. A hotel situated near the summit of the pass was burnt down in 1976. A path at the hotel site marks the start of a superb 6 km walk to Baviaanskloof. Several connecting footpaths take hikers to gorges and waterfalls.

Further down the valley is Tweede Tol, a popular camping and picnic spot (30 picnic sites and 20 camping sites) on the banks of the Wit River. The campsite marks the end-point of the Boland Hiking Trail's Limietberg Section as well as the start of shorter trails into the surrounding mountains. Beautiful pools, a rich variety of

fynbos and exceptionally beautiful scenery are among the attractions of this area. For further information, write to The State Forester, Hawequas State Forest, Private Bag X14, Huguenot 7645 (telephone Paarl 62-3172).

Beaverlac Nature Reserve

To the east of the small village of Porterville lie the Olifantsrivierberge, famous for their striking rock formations and wild flowers. The Beaverlac (private) Reserve is situated at the crest of the Dasklip Pass, at the summit of the mountain. It comprises four farms (about 15 000 ha) which are crossed by the Ratel and Olifants rivers. The rock formations have channelled the rivers into clear deep pools, waterfalls and caves, which are decorated with several San paintings, including one of a ship (only two of this type are known to exist).

The area is a sanctuary for fynbos and several antelope species: rhebok, klipspringer, grys-

Cederberg Tourist Park

Situated on the southern end of the wilderness of the Cederberg, this park is part of the farm Kromrivier, owned by the Nieuwoudt family. There are 12 bungalows, 10 campsites and 13 caravan sites in the park, which serves as a base from which to explore the area around the Sneeuberg, Apollo Peak, the Maltese Cross, San paintings, Stadsaal Rocks and Wolfberg Cracks. The Nieuwoudt family is well acquainted with the area and will provide maps and information on the more interesting walks.

There are several footpaths in the park from which you may spot caracal, dassie, rhebok and perhaps even leopard. Visitors may swim in natural pools fed by mountain streams.

The park has a shop that supplies fresh milk, eggs, bread and other necessities. Visitors need only take food and bedding, as the bungalows are well equipped (there are electric fridges and stoves, hot water showers and toilets). The great attraction of this park is its wilderness atmosphere.

The park is reached by way of the Clanwilliam-Citrusdal road. About 23km from Citrusdal, turn right towards the Cederberg. Follow this road for about 57km, and turn right at the 'Kromrivier' signpost. To book a bungalow or campsite, write to Mrs O. Nieuwoudt, 'Kromrivier', P.O. Box 284, Citrusdal 7340 (telephone Clanwilliam 1404).

Cederberg Wilderness Area

Running from north to south between Pakhuis Pass and the Middelberg Pass is the Cederberg region, of which 71000ha has been declared a wilderness area.

It is easy to reach: take the road from Citrusdal to Clanwilliam and take the right turn-off to Kriedouw. This road crosses the Olifants River, then the Nieuwoudt Pass, and reaches the Algeria Forest Station, where a forester issues permits to enter the wilderness area.

The Cederberg range takes its name from the rare Clanwilliam cedar trees (*Widdringtonia cedarbergensis*) which once covered the mountains. Unfortunately these were burnt or felled during the early pioneer years, and only a few remain in the higher altitudes.

Part of the fascination of the Cederberg is its unique rock formations, carved by many centuries of wind and erratic weather. On the slopes of the Sneeuberg, the highest peak in the range (2082m), is one of the better-known rock formations – the Maltese Cross. Other well-known formations include the Wolfberg Arch, Cathedral Rock, the imposing Pulpit and Finger Rock.

The flora of the Cederberg – varying from spring annuals to fynbos to indigenous forest – is fascinating in that some species are unique to the area. The snow protea (*Protea cryophi-*

la), found on the higher and more remote parts of the Cederberg, occurs nowhere else in the world. The rocket pincushion (*Leucospermum reflexum*) also occurs naturally in this area. The large red disa (*Disa uniflora*) is found along some of the mountain streams.

More than 30 species of mammal have been recorded in the Cederberg, and visitors may see such animals as baboon, klipspringer, rhebok (their numbers have increased in the last few years), dassie, steenbok, duiker, grysbok, wild cat, caracal, bat-eared fox and black-backed jackal. Leopard and aardwolf are also present, but are rarely seen.

As with all fynbos areas, there are relatively few birds in this region. The most common are sugarbird, various sunbirds, Cape canary and francolin. A pair of black eagles (*Aquila verreauxi*) is seen occasionally.

The Olifants River system contains several species of fish, including one so rare – the Twee River redfin – that it is found only in a small stream above a waterfall in the Cederberg. There are several hiking trails of varying lengths in the Cederberg. Overnight huts (with primitive facilities) are provided.

The Algeria station boasts a magnificent picnic site beside the Rondegat River, between the peaks of the Cederberg. There are also 40 caravan and camping sites and ablution blocks with hot and cold running water. Visitors may

swim in a natural pool in the Rondegat River. The campsites and hiking facilities should be reserved three months in advance by contacting The Forester (telephone Clanwilliam 3440) during office hours from 8a.m. to 4.15p.m. Monday to Friday. The Directorate of Forestry has compiled an excellent map of the Cederberg, and this should be made an essential piece of equipment on a hike.

The Ribboksvlei picnic site and a camp at Kliphuis, on the Pakhuis road – about 12km from Clanwilliam – also cater for visitors. Camping facilities and furnished bungalows can be hired on several farms bordering the wilderness area and details are available from The Publicity Section, Clanwilliam Municipality, P.O. Box 5, Clanwilliam 8135 (telephone Clanwilliam 28 or 215). Permits to enter the wilderness area, are available from the Forester at Cederberg Station.

Ceres Nature Reserve

As you enter Ceres from Michell's Pass, there is a sharp curve in the road just before the Dwars River. On the left, under poplar trees and pin oaks, is the entrance to the Ceres Nature Reserve. The reserve covers an area of 30ha on the slope of the Skurweberg, and was created by the municipality for the preservation of the flora (principally protea and erica) which is indigenous to the area.

ON THE EDGE OF EXTINCTION

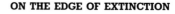

One of the rarest reptiles in the world is the tiny, prettily marked geometric tortoise (*Psammobates geometricus*), so named for the symmetrical 'starred' pattern – black or dark brown on white or yellow – of its shell. These ornate dorsal shields are raised into little cone-like mounds on the tortoise's back, from which brilliant streaks of yellow – alternating with black – radiate downwards. Its natural habitat is renosterveld: the low-lying, level areas of the western Cape – land much in demand by farmers, wine growers and urban developers.

In earlier years the geometric tortoise was much sought after for its highly decorative shell

– which ended up on many a mantlepiece.

The eggs of the tortoise have always been vulnerable to predators, and even once hatched, the baby tortoises run the gauntlet of predation by jackals, yellow mongooses and the sharp-eyed secretary bird.

It is not known how many geometric tortoises now survive in the wild (very few, it is thought), but the Cape's Department of Nature and Environmental Conservation has created three special tortoise reserves – Eensaamheid, Harmony Flats and Voëlvlei. There is also a private reserve near Gouda. Together, the protected areas shelter about 2000.

Some of the flowers, such as a subspecies of *Lithops comptonii*, are found nowhere else. There is a network of footpaths in the reserve, but there are no other facilities. It is open daily from 7 a.m. to 6 p.m., and is clearly signposted from the road. For more information contact the Information Bureau, Ceres Public Library, Voortrekker Street, Ceres 6835 (telephone Ceres 2-1177).

Clanwilliam Yellowfish Station
Established by the Cape Department of Nature and Environmental Conservation in 1976, this station serves as a hatchery where experimental breeding programmes are undertaken to breed the rare Clanwilliam yellowfish (*Barbus capensis*) and seven other rare fish found only in the Olifants River system. These fish are threatened by the destruction of their habitat and by exotic fish predators like bass.

The station also serves as a base from where the Olifants River system is studied. It can be reached by taking the turn-off from the N7 to Clanwilliam. Just before entering the town a gravel road (not signposted) leads to the station about 500 m away. The station is open from 9 a.m. to 4 p.m. on weekdays.

It is a good idea to arrange your visit in advance to ensure that someone there will be on hand to show you around. You should contact The Officer-in-Charge, Clanwilliam Yellowfish Station, P.O. Box 83, Clanwilliam 8136 (telephone Clanwilliam 4003).

Columbine Nature Reserve
About 3 km south of the whitewashed village of Paternoster is the Columbine Nature Reserve, run by the Vredenburg/Saldanha Municipality. It covers an area of 263 ha, and was established to protect the Sandveld fynbos indigenous to the region. Part of the reserve faces the Atlantic Ocean and takes in a number of bays, the most popular being Tieties Bay, set in an amphitheatre of sand dunes.

The best time to visit the reserve is in the spring (especially September), when the flowers are in glorious bloom. To get there from Vredenburg, take the road to Paternoster and continue south until you reach the gates of the reserve.

There are 60 campsites with basic facilities. For bookings apply in writing to The Town Clerk, Vredenburg/Saldanha Municipality, Private Bag X12, Vredenburg 7380. Columbine is accessible at all times during the day.

Groot Winterhoek Wilderness Area
The sight and sound of the Vier-en-Twintig River surging through dark cliffs and cascading into a deep cool basin, thrill visitors to Die Hel Valley – one of the most beautiful areas in the Groot Winterhoek Wilderness Area.

Above: *Phaenocoma prolifera* in the Ceres district of the Boland. This attractive flower, also known as pink everlasting, is an evergreen perennial. **Right:** Spring in the Cederberg mountains, with *Euryops speciosissimus* in the foreground of the picture.

But because many of the 90 km of footpaths are unmarked, only the most intrepid, experienced hikers should venture through this rugged, rocky wilderness. It is advisable to accompany someone familiar with the area and to take along a compass and map.

No more than 40 people, in groups of up to 12 each, are issued permits for the area at one time. In addition the two-day hike to Die Hel is limited to 20 people each day.

Although summers are usually dry and hot, the temperature often drops to far below freezing point in winter, when heavy snowfalls are common on the prominent Groot and Klein Winterhoek peaks.

Such is the diversity of mountain fynbos in this area, that locals say there is a fresh flower in bloom every day of the year.

Birdlife is prolific and includes the peregrine falcon, rock kestrel and jackal buzzard. Among the smaller birds are Victoria's warbler, the protea canary and the Cape sugarbird, which breeds in the mountains between February and August.

The wilderness area is reached via the Dasklip Pass above Porterville. For bookings and enquiries write to The Forester, Groot Winterhoek State Forest, P.O. Box 26, Porterville 6810 (telephone Porterville 2900).

Heerenlogement Cave
The cave (also known as Gentleman's Lodging) is situated about 32 km north of Graafwater, on the gravel road to Klawer. It was once occupied by men of the late Stone Age, but from about 1682, when explorer Olar Bergh 'discovered' it, it was used as a shelter by probably hundreds of European travellers. The cave features a fine collection of historical signatures (some badly faded) carved into the quartzite walls. These include famous names such as Bergh, the French explorer, Francois Le Vaillant, and road-builder Andrew Geddes Bain. The cave was declared a national monument in 1939. Of special interest is a Namaqua fig tree (*Ficus cordata*) – believed to be more than 200 years old – that grows from a fissure in the rocks and hangs over the top of the cave.

Paarl Mountain Nature Reserve
Towering granite domes, resembling enormous pearls when they glisten with moisture, are striking features of this 2 000 ha sanctuary west of the town of Paarl. Among the attractions of its scenic drives – narrow, sharply twisting mountainous routes – are breathtaking views of Paarl Valley and the Berg River to the east and Table Mountain, False Bay and the Atlantic to the west. There are picnic sites, and angling is permitted in the three dams on top of Paarl Mountain (a licence is required). The reserve also offers the Klipkers Hiking Trail.

The reserve is open daily from 6 a.m. to 6 p.m. To get there from Paarl, turn into Jan Phillips Mountain Road and follow the signposts. The small Meulwater Wild Flower Reserve is situated within the Paarl Mountain Nature Reserve, and hosts about 200 indigenous plant species, including protea, erica and pincushion.

Ramskop Nature Reserve
This 54 ha municipal reserve, incorporating the Clanwilliam Wild Flower Garden, is the natural habitat of small mammals such as buck, hare

and dassie, as well as several species of snake and lizard. No vehicles are allowed, but there is a circular footpath which leads to the highest point of the reserve: from here visitors have panoramic views of the Cederberg peaks, the Olifants River, the Clanwilliam Dam, Pakhuis Pass and the town itself.

Situated within the reserve is the Clanwilliam Wild Flower Garden, which features some 200 indigenous species, and the display attracts a large number of visitors in spring every year.

The garden was created in May 1967 by a few local women, and has been subsidised by the Department of Nature and Environmental Conservation of the Cape since 1972. Every year, a five-day flower show is held in the 'Old Dutch Reformed Church' in Clanwilliam's main street. The exhibits represent the large variety of flowers in the garden and the district. The only plants cultivated in the garden are those indigenous to Clanwilliam and the Namaqualand area.

While there are no facilities in the reserve or garden, the recreation area at the adjoining Clanwilliam Dam has camping, caravanning and picnicking facilities. The reserve and garden are open from 8 a.m. to 5 p.m. on weekdays and during the season (July to mid-September) they are also open at weekends (from 9 a.m. to 5 p.m.). The garden is clearly signposted on the Clanwilliam/Cape Town road.

Riverlands Nature Reserve
Over 500 species of Lowland Fynbos occur at Riverlands Nature Reserve near Malmesbury. Of these 20 are listed as rare – threatened by ploughing, development and the invasion of alien species.

The 1 297 ha reserve was proclaimed in 1986, and while no facilities exist at present, visits to the reserve can be arranged by contacting The Officer-in-Charge, Riverlands Nature Reserve, Private Bag X8, Malmesbury 7300 (telephone Malmesbury 3687).

Rocher Pan Nature Reserve
Rocher Pan is a 390 ha breeding ground and sanctuary for waterfowl. The seasonal pan, fed by the Papkuils River and full for seven months of the year, attracts as many as 150 species at any one time, notably the Cape teal, Cape shoveller, red-knobbed coot, yellowbill duck, Egyptian goose and dabchick. Waders and seabirds also forage and make their homes at the pan, and the scrubby surrounding bush supports an impressive variety of other bird life.

The best time to visit is in the spring, when wild flowers cover the ground and the bird population is at its densest. There is a winding gravel track, picnic sites (but no camping facilities), and two observation platforms. The sanctuary is open from 7 a.m. to 6 p.m. year 244

round. To get there, take the west coast road from Cape Town through Velddrif, Laaiplek and Dwarskersbos, 12 km beyond which is Rocher Pan's signposted gate. For permits and further information, write to The Officer-in-Charge, Rocher Pan Nature Reserve, Private Bag, Velddrif 7365 (telephone Velddrif 727).

Steenbokfontein and Wagensdrift Pans
South of the tiny fishing village of Lambert's Bay, on the road to Leipoldtville, is a chain of pans hosting countless birds, including an impressive flamingo population.

Tienie Versveld Flora Reserve
In 1956, farmer Tienie Versveld donated a piece of land near Darling to the National Botanic Gardens of South Africa to protect the indigenous flora and natural beauty of the Sandveld. Dominant species in the sanctuary are bulbous plants such as *Babiana*, *Spiloxene*, *Geissorhiza*, *Lachenalia* and several annuals. The reserve is also known for its spring carpet of chincherinchee and the sundew (*Drosera*) – an insectivorous plant. There is a network of footpaths in the reserve but no other facilities. The flora is best viewed in spring. For further information, write to The Garden Director, National Botanic Gardens, Private Bag X7, Claremont (telephone Cape Town 76-21166).

Tygerberg Zoo
This privately owned zoo specialises in the breeding of endangered species such as chimpanzee and the extremely rare Rothschild's

mynah (only some 600 of these birds remain in the world). There are about 300 species, including tigers, jaguars, the European brown bear, hog deer and the gibbon. Of interest is a children's farmyard. The layout of the zoo is informal, with rolling lawns (a good picnicking area) and a car park with braai facilities. A tea-room serves light meals and refreshments.

The zoo is open every day of the year from 9 a.m. to 5 p.m. To get there, take the N1 highway to Paarl and turn off at exit 15 to Stellenbosch/Klipheuwel, turn left at the stop street and then left again at the signpost. The zoo is directly ahead.

West Coast Islands
Soon after Jan van Riebeeck landed at the Cape, he dispatched a group of sailors to explore the west coast. They found a host of small islands – mostly in the area of Saldanha Bay – teeming with seal, penguin, cormorant, gannet and other forms of life.

Dassen Island, the largest of the islands, has a population of some 60 000 jackass penguin; it is also the only breeding ground in the Cape of the great white pelican. Several other species of bird are also found there, such as the Egyptian goose, cattle egret, oystercatcher, ibis, gull and a variety of land birds.

There are six other islands in Saldanha Bay: Vondeling Island is a small, rocky outcrop just south of the entrance to Saldanha Bay; in the entrance to the bay itself are three more islands (Jutten, Malgas and Marcus) and there are two more in the southern part of the bay – the

Far left: White storks in the Tygerberg Zoo. Some years ago, white storks featured in a fascinating experiment on migratory habits. It was known that white storks in eastern Europe and central Asia flew south-east before entering Africa across the Suez Canal and Sinai Peninsula. In western Europe, however, they flew south-west before entering Africa over the western Sahara or west coast. These routes enabled both populations to avoid such obstacles as the Alps, the Sahara and the Mediterranean. Eggs from eastern storks were hatched and raised by foster parents in the west, and when the time came to migrate, their genetic memory caused them to fly south-east, where they encountered the Alps and became thoroughly disorientated. **Left above:** A grysbok in the Tygerberg Zoo. **Left below:** The Clanwilliam Wild Flower Garden. **Right:** Jackass penguins jump into the sea from Malgas Island in the vicinity of Saldanha Bay. Nearby Dassen Island is the breeding area for this species of penguin.

Schaapen and Meeuwen islets. All have large colonies of seabirds, and all are closed to the public. At last count there were 17 species of breeding birds in the bay.

The seals have disappeared from these islands, and only one colony (about 2 000 strong) remains on a small rocky island called Robbesteen, just north of Melkbosstrand. These seals are protected.

West Coast National Park

The unforgettable sight of fields of brightly coloured flowers set against the clear, blue waters of the Atlantic Ocean draws thousands of visitors to West Coast National Park's Postberg Section for a brief period each spring.

For the rest of the year the focus shifts to Langebaan Lagoon. This 15 km-long by 2,5 km-wide expanse of clear, warm water is widely acknowledged as one of the great wetlands of the world and teems with life.

Tiny creatures that live in its mud, said to contain 60 million bacteria in every cubic centimetre, serve as a vital food source for large numbers of birds. During summer, up to 55 000 migratory birds leave their Arctic breeding grounds and fly south from Siberia and Greenland to transform the lagoon into a birdwatcher's paradise. It is estimated that local bird populations consume some 150 tonnes of invertebrates annually (15 per cent of the annual invertebrate population of the lagoon).

The off-shore islands of the system are, by virtue of their inaccessibility, bird sanctuaries in their own right, and here large populations roost and brood in safety. Schaapen Island, for instance, is home to one of the largest breeding colonies of kelp gulls, while Malgas Island is populated by thousands of Cape gannets. Public access to these islands is forbidden.

Fishing in the lagoon is less favourable due to the many filter feeders which are found here. Species such as red bait, mussels, clams and sea cucumber deplete the water of the nutrients necessary for the survival of large numbers of fish. The result is crystal clear water that affords a boating playground instead.

The lagoon and the islands of Malgas, Marcus, Jutten and Schaapen were originally proclaimed as Langebaan National Park on 30 August 1985. Subsequently further land areas, including the Postberg Nature Reserve, were added increasing the park's area to over 18 000 ha. Effectively, the park now forms a continuous strip of coastline, lagoon and sandveld from the village of Langebaan to the sleepy town of Yzerfontein in the south.

It is interesting to note that the area around Langebaan contains some of the richest fossil deposits in South Africa. Although, not as yet part of the national park, these deposits are protected by law, and include the remains of an extinct bear, sabre-toothed cat, a short-necked giraffe and a three-toed horse.

WEST COAST NATIONAL PARK AT A GLANCE

When to go The Postberg section is open during the flower season, which lasts from the beginning of August to the middle of September (watch the newspapers, or contact Satour, Cape Town for information). Remember to choose a sunny day when the flowers will be open. Summer is the best time for bird-watching, boating and swimming in the lagoon.

Reservations and information For further information contact the National Parks Board, P.O. Box 787, Pretoria 0001 (telephone Pretoria 343-1991) or the National Parks Board, P.O. Box 7400, Roggebaai 8012 (telephone Cape Town 419-5365) or the National Parks Board, P.O. Box 774, George 6530 (telephone George 74-6924/5). There is an information centre at Langebaan Lodge.

Getting there Langebaan village is signposted on the West Coast Road (R27) 130 km north of Cape Town. To reach Postberg turn left off the R27 at the Donkergat sign, some 84 km from Cape Town. Turn left again at the Churchhaven/Donkergat sign – follow this road to Postberg. An entrance fee is charged at the entrance gate of Postberg.

Accommodation There is overnight accommodation at Langebaan Lodge. A limited number of moorings for yachts are available for hire on a daily basis. Prior reservation is essential. The National Parks Board plans to build houseboats for use at Kraalbaai, which will ultimately be available for hire on the same basis as rest camps in other national parks. No camping is allowed in the national park reserve, but Langebaan village offers camping sites.

Eating and drinking An à la carte restaurant is available at the Langebaan Lodge, as well as at Club Mykonos, with shops and restaurants in Langebaan village. There are three picnic spots with braai facilities in the Postberg section. Wood is on sale at the entrance gate.

Getting around The reserve has approximately 30 km of hard gravel roads with demarcated areas where visitors may leave their vehicles. Well equipped toilet facilities are available at picnic spots. The Vlaeberg range in Postberg affords panoramic views over lagoon and sea.

Hiking trails, canoe routes and horseback riding are being planned. Boating, boardsailing, sailing, and power-boating are popular lagoon activities. The lagoon is regulated by the National Parks Board, and is zoned into three areas for specific purposes (consult the information centre and Langebaan Lodge).

Boats may be launched at Langebaan Yacht Club, Club Mykonos or from the hard sand of Langebaan beach at the end of Alabama Street. Petrol is available at Langebaan village.

Wildlife Some 55 000 birds may be found in the area during summer. Among these are cormorant, gull, common sandpiper, sanderling and flamingo.

Postberg is stocked with bat-eared fox, eland, zebra, kudu, hartebeest, blue wildebeest, black wildebeest, gemsbok, springbok, bontebok and many others. Predators include caracal, Cape wildcat, genet, Cape grey mongoose and black-backed jackal.

Various species of fish occur in the lagoon, with skate, ray, sand shark and mullet being common.

Taking to the water

Sailing is fast becoming one of the most popular outdoor pastimes in Southern Africa as an increasing number of enthusiasts take to lagoons, lakes and dams in a variety of craft. Dinghy sailing offers enjoyment for the whole family, and need not cost a fortune.

Designs vary from small children's boats to 6m racing craft demanding a high degree of skill. The beginner should choose a boat which belongs to a recognised class: this provides him with a reasonable assurance of quality and a guaranteed resale value. Since he may not always have someone on hand to 'crew' for him, the novice is advised to opt for a boat which can be operated single-handed.

The size and weight of the boat is another important factor. If the boat is too large or heavy for a car roof rack, it will need a trailer, which in turn needs to be licenced and insured. A fibreglass boat does not require repainting every year (as do most wooden hulls), whereas some people find the wooden hull irresistible.

Whatever design you choose, certain equipment *must* be carried whenever you go sailing. This includes:

● Life jackets for everyone on board
● A basic tool kit (knife, screwdriver and pliers)
● A tow line
● A paddle (for returning to shore if the wind fails or the boat is dismasted)
● A hand bailer (even a tin can)
● Spare shackles

The art of sailing is best learnt through practice. You will learn more by joining a club and going out with an experienced yachtsman than by reading a dozen manuals. Stick to the rules, and for safety's sake, wear a lifejacket whenever you go out.

Sailing terminology can be somewhat daunting for the novice, but he will quickly pick up the basics. There are many rules relating to sailing, all derived from practical experience. If you are on starboard, for example (with the boom over the port side), you have right of way over a port tack boat. Do not insist on your right of way if an ignorant or inexperienced yachtsman fails to change course: besides the danger involved, your self-righteousness could cost both of you a lot of money.

Paddling through Southern Africa

A canoe trip along one of Southern Africa's hundreds of rivers provides a complete and thoroughly satisfying change from the bustle

Above: Sailing Fireballs on Goreangab Dam, near Windhoek.
Below: The popular Laser II.
To contact any of Southern Africa's many sailing clubs and associations, you should write to The South African Yacht Racing Association, Private Bag 1, Saxonwold 2132.

of everyday life. And although you may well end your day on the water with aching muscles, you will have experienced the pleasure of a totally different leisure activity.

Numerous rafting and canoeing companies offer expeditions on the Orange, Doring, Tugela, Vaal and Breede rivers. These trips have been designed to cater for a wide range of people from children aged five years to dedicated professionals.

Whether you choose the white waters of the Tugela River or a family-orientated cruise down the Orange River, chances are you'll soon be back for more.

If you intend to buy or build a canoe, select a design most suited to the conditions in which you intend to use it. Obtain advice from a friend with canoeing experience or from a canoe club (you can make contact with a canoe club through most universities). Competitive canoeing is controlled by the South African Canoe Federation, P.O. Box 11118, Dorpspruit 3206.

When planning a canoe trip, decide where to start, and how far to go – having a set objective usually adds to the enjoyment. For longer trips, try to obtain a map of the river – these may be available from shops or clubs. Useful 1:50 000 scale maps are obtainable from the Government Printer. Check beforehand whether canoeing is allowed along the entire route you intend to travel.

Rain in the catchment area, which may be hundreds of kilometres away, can seriously affect your enjoyment – and your safety. Seek advice, and try to obtain a long-range weather forecast: gently flowing rivers could become raging torrents with little or no warning.

Choose the right canoe for your needs: it should not be too heavy to carry.

● You should avoid canoeing on your own, but if you must have solitude then tell someone where you intend to go, and how long you will be away.

● As a canoeist, you will need a high degree of 'water confidence'. When you capsize (and it is certain to happen at some stage), you should be able to relax, press your hands on the cockpit coaming and ease your way out. Your canoe will usually act as an additional life-belt, so you should always stay with it – even in a rocky channel. Control the canoe from the upstream end, or you may be trapped against a rock. Lie on your back in the water with your legs lifted up and forwards. As a general rule, do not try to right a canoe unless you have a secure foothold in shallow water; rather float downstream with your craft until you can reach the bank easily.

● Never enter a canoe unless you can swim. Ideally, you should be able to swim at least 50m in your canoeing clothes (an important safety rule in training).

● Practise 'laying out' sideways and returning the canoe to a balanced position by pressing your paddle blade on the water (this is known as 'bracing'). It is a good idea to try a few deliberate capsizes and practise getting out of the canoe – on both the left and right sides – and then recovering it.

● Learn to read the surface of the water: the waves and ripples can tell you a lot about the river bed.

● An occasional light bump will not do any harm, but you should try to avoid grounding. If it is safe to do so, get out before the canoe touches bottom. But be careful: the force of the current is often deceptive, and you may be knocked over.

● Never try to paddle through a shallow, rocky section, as there is a risk of damaging the hull on spurs of rock. If you cannot use the technique of 'lining down' or controlling the canoe through the hazard by means of the painter, you may have to unload and carry both canoe and cargo to safer water. The occasional 'portage' is a necessary part of most canoe trips.

● Always have your paddles ready, for bracing yourself or steering. Remember, unless you are travelling faster or slower than the current, you have very little steering control.

● Do not change places with your companion, and avoid overloading the canoe.

● Keep clear of other craft, and stay away from weirs and waterfalls – the current may be stronger than you realise.

● If you observe these basic safety precautions (there are many more), a holiday trip by canoe could be one of the cheapest and most rewarding you will ever experience.

When selecting your canoe, it is essential to deal with established and reputable companies. **1 and 3** Canadian-style fibreglass canoes with flat bottoms are ideal weekend touring canoes. **2** This single-seater canoe is designed to move through the water (including rough water) cleanly and quickly. **Above left:** The smaller lifejacket is suitable for canoeing, board-sailing, paddle-skiing and water-skiing, while the one on the right is used only for sailing. **Above right:** The shorter jacket is suitable for waterskiing and board-sailing; the other for sailing and fishing. Anyone who participates in watersport should wear a lifejacket.

Casting a line

Angling is South Africa's most popular sport, with even more participants than either rugby or soccer. The freshwater angler may choose from hundreds of safe fishing points where he can be reasonably sure of success.

There are two basic types of freshwater fishing — bait or coarse fishing (barbel, kurper, tiger-fish and others) and trout fishing. The first type is something of a gamble in that the angler is never quite sure what will take his bait, whereas in trout fishing he knows exactly what he wants.

Hooking it is only part of the fun, and fishermen tend to derive the most pleasure from playing their catch. This is where skill is important — particularly in fly-fishing, where the flexible rod and very light cast allow the fish a fairly good chance of winning the battle.

Whatever method you choose, remember that fish are expert at recognising food — and danger. They are rarely fooled by bait which moves unnaturally in the water. One answer to this and to many other requisites for successful fishing, is practice. You should also take the advice of experienced fishermen — they have probably tried everything — and join a club or society.

Learning the basics

Fly-fishing is a very skilful form of the sport. Dry and wet flies (the latter type sinks beneath the surface) are fashioned from a range of materials including feathers, fur, tinsel and artificial silk thread, and simulate adult, nymphal and larval insects, shrimps and other creatures likely to attract fish.

When casting a dry fly, great care should be taken to avoid disturbing the water's surface. If there is a current, cast the fly upstream and allow it to float down (the line also floats on the surface). Cast a wet fly across the current or slightly downstream, letting it run with the current until it reaches the end of the line; then cast again.

A third technique, known as nymph-fishing, employs an artificial lure designed to resemble a nymph which is cast over the position of the fish and made to 'float' just beneath the water's surface.

Although some fish do not have good eyesight, they are always sensitive to movements both in and out of the water. Wear neutral-coloured clothing that will blend with the background and try to avoid casting a shadow on the water. Trout, in particular, are

A 'coarse' fisherman enjoys a leisurely day at Roodepoort Dam, Transvaal. It is important that you maintain your equipment with care. Keep your reel free of dust and sand and its movable parts oiled — or preferably greased (mix lubricating oil and paraffin wax in the ratio of 1:2); check regularly for wear to the moving parts, the rod tip and the rings. Damage to these will quickly fray the line.

sensitive to vibrations caused by movements on the bank, so you should approach the dam or river carefully. If the water is clear, and there is no cover on the bank, fish from a kneeling position, holding the rod low.

Three types of trout are found in the waters of Southern Africa: brown trout, rainbow trout (the most common) and tiger trout (a hybrid). Brown trout are generally caught more easily on a dry than a wet fly. They grow larger than rainbow trout, and may develop different feeding habits. Some feed on the bottom (an imitation dragon-fly nymph is recommended), while others establish permanent territorial boundaries within which they will prey on minnows and other small fish (occasionally moths and even mice).

You need not be disheartened if you feel the fish take but the rod does not bend, as it will often make another attempt to take the fly. When you finally manage to hook a fish and bring it to the surface, try to keep its head above the water by raising the rod.

Never try to lift a large fish out of the water with your rod. Instead, make sure that the landing net is at hand when you cast, and guide the fish in over the net (a fish netted tail-first is likely to jump out of the net).

Remember that your success as an angler is not related to what you spend on equipment, but rather to practice and patience.

The rules of freshwater fishing

The inland fisherman is subject to more controls than the sea angler, but the rules are not onerous and are designed to maintain a balance between sport and conservation. All freshwater anglers must have a licence, which is renewable annually. Licences cost only a few rand and are obtainable from revenue offices and magistrates' courts.

They are valid only in the province in which they were issued. An additional fee is payable for a trout licence in Natal and the Transvaal.

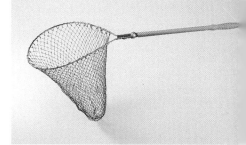

This cotton cord thread net, favoured by many freshwater fishermen, is collapsible and easily stored. However, most of today's nets are made of synthetic fibres such as nylon.

Separate permits must be obtained to fish in State forestry reserves. The licence allows you to fish in any fresh water — private or public — within the province of issue, subject to certain conditions. These conditions include restrictions on minimum size and mass, and sometimes a daily 'bag limit' per species.

Access to fishing water always depends on obtaining permission from the owner of the land on which the water is situated. In the case of rivers, you should speak to the riparian owner — whether State department, local authority or private individual. In some instances you may need clearance from an angling club, which will usually extend temporary membership to visitors at a nominal charge.

You should always have your licence with you when you go fishing, because it must be produced on demand to any person who is authorised to examine it.

Under-sized fish must be returned to the water immediately and carefully. Fish should be measured with a rigid rule, from the tip of the snout to the fork in the tail. Before handling a fish which is to be returned, make sure that your hands are wet, or you may remove the natural layer of protective mucus, making it susceptible to a fatal fungal infection.

Fishermen and the weather

The weather plays an important part not only in the comfort of the angler, but in all aspects of a fish's existence. During the winter, fish usually go off the bite and move to deep water, but during a cold snap in summer they are more likely to be found in the shallows.

In the summer months, when the water is warm, fish may go to colder, deeper water, or may also be found near rapids and other areas of turbulence where the water is more highly oxygenated.

During flood seasons, fish seek the slowest water. Floods often wash away the weeds and insects on which the fish feed, so they are likely to bite readily once the floods have subsided. Dams and slow rivers are usually poor fishing-grounds during periods of drought, when an overgrowth of weed and increase in the insect population supplies the fish with adequate food.

The fishing is usually better on a windy day. Wind and water movement dislodges weeds and insects, and fish are likely to feed. Barometric pressure can play a significant part in the movements of some species, such as trout.

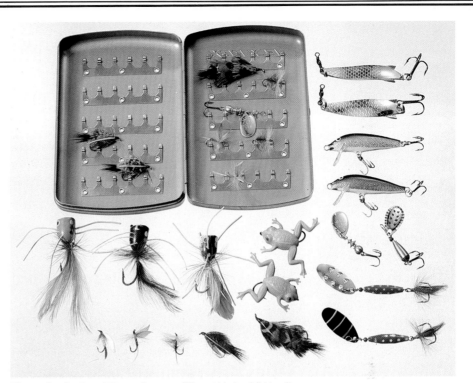

Above: A selection of flies and lures. **Below:** Rods for bass (upper) and trout (lower); a spinning reel (bottom right) — occasionally used for trout fishing — and fly reel (bottom left); and a few of the many different kinds of fishing lines available to the South African angler. If properly cared for, the nylon line is likely to be the most durable. Keep it away from direct sunlight, which makes it brittle.

THE INTERIOR

Khoikhoi described the Cape Province's interior as the Karoo, meaning 'the thirstland'. Even more than the Little Karoo south of the Swartberg Mountains, the Great Karoo is a land of raw koppies, stony plains and hardy vegetation that somehow survives the baking sunlight of high summer and frosty bite of winter nights. In earlier times the Karoo plains held large herds of game, but ruthless slaughter in the 19th century drove them to the edge of extinction.

Today, Karoo game is making a comeback on private farms and in several sanctuaries, in particular the Karoo National Park at Beaufort West and the provincial Karoo Nature Reserve at Graaff-Reinet. There are more reserves in the Namaqualand region to the west, another near-desert whose annual display of spring flowers is one of the marvels of Southern Africa. North of Namaqualand lies the Richtersveld, a wildlife paradise of open spaces and quiet which extends to the Orange River.

Upstream, the Orange River tumbles over the spectacular Augrabies Falls, centrepiece of a national park. To the north are the sandy plains of the Kalahari, another 'place of great dryness' in the language of the Khoikhoi. South Africa's famous Kalahari Gemsbok National Park adjoins a sister sanctuary in Botswana, and only a line of beacons separates them – allowing game to migrate back and forth across the international boundary as it has for millennia. In this place, at least, old Africa survives undisturbed.

Springbok graze in the arid veld of the Kalahari Gemsbok National Park. This graceful and strikingly coloured gazelle, adopted as South Africa's national and sporting emblem, once swarmed in huge herds throughout Southern Africa.

The legacy of Southern Africa's first game reserve

Early travellers knew today's Namaqualand as 'Little Namaqualand', while 'Great Nama-qualand' lay north of the Orange River in today's Namibia. For some, 'Little Namaqualand' embraced all the land between the Orange River and Garies and even Vanrhynsdorp to the south, extending eastwards to a longitude beyond Calvinia.

More often, travellers divided the area into regions with names like 'the Roggeveld', 'the Sandveld' and 'the Richtersveld' in the north, and 'Bushmanland' to the east. Then, as now, Bushmanland was flat and much more arid than its neighbours to the west.

In 1892, the legislature of the old Cape Colony proclaimed a large game reserve in Bush-manland – the first such reserve in Southern Africa. Details are sketchy, but it is known that among those behind the reserve was a Namaqualand magistrate, W.C. Scully, one of South Africa's earliest conservationists.

A part-time game ranger named Andries Esterhuysen tried unsuccessfully to stamp out poaching in the reserve. The chief culprits were local farmers who shot the game ruthlessly, and saw no purpose in the reserve: they wanted it deproclaimed and shared among them.

It is said that when they spotted Esterhuysen while poaching, they sent messages to one another by smoke signals. The slaughter continued – virtually unchecked – and animals died by the thousand. After the game was wiped out, the reserve's land was whittled away, and the last fragment was deproclaimed in the late 1920s. Those familiar with the story urged the creation of two new Bushmanland-style reserves on the banks of the Orange River – one in the Richtersveld and the other east and south of Vioolsdrift.

However, new reserves take time to create, so for the moment nature-lovers must content themselves with a modest few reserves.

The National Parks Board has recognised the area's potential and has proclaimed the Tankwa Karoo National Park. However, it is still being developed and it will be many years before it is open to the public. Reserves that are open to the public are Hester Malan Nature Reserve near Springbok, Akkerendam Nature Reserve, near Calvinia and three reserves near Nieuwoudtville. The trio comprises Nieuwoudtville Nature Reserve, Oorlogskloof Nature Reserve and Nieuwoudtville Waterfall Nature Reserve.

Akkerendam Nature Reserve
The little town of Calvinia has two attractions for nature-lovers. The first is the annual display of spring flowers, as dramatic as anywhere in Namaqualand (though local people insist that Calvinia must be seen as part of Bushmanland or even the Great Karoo). The other is Akkerendam Nature Reserve, proclaimed in 1962 and covering 2 301 ha of the spreading flats

Above: In spring a sheet of colour spreads across wide stretches of Namaqualand, turning the once barren veld into a floral wonderland of almost every imaginable hue. These Namaqualand daisies (*Dimorphotheca sinuata*) are typical of the flowers in this region (though they are found in all parts of South Africa with the exception of Natal).
Left: A group of Hartmann's mountain zebra in the Akkerendam Nature Reserve. This zebra grazes on tufted grass and tends to favour arid conditions.

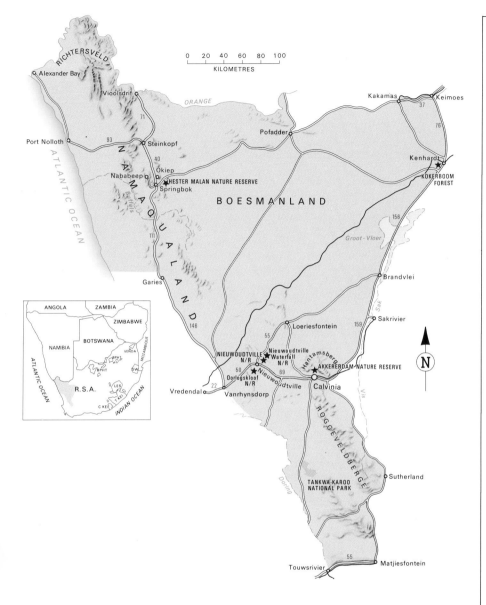

ABSORBING WATER LIKE A SPONGE

In spite of its name, the Namaqua sandgrouse is found all over the western half of Southern Africa and particularly in arid areas with short grass. You are most likely to see it at a waterhole in the Kalahari or Namib Desert where it announces its presence with the characteristic, melancholy *kelkiewyn* call. The dovelike sandgrouse feeds on small dry seeds on the ground. During the winter nesting period, the sandgrouse lays two or three eggs in a mere scrape in the ground between the tufts of grass, and the male and female take turns sitting on the nest. The male takes his turn at night, while the female remains on the nest throughout the hot day: if she left her post the embryos would quickly be killed by the searing heat (surface temperatures can reach 50°C).

She resists the heat by puffing up her feathers to create extra insulation between her body and the air outside. Meanwhile, the male is free to join his fellows in a highly organised quest for water and food that may take them on a round trip of more than 80 kilometres. Starting after sunrise, small flocks of Namaqua sandgrouse fly to a favoured waterhole where they rendezvous with flocks from other areas. Two hours after sunrise, there may be a gathering of hundreds or even thousands.

When her chicks have hatched, the female rejoins the morning flight to water. The chicks need water too, and now it is the male who comes into his own.

Each morning at the waterhole he dips his belly feathers under the surface and allows them to absorb water like a sponge: each gram of feather can absorb up to eight grams of water. With his cargo complete, he flies back to the chicks, and they drink water directly from his breast feathers.

north of the town and parts of the Hantam mountain range. Before becoming a municipal nature reserve, the area was part of the farm Akkerendam, which was once owned by South African Railways. Akkerendam's five boreholes provided the town's water supply and the farm was the obvious site for a town dam.

Today, Akkerendam and two older farm dams are attractive features of the nature reserve – which has become a bird and flora sanctuary. There is a picnic area close by and the reserve's 12 km of roads pass close to the dams, taking visitors to the higher ground that overlooks them.

The entrance to Akkerendam is just over 1 km from the town centre and is signposted (visitors should leave the town by the road that passes the hospital). It is open year-round.

Visitors are normally required to remain in their cars, but they may apply for permission to hike on one of two trails which lead through the reserve. The Kareeboom Trail along the Hantam Mountain slopes is a 2 km (1-2 hour) hike that was designed with special consideration for the needs of senior citizens. A longer and more strenuous route is provided by the Sterboom Trail which takes 6-7 hours to complete. Both trails provide an opportunity to discover the magical flora found only in the Hantam, including the orchid *Desperis purperata* and the geophyte *Romulea hantamensis*. For permits and more information contact The

Town Clerk, Calvinia Municipality, P.O. Box 28, Calvinia 8190 (telephone Calvinia 11/241).

Hester Malan (Goegap) Nature Reserve

In 1960 the Okiep Copper Company of Namaqualand donated 4 600 ha of rugged farmland to the Cape Provincial Administration to be developed as a wildflower sanctuary. The farmland was within 10 km of Springbok, and the province recognised a chance to establish a fully fledged nature reserve featuring a good variety of flora and fauna. In 1966 the administration proclaimed the area as the 'Hester Malan Nature Reserve' in honour of the wife of the late Administrator of the Cape, Dr Nico Malan.

In 1980 the copper company donated an extra 1 900 ha to make a total of 6 500 hectares. Eight years later the adjoining farm 'Goegap' was acquired by the Chief Directorate of Nature and Environmental Conservation of the Cape and increased the reserve's size to approximately 14 860 hectares. The reserve now includes broad grass plains dotted with koppies and is an excellent example of a wide range of Namaqualand habitats.

The reserve is well worth a visit during the spring months when the plains are normally covered with a variety of seasonal Namaqualand flowers (ephemerals). During the rest of the year visitors still enjoy the beautiful scenery and there is also an interesting display of Namaqualand succulents at the office complex.

Some 45 species of mammal, 29 species of reptile and three species of amphibia have been recorded in the reserve. Major game species present are Hartmann's mountain zebra, gemsbok, springbok, klipspringer, duiker and steenbok. Among the 47 bird species which have been recorded in the reserve are ostrich, black eagle, karoo korhaan, spotted dikkop and ground woodpecker.

Unfortunately, at present, road quality restricts the visitor to those areas of the reserve accessible via the main entrance road leading to the offices and the 8-9 km circular route. By far the best way to explore it is on the Ian Myers Hiking Trail which leads through the koppies from the parking area near the picnic site. This is a trail of 7 km (shorter routes can also be chosen). No accommodation is available.

The reserve is about 14 km from Springbok and adjoins the airport. It is signposted from the outskirts of the town. The reserve can be visited from 8.00 a.m. to 4.00 p.m. every day. For more information, the person to contact is The Officer-in-Charge, Hester Malan Nature Reserve, Private Bag X1, Springbok 8240 (telephone Springbok 2-1880).

Kokerboom Forest

Namaqualand San needing quivers for their poisoned arrows cut branches from the pic-
254

IN SEARCH OF CONOPHYTUM

Conophytum intrepidum flourishes on a mountainside near Port Nolloth. When not in flower, these hardy succulents resemble a row of pebbles.

Anthony Mitchell is a lean, tough and slightly sunburnt Briton who could think of nothing more exciting than to cycle through the wastes of Namaqualand in search of a humble succulent. Some people, he concedes, might think him a little crazy.

Yet this latter-day Don Quixote (he tilts at indifference rather than windmills) is determined to continue his fight for the popular recognition of *Conophytum*, a large and relatively obscure genus of succulent found chiefly in Namaqualand. Says Mitchell: 'During my first visit to South Africa in 1973 I was amazed at the amount of work still needed to be done on this vast genus — for long the happy hunting-ground of amateur and retired botanists who would often classify — independently — specimens deriving from a common source. The result was a proliferation of spurious names.'

His favourite plant, says Mitchell, is *Conophytum marginatum*, which resembles a rock-bound cluster of tiny, jade-green crystals edged with amethyst. 'But in the main, these plants are unlikely to attract much popular attention until their taxonomy [classification] is sorted out.' Bound only by his endurance, and working to a limited budget (though flexible timetable), Anthony Mitchell has traversed thousands of kilometres of Namaqualand's primitive roads and sandy tracks in his field survey. His travel-scarred bicycle and sturdy, self-made camera bag go everywhere with him. The going can be arduous, he explains, but he sees more by going slowly.

Right: *The Quahkah*, an aquatint by the artist and traveller Samuel Daniell, reproduced in *African Scenery and Animals* (published in two parts in 1804-5). Daniell's painting captures a distinctive feature of the old Karoo landscape that will never be seen again — large herds of the now extinct quagga. When the botanist William Paterson travelled through the Karoo in the late 1700s, the quagga was still one of the most common animals in the area. But within a century it had been hunted to extinction. Historical records indicate that the quagga was a gregarious animal, much like the zebra, and was often to be found in mixed herds along with black wildebeest (and even ostrich). The only specimen in Africa (there are several in Europe) is preserved at the South African Museum in Cape Town.

turesque 'tree aloe' that grows all over the north-western Cape and south-western Namibia. Then they hollowed out the branch's fibrous interior, sealed the bottom and attached a carrying strap. To this day the tree aloe is known as the 'kokerboom' or 'quiver tree'. The species (*Aloe dichotoma*) has been known to scientists since 1685, when it was discovered during Simon van der Stel's expedition to Namaqualand in search of copper. This slow-growing, smooth barked tree has greyish-green leaves and yellow flowers. It survives harsh conditions by soaking up water and storing it in the trunk.

Kokerboom trees were once used for cooling primitive homes, too. People cut the trunks into squares and used them to construct walls: water was fed into the fibrous wood from a tank at the top. Swarms of birds and locusts are drawn by the sweet nectar of the kokerboom's

Left: The beautiful spread of wild flowers that attracts thousands of visitors to Namaqualand in spring. With an average annual rainfall of only 120mm, Namaqualand is one of the dryest regions of Southern Africa. The spring flower bonanza begins in mid-July.
Above: A puff-adder in the process of swallowing a meal.

flowers, and baboon have been known to strip off the blossoms in search of the liquid.

Individual quiver trees can be seen in many locations in Namaqualand and Bushmanland, including the Hester Malan Nature Reserve. But close to the little town of Kenhardt is a 'kokerboom forest' consisting of at least 700 kokerboom growing up to 4m high. Most are on a range of koppies that straddles the municipal boundary. To reach the forest, drive 7km from Kenhardt on the road to Brandvlei. The forest can be seen from the road and offers visitors some attractive picnic sites and plenty of interesting walks.

Nieuwoudtville Nature Reserve
In 1973 the Nieuwoudtville municipality set aside a small nature reserve of 66ha, 2km east of the village adjacent to the Calvinia road. Half of the reserve is flat, while the other half consists of dolerite koppies which provide fine views of the surrounding 'Bokveld'. Nieuwoudtville's chief pride is its unique spring flora, and in particular some spectacular endemic species. The reserve is open at all times and the municipality plans to establish a parking area and picnic site on the higher ground.

Nieuwoudtville Waterfall Nature Reserve
After heavy rainfall the 70-metre high Nieuwoudtville Waterfall changes from a trick-le into a surging rush of water and a spectacular experience of sight and sound. The scenic falls are surrounded by a tiny 11ha nature reserve, which was proclaimed in 1987 and includes a wide variety of mountain fynbos and succulents.

The falls are on the Klippers River, which rises in the Bokkeveld Mountains near Nieuwoudtville and flows northwards, plummeting into the reserve's deep, circular pool. Colourful rocks, pitted by erosion lie scattered over the riverbed.

The reserve is located within the Bokkeveld Mountains in an area often dubbed 'the Boland of the Karoo', because the peninsula-shaped plateau near Nieuwoudtville is far more fertile than the arid Knersvlakte surrounding it.

The reserve, which has no facilities, can be reached 6km north of Nieuwoudtville on the road to Louriesfontein. For further information on the reserve write to the Secretary, Northwest Regional Services Council, P.O. Box 99, Calvinia 8190 (telephone Calvinia 80).

Oorlogskloof Nature Reserve
San paintings, breathtaking views and interesting rock formations are the main attractions of the 5070ha Oorlogskloof Nature Reserve, 10km south of Nieuwoudtville, on the edge of the escarpment between the inland Karoo and the coastal plain.

Although there are no buildings nor roads within the reserve, a 25km hiking trail includes parts suitable for camping.

Access to the reserve is over private property, so in order to arrange a visit first write to The Officer-in-Charge, Oorlogskloof Nature Reserve, Nieuwoudtville 8180 (telephone Nieuwoudtville 8-1010).

Tankwa Karoo National Park
Despite covering large parts of South Africa, the sparse scrub that is so typical of the Karoo, is not as hardy as it looks. Overgrazing and other bad farming practices have destroyed much of the original character of the area often leaving only semi-desert behind.

In a bid to restore part of the Karoo to its original splendour Tankwa Karoo National Park, a 27064ha area, 95km south of Calvinia and 145km north of Ceres was proclaimed in 1986. However, it will take some years for the original vegetation to re-establish itself – and in the meantime there is little to attract the visitor except solitude and some smaller animals. No facilities have yet been built.

Tankwa is very dry and receives an average of only 50mm of rain a year with a maximum of 100 millimetres. When the occasional rains do fall however, the park is transformed and the plains come alive with dazzling displays of colourful flowers.

Eye-catching twins of the Great Karoo

Fortunately for nature lovers, Southern Africa's parks and nature reserves tend to have distinctive names and there are few problems in telling them apart. Of course, there are exceptions. The eastern Cape has the Mountain Zebra National Park near Cradock and the Mountain Zebra Nature Reserve on the Gamka, while the northern Cape's Kalahari Gemsbok National Park is easily confused with the adjoining Gemsbok National Park in Botswana. Even worse, there are three separate reserves named after the Karoo.

One of the three, the Karoo National Botanic Garden at Worcester, is in a class of its own. The others, the Karoo National Park at Beaufort West and the Karoo Nature Reserve at Graaff-Reinet, are twins in more than name. Both came into being through the initiative of the S.A. Nature Foundation, a charitable trust backed by South African private enterprise and linked with the World Wildlife Fund. The Foundation specialises in providing funds to help conserve endangered species and habitats.

Early in the 1970s, the foundation began campaigning for parks or reserves in the Great Karoo, which until then had been starved of conservation areas. The public response was so strong that the foundation arranged to help bring two such areas into being – one at Graaff-Reinet, to be run by the Cape Provincial Administration, and the other at Beaufort West, to be run by the National Parks Board. The provincial reserve was proclaimed in 1975 and the national park in 1979.

The 'Karoo twins' have been friendly rivals from the beginning and keep a watchful eye on one another's activities. To the east, there are twins of a different sort: the provincial reserves Rolfontein and Doornkloof, which are near neighbours on the shores of the P.K. le Roux Dam on the Orange River. In the heart of the Cape, the Carnarvon and Victoria West municipalities support small reserves on their commonages, and the region's tally is completed by Strydenburg's tiny Aalwynprag Nature Reserve on the slopes of a roadside koppie.

Aberdeen Municipal Nature Reserve

Springbok and kudu roam the koppie-studded plains on the fringes of the Karoo town of Aberdeen, in a 1810ha municipal nature reserve. Waterbirds are also common, particularly around the reserve's spring – where clean, clear water bubbles from the earth all year round. You can enjoy a day in the open at one of the picnic sites where braais have been laid out in a shady area nearby.

Leading from the spring and passing through low acacia bush and scrub is a 15km road, which provides a pleasant walk or drive. If you proceed quietly, you will have an excellent chance of spotting game. Besides springbok and kudu there are ostrich, steenbok, monkey and jackal in the area.

The reserve, which is signposted from the Willowmore-Graaff-Reinet road lies some 300m outside the town.

For more information contact the Town Clerk, Aberdeen Municipality, P.O. Box 30, Aberdeen (telephone Aberdeen 14).

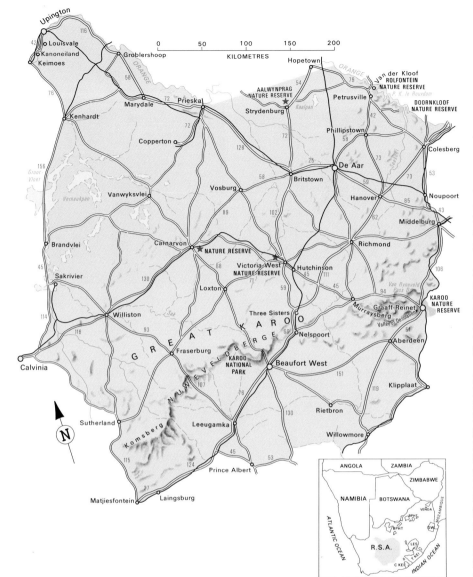

Carnarvon Nature Reserve

At the suggestion of the former mayor, Dr A.P ('Appie') van Heerden, the Carnarvon municipality set aside 670 ha of the town commonage for a nature reserve, which was proclaimed in 1971. Hartmann's mountain zebra, black wildebeest, eland, blesbok, springbok and ostrich were re-introduced and today the game population is so strong that each year the municipality sells surplus springbok to local farmers.

Roughly half of the reserve is low and flat, while the remainder consists of rough terrain at a higher elevation. Each species has its favourite habitat: the blesbok and springbok seek the plains while the black wildebeest lurk far off in the krantzes.

To reach the reserve, drive 1 km out of Carnarvon on the road to Loxton. Most sections are served by good roads. The reserve may be visited from 8 a.m. to 5 p.m. (seven days a week) by arrangement with the municipality. For more information contact The Town Clerk, Carnarvon Municipality, P.O. Box 10, Carnarvon 7060 (telephone Carnarvon 12).

Doornkloof Nature Reserve

Like Rolfontein, Doornkloof was one of the Orange River farms bought by South Africa's Department of Water Affairs in the 1960s as it prepared to flood the valley of the P.K. le Roux Dam. Part of the old farm is today under water, but for years the higher ground was rented to neighbouring farmers as grazing land. Then in 1980 the Government handed Doornkloof to the Cape's Department of Nature and Environmental Conservation, which prepared to turn it into a nature reserve.

Doornkloof's veld was allowed to recover from years of over-grazing. Then a game-proof fence was erected – a big job, for the reserve covers 8 765 ha. Even before putting in any game, wilderness trails were established through Doornkloof, which in many ways is more beautiful than the sister reserve on Rolfontein. For one thing, Doornkloof has 10 km of the Seekoei River, one of the most important tributaries of the Orange.

It would be easy to combine Doornkloof and Rolfontein as a single super-reserve. 'They are linked by a strip of shore under our control and covering about 2 500 ha,' says an official. 'In total, the three areas cover more than 16 000 ha – and that doesn't include the surface area of the dam, which we regard as a conservation area. But we believe Doornkloof and Rolfontein will be more interesting if we keep them apart. To give only one example: on Rolfontein we have white rhino, but on Doornkloof we'll have black.'

The veld in both Doornkloof and nearby Rolfontein is classified as False Upper Karoo, but it also contains vegetation typical of the Orange

Right: An armoured ground cricket feeding on a Karoo flower. These insects are omnivorous, feeding on both plants and other insects. **Opposite page left:** *Cliffortia arborea*, a hardy tree with needle-like leaves, growing in the Nuweveld mountains, in the Karoo National Park. **Opposite page right:** A pair of blesbok grazing in the Carnarvon Nature Reserve. The species mates between March and April, usually producing one active calf (the female reaches sexual maturity at about two and a quarter years). Its natural habitat is open grassland, where males will establish their own territory.

Above left: A dusky sunbird, its head dusted with pollen, searches for nectar on an aloe in the Karoo National Park. **Above right:** Renosterbos flourishes in the harsh climate of the Karoo, where little rain falls from year to year. Renosterbos (*Elytropappus rhinocerotis*), sourgrass and shrubs such as harpuis are characteristic of the cooler southern slopes of the mountains in the park. **Opposite page:** An engraving of a quiver tree trunk (*Aloe dichotoma*) from a book (published in 1789) by the botanist William Paterson, entitled *A Narrative of Four Journeys into the Country of the Hottentots, and Caffraria.*

River broken veld. Wild olive, sweet thorn and karee can be seen in the kloofs; camphor bush, cabbage trees and swarthaak cover the mountainous ridges. More than 50 different species of grass thrive on the plateaus and elsewhere in the area.

Karoo National Park

In 1973 the National Parks Board decided to create a park in the Great Karoo, and began looking for a suitable site. The news was greeted enthusiastically throughout the region, and no fewer than 17 municipalities offered parts of their commonages to start the new park on its way. The board's researchers looked into all the possibilities and recommended that the park should be at Beaufort West, since it was surrounded by typical Karoo scenery. It was central, and easily accessible to visitors. Ideal-

ly, we wanted an area that was 80 per cent plains and 20 per cent mountains,' explained Bruce Bryden, the first warden of the Karoo National Park. 'That's the balance you find in the Karoo as a whole. But when I arrived there in 1977, all we had was the commonage donated by Beaufort West municipality and the farm Stolshoek, bought for us by the S.A. Nature Foundation – a total of about 14 000 ha, and consisting chiefly of mountains.'

A year after Bryden's arrival the Parks Board bought a small farm adjoining the commonage and afterwards another farm set in the mountains. The park's size was doubled, but still the mountains outweighed the plains.

During 1981 three big manufacturing concerns joined forces to sponsor a major fundraising competition with the title 'Karoo 2000' – an effort aimed at buying more land for the park and restoration of the area to what it was like two centuries earlier. It made sense to use the money to acquire land on the plains.

Bruce Bryden's first task was to tear down the old farm fences and remove alien vegetation. At least on the commonage the veld was in good condition, for the area had lain fallow for five years. 'Once everything was cleaned up I began a survey of small mammals in the park and began looking at birds and reptiles too,' said Bryden. 'At the same time I did some bookwork to see which species used to live in the area in the old days. As a result we soon re-introduced a number of springbok, black

wildebeest, red hartebeest, gemsbok and Cape mountain zebra.'

The people of Beaufort West were delighted by these developments but the farmers whose land bordered on the park were less cheerful. 'They saw the park as a refuge for predators, especially caracal,' said Bryden. 'They were convinced our caracal would raid their sheep. Instead, they've had less trouble than before. The caracal's chief food is small mammals. As the ground cover has increased so has the population of small mammals, and the caracal have no need to go hunting outside.' The park staff has electrified the perimeter fence to deter the jackal and caracal from encroaching on neighbouring farms.

Antelope species such as mountain reedbuck, grey rhebok, grey duiker and klipspringer have always inhabited the Beaufort West locality and are well represented in the park. One may also see baboon, bat-eared fox and jackal. In addition, a number of kudu have entered the park of their own accord, perhaps realising that they are safe from hunters there.

The Karoo National Park consists of three basins and the Nuweveld mountain range to the north of Beaufort West. It is an area of mountains, plains, koppies and chasms – typical characteristics of the Great Karoo.

The park has three main vegetation zones determined by elevation – high, middle and low. The plains on the lowest levels bear typical Karoo vegetation of mixed grass and shrubs

A GRAVEYARD FULL OF MISSING LINKS

Dicynodont skeletons found at Beaufort West. These herbivorous, mammal-like reptiles lived about 230 million years ago.

To many a traveller the Karoo, with its dry, desert-like landscape stretching to the horizon, must seem one of the emptiest regions on earth. But a look at the same landscape through the eyes of a palaeontologist changes its character completely: suddenly it becomes a densely populated territory. In fact the Karoo is one of the world's largest natural graveyards, containing an immensely rich collection of fossils from the Age of Reptiles. Scientists regard it as one of the great natural wonders of the world.

By far the most important fossils in this ancient treasure-house are those belonging to the order Therapsida, the mammal-like reptiles which link primitive reptiles with the first true mammals.

About 250 million years ago, the Karoo was a shallow depression covered by a thick sheet of ice. But then the climate grew warmer and the ice retreated, turning the depression into a large and generally swampy basin. With the passage of the millennia this extensive swampland became richly populated with primitive plants and reptiles, their remains settling into the sand or mud. Their skeletons were petrified as the layers of sediment gradually hardened into stone, and within 50 million years the original floor of this extensive and gradually sinking region had become carpeted with layer upon layer of fossil-bearing sandstone and mudstone — in places several thousand metres deep.

This fossil record was imprisoned in stone for many more millions of years, but immense forces beneath the planet's crust began to lift the ancient lowlands, turning the Karoo basin into a plateau. Then the weathering and erosion began. Over millions of years, the sun, wind and water began to cut deep valleys into this great layer-cake, exposing the long-hidden fossils.

Although similar sequences of events have occurred elsewhere in the world, the Karoo is remarkable in that its rock strata contain a virtually unbroken record of species through a complete 50 million-year period (from 240 to 190 million years ago). This was a particularly important period because it saw the evolution of the first mammals.

which include skilpadbossie, honey-thorn and sweet thorn, the well-known *Acacia karroo*.

Sour grasses and renosterbos dominate the mountain slopes, and the plateau on the topmost level features a harsher sourveld, characteristic of Karoo mountains with their slightly higher incidence of rainfall.

As may be gathered from the type of vegetation, this is a dry, dusty land. Frequent and longlasting droughts are experienced (the average annual rainfall in the area is under 250 mm), but occasionally there are dramatic changes in the weather, and the heavens open up.

In 1977 the park covered an area of just under 15 000 hectares. Since then it has steadily increased in size and now covers more than 33 000 ha of the Nuweveld Mountains and the surrounding plains.

Bryden's wife Helena is herself a zoologist, and while her husband concentrated on mammals she began mounting a collection of Karoo insects which is today one of the attractions of the park. The couple lived in the spacious Stolshoek farmhouse, soon adopted as the park headquarters. There were already rudimentary roads across the surrounding area but they were not suitable for ordinary vehicles. Yet rather than improve these routes for the use of tourists, Bryden concentrated on developing a three-day 'Springbok Trail' for hikers.

At one stage (before it was expanded) the park consisted mainly of mountains, and the best way to explore it was on foot. The one essential was comfortable overnight huts. The Brydens built two of them from local stone with the design based on Karoo cottages of the old days – the front door flanked by two windows with shutters, a flat roof sloping backwards, and an outside chimney.

Bruce Bryden left the Karoo in 1980 and was succeeded as warden by Pierre van Rooyen, who reversed the three legs of the Springbok Trail and began planning extensions to take in higher elevations. 'The highest point in the Nuweveld range is more than 1 000 m above Stolshoek,' he said. 'It can get very cold on top; it's not unusual to have snow up there during winter. Even so the hikers all ask: "Can we go to the top?" 'If that's what they want, we'll have to provide a hut for them.'

Karoo Nature Reserve

According to one theory, the perfect nature reserve consists of a series of concentric rings with an undisturbed wilderness at the heart, an area of limited tourist access around it and development confined mainly to the outer edge. Graaff-Reinet's reserve is quite the opposite: the Karoo Nature Reserve encircles the town, first hugging the contours of a great oxbow in the Sundays River as it meanders through the flat-topped mountains of the Sneeuberg, then completing the ring by spreading across rising ground to the east.

Despite its unorthodox design, Graaff-Reinet's nature reserve is one of the most pleasing in Southern Africa. Graaff-Reinet itself is an exquisite centre-piece, though much of its thunder

KAROO NATURE RESERVE AT A GLANCE

When to go The Graaff-Reinet area is at its best in spring, between September and November. Between March and May is also a good time to visit – not too hot or too cold. The Valley of Desolation and the near shore of the Van Ryneveld's Pass Dam are open at all times. Other parts of the reserve are accessible to hikers in possession of a permit and by way of a controlled gate entrance.

Reservations To hike on a wilderness trail, write to The Officer-in-Charge, Karoo Nature Reserve, P.O. Box 349, Graaff-Reinet 6280 (telephone Graaff-Reinet 2-3453). Bookings for the Camdeboo Conservation Education Centre may be made by writing to The Co-ordinator, Environmental Education, Department of Nature and Environmental Conservation, Private Bag X9086, Cape Town 8000 (telephone Cape Town 45-0889/888 or Graaff-Reinet 2-3453).

Getting there The reserve encircles Graaff-Reinet. To reach the Van Ryneveld's Pass Dam and the Valley of Desolation, drive out of town on the road to Richmond and Murraysburg. The dam is readily visible just outside the town and the turn-off to the Valley of Desolation is on the left, about 5 km further on. To reach the game-viewing area take a right turn 4 km further along the Murraysburg road.

Accommodation There is accommodation for a maximum of 12 hikers at the Waaihoek trail hut. The Camdeboo Conservation Education Centre accommodates groups of 40 students and their teachers/lecturers. There is also ample accommodation in Graaff-Reinet, including rondavels and a fine caravan and camping site at Urquhart Park near the Van Ryneveld's Pass Dam.

Getting around The only surfaced road in the reserve is the tarred route to the Valley of Desolation. On the way, stop at the look-out point commanding fine views of Graaff-Reinet and of Spandau Kop, which ranks as one of the finest examples of Karoo koppies. There are three picnic sites: Picnicbos on the Van Rhyneveld's Pass; Impunzi on the game-viewing circuit and Ribbokberg on the way to the Valley of Desolation. A route map with numbered points along the way is a useful aid if you intend driving through the game-viewing area.

Wilderness trails lead through the Driekoppen area to the east of the town and may be tailored to the capabilities of the hikers taking part. There is no charge, but the trail hut may not be occupied for more than two consecutive nights. Three short, self-guided trails have been laid out in the west near Spandau Kop, in the Valley of Desolation.

Wildlife Besides indigenous species such as kudu, mountain reedbuck, grey duiker, steenbok and caracal, the reserve contains species introduced from elsewhere – Cape mountain zebra, black wildebeest, blesbok and springbok. There is an abundance of bird life, not least in the Valley of Desolation and at the Van Ryneveld's Pass Dam.

THE BUCK THAT SEEMS TO JUMP FOR JOY

An etching by Robert Batty (1789-1848) entitled 'The Springbok'.

Early settlers knew most Karoo springbok as 'trekbokke' because of periodic migrations in which perhaps thousands of them came together to move from one area to another in a single body. Those that stayed put were known as 'houbokke' and treated as a distinct species. The last of the great migrations took place in the Prieska district in 1896, and the phenomenon is not likely to be seen again (today's biologists suggest that the migrations were prompted by drought).

Instead, the 'trekbok' of the early days has become the 'springbok' of today in reference to a more playful side of its character. Like the impala, the springbok is able to leap three metres into the air and seems for a moment to hover there, like a bird. Unlike the impala, the springbok also 'pronks' (prances) by leaping with its legs held stiff — behaviour that was beautifully described by the hunter and former Indian Army officer William Cornwallis Harris in his *Portraits of the Game and Wild Animals of Southern Africa*, published in 1840.

Cornwallis Harris waxed eloquent on the startling agility of South Africa's national animal: 'Unfurling the snowy folds on their haunches so as to display around the elevated scut, a broad white gossamer disk, shaped like the spread tail of a peacock, away they all go with a succession of strange perpendicular bounds, rising with curved loins high into the air, as if they had been struck with battledores, — rebounding to the height of ten or twelve feet with the elasticity of corks thrown against a hard floor; vaulting over each other's backs with depressed heads and stiffened limbs, as if engaged in a game of leap frog; and after appearing for a second as if suspended in the air, — clearing at a single spring from ten to fifteen feet of ground without the smallest perceptible exertion — down come all four feet together with a single thump, and nimbly spurning the earth beneath, away they soar again, as if about to take flight . . .'

is stolen by the towering Spandau Kop which overlooks it from the south-west – a spectacular, double-ringed Karoo koppie named by an early Prussian settler who was reminded of Spandau Castle near Berlin. Spandau Kop is within the western section of the reserve, related to an equally impressive formation known as the Valley of Desolation.

The 'Valley' is really more of a gorge or canyon, a deep, steep-sided cleft that cuts through the Sneeuberg and reveals a glimpse of distant plains and cone-like koppies on the horizon. In 1953 the Valley of Desolation was proclaimed a Scenic National Monument.

The Valley of Desolation was the original focus of the S.A. Nature Foundation's efforts to create a Karoo reserve at Graaff-Reinet, and it is being developed for tourists with a tarred access road, picnic sites and marked walking trails. At an early stage, the project was extended to take in the nearby Van Ryneveld's Pass Dam, which already showed promise as a bird- and game-viewing area.

Situated at the foot of Spandau Kop in the Valley of Desolation is the Camdeboo Conservation Education Centre. The centre offers groups of up to 40 students courses on aspects of conservation with emphasis on the geology, birds, animals and plants of the area.

The reserve contains five distinct veld types; partly the result of the variations in elevation but mainly because Graaff-Reinet is located in a transition zone where Karoo scrub meets vegetation typical of the Cape's east coast.

The reserve was established in 1975 and covers 16 500 ha, of which about 1 000 ha is taken up by the Van Ryneveld's Pass Dam. Angling is permitted in certain sections of the dam and barbel are the most common fish to be caught. On the dam's western shore conservation officers have built a game and bird-watching hide. At the same time they have pioneered wilderness trails on the rising ground east of the town, which takes in another landmark known as Driekoppen ('Three Peaks'). Before being incorporated into the park the land was

leased to local people for grazing, and it still shows the effects. However, it is slowly recovering and supports a large herd of Cape mountain zebra introduced from the national park at Cradock.

On the map, the Karoo Nature Reserve appears to surround Graaff-Reinet without a break, but in fact it is divided into east and west sectors by the roads that enter the town. The conservation officers manage these areas separately. Cape mountain zebra have been introduced to the mountainous east section and black wildebeest and springbok to the west section. Cape buffalo, red hartebeest, gemsbok, black wildebeest, blesbok and eland have been introduced to the game-viewing area around the Van Ryneveld's Pass Dam.

Rolfontein Nature Reserve

The original Rolfontein was one of the Orange River farms partly flooded by the P.K. le Roux Dam. In 1970, what remained was handed over to the Cape's Department of Nature and Environmental Conservation to be developed as a reserve. For the next five years Rolfontein's largely mountainous terrain was left fallow, and then work started in earnest: a game fence was erected, a road system established – and animals re-introduced.

The aim was to restore the area's original character. Some species were already there: kudu, mountain reedbuck, duiker and steenbok. Early travellers' records were checked, and a variety of other species brought in, including eland (the reserve is now thought to have one of Southern Africa's biggest eland populations), gemsbok, black wildebeest, red hartebeest, warthog, springbok, Burchell's zebra, white rhino and, later, cheetah and brown hyena. Archaeological finds indicate that the Cape buffalo and warthog were once indigenous, and these too will be re-introduced.

Rolfontein is a 15 000 ha expanse of grassy flats, dolerite koppies and densely wooded kloofs that will delight any visitor. Although the vegetation is classified as False Upper Karoo, it features vegetation types typical of the mountainous valley through which the Orange River flows. Karee trees, sweet thorn and wild olive may be seen in the kloofs, while cabbage trees, swarthaak trees, sweet thorn, assegaai grass, rooigras and camphor bush are distributed among the mountainous ridges. Antelope feed on most of the area's 40 grass types.

The reserve was established to preserve a mountainous Karoo ecosystem, with all its animal and plant life, and to provide facilities for outdoor education and recreation. One way of seeing Rolfontein and its game is through the windows of a car, but walking in the reserve is probably more rewarding. Members of its staff will, on request, arrange wilderness trails.

Above: A white rhino bull stalks the Rolfontein Nature Reserve, a mountainous sanctuary beside the P.K. le Roux Dam. **Right:** The secretary bird, a large and powerful bird found throughout Southern Africa, though not in forest and mountain areas. Its feathered crest is reminiscent of the quill pens which secretaries tucked behind their ears many years ago. It is a ferocious snake-killer. **Below:** The crag lizard *(Pseudocordylus microlepidotus),* shy inhabitant of the Karoo's mountainous regions.

An eland bull in the Victoria West Nature Reserve. These large animals (they may be the size of an ox) were once widely distributed through Southern Africa, but are now found only in game parks and nature reserves. Mothers have been known to drive away predators such as hyenas, leopard and cheetahs when their calves are threatened.

There is no set route – the guide follows a path tailored to suit the party, though invariably he will take hikers to the dam. Here they board canoes and go paddling for a stretch. Visitors are asked to keep to the roads and paths.

In his years at Rolfontein, one conservation officer, Ken Coetzee, developed a computerised 'data bank' to help monitor the various species, 'At first we concentrated on game, but now we cover birds and vegetation too,' he said. 'I've divided the reserve into four-hectare squares and these are logged on a grid chart together with the three overall vegetation patterns – plateau, slope and riverine. Each species is given its own chart, and when we spot it in a new area, we make an entry on the grid and write up all the details; thus a habitat preference and distribution pattern emerge.'

As the data bank grows, observations become more sophisticated. 'For instance, if we come across a dead animal we analyse its stomach contents to see what it's been eating,' explained Coetzee. 'Its diet may vary greatly from season to season. A researcher may ask where the bat-eared fox goes in summer, or how vegetation re-establishes itself after a fire. Our data will help to provide answers.' Their success was gratifying,' added Coetzee. 'Six other Cape reserves have adopted the idea and our combined data are stored in the Provincial computer in Cape Town.'

Strydenburg Aalwynprag Nature Reserve
The smallest municipal nature reserve in the Cape Province is Strydenburg's 2ha 'Aloe Mountain' – actually the eastern slopes of the prominent koppie divided by the national road as it bypasses the town.

Proclaimed in 1977 and subsidised by the Department of Nature and Environmental Conservation, the reserve contains a fine collection of Karoo aloe and other succulents. It is located opposite Strydenburg's hotel, close to the southern exit from the national road.

Victoria West Nature Reserve
Just outside Victoria West, on the road to Loxton, are two attractive picnic sites overlooking the town dam – the haunt of flamingo, Egyptian goose and other water birds. The nearby Victoria West Nature Reserve accommodates Burchell's zebra, black wildebeest, eland, gemsbok, blesbok, springbok and ostrich. The game has done so well that the municipality almost doubled the reserve's size: it now covers nearly 700 hectares.

Permission to enter (and the key to the gate) may be obtained at the town hall. Alternatively, there are pleasant picnic spots outside the perimeter from which visitors can spot game.

There are plans to introduce a large variety of animals to the reserve, and to re-establish regular visiting hours.

Heading north to the red Kalahari

North of the Orange River, the Cape Province retains some of the typical features of Bushmanland and even the Great Karoo – but above all – it is Kalahari country. Some parts may go without rain for years on end, and large areas are flat and virtually featureless. Yet there is always water beneath the sand and abundant vegetation on the surface, and several mountain ranges break up the seemingly endless expanse of nothingness. Among them are the Langeberg and Korannaberg ranges, which run north to south. In fact they are really separate parts of the same range.

As yet, the eastern sector of the Northern Cape accommodates few nature reserves, though the impressive Augrabies Falls and Kalahari Gemsbok national parks to the west help to remedy the omission. Existing reserves include ambitious municipal schemes at Kuruman and Vryburg, smaller projects at Barkly West and Prieska (on the Orange's south bank, but forever linked with the north because of its importance as a crossing-place), the Ganspan Waterfowl Sanctuary, and the intriguing Sishen Nature Reserve – created by the South African Iron and Steel Corporation and stocked with such game as white rhino, gemsbok, eland and red hartebeest. The 22 697 ha Vaalbos National Park, which was established in 1986, is likely to be a major attraction, although it will be a while before the necessary infrastructure has been developed for tourists to visit the park.

Canteen Koppie Nature Reserve

Barkly West's Canteen Koppie is a 7 ha national monument – the focal point of the Klipdrift alluvial diamond diggings that in 1869 attracted fortune-hunters from far and wide. The diggers stripped the koppie of its vegetation and left deep holes and piles of debris that still exist. These features make the koppie a most unlikely nature reserve, but against that it is interesting to see how trees, bush and grass have successfully invaded the abandoned diggings, promising to restore the koppie's original beauty.

Canteen Koppie is within Barkly West's town commonage and is run by the municipality. To reach it, drive 1 km out of Barkly West on the road to Kimberley and watch for the 'National Monument' signs on the side of the road. The gate is on your left and the reserve is always open. There are no facilities.

Die Bos Nature Reserve

In pioneer times, certain families of the Prieska district spent every Christmas and New Year beside the Orange River in a lush wood, known simply as 'Die Bos', about 2 km east of the town. Die Bos remains a favourite picnic spot today, and since 1953 it has been a municipal nature reserve covering roughly 60 ha. The reserve is not fenced for game, but vervet monkeys swing from the trees and there is a wealth of bird life both in the trees and on reed-grown islands in the river.

Die Bos encompasses a network of roads and a group of rondavels available to visitors throughout the year. To book, write to The Town Clerk, P.O. Box 16, Prieska 8940 (telephone Prieska 3-1113/4 or 3-1375). The road to the reserve is poorly signposted, so it is wise to ask a local resident for directions.

Eye of Kuruman

At Kuruman, an underground river runs into a barrier of dolomite and is forced to the surface. Each day up to 20 million litres of water rise from a deep cave and fill the picturesque 'Eye', a large pond that supplies Kuruman's domestic water, feeds the Kuruman River and fills two 7 km irrigation canals. In the 19th century the Eye was a malaria trap, but the problem was overcome and today the pond is part of a municipal park close to the heart of the town.

Above: A swallow-tailed bee-eater. This species makes burrows in sand banks, usually laying three or four eggs. They have been seen roosting on top of each other — three or four deep! **Left:** Blesbok preparing to mate in the Kuruman Nature Reserve. The blesbok was once distributed in large numbers throughout the Northern Cape, Free State and parts of Natal and the Transvaal, but the population decreased considerably as more and more land was settled.

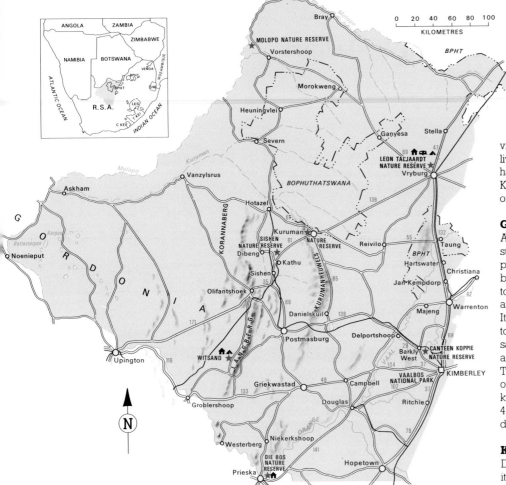

The Eye's exceptionally clear water allows visitors to see the large carp and barbel that live in it — but fishing is not permitted. The park has picnic places and a drive-in tea-room, and Kuruman's fine caravan and camping site is only a stone's throw away.

Ganspan Waterfowl Sanctuary

A shallow pan covering an area of 100ha and surrounded by flat, bush terrain is the centre-piece of a 180ha bird sanctuary set aside by the Jan Kempdorp Municipality. It is open to visitors daily from 6a.m. to 6p.m. and there are picnic places and overnight camping sites. It is not necessary for campers and other visitors to make prior arrangements to visit the sanctuary. There are also facilities for fishing and yachting, and there is one ablution block. To reach the sanctuary, leave Jan Kempdorp on the road to Ganspan and drive for two kilometres. Turn right and travel for another 4,5km on a gravel road (which is in a fair condition throughout the year).

Kuruman Nature Reserve

During the mid-1970s the Kuruman Municipality ringed 850ha of flat, well-vegetated com-monage with a game-proof fence, and in 1979 turned it into a game reserve. Smaller species such as grey duiker, steenbok, porcupine and aardvark were already well represented but larger animals had disappeared from the region and had to be reintroduced. The municipality brought in rhino, eland, gemsbok, red hartebeest, blesbok, springbok, kudu, impala, steenbok, duiker and ostrich: in each case the species thrived and increased.

For two years after its creation the reserve was closed to the public to enable the animals to get used to their new home. In 1981 the reserve was opened for three hours each Sunday afternoon (2.30p.m. to 5.30p.m. in winter, 3.30p.m. to 6.30p.m. in summer) and visitors had the chance to explore the network of red sandy roadways that criss-crossed the bush. Out-of-town visitors wanting to see the reserve at other times can make arrangements with municipal officials at the town hall. To reach the reserve, drive 1 km out of Kuruman on the road to Sishen: the gate is on the right.

Leon Taljaardt Nature Reserve

In 1968 the community of Vryburg unveiled an 857ha nature reserve on the municipal com-monage north-west of the town and named it in honour of their mayor, Dr Leon Taljaardt. The

Right: Twice a week, Kuruman's municipal officials make a full circuit of the fence surrounding the town's small nature reserve — on the lookout for tunnels under the wire dug by itinerant aardvark (or sometimes by porcupine). Such tunnels pose two problems: they are a thoroughfare for black-backed jackals seeking escape from the reserve, and they let in stray dogs that wreak havoc with the game. The aardvark digs only by night, and in the daytime it shelters in a deep burrow. The results of the aardvark's labours suggest it is a highly efficient digging machine — and so it is, though its appearance is a surprise. Its claws are predictably steel-strong (they can leave a mark on concrete) and its legs are short and powerful, like a bear's. But otherwise the aardvark is a strange mixture of kangaroo's tail, pig's snout, a worm-like tongue and donkey's ears that fold over its eyes when it is digging. Scientists place the aardvark in an order all its own (Tubulidentata).

264

reserve neighbours the municipality's Swartfontein Pleasure Resort, which offers luxury 'squaredavels', a swimming pool and caravan and camping sites. The two attractions lure tourists to Vryburg and are much appreciated by those local residents who want to escape from the town for a quiet weekend.

Step by step, the reserve was stocked with a wide variety of species – not all of them indigenous, for the main aim is to satisfy tourists. Thus Leon Taljaardt contains both black and blue wildebeest and both Burchell's and mountain zebra, though in nature the species' territories seldom overlap. The reserve also contains eland, gemsbok, red hartebeest, blesbok, Cape buffalo and white rhinoceros. However, its population of waterbuck could raise purists' eyebrows, because the species does not belong so far to the west.

Leon Taljaardt's terrain is mostly flat and featureless but in places the bush cover is so thick that it is difficult to see game. The reserve is open during daylight hours.

To reach the reserve take Molopo Road from the centre of Vryburg and drive for about five kilometres. The reserve and the pleasure resort are on the left.

Molopo Nature Reserve
The Molopo River, which follows the South Africa-Botswana boundary, is the focus of this 14 800 ha reserve. Despite being very arid – the river is usually dry – the dry thornveld and bushveld of this northern Cape region supports a surprising amount of wildlife, including gemsbok, eland and red hartebeest.

Nine pairs of white-backed vulture breed at Molopo, and you can see their large, stick nests built in the tops of trees. These, the most common of Southern Africa's vulture, feed with such enthusiasm that a flock of 50 birds can devour an impala in 10 minutes!

Molopo lies 14 km north-west of the small town of Vorstershoop, some 250 km from Vryburg. It was proclaimed in 1988 and is administered by The Department of Nature and Environmental Conservation.

The reserve is still being developed, but any prospective visitors can make arrangements with The Officer-in-Charge, Molopo Nature Reserve, P.O. Box Vorstershoop 8615 (telephone 0020 ask for Vorstershoop 1322).

Prieska Koppie Nature Reserve
When Prieska's Die Bos became a nature reserve in 1953, so too did the prominent koppie that dominates the town and provides the best views of the surrounding district. The reserve covers 32 ha and is open all the time. On top is a small fort built by British forces during the Anglo-Boer War, and the slopes feature a variety of aloes and other succulents. An even

Above: A flap-necked chameleon moves gingerly along a thorn-studded acacia branch in the Northern Cape veld. Chameleons differ from their faster-moving lizard cousins in several major respects: one is their ability to change colour to regulate their body temperatures; another is the slow pace at which they move. **Below left:** An African monarch butterfly emerges from its chrysalis. This species, which is also known as the milkweed butterfly, is one of the more common to be found throughout Southern Africa. **Below right:** A cluster of bright flowers on *Tribulus terrestris*, an annual herb.

bigger selection of succulents may be seen at the Ria Huysamen Garden in Du Toit Street – the creation of a retired schoolteacher and his wife who also care for the plants on the koppie.

Sishen Nature Reserve
The South African Iron and Steel Corporation (ISCOR) has been mining iron ore at Sishen since the 1950s. As its operations have grown, so too have the numbers of people living in Sishen's Dingle township and the newer and larger Kathu township to the north. In 1975 ISCOR decided to boost Kathu's recreational assets by developing a 2 248 ha game reserve on flats north-west of the mine, and with it a picnic area and fishing pans. To run them, the corporation brought in Piet Schuurman, an experienced game ranger from the Transvaal.

As Schuurman explains, Kathu already held a nucleus of game on an ISCOR-owned farm. 'It gave us a flying start. Once our fences were up, we transferred eland, gemsbok and springbok from the farm to their new home. We also transferred some camels – technically they don't belong, but they're an essential part of northern Cape history because the frontier police rode camels when they went out on Kalahari patrol.'

Next, Schuurman turned to ISCOR's nature reserves at Thabazimbi and Vanderbijlpark (since closed because the land was needed for industrial development).

'Thabazimbi gave us kudu and impala. Again, impala aren't necessarily indigenous to Kathu but our chief objective is to please our visitors, and they like variety.

'Vanderbijlpark gave us black wildebeest and white rhino. And then we turned to private sources and introduced red hartebeest, blesbok and Burchell's zebra. The smaller mammals were already in place.'

To give his visitors the greatest accessibility possible, Schuurman has developed an intricate network of roads that lead to every corner of the reserve. To the east, they enter the ancient Kathu Forest consisting of stately camelthorn. In the west they run through typical Kalahari veld, most of it so thick that much of the growth is being removed to improve the veld's carrying capacity – the number of animals that the vegetation can support. This objective has been kept in mind in stocking the reserve with game.

Sishen Nature Reserve is open daily between 7 a.m. and 7 p.m. from 1 October through to 30 April and between 7 a.m. and 6 p.m. from 1 May through to 30 September.

To reach the reserve, take the road to Dibeng that branches off the main provincial road between Kathu and the north. The picnic place and fishing pans are on the right and the nature reserve is behind them. A small shop stocks snacks and souvenirs and issues maps of the road system.

The Witsand

One of the traditional pleasures of the Northern Cape is an outing to the 'Roaring Dunes' of the Witsand south-west of Postmasburg, a 2 500 ha island of dazzling white sand encircled by a sea of Kalahari red. This great tract of white sand overlies abundant water in the barren reaches of an inhospitable desert.

According to geologists who have surveyed the region over the years, the Witsand owes its existence to an isolated range of koppies, which now lies buried beneath the dunes. Ordinary Kalahari sand was caught by the koppies, then relieved of the oxidised iron coating that made it red by the action of water springing from the rock. Although the dunes hold a considerable amount of water, the surrounding area is very much drier.

For generations, northern Cape farmers and their families have regarded the Witsand as a recreational area where they can toboggan down the slopes. In the process, they try to set up a deep reverberating hum that results when

Left. The Witsand of the Northern Cape is an island of white sand encircled by the ochre sands of the Kalahari. **Bottom:** The milkweed stink locust shares the bright colours of other members of the stink locust family. **Below:** The white-backed vulture is the commonest and most widespread vulture in Southern Africa. Individuals cruise at about 60 km/h, scanning the terrain below for clues which may lead them to a carcass. Other scavengers, such as crows or hyenas, often serve as beacons, leading white-backed vultures to sought-after carrion. **Opposite page:** An alert gemsbok in the Leon Taljaardt Nature Reserve.

the countless millions of sand grains rub together. According to local tradition, the dunes roar only in the months spelt with an R (in other words from September to April), but a more likely explanation is that they 'perform' only when the sand is hot and dry.

If there should happen to be a thunderstorm, the dunes will be mute for several days afterwards and visitors will be more than likely to return home disappointed.

The Witsand is well signposted both from Postmasburg, which is situated about 80 km to the north-east, and from Groblershoop, which is situated about the same distance to the south-west.

Accommodation is available in modest rondavels and camping sites at the Witsand Holiday Resort on a farm adjoining the dunes. The resort is open all year round and visitors should expect to provide their own amusement.

To book, write to Mrs E.M. Maritz, Witsand Holiday Resort, P.O. Box 327, Postmasburg 8420 (telephone Bermolli 7-2373).

Vaalbos National Park

In the northern Cape, south of the Vaal River between Barkly West and Kimberley, the 22 697 ha Vaalbos National Park represents an interesting mix of plants and habitats. These include typical Karoo, Kalahari and grassveld. The name of the park originates from the popular 'vaalbos' or camphor tree (*Tarcanantus camphoratus*), which is dominant in a large area of the park.

Apart from endemic small mammals, other established populations of springbok and hartebeest may be found, and species such as buffalo and black rhino have been reintroduced.

At present the National Park's Board is conducting biological studies at Vaalbos, the results of which will enable them to determine future management strategies. As the park is still in its infant stages, it will be some time before the necessary infrastructure is created. However, the area as a whole holds great promise for the future.

The place of great noise

Below Prieska, the Orange River flows north-west to Upington, then loops south and heads for the awesome Augrabies Falls, where it plunges 91 m in several small steps and one giant leap. The name Augrabies derives from a Khoikhoi word translating as 'the place of the great noise', and to early Khoikhoi the majestic cascade had near-sacred significance. It remains a sanctuary today, for since 1966 Augrabies and the area surrounding it has enjoyed the status of a national park.

In its original form, Augrabies Falls National Park consisted of 3750 ha on the Orange River's south bank (today it covers 9000 ha). There were adequate views of the main falls and other landmarks, but anyone wanting to see the falls from the north bank had to travel far upstream to reach a safe ford across the river. The only alternative was to walk downstream, clamber to the bottom of the Augrabies gorge, and climb up again on the other side.

The north bank has recently been made accessible by means of a narrow suspension bridge that spans the channel immediately above the main cascade. The bridge has opened the way to spectacular new views of the falls and of the exquisite 'Bridal Veil' that spouts from high on the gorge's north wall.

Augrabies is usually thought of as a remote corner of South Africa, but several communities are within easy reach. Among them are Upington and Keimoes, both of which have nature reserves of their own.

At Upington, Spitskop Nature Reserve covers 3000 ha of the municipal commonage and boasts game such as eland, gemsbok and red hartebeest. It even boasts a pair of camels. Tierberg, a mountain overlooking the town of Keimoes in the lower Orange River valley, is well known for the panoramic views it offers over the surrounding countryside.

Augrabies Falls National Park

Nowhere is the Orange River more impressive than at Augrabies Falls, which rank among the

Above: The boiling waters of the Orange River below Augrabies Falls. **Left:** Tons of water rush over the main fall and the Bridal Veil fall (left) every second, crashing into the gorge with the sound of continuous thunder. During exceptional floods, the flow has exceeded that of the Victoria Falls. Some geologists believe the gorge to be the world's most interesting example of weathering of granite.

world's greatest cataracts on a major river. First the water gathers speed over the series of cascades and rapids that provide a drop of 91 m. Then it hurtles through a narrow dog-leg channel and approaches the lip of the main cascade. There it shoots into space, plunging 56 m before it strikes the turbulent surface of an immense circular pool walled by towering cliffs of sheer granite.

The main falls account for more than 90 per cent of the water that flows over Augrabies, but there are several secondary falls channelling stray branches of the river that have escaped the main stream. One of these branches goes underground near the northern lip of the gorge, then gushes from its side as the Bridal Veil. Another creates Klaas Island which provides spectacular views of the main cascade, then enters the gorge by Twin Falls.

The quantity of water flowing over Augrabies varies greatly depending on the season. In times of drought the stream may diminish to a trickle. If there have been storms inland, the river may rise to the point where it bursts from its regular channel and hides the whole of the end of the gorge behind a curtain of water. In 1974, so much water was on the move that the gorge was filled to the brim and the park headquarters on Klaas Island was marooned for 14 days. The incidence of such floods may lessen because the course of the Orange has been blocked by major dams such as the Hendrik Verwoerd and the P. K. le Roux, which have made the river's flow more consistent.

Below the main falls, the stream careers down rapids at the bottom of the gorge. It can be seen to advantage at beauty spots such as the Arrow Head, reached by means of an easy

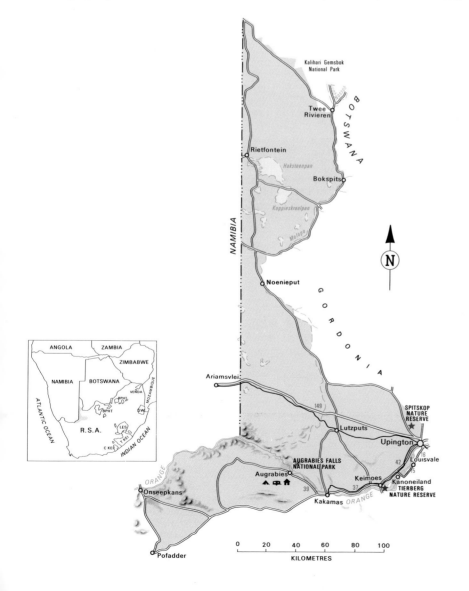

AUGRABIES AT A GLANCE

When to go The park is open throughout the year, but the falls are most impressive between October and January. The Klipspringer Trail is open from April to October. The park's gates open at sunrise and close at sundown, and visitors are welcome throughout the year.

Reservations and information Enquiries and applications for accommodation should be addressed to National Parks Board, P.O. Box 787, Pretoria 0001 (telephone Pretoria 343-1991) or National Parks Board, P.O. Box 7400, Roggebaai 8012 (telephone Cape Town 419-5365) or National Parks Board, P.O. Box 774, George 6530 (telephone George 74-6924/5) unless the accommodation is required within 12 days. For bookings at shorter notice you should contact The Tourist Office, Augrabies Falls National Park, P.O. Box 10, Augrabies 8874 (telephone Augrabies Falls call office). A small information centre next to the office tells the park's story and introduces some of its wildlife. Ask at the office for a map of the road system and 'Klipspringer Trail'.

Getting there The falls are 112 km west of Upington and 39 km north-west of Kakamas. Drive to a turn-off on the Kakamas-Springbok road about 8 km from Kakamas, then travel another 31 km to reach the park.

Accommodation Augrabies has a small number of self-contained bungalows (four beds and bedding, kitchen with eating and cooking utensils, and shower); and 'double huts' (sharing a bathroom). There is a large caravan and camping site with ablution blocks.

Eating and drinking The park cafeteria serves meals and refreshments (popular with day visitors). In front of the cafeteria is a garden containing about 100 species of aloe and other succulents. The park shop sells groceries, fresh meat and firewood. There are braai facilities at the bungalows and at the caravan and camping site.

Getting around The access road to Augrabies is tarred as far as the rest camp. Inside the park, a 30 km network of gravel roads takes visitors to major attractions like Oranjekom, Echo Corner, the Fountain and Moon Rock. There is a filling station at the rest camp. The Klipspringer Trail in the southern section of the park has two overnight huts. For a less strenuous walk, take the 2,5 km bridle path from the caravan site to the Arrow Head.

Wildlife At Augrabies' rock and water take precedence over flora and fauna but the wildlife includes klipspringer, springbok, steenbok, dassie, porcupine, leopard, baboon and vervet monkey (a group of monkeys make daily raids on the caravan site). A breeding herd of black rhino has been translocated to Augrabies from Etosha National Park. Some 140 bird species have been recorded.

Special precautions Visitors are advised to take anti-malaria tablets during their stay in the park. These are available from any chemist.

walk along a 2,5 km bridle path, or Oranjekom, which is accessible by road and offers a sheltered look-out.

Many of those who visit Augrabies are content to admire the main falls and go on their way but others find it worthwhile to drive through the park and explore its wild scenery and strange vegetation. At Moon Rock, visitors may clamber onto an immense granite dome that provides spectacular views across the whole park. At the Fountain, the attraction is a drink from a picturesque spring. And at Echo Corner on the river they experiment with loud cries that produce a strong echo after a four-second delay.

During 1775 a young Swedish-born soldier stationed at the Cape ran into trouble because of gambling debts. The soldier was Hendrik Wikar, and to escape his problems he deserted from the Dutch East India Company, heading into the interior. For the next four years he roamed the Orange River and kept a journal in which he recorded his impressions of Augrabies Falls: 'When the weather is favourable one can hear the noise like the roar of the sea from the distance of one stage away' (a day's journey by wagon).

Wikar mapped the falls and made many other discoveries on the Orange, as a result of which the Dutch East India Company agreed to overlook his desertion, and welcomed him back to Cape Town. But his achievements were forgotten until his journal was published in 1916. In the meantime, the credit for discovering Augrabies was given to a Cape Town merchant, George Thompson, who, after seeing them in 1824, named them 'King George's Cataract' after the reigning monarch, George IV.

George Thompson was a man of many parts – one of his claims was that he was the first man in Cape Town to smoke cigarettes. He was an enterprising and well-informed explorer and his *Travels and Adventure in Southern Africa* is one of the best books of its kind. In it he records that a party of Khoikhoi led him to the brink of the falls, even though 'the sight and sound of the cataract were so fearful, that they themselves regarded the place with awe, and ventured but seldom to visit it'.

Standing on a cliff opposite the top of the cascade, Thompson had a perfect view. 'The beams of the evening sun fell full upon the cascade, and occasioned a most splendid rainbow,' he wrote, 'while the vapoury mists arising from the broken waters, the bright green woods which hung from the surrounding cliffs, the astounding roar of the waterfall, and the tumultuous boiling and whirling of the stream below, striving to escape along its deep, dark and narrow path, formed altogether a combination of beauty and grandeur, such as I never before witnessed'.

270

'King George's Cataract' found its way on to maps and the name survived well into the 20th century – though local farmers usually talked of the 'Groot Waterval' and the traveller Guillermo Farini suggested the rapids and cascades should be named 'The Hundred Falls'. Meanwhile, local tribesmen continued to talk of 'Augrabies' just as their ancestors had done, and that is the name everyone uses today.

Strange tales are told of the great pool that lies at the foot of the main falls. Although its depth has never been plumbed, some authorities suggest that the water conceals a fortune in diamonds washed down the Orange River from sources far inland, but the sheer weight of water cascading down the cataract prevents them from investigating.

Andries de Bruin, a park employee whose family has lived near Augrabies for generations, says that his relatives remember a severe drought that occurred in 1934. The main falls dried up and for the only time in recorded history the pool at the bottom was exposed. 'That would have been a perfect opportunity to look for diamonds,' says De Bruin, 'but the people were afraid. Some thirsty cattle walked up the riverbed to drink at the pool when suddenly a strong wind blew them over the edge. They were never seen again.'

The disappearance of the cattle reinforced an old legend. Local residents still believe the pool is the haunt of a terrifying 'water monkey' that is liable to emerge in search of food. Zoologists speculate that the 'water monkey' legend is prompted by sightings of giant barbel that are sometimes washed over the falls. Such fish run to lengths of 2 m or more, and their long 'whiskers' and hideous faces make them appear to be formidable monsters.

In spite of this explanation, local people are convinced that the 'water monkey' means business. During 1980 strange tracks were discov-

ered around the Augrabies restaurant and there was near-hysteria as park workers reported that the monster had left the pool. Officials took photographs of the tracks and sent them to Pretoria for identification, but before the results came back the 'monkey' was identified as an otter.

The menace of the 'water monkey' may be a myth, but Augrabies itself has claimed many victims. Since the park was proclaimed in 1966 at least 16 people have lost their lives, most of them because they lost their balance on the lip of the gorge and tumbled to the river far below. Today there is a chest-high protective fence fronting the most popular vantage points on the south bank – but there are always foolhardy tourists eager to clamber over it.

In 1979 a Scandinavian visitor overbalanced on the lip of the gorge and tumbled over the edge. As he slid down the sheer rock face, the friction ripped off all his clothes – even his belt and underpants. The rock also badly lacerated his flesh, and when he hit the river several bones were broken. But the man was still alive and was able to scramble to a submerged rock, where he sat in 30 cm of water.

'That day I was on the point of setting off for a spot of leave,' recalled park warden Dries Duvenhage. 'My men told me there was someone in the river. At first I couldn't believe he had survived but we could see him sitting on the rock, so we let down a rope and one of my men climbed down and rescued him. He was severely injured and an ambulance came and took him to hospital.' As far as Duvenhage was concerned, the incident was over.

'But when I came back from leave, the man was back at the park, all covered in bandages. He said he wanted his holiday money; he'd lost his wallet when falling down the rock face. I took my binoculars and scanned the cliff, and I could see pieces of the man's clothes. Then

Left: The *Acacia karroo* is typical of the Augrabies area. It has many uses: the bark is used in tanning, the inner bark is used for ropes, the leaves, flowers and pods are useful fodder, the gum makes an adhesive and the thorns are used as needles. **Right:** A view of the gorge from the rock known as 'Ararat'. In his book *To the River's End*, author Lawrence Green described his impressions of Augrabies: 'It is the rock that remains vivid in the memory, the masses of black and grey granite, the steep rock walls of the canyon. Mile after mile of gigantic rock faces, washed and polished by the floods of centuries, naked, slippery, steep and deadly.' **Below:** Springbok graze in the sun-baked surroundings of Augrabies, where the vegetation is dominated by kokerboom and wag-'n-bietjie. The springbok is a prodigious athlete, and can easily clear 3,5 m at a leap. At full gallop it can reach a speed of nearly 90 km/h.

A PARADISE FOR DASSIES

Although the Augrabies Falls hiking trail is named in honour of the klipspringer, by far the most common mammal in the park is the dassie (also known as rock rabbit or hyrax). Dassies are seen everywhere, sunbathing on rocky ledges or scurrying for shelter in deep crevices. Some of the boldest dassies even invade the camping site and frolic on the lawns.

At first sight the dassie resembles a giant guinea-pig, but otherwise it has little in common with rodents and is instead classified among the ungulates or hoofed creatures. Absurdly, its nearest relative could be the elephant — its front teeth are tiny tusks that curve from the skull, and like the elephant, its toes have blunt plates for nails (four in front and three behind).

Of course, the dassie has evolved very differently from the elephant and nature has given it a unique way of scaling the sheer cliffs that are its favourite habitat. Its feet rest on moist pads which can be contracted and are thought to serve as suction cups. With their help the dassie can make light work of near-perpendicular cliffs — and if it wants to descend in a hurry to escape an enemy, it can tumble 15 m or more without apparent harm.

I saw something flapping. One of my men went down on a rope to have a look and it was the wallet, completely torn but with the money still inside. There was more than R400. Now that was something out of heaven.'

Klipspringer Trail

One of Augrabies' greatest attractions, the three-day 'Klipspringer Trail' was designed to take the hiker to all the major landmarks in the southern section of the park. Although regarded by some as being a long hike, the schedule is, in fact, not too demanding. Overnight facilities on the route consist of two huts, each equipped with 12 bunks.

The trail takes its name from an animal that seems particularly suited to the rocky Augrabies habitat – the klipspringer or 'rock jumper'. This small antelope has near perfect balance and is often seen perched motionless on a rock, with all four feet bunched together. The klipspringer is capable of phenomenal leaps and can scale almost sheer cliffs with great speed.

Another creature of the rocks often seen at Augrabies, is the Cape red-tailed rock lizard (*Platysaurus capensis*). In fact, only the males have red tails – the females are a uniform grey-green.

Spitskop Nature Reserve

Upington's Spitskop is a spectacular granite koppie some 13km north of the town, reached from a turn-off on the main route to Kalahari Gemsbok Park. In 1967 the municipality proclaimed a nature reserve on the sandy flats adjoining the koppie and introduced gemsbok, springbok, ostrich, eland, red hartebeest, Burchell's zebra and even a pair of camels brought from the Kalahari.

Originally the reserve covered only 1300ha, but the animals did so well that in 1980 the area was more than doubled in size to 2813 hectares. The reserve is open daily between 7 a.m. and 7 p.m. The Spitskop itself is surmounted by a sheltered look-out equipped with a telescope. At the foot is a picnic area.

Tierberg Nature Reserve

Overlooking Keimoes is the squat bulk of Tierberg, the focus of a small municipal nature reserve covering some 160ha. On Tierberg's summit is a sheltered look-out, and the slopes and foot are notable for a prodigious growth of aloes and other succulents. The most numerous species is *Aloe gariepensis*, named after the Gariep (the old Khoikhoi name for the Orange River). It blooms in August and September and produces vertical red flowers that appear to bristle like spears. Tierberg is open all through the year and is accessible by a 4km drive from the centre of Keimoes.

Above: A toad grasshopper (*Trachypetrella andersonii*) is almost perfectly camouflaged among rocks at Augrabies, its squat body resembling the horny back of a toad. The female toad grasshopper, twice the size of the male, is wingless (most males have wings).

Right above: A female Cape red-tailed rock lizard (*Platysaurus capensis*) suns itself on a rock in the Augrabies Falls National Park.

Right below: Although it belongs to the same species, only the male has a red tail. Lizards are highly adaptable creatures whose size and shape are a match for widely varying conditions. Some have limbs provided with sharp claws, some have limbs ending in a fringe or web, and others have no limbs at all. In most lizards the teeth are conical and rather blunt, and too small to pierce human skin. Despite the horrifying appearance of some species, no lizard in Southern Africa is poisonous (the only poisonous lizards in existence are the 'Gila monsters' found in Mexico and the United States). The tongue is generally flat and slightly notched at the tip, though a few species – such as the leguaan – have forked and retractile tongues similar to those of snakes.

A tale of two rivers

About 250 km north of Augrabies Falls, two rivers named Auob and Nossob enter the same channel and flow southwards to join the Molopo. The 'rivers' scarcely seem to justify the description, for the Auob remains dry for years at a stretch and the Nossob flows perhaps once in a century. But down the ages the two watercourses have carved impressive valleys through the red dunes of the southern Kalahari, and the hidden water retained in their sandy beds helps to support a rich growth of vegetation.

Between the rivers is a wedge of land that on maps resembles part of a finger pointing north from the Cape Province. West of the finger is South Africa's border with Namibia, a straight line drawn along the 20th meridian. To the east is Botswana, divided from South Africa by the bed of the Nossob. The three territories meet at a point named Union's End –

so remote that it still evokes memories of a South Africa that has long since passed away.

Since 1931, Union's End and the unspoilt wilderness to the south have been conserved in a vast national park originally created to protect the gemsbok and indeed all the region's game. Today, the Kalahari Gemsbok National Park covers an area of 960 000 ha, (roughly half the size of the Kruger National Park) including the whole of the wedge between the rivers and

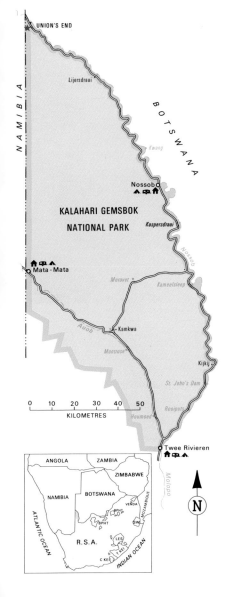

Far right above: The tsamma melon is an important source of food and especially moisture in the Kalahari. **Far right below:** A bat-eared fox. These cautious omnivores live on small animals, insects, birds and their eggs, fruit and various roots. They are thought to be monogamous, usually living in family units. **Right:** A gnarled tree overlooks the dusty bed of the Nossob River, in the Kalahari Gemsbok National Park. The discovery of Stone Age artefacts in the area indicates that the basin of the Nossob was once fertile.

THE CUNNING GOSHAWK

Clem Haagner, so frequent a visitor to the Kalahari Gemsbok National Park that a borehole has been named after him, tells the story of a chanting goshawk that discovered a novel way to prey on sandgrouse. The bird used to sit on a telegraph pole near Twee Rivieren and wait until a flock of sandgrouse began drinking at a small pool next to a fence. Then the bird swooped — not with hopes of snatching sandgrouse on the wing, but to panic some of them into flying against the fence and knocking themselves senseless.

The chanting goshawk's light blue-grey feathers and long orange legs make it quite easy to identify, but it is only one of a large number of raptor species (birds of prey) that help to make the park a paradise for bird-watching. About one-sixth of the park's many bird species are raptors preying on insects, reptiles, smaller birds or small mammals. They range from martial and tawny eagles to white-backed and lappet-faced vultures, from secretary birds to giant eagle owls.

According to Clem Haagner, February, March and April are the park's best months for raptor-spotting; particularly if the rainfall has been better than average. Fortunately for visitors, the rain encourages rapid plant growth in the riverbeds and adjoining areas, and the whole food chain is stimulated.

also a strip of land south of the Auob. Connoisseurs rank the Kalahari Gemsbok as one of the great parks of Africa — not least because it shares an unfenced boundary with a larger and equally rugged wildlife sanctuary across the Nossob in Botswana.

There was a time when small bands of San were the only human beings to venture into the area now occupied by South Africa's second largest national park. That all changed in the 19th century, when explorers discovered that the Auob and Nossob made fine transport routes. Water sources were few and far between, but teams of oxen were much more effective on the flat river beds than in the rolling sand of the dune country. Besides, there was plenty of game for the pot — an important factor for travellers in a country so harsh.

Above: The Kalahari lion kills an average of 47 animals a year – more than three times the rate of kills in the Kruger National Park. Experts explain that although prey is more scarce in the Kalahari Gemsbok National Park, and kills are made more difficult by the terrain, 50 percent of the Kalahari lion's kills are made up of small mammals.

For years, the region of the two rivers was a land beyond frontiers, and no government laid claim to it. Then at last it became attached to the old Cape Colony, which from 1897 began surveying large farms for the benefit of white settlers. Even then the region was largely a no-man's-land, and in 1904 the authorities in German South West Africa sent soldiers to block-ade Nossob waterholes and force Khoikhoi rebels to submit. The ploy backfired, and in a bloody fight at Grootkolk an entire German patrol was slaughtered.

White settlers were slow to take advantage of the new farms in the north, so the Cape authorities gave them to coloured farmers in-stead. The farms had names like Kÿ Kÿ, Kameelsleep, Kasper's Draai and Kwang – many of them recalled in the names of today's park waterholes. Then, in 1914, South Africa went to war against Germany and prepared to invade German South West Africa. As part of the invasion strategy, the South Africans sank strings of bore-holes for the benefit of soldiers and their mounts.

The invasion went off without a hitch, and when it was over the South African Government employed a number of 'bore-hole watchers' to keep an eye on the installations. The watchers and indeed the farmers were expected to live off the veld – with alarming consequences for the once abundant game.

Biltong hunters from the south also made their mark. By the late 1920s a number of species were in danger of extinction, and two North-ern Cape conservationists invited the Minister of Lands, Piet Grobler, to inspect the region.

Piet Grobler had piloted the National Parks Act through Parliament and played a major role in the proclamation of the Kruger National Park in 1926. His trip to South Africa's most remote corner convinced him that the area would make an ideal national park – not least be-cause it was associated with the gemsbok, which, with the springbok, supports the shield

Top: The imposing martial eagle (*Polemaetus bellicosus*), portrayed in a lithograph from the book by Sir Andrew Smith, *Illustrations of the Zoology of South Africa*. This large eagle preys on small animals like ground squirrels and suricates as well as game birds. It is threatened in some parts of Southern Africa — partly by farmers who resent the loss of their chickens. **Above:** A pair of white-faced owls — among the most appealing of the park's many bird species. These owls 'growl' when anyone comes too close, puffing themselves up and spreading their wings menacingly. **Left:** Red hartebeest fencing in the Kalahari Gemsbok National Park.

of the provinces on South Africa's coat of arms. He lobbied extensively in both Pretoria and Cape Town, and as a result the Kalahari Gemsbok National Park was proclaimed in 1931.

The new park's first ranger was Johannes le Riche, the son of a local trader. Le Riche and his family moved into a primitive hut vacated by one of the 'bore-hole watchers' who, like the few farmers in the park, were soon provided with new homes outside its boundaries. Hunt-

ing in the park was now strictly forbidden. The main task facing Le Riche and his assistant Gert Januarie was to intercept poachers and bring them before the magistrates.

For three years Le Riche and Januarie patrolled the park on horseback, but their efforts were hampered by a serious drought. Then, in 1934, came rains so abundant that both the Auob and Nossob came down in flood – the Nossob for the first time in this century. The

rains should have been cause for celebration – but they exacted a terrible penalty. Mosquitoes flourished in the area, Le Riche and Januarie contracted malaria, and both men died. A few days later Le Riche's brother Joep was appointed ranger in his place.

Joep le Riche's involvement with the Kalahari Gemsbok was supposed to be temporary, but he ended up staying for 36 years. He and his assistant, Gert Mouton, took conservation a step further when they set out to recommission the old bore-holes in the river beds. That way, reasoned Le Riche, he might persuade game animals to remain inside the park and not wander beyond its unfenced boundaries, where they were at the mercy of hunters.

Step by step, the position improved. In 1938 the British Government proclaimed a huge new game reserve across the Nossob in what is today Botswana, and Joep le Riche was put in charge. During the Second World War, would-be poachers were short of bullets, and the game population increased dramatically. After the war, game fences were built along the park's western and southern boundaries. From the 1950s, more emphasis was placed on tourism, and visitors began to arrive in increasing numbers. The wilderness that was the Kalahari Gemsbok began to earn its keep.

The first tourist accommodation in the Kalahari Gemsbok was a trio of rondavels built in 1940 near the confluence of the Auob and Nossob. Today the park has three well-equipped rest camps – Twee Rivieren at the southern entrance, which doubles as the park's headquarters; Mata Mata up the Auob, on the border with Namibia; and Nossob to the north-east, well on the way to Union's End. To reach the satellite camps from Twee Rivieren, the visitor has only to stick to the river beds.

Few travellers relish the prospect of long drives over sand roads, but in the Kalahari Gemsbok it is no great ordeal. Grading crews keep the roads in fine order, and patches of loose sand are rare. A gravel road which crosses the dunes to connect 'halfway house' picnic spots cannot be faulted.

Only 120km separate Twee Rivieren from Mata Mata, and there is a 166km drive between the main camp and Nossob (there is no thoroughfare at Union's End or Mata Mata). The authorities have laid down minimum legal times for the completion of these distances, but most visitors prefer to make a day of it and dawdle along in hopes of spotting unusual species or activity. For many visitors, the greatest thrill is to come upon a pride of Kalahari lions dozing by the roadside, or perhaps a cheetah running down a springbok to feed her cubs. Some people like to keep count of the various species they see, comparing tallies after each safari. Visitors often derive the most pleasure from spotting the smaller, less obvious mammals.

Gemsbok, red hartebeest, blue wildebeest and springbok are all fairly common in the riverbeds, whether as solitary bulls or rams rooted by breeding or by the territories they have marked out, or bachelor and breeding herds that are always on the move. Occasionally visitors see a group of eland, though the species tends to keep to the dunes and visits the river beds only in passing. The little steen-

THE CHEETAH SHOW

Vehicles and people have become so commonplace in the Kalahari Gemsbok that many animals simply accept them as part of the environment. Motorists often find their path blocked by herds of springbok that show no inclination to break ranks. Lions sometimes see cars as playthings, and may try to bite their tyres or swat their headlights with a massive paw. But the strangest reaction is that of the cheetah, which seems to turn a blind eye to people and behaves as if they are not there.

There are only about 60 cheetahs in the park, but these angular cats contribute some of the liveliest action that tourists are likely to see. Lions and leopards do most of their hunting at night, when visitors are in rest camps, but cheetahs hunt by day, and because their favourite prey is the springbok they conduct their campaigns in the river valleys. The more fortunate tourists can watch them every step of the way, from the time they begin stalking until they make their run and knock a springbok into oblivion. Typically, the hunter will be a

female cheetah who must satisfy her own needs as well as those of two (sometimes as many as five) cubs.

To begin with, her prey may be several hundred metres away. She will leave her cubs hidden as she prepares to take advantage of every scrap of cover. With her body flat and her ears laid back she inches closer to her prey — and it may be a matter of hours before she comes within range. Throughout that time her eyes remain fixed on her target, until finally, with a devastating sprint, she makes her attack.

Sometimes all goes to plan and she makes a kill. But more often the prey is too agile for her, and showing her resignation, she slows to a trot with her tail held high. On occasion she varies her prey and attacks the calves of larger antelope, or perhaps small mammals. But the existence of the cheetah and her family is precarious, for she is forced to compete with powerful predators, and without food her cubs will weaken and perhaps fall victim to spotted hyenas or leopards.

bok is another creature of the dunes and may be spotted close to the gravel road connecting the 'halfway house' picnic sites.

Diminutive suricates and black-backed jackals are common, as are the little bat-eared foxes often seen grubbing for insects in the late afternoon. Spotted and brown hyenas are rarely seen during the day.

The Cape fox and caracal are real collector's items, and if any of the visitors report seeing a leopard, impala or kudu, even park rangers sit up and take notice.

Running along the bed of the Nossob is a line of discreet beacons marking South Africa's border with Botswana. Otherwise there is no barrier between the two states, and the Kalahari's animals can roam from country to country as they please.

Botswana's Gemsbok National Park is even larger than South Africa's and together these great reserves of the sub-region comprise one of the least spoilt wilderness areas on the continent. This makes both of them extremely valuable to zoological researchers.

The best-known research project carried out in the Kalahari Gemsbok has been the University of Pretoria's study of the Kalahari lion – not a different species from the lion found in the Kruger Park and elsewhere, but certainly adapted to very different conditions.

The researchers found that a Kalahari lion may be expected to kill 47 animals a year – more than three times as many as its counterpart in the Kruger Park – even though prey is scarcer in the Kalahari, and the terrain makes it more difficult to catch.

As the researchers discovered, the disparity is a matter of scale. As much as 50 per cent of a Kalahari lion's kill is made up of small mammals, whereas in the Kruger Park the proportion is only one per cent. Given the opportunity, a Kalahari lion prefers to dine on ambitious fare such as gemsbok, blue wildebeest or red hartebeest. Sometimes, however, it is reduced to eating springhares, bat-eared foxes and porcupines merely to stay alive (porcupines represent one-quarter of their prey).

A biologist named Gus Mills arrived at Kalahari Gemsbok National Park in 1972 with the intention of gathering as much material as possible for a thesis on the little-known brown hyena (he later became full-time research officer at the park).

When the moon was full Mills drove through various sections of the park to watch brown hyenas on their solitary long-distance foraging expeditions. To make them easier to follow, several were fitted with 'radio collars' and located by a mobile receiver.

'The first job was to home in on an animal by using radio-tracking kit,' explained Gus Mills. 'Once we'd found one, I put the radio kit away and followed the green lights on the back of the collar – I didn't need to use headlights. Probably the most interesting thing I discovered about the species was that it's the females who have territories.

'Their offspring can remain as long as food is plentiful, but males have the option of going off on their own as nomads. They wander from area to area till they find a female in heat. After mating, they resume their nomadic existence leaving the task of feeding the cubs to the females and group-living males.'

Top: The magnificent horns which may have given birth to a legend: in profile the gemsbok resembles the mythical unicorn. The gemsbok's horns are used with deadly effect against would-be predators in the Kalahari, particularly lions. **Left:** A thunderstorm looms over the Nossob rest camp.

Top: Leopards are among the most agile and powerful of the park's predators. They are also masters of concealment. In his book, *Song of a Dry River*, Brian Barrow describes the leopard's ability to adapt to almost any environment: '. . . there are trees with dense foliage, patches of dense shrub and outcrops of calcrete rock: in any of these leopards can hide themselves so successfully that they are very seldom seen during the day.' **Above:** The caracal was once trained in Persia (now Iran) and India for hunting hares and game birds. **Left:** Wildebeest grazing on the sparsely vegetated plains of the Kalahari Gemsbok National Park.

Star-gazing

A composite picture shows the *Telstar I* experimental communication satellite, launched by NASA in 1962, against a tapestry of stars photographed from the observatory on Mount Palomar.

Discovering the universe can be a humbling experience. City-dwellers whose night sky is blotted out by tall buildings, glaring street lights and smog are missing an awe-inspiring display of celestial fireworks on a scale so vast that it defies understanding.

The immeasurable expanse of the cosmos accommodates many billions of stars and galaxies of many types. Each of the galaxies contains millions of suns, and many of these could conceivably be orbited by solar systems similar to our own 'family' of nine planets.

Yet in spite of this huge mass of cosmic matter, the universe is composed mostly of a vacuum. The Milky Way galaxy, of which our system forms an infinitesimal part, contains an estimated 100 000 million stars in a volume of approximately 200 million million cubic light years (a light year represents the distance light will travel in 365 days, and equals over nine million million kilometres).

This concept may best be explained by visualising the galaxy as a cube with sides of 100 km: if the 100 000 million suns were packed tightly together, they would occupy a space of only one cubic millimetre! Even the nearest star, Alpha Centauri, is 4,2 light years away, which means that a spacecraft travelling at today's speeds would take 80 000 years to reach its destination.

Astronomy, the science and study of heavenly bodies, is an exciting, rewarding activity which has gripped man's imagination for thousands of years — and it is for everyone. Your observations need not be on a galactic scale, either: even the familiar, unchanging face of our moon has conjured up a hundred legends.

The amateur astronomer may use a telescope, a pair of binoculars or even the naked eye to identify the Southern Cross, Orion Nebula and the magnificent sweep of the Milky Way galaxy (of which our solar system forms only a tiny part). The night sky in the Southern Hemisphere is a rich and ever-changing pageant.

Because the earth rotates in its orbit around the sun, the stars rise and set four minutes earlier on successive nights. All stars appear to rotate about a fixed point in the sky (in our case the South Pole). For this reason no two nights will be the same for the astronomer.

Avoid trying to see too much in one night. Instead you should focus on one part of the sky at a time and familiarise yourself with the posi-

Left: A meteorite found near Kouga in the Eastern Province. The 'shooting stars' spotted by amateur astronomers may be man-made satellites weighing several tons, or meteors ranging in size from pebbles to huge chunks of rock and metal. Although a great deal of space debris strikes the earth's atmosphere every day, little penetrates to produce noticeable craters on the surface. All meteorites are protected by law, and may not be removed. Occasionally an even larger body – a comet – passes through our solar system, trailing gases and dust for millions of kilometres. Some comets return at regular intervals: the famous Halley's Comet will next appear in 2061. **Right:** A 'Planisphere' is useful in identifying stars and constellations at a particular time and date.

PHILIPS' PLANISPHERE SHOWING THE PRINCIPAL STARS VISIBLE FOR EVERY HOUR IN THE YEAR From Lat. 35° South

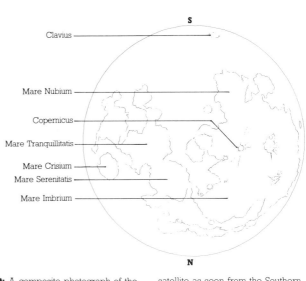

Clavius

Mare Nubium

Copernicus

Mare Tranquillitatis

Mare Crisium

Mare Serenitatis

Mare Imbrium

S

N

Left: A composite photograph of the moon (one exposure made at half-waxing and another at half-waning to provide relief) shows the earth's satellite as seen from the Southern Hemisphere. **Above:** The principal features on the visible side of the moon.

tions of some of the stars and constellations. A simple star chart would be a good start: it may consist of only one 'map' of the sky, showing the better-known stars, or it may show the positions of the stars in the Southern Hemisphere at certain times of the year.

Another useful item is the 'star wheel' or 'planisphere', which is set to the appropriate date and time by rotating a disc or mask on a star chart. This blocks out parts of the sky not visible at that time (see photograph). The planets move continually among the stars, and their

A powerful telescope reveals many more stars — some of them unimaginably distant — than would be visible to the naked eye.

relative positions are always changing. To study these movements you should consult an astronomical handbook or the astronomy column in your local newspaper.

Once familiar with the night sky, you may decide to make a closer study of the stars and planets. A good pair of binoculars would be a start, but you should exercise caution: do not buy an expensive instrument which your growing enthusiasm will make redundant within a few weeks.

You should use a steady 'rest' or mount your binoculars on a tripod — otherwise the stars will wheel about your field of vision, making it virtually impossible to focus on a particular point. Many star clusters and nebulae will become visible with even a low-power pair of binoculars, and the craters of the moon will be brought into sharp relief.

More serious amateurs may choose to buy a telescope. There are many types and sizes available, and you should choose the one which best suits your needs — and your pocket. Speak to someone at the Astronomical Society of Southern Africa (there are branches in several major centres) before making your choice. Some enthusiasts begin with a small *refractor* telescope, which uses lenses to collect light and focus it into an image. The *reflector* type — considered by many to be the better design for astronomy — works by focusing light reflected from one or more mirrors. A firm mount is essential for both types.

Modern telescopes usually have a small 'finder' telescope mounted on the tube. This has a wider field of view than the main telescope, and enables the astronomer to aim his instrument accurately, thus avoiding aimless sweeps across the sky. The telescope should wherever possible be placed away from incident light which may affect the image.

Long periods of observation and astronomical photography will necessitate some method of steering the telescope to keep pace with the apparent movement of the stars. An 'equatorial' mounting — preferably with a clockwork drive — is the only way this can be achieved.

There are many observatories dotted about the country, from large State-financed complexes costing millions of rand to modest, home-made observatories in back yards. Astronomical clubs and societies flourish in schools and universities.

The Astronomical Society of Southern Africa, a large organisation made up of both amateur and professional astronomers, holds regular meetings at centres in Johannesburg, Durban, Cape Town, Pretoria, Pietermaritzburg, Bloemfontein and Harare. The society welcomes visitors. Enquiries should be addressed to The Honorary Secretary, Astronomical Society of Southern Africa, c/o The South African Astronomical Observatory, P.O. Box 9, Observatory 7935, Cape.

Each year the society publishes a practical and informative handbook, entitled *Astronomical Handbook for Southern Africa*, and issues a monthly magazine providing advice for amateurs and professionals and news of space research.

A distant clap of thunder

Because Southern Africa is essentially outdoors country, the accurate prediction of weather conditions can make a great difference to your camping trip or holiday in a game reserve.

Cloud formations, wind strength and direction, temperature and other factors may warn of an approaching thunderstorm, for example — and those who have experienced the summer storms over Johannesburg and the high-lying areas of Lesotho and Zimbabwe are unlikely to forget them.

A thunderstorm is born when an updraught lifts moist, warm air into the atmosphere. As it rises, the air cools, and the condensed water vapour forms clouds. The clouds grow taller as the updraughts carry them higher into the atmosphere. Tiny water drops in the cloud become larger and heavier, and when they are too heavy to be supported by the rising columns of air, they fall as rain. The rain is accompanied (and sometimes preceded) by downdraughts.

A lightning bolt from *cumulo-nimbus* clouds. The Transvaal Highveld experiences a very high frequency of lightning flashes.

Occasionally the droplets of water in the cloud may be frozen as they are tossed about in the icy upper reaches of the atmosphere. These hailstones may acquire layer after layer of frozen water until they have reached the size of golf balls, when their weight causes them to fall — sometimes with devastating results.

Swirling currents of air in a thundercloud may build up so much static electricity that there is a massive discharge in the form of lightning, which equalises the electrical imbalance within the cloud. The lightning bolt may flash to the ground, to another cloud, or may even stay within the same cloud.

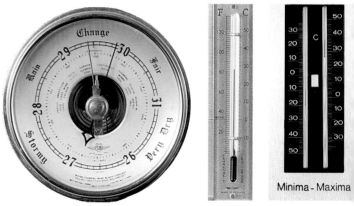

Minima - Maxima

Above left: An aneroid barometer. This instrument is far more compact than the mercury barometer used by professional meteorologists, and its pointer is activated by the expansion and contraction of a metal bellows as the air pressure changes. The words printed on the face of the barometer ('Fair', 'Stormy', 'Change') are more traditional than useful: what matters more is a *change* in the reading. Generally speaking, a drop in pressure indicates that a storm is on its way, while steady or increasing pressure usually predicts fair weather. Barometers should be mounted away from heat sources and draughts, as these could affect the readings. They should be adjusted to your elevation above sea level, and tapped lightly before use to 'unstick' the moving parts. **Above centre:** A simple thermometer, used to read the temperature at any given time. **Above right:** The maximum and minimum thermometer is used to record the highest and lowest temperatures reached during a 24-hour period. In this model, the indicators of the two extremes are returned to their original positions by pressing the button in the middle of the instrument. **Left:** A photograph of the earth taken from the Apollo II spacecraft clearly shows cloud formations over Africa.

Cirrus clouds, with Table Mountain in the distance. These clouds consist of ice particles and occur at high altitude.

Protecting yourself from lightning

Since lightning commonly strikes prominent features on earth, you should avoid high ground such as mountain ridges. Lightning currents will also follow electrical conductors such as cables, metallic pipes or fences: avoid touching or even being close to anything metallic (golfers have been injured or killed when lightning struck their upraised clubs or umbrellas).

● Do not expose yourself on a bicycle, horse or tractor during a storm. If you are caught outdoors, you should preferably sit down or crouch on some form of insulation — even if it is only a sleeping bag.

● Do not seek shelter beneath isolated tall trees, or near other tall objects which may attract lightning.

● Outdoor sporting activities — such as cricket or rugby matches, or horse riding events — should be stopped during nearby thunderstorms.

● Do not go out in a boat during a thunderstorm. If caught by a storm while far from the shore, bring down the mast to reduce the degree of exposure. In contrast, the inside of your car is a safe refuge.

● If you are in the house during a thunderstorm, avoid using electrical appliances such as hair dryers or telephones, and disconnect vulnerable items such as television sets.

● If you live in an area which experiences many thunderstorms, install an effective lightning protection system on your house.

Fleecy wisps and ragged thunderheads

The study of cloud formations can tell us a great deal about the sort of weather we may expect. These ephemeral wanderers are created by water which evaporates into the air from the earth and oceans. They are split into four major types: *stratus* (a layered form, found quite low, which is sometimes dark enough to conceal the sun), *cirrus* (a thin wispy cloud at a high altitude which is made up of ice crystals), *cumulus* (generally a low, heaped-up rain cloud or small cauliflower-shaped cloud — usually associated with fair weather, though if massed near the horizon or if in the form of a big, high cloud with many rounded heads, this type could cause sudden showers), and *nimbus* (a dark, low-lying cloud which usually means heavy rain). Cloud types· may overlap, but weather prediction may be possible after a study of three basic factors: the types of cloud, their height, and how fast they are changing.

Top left: *Cumulus* clouds are usually associated with fair weather. **Top right:** *Cumulo-nimbus* clouds are generally reponsible for thunderstorms. They are dense and dark (the base often resembles an anvil). **Lower left:** This grey cloud layer *(stratus)* may create a light drizzle. **Lower right:** *Cirro-cumulus* clouds usually mean fair weather.

NAMIBIA

North of the Orange River is the vast tract of land that Germany colonised as German South West Africa and today is called Namibia. Namib is a Khoikhoi word meaning plain, and endless plains are the key to Namibia. Some of the plains are deserts of sand, gravel and rock, some are grass-covered and provide rich grazing; others are typical savanna parkland with grass, trees and shrubs. In stark contrast are the country's tall, pastel-coloured mountain ranges and dry canyons cut deep into the barren rock.

As early as 1907, the German Governor Friedrich von Lindequist set aside three large areas of Namibia to serve as game reserves. Two of them survive today as part of the vast Namib-Naukluft Park complex in the west (4 976 800 ha), and the Etosha National Park in the north – once the world's largest game reserve.

Although it has since been greatly diminished in size, Etosha's 2 227 000 ha make it larger than the Kruger National Park, and its devotees claim it is also more exciting to visit (though not nearly as much of it is open to visitors). Besides Etosha and Namib-Naukluft, Namibia offers gems like the Fish River Canyon in the south, the Skeleton Coast in the north-west, and Waterberg Plateau and Caprivi Strip in the north-east. Wildlife is abundant almost everywhere.

A cluster of *Halenbergia hypertrophicum* brightens the northern stretches of the Namib with an all-too-brief display of colourful blooms.

A journey through forbidding territory

One of the longest and most impressive rivers in Namibia is the Fish, which rises in the Khomas Hochland Mountains south-west of Windhoek and flows 800 km before it meets the Orange River far to the south. The river's last 161 km take it through a deep canyon that is counted among the geological wonders of Southern Africa.

The Fish River Canyon is the setting of the most challenging hiking trail in Namibia, which ends at the Ai-Ais Hot Springs recreation resort. East of the Fish River are the rugged plains of Namaland, and the strange Kokerboom Forest that grows north-east of Keetmanshoop. To the west is the 'Sperrgebiet', the 'Forbidden Territory' that is closed to visitors to protect the coastal diamond industry.

Offshore is forbidden territory of a different sort – the bird paradises of the Government Guano Islands.

Ai-Ais Hot Springs

In the 19th century a Nama herdsman looking for straying cattle along the bed of the Fish River found a strong spring with water which he described as 'ai-ais' which is Nama for 'scalding hot'. Like many other such springs Ai-Ais was soon credited with medicinal properties and invalids went there in hope of a rapid cure.

Step by step a little spa developed at the spring, and during the First World War the German authorities took over Ai-Ais, building a rest and recuperation camp for sick and wounded soldiers.

Today, Ai-Ais is one of the most-visited spas in Southern Africa – not least because it is located at the bottom of the Fish River Canyon and provides an excellent base for exploring the surrounding region.

During its open season, the resort offers a fascinating mix of holidaymakers, there to 'take the waters', and sunburnt backpackers celebrating at the end of the long hike through the canyon. Traditionally hikers completing the walk leap into the large outdoor pool to cool off.

Even the winter sun makes Ai-Ais uncomfortably hot (though nights can be extremely chilly). In summer the heat becomes so oppressive that the resort closes down for a few months. 'In the heat of the day you can literally fry eggs on the rocks', says a biologist who lived at Ai-Ais for a year. 'It's so bad that from noon onwards nobody goes outside. You

Above: The magnificent Fish River Canyon, or 'Groot Kloof' as it is known to local farmers, is a deep maze of gorges and multi-layered outcrops representing aeons of relentless erosion. **Left:** The double-banded courser, with its pale plumage, may easily be overlooked by visitors to Namibia, and often it is spotted only when running. This species feeds on termites and ants – usually on open grassland or sandy veld – and lives in pairs or small flocks.

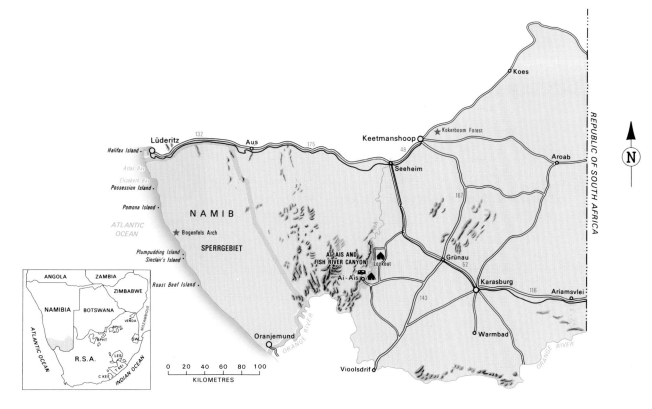

stay at home and spend the afternoon flat out in front of your air-conditioner, praying for a breeze in the evening.'

Although the heat in December and January (Ai-Ais's hottest months) can be devastating, February and March can pose an even bigger problem. 'That's when the floods may come,' says the biologist, 'though fortunately it doesn't happen often. The Fish and its tributaries drain a quarter of Namibia's surface area and all that water must come down the canyon past Ai-Ais.

'When I was there in 1974, heavy rains fell at the end of January and the river came down in flood. There was a parapet along the edge of the camping area, but the river came right over it and the whole resort below the restaurant was under water.

'The damage was terrible. All the caravans and tents were put away for the summer, but the water smashed into the brick field-kitchens and ablution blocks, and they collapsed. The pipes were broken, the borehole pump was washed away and the whole camp (including the swimming pool and tennis courts) was buried in smelly mud.

'We had to bring in drinking water from Grünau. We were just beginning to sort out the mess when in March there was a second flood, even higher than the first. Fortunately we were given warning, so we took our valuables to the top floor of the restaurant building.' The flood damage was quickly repaired.

Fish River Canyon

Ai-Ais is not the only hot spring in the bed of the Fish River. About 65 km upstream, a spring with a strong smell of sulphur trickles from the canyon wall and heats a permanent pool. During the First World War two German prisoners who had escaped from the internment camp at Aus hid at the spring for several months, and the story goes that one was cured of skin cancer and the other of asthma. The men lived partly on dates and thoughtfully planted the stones, so today there is a small grove of palm trees in that spot.

The sulphur spring and its palms provide a welcome oasis in the Fish River Canyon, which extends 161 km from the falls north of the main look-out to its junction with the Orange River. In places the gorge is up to 2,7 km wide but for most of its length it is much narrower, its course a crazy meander between steep cliffs. Its sides are a geologist's peep show, offering glimpses of varying strata, the lowest levels of which were laid down more than 2 500 million years ago.

For the first 65 km of its course towards the Orange, the Fish River's gorge is really a canyon within a canyon. An earlier version of the present river cut a wide swathe through the soft sediments of the Nama Series. The rift was enlarged when earth movements created cliffs to the west, and a geological fault had a similar effect to the east. The land tilted against the force of the stream, and in retaliation the Fish began to cut a deep channel in the bed of the original trough – much deeper, narrower, and more spectacular.

In places the canyon's floor is more than 500 m below the level of the plateau. Usually it is a silent world of placid pools and mighty boulders strewn across beds of sand, with little evidence of vegetation or wildlife.

Only rarely does the river come down in flood, but when it does the flow is so violent that rock is smashed against rock, gradually deepening the canyon with the passage of the centuries.

Before the 1960s the Fish River Canyon was little known and seldom visited, but in 1962 it was made a national monument and the area surrounding it was proclaimed a nature reserve. Since then its reputation has attracted an ever-increasing number of visitors, some content to gaze on its contortions from the security of the main look-out but others wanting closer contact by descending to the bottom. The hiking trail from the main look-out to Ai-Ais has become known as one of the most challenging in Southern Africa.

The Guano Islands

The water of the Fish River enters the Orange and is carried to the sea. There it falls under the influence of the Benguela Current, the nutrient-rich stream that originates among Antarctic icebergs and fosters an abundant growth of plankton. The plankton feed myriad fish and in turn the fish feed large colonies of seabirds including gannet, cormorant and penguin that breed on a long chain of rocks and islands off Namibia's shore. Seafarers of old knew the perilous landfalls as the Isles of Dead Ned.

The secret of who Ned was and how he came to die may be lost forever, but the isles that bore his name saw one of the strangest booms in commercial history. During the 1840s British merchants became aware that the islands held huge accumulations of seabird droppings or guano, a substance that had only recently become valuable after

AI-AIS AND FISH RIVER CANYON AT A GLANCE

When to go The hot springs resort is open from the second Friday in March to 31 October. The main look-out over the canyon can be reached all year-round but in the summer months it is best to visit it early in the morning. Hiking through the canyon is permitted only from May to the end of August. During the season the resort gate opens at sunrise and closes at sunset. Dogs and other pets are banned and so are motorcycles.

Reservations Enquiries and applications for accommodation or hiking permits should be addressed to The Director of Nature Conservation and Recreation, Private Bag 13267, Windhoek, 9000 Namibia (telephone Windhoek 3-6975/6/7/8).

Getting there From the south, take the gravel road branching north-west from a turn-off on the Vioolsdrif-Keetmanshoop road, 39 km north of Vioolsdrif (Ai-Ais is 84 km from the turn-off and the look-out is another 68 km to the north). From the east (the best approach) take the gravel road branching off the main highway 31 km south-west of Grünau (Ai-Ais is 73 km away and the look-out is 55 km from a turn-off 23 km east of the resort). From the north, approach from Seeheim on the Keetmanshoop-Lüderitz road, then 58 km north-west of Grünau take a turn-off to the look-out (48 km away). Ai-Ais is 98 km from the turn-off. Routes are signposted.

Accommodation There are campsites and ablution facilities at Hobas close to the canyon look-out, but most visitors stay in the resort itself. Luxury flats (one double, two single beds), flats (four beds) and huts (four beds) are available. In all cases bedding and towels are supplied but not cooking utensils, crockery or cutlery. There is also a large caravan and camping site, with ablution blocks. A maximum of one caravan/tent, two vehicles and eight persons are permitted per site.

Eating and drinking The resort's licensed restaurant serves meals and refreshments. A shop next door sells fresh meat, bread, butter and other groceries and also beer, wine and spirits. There are several field kitchens at the site for the use of caravanners and campers (tents and caravans are also for hire). There are braai facilities at the resort and at the canyon look-out.

Getting around There is a pleasant drive from Ai-Ais to the main canyon look-out 78 km away, and

two other look-outs are easily reached. Petrol is obtainable at Ai-Ais.

No permits are necessary for the many short walks in the riverbed and mountains close to Ai-Ais. In the past it was possible for unauthorised hikers to make a one-day hike from the main look-out to the canyon bottom and back, but this is now forbidden unless a hiking permit is obtained. The long hike from the look-out to Ai-Ais along the canyon bottom involves 86 km of walking and arduous scrambling over boulders and cliffs, and takes roughly four days (though some parties travel faster). Individual hikers are banned, the rules stipulating parties of at least three but no more than 40 people. Hikes must be booked in advance and permits obtained from The Director of Nature Conservation, Reservations, Private Bag 13267, Windhoek 9000. Applications must be accompanied by medical certificates for all members of the party to prove they are fit.

Scenic highlights The canyon is a place of rock and water but many plants have found a foothold. These include reeds and rushes in the riverbed and camelthorn and Karoo thorn trees on the banks. Watch for the kokerboom, shepherd's trees and aloes, including *Aloe gariepensis* on the canyon's walls.

Wildlife Leopard, Hartmann's mountain zebra and klipspringer are sometimes seen in the canyon, but most visitors spot only baboon and dassie. Bird life includes the fish eagle, hamerkop, grey heron and Egyptian goose. Visitors to the canyon may also spot scorpions and snakes (ranging from the black spitting cobra to the diminutive horned adder).

Special precautions When setting off on the canyon hike make sure you are carrying enough food (including emergency rations). Take along drinking water as it may not be available from the river. It is best to begin walking early in the morning, then stop at about 11 a.m. and rest until about 4 p.m., when it is cooler. Darkness falls rapidly so you should allow time to choose a campsite and prepare supper. By all means take the short cuts suggested on the trail map provided by the Director of Nature Conservation, but on no account try to invent new ones (it is easy to get lost and search parties may spend days looking for you). Take along a snake-bite kit.

---

scientists had pointed out its qualities as a fertiliser. On one island (Ichaboe) the guano was found to be more than 7 m deep in places. Ships raced south to recover as much of it as they could find.

As the months passed many hundreds of ships anchored off Ichaboe. Thousands of men camped ashore and laboured in guano pits that were pegged like mining claims. What happened to the displaced birds is not clearly recorded, though miscreant humans

Above: A large colony of cormorant inhabits Sinclair Island, off the Namib coast. The Cape cormorant, distinguished by its yellow throat and dark plumage, is by far the most abundant of the four species found on the Southern African coast, and a study made in 1956 revealed that an estimated 900 000 birds were nesting – and flourishing – on specially built platforms at Cape Cross and Walvis Bay. Cormorants feed on a variety of small fish, supplementing their diet with crabs and squid. **Right:** An engraving of Ichaboe, one of the most important guano islands, from Charles Andersson's book, *The Okavango River*. **Opposite page above:** The *Desert Rose* is a familiar sight in the Namib. **Opposite page below:** The stark beauty of the southern Namib coastline.

A RAUCOUS GLUTTON

The Cape gannet colonies on the islands off the Southern African coast are said to be among the noisiest, most crowded spots on earth (they are also rich repositories of guano, a natural fertiliser sought everywhere).

Gannets live in colonies of thousands, guarding their small nesting sites with startling ferocity: an encroaching bird is driven off with screeches and slashes of razor-sharp beaks. Because the colonies are so crowded, gannets have developed a few protective habits. Landing is as precise as possible, and a descending gannet has difficulty halting the descent of its relatively heavy body — the tail widespread, webbed feet forward, body vertical and wings beating furiously to counter its momentum. When a bird arrives at its colony, it immediately points its bill skywards, indicating to the other gannets that it is not about to attack. It is then allowed access to its nest.

Phenomenal speed and great diving skill are among the gannet's many accomplishments. It hovers effortlessly above the sea on the lookout for fish (the eyes are so placed that it can look down while in level flight), plunging into the water after its prey like a feathered arrow. Such is its momentum that it travels many metres beneath the surface.

Most gannets feed on the teeming fish stocks of the Benguela Current, which runs along the west coast of Southern Africa, sometimes following the sardine run up the east coast in June and July. They generally prey on surface fish such as mackerel, pilchard and mullet.

---

are known to have been pelted with dead penguins. By the middle of 1845 Ichaboe was stripped to the bare rock, and the process was repeated at other islands including Roast Beef, Plumpudding, Pomona and Possession. The boom faded as rapidly as it had begun, and the ships and men sailed away.

For two years the Isles of Dead Ned were left in peace. Then a Cape Town merchant wondered if the birds were producing more guano – and found they were. From that time

on, men have looked on guano as a renewable resource, allowing birds to breed on the islands and keep up their numbers.

Since 1866 the guano 'factories' have been under various forms of government protection. They were first annexed by Britain, then transferred to the Cape Colony in 1867 – which explains why today they belong to South Africa rather than Namibia. The smaller islands in this group, including Black Sophie, Sparrow-Hawk, Dumfudgeon, Eighty-Four,

Boat Rock and Marshall Reef, were not annexed by Britain and are therefore part of Namibia's territory.

The Isles of Dead Ned stretch for 350 km, from Sinclair (once known as Roast Beef Is-

land) between Oranjemund and Lüderitz to Hollam's Bird Island, which lies 160 km south of Walvis Bay. All but two fall within a strip of 100 km from Sinclair Island to Ichaboe. Some are no more than rocks poking from the sea, but at the other end of the scale there is Possession, with a surface area of 90 hectares. Perhaps the strangest of all is Mercury, so honeycombed by erosion that it vibrates when hit by a large wave.

The Isles of Dead Ned are tantalising, but access to them is strictly controlled to protect the birds and seals from human disturbance. A South African company has prospecting rights on some of the islands. The closest most visitors can come to the Guano Islands is at Lüderitz, from where they may train binoculars on Halifax Island – only 90 m from the mainland. Penguin and Seal islands, with

areas of 36 and 44 ha respectively, are clearly visible in Lüderitz Bay.

Kokerboom Forest

Early in the 1960s an extensive stand of 'quiver trees' (*Aloe dichotoma*) on the farm Gariganus, north-east of Keetmanshoop, was fenced off and proclaimed a national monument. The aim was obviously to conserve the 'forest' for posterity – but unfortunately the move backfired. Visitors went to Gariganus not merely to admire the trees; they wanted to dig up a 'quiver tree' (commonly known as a kokerboom) and take it home with them. By 1981 people had removed more than 200 young trees, ignoring the threat of heavy penalties.

Fortunately, enough of these trees remain to make a visit worthwhile. The forest is 23 km from Keetmanshoop on the road to Koes.

KEETMANSHOOP'S FLYING SNAKE

Late in 1941, strange tales circulated in the lonely sheep-farming country between Keetmanshoop and Aroab to the east. Owambo shepherds reported seeing a giant snake 'as thick as a man's thigh' that 'flew from cliff to cliff' and frightened the sheep. Another man said he had been out hunting with dogs when a huge snake attacked one of them, rolled itself into a ball and 'flew up into the cliffs', taking the dog with it. Local farmers heard the stories but dismissed them with a smile.

Then early in 1942 a farmer's son, 16-year-old Michael Esterhuise, was watching sheep near a remote koppie when he saw a large reptile peering at him from a crevice. He thought it was a leguaan or monitor lizard and threw a stone at it, upon which the creature 'growled like a dog', puffed up its throat and inflated 'fins' on the side of its head. Thoroughly alarmed, the boy rounded up the sheep and went home to tell his family.

A few days later Michael Esterhuise saw the 'thing' again, this time stretched on a ledge with its head and tail overhanging each end. It was more than 7 m long. This time he left it alone, but the next Tuesday he was watching his sheep near another koppie when he heard a sound 'like wind blowing through a pipe'. Looking up, he saw the reptile 'rolled up like a cartwheel' and flying at him from the top of the koppie. Its head protruded from the bottom and the 'fins' were extended on either side.

The boy threw himself to one side, and with a great thud the snake landed where he had been sitting. The snake skidded on the gravel, then unwound and straightened out as the boy scrambled frantically to escape.

The huge snake lashed twice with its tail, then curled it towards its head and with 'two short jerks' shot up into the air, cleared a 5 m tree and leapt back to the top of the koppie. The boy was terrified. He ran for 200 m but collapsed behind some bushes, where his father later found him.

News of Michael Esterhuise's encounter spread through the district like wildfire, and a group of farmers formed a shooting party. Pat Honeybone, in command at Keetmanshoop police station, was called to lead the hunt. He and the farmers examined the spoor at the koppie and subsequently found many traces of the snake over a large area. On one koppie they found the spoor alongside the bones of buck and sheep. But the reptile itself was not seen again, and the story was gradually forgotten.

Sarcocaulon patersonii (Bushman's candle).

The Sperrgebiet

A large area of the southern Namib (part of it known as 'Sperrgebiet' – German for 'forbidden territory') is restricted to protect the coastal diamond industry from theft and illegal prospecting. 'Diamond Area 1' stretches from the Orange River to the 26th parallel and is policed by the concession-holders, CDM (Proprietary) Limited of Oranjemund. As in much of Namibia, it is a stark, dry and sometimes searingly hot stretch of territory that would daunt even the boldest explorer.

Access to the diamond areas is severely restricted and even VIPs are not allowed in without an escort of diamond security officials. The only part of the Sperrgebiet that can be seen by the general public is the narrow strip which straddles the main road to and from Lüderitz, which goes straight through Diamond

The plants of the Namib are remarkable for the variety of ways in which they have adapted to desert conditions, not merely surviving but actually thriving in the hostile environment.

Because the Namib receives very little rain, and the heat quickly evaporates surface moisture, the indigenous plants have evolved many methods of storing water. Some species have developed small leaves (thus reducing the rate of transpiration and increasing the rate of cooling), some have leaves that drop off, and others have no leaves at all.

The mesembryanthemums have converted their leaves into water-storage tanks enclosed in leathery skin, while the Ammocharis lilies hoard their precious water supply in large underground bulbs.

One of the most common Namib plants, *Arthraerua leubnitziae,* lives through long periods of drought by shrinking. But one of the most fascinating survival methods is employed by the so-called 'ephemerals', which pack their entire life cycle into the brief spell of good growing conditions following a rare desert shower. The seeds lie dormant during the dry conditions, but suddenly spring up with the rain, burst into bloom, and release new seeds — all in a matter of days.

Above: Plumpudding Island, one of more than three dozen guano islands along the Namibia coast. Guano, a valuable fertiliser, is deposited by the large colonies of seabirds – mainly cormorant, gannet and penguin – that nest on the islands. Since these birds live on fish and other sea creatures, their droppings are rich in phosphorus and nitrogen. **Opposite page:** A colony of Cape fur seals frolic along the coast of the southern Namib. The male reaches sexual maturity at two years (three years for the female) but only becomes a fully active herd bull three or four years later.

Fenestraria rhopalophylla (window plant).

Lithops (stone plant).

Mesembryanthemum (vygie).

Sarcocaulon crassicaule (Bushman's candle).

THE SCORPION THAT SQUIRTS ITS POISON

Parabuthus villosus, one of Southern Africa's largest and most venomous scorpions, with its paralysed victim. This species produces a venom sufficiently powerful to kill a child, and has the ability to squirt venom for a considerable distance when alarmed: if struck in the eyes, its victim may be blinded.

Scorpions are arachnids, not insects, although both are arthropods. They have a capacity for survival under very harsh conditions. Desert species of the genus *Parabuthus* are so resilient that they may be kept alive in a laboratory without food or water for as long as 12 months — as long as they are given a good meal at the start!

Although a relatively primitive life form, the scorpion is lethally efficient. Its large, claw-like pedipalps hold its prey while the segmented tail is brought over the head and down to deliver the sting. The two poison-glands in the bulbous sting are surrounded by a muscular sheath which is compressed to inject the venom

through two tiny openings near the sharp tip, the dead or paralysed prey is chewed with the chelicerae (or jaws), and the soft parts are consumed in semi-liquid form.

The female scorpion, which is generally larger than the male, gives birth to 40 or more live young — each a colourless miniature of the adult, and already equipped with a gland charged with venom. The moment they are born, she gently lifts them with her pincers and places them in rows on her back, where they remain for some weeks while the mother feeds them with partly chewed portions of her prey.

All Southern African scorpions belong to one of two families. First there are the *Scorpionidae*, which have large pincers and small tails. This family relies mainly on its pincers for catching prey, and its tail sting is not especially dangerous. The second family is that of the *Buthidae*, or 'stinging scorpions', which have relatively small pincers but a larger tail and a far more potent sting.

Area 1. Because man has interfered so little with the land here, virtually the whole of the Sperrgebiet is an unspoilt wilderness and conservators see it as one of the most interesting areas in Namibia.

In spite of the harsh surroundings, brown hyena, black-backed jackal, gemsbok, springbok and ostrich seem to thrive in the area (as do seal colonies along the coast). One herd of gemsbok has turned opportunist and

292

each night steals into the outskirts of Oranjemund to graze on the diamond town's well-watered lawns.

Some tour operators want the authorities to open the Sperrgebiet to tourism (the dramatic sea arch at Bogenfels and Atlas Bay seal colony are great attractions in themselves) but it seems unlikely that any major concessions will be granted for as long as diamonds are more important to the economy.

Above, top: The kokerboom (quiver tree) of Namibia was first recorded by Simon van der Stel in 1685; he noted that San made quivers from its branches. **Above, below** The black-backed gull is primarily a coastal seabird and is rarely seen far out to sea, though it frequently follows fishing trawlers and other vessels in the hope of picking up scraps of food.

A land God made in anger

San hunters wandering through Namibia's harsh and inhospitable interior used to say: 'When God made this land, he must have been very angry.' Yet even in his anger God gave the parched land great beauty. Much of Namibia's stark grandeur still remains intact in a select group of public nature reserves and indeed in many private reserves where man's influence has been little felt.

The largest public nature reserve in the central interior is attached to Hardap Recreation Resort north-west of Mariental, which is also the home of the state-run Freshwater Fish Research Institute. Daan Viljoen Game Park – fascinating for both its flora and fauna – is 24 km from Windhoek, and the capital also has a small nature garden close to Namibia's government buildings. Gross-Barmen Hot Springs and Von Bach Recreation Resort are beauty spots close to Okahandja.

Tsaobis Leopard Nature Reserve is privately-run in the Chuos Mountains, 140 km west of Windhoek.

Daan Viljoen Game Park

It is difficult to say who appreciates Daan Viljoen more – the people of Windhoek, or visitors from outside. Windhoek's inhabitants see the park as a playground on their doorstep and flock to it over weekends and during school holidays. Out-of-town visitors generally stay at the rest camp in preference to hotels in the city. They sleep in comfortable rondavels, eat in a well-run restaurant, go game spotting in the reserve and cool off in a large swimming-pool.

The Daan Viljoen Game Park is set in the Khomas Hochland, a topsy-turvy world of rolling hills and deep ravines. The reserve covers just under 4000 ha at the eastern end of the range, and not the least of its attractions is a fine view of Windhoek – particularly impressive at sunset. With the capital so close, it is no surprise that the park's name honours the former Administrator of South West Africa, who was largely responsible for its establishment.

From a conservation point of view, Daan Viljoen is very important because it is the only nature reserve in the Khomas Hochland which is classified as one of the 15 main vegetation zones in Namibia. In places the hills support thorn scrub but for the most part they are open and grassy with a few scattered trees. The ravines have richer vegetation, and so does the Augeigas, a perennial stream that runs along the eastern boundary of the park and is dammed and landscaped at the rest camp.

Daan Viljoen's game population is made up of the species that were always common in the Khomas Hochland: mountain zebra, kudu, gemsbok, eland, red hartebeest, blue wildebeest and a few springbok. The animals roam all over the park – even in the fenced rest camp, which they enter by night to graze on the well-watered lawns. As a tourist officer reports: 'Go for a midnight stroll outside your bungalow, and you're likely to run into an eland or a zebra.'

Tourist roads are confined to a mere 600 ha of the park and the remainder is a wilderness closed to vehicles, not least because gradients

Above: Ostriches wander among the rondavels at the rest camp in the Daan Viljoen Game Park, near Windhoek. Visitors have become used to seeing a variety of animals in the camp, which is built around a dam in the rolling hills of the Khomas Hochland. Because no large predators occur in the area, visitors are encouraged to explore the park on foot. As in most reserves, there is a prohibition on domestic pets, and dogs must be left in kennels at the entrance gates. **Left:** Visitors enjoy the lush surroundings of the rest camp at Daan Viljoen.

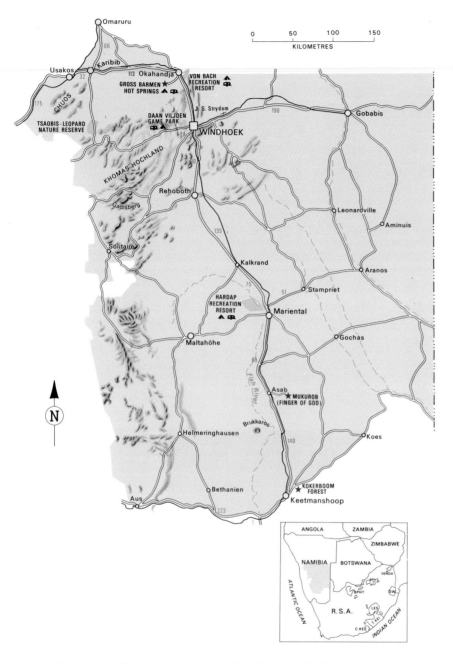

DAAN VILJOEN AT A GLANCE

When to go The park is open year-round, but the best time to visit is during the period from December to May. Try to avoid school holidays and long weekends. The park's gates open at sunrise and close at sunset, seven days a week. However, tourists staying in the park are allowed to enter and leave until 10 p.m.

Reservations and information Enquiries and applications for accommodation should be addressed to The Director of Nature Conservation, Reservations, Private Bag 13267, Windhoek 9000, Namibia (telephone Windhoek 3-6975/6/7/8).

Getting there The park is reached from a turn-off on the secondary road from Windhoek through the Khomas Hochland to Swakopmund, 21 km from Windhoek. From the turn-off there is a 3 km drive to the gates of the resort.

Accommodation Daan Viljoen's rest camp has two-bedded rondavels equipped with washbasins and kitchenettes. Bedding and towels are supplied, but not cooking utensils, crockery or cutlery. There are communal ablution blocks with hot and cold water. The large caravan and camping site has open-air kitchens and ablution blocks.

Eating and drinking A licensed restaurant serves meals and refreshments and a kiosk next door serves cold drinks and confectionery. There are braai facilities beside the bungalows, in the caravan and camping site, and at picnic places above the Augeigas Dam.

Getting around A 6,5 km gravel road takes visitors through the prettiest parts of the park.
  Many paths cross the hills and ravines that make up most of the park, and visitors are encouraged to pick their own routes.

Special attractions Among the park's many attractions are the large swimming pool (at the rest camp), Augeigas Dam with its weeping willows and thatched 'umbrellas', a ruggedly beautiful setting of ravine and precipice, and a rich variety of shrubs, trees and other flora.

Wildlife The park accommodates eland, gemsbok, kudu, red hartebeest, blue wildebeest, mountain zebra and springbok. More than 200 bird species have been reported.

are too steep for most cars. Tourists are not restricted to their vehicles, however, and are free to wander throughout the park. Two short trails of 3 km and 9 km have been laid out for anyone wishing to explore further. Visitors who want a change from mammals can look out for the many species of birds that have been reported in the park – among them the rare Damara rockjumper, Monteiro's hornbill and the beautiful crimson-breasted shrike, sometimes known as the 'Reichsvogel' because its red, black and white feathers recall the colours of Imperial Germany.

Gross-Barmen Hot Springs

In 1977 this handsome spa was unveiled on the site of an old Rhenish mission station, 24 km south-west of Okahandja. Visitors are able to pamper themselves in a large thermal pool enclosed in a glass-walled hall. The spa's modern camp offers a restaurant, a shop, fully furnished bungalows and a caravan and camping site.

There are long walks along a river bed running past the caravan and camping site, and rambles among stony koppies that overlook the resort may lead to encounters with baboon, warthog, or even a kudu or two. Gross-

Barmen's reed-surrounded dam is considered a must for bird-watchers.

The resort, reached from a turn-off 1 km south of Okahandja, is open throughout the year. Enquiries and applications for accommodation should be addressed to The Director of Nature Conservation, Reservations, Private Bag 13267, Windhoek 9000, Namibia (telephone Windhoek 3-6975/6/7/8).

Hardap Recreation Resort

One of Namibia's most unusual 'bird paradises' consists of groups of dead camelthorn trees half submerged in Hardap Dam. The trees died when the dam filled with water in 1963, but their branches have not rotted and they provide safe nesting sites for hundreds of white-breasted cormorants – the largest of the marine cormorants – that thrive on the dam's large fish population. Some of the trees hold as many as eight or nine nests – untidy constructions of twigs on which the breeding cormorants balance precariously as they dry their wings in the breeze.

Although fishermen have been known to (illegally) destroy this cormorant's eggs, supposing it to be responsible for the decimation of the fish population in dams and lakes, detailed studies have found that the white-breasted cormorant eats nearly five times as many parasites as healthy fish.

Because cormorants catch large numbers of the bottom-feeding mud mullet (rarely caught on a hook), they actually help the fisherman by making place for other species of fish. While it is widely believed that this cormorant eats more than twice its own weight in fish every day, it in fact consumes only 20-25 per cent of its body weight a day. Off the coast, it eats fish such as hottentot and steenvis.

The trees are within a 25 000 ha nature reserve surrounding the dam, though most of the reserve is on the south side, across the water from the smart recreation resort that falls within its boundaries. The resort came into being in 1964 and the reserve was proclaimed four years later, the result of the merging of several farms. Today the reserve accommodates healthy populations of kudu, gemsbok, red hartebeest, eland, mountain zebra and springbok, and also a number of cheetah that wreak havoc among its ostrich population.

Ironically, although Hardap is one of Namibia's best-known resorts, the nature reserve is unfamiliar to the large majority of visitors. Tens of thousands stay at the recreation resort each year but very few of them bother to tour the area that holds game. 'Most of them are more interested in sport,' said a tourist officer. 'We have tennis courts, a swimming-pool, fishing and boating. We tell people that there is game across the water, but not many go to see it.'

The road to the reserve runs along the top of the dam wall, and once inside the game fence it enters a world of stone and thorn, a challenging landscape of coned koppies and deep dongas created by heavy floods of the past. The road takes visitors on an 82 km circle through the reserve, and from a look-out high on a plateau they may see the great dam as a ribbon of blue on the horizon. The more adventurous leave their cars there and blaze their own hiking trail through the reserve to reach the dam's shores.

Above: *Cyphostemma juttae* (wild grape) is an attractive and hardy succulent which produces its brightly coloured clusters of 'grapes' near the end of summer. The papery skin around the thick trunk peels off continuously as the plant grows. **Right:** A black-headed heron peers across tall grass near the Hardap Dam, haven for a large variety of waterfowl. **Below:** The armoured ground cricket (*koringkriek*), a nocturnal long-horned grasshopper found throughout Southern Africa. Although non-poisonous, this insect can inflict a painful bite.

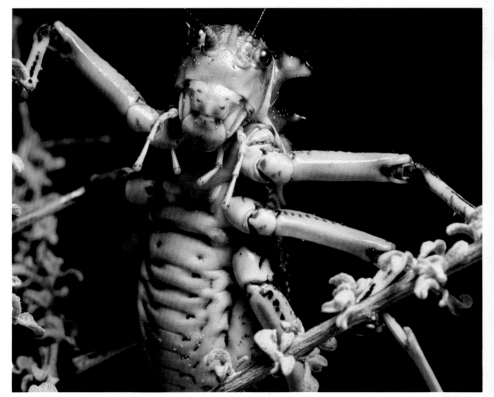

A DEMOLISHED DEITY

The spectacular rock formation known as 'Mukurob' – popularly known as 'the finger of God' – was one of Namibia's most evocative natural symbols. A vertical column of sandstone and shale strata, it stood 34 m high and perched precariously on a pedestal of Karoo slate. Nature had gradually formed it in the course of some 60 million years. Then on 8 December 1988 it was instantly toppled from its throne – probably by a strong wind and the long-term effects of creeping erosion, though some have linked the collapse to an earthquake on the other side of the world, in the USSR. Great was Mukurob's fall!

Etymologists disagree with the popular translation 'finger of God'. To the ancient Quena, or Khoikhoi, Mukurob (accent on the second syllable: mukoorob) was quite simply a term for the 'creator' or 'highest god'. It stood at the centre of Quenaland and was a religious symbol of enormous significance to the local people.

To view the shattered remains of this demolished deity, turn east onto a gravel road at Asab, on the highway between Mariental and Keetmanshoop, and drive for 24 km. In 1955 the bulbous 'finger' was declared a national monument.

Tsaobis-Leopard Nature Reserve

During 1969 a Swiss conservationist, Dr August Juchli, established a private game park on 35 000 ha in the Chuos Mountains south of Karibib. He began to breed and study the leopard, and at the same time encouraged other species, including giraffe, kudu, blue wildebeest, red hartebeest and springbok. Today there are between 25 and 30 leopard in the reserve, but visitors are warned that they are elusive and hard to spot. Visitors may go on nocturnal drives in hopes of seeing them.

One of Tsaobis-Leopard's special delights is horseback riding through the mountains, and there are horses for hire. Otherwise visitors are taken out in 4-wheel-drive vehicles (the roads are somewhat primitive, and not suitable for ordinary cars), or simply laze by the swimming pool. The park's attractive rest camp offers air-conditioned bungalows with separate living and sleeping quarters. Enquiries and applications for accommodation should be made direct to Tsaobis-Leopard Nature Reserve, P.O. Box 143, Karibib 9000, Namibia (telephone Karibib 1304).

To reach Tsaobis-Leopard (it is open throughout the year), drive to a turn-off 68 km south of Karibib on the road between Karibib and Anschluss. The camp is 10 km from the turn-off.

Von Bach Recreation Resort

Like Hardap Dam to the south, the attractive Sartorius von Bach storage dam just outside Okahandja is popular with aquatic sport enthusiasts, including yachtsmen, waterskiers and fishermen.

There are several two-bedded huts (no bedding is provided) as well as caravan and camping sites for overnight visitors. There are no cooking facilities, except braai places. Picnic sites are available for day campers and there are communal ablution blocks. Fish in the dam include blue kurper, large-mouth bass and small-mouth yellowfish. Fishing permits may be obtained at the resort office.

The resort is 4 285 ha in extent and harbours numerous kudu as well as eland, mountain zebra and springbok. Von Bach Dam is reached from a turn-off 1 km south of Okahandja on the road to Windhoek. It is open year-round, from sunrise to sunset.

Windhoek Nature Garden

The grounds of Namibia's government buildings feature a 5 ha nature garden that has a special place in the affections of Windhoek's inhabitants. The garden once held a number of large antelope, but they did so much damage to the vegetation that it was decided to remove them.

There was a storm of protest from Windhoek, so as a compromise part of the garden was restocked with small antelope, such as duiker, impala and springbok.

Among the nature garden's rich variety of plants is a collection of succulents. In time, the authorities hope, the collection will represent all the flora of Namibia. Neither the flower collection nor the game enclosure is open to the public, but both can be viewed from a high terrace set above the perimeter fence.

THE REGAL KUDU AND HIS HAREM

Windhoek's Kaiserstrasse is graced by a life-size statue of a kudu bull – a species found in nearly every part of the territory. The kudu is especially common in the hilly interior and is well represented at Hardap and Daan Viljoen.

Once settled, kudu appear to have no interest in long-distance migration. Recently, however, two natural limiting factors – drought and rabies – greatly reduced their numbers, and thousands of kudu have died.

One characteristic of the species that still puzzles zoologists is the kudu's uneven sex balance. The birth ratio between bulls and cows is nearly even, but for reasons as yet unexplained a high proportion of bulls die young. Few reach extreme old age. Overall there are probably twice as many cows as bulls, and in some areas the ratio may be even greater. One possible explanation is that hunters shoot kudu bulls for their horns and tend to ignore the hornless cows – but this cannot be the sole reason for the phenomenon, since the imbalance is found even in areas where little hunting occurs.

Recent studies in the Cape and in Namibia suggest that kudu group themselves in three combinations – mixed groups of cows and young, breeding herds of one adult bull and several females, and bachelor groups consisting of young males. Bulls over the age of five years tend to restrict themselves to 'home ranges' of a few square kilometres – not really territories, because the ranges of several bulls may overlap and they seem happy to co-exist.

A herd of cows moves through the ranges of a number of solitary bulls, and in the rutting season each bull does his best to win the cows' attentions, though usually he does not prevent them from moving on to another bull if they choose to do so.

However, while the cows are with him he may be challenged by a rival bull, and that is when his magnificent horns come into play. If he is not careful, his horns will become inextricably entangled with his rival's – and both will die. Like most fighting in the animal kingdom, however, threats are 90 per cent of the game. Actual clashes and fight-related deaths are relatively rare.

Above: The Cape wolf snake has sharp wolf-like teeth which enable it to maintain a firm grip on smooth-scaled lizard prey. **Left:** The distinctively coloured Cape white-eye, found in small flocks throughout Southern Africa, is one of the most melodious contributors to the 'morning chorus'. It lives mainly on small insects, berries and soft fruit.

Mountains and a sea of sand

In 1965 the American space capsule *Gemini V* orbited the earth for eight days with astronauts Gordon Cooper and Pete Conrad at the controls. The men circled the globe 120 times and were able to take hundreds of remarkable photographs of its surface, some so detailed that they showed the wake of ships at sea and the course of roads and railways. One of the most revealing was taken from above the dry Kuiseb River, and scanned a large area of the central Namib Desert.

In the photograph, Walvis Bay's fine harbour appears as a hook of land grappling with the blue Atlantic to the west. About 48 km to the south, the shifting sandspit that closes Sandvis (known by some as Sandwich Harbour) is a faint ribbon of pink with a large lagoon trapped behind it. Wave after wave of red dunes run parallel with the coast, forming a sea of sand that stretches 120 km inland. Yet to the north, the dunes are cut off by the Kuiseb River and give way to gravel plains.

As the photograph showed, the Kuiseb bisects the Namib to sharply demarcate the dune sea and gravel plains. Periodic floods washed away the northern tentacles of dunes before the

sand had a chance to 'walk' across the riverbed and overwhelm the other bank. Today the lower Kuiseb is a part of the Namib-Naukluft Park, which contains vast areas of the desert as well as the Naukluft Mountains, stronghold of Hartmann's Mountain Zebra. The park's total area is 49 768 square kilometres. The richest vegetation is to be found in the beds of the Kuiseb and Swakop rivers: even the dunes support several species of plants.

Because the park is so large it can be divided into three areas. The Namib section in the north includes the beds of the Swakop and Kuiseb rivers, Welwitschiavlakte (a home of the plant *Welwitschia mirabilis*), Sandvis and the Kuiseb River Canyon.

Conservationists have expressed concern at the amount of prospecting that occurs in the Namib between the Swakop and Kuiseb rivers. Although the prospecting grants are very old they are still legal – and there is little the authorities can do to stop it. The resulting damage to the environment, says one official, is readily visible to passing tourists.

The sand section from the Kuiseb southwards includes the dramatic Sesriem Canyon and Sos-

susvlei – which lies among the world's highest dunes. The Naukluft section, once a separate reserve, has some spectacular mountain formations and beautiful valleys with perennial springs. To the west of the park lies Walvis Bay, with its variety of bird life in the bird sanctuary and at the lagoon which lies on the outskirts of the town.

Namib-Naukluft Park

Although Namibia's largest park was only proclaimed in 1979, most of its components have been nature reserves for much longer. The Namib section of the north was proclaimed 'Game Reserve 3' by Governor Friedrich von Lindequist in 1907, which makes it a contemporary of Etosha National Park. The dune sea of the south was part of the Sperrgebiet for half a century before being incorporated in the park. Naukluft in the east was originally a farm that was bought by Namibia's Administration in 1960 to provide a refuge for mountain zebra.

The administration steadily enlarged 'Naukluft Mountain Zebra Park' by acquiring more farms, eventually linking the reserve with the dunes of the Namib by opening a 30 km-wide

Left: Goanikontes, an oasis on the Swakop River (47 km from the town of Swakopmund). The oasis, situated in a deep ravine flanked by dark-coloured hills, is a popular picnicking and camping spot for the inhabitants of Swakopmund. **Above left:** 'The dancing white lady'. This unusual spider, seen here digging a burrow, owes its name to its habit of rearing up aggressively when threatened. However, it is possibly even better known for its method of descending a Namib dune: it folds its legs inwards and launches itself

down the slope like a tiny, furry cartwheel. The dancing white lady hunts mainly during the night – sometimes capturing prey larger than itself. **Above right:** The sidewinding adder (*Bitis peringueyi*) has developed an unusual way of crossing the loose sand of the Namib, moving in a series of thrusts which leave the distinctive trail of parallel lines. This small adder can achieve a surprising speed with its seemingly awkward method of locomotion.

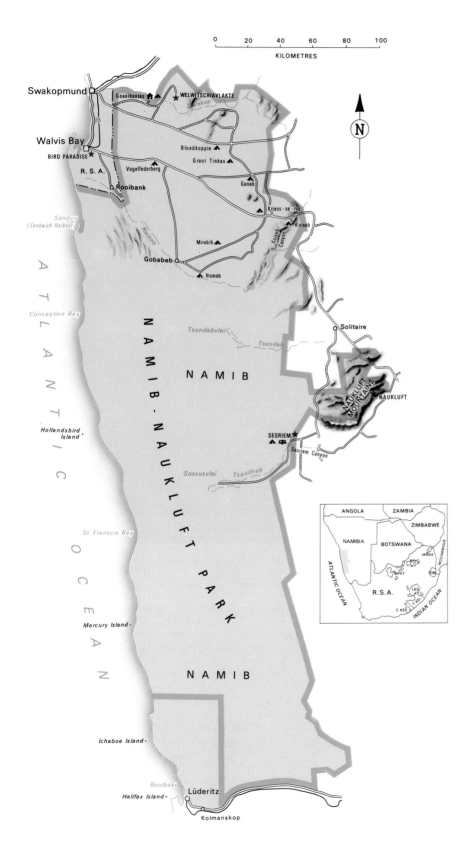

corridor. Mountain zebra and gemsbok can now migrate freely from the high plateau that tops the Naukluft to the spreading plains of the west. North and south of the corridor, the Naukluft is linked to the rest of the park by the Tsondab and Tsauchab rivers, which have their origin in the mountains and are eventually trapped among the dunes.

The rivers end at Tsondabvlei and Sossusvlei respectively, both clay floor pans in a cul-de-sac of sand that at Sossusvlei towers more than 350m above the river bed. Geographers believe that the rivers once flowed to the sea, and there is evidence that the Tsondab's water still seeps a considerable distance through the sand to emerge at Conception Bay on the coast. Tsondabvlei has a rich growth of trees which provide a haven for lappet-faced vultures, and for this reason it is closed to all visitors except scientific researchers.

Sossusvlei provides visitors with their closest view of the Namib's desert sands. At different times of day the dunes appear ivory-white, golden, ochre, orange and maroon. The road to Sossusvlei follows the dry riverbed from Sesriem ('six-thong') Canyon, so named because early travellers found that to draw water from the bottom with a bucket they needed to knot together six harness thongs (osrieme).

In spite of the rivers and the corridor, the Naukluft is inevitably the incongruity in the Namib's mélange of ecosystems. One geologist has described it as 'a mass of rock that once formed the top of a range of mountains. But somehow it slipped sideways and travelled at least 70km to reach its present position, riding over softer formations or crumpling them up and pushing them from behind. You can see the folds in the rock.'

A small campsite at the Naukluft is the starting point of the 120km (eight-day) Namib-Naukluft Hiking Trail and shorter alternatives. On winter mornings zebra can be seen sunning themselves on the slopes, standing broadside to the sun, whereas in warmer conditions they almost always face away from the sun.

Dr Eugene Joubert, one of Namibia's most respected biologists, spent three years studying the species. There was a practical reason for the zebra's preferred stance, he explained. Writing in the 1974 SWA Annual, Dr Joubert made the point that dark surfaces absorbed more heat than lighter-coloured areas.

A Hartmann's zebra standing broadside on displayed a body surface with a light to dark ratio of 1:3, whereas the ratio changed to 3:1 when it faced away, thus reducing the exposure of areas which absorbed the most heat. 'This fact,' wrote Dr Joubert, 'combined with the difference in total body surface when viewed laterally and posteriorly, makes the orientation of body surfaces to physical stimuli an impor-

tant factor in the adaptation of the Hartmann zebra to its environment.'

Dr Joubert made equally fascinating discoveries about the zebra's social life. In an article in the 1972 *SWA Annual*, he described a typical family unit, consisting of an adult dominant stallion, one or more mares and their foals. The stallion was nominally the head of the group's social organisation, wrote Dr Joubert, but played no conspicuous role in the daily social organisation of the family unit.

'His role is mainly directed outwards, protecting his family group against predators and other encroaching stallions. Any one in the family group – most often it is a mare – gives the alarm when danger threatens. The male then usually takes up a position between the source of danger and the rest of the family group.

'When the family group moves away the dominant stallion shows a tendency to bring up the rear. The advantage of this behaviour to the survival of the species is clear. It allows the mares who are important for breeding purposes a greater margin of safety.'

The pecking order is most obvious at a dust-bath, where the mares take turns to wallow in strict order of seniority. But in spite of the occasional bad feeling, it takes more than an encroaching stallion to split the family. 'Once I watched a young stallion make a successful challenge for a group of four mares. He forced out the stallion who had formed the family but was only interested in two of the mares and tried to lose the others. They refused to leave and he ended up having to accept all four,' says Joubert.

Namib-Naukluft: Gobabeb
The footprints occasionally seen in the canyon could have been made by Topnaar Khoikhoi who have lived in the river valley downstream for generations. These tribesmen farm goats and cattle and form a permanent population in the Namib-Naukluft Park.

Their numbers are not great, but their stamp on the Namib is indelible. Part of their rich heritage is evident in the scores of curious place names like Gobabeb, 'the place of the fig tree'. They refer to the moaning west wind as 'soo-oop wa'.

In 1963 Gobabeb was selected as the site for a permanent research station, as it has access to the central Namib's three main ecosystems – dunes, riverbeds and gravel plains.

Today the Namib Research Institute, with its small staff of scientists and conservationists, attracts researchers in many fields from all over the world. They live here in bungalows and caravans clustered around a block containing offices and laboratories.

Right: A white-backed vulture, the most common vulture in Namibia. This species builds its nest in a tree, laying only one egg, which is incubated by both parents for about two months. Like other vultures, this (summer-nesting) species does not require rain as a stimulus for breeding. The adult vulture is distinguished by its white back and wing-coverts, which are darker than the widely spread Cape vulture.

Left: Flamingoes make their graceful way over the tall dunes at Sandvis. These beautiful birds, with their red and black wings and pink bills (tipped with black), provide an unforgettable sight as they soar in formation over the desert. Sandvis was visited twice by ships of the Dutch East India Company in the 1670s, and centuries later (between 1904 and 1906) was used to route smuggled arms to Khoikhoi and Herero rebels.

There may be more than 30 people living at Gobabeb at any one time. Perhaps ten will be scientists – geologists studying the dunes, archaeologists looking for signs of ancient man, ornithologists, botanists, zoologists observing reptiles and, above all, entomologists, there to examine the rich insect life of the three ecosystems. The others include research assistants assigned to help the individual scientists and two nature conservationists who man a significant weather station for Namibia's administration.

At the heart of this community is the Desert Ecological Research Unit, established in 1966 through the foresight of a famous Austrian entomologist, Dr Charles Koch, and funded by South Africa's Council for Scientific and Industrial Research (CSIR) and the Transvaal Museum, which share responsibility for the station with Namibia's Department of Agriculture and Nature Conservation. The unit's director, American-born ecologist Mary Seely, did much to make Gobabeb world famous. In the past its growing reputation attracted curious tourists who seriously disrupted the research work in progress, with the unfortunate result that casual visitors have had to be banned.

Virtually every day at Gobabeb, some of the residents will climb on to motor tricycles with especially wide tyres (these help to spread the load on loose terrain) and zoom down the hill to the dry riverbed, across the grey sand at the bottom and up into the red dunes on the other side. There they will scatter to work with the astonishingly rich bounty of insect and animal life that is the Namib's chief treasure – life in miniature, so varied and abundant that scientists regard the Namib dunes as one of the most fascinating ecosystems on the planet.

In many ways, the sand environment has more in common with the sea than with conventional solid ground.

When disturbed by the wind, the sand flows and ripples like water, and the cloud of sand 'smoke' sometimes blown from the top of a dune is like a cloud of spray.

Many desert creatures have webbed feet or paddles that help them 'swim' through the sand, and even the food chain that supports them is like the chain in the sea: wind-blown detritus takes the place of plankton, primary feeders (insects) eat the detritus, and predators eat the primary feeders.

From the west comes a breeze cooled by the Benguela Current off the coast, and with it frequent fogs that creep inland and blanket the dunes. The fog brings moisture that in the right conditions condenses in tiny drops on detritus, sand grains, the sparse vegetation, even the desert creatures, and many of them have evolved special methods of capturing it. The most inventive are four species of beetle.

NAMIB-NAUKLUFT AT A GLANCE

When to go The park is open year-round, but beware of high temperatures in summer (October to March). The Naukluft section is open to only one group of campers at a time and a group must consist of at least three and not more than 40 people. The same rules apply at Sossusvlei, except that more than one group is admitted at a time. Otherwise there is no limit on access to the park. The Namib Research Institute at Gobabeb may not be visited without special permission.

Permits and information If you stick to the proclaimed main roads you may drive through the park without a permit. If you want to see more, apply for a permit from the Director of Nature Conservation, Reservations, Private Bag 13267, Windhoek 9000, Namibia (telephone Windhoek 3-6975/6/7/8). You may also apply to the Department of Agriculture and Nature Conservation in Swakopmund.

The Department issues a sketch-map of the Namib section of the park: ask for it in Swakopmund or Windhoek.

Getting there From Windhoek, the most popular approach is by the main road to Swakopmund, but a more scenic route crosses the Gamsberg Pass before continuing through the park to Walvis Bay. To reach Naukluft and the southern dunes, drive by way of Solitaire (249 km from Windhoek), then south on the road to Sesriem.

Accommodation There is no permanent accommodation in the park (though Walvis Bay and Swakopmund are close) but there are a number of official overnight camping sites equipped with picnic tables and toilets. The sites include Homeb (in the bed of the Kuiseb River, 20 km up river from Gobabeb); Ganab (near a watering point that is a good place to watch game); Welwitschiavlakte

(best known for the fascinating *Welwitschia mirabilis*); Naukluft (available only to those with reservations) and Sesriem (the most 'organised' caravan and camping site).

Eating and drinking Take all the food and water (extremely important) you will need, and emergency supplies in case your vehicle breaks down. You should also pack your own firewood (you are not allowed to collect firewood in the park).

Getting around Petrol is available at Sesriem and Solitaire but otherwise motorists should fill up at Walvis Bay or Swakopmund.

The 120 km Namib-Naukluft Hiking Trail takes eight days, although a shorter four-day route is also available. Hiking is permitted between 1 March and 31 October. Groups must comprise a minimum of three and a maximum of twelve persons. Only water, toilet facilities and basic shelter are provided. Bookings may be made up to 18 months in advance. Day trails through the Naukluft include the seven-hour Waterkloof Day Trail and the five-hour Olive Day Trail.

The four-hour Welwitschia Drive can be explored using a brochure, which corresponds with numbered beacons at various points of interest along the route.

Fishing Angling spots may be found down the coast between Walvis Bay and Sandvis (but you will need a 4-wheel-drive vehicle to reach them). Obtain permits to enter the coastal area of the park from filling stations in Walvis Bay.

Wildlife Gemsbok, springbok and ostrich are the most visible species on the gravel plains. Mountain zebra abound in the Naukluft. In the dunes and the Kuiseb, watch for beetles and listen for the barking gecko at sundown.

Far left: A river frog in the Namib-Naukluft Park. Frogs are easily the most numerous of land vertebrates, and they are found in virtually every part of Southern Africa – including mountaintops, deserts, forests and sea shores. **Left:** The blister beetle's striking colours serve as a warning to predators: its body contains the poisonous chemical cantharadin. This specimen, perched on a nara plant, is coated with droplets of condensed fog. **Right:** Hartmann's Mountain Zebra in the Namib-Naukluft Park.

THE ENTERPRISING ANT

Ants of the species *Camponotus detritus.*

Studies of desert ants have revealed that they are one of the most abundant and ecologically important groups of animals. In fact in almost all terrestrial ecosystems, social insects such as ants, wasps, bees and termites are frequently the ecologically dominant animals.

It is a remarkable but little-known fact that in terms of biomass and food consumption the social insects exceed all the vertebrates (mammals, reptiles and birds) put together. In other words the weight of all the lions, elephants, antelope, rodents, lizards, snakes, eagles, owls and sparrows, to mention but a few of the vertebrates that occur in a natural ecosystem such as Etosha Pan, would fall short of that of all the social insects in that area! The possible importance of ants in the Namib desert has resulted in two scientists devoting their sojourn at Gobabeb to the study of ants.

It has been discovered that the ant known as *Camponotus detritus* is the predominant species in the dunes. It is a large ant and lives in colonies of up to 20 000 individuals. This ant is found at the base of sand dunes, where it spends much of its time climbing the typically sparse vegetation of that zone (usually grass) in search of scale insects. These insects secrete a sugar-rich fluid known as honeydew, and this forms the ant's staple diet.

It is an aggressive species of ant, sometimes biting and squirting formic acid at creatures which happen to disturb it. Excavating nests to determine the number of individuals is consequently an uncomfortable experience for the investigating scientist. The ant is also highly aggressive towards rival colonies of its own species and stray ants are frequently waylaid and killed, literally by being torn to pieces.

Many ant species have been found on the gravel plains. Up to 11 species live together in any one area and scientists are trying to discover how so many species co-exist and find sufficient food in this apparently barren and harsh habitat, where little vegetation survives the long periods of drought.

Ant nests are located by setting out bait and then following ants as they carry it back to their nests. These nests are then marked to enable the scientists to make detailed observations of ant behaviour.

Three of the species belong to one genus, *Lepidochora* (sometimes known as 'flying saucers'). Normally they remain below the surface of the dune until sunset, when they emerge to search for detritus, but on a foggy morning they appear in great numbers and plough a narrow trench – up to a metre in length – in the damp sand. On either side is a ridge which catches extra moisture and the beetles then extract this moisture from the damp ridges. The beetles bide their time until droplets form, then move down the trench and gather the moisture.

The most celebrated Namib beetle is *Onymacris unguicularis*, which has been described as a living condensation unit. During the night it shelters in the slip-face of a dune, but on a foggy morning it climbs slowly to the top and virtually does a handstand, with its head down and its back near-vertical and facing the wind to collect moisture. The fog condenses and little droplets roll down the beetle's back, eventually reaching its mouth. Then the beetle drinks its fill.

Namib-Naukluft: Hiking Trail
The Naukluft is one of the most varied areas of Namibia and this trail takes you through its mountain passes and deep ravines, where you will discover huge caves and refreshing perennial streams.

The eight-day trail covers 120 km but there are also seven- and four-day trails. Hiking is only permitted between 1 March and 31 October because of soaring summer temperatures, and groups must consist of a minimum of three and maximum of 12 people. For more information and reservations contact the Director of Nature Conservation, Private Bag 13267, Windhoek 9000 (telephone Windhoek 3-6975/6/7/8).

Namib-Naukluft: Kuiseb River Canyon
About 70 km north-west of the Naukluft is another geological phenomenon, the great canyon of the Kuiseb River. Like the Fish River in the south, the Kuiseb must once have been far more powerful than it is today – it has

gouged a deep trough in the soft rock of the interior plateau. Seen from above, the inside of the canyon is a bewildering hotch-potch of domed hills and long ridges that enshrine a kaleidoscope of eroded sediments. Far below, the present river bed meanders along the bottom as a narrow ribbon of sand and vegetation.

The canyon, with walls so broken and precipitous that there are few tracks to the bottom, could hardly be more desolate. At the outbreak of the Second World War, two German geologists named Henno Martin and Hermann Korn decided to use the loneliness to their advantage. If they stayed in Windhoek, they reasoned, they might well be interned as aliens. By hiding in the desert, they could live as they liked while the world went mad around them.

In his book, *The Sheltering Desert*, Henno Martin tells how they loaded a truck with petrol and supplies and set off on a circuitous route to the canyon, hoping to confuse possible pursuers. Once there, they found to their surprise that carp had populated a shallow pool in the riverbed, and deduced that floods had washed them from sources far upstream. They located a rock overhang high up the canyon wall which they named 'Carp Cliff' in recognition of their good fortune. With their few possessions dispersed about the hideaway, they planted vegetables beside the pool and went out hunting for the pot.

For more than two years the two men lived as Robinson Crusoes of the desert, surviving off the land and its wildlife and facing drought, flood, hunger and illness with equanimity. A radio kept them abreast of the latest war news, but throughout they were nagged by the worry that the authorities would come looking for them. They went to elaborate lengths to construct traps for trucks (nearly falling victim with their own vehicle). Twice the resourceful fugitives changed their abode to make detection even more difficult for their pursuers.

The nastiest moment of the long sojourn came when they found fresh 'Man Friday' footprints in the sand of the riverbed. They were certain the intruders had spotted their vegetable patch, and were sure they would be reported, but then realised the strangers must have passed by night, and could not have seen anything. In the end Korn fell seriously ill, and Martin persuaded a farmer to take him to Windhoek. Martin wanted to remain in the desert, but Korn believed his friend could not survive alone, and revealed his whereabouts to the police.

Namib-Naukluft: Welwitschia Drive

This drive through Namib-Naukluft Park's Welwitschia Plains lets you discover fascinating specimens of this unusual plant. To get there turn off the tarred Swakopmund-Karibib road (B2), just beyond the Martin Luther steam

THE NARA PLANT

Of all the intriguing items in the Namib's natural larder the one that has proved among the most precious to man since prehistoric times is surely the remarkable nara plant (*Acanthosicyos horrida*). Many tribesmen must have owed their survival at one time or another to the life-saving supply of water stored within its hard and knobbly outer shell.

The nara, a member of the pumpkin family, survives in the desert by sending its twisted root deep down through the sand to a hidden reserve of water, while up above, in the sunshine, the adult plant minimises the loss of water through evaporation by simply discarding its leaves – instead growing a multitude of thorns. It seems that these thorns (and the stems on which they grow) contain all the green chloroplast cells that the plant needs for photosynthesising its food from the carbon dioxide absorbed from the air.

This essential function is normally performed by the leaves. For much of the year the plant resembles a great tangle of grey-green barbed wire. But then yellow flowers spring from this bundle of thorns, to be followed in due course by the melon-like fruit. The fruit has the tough outer skin that is typical of its kind but inside it is a treasure of fairly bitter, watery pulp with a taste reminiscent of cucumbers. When dried, the plant's seeds have a taste much like that of almonds, and in good years a fair quantity is exported to overseas markets.

Top: Beetles of the genus *Lepidochora* dig a trench in the desert sand to catch condensed fog. **Above:** White pelicans in a Namib Desert coastal vlei. **Left:** The Kuiseb River Canyon. **Opposite above:** A variety of seabirds congregate at Walvis Bay Lagoon. About 50 000 greater and lesser flamingoes live in this sanctuary.

engine, into the Khomas Hochland road (C28) and then turn left at the sign for Goanikontes. Continue to the first of 13 numbered stone beacons. Four hours will leave you time to explore the area around all the beacons with the aid of a brochure. Permits are necessary and are obtained by writing to The Director of Nature Conservation, Private Bag 13267, Windhoek 9000 (telephone Windhoek 3-6975/6/7/8).

Sandvis

The Kuiseb leaves the park about 100 km downstream of the canyon and enters the enclave of Walvis Bay. There it loses itself in a wide sandy delta that very seldom flows with

water (though there is plenty beneath the surface). Geologists surmise that near the coast the dunes have gradually pushed the Kuiseb's delta towards the north. Yet some of the water continues to flow in the old bed beneath the dunes and eventually seeps to the surface at the edge of the great lagoon known as Sandvis.

In the 18th and 19th centuries, Sandvis was a well-known refuge on the dangerous Atlantic coast and many ships anchored there to shelter and refit after storms. According to an old story, a sailing ship carrying a great treasure was stranded in the lagoon in 1770 and abandoned to the sand. But in spite of frequent searches, neither the ship nor the treasure has

come to light. In the 19th century the bay was used by whalers, and from 1910 to 1947 it was exploited by a series of guano diggers.

The diggers exploited guano deposited on a group of small islands in the lagoon, but the entrance silted up periodically and the water inside became much shallower. Fewer fish entered the lagoon, with the result that the bird population decreased considerably.

In 1941, even before guano digging came to an end, Sandvis was made part of Game Reserve 3. The reserve was proclaimed to keep out independent fishermen.

Today the birds have even more privacy, for the entrance to the lagoon is fenced off from

the rest of the park. No vehicles are allowed, and this haven may only be visited on foot (with a permit). Flamingoes, pelicans, cormorants and more than 100 other species have the reed-encircled lagoon virtually to themselves, sharing it only with the occasional bird watcher.

Sandvis is also the breeding ground of vast numbers of fish. This attracts large flocks of birds that live off the young fish trapped in shallow waters by the outgoing tide.

Walvis Bay bird sanctuaries
Like the offshore Guano Islands along the west coast of Namibia, the Walvis Bay enclave (with an area of 1 124 km²) belongs to South Africa rather than Namibia.

The enclave is noted for its abundant bird life, of which 75 different species have been identified. Although shorebirds such as the white pelican, greater flamingo, curlew sandpiper, sand-plover and sanderling, as well as cormorants and gulls, are found all along the 30 km beach between Walvis Bay and Swakopmund, about 50 000 greater and lesser flamingoes and large flocks of pelicans can be found in the bird sanctuary known as the Walvis Bay Lagoon. This shallow wetland, which is surrounded in the east by the shifting sand dunes of the Namib Desert and in the west by the Atlantic Ocean, provides a natural habitat for a large variety of birds. It is situated within the township boundaries.

The second bird sanctuary in the enclave is known as the 'Bird Paradise' – a series of small lakes between the dunes adjoining the sewage disposal works.

The sanctuary's waterbeds, which are fringed by green grass, reeds and sandbanks, attract pelicans, flamingoes and various other species of birds. Several gravelled access roads have been built, enabling the visitor to approach within a few metres of the birds.

STUMBLING ACROSS THE WORLD'S ODDEST PLANT

In 1860 the explorers James Chapman, a photographer, and Thomas Baines, an artist, teamed up to travel from Walvis Bay to the Victoria Falls. They were not far up the sandy Swakop riverbed when they came upon a large plant which resembled nothing they had seen before.

The two men were fascinated: Baines promptly sat down to sketch the plant, and later sketched himself sketching, while Chapman set up a stereoscopic camera to capture a double image that through a special viewer would appear in three dimensions.

The plant was a *Welwitschia mirabilis*, hailed by Charles Darwin as 'the platypus of the Plant Kingdom'. This strange plant, which can live for a thousand years, produces only two leaves in its lifetime. They grow continuously, but the sun and wind-driven sand wither and shred the outer tips.

Botanists say the welwitschia should be found in a tropical rain forest rather than in the harsh Namib. However careful study has begun to reveal at least some of this plant's secrets: scientists have found that it can close its millions of leaf pores during the day, thus minimising evaporation. When the air cools, the pores re-open, and it is believed the leaves absorb moisture from fog in some way.

A plant dug up by Baines and Chapman weighed more than 100 kg and had a single long tap-root (though today's botanists say the roots are branched). Baines packed sketches and some specimen cones in a box and sent them to the coast to be forwarded to Kew Gardens in London. It was months before they arrived and by then the cones were rapidly decomposing. Even so they were eagerly examined by Sir William Hooker, director of the Gardens and Britain's leading botanist.

Hooker later described the plant as 'the most wonderful in a botanical point of view, that has been brought to light during the present century'. But he had a feeling that it might be the same as a specimen described in a letter he had just received from an Austrian-born botanist working in south-western Angola. Further enquiries showed that this was the case. The Austrian was Friedrich Welwitsch, and as he was technically the first to report the wonderful plant it was named *Welwitschia mirabilis* in his honour.

Coastal fog and mountain dew

Few places in Southern Africa sound more forbidding than the Skeleton Coast, that lonely stretch of shore between Swakopmund and the Kunene River on Namibia's border with Angola. The Skeleton Coast is the graveyard of many fine ships – and the men who sailed them. Relics of one wreck have been dated to the 15th century, and more recent victims include passenger liners.

Even a few aircraft have met their end on these shores, and few years pass without fresh additions to the grim list of casualties.

For the mariner, the Skeleton Coast is a nightmare, but it can also be a revelation for those who want to share nature's secrets. The barren coastline's mood seems to change continually as fog battles with sunshine and the wind plays games with the sand. Wide horizons delight the eye and the desert's solitude and tranquillity are treats for the soul. That is the essence of Skeleton Coast Park, a strip of land roughly 40 km deep that hugs the shore from the mouth of the Ugab River to the Kunene in the north.

Inland from the coast are the mountains of Damaraland and Kaokoland. Both regions are linked with the sea by dry riverbeds. Wildlife, including lion, elephant and black rhino, use the riverbeds as corridors when they move from east to west and back again in their search for food and water. This pattern of migration has probably continued unchanged for thousands of years. Kaokoland Nature Reserve covers 1-million hectares and was established to protect wildlife, such as rhino, from the poachers of Damaraland and Kaokoland. This vast reserve also contributes greatly to this area's ecological unity.

All of Damaraland is beautiful, but a few sites have special status. The Brandberg, with its thousands of ancient rock paintings is one of these. Twyfelfontein's rock engravings of rhi-

Above: Ancient San paintings on a cave wall on the slopes of the Brandberg. The curiously named 'White Lady' is the striding figure at centre right. Despite its name, the figure is thought to be neither white nor female. **Left:** The impressive Brandberg, on the eastern edge of the Namib Desert. Relics such as stone tools, grinding-stones, fragments of pottery and arrow heads have been found on the Brandberg, indicating that Stone Age man lived there. **Right:** A colourful display of blooms on the Namib edelweiss (*Helichrysum roseo-niveum*), an annual with thick, downy leaves.

DAMARALAND AT A GLANCE

Note: Damaraland's attractions are spread over a large area but many visitors devise a 'grand tour', basing themselves in Khorixas, which is the region's capital.

When to go The attractions may be visited all year round, but the months from November to March are extremely hot. The Khorixas rest camp is closed in December.

Reservations Enquiries and applications for bookings at Khorixas rest camp should be addressed to The Regional Manager, Corporation for Economic Development, P.O. Box 2, Khorixas 9000 (telephone Khorixas 1503).

Getting there Khorixas is in the middle of Damaraland and can be reached from the north, south, east and west. From Windhoek or the Etosha National Park, drive to Outjo, then 132km to the west. From Skeleton Coast, drive 238km east from Torra Bay. From Walvis Bay and Swakopmund, drive via Hentiesbaai and Uis. The rest camp is 4km from the centre of the town.

Accommodation Khorixas rest camp was opened in 1977 and offers self-contained rondavels with bedding and towels and a caravan and camping site with ablution block.

Eating and drinking The licensed restaurant at Khorixas rest camp serves meals and refreshments. Shops are few and far between in Damaraland and campers should stock up at Khorixas, Uis or Omaruru.

Getting around Most of Damaraland's roads are rudimentary at best, so visitors should prepare themselves for clouds of dust and long stretches of corrugations. Petrol can be obtained at Khorixas, Palmwag, Uis and Omaruru.

Wildlife Northern Damaraland still has a significant population of lion, elephant, black rhino, leopard, large antelope and mountain zebra, but in the southern farmlands only antelope and zebra are common.

no and other species are said to be among the finest in Africa. The Petrified Forest near Khorixas is also well worth a visit. Back on the coast, the Cape Cross Seal Reserve, situated 78km south of the Ugab River, is another appealing spot – though entrance is restricted for most of the year.

The Brandberg

The highest mountain in Namibia is Königstein, a 2573m peak among several others on the mighty plug of granite known as the Brandberg. Together with its spreading foothills, the Brandberg occupies a huge oval at the edge of the Namib, nearly 30km from west to east and 23km from north to south. The mountain leaps 2000m above the surrounding plains and

THE NAMIB'S PAINTED ROCKS

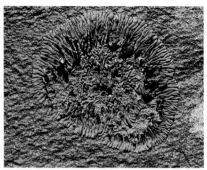

Where the sand has been swept away by the wind, the Namib's rocky hills often appear to be coated with great splashes of white and orange paint, now peeling in the sun — seemingly the work of some well-intentioned but artless giant who sought to add a little colour to this otherwise barren landscape. Closer inspection reveals that the 'paint' consists of colourful lichens growing on the rocks.

A lichen is not a single plant, but a very close partnership between an alga and a fungus. These elementary life-forms join in a co-operative venture, forming what we call a lichen. It is an extremely hardy combination: lichens are among the first signs of life to appear on a mountainside scarred by an avalanche, and are often the only sign of life to be seen in many a polar waste.

The basic framework of the joint enterprise is generally provided by the hair-like structures of the fungus. These form a microscopic jungle inhabited by the tiny green algae, which are able to use sunlight to photosynthesise sugars to the mutual benefit of both organisms.

The Namib is basically a harsh environment, but the coastal fog that so often blankets the shoreline seems to deliver just the right amount of shade and moisture to make the coastal strip ideal lichen country. As a result, the Skeleton Coast Park is home to over seventy different lichen species, and ranks as the richest concentration of lichen fields in the world.

Right: A snarling cheetah, the fastest creature on four legs. This greyhound-shaped carnivore, though essentially peaceful and easily tamed, becomes a spotted demon when pursuing its prey. **Far right:** A black rhino and her calf on the rugged plains of Damaraland. This species has a gestation period of about 15 months and the single calf is suckled for at least a year. Black rhino live for up to 40 years. **Below:** Chunks of fossilised trees in Damaraland's Petrified Forest. **Below right:** Basking seals on the rocks in the large colony at Cape Cross. Their hearing and underwater sight are good, and their sense of smell is sufficiently well developed for them to scent people from a considerable distance.

serves as an island in the desert, a refuge for flora and fauna and indeed for primitive man over many thousands of years.

It is not clear how the Brandberg earned its name. Perhaps it recalls the early traveller Pieter Brand, who was in the area in 1792. Perhaps it means 'Burnt Mountain' and refers to the peaks' red glow in the setting sun, or to blackened rocks in the foothills. From a distance the granite mass seems lifeless and desolate, so it is a surprise to find that it contains many hidden reservoirs of water trapped in hollows and sediment. Mountain zebra, klipspringer and leopard occur on the Brandberg's rock.

The Brandberg holds many secrets, the most intriguing of which is the origin of thousands of rock paintings that adorn boulders and overhangs in sheltered ravines. The most famous is the 'White Lady' discovered in 1918 and later studied by the Abbé Breuil — but today's scholars say the figure is neither white nor female. They believe it is wearing bead ornaments of the sort that can still be seen in Kaokoland, and suggest that the artist had seen a band of Herero pastoralists.

A staff archaeologist at the State Museum in Windhoek and authority on the Brandberg says there are several hundred rock art sites on the

mountain — most of them in shelters. 'It's revealing to count the figures to see which are emphasised,' he says. 'Giraffe and springbok appear most often, followed by gemsbok and ostrich. There are more human than animal figures. A lot of the paintings probably illustrate myths, but as we don't know who painted them we can't understand their significance.'

Once the whole of the Brandberg was a proclaimed nature reserve, but today its only safeguard is its status as a national monument. Inevitably the 'White Lady' remains the top attraction, though it has had to be fenced off because thoughtless vandals have hastened its

decline by throwing liquid over it (even beer and cold drinks) to bring up its colours. To reach the mountain, take the gravel track leading 28 km from a turn-off on the road between Uis and Khorixas, 14 km from Uis.

Cape Cross Seal Reserve

There are 23 breeding colonies of the Cape fur seal along the coasts of South Africa and Namibia, and one of the largest is at Cape Cross, reached from a turn-off on the coastal road 119 km north of Swakopmund. There are seals at the colony throughout the year but the busiest time is November and December, when up to 200 000 gather there for the breeding cycle. The cows give birth to pups conceived a year earlier, and within a week they mate with a bull who is likely to have fought off more than one rival for his small but inviolate piece of territory – and his harem.

Though Cape Cross is uninhabited, from a distance the seals lounging on the rocks can easily be mistaken for people. Historians speculate that in 1484 the seals caught the eye of the Portuguese navigator Diego Cao, who landed at the Cape and erected a cross or *padrao* on behalf of the Portuguese monarch. As far as is known, Cao and his men were the first white men to set foot in Southern Africa. The original cross was taken to Germany in 1893, but a replica now stands in its place.

As at other seal colonies, each year a number of young seals are culled for their sleek under-fur and carcasses – turned into meat and bone-meal. The practice has aroused considerable controversy over the years. Since seal harvesting and tourism are hardly compatible, the reserve is closed from July to December – except on Tuesday and Wednesday afternoons. However it is open every day from sunrise to sunset during the December and January school holidays, the Easter school holidays and over weekends to the end of June.

Kaokoland Nature Reserve

Separated from the Atlantic by the Skeleton Coast Park, the Kaokoland Nature Reserve covers some 1-million hectares of rugged, unspoilt terrain in north-western Namibia. This region was first described by explorer Charles Andersson in 1858 as 'the finest and most peculiar hill-scenery I have ever seen'. Wide plains alternate with mountain ranges whose cliffs resemble fortifications, or crumbling pieces of Gothic architecture.

Wildlife in this harsh but beautiful location includes elephant, black rhino, giraffe, springbok, oryx, ostrich and the occasional lion (almost exterminated in the highlands but still surviving to the west), as well as assorted smaller vertebrates. Vegetation is thorn and mopane scrub savanna, becoming sparser towards the west.

This is not a nature reserve for ease-loving tourists but rather for those who appreciate the bundu. Groups should have at least two 4-wheel-drive vehicles, and be equipped with spares, fuel, water, food, camping equipment and first-aid supplies. Camping takes place mainly in riverbeds (in the dry season), but because of the sensitivity of the flora and fauna certain riverbeds are out of bounds. There are plans to establish two camps which will cater for a maximum of 15 people. For more detailed information, write to The Director of Nature Conservation and Recreation Resorts, Private Bag 13267, Windhoek, 9000 (telephone Windhoek 3-6975/6/7/8).

The Petrified Forest

Damaraland's Petrified Forest looks like a fossilised lumber yard. The veld is strewn with brittle chunks and chips of 'wood' and many complete 'trunks' are embedded in the soil. Palaeontologists estimate the fossils are 200 million years old, but say there is no evidence that there was ever a forest on the site. It has been suggested that the trees grew elsewhere and were uprooted and swept away in a flood.

The Petrified Forest, a national monument, offers a number of pleasant walks with views of the surrounding mountains. It is located 24 km west of Khorixas, on the road to the sea, and is signposted.

Skeleton Coast Park

Not only ships have come to grief along the Skeleton Coast. For decades men have dreamed of uncovering great storehouses of diamonds like those at the mouth of the Orange River – and they have failed. Certainly diamonds have come to light, and small mines have been established – but in at least three cases they have been spectacular failures. One of these mines was situated at Terrace Bay, between the Uniab and Hoanib rivers. When the company concerned went bankrupt, it surrendered its buildings to the country's.

The windfall could not have been more welcome. The Skeleton Coast Park had been in existence since 1971, but all it could offer in the way of tourist accommodation was a camping site at Torra Bay to the south, open only in December and January and catering for fishermen

Top: A wrecked ship is dwarfed by towering dunes along the notorious Skeleton Coast, where the constantly shifting sands keep changing the shoreline. This treacherous shore claimed many such vessels which still litter the coast. **Above:** A cluster of everlastings at Twyfelfontein. **Right:** An ancient menagerie engraved by San at Twyfelfontein.

and their families. Terrace Bay had the makings of a first-rate tourist camp, and nature conservators had visions of a brisk stream of appreciative visitors who would be drawn to the park by its beauty.

However, visitors to Terrace Bay are restricted to an area 30 km long and 5 km wide along the coastline, stretching 15 km above and below Terrace Bay.

'There's nowhere else like it,' says a nature conservator. 'You can go from lions and rhinos to seabirds, all in one park. You can go from dolphins to giraffes. If you're lucky within five kilometres of seeing an elephant you may see a seal. You find springbok and gemsbok and on occasion even mountain zebra right down by the sea – a lion may even kill a gemsbok on the beach. There are greater and lesser

Left: The palm-fronted banks at the Kunene River at the Epupa Falls, about 129 km downstream from the larger Ruacana Falls. The Epupa Falls lie in the mountainous regions at the northernmost limit of the Kaokoland Nature Reserve. This one million hectare nature reserve is separated from the sea by the Skeleton Coast National Park. The nature reserve has an abundance of game, which includes lion, elephant, black rhino, giraffe, springbok, oryx and ostrich.

THE DAY OF THE JACKAL

Black-backed jackals – those cunning and resourceful scavengers recognised by the dark mantle on their backs – are to be seen all along the coast of Namibia and visitors often wonder how they find enough to eat. At Terrace Bay they shadow the fishermen, waiting in the wings as they clean their fish and throw aside the offal. Elsewhere they must forage for dead fish, sick birds, dying seals or whatever else they can find – even shellfish on occasion. At Cape Cross, they have been known to disembowel a sick seal.

The jackal's only competition on the Skeleton Coast is the brown hyena, which lives in burrows in the dunes and usually emerges at night, whereas jackals scavenge by day and night. At times jackals work together, but most – except when they mate – are loners. The female weans her cubs in a burrow in the dunes, and while they are still young she takes them on their first scavenging expedition. To give them a taste for flesh, she swallows, then regurgitates it so they can feed in their turn.

flamingoes in the vleis at the river mouths, and inland you'll find eagles and vultures...and all this is within our boundaries.'

As yet, visitors heading for Terrace Bay and Torra Bay must keep to the road, thereby missing many of the beauty spots along the way. However, some fascinating areas are open to hikers, including a 6 km trail at Uniab River Delta, where a waterfall lies hidden among the dunes. Hikers undertaking the three-day Ugab Trail are led by a nature conservator along the the Ugab River, which forms the southern boundary of the park.

Besides these pockets, which are open for exploration the only 'wilderness experience' offered in the Skeleton Coast Park has been the result of private enterprise. Explains an official: 'A part of the wilderness concept is the knowledge that you or your group are alone in a vast territory. This aspect would be lost if all sorts of additional areas are opened to tourists. This is why only one firm has been allowed to operate safaris – despite pressure for more.'

Louw Schoeman, a Windhoek lawyer, had business interests on the Skeleton Coast for years, and in 1977 was given permission to organise fly-in safaris. In the beginning he flew clients to an old amethyst mine near the coast, but he found the area wet and foggy, and unsuitable for his needs.

So he moved camp 35 km inland to a riverbed lush with green vegetation and set against mountains. There his clients sleep in igloo tents and dine under a tree. The accent is on open spaces, and the fascinating variety of creatures that inhabit them.

'The safari lasts five days,' Louw Schoeman explains. 'One day we'll drive north up the beach to the seal colony at Angra Frio. Another time we'll go to the Hoarusib Canyon, which is rich in wildlife – though I emphasise that in this park it's the landscape that's important far more than the animals. It seems to change round every corner.'

Twyfelfontein

'Doubtful Spring' (its flow has always been erratic) is set in a long shallow valley flanked by gently sloping hills. The hills contain more than 3 000 rock engravings, comprising the richest such collection in Africa. The engravings have been chipped out of hard rock, perhaps with a quartz hammer. Experiments using one of these crude tools have shown that a typical engraving would have been completed in as little as 30 minutes.

A staff archaeologist at the State Museum in Windhoek has pointed out that Twyfelfontein's engravings have a different emphasis from the rock paintings in the Brandberg and indeed from engravings found in South Africa. The more numerous of the larger species are giraffe, rhino, zebra and ostrich, while springbok and humans are only poorly represented. There are also engravings of animal spoor.

Twyfelfontein's engravings were discovered early this century, but it is only since the 1970s that they have become a tourist drawcard. To view this ancient and fascinating art, follow the signs from turn-offs on the road between Khorixas and the sea. The two turn-offs are situated 46 km and 78 km respectively from Khorixas.

The lake of a mother's tears

An old San legend tells of a party of strangers that strayed into Heiqum territory. A band of hunters surrounded the intruders and killed the men and children, but allowed the women to live. One young mother was inconsolable. She sat under a tree and rocked her dead infant in her arms, weeping so bitterly that her tears formed a huge lake. The sun dried the tears, leaving the ground covered in salt. That, say the Heiqum, was the origin of Etosha Pan – lake of a mother's tears.

The Heiqum (widely known by the misnomer 'Bushmen') have lived around the pan for a thousand years or longer. Their forebears were hunters and gatherers, preying on the mighty herds of antelope that fed on the savanna plains around the pan and drank at the perennial springs that oozed through cracks in its rim. They were familiar with the three great seasons of Etosha's year: four cold and dry months, four hot and dry months, and four hot months wet with the tears of the grieving mother.

Until the 1890s the Heiqum and their game were undisturbed. But then came the outbreak of rinderpest that affected all Southern Africa, killing both game and domestic cattle. In an attempt to contain the disease, the German authorities in Windhoek quickly developed a stock-free zone along the southern edge of the pan. Several small military detachments were sent to enforce the stock ban and prevent cattle smuggling, and two of them were based at remote locations named Okaukuejo (pronounced 'Oka-koo-yoo') and Namutoni, where the men were housed in tiny forts.

In 1907 Governor Friedrich von Lindequist proclaimed three large game reserves. One was north of Grootfontein, another covered a large area of the Namib Desert, and the third the 'Etosha Game Park', included the area around the pan and much of the Kaokoveld.

At one stage the park covered 99 526 km² (it was the largest natural reserve in the world), but in 1967 it was cut back to make room for tribal homelands, and became the Etosha National Park – one of the best-known and most fascinating natural sanctuaries in the world. The park's present area is over 23 000 km².

Above: A kori bustard in the shade
of an acacia. These large birds live
on small mammals or reptiles,
seeds, insects and carrion. **Left:** A
herd of gemsbok approaches the
Kapupuhedi waterhole, near the
south-western edge of the pan.
Territorial males mark their
boundaries with piles of dung.
Right: The park has a relatively
small cheetah population – largely
because they face stiff competition
from other predators such as lion
and hyena.

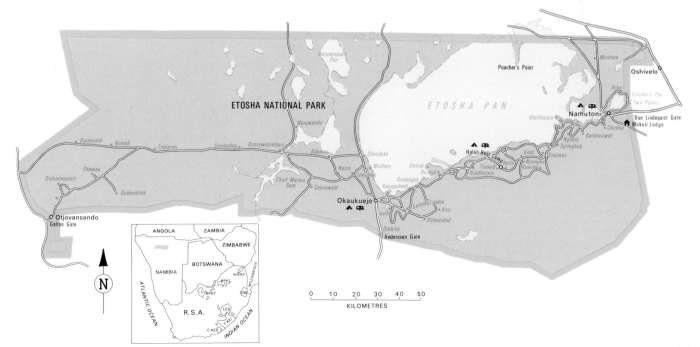

ETOSHA AT A GLANCE

When to go The park is open all year round except for Halali which is only open from the second Friday in March until 31 October. The best months for game-viewing are August and September, when the animals concentrate around waterholes. Try to avoid school holidays, when the rest camps are full. Etosha's three rest camps open at sunrise and close at sunset, so tourists arriving at the entrance gates should leave enough time to drive to the camps. Mokuti Lodge, outside Lindequist Gate, is open 24 hours a day throughout the year. Dogs and other pets are not allowed in the park but may be left in cages at the entrance gates (their owners are responsible for them). Firearms must be declared at the entrance gates and will be sealed on arrival.

Reservations and information Enquiries and applications for accommodation should be addressed to The Director of Nature Conservation, Reservations, Private Bag 13267, Windhoek 9000, Namibia (telephone Windhoek 3-6975/6/7/8). Bookings for Mokuti Lodge may be made by writing to Central Reservations Windhoek, Namib-Sun Hotels, P.O. Box 2862, Windhoek 9000 (telephone Windhoek 3-3145).

Okaukuejo has an information centre with interesting displays of the park's activities. Namutoni's history is told in a museum inside the fort's look-out tower. A map of the park is on sale in the rest camp offices and booklets can be bought in the rest camp shops.

Getting there By the eastern route Etosha is 553 km north of Windhoek. Drive to Von Lindequist Gate via Otjiwarongo and Tsumeb, then to Namutoni rest camp, which is 11 km inside the park. The road is tarred all the way. The southern route is shorter (447 km) but the last 109 km are not tarred. Drive to Andersson Gate via Outjo, then to Okaukuejo rest camp, which is 17,5 km inside the park boundary.

There is a road to Galton Gate in the far west of the park (233 km from Outjo) but as yet there is no tourist accommodation at Otjovasandu camp, where conservators carefully nurture rare and endangered species.

There are airstrips at Namutoni, Okaukuejo and Halali, and a private operator based in the park organises transport for those who arrive by air.

Mokuti Lodge, 500 m from the Van Lindequist Gate is accessible by tarred road. It has hangar facilities and a modern runway.

Accommodation The park has three rest camps: Okaukuejo in the west, Namutoni in the east and Halali in the middle. Okaukuejo has luxury rondavels clustered around a waterhole (five beds in two bedrooms, kitchen, shower and toilet); bungalows 'with amenities' (six beds in a bedroom, diningroom, shower and toilet); ordinary bungalows (two beds in a bedroom, washbasin); 'bus quarters' for coach tourists (two beds in one bedroom, bath and toilet); dormitories (eight beds) and tents (four beds). There is also a large caravan and camping site with a number of ablution blocks.

Halali offers luxury bungalows (five beds in two bedrooms, kitchen, shower); bungalows (three beds in a bedroom, washbasin and communal ablution block); dormitories (ten beds); and tents (four beds). As at the other rest camps, towels and bedding are provided, but not cooking utensils, crockery and cutlery. There is a large caravan and camping site.

At Namutoni, visitors stay in the fort or at the adjoining campsite. In the fort are rooms with washbasins (three beds and furniture); ordinary rooms (two or three beds and furniture); and dormitories (four, six or 12 beds and furniture). In the campsite are 'ski' huts (two beds) and 'bus quarters' for coach and other tourists (mobile homes). The campsite also has a large area for camping and caravanning.

Guests at Mokuti Lodge stay in luxury chalets (two or five beds) or in tourist units (two beds). All accommodation is air-conditioned with *en suite* bathrooms. There is a swimming pool for taking it easy and cooling down.

Eating and drinking There are restaurants at all three rest camps and all are licensed. Each camp has a tourist shop selling a limited variety of groceries including frozen meat, wine, beer, spirits and bundles of firewood. There are braaivleis facilities beside the bungalows and at the caravan and camping sites, while out in the park are picnic tables at rudimentary 'toilet stops' protected by game-proof fences. Mokuti Lodge has restaurants and bars.

Getting around The park has an intricate road system linking the rest camps with more than 30 waterholes (though some of them may be closed – check with tourist officers at the rest camps). All the roads are surfaced with gravel and grading crews try to keep them in good order, but sharp stones cause many punctures. Petrol pump attendants at the rest camps can mend punctures. Cars that break down can be towed to the nearest rest camp. There is a qualified mechanic at Okaukuejo but for major repairs vehicles may have to be towed to Outjo or Tsumeb.

Wildlife Much of the park is closed to visitors but the species commonly seen from tourist roads include Burchell's zebra, kudu, red hartebeest, blue wildebeest, eland, gemsbok, springbok, blackfaced impala, Damara dik-dik, steenbok, blackbacked jackal, lion, elephant, ostrich and giraffe. More than 300 bird species have been reported. Visitors at Okaukuejo's floodlit waterhole may see nocturnal visitors such as spotted hyena, brown hyena and black rhino as well as other species seen during the day.

Special precautions Before entering the park you should embark on a course of anti-malaria tablets. When driving in the park, make sure you take water and emergency rations in case your vehicle breaks down, If it does, stay in your vehicle. You may have a long wait before somebody drives past, but rather that than be eaten by lions as you walk for help.

Top: A red-eyed bulbul in one of its favourite haunts. Its shallow nests are often built in thorn trees. **Right:** A magnificent kudu bull at Etosha. It takes about six years for the horns of the greater kudu to spiral to their maximum length. **Below:** A southern bird snake (sometimes known as a twig or vine snake) in the Etosha National Park. When this snake lies motionless, it resembles a twig. **Bottom:** An adult Bushman arrow poison beetle, one of several species of leaf beetles whose larvae are used by the San to poison their arrows.

Even inexperienced bird-watchers find it easy to recognise members of the hornbill family. Their long, curved beaks are unmistakable, and so is their awkward flight of a few flaps followed by a long glide. There are nine hornbill species in Southern Africa and Etosha accommodates four of them.

Quite often, hornbills of different species can be seen close together, raiding bushes for fruit, termites or other insects and running or hopping along the ground with their perky tails held high. They seem a sociable family — which makes their breeding behaviour all the stranger. No other birds go to such lengths to isolate themselves.

When she is ready to lay eggs, the female hornbill immures herself in a hole in a tree. She seals the hole (occasionally with help from the male) at a time of her own choosing, using mud or her excreta.

The hornbills leave a small vertical slit in the wall through which the male passes food, but otherwise the female is cut off from the world. Inside, she moults most of her wing and tail feathers and either pushes them out of the cavity or places them in crevices.

To keep the nest clean, she defecates through the small slit. She remains inside until the chicks are 25 days old, by which time she has new feathers. She then breaks out (with the male's help) and helps to find food.

With their mother gone, the chicks re-seal the nest and remain inside for another 20-25 days before they are ready to emerge. All this time they are fed by both parents. At last the nest is abandoned, and the hornbills return to their socialising. The species may be told apart by looking at their bills — black for the male grey hornbill (maroon and cream for the female), red for the red-billed, yellow for the yellow-billed and a red, heavy bill for the Monteiro's.

The first white travellers to see the great pan were two young explorers, Francis Galton of Britain and Charles Andersson of Sweden, who passed its eastern edge in 1851 on their way to the land of the Owambo.

Galton was a cousin of the famous naturalist Charles Darwin, and was later to devise the system of fingerprint identification used by the world's police forces. In his book *The Narrative of an Explorer in Tropical South Africa* he wrote of Etosha: 'It is very remarkable in many ways. The borders are defined and wooded; its surface is flat and effloresced, and the mirage excessive over it.'

It was the pan's mirage or glare that intrigued Owambo tribesmen who saw it – Etosha means 'the big white place'. But for Galton and Andersson it was a disappointment. They had been told that Etosha held a great lake yet they found it was bone dry. They even misunderstood its size. Galton wrote: 'It was about nine miles [14,5 km] in breadth, but the mirage prevented my guessing its length; it certainly exceeded fifteen miles [24 km].' In fact the pan is up to 129 km long and 72 km wide. The pan is remarkable by any yardstick, but geologists point out that it is merely a part of a much larger phenomenon – the Etosha Basin, which includes not only the plains around the pan but all of Owambo to the north. A likely theory on

BEWARE THE BLACK-TEMPERED RHINO

Etosha's nature conservators say that one of the best ways of learning about the park is to tour with a coach party, because the courier will know where to find the most exciting animals. One such party got more than it bargained for when it stopped to view some blue wildebeest. Suddenly there was a loud bang from the rear and the coach lurched forward. It had been butted by an enraged black rhino.

As recently as the 1960s, black rhino were rare in Etosha, and indeed in all of Namibia. Most of those that remained were in the mountains of Damaraland and Kaokoland. To make sure the species was saved, 40 of them were moved to the mountainous region around Otjovasandu in the west of the park, where they were set free and allowed to mingle with the rhino already there. Since then, black rhino have spread over most of the park, and now there are more than 300 of them.

Most of Etosha's rhinos like to escape the heat of the day and emerge only at night. At Okaukuejo, visitors watching at the floodlit waterhole stand a good chance of seeing one come to drink, though they may sometimes have a long wait. Elsewhere, nature conservators have watched with amusement as rhino, irritated by the presence of other animals and indeed of other rhino, set out to drive them away. A nature conservator at Halali rest camp

once watched a remarkable duel at a waterhole far from the tourist road. 'There were several rhinos in the vicinity, but one of them was dominating the hole,' he says. 'Then another rhino arrived, smaller, but with longer horns and looking as if he had come from a long way away. He wanted to drink but the first rhino interfered and they began to fight. For the next three hours there wasn't more than a metre between them.

'I've never seen anything so exciting. The animals stood nose to nose with their horns lowered and took it in turns to lunge and charge and kick. You could hear a sharp crack as they came together. With all that weight behind their shoulders they were hurting one another – the head's not very sensitive to pain, but I could see deep cuts under their bodies. From time to time, one of them was thrown right off balance. Then at last the first rhino had had enough – he backed off, then sat on his haunches.

'Then as I watched, he keeled over. I thought he was dead. The other rhino, the one that had been challenged, stood and watched him for a while – then he keeled over as well. I thought, now we've got two dead rhinos. But after a while the victor recovered and went off to drink. After another ten minutes, the loser felt better too... and trotted away into the veld.'

If the predators do come within striking distance, the chicks not yet old enough to be fully mobile will be abandoned to their fate. Those that can will try to walk to a safer place – but there are long odds against their arrival, for there are many dangers. The sight of helpless chicks spread over a wide area of the parched earth is one that few observers can forget. Lately, park officials have saved stranded chicks by sending them to zoos in South Africa.

The long road between the Okaukuejo and Namutoni rest camps offers many views across the pan. A number of turn-offs lead to waterholes at its rim, and often visitors are astonished to find not only a variety of antelope but also elephant or giraffe quenching their thirst within metres of the salt.

There is plenty to see. At one waterhole will be zebra, at another kudu, at a third springbok, red hartebeest or gemsbok. There should be no difficulty in tracking down a herd of elephant – but if it is a breeding herd with babies, go cautiously – the matriarchs have notoriously short tempers. Giraffe are seen among the trees and perhaps there will be a pride of lions, lying in ambush for antelope or zebra or merely dozing while they digest their last meal.

Towards the end of the season, Etosha's roads are hot and dusty, and nature conservators caution visitors against driving from waterhole to waterhole as they might do in other parks.

'Better to stick to one,' advises a senior park official. 'Take binoculars and refreshments and maybe a book and, if it's possible, park in the shade. At times there'll be nothing happening, but the animals must come to drink and by the end of the day you'll be surprised how much you've seen.'

Tourist officers at the three rest camps will offer advice on the best waterholes to visit but some visitors don't take long to learn that they can see most of what Etosha offers without setting foot out of Okaukuejo. The rest camp has been built beside one of the park's most spectacular waterholes, and visitors can sit and watch the activities of the animals from behind a low stone wall less than 30m from the water's edge.

As an added bonus, the waterhole is floodlit all night long. Although one would expect animals to avoid the bright lights, they have gradually become accustomed to them, and do not appear to be disturbed by the observers. The procession of game arriving at the waterhole would have been a credit to Noah's Ark.

Okaukuejo camp is Etosha's headquarters. It is from there that the team of nature conservators, described by officials as 'the eyes and ears of the park', is directed.

Among the conservators is a 'problem animal' officer who must deal with elephants

Etosha's origin suggests that there was once a great lake in the basin, but climatic changes led to evaporation at the rate of 3000mm a year. Gradually the lake shrank until all that remained was the sandy clay on the bottom, so encrusted with salt that no vegetation could take root in it.

During most of the year the great pan appears barren and desolate, but for a brief period of time Etosha offers an illusion of its former splendour. From November onwards, the rains that fall over the park begin to fill the cracks in the clay, and everywhere there are muddy pools. Then lazy streams flowing almost imperceptibly from the plains to the north bring floodwaters drained from neighbouring Owambo and Angola. In exceptional years much of the pan once again becomes a lake – though in only a few places is it more than a metre deep, and for the greater part is only a few centimetres in depth.

The floodwaters bring life. Micro-organisms flourish, providing food for thousands of greater and lesser flamingoes that come to the pan to breed on elevated areas where they will be safe from predators. They have little time: their chicks must grow up before the water evaporates and the predators can come close.

Above: An Etosha lion in a familiar pose. He is essentially a lazy creature, allowing the lionesses to do most of the hunting. **Top left:** A lilac-breasted roller, one of the park's most beautiful birds. It is said that the king of the Ndbele, Mzilikazi, reserved this bird's feathers for his exclusive use and it is widely known as 'Mzilikazi's roller'. **Left:** The Etosha Pan at sunset. It is the centre of one of the greatest game parks on the African continent. **Below:** A quizzical look from a blue wildebeest. Their principal enemies are lion, leopard, cheetah, spotted hyena, wild dog – and anthrax, to which they are particularly vulnerable. Sometimes blue wildebeest will follow the sound of thunder, or perhaps the sight of rain clouds for kilometres, until they reach the freshly fallen rain. On their massive migrations, territorial bulls are known to relegate the younger males to the perimeter of the herd, where they are always alert to danger.

that break through the perimeter fence. There are also three conservators at Otjovasandu in the far west, where the park maintains a large predator-free area for rare and endangered species such as the black rhino, black-faced impala, roan antelope and tsessebe.

Much of an Etosha conservator's work is routine. Each has an area of his own, and he and two Heiqum assistants check fences, clean roads and firebreaks, mend ailing wind-pumps and keep an eye on tourists. But one part of his work is special: he is expected to spend a good part of each month on horseback, which will give him the chance to patrol deep into his area and observe the game at close quarters. Each conservator has two horses – one for himself and one for a Heiqum assistant – and the men will spend days out of camp.

Although they are trained to take precautions, things may sometimes go wrong. One night a nature conservator at Halali woke up to find himself staring at a lion. He described his experience: 'I'd seen him in the daytime – an old male by himself. There wasn't time to get out of my sleeping bag before he jumped onto one of the horses. Luckily it broke free and escaped. But the lion then pounced on the other horse, which ran off with the lion clinging to its back. It eventually shook him off, but it was three days before we caught up with the horses and calmed them down.'

Another conservator had an even more frightening encounter. When out on patrol he was charged by an elephant cow. He tried to escape but his horse stumbled and threw him onto the ground, then ran off. The elephant made a mock charge, then turned away and rejoined the herd leaving the conservator shaken but unhurt.

In the hot, dry season that precedes the rains, Etosha's great herds of game must converge on the perennial waterholes ringing the pan. There they run the gauntlet of lions and other predators that have only to lie in wait, knowing that their prey will have to drink. But sometimes they have an alternative: heavy rains fill shallow depressions on the plains and create hundreds of new waterholes.

This has long been Etosha's traditional cycle – but since the 1950s there have been major changes. The park's populations of blue wildebeest and Burchell's zebra have slumped alarmingly while the numbers of lion, elephant, wildebeest, zebra and giraffe have shot up. A senior biologist at Okaukuejo's Ecological Institute investigated these swings and found that they were all the result of man's well-meant but misguided attempts to improve on nature. Fortunately, he feels, it is not too late to remedy the mistakes.

'Take the elephant,' he says. 'In 1955 there were between 50 and 100 elephants in the

HIGH SOCIETY

A coloured lithograph by Sir Andrew Smith depicts the sociable weaver against a background of somewhat stylised nests.

Most birds are fairly discreet in building their nests, and few visitors manage to locate them. One exception is the sociable weaver (*Philetairus socius*), whose nest could not be more obvious. The sociable weaver's home is a vast edifice of straw resting on the sturdy branches of certain acacia trees – quite possibly the work of generations of weavers that kept it in a fine state of repair and steadily added to it as their colony grew over the years. The large communal nest keeps the birds warm in winter and cool in summer.

To build such a home, adult weavers begin by pushing individual twigs into cracks and crevices in the bark of an acacia. Before long, the twigs are packed together so tightly that they provide an anchor for more straw, and gradually the weavers thatch a roof. Meanwhile, some of the birds begin to make rounded nesting-chambers – suspended from the roof but thatched together to form a solid mass. Each chamber has a near-vertical tunnel connecting it with the nest's underside.

In the breeding season, each pair of sociable weavers has a nesting chamber to itself, but sometimes several (non-breeding) birds share a chamber. The arrangement seems to suit them well, for weavers like doing everything together. Early in the morning the birds leave the nest to go feeding. Towards midday they all return for a rest, and later they go feeding again. At dusk they disappear into their nesting chambers, which serve as their homes all year, whether or not they are breeding.

Like most thirstland birds, the weaver will not breed unless there have been adequate rains. When that happens, the drive to reproduce is accompanied by an urge to build new nesting chambers, and the colony's home may be greatly extended. But on occasion these winged engineers make mistakes: sometimes the nest becomes waterlogged and too heavy for the branch that supports it, and parts of or even the whole structure may crash to the ground. When that happens, the weavers simply begin all over again.

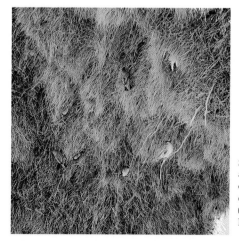

Sociable weavers at work on their elaborate communal home (viewed from below).

Opposite page: The Damara dik-dik (*Madoqua kirki*) is the only species of dik-dik occurring in Southern Africa. **Top:** The graceful steenbok is monogamous, and pairs for life (though the male and female occasionally separate for short periods). The adult male marks out his territory with a system of dung heaps and secretions from a throat gland – unique to the steenbok.
Above: *Moringa ovalifolia* is one of Etosha's most fascinating trees. Its bark, stem and roots are eaten by a number of animals.

park. Now there are 2500. They feed on trees that in the past would not have been here because they'd have burnt up in veld fires. Then man stepped in and controlled the fires, which meant that the focus of the ecosystem switched from savanna to woodland.

'The giraffes have appreciated it as much as the elephants. But now we clearly understand the importance of veld fires to the ecosystem, and when they are started by lightning we usually leave them alone to burn as far as the surrounding fire-break.

'Another form of tampering has been the erection of boundary fences. The idea of the fences is more to keep domestic animals out of the park than to keep our animals in. But nobody realised the effect they would have on migration patterns.

'Blue wildebeest used to migrate all the way round the pan in their search for grass. Then their path was blocked by the northern fence, which at one point cut straight across the pan. In 25 years the wildebeest population dropped from 25000 to 2300.'

The Department of Agriculture and Nature Conservation would like to see the park's boundaries extended northwards so that the old migration patterns which existed before man intervened can be resumed – but even then the beleaguered wildebeest's troubles would not be over.

To provide gravel for tourist roads, the park authorities have had to dig scores of deep lime-pits which fill with water after the rains. Many of the pits have become infected with anthrax, a disease fatal to the herbivores that drink the water – mostly wildebeest and zebra. The sick and the dead provide easy meals for the many prowling lions.

'And so the chain goes on,' says a researcher. 'In the past, the lions would have gone hungry in the wet season and many of their cubs would have died. Now they thrive, and the extra lions are competing with cheetah for living space, robbing them of their prey, and killing young cheetah when they find them. Consequently we have a greatly reduced cheetah population.' It was obvious that the lions should be contained, but it would not help to shoot them. 'Nature has a way of over-compensating in retaliation.'

Instead, the department is strongly committed to an experiment that is the first of its kind in the world.

Ten of Etosha's lionesses have been put on contraceptive injections and the authorities are waiting to see the results before deciding whether or not to treat other lionesses in the same way. This method of controlling the lion population appears preferable to the slaughter of entire prides with rifle bullets, say conservators. Moreover, it does not destroy genetic material, which culling certainly does.

Top: A yellow mongoose surveys his small slice of Etosha territory. This species is very similar to the slender mongoose. **Left:** Giraffe at the Klein Namutoni waterhole. **Above:** A female black-faced impala. These medium-sized antelope are gregarious animals and tend to move in herds.

East to the water country

Attached to Namibia's north-east corner is the odd pan-handle known as the Caprivi Strip, 450 km from west to east and nowhere more than 100 km wide. The strip is named after a former Imperial Chancellor of Germany, Count Leo von Caprivi – but those who live in the area know it as Linyanti, the Water Country.

Since Namibia's independence in 1990, the withdrawal of troops has restored Caprivi's tourist potential and two reserves, The Caprivi and Mahango Game reserves, are being developed on opposite banks of the magnificent Okavango River. Although there is no overnight accommodation in either reserve, nearby Popa Falls has a rest camp and is an attraction in itself. There is also accommodation at a number of private resorts in northern Namibia.

In the early 1970s the bush war was sufficiently fierce to raise grave questions about the future of scarce species such as Caprivi's sable. This led to the authorities proclaiming a new park on Waterberg Plateau, 60 km east of Otjiwarongo. Visitors to the park stay in Bernabé de la Bat Rest Camp from where scenic game-viewing tours are arranged.

The savanna vegetation is much like Caprivi's (though not so rich) and the top of the plateau makes a perfect sanctuary, not only for animals but for other scarce species as well. Waterberg's game population ranges from buffalo to rhino, from giraffe to roan.

The plateau's water is in the form of contact springs that bubble from the sandstone on the plateau's sides (a contact spring is formed by a top layer of porous material through which rain water seeps until it makes contact with an impervious layer of rock. The water finds its way to the edge of this layer, where it gushes out in the form of a spring). These springs have long made Waterberg an important focus of settlement. There is an impressive body of water at Lake Otjikoto, a large dolomite sinkhole lying 170 km to the north.

In remote eastern Kavango the Kaudom Nature Reserve offers an unspoilt wildlife experience. The reserve, reached only by 4-wheel-drive vehicle, has two camps, Sikereti and Kaudom.

Various private resorts in northern Namibia offer visitors accommodation as well as a personalised wildlife experience.

Left: A sable wanders in a grove of Rhodesian teak in Caprivi. Sable usually congregate in herds of up to 15, although they do form temporary groupings of 50 or more. Adult bulls establish their own territory, and during the mating season aggressively defend it.
Below: Oxpeckers swarm over a wild donkey in Caprivi. These birds live mainly on blood-gorged ticks. Their sharp claws, stiff tail feathers (used to prop themselves against their host's body) and flattened bills are well suited to their feeding habits.

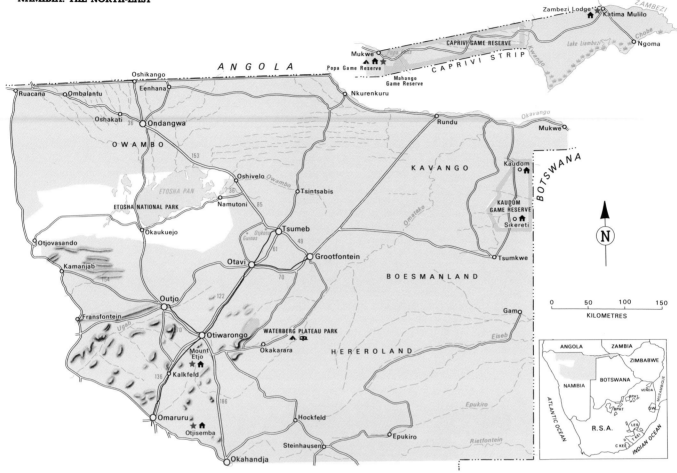

Above: A strangler fig clasps a mopane tree in an unbreakable grip that may eventually kill the tree. The strangler fig grows from a seed (dropped by a bird or mammal) in the branches of the host tree. When the seeds germinate, they extrude long 'roots' which wind around the tree trunk.

Right: A white-headed vulture. This carrion-eater (it also feeds on live birds and mammals) is found principally in savanna bushveld across Southern Africa.

Caprivi Game Reserve

In 1966 the ecologist Ken Tinley was asked to appraise west Caprivi for Namibia's Administration. Was it a good idea to open the area for agricultural settlement, as was happening in east Caprivi?

After analysing the soils Tinley advised against it, instead recommending that west Caprivi should be left in its natural state as a haven for wildlife, and an ancient homeland for the indigenous San hunter-gatherers.

Before any decision was taken, Caprivi was plunged into the bush war that lasted until 1989. Although Caprivi's development as a wildlife sanctuary has been suspended – the ingredients remain – and in the future it seems set to become a major wildlife attraction.

In the future the focus for visitors to the reserve is likely to be the former army base at Buffalo, on the banks of the Okavango. Game-viewing, fishing and bird-watching are excellent here. Visitors can expect to see elephant, hippo, buffalo, crocodile, lechwe, sable, roan, reedbuck and a host of waterbirds.

There are no facilities in the reserve at present, but a new all-purpose gravel road runs from west to east and handsome new bridges cross the Okavango and Kwando rivers. Enquiries about the reserve may be addressed to the Director of Nature Conservation, Private

Bag 13306, Windhoek 9000, Namibia (telephone Windhoek 3-6975/6/7/8).

Kaudom Nature Reserve

Despite its out-of-the-way location in northern Namibia, on the Botswana border, the rich wildlife and beauty of the 384 000 ha Kaudom Nature Reserve is still within the reach of adventuresome outdoor enthusiasts.

Two islands of civilisation, Sikereti and Kaudom, have huts, campsites and ablution facilities. The camps are linked by tracks which cross Kalahari sand dunes and dry riverbeds called 'Omurambas' – meaning 'ill-defined drainage lines'. Along the length of the omurambas are springs and waterholes, which are the most advantageous spots for game-viewing. During the dry season (June to October), the waterholes are frequented by lion, elephant, giraffe, gemsbok, wildebeest, eland, kudu and even wild dog.

OTJIKOTO FOUNTAIN.

Left: An early representation of Lake Otjikoto in Charles Andersson's book, *Lake Ngami*. **Below:** A modern view of Lake Otjikoto. 'So effectually [sic] is it hidden,' wrote Andersson, 'that a person might pass within fifty paces of it without being aware of its existence.' He could not resist investigating further. With his companion Francis Galton, he swam into a cavern. 'In this mysterious spot, two owls, and a great number of bats, had taken up their abode. On approaching some of the latter, which I saw clinging to the rocks, I found, to my surprise, that they were dead; and had probably been so for many years . . .'

Kaudom's vegetation is quite different from other parks in Namibia. On the dry woodland savanna areas there are leadwood and acacia, while the dunes are dotted with kiaat, Rhodesian teak and false mopane.

The reserve is about 60 km north of Tsumkwe, where petrol is usually available. The park can also be reached from the north by a turn-off on the Rundu/Mukwe road. Because of sandy roads, driving is slow and plenty of time should be set aside to complete your journey. Visiting groups must have at least two 4-wheel-drive vehicles and be well equipped with petrol, water and food. Enquiries and application for accommodation should be addressed to the Director of Nature Conservation, Reservations, Private Bag 13267, Windhoek 9000 Namibia (Windhoek 3-6975/6/7/8).

Lake Otjikoto

In his book, Lake Ngami, the explorer Charles Andersson described Lake Otjikoto as 'the most extraordinary chasm it was ever my fortune to see'. He and Francis Galton arrived on its cylindrical brink during 1851 and, having plumbed its depths to some 72 m, astonished their Owambo guides by plunging in head first. They swam into a half-submerged cavern

EXPLORING A HELL ON EARTH

Even today, a land journey from the coast of Namibia eastwards to Lake Ngami is not lightly undertaken. Back in the 1850s it was the nearest thing to hell on earth.

The mysterious 'Great Lake' Ngami had been a lure to explorers since missionary David Livingstone sighted the lake a few years previously. Livingstone had travelled north from near Kuruman. Now the race was on to find a way to the lake from the west.

On August 20, 1850 two men – Francis Galton (above right), an Englishman, and Charles Andersson (above left), a Swede – landed at Walvis Bay determined not only to find a way to the lake, but also to 'fill in the empty space on the map between the Cape Colony and Portuguese settlement in the west'.

Enlisting the help of a local missionary, the explorers and their party headed east through the dangers of wild animals and crushing heat. Windhoek was reached before the party turned north, to discover Lake Otjikoto at Tsumeb and Owambo. Further travel was then blocked by the paramount chief Nangoro and

the party returned to the coast.

Undaunted, Galton and Andersson set out again, this time reaching beyond present-day Gobabis. But again Lake Ngami eluded the pair – Galton returned to Cape Town and England, leaving Andersson alone to unlock the secret of a westerly route to the lake in 1853. Both men left extensive records of their adventures, particularly of the wild animals that once roamed the Kalahari.

In *The Narrative of an Explorer in Tropical South Africa*, Galton recalled his near brush with a lion that suddenly appeared, crouching, a few feet above his head on a rocky outcrop. 'I did feel queer, but... I walked steadily down the rock, looking very frequently over my shoulder; but it was not till I came to where the men stood that I could see the round head and pricked ears of my enemy, peering over the ledge under which I had been at work.'

Heat was another problem. Andersson began to feel giddy on a hunting expedition and realised he was suffering from heatstroke. The temperature was 69°C.

which sparkled like crystal in the reflected sunlight: 'The transparency of the water, which was of the deepest sea-green, was remarkable.'

The travellers' explorations of the lake were free of incident, but in later years strange tales were told of Otjikoto. It was said the lake was haunted: when the Germans dumped munitions into the water in 1915, a trooper was snagged in a harness line and drowned. It was also suggested that the lake was bottomless, and hid a treacherous whirlpool – in 1927 the Tsumeb postmaster dived in and was never seen again. Today such tales are discounted, and it is accepted that the lake is a dolomite sinkhole.

For scientists, Otjikoto's chief attraction is its population of fish. Charles Andersson commented on the large numbers of dwarf bream, whose descendants now live on the lake's rubbish-strewn bottom. They have been driven there by an alien species somehow imported from a larger sinkhole named Lake Guinas, 19km to the west.

The *Tilapia guinasana* have multiplied enormously in their new home, so much so that they are now known as 'Otjikoto cichlid'. In 1980, Mozambique or blue tilapia were introduced (illegally) into Otjikoto. They too multiplied rapidly, with the result that the lake's population of Otjikoto cichlids has been reduced.

Lake Otjikoto has been a national monument since 1972, and for many years its water has been used to irrigate local farmland (which explains the quaint pumping platform that hangs from the rim). Most of the lake is fenced off to prevent animals from falling in, but there is an adequate viewing point within this area from a tree-sheltered cliff close to the road. To reach the site, drive north east from Tsumeb on the road to the Etosha National Park. The lake is next to the main road.

Mahango Game Reserve

The wide, lushly-vegetated plains of the Okavango River is the setting for the idyllic 25 000 ha Mahango Game Reserve. Wild dates and huge baobabs thrive in the fertile soil of the floodplains and provide a dense habitat for a profusion of birds and animals.

324

Game-viewing is best during the dry season (June-October). Besides elephant, visitors may see lion, buffalo, kudu, bushbuck, reedbuck, warthog and waterbuck. Despite the heat, summer is the best time for bird-watching. Fishing is not permitted.

Mahango is bisected by two routes. One, a gravel road, is suitable for all motor cars. The second, however, should only be used by 4-wheel-drive vehicles.

Visitors are permitted to picnic at a site that has been established on the river bank, but be cautious at all times and swim at your own peril. Although the shimmering water looks inviting it could easily hide a hungry crocodile! If you look out over the far side of the river you might see a herd of elephant from Caprivi Game Reserve converging on the bank to drink their fill. There are no overnight facilities, but Popa Falls, which has a campsite and bungalows, is located about 15km north of the entrance. Any enquiries should be addressed to the Director of Nature Conservation, Reservations, Private Bag 13267, Windhoek 9000 Namibia (Windhoek 3-6975/6/7/8).

Mount Etjo Safari Lodge

Conservationist Jan Oelofse owns a private nature reserve that boasts the ultimate in safari attractions: not only abundant wildlife – including white rhino, elephant, lion and giraffe – but animal tracks and fossils from prehistoric times. The past is evocatively conjured up, too, by caves that were once the dwelling-place of the hardy San.

Mount Etjo Safari Lodge nestles in this spacious reserve, east of Kalkfeld on Route 2483. Visitors can view game from open safari vehicles, on foot or – most leisurely of all – at a hide beside a waterhole. If you are feeling adventurous you can even spend a night in a comfortable tree-top hide next to one of these wildlife watering-places.

The safari lodge complex includes a swimming pool and conference facilities, and there's an airstrip for guests who wish to arrive by aeroplane (Windhoek is 240km away). All bedrooms have their own bathrooms.

For further information and bookings write to Mount Etjo Safari Lodge, P.O. Box 81, Kalkfeld, 9205 Namibia (telephone Kalkfeld 1602).

Otjisemba

In the Herero language Otjisemba is the 'place of beauty'. Visitors to the safari lodge here – it lies on Route 2110 between Okahandja and Omaruru – have professional trackers and rangers to lead them on game trails and game drives through the unspoilt bush. And in addition to the plentiful attractions of fauna and the flora in the wild, rare San rock engravings provide further appeal.

Above: The small (about 1 cm) fruit of a wild fig in Caprivi. This widely distributed species may vary in size (it has been known to reach almost 20 m in height). **Right:** Openbill storks migrate to Southern Africa from the African tropics. This stork has a gap between its closed mandibles, and this is believed to be an adaptation to its staple diet of freshwater mussels. The openbill has been seen to carry mussels from the water into the hot sunlight and wait until they open. **Opposite page top:** A grove of *Lonchocarpus capassa* (apple-leaf), a typical tree of the region. It produces sprays of pale blue, violet or lilac flowers in December and January. **Opposite page below:** The widespread rock hyrax, or dassie, is an outstanding climber, being able to scramble up and down trees and rocks with surprising rapidity. It usually sunbathes in the morning.

Accommodation is in modern chalets. There is a swimming pool, and the convivial amenities of the central lodge include a bar and a lounge with open stone hearth, while the cuisine features local game dishes. For further information and bookings write to Otjisemba (Pty) Ltd, P.O. Box 756, Okahandja, 9000 Namibia (telephone Okahandja 8-2103).

Popa Falls Game Reserve

Rapids, rather than falls, would be the best way to describe this stretch of white water on the Okavango; but don't be disappointed – there is a feast of activities to keep almost everyone happy: from serene and beautiful sunsets and enriching walks to enjoy to the ultimate in freshwater angling – tiger-fishing!

The water-level drops during the dry season, allowing you to reach some of the smaller islands in the river using the exposed rocks as stepping stones; while the larger islands can be reached via a series of footbridges. The islands are well-worth exploring as their forests hide myriad birds. You will also come across distinctive paths steamrolled by hippo during their nocturnal wanderings in search of food. Crocodile are occasionally seen in the main section of the river.

Besides its own varied attractions, Popa is also an excellent base from which to explore Mahango and Caprivi game reserves.

Accommodation comprises four-bedded rustic huts, a caravan site with ablution facilities, a field kitchen and braai sites. If you like angling, a private safari camp nearby arranges fishing expeditions and offers meals. There is a kiosk which sells cigarettes, cooldrinks, tea, coffee and tinned foods.

Access is via a gravel road (suitable for all vehicles) which follows the Okavango River from Rundu in the west to the bridge crossing the river into the Caprivi Game Reserve. Take the right fork to follow the river to Popa Falls, a distance of about 5 km. Reservations and enquiries should be addressed to The Director of Nature Conservation, Reservations, Private Bag 13267, Windhoek 9000, Namibia (telephone Windhoek 3-6975/6/7/8/).

Waterberg Plateau Park

The Karoo is a long way from northern Namibia, but Waterberg Plateau is a typical Karoo formation and features close similarities to the Orange Free State's Golden Gate. The southern point of the plateau's hard sandstone looms 100 m above the surrounding plain, and to the east and west are near-vertical cliffs that impose natural boundaries on the Waterberg's treasured wildlife species. Only in the north is there any need for a fence, for there the plateau gradually widens and dips until it becomes one with the plain.

Right: Carmine bee-eaters nesting on a bank of the Chobe River in Caprivi. This attractive and energetic bird (the young have pink or pale bluish throats) eats beetles, grasshoppers and other insects.
Opposite top: Blister beetles, with their striking coloration, are members of the fascinating family Meloidae. Their blood contains a poisonous substance, cantharadin, which is widely believed to be an aphrodisiac (it is the basis of 'Spanish Fly'). However, doctors point out that cantharadin merely irritates the urinary tract – and can be extremely dangerous. The beetles were also used to a limited extent in medicine, in cases where it was thought necessary to cause blisters on the patient's skin.
Opposite right: *Belenois aurota*, a very common butterfly in the Waterberg Plateau Park and elsewhere in Southern Africa. It has a wingspan of 4 to 6 cm.
Opposite left: *Hibiscus calyphyllus* on the Waterberg.

MUSCLE, TOOTH AND CLAW

Although the lion is usually looked upon as the king of the carnivores, he certainly is not the bravest. Some believe that this title goes to a mighty little bundle of energy that goes by the name of honey badger, or ratel.

Although a relatively small mammal and seldom more than 75 cm from the tip of his nose to the base of his stubby tail, the honey badger is very powerfully built – a compact 12 kg of muscle, sharp teeth and lethal claws.

Although classified as a carnivore, he actually eats a variety of roots, bulbs and fruit as well as insects, rodents and snakes. His long, curved claws are perfectly designed for flipping over stones and ripping the bark off dead tree trunks in search of various insects.

These formidable claws also come in useful for 'burgling' the nests of wild bees, for the honey badger, as his name suggests, has a particular fondness for honey. The bees attack him ferociously when he tears open their nests, but his thick hide makes him largely immune to their stings. This liking for honey has apparently led him into an habitual association with the little bird known as the honeyguide, which leads him to bees' nests with its chattering displays, and then eats the titbits exposed when the honey badger breaks open the nest.

The top of the plateau features typical savanna vegetation but in places there has been severe bush encroachment because the natural fire pattern has been disturbed from time to time (though this is being reversed). Below the plateau the vegetation is more wooded.

Even before the plateau became a park it held an impressive population of eland and several other species of antelope, and the Administration's original idea was to create an eland reserve.

The first animals introduced to the plateau from outside were eland captured on farmland north-east of Etosha. The eland adapted well, so the Administration prepared to restore the plateau to what it had been in the old days. To make sure of their facts, researchers examined the descriptions given by early travellers like Galton and Andersson.

Giraffe were brought from the north, blue wildebeest from Daan Viljoen, duiker from around Tsumeb and red hartebeest from a local farm. White rhino and impala came from Natal and Cape buffalo from Addo Elephant National Park in the eastern Cape. In two cases, animals arrived after periods in quarantine near Etosha's Otjovasandu – roan from Kavango in north-eastern Namibia, and sable and tsessebe from Caprivi. In 1989 black rhino were relocated here from Etosha and Damaraland to safeguard them from the waves of poachers coming into these areas.

A nature conservator at the plateau explains that when new animals arrive from other areas, they first have to spend three weeks in a 12 ha quarantine camp to make sure they will not introduce disease into the park. 'I check on them daily,' he says. 'When they are ready, I let them into a 1 000 ha acclimatisation camp where they'll spend up to three months. There they are safe from predators and have ample opportunity to get used to Waterberg's climate and vegetation.'

From the camp, the animals graduate to the park proper – in total some 40 000 ha (though not many of the animals will ever descend the cliffs to its lower levels). Some species take a long time to adjust. 'We introduced eleven white rhino in 1977,' says the conservator.' They spent more than three years exploring the territory before they were ready to breed.'

'Then in 1981 four cows produced calves.' This was greatly encouraging. 'We took it as proof that the rhino have accepted Waterberg as their permanent home.'

Bernarbé de la Bat Rest Camp is a modern well-equipped complex accommodating visitors in bungalows and campsites. It is the start of a network of trails of varying lengths. One of these at the foot of the plateau leads to a lookout – the site on which the Germans stationed a heliograph during the 1904-7 Herero uprising.

Zambezi Lodge

Towering indigenous trees and lush tropical gardens provide the atmospheric setting for the Zambezi Lodge, situated on the Namibian side of the great river 2 km from the little town of Katima Mulilo. For bird-watching expeditions or fishing trips on the Zambezi you can hire a motorboat or, more adventurously, a 'mokoro' (traditional dugout canoe). Chobe Game Reserve, famous for its elephant and lechwe herds, is just to the south in Botswana.

Accommodation at the lodge comprises 17 double and two single bedroom units and six family units, each with its own bathroom. There's a floodlit swimming pool, floating bar, restaurant, gym, sauna and nine-hole golf course (onto which free-ranging herds of hippo occasionally stray in search of grazing).

Turbo-prop aircraft fly to Katima Mulilo from Johannesburg and Windhoek and good tarred roads lead most of the way to Zambezi Lodge (on the Windhoek road the tar ends at Bagani, while on the Johannesburg road the last 130 km from Francistown is untarred). For further information and bookings write to Alta Visagie, P.O. Box 98, Katima Mulilo 9000, Namibia (or telephone Katima Mulilo 203/149).

Through the lens

These two photographs, taken from the same position, illustrate the effects produced by a variety of lenses. The wide-angle lens (left) captures a broader expanse of territory, while the standard lens reproduces the view as the human eye sees it.

Southern Africa offers generous opportunities for the average photographer to 'shoot' wild animals in their natural surroundings. Patience, practice and attention to a few fundamental principles are all that you require, with even a relatively inexpensive camera, to create a permanent record of the scenes you observed and enjoyed.

If you go out on foot, wear drab-coloured clothing – you are less likely to scare away your subject. You may have to sit quite still for a long time while waiting for the right moment, so be sure that your clothes are also comfortable. Take a field guide on the birds or animals you want to photograph, as well as a notebook and pencil. Make a note of light conditions, film speed and camera settings for each exposure.

Dust and moisture can be harmful to your equipment, and proper precautions should be taken. Protect your lenses against accidental scratches by fitting them with lens caps or ultraviolet (UV) filters. Keep lenses clean with lens paper (take care not to scratch the surface) and a blow-brush. All equipment should be kept under cover – preferably in an insulated and well-sealed bag or case – until it is used. Remember that heat can be your worst enemy. Do not leave your camera in a hot vehicle or in direct sunlight, and store all film (especially after it has been exposed) in a 'cool' bag or ice bucket, making sure that it is insulated from moisture. Process the film as soon as possible. When working in particularly dusty conditions, wrap your cameras and lenses in plastic bags – grit could cause havoc in their delicate mechanism.

Because of its lightness and versatility, a 35mm single lens reflex (SLR) camera is the most convenient for use in the field. In addition to the standard lens (usually about 50mm), a telephoto lens of 100mm to 400mm is ideal for capturing candid wildlife shots: without it you may not be able to get close enough for a good study of a shy or dangerous animal.

Some useful accessories
● A 2X ('two-times') converter is a useful and inexpensive accessory: it doubles the focal length of your lenses and brings otherwise unreachable subjects into the viewfinder (the converter is cheaper than a telephoto lens, but some photographers regard this as being an unacceptable short cut). Make sure that the converter matches the lenses with which you intend to use it.

● The standard lens may suffice for landscape studies, but you might care to experiment with a wide-angle lens. One of about 28mm is suitable for most situations. When using a wide-angle lens, remember that although it gives prominence to the foreground, it reduces the impact of distant objects, such as trees and mountains. Because of the distortion produced by this type of lens, the camera must be held absolutely upright – otherwise tall objects will appear to lean over in your picture. However, the most versatile lenses for nature photography are the 'zoom' and 'macro-zoom' types. These have a variable focal length, and can be used for close-ups as well as telephoto work.

Use of a telephoto or 'zoom' lens, which generally reduces the depth of field (range of focus), dictates a fairly fast film. A (black and white) film speed of 400 ASA is often fast enough to 'freeze' movement, even with the longer lens. Under bright light conditions, colour film with an ASA rating of between 50 and 160 should be adequate, especially for static subjects such as landscapes and flowers. When photographing animals, use shutter speeds of 1/125 second – 1/250 second to stop movement, and remember that 'panning' (tracking the subject in the viewfinder) will help to keep the animal in focus. Before you buy a lens, find out whether you can hire what you need from photographic dealers.

● If your camera is not fitted with a through-the-lens (TTL) light metering system, you will have to remember to alter settings when you use a converter or telephoto lens – they admit less light to the film.

● Your camera will be difficult to hold still when an extended lens is fitted. Even with a high shutter speed, 1/250 second, a camera with a 300mm lens will probably have some 'shake', resulting in a blurred photograph. If you are photographing from a car, use a folded towel on the window sill as a rest for the lens. If you are on foot, take a tripod or monopod. You can give a tripod extra rigidity by hanging a weight from its centre-pole: use a cable shutter release to avoid vibration.

● A lens hood is an inexpensive accessory, and is essential in reducing 'flare' when shooting towards the sun.

● For bird or insect photography you will almost certainly need a flashgun. Nests are often in deep shade in a bush, and without a flashgun you may not be able to take a photograph at all.

● A motor drive and remote shutter-release device would enable you to operate your camera, if it has been pre-focused, at distances of up to about 100m. This system works satisfactorily, but using a camera in a 'hide' probably gives consistently better results, and is less expensive. Your car may also be used as a hide. Animals will often accept the presence of a vehicle, but feel threatened by the sight of a man on foot.

Stalking your subject You can conduct a leisurely and nearly always rewarding 'photosafari' in your own garden, with birds, flowers, butterflies or trees as your subjects. But when you are in the field after game it is often a matter of luck whether or not your quarry appears within the effective focal length of the lens you have fitted. When you are certain you have a good picture, 'bracket' the exposure to make sure you have it (expose the scene at one f-stop above and one below the original exposure). Prepare your camera so that you can shoot as soon as you see your subject: with this picture in hand, you can then try other adjustments.

A low-power telephoto lens cuts out some background, but retains the tree-top to indicate the presence of living vegetation.

The medium telephoto lens changes the mood, giving more emphasis to the animal subject and reducing the impact of its surroundings.

In this picture the elephant is clearly intended to dominate (remember: the more powerful the telephoto lens, the smaller the depth of field).

When the animal is within the correct range, track it for a while through the viewfinder. It may yawn, growl,' look directly at you or do something that will give you a truly appealing picture rather than one that is just a good record of a species. Placing the subject in the exact centre of the frame sometimes gives the picture a posed look. Make sure that the whole animal is in the viewfinder unless you have a good reason for doing otherwise.

Depth of field is more difficult to control with a telephoto lens than with a standard lens but a 'head only' shot looks more effective with the background slightly out of focus and the features of the head sharp and clear. When photographing the whole animal keep the surroundings in focus. Closing the aperture to

increase the depth of field means that you will have to use a longer exposure, and unless you have a tripod or a firm 'rest', there is a risk of a blurred picture.

When you have only a few exposures left on a film, it is sometimes a good idea to rewind and load with a new film while you have time. You may be wasting a few frames, but you will have a full roll of film to use on a once-in-a-lifetime opportunity that may crop up at any moment – especially in game reserves.

The best natural light is provided by the low sun of early morning and late afternoon, but you should remember to check your light meter every minute or so because the light values change rapidly at those times. Keep an eye open for man-made features which might jar

in a nature picture: motor cars, telegraph poles and even a discarded bottle could ruin a beautiful setting.

'Bad' weather often provides the most dramatic light for outdoor photography – the subdued tones of an overcast sky are ideal for landscapes. Resist the temptation to economise by combining the scenic shot with a family portrait. Both subjects will be diluted and the picture will do justice to neither.

Preoccupation with the interest or beauty of a nature scene can easily lull you into carelessness, a state of mind in which you feel there is little to do but 'point-and-press'. But nature will not do it all – your practice and expertise are as important as the subject. A final word of advice: take plenty of film.

Left: This underwater camera can be taken to a depth of 50 m without a special housing. It is coupled to a powerful electronic flashgun.

Above: Mushroom Rocks in the Golden Gate National Park, taken without a polarising filter (and **above left**) with a filter.

On safari

The simplest and probably the least stressful way to view Southern Africa's wealth of game parks and nature reserves is by signing on for an organised tour. Today there are 'package' safaris to suit just about every adventurer's dream – and most budgets.

At the inexpensive end of the spectrum are the many half-day excursions by bus, while at the other extreme is the two-week grand tour by chauffeured 4-wheel-drive through some of the world's most exclusive (and expensive) private game parks.

Some holidaymakers might prefer an even more unusual excursion, like skimming over the Magaliesberg in a hot air balloon, or joining a hiking party and exploring the awesome Fish River Canyon. Whatever your choice of safari, remember that somebody is likely to have done it that way before. Ask for advice and take the advice. Established safari operators will, if they wish to maintain a good reputation, be candid about the advantages or otherwise of your proposed route.

The first benefit of the organised safari is immediately apparent: you know in advance roughly what your holiday will cost you (you may even be able to pay for it in instalments). Benefit number two is the carefree character of the adventure.

You can relax in the knowledge that should your vehicle suffer a mishap or breakdown – it is someone else's problem.

A third advantage is the tour guide, who is likely to have been there many times and can therefore speak with authority on virtually every aspect of the park or reserve. He will take you along the best route and point out sights you may normally have missed.

Most cities and large towns in Southern Africa have a complement of tour operators and tourist bureaus staffed by people with an intimate knowledge of local attractions – and the best way to see them.

Doing it your way

You may, of course, be one of those independent and adventurous spirits who despise the predictability and 'guaranteed success' of an organised tour. For you the essence of an adventure is the freedom to explore a place whenever you like, content in the knowledge that surprises may lurk around any corner. If you would rather organise your own safari, you are advised to follow these practical suggestions:

330

Top: Negotiating a dusty, primitive track in Damaraland. On routes such as this, conventional vehicles are useless. Safaris should be planned with care, and provision should be made for such important factors as the type of terrain, weather, distance between water points, availability of fuel and, where applicable, the physical fitness of the participants in the expedition. **Above left:** This reasonably priced compass is flat and compact, with calibrated edges to facilitate map measurements. The housing carries an arrow which indicates the direction of travel.
Above right: This simple compass is suitable for precision aiming on land and water (the compass is placed on a map and used to take bearings on objects). It is a lightweight design, and comes equipped with a safety cord. The ability to read maps will stand the more adventurous tourist in good stead in the wilder parts of Southern Africa.

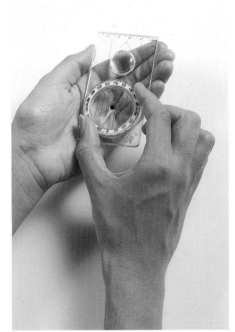

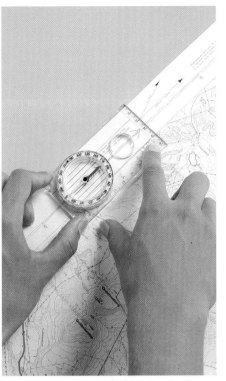

Above: These three photographs indicate a simple way of setting a map with the use of a compass. **Step 1** Turn the 'N' of the compass housing until it is aligned with the direction-of-travel arrow on the baseplate. **Step 2** Place the map on a flat, non-magnetic surface. Align the edge of the baseplate of the compass with the North line shown on the map. **Step 3** Turn the map, holding the compass firmly to it and with the baseplate edge in constant alignment with the map's North line, until the North point of the compass needle points to the 'N' of the compass housing. You can now put the compass away, as the map is set. This means that directions on the map are the same as directions on the ground. In other words, if you can identify where on the map you are now (call this point 'A'), and another point ('B') where you want to go, you could find the direction in which to walk by projecting the line from 'A' to 'B' on the map (as shown in the figure). For practical reasons, it is a good idea to familiarise yourself with some of the more common map symbols before setting out on your safari.

● If you cannot afford to buy such a vehicle, consider renting one.

● Ask the tour companies for advice on suitable spares and equipment. The Automobile Association will also give advice.

● Find out in advance where you will be able to stock up with supplies of food, water, and petrol, and where you could have your vehicle repaired should it become necessary. Also ascertain well in advance which special permits and inoculations are required. Contact the Automobile Association for information.

● If you are travelling to remote areas, remember that the water may be polluted. There are a number of chemical purifiers on the market, and a new invention – known as a 'survival straw' – can produce pleasant-tasting, bacteria-free water from raw municipal sewage and stagnant pond water.

● Always ensure that somebody at home knows your destination and estimated time of arrival. Contact them when you arrive and let them know when you expect to return home.

● You will need valid passports and possibly entry visas for the country or countries you intend visiting. Re-entry permits may be required for foreign passport holders. It is also advisable to take a supply of the relevant currency, but you should first seek advice from the relevant authorities.

For information on safaris in Southern Africa, write to the following addresses:

South Africa The Director of the South African Tourist Corporation (SATOUR), Private Bag X164, Pretoria 0001 (telephone Pretoria 348-9521).

Botswana The Tourist Officer, Department of Wildlife and National Parks, P.O. Box 131, Gaborone (telephone Gaborone 37-1405).

Namibia Director of Nature Conservation, Reservations, Private Bag 13267, Windhoek 9000 (telephone Windhoek 3-6975/6/7/8).

Zimbabwe Zimbabwe Tourism Development Corporation, P.O. Box 8052, Causeway, Harare (telephone Harare 79-3666).

Lesotho Lesotho Tourist Board, P.O. Box 1378, Maseru (telephone Maseru 32-2896).

Swaziland The Government Tourist Office, P.O. Box 451, Mbabane (telephone Mbabane 4-3201).

Ciskei Department of Tourism and Aviation, Private Bag X0026, Bisho (telephone Bisho 91121).

Transkei Department of Agriculture and Forestry, Private Bag X5002, Umtata (telephone Umtata 2-5191).

Venda Venda Development Corporation, P.O. Box 9, Sibasa, Venda (telephone Sibasa 2-1131).

How to use a compass

When straying from the beaten track, you may need to make use of a compass. An orienteering type is considered the best for beginners, who may choose from a range of instruments with direction-finder, transparent base and liquid-filled housing for rapid (and accurate) readings. In using a compass, learn to differentiate between *true* or geographic north (to which maps are drawn) and *magnetic* north (the direction in which the magnetised needle points). The difference between the two, called declination, is measured in degrees.

● To follow a compass reading, first determine the degree direction (for example, 10 degrees NE) on the compass rim. Hold the compass at waist level and turn around until the red tip of the needle lies directly over the orienteering arrow (within the housing). Then look straight ahead, pinpoint a landmark such as a tree or mountain peak, and walk towards it.

● To take a bearing, face the desired direction and turn the housing until the needle points to 'N'.

● To set a direction, align the compass edge with your present position and your destination on a map. Turn the compass housing until the orienteering arrow is parallel to the meridian on the map.

BOTSWANA

Botswana is Southern Africa's largest and most authentic wilderness, a country of harsh contrast and matchless beauty: once seen, it will never be forgotten. This is Van der Post country, a parched expanse of sand, sweet grass and teeming game that conjures up a hundred adventure stories.

Once the exclusive haunt of indigenous tribesmen, hunters and adventurers, Botswana is today an exciting mixture of cultures and lifestyles. The lean, sunburnt hunters still exist, but they rub shoulders and share sundowners with more conventional tourists – and sometimes with conservationists, a multi-talented body of people dedicated to the preservation of the Kalahari's wildlife heritage.

There are many privately owned lodges and camps throughout Botswana, and facilities and accommodation vary widely: some are primitive and relatively cheap, while others are unabashedly luxurious and expensive. Visitors may fly in or explore the country in 4-wheel-drive vehicles; in the vast and beautiful Okavango Delta they navigate the shallow water in dugout canoes.

Whatever the medium of transport, however, it should be remembered that Botswana is big, untamed and potentially dangerous: do not attempt to explore its sandy wastes in a conventional car (in most areas the authorities recommend two 4-wheel-drive vehicles as a precaution), and do not stray from the roads and tracks.

Elephants drinking at the Savuti Channel, an abrupt offshoot of the Linyanti River, in Botswana's Chobe National Park. Wildlife is drawn as if by a magnet when the channel is in flood.

333

Wild and misty waterways

In the waterways of the Okavango, one of the world's last great wildernesses, scented water lilies, yellow, white, pink and lilac, shimmer on the water. A dragonfly hovers, a jacana bird trots across the lily leaves in search of its food. At water level in a nearby water-rooted fig, where the sacred ibis, cormorant, darter and egret huddle, spiders weave delicate filigree webs and cocoons of incredible complexity. On and around islands of tufted grass snakes keep company with turtles and thousands of colourful, noisy frogs. As the dugout canoe cuts its way silently through the reeds, the lily leaves – green to the sun and red to the tigerfish below – trail on long stalks.

On a floating papyrus bed, a tiny crocodile basks open-mouthed in the sun, its hide glistening, needle-sharp teeth bared in unconscious menace. Round the next bend – and there are many bends in the labyrinthine meanderings of the delta – a scrum of hippo huff, snort and lower their corpulent bodies beneath the water. When the flood comes in mid-winter, the water is crystal clear and fast-running: later, the current may be barely discernible over the flats, making navigation difficult for the inexperienced explorer. Water creeps down the

dry riverbeds and across the dusty floodplains, obliterating stagnant pools and dispersing the thousands of animals which concentrated upon them in the drier times.

Born in the uplands of western Angola, where the coffee grows, the Okavango is a great and troubled river (the third largest in Southern Africa). It flows not to the sea, but east into the fiery heart of the Kalahari Desert – and there, in a fragile, tremor-shaken depression, it slows, stretches and dies. But its grave is a delta extending for 15 000 km – a natural symphony of rivers, lagoons, islands and forests. To those who have been there, the Okavango is beautiful beyond words.

Protected by the presence of tsetse fly and by its very size, the delta has until recently remained largely unconquered by man's marauding rifles, ever-expanding habitations and herds of cattle.

The large variety of game in the delta includes some 20 000 buffalo and the elusive sitatunga, whose splayed hoofs enable it to walk through the swamps without getting bogged down.

There are several safari camps, some accessible only by air from outside the delta. Maun is the main springboard to the delta and serv-

ices some of the camps by road and air. It takes about 12 hours in a 4-wheel-drive vehicle to cover the 380 km journey from Maun to Shakawe in the north. The normal route from Namibia is via the border post of Mamuno, some 200 km (six hours) of deep sand (4-wheel-drive only) to the cattle centre of Ghanzi.

There are flights from Johannesburg to Gaborone which link up to internal flights to Maun. For further information, write to Maun Office Services, P.O. Box 448, Maun, Botswana (telephone Maun 260222) or Travel Wild, P.O. Box 236, Maun, Botswana (telephone Maun 260493).

Chief's Island

Named after Moremi, chief of the Tswana, Chief's Island in the Okavango Delta, 100 km long and 15 km across its widest point, is a great tract of woodland and savanna rich in game, hidden waterways and bird life. It is flanked by two of the delta's largest rivers, the Boro and the Santantadibe, both of which flow into the Thamalakane River, not far from Maun. It forms a good third of the Moremi Wildlife Reserve. No camps or human habitations are permitted on the island: consequently the overwhelming sense of wildness is complete.

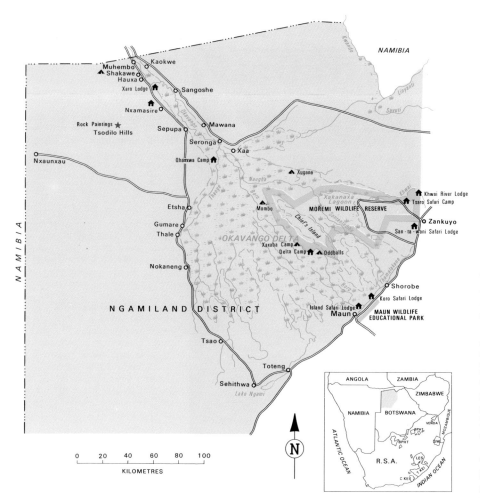

Opposite page left: A bird's-eye view of the Delta. The Okavango River is Southern Africa's third largest. **Opposite page right:** A nymphal foam grasshopper belonging to the family Pyrgomorphidae. Although it possesses wing pads, this species has flightless adults. For self-protection, these large grasshoppers, or bush locusts, depend very much on their striking 'warning' colours, which advertise their toxic nature to vertebrate predators. In response to an attack by a predator they release foul-smelling, poisonous fluids from various points on their bodies. Some species propel the fluid in a jet from special glands; others produce a foam composed of irritants mixed with their own blood. **Right:** Little bee-eaters huddling together at night in the depths of an Okavango reed bed. Although these birds are (for obvious reasons) unpopular with apiarists, bee-eaters do in fact feed on many types of flying insect other than honey bees.

There are several (tented) photographic safari camps fringing Chief's Island – all accessible from Maun by small aircraft or by boat with a guide. From Maun it is 70 km by air to these camps. For further details, you should write to Maun Office Services, P.O. Box 443, Maun, Botswana (telephone Maun 260222); or to Travel Wild, P.O. Box 236, Maun, Botswana (telephone Maun 260493).

Delta Camp

Situated outside the Moremi Wildlife Reserve, and accessible only by light aircraft from Maun, Delta Camp is a remote bush camp accommodating 4 people (the accommodation consists of a four-bedded family hut). The camp is on Noga Island, and is a week's lazy travel (by water) from Shakawe. The camp is visited by a host of birds and animals, including barred owls, bearded woodpeckers, baboon and porcupine, amongst others.

Built around some magnificent trees, the camp abuts onto Chief's Island. Excursions are undertaken in mokoro and on foot – particularly on Chief's Island, which hosts a large variety of game, both big and small. The winter months are the busiest, but summer is also a delight for naturalists and bird-watchers. Chief's Island lies approximately 60 km west-northwest of Maun (the distance by river is about 80 km).

For more information, write to Okavango Tours and Safaris, P.O. Box 52900, Saxonwold 2132 (telephone Johannesburg 788-5549), or you could write to the Botswana address of Okavango Tours and Safaris, P.O. Box 39, Maun (telephone Maun 260220).

Fish Eagle Trail

The trail is run by Educational Wildlife Expeditions, part of the Transvaal-based organisation known as the Endangered Wildlife Trust. Groups of up to eight people are taken walking and by dugout canoe into the Okavango Delta, where they camp for three nights before continuing to Savuti Channel in the Chobe National Park. The participants leave from Johannesburg on Fridays by light aircraft, and return on a Tuesday. For further information, write to Fish Eagle Trail, P.O. Box 645, Bedfordview 2008 (telephone Johannesburg 53-1814).

Khwai River Lodge

The Khwai River (in the north-east of the Okavango Delta) is one of the major rivers of the delta though it occasionally all but dries up, leaving a few hippo pools to await the fresh waters of the new season. It forms the northern border of the Moremi Wildlife Reserve and is host to several lodges and photographic safari camps, among them the Khwai River Lodge (operated by Gametrackers) near the reserve's northern entrance gate.

The lodge, with its flat-topped acacia shade trees and huge sycamore fig trees, thatched chalets, pool and patio overlooking the river and Moremi forest, was built in 1966 by Ker, Downey and Selby – professional hunters. A herd of red lechwe gallops through the reed beds in the early morning, pauses to browse, then gallops away. The nocturnal 'chorus' includes hyena, lion, baboon and crickets, but is inevitably dominated by the grunting and snorting of hippo – hardly tuneful, but certainly authentic Africa.

The lodge offers all day Land-Rover trips into the Moremi (travelling as far as Xakanaxa Lagoon on the edge of the permanent water), sundowner game drives, and 5 km early-morning bush walks. These end with breakfast in an open-air thorn boma over which a high fish eagle's nest presides.

From Maun it is 140 km or four hours by 4-wheel-drive to Khwai River Lodge (the Shorobe road runs along the east bank of the Thamalakane River). Take the first turning to the left after Zankuyo village and head for the Moremi reserve's north gate. The lodge is 10 km east of the gate on the north bank of the Khwai River. There is an airstrip, and the Gametrackers' light aircraft will fly you straight in from either the Victoria Falls or Johannesburg (via Maun). From the Kazungula border post on the Zambezi, 70 km from the Victoria Falls, visitors face a rough drive of approximately 280 km to Khwai River Lodge.

For further information, write to The Manager, Khwai River Lodge, P.O. Box 66, Maun, Botswana. Gametrackers have a central reservations office in South Africa: address enquiries to Safariplan, P.O. Box 4245, Randburg 2125 (telephone Johannesburg 886-1810).

Koro Safari Lodge

Beside the Thamalakane River and 20 km north of Maun, on the road to Moremi, lies Koro Safari Lodge. It is at the perimeter of the Okavango Delta; safaris into the delta itself, either by vehicle or boat, can be arranged.

Accommodation at the lodge is in thatched-roof brick chalets, some with their own showers. (Booking is not essential.) The last 5 km of the road to Koro Safari Lodge are sandy, and a 4-wheel-drive vehicle is recommended. For further enquiries you should write to Private Bag 22, Maun, Botswana (or telephone Maun 260205 or 260222).

Lake Ngami

The legendary Lake Ngami is like a great blue mirage on the edge of the dry grassland of the Okavango Delta, about 70 km from Maun. This lake attracted (among others) David Livingstone in 1849, and its shores are now the home of Yei fishermen and colourful Herero pastoralists. In

Left: A sharp-eyed Pel's fishing owl (*Scotopelia peli*) watches the Okavango waters for signs of its prey. One of the rarer species of owl (though fairly common in the wetlands of Botswana), it has bare legs and long, strong claws.
Opposite page above left: A semi-aquatic antelope related to the waterbuck, the red lechwe lives mainly in the flood plains of the Okavango, western Zambia and southern Zaire. Water is both its sustenance and its defence: the species feeds on wetland grasses and aquatic plants, retiring to deeper water (slow-footed on land, it is a competent swimmer) when threatened. Lechwes are gregarious animals, sometimes gathering in herds of a thousand and more.
Opposite page above right: *Nymphaea caerulea*, a delicately attractive species of water lily that thrives in the Okavango area.
Opposite page below: Tsessebe in the Moremi Wildlife Reserve. Normally these antelope live in small groups of eight to 10 (though single bulls are occasionally seen in the company of other species such as blue wildebeest and zebra), but come together in herds of up to 200 in the dry season. Not only is the tsessebe the swiftest of all Southern Africa's buck, but it also has stamina to match its speed — it can maintain its full pace for anything up to five kilometres.

some years it is a dustbowl, but for decades on end can be a shallow lake 45 km long and up to 16 km wide.

Countless birds wheel, dive and feed in the water, in the air and on the shores: colonies of breeding pelicans, gulls, storks, greater and lesser flamingoes, herons and many other species throng the shallows. October to March is the best time to visit. Ornithological safaris are operated to the lake from Maun.

Maun

Patched-up Land-Rovers, compressed sand, floodplains and whisky: Maun is all this and much more, an appealing anachronism whose residents (some of them, anyway) appear to have walked out of the pages of a Wilbur Smith novel. Maun is Botswana's tourist centre and jump-off point for the Okavango. There are several companies with whom most of the photographic safari operators deal: Merlin Travel (telephone Maun 260351), Travel Wild (telephone Maun 260493), Okavango Tours and Safaris (telephone Maun 260220), and Bonaven-

ture Botswana (telephone Maun 260222). Riley's Garage (P.O. Box 20, Maun; telephone Maun 260203) and Riley's Hotel (P.O. Box 1, Maun; telephone Maun 260204) are more or less 'national monuments'. Maun is one hour by air from Victoria Falls, and three hours from Lanseria airport in Johannesburg.

Apart from Riley's Hotel, there are three other lodges and camps: Okavango River Lodge (telephone Maun 260298), Okavango Swamps Crocodile Farm (telephone Maun 260570) and Island Safari Lodge (telephone Maun 260300). All are on the Thamalakane River (just north of Maun) and all feature thatched chalets and campsites. Activities include wildlife and Okavango Delta safaris (visitors travel in 4-wheel-drive vehicles and boats). Boats may be hired, and guides are available. Island Safari Lodge shows films four times a week. You can drive a normal saloon car the whole distance from Francistown (on the Cape-Zimbabwe highway) to Maun. The first 188 km is on tar. For further information contact Maun Office Services or any other travel agent.

declaring 1800 km² of their tribally owned land in the Okavango Delta a game reserve. Today its floodplains offer a rich variety of game, magnificent mopane forests, islands of tall fan palms, crystal-clear Okavango waterways and practically every wildlife habitat. Even a short drive into the reserve results in a dozen sightings: impala, roan, lion, tsessebe, kudu, elephant, buffalo, lechwe, warthog and legions of baboon.

Huge strangler figs, with roots resembling snakes, enmesh the kigelia sausage trees, while in the distant vlei hundreds of tsessebe graze. The bird life in Moremi is rich to the point of extravagance: rollers, hoopoes, kingfishers, owls and woodpeckers are the most common, while a bend in the Khwai River offers a view of birds such as wattled cranes, spur-winged geese, saddlebill storks and herons.

For further information on Moremi, write to The Senior Warden, Department of Wildlife and National Parks, P.O. Box 11, Maun, Botswana (telephone Maun 260230).

Oddballs

Oddballs is one of the Okavango's budget camps. Booking is not essential, and campers are expected to bring their own food (but the complex includes a restaurant and a shop stocking a limited range of tinned foods). Visitors are brought to Oddballs from Maun, about 50 km away, by air or boat. Once there, the delta and its fauna can be explored at leisure by 'mokoro' – dugout canoe. For further information write to P.O. Box 39, Maun, Botswana (telephone Maun 260220).

Qhaaxwa Camp

The reed chalets of Qhaaxwa Camp are clustered on a tranquil island, opening onto a papyrus-fringed lagoon, at the southernmost end of the Okavango Delta's 'panhandle'. It's a place for surveying the abundant bird life – fish eagles, slaty egrets, Pel's fishing owls, African skimmers, swamp boubous and many others – or for boating in mokoro or powerboats through placid, translucent waters that are home to bream and tigerfish, not to mention the occasional hippo. Water-loving lechwe and the elusive sitatunga are the main inhabitants of the area's floodplains.

The camp takes up to 16 guests in chalets with *en suite* washing facilities. Further enquiries can be made to Gametrackers, P.O. Box 4245, Randburg 2125 (telephone Johannesburg 886-1810).

San-ta-wani Safari Lodge

San-ta-wani is named after a mythical fox (as opposed to the bat-eared fox, symbol of Botswana's Department of Wildlife, National Parks and Tourism), whose footprints are, according to legend, purple in the dew.

Maun Wildlife Educational Park

The only fenced game park in Botswana lies alongside the Thamalakane River near Maun. At the entrance gate, a board informs visitors that this sanctuary, 2 km long and 1 km wide, was established to teach people about wildlife conservation and management. The park contains vegetation typical of the area where the Okavango and Kalahari meet. A variety of game, including giraffe, kudu and wildebeest, has been reintroduced.

The park is ten minutes by car from Riley's Hotel in the village: you let yourself in by pushing aside some dusty poles. For further information, you should write to The Senior Game Warden, Department of Wildlife and National Parks, P.O. Box 111, Maun, Botswana (telephone Maun 260230).

Mombo Camp

You might be lucky enough to spot an albino lechwe when you're game-viewing in the area surrounding Mombo Camp; these unusual animals are a local feature. The tented camp is in the western delta of the Okavango and is reached by air (normally from Maun). In addition to game safaris, fishing and walking trips are organised. Mombo sleeps 12 people. For further information you can write to Nemesis (Pty) Ltd, P.O. Box 201, Maun, Botswana (or telephone Maun 260351).

Moremi Wildlife Reserve

Botswana is a magnet for hunters, and has been so for centuries. It was the decimation of the game that prompted naturalists Robert and June Kaye to rally the Tswana people into

OKAVANGO AT A GLANCE

When to go The best time to visit this rugged and beautiful area is from late May through to October, when the Okavango River floods the delta. December to February is the wet season, and not recommended. The Moremi Game Reserve in the delta is open year-round, except when the rains occasionally necessitate closure. The later in the year (before the onset of the December rains), the better the game-viewing.

Reservations and information To reserve accommodation in the two chalet camps at Khwai River and San-ta-wani (on the eastern fringe of the delta), write to Gametrackers, c/o Safariplan, P.O. Box 4245, Randburg 2125 (telephone Johannesburg 886-1810).

The travel contacts in Maun are: Merlin Travel (telephone Maun 260351), Travel Wild (telephone Maun 260493), Okavango Tours and Safaris (telephone Maun 260220), and Bonaventure Botswana (telephone Maun 260222).

Another travel contact is Maun Office Services, P.O. Box 443, Maun, Botswana (telephone Maun 260222).

For information on the Okavango Delta, you should write to the Department of Wildlife and National Parks, P.O. Box 111 Maun, Botswana (telephone Maun 260230)

Getting there Maun is the springboard for most trips in the Okavango Delta. It is accessible by road and by air.

Accommodation There are government camping sites in the Moremi Wildlife Reserve, and numerous (privately run) photographic, fishing and bird-watching safari camps in the Okavango. Nearly all offer all-inclusive tented camp facilities.

Eating and drinking All foodstuffs and drink are supplied at photographic safari camps. Because the Okavango is a true wilderness, there are no shops or petrol stations. Visitors intending to camp should bring their own food, petrol, spares and water. Maun is the nearest shopping area.

Getting around Aircraft are an obvious form of transport in the Okavango Delta. Air Kavango (P.O. Box 169, Maun, Botswana; telephone Maun 260393) operates three (single-engined) six-seater aircraft. Most safari operators have their own aircraft. Four-wheel-drive vehicles are recommended, although experienced drivers familiar with the terrain sometimes use conventional vehicles. Vehicles can also be hired in Maun. A variety of companies operate safaris into the Okavango, and they usually include the Savuti Channel area of the Chobe National Park in their itinerary. There is a rustic bus service from Francistown to Maun.

Special attractions A trip on a mokoro at Xaxaba, Xakanaxa, Xugana or from Maun or Shakawe is an unforgettable experience. The limestone Gcwihaba Caverns, 150km west of the delta, are worth a detour. The Tsodilo Hills, 50km west of the Okavango, and rising 400m above the surrounding Kalahari plains, are studded with endless small samples of prehistoric rock art. This is the only place left in Southern Africa where San still live near the rock art of their forefathers.

Wildlife Hippo, crocodile, python, lion, elephant, lechwe, baboon, wildebeest, buffalo, warthog, bat-eared fox and hundreds of species of birds are represented in the Okavango Delta.

Fishing The Okavango is not a swamp. Its waters are crystal clear and teem (at the edges) with bream and tigerfish. The best fishing is from September to April (tackle can be hired in the camps). Fishing licences or permits are not required in the delta, but they are in the game reserves.

Special precautions Anti-malaria precautions and a snake-bite kit are essential. Use mosquito nets at night. A first-aid kit should be carried. Beware of crocodile when swimming. Sluggish water in Maun may be infested with bilharzia-carrying snails. There is tsetse fly in the delta, but sleeping sickness is rare. Permission is needed to camp in the reserve. A guide is recommended.

Shakawe

Shakawe is in the far north-west corner of Botswana, 15km from the Caprivi Strip. Permits are necessary from the South African authorities to enter via the western Caprivi (Shakawe), or the eastern Caprivi (Ngoma).

Situated beside the Okavango River, Shakawe is a sprawling conglomeration of huts, reeds, dugout canoes and anthills. It is here, in the forests of the Okavango River floodplain, that the giant mokutshumo trees are felled by the Mbukushu people to make dugout canoes, the taxis of the Okavango. Here, too, is one of Botswana's best tigerfishing spots.

The Shakawe Fishing Camp, run by Okavango Fishing Safaris (P.O. Box 446, Francistown, Botswana); and Nxamasire Fishing Camp, P.O. Box 236, Maun (telephone Maun 260493 or Johannesburg 53-1814) offer accommodation with all facilities for visitors. There is a campsite at Shakawe fishing camp with ablution blocks; running water and firewood. The best fishing is in August and September. The distance by road from Maun is 370km, and can only be covered in 4-wheel-drive vehicles. Further information is available from Maun Office Services, P.O. Box 448, Maun, Botswana (telephone Maun 260202) or Travel Wild at P.O. Box 236, Maun, Botswana (telephone Maun 260493).

Sitatunga Safaris

About 15km south of Maun – on a gravel road that's negotiable by 2-wheel drive vehicles – is the budget-price Sitatunga Safaris camping site, laid out in a well-wooded location. The various facilities available include a provision store, tapped water, firewood, bucket-showers and toilets that (like the showers) are reed-enclosed and open to the skies for an extra 'outdoor experience'.

Nearer to the Thamalakane River is a tented camp, where showers and toilets are brick-walled. A pleasant restaurant situated on the bank overlooks the river. For further enquiries write to Private Bag 47, Maun, Botswana (or telephone Maun 260570).

Tsaro Lodge

Tsaro is a luxurious safari camp on a 6ha floodplain island on the northern edge of the Moremi Wildlife Reserve, situated near Khwai River Lodge. It is 160km from Maun and 10km from the reserve's north gate. There are eight thatched rondavels with *en suite* facilities, which have been built beneath giant trees – motshaba figs, leadwood trees, crotons and knobthorns overlooking the Khwai River. There is also a swimming pool, a fully stocked bar and conference facilities for up to 16 people.

For further information about Tsaro, write to: Okavango Explorations, P.O. Box 69859, Bryanston 2021 (telephone Johannesburg 708-1893).

The lodge is situated south of Moremi Wildlife Reserve's south gate, 74km from Maun. Turn left at a junction about 7km from Maun and 20km beyond Shukumukwa Village on the 'great north track' to the Chobe National Park and Victoria Falls. It should be noted that the lodge does not accept casual visitors.

There is an airstrip beside a nearby lagoon formed by the Mogogelo River, and the game-viewing is excellent: visitors are likely to spot elephant, wildebeest, kudu, zebra, hyena, buffalo and myriad birds of many species.

Gametrackers operate San-ta-wani lodge. As with all Gametracker camps, it is closed from 1 January to 28 February. Canoes on the waterways are a speciality. For further information write to Gametrackers, c/o Safariplan, P.O. Box 4245, Randburg 2125 (telephone Johannesburg 886-1810), or telephone Gametrackers Botswana at Maun 260302.

Left: A flight of squacco herons on the papyrus-lined Okavango River – a fairly rare sight because, although the species is common in the wetter regions of Southern Africa, it tends to be a solitary bird, spending much of its time standing almost motionless among the marsh reeds. The squacco heron is a shy and skulking bird. You won't spot it very easily because it is well camouflaged and can be over-looked. It tends to roost communally, sometimes with other waterbirds. It forages by stalking slowly in shallow water. **Above left:** The blood lily brings a splash of strident colour to the delta countryside. **Above:** The nocturnal scrub hare is larger (the males weigh up to 2 kg) and longer-eared than other Southern African hares. The species thrives throughout the subcontinent – though it tends to avoid forest – and, in many areas, encroaches on cultivated lands.

Xakanaxa Lagoon

Fifty kilometres from Khwai River Lodge and 160 km from Maun, in the north of the Moremi Wildlife Reserve along a sandy road through dense forests of mopane, is Xakanaxa – a crescent-shaped and crystal-clear lagoon on the Muanachira River. Here, on the permanent water of the Okavango (as opposed to the flood-plains), is a comfortable camp run by Moremi Safaris. It is among the most attractive camps in the delta and has eight walk-in tented rooms with built-in ground sheets and mosquito netting. There is hot and cold running water, flush toilets and showers. Huge sausage trees overhang the tents at the water's edge, and there is a communal reed-walled dining room.

Xakanaxa specialises in boat trips through the Okavango waterways: underwater hippo paths and tigerfish are clearly visible beneath the boat. Game-viewing is not good during the mid-November to March rainy season. July to October are the months to see nesting marabous and yellow-billed storks. The minimum stay is four nights (children pay adult rates). Liquor and transport by 4-wheel-drive vehicle are included in the tariff. There is an airstrip at Khwai, 50 km distant. The camp caters for 12 people. For further information, write to Moremi Safaris, P.O. Box 32, Maun, Botswana.

Xaro Lodge

An ideal retreat for anglers, Xaro Lodge lies on a peninsula jutting out into the fast-flowing Okavango River, on the western side of the delta's panhandle. There's bird- and game-watching too; while an unusual attraction is an outing – by road or air – to the nearby Tsodilo Hills, where more than 2 500 rock paintings are to be found. (The area is still inhabited by San.)

Xaro Lodge sleeps 4, in luxury double tents, with a bathroom near each pair of tents. There is hot and cold running water, flush toilets, a fully stocked bar and a lounge and dining room. For further enquiries you should write to P.O. Box 8523, Edenglen 1613, (or telephone Johannesburg 609-2464).

Xaxaba Camp

Paul and Penny Rawson's bush camp is situated beneath riverine forest trees, 8 km from Chief's Island in the southern Moremi Wildlife Reserve and on the banks of the Xaxaba flood-plain lagoon in the Okavango.

Xaxaba is 67 km from Maun, and is open year-round. It has its own light aircraft and airstrip, and offers photographic safaris for up to 22 people, game-viewing excursions by land and water, boat hire, fishing tackle and camping sites. The food is excellent. Educational Wildlife Expeditions use Xaxaba as a base on their Fish Eagle Trail. Further information is obtainable from Xaxaba Island Camp, P.O. Box 147, Maun, Botswana (telephone Maun 260205).

Xugana

The word *xugana*, which means 'kneel down to drink', was given by the ancient San to one of the most idyllic and secluded locations in the northern reaches of the Okavango Delta. This beautiful camp on the shore of an ox-bow lagoon offers eight luxury tents within a vault of wild fig, garcinia and mokutshumo trees. The showers, toilets, bar and dining room are of brick and thatch construction. This is one of the few lodges in the Okavango which offers a full range of delta experiences: boating, mokoros, nature drives, fishing and walks. Xugana is owned by Mr and Mrs David Hartley and lies some 70 km from Moremi Wildlife Reserve's north gate (by air 115 km north of Maun). No casual visitors are accepted and one can only get there by flying to the private airstrip one kilometre from the camp.

For further information, write to Okavango Explorations, P.O. Box 69859, Bryanston 2021 (telephone Johannesburg 708-1893). Alternatively, write to P.O. Box 180, Caledon 7230 (telephone Caledon 2-2463; telex 5721323).

A sunburnt wilderness

There is no such place as the lost city of the Kalahari – but it is all too easy to get lost yourself in this vast grassland. The Kalahari is a flat, seemingly endless expanse of land where the days are scorching hot and the nights can be very cold. Four of Africa's most remote game areas are here: the Central Kalahari, Khutse, Mabuasehube and Gemsbok.

At 65 000 km² these regions cover a land mass three-quarters the size of Natal. The Kalahari is home to the few remaining hunter-gatherers of Southern Africa, the San. There are lion, leopard, cheetah, caracal, wild dog, bat-eared fox, gemsbok, herds of wildebeest up to 40 000 strong – and practically no water. It is a harsh land, where only the strong and the clever can survive.

There are around 30 000 San in Botswana (with possibly another 25 000 in neighbouring territories) – remnants of a once-prolific population that, in the later Stone Age, hunted game and gathered the fruits of the earth and sea throughout the Southern African subcontinent.

Negroid migrants arrived from the north and intermarried with the local Khoikhoi and San, and (much later) white settlers from the south oc-cupied the fertile lands, pushing what remained of these distinctive and, in many ways, remarkable people to the most inhospitable regions of the interior – to the wastes of Namibia and the Kalahari.

Small, fleet of foot and keen of eye, the San is a superb tracking hunter. His weapons are the spear, the knobkerrie and, most often, the bow and arrow: he tips the shaft behind the arrow head with poison derived from the plants of the semi-desert, from the beetle *Diamphidium*, and from various spiders. The poison works slowly, and the prey usually rejoins the herd, which is then shadowed by the hunters, perhaps for three days. When the animal is too weak to keep up any longer, the San close in for the kill.

Game meat, though, supplements rather than makes up the San's diet. The hunt has a social significance, more important than the food it brings. For the most part San communities subsist on the small animals and the insects of the Kalahari: snakes, birds and their eggs, frogs, rodents, tortoises, porcupines, locusts and termites. For energy, some proteins and vitamins the San depends on 'veldkos' – gathered food. The region, arid wasteland though it may seem, supports an impressive variety of edible plant life.

Water is the perennial problem, especially in the southern Kalahari. There are a few permanent springs, occasionally ground water near the surface, and the seasonal rains bring sudden relief. But sometimes the rains do not come at all, and drought is the normal condition. Over the generations the San have learnt how to survive these long waterless periods. When the rain does fall, they fill calabashes and ostrich egg shells and bury the water in the cooler depths of the earth.

In a rainless year they will dig for water and suck it from the soil through grass-filtered reed pipes, or seek out water-storing plants such as the tsamma melon and the gemsbok cucumber. One large specimen of the *Tylosema esculentum*, found in the 1970s, weighed 260 kg and contained over 100 ℓ of liquid.

Highly mobile as a result of being forced to travel long distances for food, the San's personal possessions are few and restricted to those things he can easily carry – tanned skins, his bow and arrows, spear and throwing stick, skin bag,

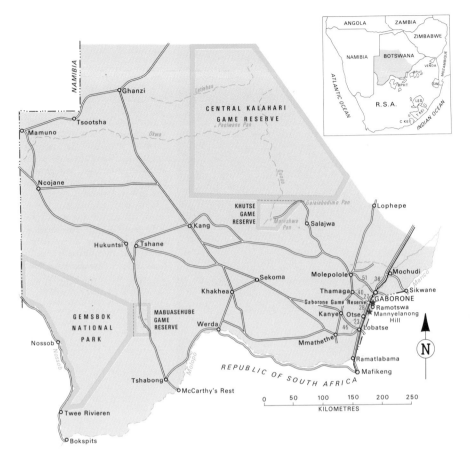

ostrich eggs enclosed in a net. His shelter is a simple, temporary affair of branches and grass.

The northern parts of the Kalahari are richer in water, vegetation and game; the semi-desert gradually becomes woodland savanna, able to support larger groupings of hunter-gatherers than the wilderness thirstlands to the south. The San's is a hunting economy and the size of a group at any given time is dictated by several factors – the season of the year, the availability of water, the terrain. But generally a group will number from 20-50 individuals in the better-provided northern regions; as few as four families in the most desolate southern areas.

These are the San beloved of Sir Laurens van der Post: touched but largely unspoilt by other cultures, living the life of their ancestors. Their numbers are slowly growing, but increasing contact with farmers and pastoralists has eroded their traditional ways.

Many are at a transitional stage: although still mobile, they now move around the countryside with a few goats and chickens and goods such as cooking pots and knives. Many thousands of others have settled on farms and are integrated into the modern rural economy.

Central Kalahari Game Reserve

Passing through wetter and drier periods, the Kalahari has steadily become drier over the last million years. Even the name, sometimes spelt 'Kgalagadi', means 'the great drying up' or 'thirst' in the dialect of the Tswana.

Under the vast wilderness of savanna, dry grassland and fossil river beds, is some water – much of it heavily mineralised and undrinkable. It rains spasmodically in the Kalahari – and twice in the last half-century it has been known to snow, the most recent occasion being in July, 1982.

Today the reserve is primarily the home of the San who still hunt the vast herds of hartebeest, gemsbok, springbok, wildebeest and eland which graze here.

But there is a far greater danger to these great herds than the hunting needs of the San. Over the great areas of the Kalahari – including most of Botswana, parts of Angola and Namibia and South Africa south to the Orange River – fences have been erected to demarcate borders and to prevent the spread of foot-and-mouth disease among cattle. These fences now pose a threat to the herds, cutting them off from traditional grazing grounds.

The Central Kalahari Game Reserve – covering 51 800 km² – is an important haven for these threatened herds. By a miracle of nature they can exist without rivers or waterholes – by feeding at night from plants wet with dew and from succulents that gain moisture from deep root systems. The swollen underground parts of plants such as wild cucumber and aloes are favourites. After a veld fire, the herds feed on young shoots.

Opposite page left: A family of spotted hyena rests up during the heat of the day in the Gemsbok National Park. The species is probably best known for its lunatic laughter — the cry of triumph after a successful hunt — but it has many other voices. Fully 17 distinctive sounds have been recorded, ranging from a high-pitched howl when gathering for the hunt to an angry scream when competing for a carcass. **Opposite page right:** A 'dust devil', or small whirlwind, winds its erratic way across one of the park's pans. **Right:** A porcupine. This nocturnal animal spends most of the daylight hours inside its burrow, emerging occasionally, as this one has, to sunbathe. Porcupines have a highly developed defence mechanism and few natural enemies. When a predator — perhaps a particularly hungry leopard or lion — does attack, their needle-sharp quills rise and they either jump backwards against their assailant, driving home the quills, or (if chased) stop abruptly, causing the pursuer to impale itself. The porcupine does not 'shoot' its quills.

Far left: Ochre sand dunes at Twee Rivieren, main entrance to the Gemsbok National Park. **Left:** The last of the twilight in the Gemsbok National Park. **Opposite page right:** The brown hyena is smaller, shyer, and more solitary than its spotted cousin. It lives in rock fissures and thickets but most often in a burrow, which is easily recognised by the bones and feathers – the remains of many meals – that litter the immediate surroundings. **Opposite page far right:** The fork-marked sand snake, a quick-moving, diurnal species which is sometimes preyed on and eaten by its traditional enemy – the snake eagle. **Opposite page below right:** A herd of springbok on the move along the banks of the Nossob River. **Opposite page left:** A Cape fox beside its den in the Gemsbok National Park. This is the only true fox found in Southern Africa. The species has extremely good sight and hearing.

KALAHARI AT A GLANCE

When to go The winter months June, July and August are the best for visitors.

Reservations and information To visit the Kalahari and all the other National Parks and Game Reserves in Botswana a permit is necessary. More information about all reserves, permits and the fees payable may be obtained from The Director, Department of Wildlife and National Parks, P.O. Box 131, Gaborone, Botswana (telephone Gaborone 37-1405) or The Director, Tourism Development Unit, Private Bag 0047, Gaborone, Botswana (telephone Gaborone 35-3024).

Getting there There are scheduled flights into Gaborone from Johannesburg, Harare and Lusaka, and into Maun and Francistown from Gaborone. Photographic safari operators offer 4-wheel-drive vehicles, aircraft and guides – most operating from Maun. Both the Gemsbok and the Mabuasehube reserves are best approached from the south; Khutse from Gaborone and the Central Kalahari Game Reserve from Ghanzi in the west (via Dekar) or Francistown (via Orapa).

Accommodation There is no accommodation in any of the game parks. Camping is permitted but facilities are non-existent or minimal.

Eating and drinking All food supplies and water should be carried. Count on 8ℓ of water per person per day for drinking and washing.

Getting around A guide should accompany your party and a compass should be carried. For safety, take two 4-wheel-drive vehicles.

Wildlife Practically every species of game, with the exception of elephant, can be found in the Kalahari. There are 3 000 giraffe alone in the Central Kalahari Game Reserve. Thousands of wildebeest, hartebeest and springbok gather at the pans, attracting a variety of predators.

Special precautions A trip into the Kalahari must be carefully planned. Two 4-wheel-drive vehicles are necessary, and you should take all the spares, food and water you may require. The nearest police station should be informed of your movements. Take anti-malaria tablets. Remember that it is considered normal for people in Botswana to assist a vehicle or its passengers stranded in the Kalahari or other outback areas.

San, too, survive on some unlikely plants and animals in this harsh land. Virtually any creature is a potential meal, as Guillermo Farini discovered during his travels. In his book, *Through the Kalahari Desert*, he describes how his companion, Kert, 'went into a transport of joy at finding some "Bushman's rice" – the immature stages of certain species of termite or white ant, with broad black heads and long fat bodies...Taking a handful of these he poured them into his mouth and chewed them with the greatest gusto, smacking his lips as they disappeared down his throat'.

Permits are required and a fee is charged if you wish to enter or camp in the reserve. For more information contact The Director, Department of Wildlife and National Parks, P.O. Box 131, Gaborone, Botswana (telephone Gaborone 37-1405). This area encompasses some of the harshest territory in Botswana, so if you do intend visiting it, remember to take special precautions.

Gaborone Game Reserve

You can see white rhino right in the heart of Botswana's capital city at the small Gaborone Game Reserve. While the rhino are kept securely in a special enclosure, the remaining game in this educational reserve can roam quite freely within 4 km² of fenced-off plains. Along the reserve's eastern boundary is the heavily forested Not-

wane River, where numerous forest species of animals and birds may be found.

Among the reserve's impressive array of animals are eland, gemsbok, wildebeest, impala, springbok, warthog, kudu, and many species of bird and reptile. For more information contact The Director, Department of Wildlife and National Parks, P.O. Box 131, Gaborone, Botswana (telephone Gaborone 37-2405).

Gemsbok National Park

There are two Gemsbok parks: The Kalahari Gemsbok National Park in South Africa and the larger Botswana section, the 9 000 km² Gemsbok National Park, separated by the ancient bed of the Nossob River. The main entrance into both is at Twee Rivieren, close to the Botswana border post at Bokspits.

Normal saloon cars can be driven through this desert-like section of the Kalahari by following dried-up fossil river beds – which flow only once in 20 years or so. Game includes springbok, hartebeest, gemsbok, eland, wildebeest, ostrich and kudu, with predators such as lion, cheetah, brown hyena, leopard and wild dog.

Khutse Game Reserve

Fifteen thousand years ago, the complex of seasonal Kalahari pans that form the Khutse

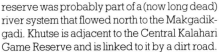

reserve was probably part of a (now long dead) river system that flowed north to the Makgadikgadi. Khutse is adjacent to the Central Kalahari Game Reserve and is linked to it by a dirt road.

Khutse can be reached by 4-wheel-drive vehicles after a 240 km drive from the Botswana capital of Gaborone. However, sufficient fuel should be carried for at least 650 km in order to tour the 2 590 km² reserve and return to Gaborone. The public campsites at Galalabodimo and Moreseve Pans have limited facilities.

In this, a true desert environment, you may see kudu, ostrich, gemsbok, hartebeest, wildebeest, springbok, eland, steenbok, caracal, porcupine, lion (fairly common), cheetah, brown hyena and spotted hyena, mongoose, black-backed jackal, bat-eared fox and ground squirrel. The reserve boasts more than 70 species of birds.

The pans usually consist of dry, white sand, with a little moisture at the lowest level.

Mabuasehube Game Reserve

The Mabuasehube reserve lies in the Kalahari approximately 150 km north of the South African border post of McCarthy's Rest near Kuruman. At Tshabong, 21 km inside Botswana, it is a good idea to notify the police before proceeding farther: the Kalahari is no place to get lost. Days may pass without a vehicle along this sand road to Hukuntsi. A store at Tshabong can supply food and other essentials, and petrol is available.

The 1 792 km² reserve consists of three large pans with a good variety of game. It lies adjacent to and east of the Gemsbok National Park. Large herds of eland, hartebeest, springbok and gemsbok can be seen, and predators such as lion,

brown hyena, caracal, Cape fox, leopard, and wild dog are active at night, when a spotlight can reveal a 'laager' of animals around the camp.

The best time to visit is from June to August.

Mannyelanong Hill

Mannyelanong, about 40 km south of Gaborone near the tiny village of Otse, means 'the place where vultures defecate' – and is today one of the few remaining nesting grounds of the Cape vulture. There were 300 pairs in 1963; by 1980 there were only about a hundred, swooping and diving above the Mannyelanong Hill face.

There are few predators left in this part of Botswana, and increasingly strenuous efforts are being made to save the remaining Cape vultures. Conservationists call this vulture 'a sail-plane, a health inspector and a refuse remover'.

Remote and burnished grassland

In the early 19th century the Boteti River area in central Botswana, was one of several regions of the country that served as sanctuary to an awesome number and variety of wild animals. Early travellers trekking across the edge of the Kalahari and the Makgadikgadi told of countless herds of wildebeest and zebra.

Then came the hunters and traders, greedy for furs, skins, feathers and, above all, ivory. During the two years following Lake Ngami's discovery in mid-century, 900 elephant were shot in the Boteti River area alone. Alec Campbell, in his *Guide to Botswana*, estimates that 'it would be a fair guess to say that each year from 1865 onwards 5000 elephant, 3000 leopard, 3000 lion, 3000 ostrich, 250000 small fur-bearing animals and probably another 100000 meat animals were slaughtered, mainly for trade. In ten years the country could have been stripped had it not been for the difficulty of penetrating some of the major wildlife areas'.

This very remoteness, and the introduction of expensive hunting licences before the turn of the century, prevented the total extermination of Botswana's magnificent living heritage.

The 12000 km² Makgadikgadi is a wilderness of salt pans, grass plains and herds of ever-moving game. There are few roads and there is usually no water. Long ago, the ancient lake was almost certainly filled by the Zambezi, Kuando, Okavango and Okwa systems, but today only severe storms deposit enough water in the pans to attract the flamingoes.

Two roads loop around the pans and link the two towns of Francistown in the east and Maun on the fringe of the Okavango Delta in the west. There are two main pans, the Sowa and the Ntwetwe. The two game reserves of the Makgadikgadi, the Nxai Pan National Park and the Makgadikgadi Pans Game Reserve, are in the west. Lake Xau lies close to the Boteti River in the south. Wildebeest, springbok, zebra and other antelope live off the grass that grows on the plains. Visitors may see lion, bat-eared fox, bateleur eagles and a host of other species.

Gweta Rest Camp

A little more than halfway along the main road from Francistown (via Nata) to Maun lies the rural village of Gweta, set among tall palms. The well-signposted rest camp, or motel, comprises thatched, brick cottages, a restaurant, a bar patronised by the local community, a shop and a vehicle workshop (but no fuel is sold). There's also an attractive, serviced camping site nearby.

To the south of Gweta are the Makgadikgadi salt pans – all that remains of a once great lake that covered much of northern Botswana – and not far west stretches the vast Makgadikgadi Game Reserve. The unfenced reserve is without facilities (water, fuel, food), and the tracks, though good, are not signposted. Game

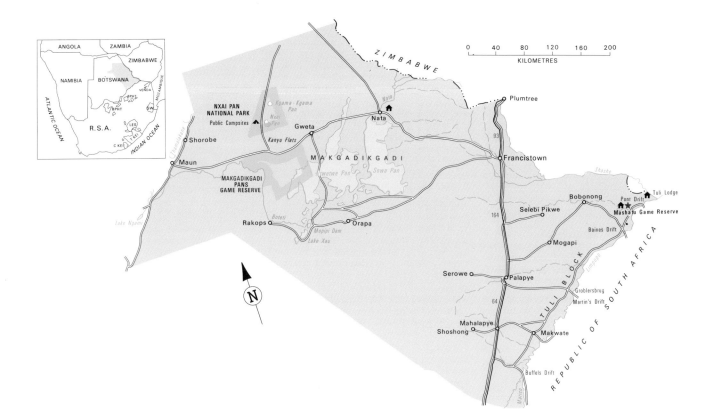

Left top: Very enlarged antennae are a characteristic of this paussid beetle, found (usually in ants' nests) all over Botswana. Ants may often be seen clustered around this beetle, stimulating it into producing secretions of which they are particularly fond. **Left below:** The shallow waters of the Makgadikgadi pans are magnets to waterfowl of many species. Although once an immense sheet of water, much of the area has dried up, leaving stretches of salt-encrusted sand as far as the eye can see. There is evidence that the pans of Makgadikgadi are all that is left of a huge lake which reached a depth of 945 m and an area of 60 000 km² — including a large part of the area now occupied by the Okavango Delta. Boreholes sunk in the area have revealed sedimentation of up to 100 m in depth. Man occupied the area of the pans in very ancient times, and many Stone Age artefacts have been found. **Far left:** Selous' mongoose (seen here beside its hole in the Makgadikgadi Pans Game Reserve). This small, slender mongoose is mainly nocturnal, though it may be seen in daylight. **Right:** Vegetable ivory *(mokolane)* palms in the Makgadikgadi Pans Game Reserve.

drives into the pans and reserve can be organised from Gweta.

For further information about Gweta Rest Camp write to P.O. Box 124, Gweta, Botswana.

Lake Xau

Lake Xau was once a large, shallow lake fed by the Boteti River, which flows out of the Okavango Delta east for 500 km into the Kalahari, carrying the last of the Okavango's water. Today, with the waters trapped at the Mopipi Dam (itself originally a pan), Lake Xau is usually as dry as its sister pans of the Makgadikgadi, on whose southern edge it lies. The reeds are still on the lake shore, but less luxuriant. Khoikhoi legend relates that the lake dried up in about the year 1800 when thousands of fish, crocodile and hippo were reported to have died and rotted in the lake bed.

In the main, the area's wildlife stays farther north and west on the grasslands between the Boteti River and the Ntwetwe Pan of the Makgadikgadi. Bird life is still abundant on the lake itself. A sand and gravel road south of the Makgadikgadi pans stretches about 350 km from Francistown to Lake Xau (240 km to Orapa). There are no facilities, petrol stations or accommodation and you must have a 4-wheel-drive vehicle. The road that runs parallel to the Boteti River from Lake Xau to Maun is 140 km of 'choose-your-track' that eventually becomes the main Maun-Nata road.

When to go June to late September are the best months for the Makgadikgadi, when nights are cool, but the grasslands of Nxai Pan only teem with game in the rainy months from January to April. The reserves are open all year.

Reservations and information There is no need to book campsites in advance. For information, write to The Department of Wildlife and National Parks, P.O Box 131, Gaborone, Botswana (telephone Gaborone 37-1405).

Getting there There are scheduled air services from Harare and Johannesburg to Gaborone, which in turn is linked to Francistown and Maun. The 350 km northern road to the reserves from Francistown is suitable for saloon cars and is tarred for the first 188 km (to Nata). However, 4-wheel-drive vehicles are essential to enter the reserves.

Accommodation There is no organised accommodation in the pans. Public campsites are available in the reserves, however.

Eating and drinking Visitors should take sufficient food and water for the duration of the trip (few campsites have boreholes).

Getting around The roads in the pans are at best tracks. Visitors should travel with two 4-wheel-drive vehicles. Essential equipment includes puncture repair kit, extra fuel in metal (not plastic) jerry cans, at least 20ℓ water, motor oil, jacks, spanners, fan-belts, inner tubes, a pump, spare coil, rotor, fuel-pump kit, regulator, condenser, plugs, points, radiator hose, nylon tubing, clips and strips of steel mesh wire (for use when bogged down in sand). A guide should accompany you in the parts of the Makgadikgadi outside the reserve. A compass could be useful.

Wildlife Wildebeest and zebra live and migrate between the Boteti River and the north-west corner of Ntwetwe Pan (Makgadikgadi Pan Game Reserve) and then on to Nxai Pan, farther north. They tend to move north and east during the rainy months to feed on the grass plains and then, as the surface water decreases in volume, they move south-west to the Boteti again – followed by lion and other predators. The Nata River flows out of Zimbabwe and eventually dries up in a delta at the north-east tip of the Sowa Pan, the smaller of the two Makgadikgadi pans. Here, you can sometimes see thousands of flamingoes lining the shore for many kilometres. One sighting was estimated at over a million birds. The flamingo's nest is a cone of mud about 30 cm high, with a hollow on top to hold an egg.

Fishing There is good fishing (bream) in the Nata and Boteti rivers (the best time is September to April). Fishing permits are required in parks and game reserves.

Special precautions Visitors are advised to start a course of anti-malaria tablets (available from chemists) before entering this region.

Four-wheel-drive vehicles are essential if you leave the roads on the open plain. Camping is permitted in the reserve.

Mashatu Game Reserve and Tuli Safari Lodge
In the populated eastern section of Botswana, the Limpopo River forms the boundary with the Transvaal. The Limpopo forms the rounded 'hat' of South Africa as it flows first north then east to the Indian Ocean. At its crown, not far to the west of Messina and Beit Bridge, it links up with the Shashe River.

In the watered, lush countryside between the Shashe and the Limpopo is a complex of several privately owned ranches and farms forming a part of the Tuli Block.

The countryside is wild and beautiful mopane woodland, broken up by koppies and granite outcrops. The rivers are lined with giant acacias and mashatu trees.

Two major attractions here are Mashatu Game Reserve and the Tuli Safari Lodge.

The largest privately owned game reserve in southern Africa, Mashatu offers game drives in 4-wheel-drive open vehicles, accompanied by Tswana rangers and trackers.

There's no shortage of game here – Mashatu provides refuge for the largest single population of African elephant on private land in the world – more than 700 animals. You can also see cheetah, zebra, giraffe, eland, impala, leopard, lion, kudu, bushbuck, baboon and more than 350 species of birds.

The reserve's main camp offers accommodation in air-conditioned, en suite chalets or rondavels, with electricity around the clock. There is a swimming pool, bar, dining terrace, and a boma overlooking the spot-lit waterhole.

In the remote northern corner of the reserve lies the Mashatu tent camp, with seven insect-proofed double tents that have en suite toilet and shower facilities. There is also a clear plunge pool, an open-sided deck under thatch for dining, and a boma. The main camp accommodates a maximum of 30 guests, and the tent camp a maximum of 14.

You can reach Mashatu by road (five-and-a-half hours from Johannesburg) or by chartered aircraft from most parts of Southern Africa. For more information contact the Rattray Reserves marketing office at Suite 4, Tulbagh, 360 Oak Avenue, Ferndale, Randburg (telephone Johannesburg 789-2677).

Tuli Lodge, revamped at a cost of R1,5 million, is also five-and-a-half hours' drive from Johannesburg, or one-and-a-half hours by air from Lanseria Airport.

Here are no fences to restrict your movement while you track elephant or lion in the bush.

Accommodation is in luxury thatched chalets with bathrooms en suite. Game drives in open

For further information, write to The Senior Tourism Officer, Private Bag 0047, Gaborone, Botswana (telephone Gaborone 353024) or to The Department of Wildlife, National Parks and Tourism, P.O. Box 131, Gaborone, Botswana (telephone Gaborone 371405).

Makgadikgadi Pans Game Reserve
The main Francistown to Maun road crosses the migratory path of wildebeest and zebra, and separates Nxai Pan National Park to the north and the Makgadikgadi Pans Game Reserve to the south at a point 350 km from Francistown.

The reserve's 4 144 km² of game-rich grasslands include the north-west section of the Ntwetwe, one of two giant salt pans that together form the Makgadikgadi Pans – reputed to be the largest in the world. In the shimmering heat of midday the pans become blinding mirages of make-believe water surrounded by burnished grasslands. When rains fill the shallow pans to the depth of a few centimetres, they attract countless flamingoes, pelicans, waders and other waterfowl.

There are animals in profusion: gemsbok, zebra, springbok, wildebeest, ostrich, lion, jackal, hyena and cheetah. In the palm trees and thickets, and silhouetted in the pale sky, are doves, rollers and eagles. The little-known palm-nut vulture is seen here.

North of the Ntwetwe Pan are huge grassy plains and strikingly beautiful (especially in a dusty African sunset) groves of mokolane palm trees (in some parts of the country, people extract, ferment and drink its juice as wine or distil it to create a powerful spirit). The fruit is known as 'vegetable ivory' for its decorative value – from it are made necklaces and the colourful heads of carrying sticks.

In the dry season and in times of drought wildebeest and zebra roam the open country between the Boteti (or Botletli) River and the north-western edge of the pan. When the rains come they migrate to these northern plains, and then return to the waters of the Boteti for the dry winter months.

Access is 30 km west of Gweta, 300 km from Francistown on the road to Maun in the west.

Left: An aardwolf in the Nxai Pan National Park. At first glance the aardwolf resembles a small striped hyena, with its slender legs, mane from neck to tail, and vertical stripes. However, it is noticeably smaller than the scavenger. **Above:** The bateleur eagle is one of the best-known raptors of the African savanna: it is easily recognised by its characteristic straight-line flight across the veld, rocking from side to side as it flies.

Land Rovers are included in the daily tariff, as well as three sumptuous meals a day.

For further information and brochures, you should write to Tuli Safari Lodge (Pty) Ltd, P.O. Box 41478, Craighall 2024 (telephone Johannesburg 788-1748/9).

Nata Lodge
Set at the edge of the Makgadikgadi salt pans, Nata Lodge is 10 km south of Nata, on the tarred road to Maun, Chobe and Victoria Falls. The bird life here is diverse and abundant. But for the travel-weary visitor the chief attraction of Nata Lodge must be its bar, its swimming pool, its restaurant and its accommodation: thatched, A-frame cottages in a setting of palms, marulas and tall thorn trees. There's a campsite too. In the holiday season booking for Nata Lodge is essential. Write to Nata Lodge, Private Bag 10, Francistown, Botswana (telephone Francistown 61-1210).

Nxai Pan National Park
The easiest route to the Nxai Pan National Park is via Francistown, the bustling little capital of the North-East District. The town lies on the main railway line and is 190 km (three hours) from Bulawayo on a tarred road. The nearest large town in South Africa is Potgietersrus to the south-east, and there is an immigration and customs post at Martin's Drift-Groblersbrug.

A road suitable for saloon cars leads west to Nxai Pan and the Okavango Delta. It is tarred for 188 km as far as the town of Nata. There is a filling station and lodge here.

The turn-off to Nxai Pan is approximately 160 km away (140 km from Maun). A 4-wheel-drive vehicle is necessary to enter the park. Turn right off the main road for 16 km to connect with the old Maun road. The pan lies another 17 km north over a sand ridge.

The 2590 km² reserve is mainly forest and savanna woodland. Nxai Pan is a fossil lake bed some 14 km wide, and covered with short grass (dotted with small islands of trees). There are many giraffe, which may be seen in herds of up to 60, scattered across the pan. This is also the playground of bat-eared fox, which scamper from one anthill to the next. These endearing animals are omnivorous (wild fruits, rodents and reptiles figure in their diet) but termites, locusts and beetles are their staple food.

Their outsize ears are sensitive to the sounds of insect movement beneath the surface and, once located, the prey (sometimes colonies of termites) is swiftly dug up, even from the hardest ground, and devoured. A colloquial Afrikaans name for the species is *draaijakkals* ('turning jackal'), descriptive of its nimbleness: it can turn and double back on its tracks at speed. It has a fluid, twisting way of running that helps it to evade predators.

During the rainy summer months (December to March), herds of wildebeest and zebra concentrate at water-filled depressions in the pan.

Bird life includes vultures, goshawks and eagles. Lion and cheetah are often seen.

The smaller Kgama-Kgama Pan, where King Khama III once had a cattle post, is 35 km to the north; while south are the Kanyu Flats, a 'billiard table' of miniature pans on the eastern fringe of which stand the 'Sleeping Sisters', five baobabs painted by artist-explorer Thomas Baines over 100 years ago and still standing with only one branch missing on one tree.

There are two public campsites; the northernmost has a borehole. Game scouts are available to assist you in planning your tour route.

Havens of the north

Chobe National Park, in the north of Botswana, is one of Africa's great national parks. Rolling grass plains, dusty mopane woodlands, the fossil lake bed of the Mababe Depression and the lush flood plains of the Linyanti and Chobe rivers – they join the Zambezi at Kazungula, meeting point of four nations – offer a variety of habitats for the herds of elephant, buffalo and zebra for which this park is world-renowned. The game provides ample feeding ground for predators such as lion, hyena and many others. Tigerfish and bream lure the fishermen to the papyrus-fringed waterways of the Linyanti.

The winter sunsets at Savuti are spectacular, while the pans of the east are host to a variety of wildlife that includes lion and elephant. The riverine forests of the north, watered by the Chobe, reveal myriad multi-coloured birds, bushbuck, lechwe, sable, giraffe, crocodile, hippo, baboon, eland, tsessebe, kudu and buffalo. Some of the 80 km of roads along the river are suitable for saloon cars, while Africa's greatest spectacle, the Victoria Falls, is only an hour's drive away.

Chobe, Kasane, Kazuma, Maikaelelo and Sibuyu forest reserves

Kasane, Kazuma and Sibuyu forest reserves stretch one after another north to south along the Zimbabwe and Hwange National Park border, and – together with the nearby Maikaelelo and Chobe forest reserves – are the only natural timber forests in Botswana.

Access is by the tarred road from Kasane village to Nata and Francistown – an old ivory trail to the Zambezi known as the Pandamatenga. It is 312 km from Kasane to Nata and another 188 km to Francistown.

The Pandamatenga border post is 100 km south of the crossing at Kazungula and 5 km from the Zimbabwe border at a point that connects with a dirt road through Zimbabwe's Kazuma Pan National Park. This road branches north to Matetsi and the tarred Bulawayo road (65 km), and south to Robin's camp, in the Hwange National Park (48 km).

There are many species of woody plants in Botswana. Larger trees in the forest reserves include Rhodesian teak and mukwa (or kiaat). A wide variety of game (both browsers and predators) moves between the forest reserves, the mopane woodlands and the unfenced Chobe National Park. The bird life is rich and colourful. There are no facilities in any of these or in the Maikaelelo and Chobe forest reserves, adjacent to the eastern and western flanks of Chobe National Park respectively. Camping is allowed only with prior permission from the Forestry Department, Ministry of Agriculture, Private Bag 003, Gaborone (telephone Gaborone 35-0500). Further information is also available from this address.

Chobe Chilwero

A blanket of thatch covers the imaginatively designed two-storey main building at Chobe Chilwero, which is situated at the northern tip of the Chobe National Park. This building is the dining area; there's a magnificent kiaat-wood dining table and, on the upper level, you will find a balcony commanding spectacular views of the Chobe River, 100 m below. Nestling around the main building are eight thatched A-frame bungalows, each with two beds and an *en suite* bathroom.

Twice-daily, professional guides lead excursions into the Chobe National Park in open 4-wheel-drive vehicles, while boating and fishing are popular alternatives.

The camp is situated just north of Kasane and is easily accessible by road. For bookings and additional information, write to P.O. Box 22, Kasane, Botswana (telephone Kasane 25-0234) or Gametrackers, P.O. Box 4245, Randburg 2125 (telephone Johannesburg 886-1810).

Chobe National Park: Kasane

Much of Botswana consists of various flood plains, sandy depressions or Kalahari-type desert. Chobe National Park, with an area of

Above: A stalk-eyed fly. This bizarre insect, with eyes and antennae at the end of stalks which may be as much as 12 mm apart, commonly found along rivers. It feeds largely on decaying plants. **Left:** The magnificent Chobe River at sunset. **Opposite page:** A young sitatunga in dense papyrus beside the Linyanti River — a typical habitat for this small, shy buck. The sitatunga's feet are adapted for running across swamps.

CHOBE AT A GLANCE

When to go The park is open all year – with the exception of the Mababe Depression and Savuti Channel area, which is closed during the rainy season (1 December to 31 March). The rains create large mudholes and travel during this period is risky.

Reservations and information Entry permits can be obtained by writing directly to the Department of Wildlife and National Parks, P.O. Box 17, Kasane, Botswana (telephone Kasane 25-0235). It is not necessary to reserve campsites.

Getting there There are light aircraft landing strips at Kasane, Savuti and Linyanti (to the west of the park). A variety of operators conduct all-inclusive safaris, the largest being the South African-based Gametrackers, which has two permanent camps at Savuti, the most densely (game) populated area of the park. The normal overland route into Chobe is via the good 69 km road from Victoria Falls in Zimbabwe to the Kazungula border post. Kasane village is 13 km west of Kazangula. There is a sand road from Maun which may be used in the dry season (4-wheel-drive vehicles only). Before setting off you are advised to get information on the condition of the road from the Department of Wildlife and National Parks.

Accommodation There are luxury tented camps at Savuti and Linyanti, chalets and camping at the Chobe Safari Lodge at Kasane, and public campsites at Savuti in the west, Serondela in the north and Nogatsau.

Eating and drinking The food and wine lists at the Gametrackers' and Linyanti Explorations' camps are impressive - as are those at the Chobe Safari Lodge in the north-east. The items on the lists are not cheap, however. Other supplies are available from various shops at Kasane, Maun or Victoria Falls.

Getting around While a 4-wheel-drive vehicle is a definite advantage, an ordinary saloon car will be more than adequate for the road between Chobe Game Lodge and Kasane. Kasane has food stores, petrol, banks and a post office.

Special attractions The elephants at Savuti, the carmine bee-eaters along the Chobe River, the forests and the papyrus waterways of Linyanti will delight the eye. The bush sunsets in the dust of winter are unforgettable.

Wildlife There are few places in the world that can equal Chobe's enormous variety of big game and bird life. The aristocrats of the wild – buffalo, elephant, giraffe, rhino, lion, impala, sable and fish eagle – are all here.

Fishing Tigerfish, bream and barbel are the principal fish caught in the Chobe-Linyanti river systems.

Special precautions A course of anti-malaria tablets should be started before visiting Chobe. Because nights tend to be chilly, a warm jacket should be packed in with other essentials. A mosquito repellent would be useful and a hat is essential during the hot daylight hours.

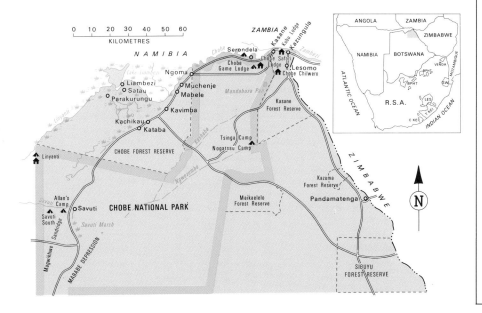

10878km², is a combination of the first three. It is named after the Chobe River – the name commonly given to a series of rivers which forms an irregular boundary between Botswana and the Caprivi Strip of Namibia.

The rivers, running east to west, start as the Kwando – which, like the Okavango, rises in Angola. It soon becomes the Linyanti, then Itenge, and finally the Chobe – which in turn is a major tributary of the Zambezi.

Kasane village, 13km west of the Kazungula border post, serves as the headquarters of the Chobe National Park. Facilities include an airstrip, a bakery, a service station, hotel, bottle store and bank. Visitors will be intrigued by a baobab tree that the colonial administration used alternately as a prison and toilet.

The northern section of Chobe offers 35km of river frontage as far as Ngoma. It has gravel roads suitable only for 4-wheel-drive vehicles, which can also be used to explore the forests and riverside paths. The animals, which come down to drink at the river from about 3 p.m. onwards include elephant, buffalo, sable, bushbuck, waterbuck, tsessebe and baboon. Visitors may see hippo and crocodile. There are also lion, leopard (very rarely seen), rhino, warthog and a variety of birds that include fish eagle, banded harrier hawk and a colony of carmine bee-eaters nesting in tiny caves on the banks of the Chobe River.

A public camping site at Serondela has ablution facilities. Camping is also permitted at the Chobe Safari Lodge, 3km from the park gate (write to P.O. Box 10, Kasane, Botswana; telephone Kasane 25-0336). Visitors may also stay at the Chobe Game Lodge (write to P.O. Box 32, Kasane, Botswana; telephone Kasane 25-0340). There is good fishing in the river (bream, barbel and tigerfish). Entry, fishing and camping permits are available at the Kasane gate, which is open from sunrise to sunset, and at Maun village (if you are entering from the southern Mababe Depression gate). A 4-wheel-drive vehicle is always necessary for travelling in this part of Botswana. The best time to visit is from June to October. From December to April (the wet season), access is limited by washed out roads and extensive mudholes. Intending visitors should write to The Senior Game Warden, Department of Wildlife and National Parks, P.O. Box 17, Kasane, Botswana (telephone Kasane 25-0235).

Chobe National Park: Nogatsau

A cluster of eight large pans and natural springs on the Ngwezumba River, surrounded by forest and mopane woodland, forms this section of Chobe National Park. It lies 100km south of the Chobe River and the Serondela campsite on the alternative eastern route (4-wheel-drive only) to Savuti.

'MR MEERKAT' — EVERYBODY'S FAVOURITE

Among the most endearing of all Southern Africa's small mammals is unquestionably the suricate (or grey meerkat), which can often be spotted sitting upright on top of a stone or antheap, surveying his little slice of real estate.

The suricate, a member of the mongoose family, is specially adapted to life in arid regions. Unlike most of its mongoose relatives, it is a very social creature, living in small colonies with as many as 50 members, and often sharing the communal burrow with families of ground squirrels and yellow mongooses. The burrows have many entrances and can easily be recognised by the mounds of excavated earth thrown up beside them. Members of the colony spend most of the day in the neighbourhood of the burrow, digging in search of insects (they also eat lizards, birds' eggs, mice, and the roots of various plants). It is said that they have an acute sense of smell, and can sniff out a bulb even when it is buried deep underground.

In the popular imagination, the suricate (and other mongooses) is renowned for fights with poisonous snakes, and this is an instance of a popular 'myth' being fully supported by scientific facts. There are reliable accounts of fights between suricates and cobras, and records of suricates killing and eating poisonous scorpions: in virtually every case the observers noted that the suricate was so nimble and quick in its attack that the snakes did not stand a chance. Often the suricate made no attempt to dodge the snake: it simply jumped straight in and killed its victim with a bite in the neck.

One fact that several of these observers noted was that although the suricate was sometimes bitten by a snake in the course of a fight, the snake's venom appeared to have very little effect. Laboratory experiments have shown that a suricate can absorb (with no apparent ill effect) an amount of cobra venom that would kill any other animals of a similar size. It seems that the suricate, over a period of time, has evolved a degree of immunity to the poisons contained in snake-venom.

The pans, including the Cwikampa, Mandabuza and Mapororo, usually contain water in varying amounts – but it is at the beginning of the wet season that they are host to herds of buffalo and elephant. Oribi, gemsbok and roan can be seen on the grass plains.

There are two campsites, Nogatsau (with ablution facilities) and Tsinga. You should write to the warden at Kasane before visiting this section of the Chobe National Park.

Intending visitors should address letters to The Senior Warden, Department of Wildlife and National Parks, P.O. Box 17, Kasane, Botswana (telephone Kasane 25-0235).

Chobe National Park: Savuti

Visitors to the Gametrackers' camp high up on a sandbank along the Savuti River Channel are quite likely to have a rude awakening as an elephant shakes a camelthorn tree beside their tent – an effective method of dislodging the tasty *mogotlho* seed pods (likened by one visitor to 'furry giraffe ears').

From June through to December the Savuti Channel carries the overspill of the Linyanti-Chobe floodwaters through the Magwikhwe sand ridge and into the Savuti Marsh at the northernmost tip of the Mababe Depression. Thousands of years ago, the Mababe, like a host of other depressions in the sandy grasslands of Botswana, was a great lake.

Very occasionally, when the rains are particularly good in the Sa dà Bandiera highlands of Angola, the Okavango Delta spills a little of its water along the Magwegqana fault line and into the Savuti Channel. The Savuti – home of dozens of baboon, stork and cormorant – was dry for 100 years; then in 1957 it flooded, drowning the giant trees that now stand stripped of their bark, grey and dead in mid-river.

Above: Papyrus and wild date palms on the banks of the Linyanti River. **Below left:** A female puku in the Chobe flood plain. Although the males are often solitary, they sometimes form small troops. Pukus are usually found in the vicinity of water. **Below right:** Purple rollers abound in the Chobe National Park. They are larger than the other rollers, and are recognised by their white eyebrows. They live on lizards, insects, scorpions and small snakes.

Late afternoon at one of these bends in the river is like a line-up for Noah's Ark. The crocodile lie motionless, jaws agape. Downstream, a dozen hippo yawn, twitch and snort. A line of elephant and their young emerge from the dusty mopane scrub to splash playfully in the water, and to drink. Sable, impala, warthog, guinea fowl and giraffe all seem to find a favourite spot. In the distance, from the direction of the Savuti Marsh comes the chilling grunt of a lion on the prowl.

The Savuti Marsh is anything but a marsh in the dry season: it is a treeless and seemingly uninhabited grass plain stretching to the horizon. But flooded it is a magnet for game: zebra, buffalo, sable, wildebeest, tsessebe, elephant and impala – literally thousands of animals venture onto the plains.

A variety of safari operators provide tours of Savuti, and there are two camps operated by a safari firm called Gametrackers: Savuti South and Allan's Camp. Savuti South features luxury tents, electricity, game drives in padded safari vehicles and candelight dinners. Allan's Camp has reed-covered tents, deck chairs and fire-side food. Each caters for up to 16 people.

For further information, write to Gametrackers, P.O. Box 4245, Randburg 2125 (telephone Johannesburg 886-1810). Lloyd Wilmot's Camp is also worth a visit.

Kubu Lodge

Once the site of the Employment Bureau of Africa (a labour recruitment office for the area), Kubu Lodge still retains a certain colonial aura – the old houses sport wide verandahs, the surroundings are ablaze with exotic trees. The lodge is about 11 km from Kasane, at Botswana's north-eastern boundary tip.

The camp comprises 10 wood-and-thatch chalets and a campsite beside the Chobe River. There is a swimming pool and a tennis court. Professional guides lead daily game-drives in open 4-wheel-drive vehicles to the Chobe National Park. For visits in the holiday season booking is essential. Write for further information to Kubu Lodge, P.O. Box 43, Kasane (or telephone Kasane 25-0312).

Linyanti

When the Kwando River has an exceptional flood, water feeds into the Linyanti River via the Magwegqana (or Selinda) Spillway, thus linking the Chobe and Okavango systems. The flood plains around the river then resemble the Okavango Delta, with a maze of little islands, reed marsh channels and meandering waterways which flow first one way, then the other – depending on the force of the incoming waters.

Strangler figs and other large river trees, conceal a collection of colourful bird life, palms and the gentle lapping of water. The twisting waterways, dotted with forest islands, that ultimately link up with the Chobe and then the Zambezi, conceal hippo and crocodile and a host of fish species, while in the nearby woodlands visitors may spot wild dog, elephant, sable, impala and lion.

There are over 300 species of birds in the area, including white pelican, African hawk eagle, scarlet-chested sunbird, tinkling cisticola and carmine bee-eater (the Linyanti airstrip colony is one of only two places where these birds are known to lay their eggs on flat land; they usually prefer to burrow into river banks).

Linyanti is on the Gametrackers' Botswana itinerary. There is an airstrip 10 km from their safari camp. There is no bilharzia in the area, but anti-malaria precautions should be taken. The fishing is excellent. It is possible to drive (4-wheel-drive vehicle) to Savuti Channel camp or Kasane Village – a five-hour run. There is a camping site 15 km distant.

For further information, write to P.O. Box 22, Kasane, Botswana (telephone Kasane 25-0234), or write to Gametrackers, P.O. Box 4245, Randburg 2125 (telephone Johannesburg 886-1810).

Taking your home on holiday

The ever-increasing cost of holiday accommodation is only one of the many reasons for the enduring popularity of caravanning in Southern Africa. Enthusiasts also enjoy total mobility, which allows them to explore virtually every corner of Southern Africa, and the freedom to eat when and what they choose.

Choosing your caravan

When selecting your caravan you should consider the size of your family and the degree of comfort you will require, how much you can spend, and whether your vehicle is suitable for towing. You will have to take into account the power of your vehicle's engine, the type of terrain you expect to encounter, and whether your vehicle's brakes and other equipment are sturdy enough to withstand the extra strain. The GvM (gross vehicle mass) of the caravan should not exceed 75 per cent of the tare (unloaded mass) of the towing vehicle.

There are many designs to choose from, and buyers are advised to consult an experienced caravanner, a caravan club or the Automobile Association before making their choice.

Hints for successful caravanning

● Do not tow a caravan with an underpowered vehicle. If the car is not driven correctly, the extra mass can place a strain on components such as engine, gearbox, shock absorbers, tyres, clutch and brakes, and excessive loading could lead to serious damage – with disastrous consequences for your holiday.

● Practise reversing your car with the caravan attached before setting out. You will find that the steering wheel has to be turned in the 'wrong' direction.

● Check that you fulfil all the legal requirements (once again, a dealer can advise you on this) and ensure that both your caravan and towing vehicle are adequately insured.

● Carry a good fire extinguisher and place it in an easily accessible spot.

● Before leaving home, have the towing vehicle properly serviced and checked. Pay particular attention to wheel alignment, tyres, suspension (a dealer may recommend fitting different shock absorbers, or stiffening the springs), cooling system and generator. It is always a good idea to carry a spare fan belt, radiator cap and hoses, and a few basic tools.

● When setting the headlights it should be remembered that the caravan's mass will probably pull the back of the towing vehicle down, with the result that oncoming motorists may be blinded by the lights.

Enthusiasts have a wide choice of caravans, ranging from very light models which may be towed even by small cars, to luxury models (left) with facilities to match. The smaller caravans feature only the bare essentials.

This 'Mobi Chalet' features a microwave oven, wall-to-wall carpets, bathroom and mirrored lounge.

The truck-mounted caravan is becoming increasingly popular among holidaymakers.

Many caravans come equipped with large tents. Families often use the tent as a living and dining area.

There are strict regulations relating to caravan ownership, and contravention of the rules could mean a fine. All caravans should be registered and licensed annually (whether used on a public road or not). When buying a second-hand caravan, you will be required to produce a roadworthy certificate before it can be transferred to your name. If you move to another town, you are obliged to inform the local licensing authority. Although reputable caravan manufacturers ensure that their vehicles comply with the legal requirements it is a good idea to contact a caravan club or the Automobile Association for additional advice. **Above and above right:** Every caravan should be fitted with side (yellow), front (white) and rear (red) reflectors at predetermined heights. The licence token should be displayed on the front of the caravan (above centre) and the registration plates at the rear (above right) not more than 1,5 m above ground level. All caravanners should carry at least two warning triangles (right), which should be placed at a distance of 45 m to the front and the rear of the caravan if it is parked in a roadway. If you have to stop in a one-way road, one triangle should be placed on the side of the approaching traffic. However, it should be noted that it is illegal to stop a caravan (or any other vehicle) within 1 m of the edge of a public road (outside an urban area) unless in a parking area.

- Tyre pressures should be adjusted to compensate for the extra load.
- Fit extendable wing mirrors (available from caravan dealers and most motor accessory stores) to give you a clear view to the left and right rear.
- Do not overload your caravan: it has been designed for a certain maximum mass. Try to pack everything into the storage space provided, and if it is necessary to use the floor, make sure that heavy items are secured. Too heavy a load in front of or behind the axle can badly affect the caravan's stability: aim for a nose weight of between 75 kg and 100 kg (measured at the jockey wheel). Some owners fit stabilisers and 'equaliser bars' to reduce sway.
- Before setting off on your holiday, ensure that everything inside the caravan is properly secured. Close the valves on all gas cylinders, raise the caravan jacks and clamp them, raise and clamp the jockey wheel, close all windows and vents, release the caravan brake, check that the coupling is properly seated, and attach the safety chain. Ask someone to check that the car and caravan lights work correctly while you operate the switches from inside the vehicle.
- Remember not to carry passengers in the caravan while you are on the road. It is both illegal and dangerous.
- Observe the speed limits and always allow yourself enough braking space, taking into consideration the extra mass of the caravan.
- Use the indicators every time you overtake or make a turn and allow for the extra length of the car caravan combination when returning to the left lane.
- Avoid hard braking (except in emergencies) and do not cut corners.
- Do not over-correct: this could cause the caravan to sway dangerously ('fishtail'). If this does occur maintain a straight course and apply brakes slowly and at short intervals (the lower the speed, the better the tyre adhesion).
- When driving down a steep hill, use the engine as a brake (engage a lower gear) to avoid overheating the brake discs or drums.
- Use lay-bys when available – it is illegal to park on the road verge except in an emergency. Always use the warning triangles when stopping beside the road (required by law).
- If your caravan is considerably higher than the towing vehicle, avoid passing too close to traffic signs, low branches and other obstacles.
- Make periodic checks of all body bolts and screws, coupling, wheel nuts, tyres, brakes and other equipment. Look out for hairline cracks on the tow bracket and at other crucial spots.
- Drive courteously, never forgetting that your manoeuvrability is reduced when towing a caravan. Try to accommodate other drivers wherever possible: the frustration of a motorist trapped behind a slow-moving caravan could provoke him to do something reckless.

Fold-up caravans are a marvel of compactness. Some models have almost as many facilities as the conventional designs. These caravans may be erected by one person in as little as five minutes.

Around the campfire

An experienced camper will never set out on his trip before consulting a comprehensive check-list of everything he may require. This may remove some of the spontaneity in which campers delight, but it certainly takes the guesswork and worry out of this increasingly popular pastime.

Outdoor living need not be synonymous with 'roughing it'. Today's specialised equipment, much of it developed for conditions which might be encountered in Southern Africa, makes camping a pleasure for the whole family. When buying your equipment, consider the size of your family, the sort of weather you may experience, the length of your trip and the size of your budget. Buy or hire the best you can afford — it will pay dividends in the long run.

Inside your tent — and out

The tent is the most important (and most expensive) item in the camper's equipment, and its size, design, efficiency and durability will determine the success or failure of an expedition. Whether you expect hot, cloudless days and warm, frost-free nights is immaterial: a tent provides comfort and security as well as protection from bad weather.

Some campers might be content with the single-room cottage design (the choice of most backpackers), but after a few days the restricted living space will make itself felt. Most campers opt for semi-frame tents, with dividing sections, or the robust full-frame tent — by far the most versatile design.

Whatever the material used, the tent should be durable, resistant to rot and mildew and large enough to accommodate its occupants

Left: A fishing camp (Shakawe) on the Okavango River, in the north-west corner of Botswana. Although these tents have been pitched on a concrete base, affording their occupants a degree of protection from damp, most modern tents are fitted with a flounce — a strip of coated fabric which is in contact with soil and water at ground level. The flounce serves to keep the tent walls clean and dry.

without sardine-like packing. For most comfort it should have a waterproof outer layer, a lightweight inner layer and a built-in groundsheet to keep out insects. Seams should be tough and the fabric closely woven to ensure a tear-resistant, waterproof shelter. An important point to remember: never fold up and store a damp tent — it will be ruined.

A well-designed tent will have a light, strong and easily assembled frame. Segmented tent poles are preferred, unless your car has a roof rack. Guy ropes should be of a synthetic material such as nylon (usually more durable than hemp ropes) and metal tent pegs of a strong design.

Where to pitch

A suitable campsite is determined by a variety of factors, including the availability of water and the likelihood of rain. Avoid camping at the foot of a slope, where water may collect in pools after a storm, or too close to a stream, where rising water may flood your tent. The best spot to pitch your tent is probably on slightly sloping ground of a consistency that will hold tent pegs firmly. Short grass would be suitable, and sea or river sand are also acceptable - though sand makes a very hard bed when compacted. If you cannot camp near water, remember to take your own supplies.

Cleanliness is one of the basic requisites of a campsite. All refuse, from cigarette butts to aluminium foil and potato peelings, should be stashed in plastic bags and taken away with you. When staying at organised campsites equipped with refuse cans, ensure that everyone in the party — especially the children — makes use of them.

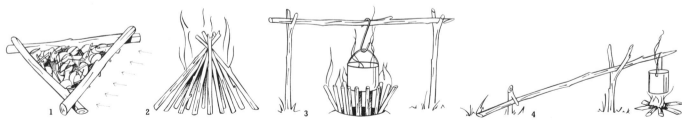

A properly made campfire can mean the difference between a successful camping trip and a disaster. Ensure that you have an adequate supply of wood before lighting the fire, and observe some basic safety rules. There are many ways of preparing a fire, and some of the basic methods are illustrated here. **1** The *basic fire lay*, in which three sticks are laid to form a triangle, with the tinder inside. The stick on the windward side is laid on top of the other sticks to ensure a draught to the tinder. **2** The *teepee fire* is probably the most popular among campers because it produces large flames. **3** To make a *stew fire*, dig a hole about 30 cm deep (and about the same across) and light a small teepee fire in the bottom. Arrange more sticks around the edge of the hole so that they are ignited by the flames: as the wood burns, the sticks will drop lower into the hole, thus ensuring a continuous blaze. If the stew pot is suspended over the flames from a 'cooking crane', the cooking will virtually look after itself. **4** One of the easiest and most effective cooking fires is the *kettle fire* — generally used for making tea or coffee. The fire is made in such a way that the flames envelop only the bottom of the pot or kettle (use a green stick about 2 m long to support it).

Where no sanitary facilities are provided, campers should build their own latrines some distance from the camp-site. Human waste should be buried as deeply as possible. Some people prefer a portable lavatory, but seasoned campers usually manage without it.

Cooking in camps and caravans

Mealtime in a caravan or camp-site could, with a little forethought and common sense, be the highlight of the day. Food prepared away from one's home environment — sometimes in downright primitive conditions — has a special appeal.

Although some campers and caravaners choose stoves designed for methylated spirits, paraffin and other liquid or solid fuels, most prefer gas appliances. Liquefied petroleum gas (LPG) is an easily obtainable, relatively cheap and clean fuel which burns with an intense heat when mixed with air.

Keeping perishables fresh is rarely a problem with the mobile camper. Some of today's compact refrigerators offer a three-way power facility which allows them to be run off the mains electricity supply at home, the car battery *en*

Right: Lamps of varying power and a selection of cooking tops (far right) may be fitted to portable gas cylinders such as these. Manufacturers also offer braai grids, toasters, 'woks' and even a fondue attachment. Gas cylinders may be recharged at literally hundreds of points throughout Southern Africa.

route, and a gas cylinder at the campsite.

Gas cooking is safe if users follow sensible guidelines, the most important of which are:
• If you smell gas (LPG for commercial use has an additive with a distinctive odour), locate the source as quickly as possible. Examine all pipes, joints, taps and other fittings (a solution of soapy water will bubble at a gas leak). Never look for a leak with a naked flame.
• Ensure that there is adequate ventilation when cooking in a caravan or any other enclosed space. Floor vents should be permanently open, as LPG is heavier than air, and will tend to collect on the floor. Although the gas is not poisonous, breathing a high concentration could

cause dizziness and headaches. When an appliance goes out accidentally, clear the tent or caravan of accumulated gas before re-lighting: failure to do so could cause an explosion.
• Gas cylinders should never be placed on a hot stove or near a naked flame, and where possible they should be shielded from the hot sun.
• Place your cooking utensil on the burner before turning on the gas and lighting it. When using a gas oven, strike a match before turning on the gas: this will prevent a build-up of gas in the oven.
• To make the best possible use of the heat: use utensils with straight sides and tight-fitting covers.
• When cooking in the open, protect the flame from the wind with a shield of flame-resistant material, and ensure that it is a safe distance from the stove.
• Tell the local police where you are going, and how long you expect to be away.
• Check that all doors and windows are locked.
• Ask the post office to hold your mail (they will also re-direct telephone calls for a small charge).
• Stop delivery of milk and newspapers.
• Turn the hot water cylinder off.
• Turn off water to outside taps.
• Disconnect all electrical appliances.
• Arrange for care of pets and plants.
• Leave a key with friends or neighbours (some people leave a light or radio switched on).
• Leave your firearm(s) with the police or in another safe place.
• Check whether malaria, bilharzia or other diseases are prevalent in the area you intend to visit, and ask your local health authority or doctor for advice on inoculation and other precautions. If you are in any doubt, make sure that you boil your drinking water, or use one of the water purifiers now on the market.

Above left: The full-frame tent, though more expensive than other designs, is far more robust and usually has more accommodation. The awning is also a useful feature.
Above right: Semi-frame tents suitable for weekend camping, generally sleeping from two to four people. Although designs vary, most can be pitched with little difficulty.
Right: Two-man tents such as this model are light, simple in design, and low-priced. This is the tent usually chosen by hikers.

ZIMBABWE

Zimbabwe is an African feast, a sweeping bounty of woodland, mountain, waterfall and grassy plain that stretches 800 km from Kipling's beloved Limpopo to the mighty Zambezi in the north – over 390 000 km² of largely unspoilt wilderness that is home to a huge variety of wildlife.

Few of the world's game sanctuaries could match the havens encompassed in the great crescent of river bank, escarpment and dusty plain that curves for nearly 1000 km from Mana Pools west to Kariba, Matusadona, Victoria Falls, Matetsi and south to the Hwange National Park. These sun-washed spaces support an enormous number of mammals, birds and reptiles – elephant, buffalo, zebra, kudu, lion, giraffe, crocodile, black eagle, sunbird and a thousand others. This is also the haunt of the tigerfish, that ferocious, ever-hungry and strikingly beautiful predator renowned throughout the angling world as a fine fighting fish. Nor could there be many grander parts of Africa than the Nyanga and Vumba ranges of the country's eastern highlands, or as awesomely strange as the ancient Matobo Hills of Matabeleland, spiritual home of the oracle M'limo and last resting place of Cecil John Rhodes.

Zimbabwe has set aside over 12 per cent of its land – some 43 000 km² – for parks and game sanctuaries. It is a unique heritage.

Small-spotted genets in typical habitat. These long-legged, mainly arboreal creatures are usually found in dense forest. This species has an elongated face and darker underparts than other genets.

North to the mighty Zambezi

In length, in height, in massive volume of water, the Victoria Falls is sheer visual splendour. In peak season an almost continuous avalanche of water 1688 m long hurls itself over the black basalt brink, seething, boiling, twisting in a fury of foam and spray down into the gorge 100 m below. There it churns through a zig-zag series of giant cracks in the lava before continuing on its way to Kariba.

The Victoria Falls, with its two national parks, is a major world tourist attraction. The falls and the palm-lined Zambezi River are the focal point of a wilderness area stretching 70 km west to Botswana's Chobe Game Park and 290 km south through Hwange – Zimbabwe's premier national park. Excluding the hunting safari areas, Hwange's 14 620 km² (two-thirds the size of the Kruger National Park) is larger than all of Zimbabwe's other national parks put together.

Hwange National Park

Evening at Nyamandhlovu pan in the northern sector of this huge park (over 14 000 km²), when the elephants come to drink, is (in the dry season) a wildlife extravaganza. There are invariably at least a dozen species of game in or near the water, or on the great plain that surrounds it.

But the highlight is the arrival of the elephant. A forerunner or two, then a herd of 50 or more (bulls, cows and young) appear in a swift dash for the water, scattering the other animals. There they will wade, splash, throw mud on themselves, gurgle, rumble, trumpet and drink. A bull can consume 250ℓ of water in twenty minutes.

There are some 21 000 elephant in Hwange. Each adult male weighs an average of 4,5 tons, and spends 12 to 18 hours a day consuming 170 kg of fresh food. Elephant live to about 70, by which time the last of their six sets of grinding teeth is likely to have worn down.

Hwange Park, known until recently as Wankie National Park, came into existence in 1928. A century earlier, the area south of it had been the royal hunting preserve of Mzilikazi, warrior-king of the Ndebele. Ruling the area at the time of Mzilikazi's arrival was Hwange Rosumbani, a Rozvi sub-chief. The word Rozvi probably comes from the Shona 'kuruzva' (to destroy) and this is what the Ndebele did to Hwange (with the doubtful compensation that the area would continue to be called after him). Others visited the Hwange area, but they were not to remember it with affection. To early Eu-

Above: The rufous-brown, white-speckled colouring of a female Sharpe's grysbok blends with its surroundings in the Hwange National Park. During the heat of the day, this small antelope seeks refuge among boulders and rocks and even in old burrows excavated by aardvarks. When on the move, it keeps its head low and, when disturbed, makes off at a scuttling run for shelter of the bush. **Left:** Purple rose ginger flowers (*Kaemferia rosea*) in the Hwange National Park. **Right:** The white-crowned shrike, found throughout the Hwange National Park, has a habit of perching on the outermost branches of trees – particularly baobabs.

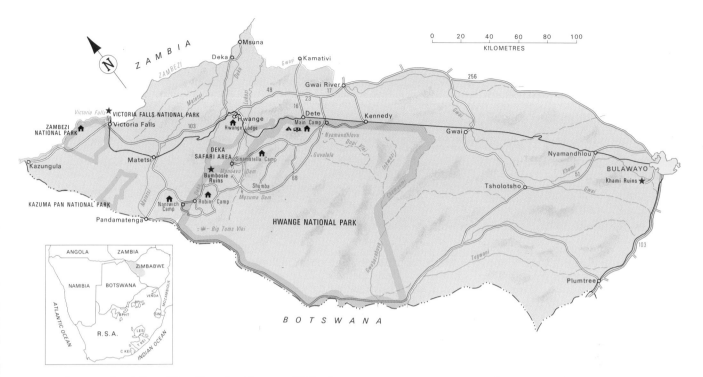

ropean explorers, as they followed the old road to Panda-ma-Tenga between Botswana and Zimbabwe, it was the 'white man's grave' – fever-ridden, hot, and populated by marauding lions. There was a time when the north of Hwange consisted of swamps and forests. However, tsetse fly was eliminated when the game herds were almost wiped out by the rinderpest epidemic of the 19th century. Half a century of conservation has allowed the game numbers to build up to present levels.

The three national parks tourist camps – Main, Sinamatella and Robins/Nantwich – are situated in the northern half of the park. There are hides overlooking pans at Nyamandhlovu and Guvalala, both of which are along the 76 km tarred road from Main Camp to the Shumba picnic site.

Hwange: Main Camp

Access to Main Camp is at the 264,5 km peg on the Bulawayo-Victoria Falls road. A 24 km tarred road leads to the camp. There are nine game-viewing drives ranging from 16 to 120 km in length, as well as other (minor) roads.

Hwange is on the fringe of the Kalahari, with the Okavango wetland lying far to the west. Millennia ago, it was a desert. From the air the

southern section of the park reveals, through its mixed scrub and Kalahari woodland, the ancient lines of fossil sand dunes. Once there were rivers, but now there are only short-lived streams created by the rains. To compensate, boreholes feed water to the 45 major pans and six dams. Hwange has one of the densest populations of game in the world. There are 750 lion, 2 500 zebra, 2 000 sable, 900 roan and 401 spe-

HWANGE AT A GLANCE

When to go The Main, Nantwich and Sinamatella camps are open all year, from sunrise to sunset, but Robins Camp is closed during the wet season (1 November to 30 April). The peak game-viewing period is the hot, dry months of September and October. Many species give birth to their young during the wet season, which begins in late November or December.

Reservations and information To make reservations or request information on all camps in the Hwange National Park, write to The National Parks Central Booking Office, P.O. Box 8151, Causeway, Harare, Zimbabwe (telephone Harare 70-6077).

Getting there Air Zimbabwe offers flights to Main Camp. Visitors may also travel by rail to Dete station, from where they take a coach to Main Camp.

Accommodation Apart from the lodges and chalets, there is accommodation of varying standard at hotels in Dete (24 km from Main Camp), Gwayi River (28 km from Main Camp) and the town of Hwange (52 km from Sinamatella Camp). The Hwange Safari Lodge, 10 km from Main Camp, has a three-star grading.

Eating and drinking There are restaurants and bars at Main Camp and Sinamatella, and facilities at hotels outside its borders are fair to excellent.

Getting around The Hwange Safari Lodge and another tour operator offer a variety of game-drives from Main Camp. Visitors may also go on foot safaris.

Special attractions These include escorted game-drives by moonlight and an impressive view of elephant at Nyamandhlovu, near Main Camp.

Wildlife Hwange has a population of 50 000 elephant, 750 lion and a variety of other game.

Special precautions Visitors should take a course of anti-malaria tablets before entering the area.

359

cies of birds. Herds of up to 500 buffalo (there are 15 000 in the park area) and elephant are commonly seen.

Accommodation at Main camp consists of lodges, cottages, chalets and camping and caravan sites which are served by a restaurant, bar and store. Petrol is available.

Hwange: Nantwich Camp

Nantwich's three fully equipped lodges are under the control of Robins Camp. They are 11 km from the camp, in a setting of splendid isolation overlooking a stretch of water.

Fire is always a threat in a game reserve. There are some 1 500 km of 100 m-wide fire breaks (or traces) in Hwange, allied to a network of fire towers, and the whole park is divided into fire-control blocks. The prevention of soil erosion and the preservation of vleis are two other functions of the park's staff, as is the maintenance – through culling, for example – of the correct 'carrying capacity' of the animal population. Displays demonstrating these aspects of Hwange's management can be seen at any one of the park's three administration centres.

Hwange: Robins Camp

A hyena managed to get himself locked in the lavatory at Robins camp not so long ago. The confused animal was released by amused wardens. It was an incident in keeping with the eccentric history of this part of Hwange National Park. The camp is named after Herbert Robins, a bachelor recluse and amateur astronomer who owned two farms, Big Toms (after hunter Tom Sadler) and Little Toms on tributaries of the Deka River. Robins used to sleep during the day, spending much of the night starwatching from a tall, square, concrete tower he built (the tower is now part of the Robins Camp administration complex). Daytime callers were, naturally, not welcomed by the half-awake Robins dressed in pyjamas and knitted sailor cap. He died in 1939, bequeathing his farms to the nation.

360

There are more lion in the vicinity of Robins than around any of the other camps, the predators appearing to favour the surrounding basalt areas here rather than elsewhere in the park. Tsessebe and reedbuck are also more common.

The 70 km road to Robins is all gravel and leaves the main Victoria Falls-Bulawayo route 48 km south of the falls. One should allow a full day to travel from Robins through the park to Main Camp. The park's staff are helpful and will, for instance, arrange for a puncture to be fixed. Accommodation comprises chalets with outdoor cooking facilities (guests must bring their own crockery and cutlery) and camping and caravan sites. There is a store in the camp and petrol is available. The tortuous game-drive to crocodile pools on the Deka River is rewarding. There is a platform at Big Toms vlei and a hide at Little Toms.

Hwange: Sinamatella Camp

Situated on a boulder-strewn ridge 55 m high overlooking the Sinamatella valley, the camp is 48 km from the town of Hwange on a gravel road via Mbala Lodge in the Deka Safari Area. There are lodges, cottages and chalets (visitors must bring food, crockery and cutlery), and a number of camping and caravan sites. The camp has a restaurant, bar, store and petrol.

The bush, with grassy vleis, is thicker here than at Main Camp, Sinamatella being north of the watershed which drains into the Zambezi. Several dams, including Detema, halfway to Robins Camp, Mandavu (both with picnic sites) and Masuma provide good game-viewing. Impala, warthog, klipspringer and leopard are more numerous here than at Main Camp.

The famous Beadle croc, raised in the former Chief Justice's goldfish pond and later transferred to Nyamandhlovu Pan near Main Camp, is probably the most photographed predator ever. There are several game-drives, including the popular Lukosi River loop. Visitors must leave Sinamatella by 2 p.m. to reach Main Camp at dusk and by 3 p.m. to reach Robins.

Hwange Safari Lodge

Four kilometres from the Hwange Park airport (follow the signposts) is the lodge, a luxury hotel fringing Hwange Main Camp, and a safari centre featuring a variety of activities that include veld walks, dawn patrols, sunset trails and one- or two-night bush camp mini-safaris. Visitors sleep in wooden tree-houses near the lodge. There is even a children's camp, complete with log-fire tales. The seven tree-houses (one with a wild bees' nest at its base) overlook the Dete vlei.

In effect, the lodge has its own game-rich reserve in the 26 000 ha conservation area of Kalahari teak and giant camelthorn that surrounds it. An elephant pan is situated in front of the lodge, and both here and elsewhere are bunker hides from which you can practically touch the elephant. For further information, write to The Hwange Safari Lodge, Private Bag 5792, Dete, Zimbabwe (telephone Dete 331).

Kazuma Pan National Park

Hwange National Park, Deka Safari Area, Matetsi Safari Area, Kazuma Pan, the Zambezi National Park and the Victoria Falls National Park form a continuous south to north belt in the top left corner of Zimbabwe. They differ widely. The Kazuma Pan National Park in the far west of the Matetsi Safari Area is a 312 km² reserve where a series of natural pans are

Far left: A herd of sable kicks up dust in this tinted lithograph from the book *African Hunting and Adventure from Natal to the Zambezi... from 1852 to 1860*, by English hunter and traveller William Charles Baldwin. The lithograph, entitled 'Chasing Harris bucks', is by James Wolf. One of Baldwin's expeditions into the interior comprised an eight-member party of raw youngsters, which the infamous 'Elephant' White led into fever-ridden Zululand one steamy January. Their journey was disastrous: only Baldwin and one other member of the party survived. **Left above:** The banded mongoose, distinguished by its striped back and short, tapering tail, lives in packs of up to 50 members. This adept rock climber will also take to the trees in an emergency, and when alarmed will usually utter a shrill warning cry. It is a courageous animal which shows little fear when cornered. Its major enemies are larger carnivores and birds of prey. **Left below:** The serval, a largely nocturnal cat, feeds on various small animals, ranging from lizards and mice to duikers. **Right:** Sable in the Chamabonda section of the Victoria Falls National Park.

seasonally flooded, attracting wildfowl. The game, which includes gemsbok, cheetah and giraffe, tend to concentrate in the more watered and tree-covered western section, the east being open grassland. Game-viewing on foot is permitted but there are no facilities, and four-wheel-drive vehicles are essential in this remote area.

To get there from Victoria Falls, turn right at the Matetsi signpost and ask, at the Matetsi Headquarters, for directions to the Pandamatenga road which runs parallel to the Zimbabwe-Botswana border to Kazuma Pan. Prior permission must be obtained from Matetsi Headquarters.

Victoria Falls National Park

The Victoria Falls National Park is the 2340ha area surrounding the falls and stretching some 500m back from both falls and river's edge. The spray of *Mosi-oa-Tunya*, or the 'smoke that thunders', reaches as high as 450m and has on occasion been seen from 80km away.

The great throb of the falls and the seething cauldron below dominate the whole area – pulling one like a magnet. In the flood season, the Zambezi River pours over the falls at the staggering rate of 545 million litres a minute.

VICTORIA FALLS AND ZAMBEZI NATIONAL PARKS AT A GLANCE

When to go Spray can obscure the falls during the peak-flow winter months, and visitors find the period between August and November the best time for photography. The Zambezi National Park's gates are open during daylight hours only, and are closed during the wet season (1 November to 30 April).

Reservations Bookings for the lodges in the Zambezi National Park and for the Kandahar, Mpala-Jena and Sansimba fishing camps should be made through The National Parks Central Booking Office, P.O. Box 8151, Causeway, Harare, Zimbabwe (telephone Harare 70-6077). Visitors who wish to book cottages, chalets, camping and caravan sites at the rest camp in Victoria Falls village should write to The Victoria Falls Town Council, P.O. Box 41, Victoria Falls, Zimbabwe (telephone Victoria Falls 210).

Getting there The falls are 439km from Bulawayo by road, and there is also a rail link with the city. Otherwise visitors may fly by Air Zimbabwe from Harare, Bulawayo and Johannesburg. The Zambezi National Park is about 6km from Victoria Falls village (take the road running past the Zambezi River and crocodile ranches).

Accommodation There are fully equipped lodges (sleeping six persons each) situated on the banks of the Zambezi in the Zambezi National Park. The primitive but appealing fishing camps, in the Zambezi National Park, may be booked by parties of up to 10 people. Each fishing camp has a central sleeping shelter and ablution block. The facilities at the rest camp in Victoria Falls village include cottages and chalets (visitors supply their own crockery and cutlery). There are camping spots in the village and caravanning sites further upstream.

Eating and drinking As with most national parks in Zimbabwe, there are no restaurants or bars within the reserves. The hotels at and near Victoria Falls village, however, provide this region's many visitors excellent facilities.

Getting around There are launch cruises up the Zambezi and spectacular flights (known as 'the flight of angels') over the falls. More adventurous visitors can actually 'shoot the rapids' in the 'boiling pot' below the falls. The Zambezi National Park can be explored by driving along the picturesque Zambezi Drive or taking either of the two other roads traversing the park.

Special attractions The Victoria Falls area features a crocodile ranch with 4000 specimens, a snake park, tribal dancing at the Victoria Falls Hotel and an Ndebele craft village.

David Livingstone, Victorian explorer and the first white man to have recorded seeing the falls, approached them on 16 November 1855 from up-river, in a canoe paddled by Kololo tribesmen. They landed him on Kazeruka Island (now Livingstone Island) perched on the very lip. It was from here, lying full-length, that he first peered over. He later wrote: 'Scenes so lovely must have been gazed upon by angels in their flight'. He carved his name on a tree – 'a weakness', as he put it, that he only once indulged in. David Livingstone's statue today gazes over the savage spectacle of Devil's Cataract.

A walk, with steps cut into the cliff, descends a third of the way down to a viewing platform, and there are view sites along the length of the falls.

A rain forest fringes the chasm, and in this fairyland of ferns, orchids and blood-lilies, the falls appear as a tumultuously moving mosaic behind a screen of spray. Vervet monkeys and the occasional scarlet-breasted sunbird chatter in the vines that loop the wild fig and the palms, the moss-covered African ebony and sausage trees. A path traces the edge of the cliff through the sun-speckled and perpetually drenched forest. There is always at least one spectacular rainbow, and the gossamer spray is tinted soft pink and gold in early morning and evening. To see the rare lunar rainbow at night is an entrancing experience.

Nearby, Victoria Falls village has some splendid hotels and a casino.

The entrance to the park is encountered just before the border post with Zambia. The park is open from sunrise to sunset. There are the usual border formalities, but once they are negotiated, viewing is possible from the bridge and Zambian bank.

Zambezi National Park

Zambezi Drive starts at the Victoria Falls and, tracing the riverbank, ends 46 km upstream at the Zambezi National Park's western boundary. The park, stretching south from the river in a wedge of the Zambezi basin 26 km deep, is 56 010 ha in area.

Along the drive are some delightful picnic sites and fishing spots (tigerfish, bream and vundu can be caught). No fishing licence is required. There are six-bedded lodges on the banks of the Zambezi River. Fishermen are also well accommodated in the Kandahar, Mpala-Jena and Sansimba fishing camps.

Two other roads traverse the park: the main route to Kazungula on the Botswana border, and the Chamabonda Drive, 6 km from the Victoria Falls on the Bulawayo road. This drive follows the small Masuwe River, with its thick vegetation opening out into large, treeless vleis where some magnificent herds of up to 200 sable have been seen.

Other large mammals in the park include buffalo, black rhino, white rhino, waterbuck, kudu, impala, elephant, zebra, lion, leopard and cheetah. Visitors may also spot crocodile and hippo in the river.

To make a reservation, write to The National Parks Central Booking Office, P.O. Box 8151, Causeway, Harare, Zimbabwe (telephone Harare 70-6077).

Left: A solitary bushbuck ewe (*Tragelaphus scriptus*) in long grass in the Victoria Falls National Park. The male of the species has spirally twisted, slightly bowed horns, and is larger than the female. **Above:** This coloured lithograph by Thomas Baines depicts the chasm at the foot of the Victoria Falls and the churning Zambezi River. Baines was prominent among the many pre-photography artists who captured Southern Africa's wild animals and scenic grandeur in a variety of art forms. In 1858 Baines joined David Livingstone on an expedition to the mouth of the Zambezi River. He was sacked by Livingstone after being accused of theft, and joined a new expedition from Walvis Bay to

Victoria Falls – becoming the first artist to paint the falls. Later in his life he won a gold-mining concession from Lobengula, the Ndebele king, that was sold after Baines's death to the British South Africa Company. In over 4 000 pencil sketches, water colours and oils, Baines vividly recorded the people, the animals, the trees, flowers and wars of the mid-19th century. And yet when he died in Durban in 1875 he had the equivalent of 25 cents in his pocket. **Right above:** 'The smoke that thunders': swathed in the permanent mist of its plummeting waters, the Zambezi River surges through the gorge at the base of the Victoria Falls.

The inland ocean of Kariba

Dawn creeps across the mist-shrouded waters of Lake Kariba. The ghostly skeletons of long-dead trees play mournful host to egret and darter. In a giant leadwood tree, a fish eagle hunches and surveys its world. As the sun appears, a buffalo heaves itself out of the mud; a goliath heron breaks and glides away. The sun clears the tree-line, its rays skim over the Matusadona Mountains and catch a malachite kingfisher spraying rainbow droplets in her morning bath. The mists writhe and vanish, and another day begins.

At Kariba on the Zambezi, where for thousands of years only the elephant and warthog paused to drink, there now stands a million cubic metres of concrete and 11 000 tons of reinforcing steel. This is Kariba Dam. One hundred and twenty-eight metres high and 617m wide, it holds back one of Africa's greatest rivers in a lake 282 km long. This inland ocean is the size of Wales – a wilderness of tigerfish and sudden storms that is unique in Southern Africa. The dam is the focal point of the Mana, Matusadona and Chizarira national parks, the Chete and Charara safari areas, and a host of smaller wildlife safari resorts.

Bumi Hills Safari Lodge

The 20 luxury rooms and chalets of Bumi Hills Safari Lodge are poised on a ridge overlooking the shores of Kariba. Far below, the lake stretches in an arc. A pair of bateleur eagles wheel at eye level, riding the thermals.

Bumi is a wild haven on the edge of Matusadona National Park where, say impressed visitors, each day begins like the dawn of creation and ends in an Armageddon of blazing blood-red sky.

Guided bushwalks and game drives are offered, while a four-day wilderness water safari up the Ume River is like drifting across a prehistoric swampland. For this, accommodation is in insect-proofed, twin-bedded water-safari craft; meals could include Chicken Nzhou smoked over dried elephant dung and mopane leaves – the chef's speciality. Binoculars and camera are essential. A twin-engined aircraft flies guests to Bumi's strip from Kariba. Bumi is open year-round. For reservations, write to Bumi Hills Safari Lodge, P.O. Box 41, Kariba, Zimbabwe (telephone Kariba 2353); or Zimbabwe Sun Hotels Central Reservations, P.O. Box 8221, Causeway, Harare, Zimbabwe (telephone Harare 73-6644).

Top: *Combretum mossambicense* along the Zambezi. **Above:** A waterbuck ram beside Lake Kariba, in the Bumi Hills region. **Left:** Kariba at dusk. The huge lake (it has an area of over 5 000 km²) is retained by a massive concrete arch, 607 m wide, 126 m high and 21 m thick. An estimated 50 000 people and countless animals were ousted by the rising waters of the dam.

Charara Safari Area

Stretching over 1 700 km² from the outskirts of
Kariba Village, Charara has a network of gravel roads (4-wheel-drive only) and there is good
game-viewing, particularly in the late afternoons when the animals trek to the lake shore.
The area is open from sunrise to sunset
throughout the year. Game-viewing on foot is
also permitted, provided a permit has been
obtained from the warden. Being served by
Kariba Village itself, there is very little
accommodation for visitors, other than
Nyanyana's 35 camping and caravan sites at
the mouth of the Nyanyana River, 28 km from
Kariba. The turn-off to the camp *en route* from
Harare to Kariba is 56 km from Makuti, followed
by 5,5 km of dirt road. There are ablution
blocks and a slipway for boats, and firewood
is sold. For further information and to reserve
camping and caravan sites write to The National Parks Central Booking Office, P.O. Box 8151,
Causeway, Harare, Zimbabwe (telephone Harare 70-6077).

Chizarira National Park

Few visitors have been into this remote
200 000 ha mountain park, 50 km inland from Binga on Lake Kariba. Access is difficult: turn right
16 km north of the Hwange Park turn-off on the
Bulawayo-Victoria Falls road. Apart from the
first 25 km, the 155 km route to Binga has a good
gravel surface, but roads in Chizarira – a
Batonka word meaning barrier – are only
suitable for 4-wheel-drive or sturdy vehicles.
The alternative route is along the rough Zambezi escarpment Hostes Nicolle Drive from Karoi,
370 km distant.

Like land falling down to the sea, Chizarira
descends in wooded ridges, mountains and
rocky valleys to the escarpment overlooking
Lake Kariba. It is a primordial land of rivers,
natural springs and perennial streams, of msasa
and Prince of Wales feather (mfuti) trees, of
sudden bush fires and rugged mountain
scenery. Chizarira's supposedly haunted Tun-
dazi Mountain rises 1 370 m above the Zambezi valley. The National Parks headquarters is
at Manzituba in the west, where there is an airstrip. There are camping facilities and bookings may be made by writing to The National
Parks Central Booking Office, P.O. Box 8151,
Causeway, Harare, Zimbabwe (telephone Harare 70-6077). The game includes some 1 000
elephant, 1 000 buffalo, 500 tsessebe, sable,
roan, black rhino, crocodile, leopard and lion.

Fothergill Island

Twenty kilometres from Kariba, and separated from the mainland by a small channel, lies
the 400 ha Fothergill Island, cradled at the base
of the Matusadona Mountains. It is named after ranger Rupert Fothergill, who launched
364

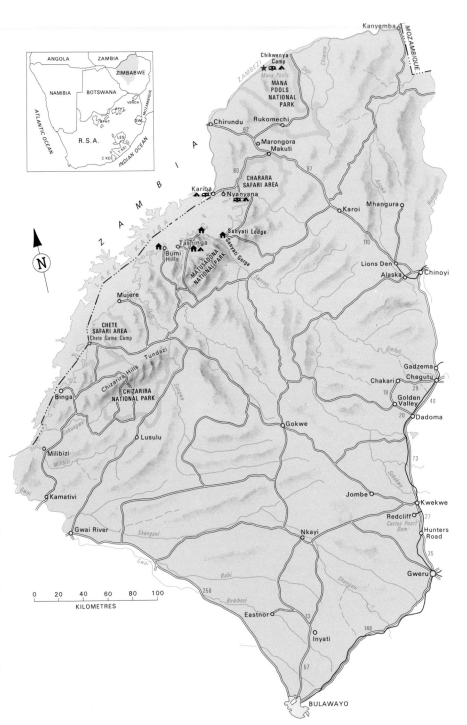

Above: Impala graze around the Bumi Hills hide on Starvation Island in Lake Kariba. The island's name recalls the crisis of many years ago when hundreds of hungry animals were rescued from the rising waters of Lake Kariba. The island is still visited by antelope and elephant, who swim across from the mainland. **Right:** Wahlberg's skink — a common inhabitant of the Kariba area. **Far right:** A black rhino in the Mana Pools National Park — a broad expanse of acacia and mahogany woodland which is regularly invaded by game during the dry season.

Operation Noah — an animal rescue operation unique in its size and complexity. As the waters of the Zambezi rose behind the new dam wall, countless thousands of animals of all sizes were stranded on ever-shrinking islands. Fothergill was among the many dedicated people who ventured on to the lake in a variety of craft to save buck, baboon, snake, porcupine, monkey and other creatures — often at great risk to themselves. The exhausted, starving victims thanked their rescuers with countless bites, kicks and scratches.

On the island is a safari lodge where twenty-five thatched chalets, with showers open to the stars, crouch around the central double-storey dining lodge and bar. Wildlife expeditions are led by guides and include safaris which may be undertaken by boat, vehicle or on foot. There are also Matusadona walking and canoe trails (for the fitter visitor) and photographic tree-hide excursions. This is elephant and buffalo country. Tigerfish and bream may be caught in the lake. Meals at Fothergill are heralded by Batonka drumming and cooked on open fires. Fothergill is open all year round. Boats can be chartered from Kariba Village to cross the lake to Fothergill Island (there is also an airstrip). For further information, write to Fothergill Island Safaris, Private Bag 2081, Kariba (telephone Kariba 2253 or Harare 70-5144).

Lake Kariba

Lake Kariba is a vast, man-made wilderness. Its shores accommodate a huge variety of game, its waters teem with tigerfish and other species, and skeletal forests in its shallows are home to thousands of nesting fish eagles. This huge inland sea covers 5 180km² of what was once the Gwembe Trough. At night its waters are speckled with the tiny bright stars of fishing boats netting Kapenta (a freshwater sardine).

Adapting to the initial flooding and annual fluctuation of the lake level, a rich variety of animal and plant species has come to flourish on the banks of the lake.

Acting as a stabiliser to the lake shore has been the explosive growth of *Salvinia molesta*, or Kariba weed, a choking water fern that deeply concerned ecologists in the early years. In due course it receded, however, and today plays a vital role as the reservoir for nutrients released by the flooded earth, and as a scaffolding for a new grassland shelter for young fish and waterfowl.

The bright green *Panicum repens*, or torpedo grass, began to colonise the lake shore in 1970, particularly in areas which had been previously cleared of trees. Originating as a swamp grass on the upper Zambezi, it has thrived on the slow annual cycle of submersion and exposure of the shoreline and has become an important source of dry-season grazing for buffalo, elephant and other game.

In the lake are sponges, jellyfish, shrimps, mussels, turtles and some 42 species of fish, including nkupe, chessa, bottle nose, vundu, barbel, several types of bream and, of course, the famed tigerfish.

One hundred thousand hectares of forest were cleared prior to flooding, but other trees drowned, rotted and broke off at the waterline as they were annually submerged and exposed. Underwater, they toughened into rockhard hazards to boats. Above the water, the trees are perches for the fish eagle, cormorant, pied kingfisher, darter, marabou and heron. The lake is also rich in crocodile, and breeding areas and crocodile farms have been established around its rim.

The lake is in effect a small inland sea: it has waves, currents and sudden storms. The rivers (Mlibizi, Zambezi, Sanyati, Ume, Sebungwe) still flow beneath it along their centuries-old courses. Yachts, powerboats, canoes, motorised double-storey houseboats, floating game-viewing hides, windsurfers, sardine-trawlers and water-skiers all ply its waters. A 22-hour voyage on the *Sealion*, one of two Kariba car and passenger ferries (one carries cargo only) that plies the 282 km between Kariba's Andora harbour and Mlibizi in the western narrows, is a journey back to the days of Bogart and the *African Queen*. Navigating the Chete Gorge by 366

radar at night, with a spotlight to pick out the red eyes of crocodile on the shore, or a mid-journey swim in the lake (with a wary eye open for crocodile), are among the highlights of a visit to Kariba. To book a place on the ferry, write to Kariba Ferries, P.O. Box 578, Harare, Zimbabwe, or P.O. Box 70, Kariba, Zimbabwe (telephone Kariba 2460).

A bushbuck ram in the Mana Pools National Park. Although normally nervous and shy, a cornered bushbuck will turn into a brave attacker. The slightly spiralled horns (found only on males) reach 52 cm and are a fearsome weapon against leopards, wild dogs and even human beings.

AN EAGLE FALLS

Lake Kariba's fish eagles (Haliaeetus vocifer) face extinction within ten years as a result of the pesticide DDT. This pesticide, of which 1 100 tons a year are used in crop spraying and in tsetse and malarial mosquito control, is not banned in Zimbabwe as it is in many other countries. It affects the beautiful birds' reproductive processes. Eggshells become thinner, vulnerable to excessive moisture evaporation, and too weak to support the weight of the brooding parent. This was discovered when national parks rangers were lowered by helicopter on to fish eagle nests atop the dead trees of Kariba's shoreline to collect clutches of eggs for analysis.

The American bald eagle population began declining when eggshell thinning reached 10 per cent: at Lake Kariba it is already 16 per cent. The peregrine falcon (Falco peregrinus) will, however, probably be the first bird to disappear, as it did in the eastern U.S.A. Also on the death list if immediate action is not taken (there are several alternative safer pesticides) are the heron, cormorant, black sparrowhawk and rare fishing owl. The lake's huge fish population is also threatened.

Kariba Village, on the heights above the dam wall, has air-conditioned hotels, camping and caravan sites, and a casino – a far cry from the rugged construction site of the fifties, where 86 men died in the building of the dam. A church honours their memory. It can be hot: the average summer temperature is 38°C. Panoramic views reward visitors to the small Peak Road Nature Reserve up Kariba Heights. The Charara Safari Area begins at Kariba Village, and Nyanyana camp lies 28 km distant. For more information write to The Kariba Publicity Association, P.O. Box 86, Kariba, Zimbabwe (telephone Kariba 2328).

The western half of Lake Kariba traditionally begins at Binga, some 155 km from the Bulawayo-Victoria Falls highway. There are no game reserves in the west, but Chizarira National Park is 50 km from Binga and Hwange National Park is a two- to three-hour drive west of Chizarira.

Mana Pools National Park

Created by the Zambezi breaking over an alluvial floodplain 12 km wide and 30 km long, Mana is rich in game, forests of giant acacia and mahogany, and a large and varied river life. Here you will see carmine bee-eaters, their nests burrowed into the river bank, rare nyala, sacred ibis and colourful dawns and sunsets – sights and experiences that will remain with you always.

KARIBA AREA AT A GLANCE

When to go The national parks and safari lodges in this region are open to visitors year-round.

Reservations For national parks accommodation at Mana Pools, Nyanyana Camp (Charara), Tashinga and Sanyati West (both Matusadona), write to The National Parks Central Booking Office, P.O. Box 8151, Causeway, Harare, Zimbabwe (telephone Harare 70-6077).

Getting there Motorists may take a fully tarred road (367 km) from Harare. Express Motorways operates coach trips from Harare. Visitors may also choose to take the Hostes Nicolle Drive, a 499 km gravel road leading from the Bulawayo-Victoria Falls highway. Charter flights are available from Harare to Bumi and from Kariba to Fothergill and Spurwing.

Accommodation The Bumi Hills Safari Lodge offers 20 luxury chalets, Charara has 35 caravan and camping sites (with other accommodation in nearby Kariba Village), Chizarira has no accommodation at all, the Fothergill Island Safari Lodge features 25 thatched chalets. The Matusadona area also has camping facilities and exclusive safari camps.

Eating and drinking The Bumi Hills Safari Lodge offers such exotic fare as chicken cooked over dried elephant dung, Fothergill Island's Safari Lodge has a double-storey dining room and bar.

Getting around Visitors may view the Kariba area in a variety of ways, but one of the most appealing is by boat down the length of the lake. Visitors may go on walking and canoe trails, photographic excursions, shoreline boat safaris and trips in a floating hide. Game-viewing trips on foot are also very popular.

Special attractions Kariba has everything the nature enthusiast could want – a sweeping, dramatic expanse of water, rich and widely varying vegetation, and very good facilities for holidaymakers.

Wildlife The area is rich in myriad game species, including just about every large Southern African mammal with the exception of white rhino, giraffe and wildebeest. There are also excellent opportunities for bird-watchers.

Fishing Boats and fishing tackle are available for hire, and all resorts have mooring and refuelling facilities for private boats.

Special precautions Visitors should take precautions against malaria. Areas such as Matusadona and Mana have tsetse fly, and bilharzia is present in the stagnant water on the lake's shores. Beware of crocodiles.

Mana means 'four', after four families who once lived here. Long Pool, famous for its crocodile, is where herds of up to 400 buffalo gather in October, and every night the roar of the lion is heard.

The 43 camping and caravan sites open from 1 May to 31 October, and two luxury camps (open throughout the year) at Mana's four camps are set at the water's edge and look across the Zambezi to the steeply rising Zambian escarpment one kilometre away. Mana Pools National Park is one of the few Zimbabwe game parks where visitors are allowed to leave their cars and walk around. Nevertheless, you are still urged to exercise a degree of caution. A maximum of 50 vehicles is permitted in the park at one time.

Mana's hinterland – a quarter of a million hectares between the Zambezi escarpment, down through mopane woodland, then jesse bush, and eventually the floodplain and river – is there primarily for the animals. There are no fences, and if an elephant bumps your tent at night or steps over your sleeping bag, the ranger is likely to express the hope that the elephant was not upset!

The river is a fisherman's dream (tigerfish, barbel, vundu, bream) but there are other aspects of this region that visitors will find less appealing: the temperature can reach a suffocating 46°C; anti-malaria precautions are essential; drinking water must be boiled; it is a tsetse area – and the Zambezi is not, as one lady wrote in the visitors' book, 'such nice, safe water for the children to bathe in'. There is a bush airstrip. Marongora, where Mana Pools permits must be obtained, is 16 km north of Makuti (the last petrol stop) and 312 km from Harare on the road to Zambia.

Leaving Marongora no later than 3.30 p.m., turn right on to a gravel road six kilometres further north, at the foot of the escarpment, drive 30 km to Nyakasikana Gate, and then 42 km to Nyamepi Camp.

Fothergill Island Safaris operate all-inclusive land and river photographic safaris from their six super-luxurious thatched chalets – known as Chikwenya Camp – at the confluence of the

ated 300 m from the spectacular Sanyati Gorge. Only a third of the park is open to the public, but if you are tired of fighting the striped tiger-fish or waterdog (*Hydrocyon vittatus*) you can literally take to the hills. This forbidding bush-land has been declared a wilderness area, and only those with special permission are allowed access to it.

There are an estimated 100 black rhino, 400 adult crocodile, 200 hippo, 1 000 elephant and several thousand buffalo in Matusadona.

Kariba Dam has not eradicated the instincts of the elephant and buffalo, which still try to fol-low the migratory routes of former years to the Zambezi, the buffalo pushing to the very edge of the land and the elephant actually swimming to Starvation Island.

In January 1982, a pair of elephant following these ancient migratory routes swam the en-tire 40 km across Lake Kariba, spending some 30 hours in the water.

Exhausted, they helped each other along, the one in front inflating his lungs for buoyancy and being pushed by the one behind. National Parks staff in boats, led by the warden, came to the intrepid elephants' rescue, guiding them gently ashore at Kariba Village.

Sanyati Lodge

After dark at Sanyati Lodge, in the isolated Matusadona Game Reserve, there's not even an electricity generator to intrude on the peace and the natural night-time sounds, for energy is provided by solar power. The lodge is on the shoreline of Lake Kariba, and a mere 300 m from the Sanyati Gorge. The area abounds with animal and bird life; the angler is well provid-ed for too.

This is a small camp, with accommodation in well-spaced stone-and-thatch chalets, with bathrooms. Meals are taken on a patio that overlooks the entire Kariba Eastern Basin.

For further information and bookings write to Sanyati Lodge, P.O. Box 4047, Harare, Zim-babwe (or telephone Harare 70-3000).

Spurwing Island

A menu highlight, wild mushroom soup, is made from huge mushrooms that grow on the ant-hills of Spurwing Island, and is typical of the imaginative way in which Matusadona Safari Lodge is run. It has 11 immaculate open chalets, tents under thatch, three cottages, two luxury lodges, generated electricity and a huge freez-er room for the day's tigerfish catch, and close-cropped green grass.

The dining room and two-storey thatched pub overlooks the lake, and occasionally visitors will see 'Fisi', the floating hide, returning from a game-viewing trip. For further information, write to Spurwing Island, P.O. Box 101, Kariba, Zim-babwe (telephone Kariba 2466).

Sapi and Zambezi rivers to the east of the Mana Pools National Park. Chikwenya is open from mid-April to the end of October.

For information and reservations write to Fothergill Island Safaris, Private Bag 2081, Kari-ba, Zimbabwe (telephone Kariba 2253 or Ha-rare 70-5144). Outside the western boundaries of Mana Pools is a similar luxurious safari camp, called Ruckomechi. For information and reser-vations write to Shearwater, P.O. Box 3961, Ha-rare (telephone Harare 73-5712).

Matusadona National Park

You can get to Matusadona's three National Parks camps by road – at least six cars a year make the effort. But unless you're a fish eagle or have a 4-wheel-drive vehicle rather take a boat from Kariba, or a light aircraft. Matusado-na sprawls across 1 407 km² between the Ume and Sanyati rivers, its tumble of wooded moun-tains falling down from the uninhabited plateau to the little bays, creeks and islands of Kariba. The Sanyati Gorge is particularly dramatic. Once the hot, narrow valley through which the
368

Sanyati rushed from the mountains to the Zambezi Valley, it has become an African fjord navigable for 12 kilometres.

Exclusive bush camps (one party at a time) accommodating up to 12 people in two fully equipped units (linen, crockery, refrigerator, gas) are available at Tashinga, the park head-quarters on the Ume River (some 55 km from Kariba by boat), and at Elephant Point, 10 km farther east. There is an airstrip at Tashinga and the road distance from Harare is 468 km. Camp-ing facilities with tents, mattresses and hot water are available at Tashinga and another camp at Sanyati West. Petrol and diesel are available – though not always – at Bumi harbour, 14 km from Tashinga. Visitors should take precautions against the malarial mosquito and tsetse fly, and drinking water must always be purified. Con-sult your doctor or chemist for advice. The camps are open from sunrise to sunset through-out the year.

Bumi, Fothergill, and Spurwing safari lodges are three privately run off-shore Matusadona base camps. A fourth, Sanyati Lodge, is situ-

The ancient land of the Shona

The imposing Mashonaland plateau of Zimbabwe is a parkland of rolling msasa woodlands between the Zambezi and Limpopo rivers. Six hundred kilometres wide, the plains and great grassy vleis are littered with granite castle koppies and weird nests of balancing rocks, some as old as 3 000 million years.

This, the land of the Shona, is rich in small game species, in bird life and in a thousand-year history of Iron Age agriculture, trade and conquest. The evenings are always cool and the summer daylight temperatures average 27°C. The rainy season is from November to March. The winter months of June and July can bring frost at night.

The north-east of Zimbabwe encompasses much of the plateau and the nation's capital, Harare. None of the country's great concentrations of big game are here, but there are numerous parks, recreational areas and sanctuaries, usually around man-made dams. Features such as the Chinhoyi Caves, Lake McIlwaine's San paintings, Ewanrigg's aloe rockeries and Epworth's balancing rocks have been complemented by private game reserves, botanic gardens, the Larvon bird sanctuary and innumerable bream-fishing waters.

Good, inexpensive accommodation is provided in the main recreational areas by the Department of National Parks and Wildlife Management, access to which is usually on tarred roads. A stay of three to five days in and around Harare, *en route* from Beit Bridge to Lake Kariba, or perhaps from Bulawayo's Matobo Hills to the Eastern Highlands, can be thoroughly rewarding.

Ballantyne and Blair Parks
These twin Harare suburban parks, with their miniature lakes, weeping willows and wild duck, are open throughout the year from 10.30 a.m. to 4.30 p.m. (closing at 1 p.m. on Sundays). To reach the parks, take the Borrowdale road, turn first right and drive past the racecourse into Whitwell Road and straight on down Addington Lane (the parks border this road). Children, who should not be allowed to paddle in the water, are entertained by duiker, rabbits, guinea fowl and peacocks while their parents fish for bream. The parks, which are some 10 km from town, are home to spur-winged geese, migratory teal, Egyptian geese and many other waterfowl.

Chinhoyi Caves Recreational Park
A sinkhole (or collapsed limestone cavern) and haunt of spirits or legendary serpent, the Chinhoyi Caves' sleeping pool, 10 km beyond Chinhoyi town on the main road to Kariba, is a fairytale sight whether viewed from ground lev-

Above: The botanical reserve in the Mtoroshanga Pass was created especially for this flame-red species of aloe *(Aloe ortholopha)*, which grows only in the chrome-rich Great Dyke in Zimbabwe. **Left:** The Chinhoyi Caves, once a refuge for warring tribesmen, are now a favourite tourist attraction. The main cave at Chinhoyi penetrates 45 m into the limestone rock, at the base of which is the 'Sleeping Pool'. The pool is 102 m deep, and divers from all over the world have plumbed its crystalline depths. **Right:** The balancing rocks at Epworth, Harare, form a natural sculpture 58 m high.

el 46m above the pool, from the steps of the 'Sloping Passage', or from the 'Dark Cave'.

The Shona know the caves as *Chirorodziva*, or 'pool of the fall'. This refers to the roof of the cave, to the unfortunate victims of Zululand's rampaging Nguni in the 1830s, or perhaps to the murderous habits of the outlaw Nyamakwere, who once made the caves his stronghold. Divers have explored the pool, now stocked with goldfish, to a depth of 102 metres. People lived in or near the labyrinth of caves and tunnels for 1500 years. Chief Chinhoyi used to retreat into them to avoid Ndebele raids 100 years ago. Today the caves' recreational park has suitable camping and caravanning facilities and a small motel.

The caves are open all year, from sunrise to sunset. For further information, write to The National Parks Central Booking Office, P.O. Box 8151, Causeway, Harare, Zimbabwe (telephone Harare 70-6077).

Domboshawa

A huge whale-backed rock which takes some 15 minutes to climb, Domboshawa ('red rock') has caves, San paintings, blasted heath-like trees halfway up, and windy panoramic views of the summit. It is situated 35km north of Harare on the Domboshawa road and 2km from Domboshawa village. It is accessible to visitors 24 hours a day.

Dutchman's Pool and Sable Park

On the one bank of Dutchman's Pool on the Sebakwe River, less than 10km east of Kwekwe in Zimbabwe's Midlands, is Sable Park, a delightful little 350ha reserve stocked with ostrich, zebra and several varieties of buck originally donated by local ranchers. It is open all year from 6a.m. to 6p.m.

There are several hides for bird-watching near the water's edge. Both Dutchman's Pool and the Cactus Poort Dam, 16km south of Kwekwe and 3km from the iron-and-steel town of Redcliff, are favourites with local yachtsmen, and the fishing is good, too. Permits are necessary to enter the park. For further information, write to The Town Clerk, P.O. Box 115, Kwekwe, Zimbabwe (telephone Kwekwe 2301).

Epworth Balancing Rocks

Although rising vegetation now partially obscures them, the Epworth Mission's 40ha of balancing rocks, 13km south of Harare and just off the Widdecombe Road, are still a delightful giant's playground. Piled haphazardly one upon the other like huge kitchen platters, these great granite slabs are the result of millions of years of heat, storms and freezing nights that crumbled the surrounding soil, leaving the boulders stark against the blue sky – an awesome sight and an occasionally frustrating

challenge to the photographer. The site remains open 24 hours a day.

Ewanrigg Botanical Garden

A 283ha garden park of brilliant aloes and prehistoric cycads set in natural woodland 41km north-east of Harare on the Shamva road, and open during daylight hours throughout the year, Ewanrigg is a psychedelic feast of colour, particularly in the springtime from June to August. Farmer Basil Christian named it after his brother Ewan, who was killed in the Second World War ('rigg' is Welsh for ridge), and donated it to the nation in 1950.

It has since been enlarged to include cacti, fuchsia, Barberton daisy and bougainvillea sections, a water garden, a bamboo and palm dell and a filigree network of footpaths through the woods, lawns and rockeries. There are no caravanning facilities, but picnic sites are available for day visitors.

Gweru Antelope Park

Gweru, on the main Bulawayo-Harare road, is the capital of Zimbabwe's midlands. The Antelope Park is 9km from Gweru, along Bristol Road past the heavy industrial sites. The buck include eland, sable, kudu, impala, reedbuck, steenbok and tsessebe, and there are lion, leopard and cheetah enclosures. The bird life is particularly prolific. A tearoom functions at weekends, and braais are allowed. It is open between 10a.m. and 6p.m. daily. There is a caravan park in Gweru. For further information, write to The Manager, Gweru Antelope Park, P.O. Box 1218, Gweru, Zimbabwe (telephone Gweru 31-2512).

Imire Game Park

This park in the Wedza area, 105km east of Harare on tarred road, is owned and run by the Travers family. Previously a tobacco farm and cattle ranch, its two 500ha sections offer exclusive accommodation for eight people in the Sable Lodge. Lion, cheetah and leopard are in enclosures, while elephant, buffalo, wild pig, black rhino, giraffe, zebra and a dozen buck species roam freely. San paintings, Shona ruins, caves, and a crocodile sanctuary are other features of this fascinating park.

Facilities exist for duck-shooting and select hunting, the price of which includes all meals, game vehicle and courier. For further information, write to Imire Game Park, Private Bag 3750, Marondera, Zimbabwe (telephone Wedza 2240).

Iwaba

Situated near the midlands town of Kwekwe on the southern bank of the Munyati River, Iwaba's private 10000ha estate caters for year-round hunting and photographic safaris. There is a wide variety of animals including elephant, cheetah, crocodile, leopard, black and white rhino and 13 species of antelope. Iwaba is also an excellent location for bird-watching, especially during summer. To reach Iwaba, leave Kwekwe on the Harare road and drive for 13km before turning right (at a crossroads) into Shamwari Road. Continue for 36km, turn left at the Iwaba sign and drive a further 10 kilometres. Guests are accommodated in thatched rondavels and prior booking is essential. For further information write to Iwaba Safaris, P.O. Box 5, Kwekwe, Zimbabwe (telephone Kwekwe 24-7723).

Lake McIlwaine Recreational Park

Lake McIlwaine, Harare's premier recreation park and Zimbabwe's fourth largest lake, lies 32km west of the capital, off the main Bulawayo road. The north bank, with access roads 16km and 29km from Harare, is a colourful sprawl of camping and caravan sites, a hotel, tea-gardens and sailing and angling clubs. The south bank road leads to the spillway with a 13km fork to the game park and rest camp. Over half of the 55000ha park is taken up by the 14,5km long Lake McIlwaine, while 1600ha are occupied by the actual game park, which

A spotted bush snake (*Meizodon semiordinatus*). This graceful snake is essentially arboreal but is also at home on the ground. Its colouring provides an effective camouflage but if cornered this non-poisonous snake becomes extremely aggressive.

THE MENACING WIDOW

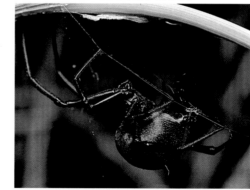

The highly venomous black widow spider (*Latrodectus mactans*).

The black widow or button spider, *Latrodectus mactans*, is one of the world's most feared spiders. Found throughout Southern Africa, this small, velvet-black arachnid has earned an undeserved reputation as a killer — for in reality fewer than five per cent of *treated* cases end in fatalities.

Victims usually suffer severe pain in the legs, arms, abdomen and chest after being bitten. The abdominal muscles tense, and there may be nausea and excessive perspiration. In rare cases, death may occur as a result of respiratory failure; the victims are usually elderly or ill people, or small children.

This spider (there is also a brown widow, which is less poisonous) bears a red stripe or stripes on the upper side of the abdomen, and there are occasionally yellow markings (in mature specimens the markings may shrink to a barely discernible red dot).

The 'hour-glass' marking usually associated with this species is found only in the American form. If molested, the black widow spider may sham death.

offers fully equipped two-bedroom lodges and lakeside chalets (the latter ranging from one to three bedrooms with bed linen but no crockery or cutlery). There are two swimming pools, two tennis courts and a children's playground. The nearest store is 13km distant and petrol 16km. There is good fishing (licences available at the Warden's office) for tigerfish, bream, yellowfish, barbel and Hunyani salmon. Bilharzia and crocodiles discourage swimming. The park is open all year from sunrise to sunset (notify the authorities in case of late arrival). Game-viewing roads with names like Tsessebe Drive and Reedbuck Vlei loop through the wooded parkland. There are zebra, giraffe, wildebeest, kudu, sable, impala, ostrich and white rhino, whose nocturnal habits regularly include a stroll past the chalets to the lakeshore. Near Bushman's Point picnic sites there is a walking area with signposted bush trails. The bird life is prolific. For further information and bookings, write to The National Parks Central Booking Office, P.O. Box 8151, Causeway, Harare, Zimbabwe (telephone Harare 70-6077).

Lake Robertson (Darwendale) Recreational Park

This recreational park, embracing an 81 km² lake, is 85km from Harare (turn off the Bulawayo road at Norton). There are camping and caravan sites available. Near the dam wall there are several boat-launching sites and open-sided rondavels (for picnickers) built picturesquely on the lakeshore in a setting of beautiful rockeries. The lake offers fishing, boating and views of natural woodlands.

Larvon Bird Garden

The Larvon Bird Garden probably provides the most enjoyable of Harare's wildlife day excursions. Harry and Marie Scott opened this

unique 3ha bird sanctuary in 1966. The beautiful dam boasts 46 species of waterfowl, while half of Zimbabwe's indigenous bird species can be seen in the sanctuaries on either side of the neat walkways, lawns and flower gardens, together with a variety of exotic feathered guests from as far afield as Russia and China. There are storks, cuckoos, inland gulls, wattled cranes, pheasants, 75 species of parrot and some 25 species of eagle and hawk, including the African hawk eagle – in all, a colourful collection of some 430 different species.

Harry Scott's family have been bird-keepers for 120 years, and this fact is widely known: at least one injured bird a day is brought to him. His food bill, which includes the cost of breeding such avian delicacies as maggots, mice, rats and fruit flies, comes to the substantial sum of Z$1 800 a month.

The garden is 17km from Harare on the Bulawayo road (follow the signs). There is an immaculate tea-garden, and the park is open from 11a.m. to 5p.m. on weekdays (except Thursday) and 9a.m to 5p.m. on Saturdays, Sundays and public holidays.

Lion Park

The late Ossie Bristow used to walk his 31 lions to their cages at night while holding 'Lazy', a favourite, by the tail. On one memorable occasion he waited patiently while four cubs were born; the mother, her labours over, picked up each cub in turn in her teeth and placed them in his open arms. South African-born Mrs Joyce Bristow has inherited the mantle of pride leader on their 500ha Harare Lion Park, situated in a balancing rock-dominated valley 24km from Harare on the Bulawayo road (turn off at the Lion Park sign).

The leopard, elephant, spotted hyena and caracal and lion of the park have featured in

several South African and American films. Many of the animals were orphans and all the cubs spent their infancy relaxing in comfort in Mrs Bristow's lounge. A tea-room is open at weekends and the park is open every day from 8.30a.m to 5p.m.

Mazowe Dam

The 400ha Mazowe Dam, 40km north-west of Harare on the Concession-Bindura road, irrigates the 21600ha Mazowe citrus estate where the oranges are said to be signed by the sun. The dam is open 24 hours a day, throughout the year. The dam is suited only for picnicking. It is a favourite angling spot, and there is usually a youngster selling worms. The dam is the headquarters of the Hunyani Rowing Club. The road cuts through the Iron Mask range of hills as it approaches the dam wall, where there is a fruit kiosk. As at all Zimbabwe's dams, visitors should take precautions against bilharzia.

National Botanic Garden

Millennia ago when, as the Shona say, the rocks were still soft, half the world formed one large continent called Gondwanaland. Botanist Tom Müller has attempted, in the Indian, Australian and South American sections of Zimbabwe's National Botanic Garden, 4km from Harare's city centre, to bridge the continental drift of 90 million years and show zonal similarities.

Seven thousand plants, divided into ecological zones from savanna woodland to rain forest, from riverine to lowveld, representing 850 indigenous and 350 imported species, grow on either side of the signposted garden trails in the 58 wooded hectares of lawn, lake and koppie. The gates open at dawn and close at sunset. The herbarium, one of the two largest in tropical Africa, houses 250000 pressed plants. To

Far left: A pearl-spotted owl at Larvon. This is the tiniest of the Zimbabwean owls, standing only 13 cm high. **Left:** A cub shelters from the sun in the Lion Park near Harare. **Top:** A panel of San paintings at Bushman Point in the McIlwaine Recreational Park. This site features a unique depiction of a man chopping down a tree. **Above:** A kudu bull tries to hide beneath a thorn bush in this work by John Guille Millais, a British artist and hunter. The illustration is taken from his book *A Breath from the Veld* published in 1895. Millais wrote several other books, including *Wanderings and Memories*, in which he recorded outdoor life south of the Zambezi. **Right:** The National Botanic Gardens near Harare, home of 850 indigenous and 350 exotic plants.

reach the garden, drive along 2nd Street and turn into Downie Avenue about 4 km from the city centre. The garden is straight ahead.

Ngezi Recreational Park

A good gravel road 34 km north of Chivhu will take you a further 56 km to the 6 326 ha Ngezi Recreational Park. A shoreline hideaway with magnificent views, the park's four fully equipped lodges (bedding, crockery, pressure lamps are supplied) must be booked 6 months in advance. Camping and caravan sites, some without ablution blocks, are also available. Fish-ing (licences are obtainable from Ngezi's senior ranger) is excellent in the 573 ha dam which lies in the lee of the Mashava Hills. Game-viewing is limited and best undertaken on foot. The park is open all year, from sunrise to sunset. Reservations are made through The National Parks Central Booking Office, P.O. Box 8151, Causeway, Harare, Zimbabwe (telephone Harare 70-6077).

Sebakwe Recreational Park

Sebakwe's 27 km² recreational park is 54 (mainly tar) kilometres from Kwekwe on the Mvuma road. Year-round coarse fishing in the 1 518 ha dam is this little park's main attraction, although game-viewing on foot, as in its sister park Ngezi, can be rewarding. There is a migratory game population which includes sable, impala and kudu. The cliff scenery is outstanding.

The park is normally open all year round, from sunrise to sunset. The nearest petrol station is at Kwekwe. There are no overnight facilities. For further information, write to The National Parks Central Booking Office, P.O. Box 8151, Causeway, Harare, Zimbabwe (telephone Harare 70-6077).

Eastwards to the frontier highlands

Zimbabwe's eastern highlands form a natural frontier with neighbouring Mozambique. They sweep 300 km from Nyanga in the north, through the Vumba Mountains near the little city of Mutare, to Cashel, to the Chimanimani range, and end south of the Chirinda forest in a tumble of green slopes.

The most striking feature of this, the grandest part of the country's highveld, is probably Mount Nyangani. Standing at its summit, 2592 m above sea level (it is an easy two-hour, three-stage climb), you look back to the lakes and forests, and to range after purple range stretching to the distant horizon. A gentle prospect, but deceptive – turn the other way and you realise you are perched on a great granite shelf. Africa's central plateau has, at your feet, come to an abrupt break in an awe-inspiring avalanche of falling rock and craggy peak.

Bridal Veil Falls

Bridal Veil Falls in California drop 189 m and vaporise. At 50 m, Chimanimani Bridal Veil Falls are nowhere as grand, but the cascades of water gently descending from one level to the next make up in beauty what they lack in size. The falls, 4,5 km from the village, are on a tributary of the Nyahodi River.

The spot is surrounded by spray-fed ferns and shady trees that make it an ideal picnic spot, attracting parties from as far away as Mutare. The twisting skyline section of the main road linking Chimanimani to the mountain village of Chipinge is one of the most beautiful in the highlands. Trek leader Tom Moodie's grave is two minutes down the skyline road and the 'Ponte Italia' bridge, built by Italian prisoners during the Second World War, is farther up the dramatic pass.

Bunga Forest Botanical Reserve

This 1558 ha forest of dense indigenous trees lies on both sides of the Vumba road, 27 km south of Mutare. Its footpaths and dappled, damp foliage are reminiscent of the Knysna forests in the Cape. Visitors are asked not to pick wild flowers or any of the interesting variety of ferns. Blue duiker and bushbuck are resident but rare, and there are bushpig and samango monkeys.

To drive from Mutare (one of the most beautifully situated towns in all of Africa) to the forest is a memorable experience. The road winds up and through the densely wooded, often misty, granite heights of the Vumba Mountains, and the views, down and eastwards over Mozambique, are breathtaking. After 9 km there is a turn-off leading to the 75 km scenic drive through the Burma Valley, taking you past scat-

Above: The long-necked darter, found near rivers and other stretches of water throughout Southern Africa, may often be seen perched on stumps or dead trees. These birds swim with their gracefully-proportioned bodies almost completely submerged. They feed on fish and frogs. **Left:** Bridal Veil Falls, near the town of Chimanimani. **Right:** Autumn colours on the firebush (*Hymenodictyon floribundum*). This thin-barked tree is very susceptible to fire, and is therefore often found growing in cracks, fissures in rock and other spots where fires are unlikely to affect it.

tered coffee, cotton and banana plantations and the Nyachowa Falls.

There are a number of hotels, caravan and camping sites in and around Mutare and the Vumba. For further information, write to The Manicaland Publicity Association, P.O. Box 69, Mutare, Zimbabwe (telephone Mutare 6-4711).

Cecil Kop Nature Reserve

Cecil Kop Mountain overlooks Zimbabwe's eastern gateway city of Mutare. The city is now home to the country's newest game reserve, 1 740 ha of natural mountain grassland, forest, open woodland and vlei, 3,5 km from its centre.

Phase one of the three-stage development – brainchild of the Wildlife Society of Zimbabwe – was the fencing of a 400 ha game-viewing area overlooking a water hole. The game includes elephant, two white rhino donated by the Natal Parks Board, zebra, sable, eland, tsessebe, wildebeest and, on the dam, Egyptian goose, cormorant, grey heron, darter and numerous other species of waterfowl. Visitors see the game from the outside – an elevated area on which there are two thatched viewing platforms, one of which also serves the two-

storey Rupert Fothergill open-air wildlife classroom. Future plans include game-viewing by car through the mountain reserve, a wilderness area for pony and walking trails and the opening of 'Thompson's Vlei', with giraffe, reedbuck, nyala and buffalo.

A tea kiosk operates at weekends. The reserve, which is open daily from 7 a.m. to sunset, is reached by driving north along Main Street and then into Arcadia Road.

THE IMPREGNABLE LAIR OF THE BIRD OF DOOM

To many tribesmen, one of the most feared birds is the odd-looking hamerkop. It is often seen standing in shallow water, deep in concentration as it watches for fish and frogs. The tribesmen say that to disturb it will bring disaster. A displeased hamerkop will cry as it flies over a kraal, supposedly a signal that tragedy will soon strike.

This so-called 'bird of doom' is, however, one of nature's cleverest architects. Its monumen-

tal nest is virtually impregnable and so well disguised that many potential enemies will never realise it is there. Usually sited on a ledge or in a tree, it resembles a heap of haphazard sticks and rubbish. Inside, though, there is a neat dome roof plastered with mud – so strong that it can bear the weight of a person. It has three chambers, one for the parent birds, one for fledgelings and a reception area, reached by a concealed outside entrance.

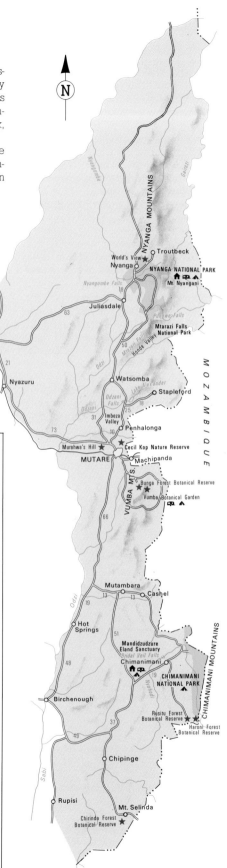

Chimanimani Eland Sanctuary

The 1 800 ha eland reserve is adjacent to the village of Chimanimani. There have always been wild eland in the forests of the area, the species being the only large antelope to adapt to the artificial environment of pine plantations. They ceased their normal migratory habits and learned to feed off the buds and bark of the young pine trees. Much damage was caused, so the buck were captured and placed in the reserve, funds for which were provided by the small Chimanimani community and the Conservation Trust of Zimbabwe.

Eland are Africa's largest antelope, weighing up to 800 kg and standing nearly two metres high. Their meat is comparable to lean beef. The Department of National Parks maintains an experimental herd at Mushandike near Masvingo, as the species has potential for domestication. There are few eland left in the Chimanimani sanctuary, but there are waterbuck and zebra. Two roads lead into the reserve, one twisting up the 1 992 m Pork Pie, or *Nyamzure*, Mountain.

The eland reserve has no facilities. Several interesting drives start from the village of Chimanimani, including the 70 km scenic drive to the farming community of Cashel. It passes the Chimanimani pincer-gap through which the Musapa River flows, and there are some magnificent msasa forests on the way.

Chimanimani National Park

Of all mountains of Zimbabwe, the Chimanimani are probably the loveliest. Raw beauty on a vast scale, they stretch some 48 km to form the southern bastion of the eastern highlands.

The Portuguese were not the first outsiders to make their way through what must have been a daunting barrier. Centuries earlier, Arab traders used the Chimanimani gap, or 'pincers', through the range to reach the interior and Great Zimbabwe. The original name for the Chimanimani may have been 'chimwenjemwenje', after the flashes of sunlight sparkling off their heights.

The eastern highlands, backbone of Zimbabwe, are part of that seemingly endless series of mountains fringing Africa's plateau, a range stretching from the ancient uplands of Ethiopia through to the rugged Drakensberg of Natal. Geologists refer to it as the Frontier System. The Chimanimani section, 2 400 m at its highest, came into being some 1 600 million years ago when the white quartzite massif was forced against the plateau, shattering in folds over its leading edge.

The 171 km² of the Chimanimani National Park is subject to sudden storms and mists that create a startling landscape of scarred and splintered rock, twisted in shape and multi-hued with lichen. But just as suddenly the great

humped range is bathed in sunlight that seeks out the shadowed green folds and glistening wet rock faces.

Ferns and orchids grow in profusion beside the streams. In the foothills and valleys, proteas and wild fig trees abound, mingling in the evergreen forest with cedars and yellowwood, Howman's cliff aloe, wild sweet pea, mountain hibiscus, travellers' joy and the familiar Zimbabwe creeper.

No roads spoil the tranquillity of the Chimanimani. The mountains are haven to bird and wildlife; and of course to the mountaineer, the outward-bound enthusiast and the explorer.

There are mountain lakes, rivers with trout pools and waterfalls, one of the loveliest being near the old Outward Bound School. Another is the 120 m high Martin's Falls on the eastern side. Eland, sable, bushbuck and blue duiker are seen regularly; klipspringer and leopard less often. The bird life includes purple-crested loeries, malachite sunbirds, laughing doves, trumpeter hornbills and francolins.

Zimbabwe's Department of National Parks operates a base camp and information office known locally as 'Dead Cow Camp'. Proceed along the road in front of the Chimanimani Hotel for 14 km, ignoring both the Orange Grove and Tilbury turn-offs, and at the Outward Bound School fork turn right and continue a further 5 km until the camp's entrance is reached.

All visitors must report at the school, or to the Senior Ranger's office in the Eland Sanctuary,

---

NYANGA AT A GLANCE

When to go The park is open to visitors throughout the year (from sunrise to sunset), but Nyanga can be bitterly cold during the short winter months. Summer days can be extremely hot, though the nights are generally cool.

Reservations and information Enquiries and applications for accommodation should be addressed to The National Parks Central Booking Office, P.O. Box 8151, Causeway, Harare, Zimbabwe (telephone Harare 70-6077).

Getting there The park is 275 km of tarred road eastwards from Harare, via Rusape; 99 km north from Mutare.

Accommodation There is one hotel in the park and at least six nearby. A private holiday cottage to rent in Nyanga is a much sought-after prize, and it would be worth your while to locate one. National Parks offer fully equipped and serviced lodges at the Rhodes, Mare and Udu dams. The Udu has an 'orthopaedic' lodge which is designed

to cater for visitors in wheelchairs. Park accommodation should be booked well in advance. There is a caravans-only site at the Mare River, and a camping and caravan site at Nyangombe River on the Nyanga village road, 2 km past the Rhodes Dam turn-off.

Eating and drinking Meals are available at the hotel in the park. Visitors must supply their own food for braais and picnics.

Wildlife Nyanga is essentially a mountain-scenery area. You may, however, see kudu and other, smaller, antelope.

Special attractions Mount Nyangani, on the circular drive, is well worth climbing for the magnificent view from its summit – unless of course the weather is cloudy, in which case it would be unwise to attempt the walk. A visit to Rhodes Museum is also recommended. Scattered throughout the park are the ruins of scores of stone enclosures, popularly believed to have been 'slave pits' (in reality they were probably small cattle pens, built by long-ago Karanga tribesmen). Guided pony trails, lasting one-and-a-half hours, operate twice daily. There is swimming at Nyangombe rock pool.

Fishing The park is very popular among trout fishermen. Trout licences are available from the Udu, Mare and Rhodes offices. These dams are open throughout the year, and rowing boats can be hired. Purdon Dam and Lake Gulliver are open between 1 October and 31 July, while the reserve's 80 km of rivers are accessible to anglers from 1 October to 31 May.

Special precautions There is no bilharzia at Nyanga, but tiny ticks in the park's long grass during winter can be an irritant.

Opposite page: The Vumba Botanical Garden, situated in an extensive woodland reserve, attracts many visitors with its multi-coloured display of flora and its network of footpaths that wind through beautiful countryside. **Above:** The giant kingfisher *(Megaceryle maxima)* is a widely dispersed species which frequents lagoons, rivers, streams and coastal pools. Its long bill aids the kingfisher in holding its slippery prey which is turned head-first before it is swallowed. **Right:** The msasa tree has several practical uses: tannin is extracted from the bark, a substance in the roots is used to alleviate the symptoms of dysentery, and the wood is used as fuel.

Chimanimani. The office is closed from 12.30 p.m. on Saturday to 6 a.m. on Monday. A three-hour walk brings you to a rustic refuge hut overlooking the Bundi River. Camping is allowed in the park.

For further information, you should write to The National Parks Central Booking Office, P.O. Box 8151, Causeway, Harare, Zimbabwe (telephone Harare 70-6077).

Chirinda Forest Botanical Reserve

The Chirinda Forest Botanical Reserve, of 949 ha and with more than 100 tree species, is a good example of primeval subtropical forest and is an entomologists' mecca. The name means 'place of watching' or 'refuge': many years ago, local inhabitants would hide from raiders in the forest and keep a watch from the trees, one of which is the country's tallest – a 1 000-year-old

red mahogany *(Khaya nyasica).* Nearly 16 m in circumference, it stands 58,5 m high, its lofty branches providing a home for at least one pair of trumpeter hornbills.

The forest is 32 tarred kilometres south of Chipinge, Zimbabwe's tea and coffee farming centre, 183 km from Mutare and 230 km from Masvingo. Turn into the forest just before the American Mount Selinda Mission.

It is a whisper-world of ironwoods, parasitic creepers, figs, ferns, butterflies (including lilac beauty), the rare pink or lilac orchid *(Calanthe natalensis),* samango monkeys and the occasional cough of a leopard. Features include the 'Valley of the Giants', a picnic site, and a memorial tablet to the British naturalist Charles Swynnerton, who lived in the forest at the turn of the century and recorded its wonderland of insects, squirrels, birds and butterflies.

Lake Lesapi

Completed in 1972, the dam on the Lesapi River supplies water 200 km downstream to the Middle Sabi irrigation scheme. The 80 ha park surrounding the dam lies just outside the town of Rusape, 'the place of sandy soil', 170 km east of Harare on the Mutare road, the best route to the Nyanga National Park. It has an attractive camping and caravan site situated among koppies and balancing rocks, and the fishing (bass and bream) in the 615 ha dam is excellent. The shoreline has numerous coves, while near the dam wall scenic walks lead to landscaped gardens. There are some magnificent rock paintings which can be seen on Diana's Vow Farm, some 30 km from Rusape off the Nyanga road.

For further information, and to reserve campsites, write to The Department of Water

Resources and Development, P.O. Box 229, Rusape, Zimbabwe (telephone Rusape 28-1515).

La Rochelle

A white Huguenot tower dominates the beautiful La Rochelle gardens, the 14 ha former home of the late Sir Stephen and Lady Courtauld, in the green, wooded Imbeza Valley of Penhalonga, 13 km north-west of Mutare. The landscaped estate is a blaze of formal colours, exotic trees, rare orchids and ornamental shrubs among the waterfalls, fountains and ponds. A furnished two-bed cottage is available on the estate. For further information, write to The Horticulturist, La Rochelle, P.O. Box 38, Penhalonga, Zimbabwe (telephone Penhalonga 250). The gardens are open all year, from 9 a.m to 5 p.m.

Penhalonga was named after one of the several aristocratic adventurers who came to Manicaland in the late 19th century in search of gold. Near Penhalonga is Lake Alexander (Mutare's water supply), the Odzani Falls, Stapleford Forest Reserve and, on a hill summit dividing Zimbabwe and Mozambique, a plaque marking the spot at which Cecil John Rhodes first entered Zimbabwe.

Murahwa's Hill

One of two breaks in the eastern highland range is at Mutare. It was through this gap, up the hot steaming valley, that the Portuguese traders came in search of gold 400 years ago.

Hidden in a bowl of wooded hills, Mutare, 262 km east of Harare, straddles the access route to Beira on the coast. Evelyn Waugh once said of the place: 'There is neither snow nor sea, but there is everything else'. To the right of Christmas Pass, as one descends into the town, is a small nature reserve known as Murahwa's Hill, named after a Nyika sub-chief. It has arguably the greatest diversity of trees of any one spot in Zimbabwe: at least 132 have been identified. It is also an ideal habitat for birds, butterflies and wild orchids. Entrance gates are at Christmas Pass, and down near the showgrounds on Jan Smuts Drive.

Nyanga National Park

'Nyanga is much finer than you described,' Cecil John Rhodes wrote to his agent James McDonald. 'Before it is all gone, quickly buy me up to 100 000 acres.' At his death Rhodes bequeathed this spectacular piece of land to the nation.

Nyanga and the Mtarazi Falls National Park, some 28 900 ha and 2 495 ha respectively, are administered as one unit, a giant 2 000 m-2 300 m-high plateau of downs, heather-scented air, lakes, evergreens, waterfalls and rippling streams on Zimbabwe's eastern border mountains. Much of Zimbabwe's fruit (apples in particular) is grown in the vicinity of the reserve. The air is bracing, and comfortable nights spent in the thatched lodges are tailor-made for roaring log fires.

Well-tended gravel roads link the many mountain view sites with the Mare, Rhodes and Udu dams, which are all well-stocked with rainbow, brown and brook trout.

Just outside the park, 5 km west of the main Nyanga road past Udu Dam, are the attractive Nyangombe Falls. They lie in the Claremont estate (John Moodie, renegade member of the 1892 Gazaland Trek, named his farm Claremont, where his wife Margaret once lived in the Cape). You can climb part of the way down the dramatic falls.

Nyanga's high plateau is the birthplace of many a river. The Pungwe, Odzi and Gairezi start here as gently bubbling streams beneath the marsh grass. And some, such as the

Above: A gorgeous bush shrike (*Telophorus quadricolor*), photographed near Mutare. This beautiful bird builds its nest with twigs, arranging them loosely in the form of a shallow bowl and lodging the structure low down in a bush or tree. Because of its shy, retiring nature the gorgeous bush shrike is rarely seen. The young of this species has a yellow throat and green tail. **Left:** The La Rochelle gardens near Mutare provide visitors with a wealth of flowers, trees and shrubs (both indigenous and exotic). **Right:** *Bauhinia galpinii*. This plant is also commonly known as camelsfoot — a name derived from the belief that its leaves (when laid flat) resemble the footprint of a camel.

Pungwe, Nyangombe and Mtarazi, leap off the plateau in spectacular waterfalls. In the 2 495 ha park, now part of the Nyanga National Park, a narrow track parallels the plateau shoulder to the point where the river cascades in a ribbon of silver 762 m down the cliff face and into the Honde Valley. It is converted into glistening mist and spray *en route*, and moistens a luxuriant rain forest, home of the rare blue duiker, immediately beneath it. A picnic and braai site is situated at the car park 200 m from the final walk to the falls.

Just beyond the Rhodes Hotel, in the Nyanga National Park, a scenic drive through rolling mountain moorland, wattle and pine plantations, past the Pungwe Falls and Honde view sites, leads to the Mtarazi Falls.

The view of the falls from the semi-tropical Honde Valley far below is just as spectacular as the view from the top.

Nyanga: Nyamziwa Falls and Pungwe Falls

What might be the perfect picnic spot can be found on the banks of the little Nyamziwa River in Nyanga, within earshot of the sparkling falls of the same name. Among its attractions are riverside walks and the sweeping vista of distant Mount Nyangani – at 2 593 m, Zimbabwe's highest mountain. It lies 11 km from the Rhodes Dam tourist office, *en route* to the mountain.

The view site overlooking the Pungwe Falls balances on the edge of a precipitous drop, enabling photographers to capture the full, breathtaking beauty of the huge cascade of water winding its way seawards through the jungle-green gorge. A 20 km scenic drive, starting at Rhodes Dam Hotel, leads to the Pungwe. The river rises at the foot of Mount Nyangani in the national park and, joined by the Matenderere and at least two other tributaries, slices through highland for 30 km before plung-

ing 240 m into the 10 km long gorge. After its long, winding journey, the Pungwe River reaches the Indian Ocean near Beira. Two riverside National Parks cottages are sited at the Pungwe Drift near the falls.

Rusitu Forest Botanical Reserve

You need a detailed map and the assistance of the Forestry Commission to reach this 150 ha area of low-altitude dense forest, 50 km due south of Chimanimani on rough gravel roads. There are no facilities at all, but if you are a botanist or collector of butterflies, you will enjoy it. The deadly gaboon adder (*Bitis gabonica*) is found in the Lusitu Valley area. For directions and further information, write to The Forestry Commission, P.O. Box 40, Chimanimani, Zimbabwe (telephone Chimanimani 440).

Vumba Botanical Garden

This 200 ha indigenous woodland reserve, of which 76 ha is a landscaped botanical garden and forest walk, is 32 km from Mutare off the Chimanimani road. Originally this was a small private garden around an ornamental lake. The gardens are at an altitude of 1 524 m and overlook the plains of Mozambique 1 000 m below. Its high annual rainfall of 1 676 mm nourishes lush flora (including tree ferns), while thousands of fuchsias, azaleas, hydrangeas, and annuals of all hues and blossoms have been planted. The garden is open all year, from sunrise to sunset.

Twenty-four kilometres of footpaths wind through the banks of flowers, across small streams and into woodlands. The camping and caravan site is well equipped (including ablution blocks, firewood and swimming pool), and there are some excellent holiday hotels in the Vumba 'mountains of mist'. Leopard Rock, a rambling, Scottish castle-like inn with golf course and tennis court, is 5 km away.

Petrol and stores are available in Mutare. To reserve camping and caravan sites write to The National Parks Central Booking Office, P.O. Box 8151, Causeway, Harare, Zimbabwe (telephone Harare 70-6077).

World's View

Bracken and heather moorland surround the Connemara lakes *en route* to World's View, the northernmost edge of the Nyanga range – a drop of some 1 000 metres. World's View is part of a 92 ha National Trust estate.

The cliff-edge paths offer windswept picnic spots and, of course, spectacular views. Turn left just before the Troutbeck Inn for the 7 km drive to the summit, a road that continues around the three lakes to Eagle's View and down again. The westward slopes of the Nyanga park support msasa trees which turn the mountains red and gold during spring.

The place of the elephant

Defeated by Shaka in 1819, the Zulu-speaking Ndwandwe fled north in the direction of Delagoa Bay under their generals Nxaba, Zwangendaba and Soshangana. Soshangana proved the most militarily efficient, turning on his rival generals and subjugating the Tsonga people of Gazaland, across the Limpopo. Part of the territory he captured is today Zimbabwe's second largest national park, the 4 964 km² Gonarezhou ('Place of the Elephant') National Park, stretching for over 100 km along the country's south-west lowveld boundary with Mozambique.

Masvingo, 286 km from Beit Bridge and close to the ruins of Great Zimbabwe and Lake Kyle, is the centre for this area.

Bangala Recreational Park

The south-east lowveld, nourished by a network of irrigation canals and dams such as Kyle, Bangala and MacDougall, is the granary and sugar storehouse of Zimbabwe. The Mtilikwe River near Great Zimbabwe is dammed by the Kyle and farther south by the Bangala dams to create a still undeveloped 28 km² park where boating and fishing are permitted. From the Es-quilingwe weir on the Mtilikwe, a system of canals carries water 55 km to sugar and fruit estates at Triangle and Hippo Valley. The park is 147 km south of Masvingo (24 km of gravel road). Turn left at Ngundu Halt, which lies 95 km to the south, and proceed for 28 km on the Chiredzi road before turning left again. There are no facilities in the park, which is open 24 hours a day.

Gonarezhou National Park

This park is wild, hot, remote and full of game – particularly elephants, which have become somewhat cantankerous thanks to the activities of hunters and poachers before the area was declared a reserve. Tsetse fly control operations in surrounding areas took a heavy toll of the park's game population, and some 55 000 animals were shot, including 12 000 kudu and 15 000 duiker. But since being declared a park, the area has improved vastly. It became a game reserve in 1968, and a national park seven years later.

Gonarezhou is 40 km wide and forms a natural migratory triangle with the game populations of Kruger National Park in South Africa and the Mozambique game area bordering on Gonarezhou. Eight hundred Kruger Park eland are known to have crossed into the Gonarezhou region, as well as several herds of elephant. There are 6 000 elephant in Gonarezhou, 4 000 buffalo, 160 black rhino, 1 000 nyala (the country's greatest concentration), kudu, lion, leopard, hippo and a host of other animals.

The park is divided into the Chipinda Pools and Mabalauta areas in the north and south respectively. There is no road (within the park) linking them and the vast central section is an untouched wilderness area.

The park is open only in the dry season (1 May to 31 October). If you intend visiting the park it is essential to get prior permission from The National Parks Central Booking Office, P.O. Box 8151, Causeway, Harare, Zimbabwe (telephone Harare 70-6077).

Gonarezhou: Chipinda Pools

In summer it is uncomfortably hot (40°C) and humid at Chipinda, a series of hippo and crocodile pools on the Lundi River and site of the Gonarezhou National Park headquarters. Access is via Chiredzi, 59 km distant on a gravel

Above left: The 19th-century hunter and explorer William Baldwin. He came to Natal in 1851, and made several hunting trips to Zululand before travelling to the Transvaal and farther north. He met David Livingstone at the Victoria Falls in 1860, and claimed to be the second white man to reach the Falls. Baldwin covered vast distances on his trips through Southern Africa.

Above right: The Zimbabwe creeper (*Podranea brycei*) is fairly widely distributed throughout that country, and differs from the South African species (Port St Johns creeper) in that the corollas are slightly compressed at the mouth.
Left: The Sabi River — one of the crucial arteries in Zimbabwe. Animals are drawn by the thousand to its verdant banks.

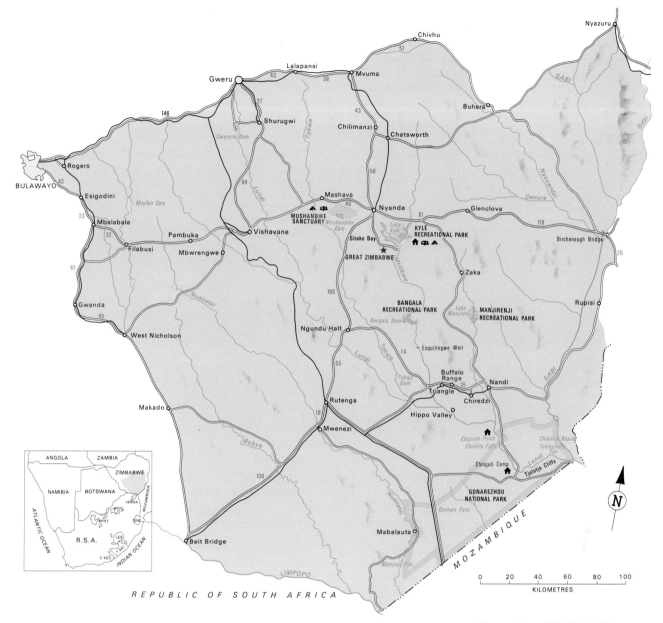

road (the last point for petrol and stores). Chipinda Pools covers about half of the 5000 km² park and is open between 1 May and 31 October, from sunrise to sunset.

There are a number of campsites spread out over 100 km of the Lundi River. Those at Chipinda Pools itself and Chinguli camp have an open-air dining rondavel and ablution facilities, while the others, which are for hire on a weekly basis, are single party (up to 10 persons) bush camps with no facilities other than a primitive lavatory, rubbish pit and braai area. There is a variety of picnic sites suitable for day visitors, the farthest being 30 km distant at Tjolotjo cliffs – which stretch 32 km along the Lundi. A 4-wheel-drive vehicle is recommended on most of the 200 km of game drives and to reach the bush camps. Anti-malaria precautions should be taken. The river is infested with bilharzia.

Chipinda is a good fishing area (tigerfish and black bream). There is plenty of game, however, including lion, giraffe, elephant, buffalo, Lichtenstein's hartebeest and nyala. There is also rich riverine bird life, but bird-spotting is more difficult than at Mabalauta because the bush is thicker.

Gonarezhou is the only Zimbabwe game park situated astride a major river. The Lundi links up with the Sabi River at the border with Mozambique to form the Tamboharta Pan, which stretches the full 8 km between the two rivers in times of flood. On the Sabi are the impressive Chivilila rapids, which can be approached only on foot. Permission is needed to visit the area. For further information, and bookings write to The National Parks Central Booking Office, P.O. Box 8151, Causeway, Harare, Zimbabwe (telephone Harare 70-6077).

Gonarezhou: Chivilila Falls

Two kilometres south of the Chipinda Pools tourist office, the Lundi River has carved a path along a rocky gorge through which the water courses in a series of 10 m drops. This is Chivilila Falls, one of the many attractive Lundi River campsites in the Gonarezhou National Park. Fishing is permitted here (as it is all along the Lundi) although there are strictly enforced rules relating to the number of fish that may be caught or removed from the park. Visits are only permitted with the permission of the Department of National Parks.

Gonarezhou: Gorhwe Pans

This series of at least four pans is situated in the wilderness area some 30 km north of Mabalauta, between the railway line and the Guluene River in the Gonarezhou National

381

Park. They are accessible only by 4-wheel-drive vehicle along an old tsetse 'cut' (with the permission of the Department of National Parks). Elephant and other game are attracted to the pans when they are filled with water.

Gonarezhou: Mabalauta

The Nuanetsi River marks the southern boundary of the 2 000 km² Mabalauta section of the Gonarezhou National Park. Mabalauta is the Shangaan name for the local *Ficus capreifolia* tree, the leaves of which are sufficiently rough to be used by tribesmen as sandpaper for smoothing down the wood of their bows and arrows. This is the land of the big elephants, some with tusks weighing up to 45 kg each.

The park rest camp, Swimuwini 'the place of baobabs', is sited on a cliff overlooking the Nuanetsi River's Buffalo Bend which, in the dry season, is a vast snake-like sweep of yellow sand. The camp's chalets are named in Latin after trees in the area (*Trichilia, Albizia*) and all are sited beneath giant baobabs.

The park's wildlife is very much in evidence: visitors invariably speak of hearing lions roaring near the camp at night. The park's tourist office, to which all visitors must report on arrival, is situated 8 km away. Five camping and caravan sites have been opened along the river, and two light aircraft landing strips serve the area.

A half-hour drive at midday can easily result in close-up sightings of a dozen species of game including nyala, black-backed jackal, waterbuck and elephant, while in the evening lion may be seen stalking the herds of antelope that amble down the many game trails to the water. You can leave your car at any of the four viewpoints overlooking the Nuanetsi. One of these, a thatched shelter perched on a cliff edge, looks right down on the Mwatombo crocodile pools. There are over 180 km of game drives, including Soshangana, named after the old warrior chief, and half a dozen pans – the best of which, Manyanda, features a game-viewing platform. There is also a four-day wilderness trail through the area.

Mabalauta's wild beauty attracts all sorts: the South African singing group 'Four Jacks and a Jill' had a small house nearby, seeing the area's wild beauty as a source of inspiration. It still stands today, empty and a little overgrown, beside the river.

Gonarezhou: Manjinji Pan

Manjinji Pan, on the southern bank of the Nuanetsi River in the Mabalauta area of the Gonarezhou National Park, and some 25 km from the park's office, was once the focal point of a substantial bird community – particularly strong in waterfowl. But it was to some extent artificial: a local resident, an amateur ornithol-ogist, used to pump water into the pan from the Nuanetsi River. Now that he has abandoned the scheme, however, the pan is silting up – and cattle predominate. No access is permitted without the permission of the Department of National Parks.

Great Zimbabwe

The sheer size of Great Zimbabwe is awe-inspiring. These great *dzimba dzemabwe*, or houses of stone, 27 km south-east of Masvingo were built by the Karanga, ancestor's of today's Shona, between the 11th and 15th centuries as the royal capital of a state that dominated the central plateau and gold trade to the coast. Great Zimbabwe itself may have been a city of 30 000 people.

A solid stone conical tower akin to a giant grain bin, symbol of the king's largesse and repository of tribute, forms the centre-piece of a huge elliptical building, a wall and hut complex. The outer wall is 249 m in circumference and in parts over 10 m high and 5 m thick.

Eight kilometres by road from Kyle's lakeshore, Great Zimbabwe is set in a rugged koppie-strewn valley with a site museum and 4 ha of colourful aloe gardens. This national monument is open until 5 p.m. daily. The 43-room Great Zimbabwe hotel is a ten-minute walk from the complex. For further information, write to The Director, National Museums and Monuments, P.O. Box 8540, Causeway, Harare, Zimbabwe (telephone Harare 70-7202).

Gwenoro Dam

The dam is 40 km from Gweru on the Bulawayo road (the turn-off is 6 km south of Gweru). Gwenoro Dam is noted for its bass and bream fishing, and is also popular with yachtsmen – many from the nearby chrome mine, which operates a club on the shore. Caravanning and camping facilities are available among the rolling hills of Ferny Creek, 2,5 km from the town of Shurugwi. Near Gwenoro Dam is the new Amantongokwe Dam, the largest of the area's three dams. Picnicking and fishing are allowed.

Kyle Recreational Park

'A river with crocodiles is ecologically balanced', a display inside the Kyle park's wildlife museum informs visitors. Lake Kyle, Zimbabwe's second largest stretch of water, at the confluence of the Mshagashe and Mtilikwe rivers, certainly has crocodiles. Four confirmed man-eaters, including the infamous 'Cripple Koos', actually live in the park's crocodile pond.

The lake is part of the 169 km² Kyle Recreational Park, 32 km east of Masvingo on the Birchenough Bridge-Mutare road. The park, on the northern shore of the lake, offers white rhi-

---

MABALAUTA AT A GLANCE

When to go The park is open only from 1 May to 31 October, the region's dry months. Visitors should not arrive later than 5 p.m.

Permits Visitors to all areas of Gonarezhou, including Mabalauta, should note that it is essential to check with the booking office before undertaking a visit as restrictions apply and sometimes temporary closures are enforced.

Reservations and information Reservations should be made through The National Parks Central Booking Office, P.O. Box 8151, Causeway, Harare, Zimbabwe (telephone Harare 70-6077).

Getting there Access to Mabalauta is by road from Ngundu Halt (on the Beit Bridge road) to the sugarcane town of Chiredzi, and then along a 160 km gravel road which follows the western edge of the park. There is also an untarred road (116 km) leading from Nuanetsi.

Accommodation There are five chalets at the Swimuwini rest camp, with a total of 21 beds. Each chalet has a refrigerator/deep freeze, cooking utensils and linen, but no crockery or cutlery.

Eating and drinking There are no restaurants, shops or bars at Mabalauta. Visitors in chalets or at the campsites should bring their own supplies.

Getting around All visitors should report on arrival to the tourist office, situated 8 km to the north of the rest camp. Private aircraft charters are available (write to Cane Air, P.O. Box 20, Chiredzi, Zimbabwe or telephone Chiredzi 643). There are many game drives, and there are plans to introduce wilderness trails. There are no petrol pumps, and visitors should make allowance for this when planning their routes.

Special attractions These include a shelter offering a bird's-eye view of the crocodile pool and a game-viewing platform at Manyanda Pan.

Wildlife Visitors may see a wide variety of game, including elephant, lion, black-backed jackal, waterbuck, nyala and several other antelope.

Fishing You may not fish in the Nuanetsi River.

Special precautions Visitors should proceed with caution when encountering elephants – they are unpredictable creatures. You should take a course of anti-malaria tablets before entering the area. These are available from any chemist without prescription. However, because specific precautions may be necessary for certain strains of the disease, intending visitors should seek medical advice. There is bilharzia in the Nuanetsi River. Most family cars could reach Swimuwini without difficulty, but some game drives require a pick-up or 4-wheel-drive vehicle (to traverse the sandy areas). Visitors must make sure they are in camp by sundown.

Above: *Anomatheca grandiflora*, photographed in the Kyle Recreational Park. **Left above:** Lake Kyle (also known as Kyle Dam), the second largest body of water in Zimbabwe, is one of the country's most popular tourist spots. **Left below:** A brown-hooded kingfisher. Unlike some other species of kingfisher in Southern Africa, this bird hunts insects in bush country. **Right:** A female grey duiker. The males of this species are very pugnacious, marking their territory (with the preorbital gland's secretions) on the tips of twigs, and defending it with vigour.

no, reedbuck, tsessebe, giraffe, oribi, nyala and many other species. Visitors may explore the park on foot or on pony trails, and the lake is renowned for its bass fishing.

The hills of Great Zimbabwe can be seen from the 10 fully equipped lodges overlooking the lake. There are two caravan and camp sites (the site on the south bank at Sikato Bay is reached via the Masvingo-Great Zimbabwe road). The park is open throughout the year between 6 a.m. and 6 p.m. There are holiday hotels on the lakeshore offering chalets, lodges and camping. For further information, write to The Publicity Bureau, P.O. Box 340, Masvingo, Zimbabwe (telephone Masvingo 2643). Bookings and enquiries should be addressed to The National Parks Central Booking Office, P.O. Box 8151, Causeway, Harare, Zimbabwe (telephone Harare 70-6077).

Manjirenji Recreational Park.
Boating and fishing are permitted in this scenically attractive and remote 35 km² park, which encompasses Lake MacDougall, a lowveld wheat irrigation dam on the Chiredzi River. Tom MacDougall is a legendary lowveld figure who pioneered sugar farming in the area with the use of irrigation tunnels, one of which, in the Triangle area, burrows 472 m through a granite hill (it is now a national monument). The park is situated 65 km north of Chiredzi on the Zaka-Nyanda road, and is open 24 hours a day, throughout the year.

Mushandike Sanctuary
There are only camping and caravan facilities (with an ablution block) in Mushandike, a 129 km² park surrounding the small (417 ha) mountain-ringed Mushandike Dam, 26 km west

of Masvingo on the Zvishavane-Bulawayo road. The access roads and internal (gravel) roads can be negotiated by all types of vehicles, although the internal routes may be subject to seasonal flooding. Prospective visitors are advised to seek the Warden's advice. The game includes a number of white rhino, leopard, sable, waterbuck, wildebeest, zebra, impala and grysbok. Waterfowl in the dam area includes red-billed teals, Egyptian geese, knobbilled ducks, herons and cormorants. Fishing is permitted in the dam, and anglers may catch black bass, tilapia and barbel. The sanctuary is open all year, from sunrise to sunset. However, the eland research station within the park is closed to the public. Bookings should be addressed to The Warden, Mushandike Sanctuary, Private Bag 9036, Masvingo, Zimbabwe (telephone Masvingo 29-4513).

Brooding home of the oracle

Zimbabwe has some of the oldest rock formations in the world, and some of the most exposed. Especially dramatic are those in the 54 200 ha Matobo National Park, 54 km from the country's second largest city, Bulawayo. Here, horizon follows horizon of granite domes and giant balancing rocks – an immense and brooding place which, it is said, is haunted by the spirits of the ancients, their words of wisdom and warning spoken through the 'Mlimo', oracle of Malindidzimu Mountain.

The Matobos, in fact, are by far Bulawayo's most impressive wilderness attraction, and south-west Zimbabwe's only game park other than the Tuli safari area (reserved for hunting) on the Botswana border.

Bulawayo is served by Air Zimbabwe and South African Airways to and from Johannesburg, Harare and Victoria Falls. There are similar rail links. Express Motorways operate daily coaches to and from Harare and, in association with South African Railways, three services a week to and from Johannesburg.

There is an excellent 322 km tarred road leading to Bulawayo from Beit Bridge, the border post between Zimbabwe and South Africa.

The city has pleasant hotels and motels, and there are some beautifully situated camping and caravan sites in the municipality's Central Park (P.O. Box 2034, Bulawayo, Zimbabwe. Telephone Bulawayo 7-0111).

Centenary and Central Parks

South-east of Bulawayo and within walking distance of the city centre is a green belt through which the small Matsheumhlope River runs. It stretches from the Hillside Dams 6,5 km away, through the Bulawayo Golf Course to the National Library, the municipal caravan park, and eventually the twin Central and Centenary parks, divided east to west by Selborne Avenue, which leads to Johannesburg.

Covering an area of 45 ha, these two parks (three if one includes the tiny Princess Park) – with their superb gardens, fountains, bougainvillaea, lily pond featuring a concrete map of the Cape Peninsula, giant date palms and lush evergreens, are rated among the best city gardens in Zimbabwe (after the National Botanic Garden in Harare).

Centenary Park has an aviary, a miniature railway for children (open weekends) and an open-air amphitheatre in which concerts are held. The Natural Museum of Zimbabwe, which contains exhibits illustrating the history, mineral wealth and wildlife of Zimbabwe, is situated in the park. The displays include the second largest mounted elephant in the world. The 75 000 specimens of mammals and 60 000 specimens of birds make it the largest and most comprehensive collection in the southern hemisphere, and it is a magnet to ornithologists and research scientists the world over.

It is open daily, including Sundays and public holidays (except Christmas Day and Good Friday), from 9 a.m. to 5 p.m. For further information, write to The Director, Bulawayo Publicity Association, P.O. Box 861, Bulawayo, Zimbabwe (telephone Bulawayo 6-0867).

Left: A black eagle (*Aquila verreauxii*) with its month-old chick high up in Zimbabwe's Matobos. These hills accommodate one of the densest eagle populations in the world. **Below:** A blue-eared glossy starling. In Zimbabwe this species breeds from September to January. **Right above:** Spectacular blooms on a broad-leaved erythrina. The bark of this tree is used in tribal medicine: it is burnt, reduced to a powder and used to treat open sores. **Right below:** Veld violets sometimes form a dense mat on the surface of the ground.

If Frederick Courteney Selous were to-day he would be the constant target of attack from wildlife conservationists. Just how many elephants dropped in his sights during his hunting expeditions in Southern Africa is not known for sure, but in the three seasons from 1872-1874 he personally recorded killing 78.

Selous was the legendary figure of Queen Victoria's Empire; a gentleman adventurer who was regarded as the model for the hero of Rider Haggard's King Solomon's Mines, Allan Quatermain.

Selous was born in London in 1851. After completing his schooling in England, Switzerland and Germany, he made his way to Delagoa Bay determined to find adventure, and live the free life of a hunter.

Selous soon earned a reputation in Southern Africa as a deadly shot. At the end of one expedition, between the Zambezi and Gwai rivers in 1873, he and a hunting companion carried off 2 300 kg of ivory.

His exploits with a gun earned Selous both envy and scorn. The explorer Henry Morton Stanley held Selous in the utmost contempt, and labelled him as an unnecessary slayer of lion and various other animals. Selous' defence was that he killed animals in Africa only to support himself while collecting objects of natural history.

But even his critics had to admit that Selous had guts: his coolness in the face of a charging elephant was legendary. This man was later to play an important role in the colonisation of what is today Zimbabwe.

Selous died during Smuts' invasion of German East Africa in 1916-17. He was watching enemy movements through binoculars when a German bullet struck him in the head.

So died the man who has been described as 'the last of the big-game hunters'.

Chipangali Wildlife Orphanage

Chipangali means 'open friendly country' and is named after the Chipangali area of the game-rich Luangwa Valley in Zambia, where Vivian Wilson spent many years. Writer, zoologist, former curator of Bulawayo's National Museum and founder (in 1974) of Chipangali, a genuine African wildlife orphanage, Viv and his artist wife Paddy are true friends of the wild.

They know that many animals orphaned when young or raised as pets, injured on roads, or in game-poacher's traps, can never be returned to the bush. Treated and brought back to health in Chipangali's hospital, they enable the Wilsons to fulfil their five basic aims. These are conservation of wildlife, education of the young, appreciation of the environment, the provision of recreation for city dwellers, and research – for example, into the breeding of endangered species.

Chipangali's 81 ha, on the Johannesburg road 25 km from town and facing the Matobos, are home to 41 species of mammal, in all some 250 animals, including thick-tailed bushbaby, leopard, cheetah, black rhino and black-backed jackal.

There are also seven rare brown hyena, serval, duiker, steenbok, klipspringer, elephant, porcupine and crocodile. The wildlife orphanage also accommodates 70 species of

Above: A rock painting in the Matobos shows a hunting scene. **Left:** The black mamba is regarded as one of Southern Africa's most dangerous snakes. Although its venom is not as potent as that of some cobras, the black mamba has a greater reserve of venom, and is very quick to attack when disturbed. This large snake almost invariably confines itself to a particular locality, where it makes its home in an abandoned termite mound, among rocks or perhaps in an animal hole. **Opposite above:** A zebra in the Matobo National Park.

birds, including the lesser flamingo, bateleur eagle and crested crane. The animals are securely housed in open paddocks or large wire enclosures.

Visitor facilities at the orphanage, which is open daily from 10 a.m. to 4.30 p.m. (closed on Mondays) include a tea garden, a crocodile pool and a bird garden. Feeding time is 3.30 p.m. The food bill is Z$20 000 a year, and to help offset costs, animals can be 'adopted' for a monthly fee ranging from $5 for an egret to $40 for a lion. A plaque carrying your name is placed on your orphan's enclosure.

For further information, write to Chipangali Wildlife Orphanage, P.O. Box 1057, Bulawayo, Zimbabwe (telephone Bulawayo 7-0764).

Hillside Dams

Two small dams in Bulawayo's attractive Hillside suburb, 6,5 km from the town (travel south on Grey Street and follow the signs) form a small nature reserve and bird sanctuary run by the municipality. In Matabeleland, noted for its dry climate, the dams, with their tree-shaded lawns, rockeries, aloe and flower gardens and island-dotted expanses of water, are refreshing spots for walking and picnicking.

Migratory duck and other waterfowl nest in the reeds at the water's edge and fishing (bass, bream, barbel) is permitted in the upper dam. The dams feature an attractive braai area. They are open 24 hours a day.

Matobo National Park

The Matobos, ancient hills of history, are the spiritual home of Mzilikazi's Khumalo warriors, of Cecil John Rhodes and of the San, those dancing hunter-gatherers of the caves. This great boulderland – 43 200 ha of balancing rock overhangs, secret caves and wooded valleys – lies 54 km south of Bulawayo. It has a haunting, ethereal grandeur. High above the castle koppies and wild fig trees soar the black eagles, guardians of ancestral spirits. The Matobo Hills is their last stronghold in Africa.

Geological faults have created the great whale-back domes, or *dwalas*, sometimes with huge boulders isolated on their smooth pates as if ready to be rolled down on invaders. Candelabra euphorbias, golden-flowered umsehla (*Peltophorum africanum*) and *mnondo* trees clothe the feet of all this 'chaotic grandeur', as Rhodes described it.

The park is divided into the Northern, the Bambata, the Togwe, the Maleme and the Central wild region, the Hazelside recreational area (encompassing Matobo Dam) near the entrance, and the 16 500 ha game reserve in the Whovi wild region.

Animals in the game reserve (which opens just before sunrise and closes just after sunset) include white rhino, 200 buffalo, one of the country's biggest leopard populations, giraffe, eland, sable, zebra, impala, steenbok, crocodile, hippo and warthog.

The entrance to the park is 62 km from Bulawayo. There is also plenty of game in the wild areas outside the reserve, and there is a thriving population of highly venomous black mambas throughout.

Caves in or near the park include Nswatugi, its walls adorned by multi-coloured giraffes; Bambata, the first cave in Africa to be excavated; Silozwane, once used by the Ndebele for rainmaking ceremonies; Gulubahwa, with its 4,5 m drawing of a snake carrying people on its back, and Pomongwe Cave and site museum. The park was Cecil Rhodes's gift to the people of Bulawayo – given to enable them to 'enjoy the glory of the Matobos from Saturday to Monday'.

Visitors using the caravan site at Maleme Dam are warned that the approaches are very steep. A tow service is available on request during office hours. Fishermen and boating enthusiasts should note that all waters in the park are infested with bilharzia. The Matobos region is generally very hot in summer and very cold in winter. For further information and enquiries, write to The National Parks Bulawayo Booking Agency, P.O. Box 2283, Bulawayo, Zimbabwe (telephone Bulawayo 6-3646).

Matobo National Park: World's View
Cecil John Rhodes, the diamond magnate, visionary, imperialist, philanthropist, instigator of the Rhodes scholarships at Oxford, Prime

NATURE'S LIVING 'LIGHT BULBS'

The female glow-worm emits a steady light. The firefly is the male winged beetle.

Glow-worms and fireflies, closely related to each other, are misnamed. They are in fact neither worms nor flies, but species of beetles belonging to the family Lampyridae. These remarkable creatures are distinguished by their ability to create light.

The light-producing organ, situated at the lower end of the abdomen, is a highly efficient mechanism that directs the chemical reaction between a substance called luciferin and the enzyme luciferase. The interaction produces rays which are confined to the visible part of the spectrum (that is to say, almost no heat is generated), which is the kind of pure light source that scientific man perfected only after decades of experiment.

The beetles' lights are essential to the courtship and mating process, serving as recognition signals between males and females of the same species. The male firefly's light, stronger than the largely sedentary female's, flashes as he flies about the night. Among glow-worms, however, it is the female that shines the brightest — she emits a steady light (as against the flickering of the male firefly) from her static position on the ground.

Entomologists, curious to find out how an adult male *Luciola* can distinguish a female in the dead of night, have established that the male recognises the flash frequency of his own species. Despite the fact that the interval between each flash may be altered with a change in the air temperature, the males seem to be able to compensate for this phenomenon, as no cross-breeding seems to occur between species.

Minister of the Cape and founder of Rhodesia, wrote in his will: 'I admire the grandeur and loneliness of the Matopos in Rhodesia, and therefore I desire to be buried in the Matopos on the hill 'Malindidzimu' which I used to visit and which I called the 'View of the World', in a square to be cut in the rock on the top of the hill, covered with a brass plate with these words thereon: 'Here lie the remains of Cecil John Rhodes'. On 10 April 1902, to the roar of 'bayete' from thousands of Ndebele warriors, this is what happened.

The turn-off to the huge granite dome of World's View, with its panorama of range after range of hills, lies 44 km from Bulawayo within the Matobo National Park. There is an easy climb to the summit from the car park, where there are braai sites and a pictorial history of Rhodes. The park's ranger salutes as he hands you the visitors' book to sign. Enquiries should be sent to The Warden, Matobo National Park, Private Bag K5142, Bulawayo, Zimbabwe.

Tshabalala Sanctuary
At the 10,5 km peg on the Matobo road (Grey Street extension) is the attractive Tshabalala Game Sanctuary – which you can easily identify by the wrought iron animal silhouette gates. This 1 215 ha sanctuary is for non-dangerous game such as zebra, wildebeest, tsessebe, giraffe, kudu, sable and a variety of smaller mammals.

Tshabalala is run by the Department of National Parks as an interpretative educational sanctuary and as a recreational area for the people of Bulawayo. You can walk, ride, cycle and even drive your motor vehicle in it. It is open from 6 a.m. to 6 p.m.

Umzingwane Recreational Park
This small 12 km² park has no facilities. It is situated 55 km south of Bulawayo and 267 km north of Beit Bridge (near the main highway). Fishing, boating and unspoilt scenery are its attractions. It is open 24 hours a day.

IDENTIFYING THE SPECIES

Southern Africa's huge variety of plant and animal life makes it one of the richest natural treasure-chests in the world. This is the home of the baobab tree, that ancient and corpulent giant of a dozen legends; lair of the magnificent bateleur eagle and hunting-ground of Africa's largest predator — the shaggy-maned, deceptively lazy and immensely powerful lion.

Sweeping expanses of desert and savanna, dense forests, tall mountains and a hundred other habitats accommodate countless living things. Myriad birds of all sizes wheel and dart through our skies while below them, mammals and reptiles by the million play out their roles in the food chain.

At their feet, largely unnoticed, insects crawl and scuttle in blind obedience to instinct evolved over millions of years. Insects are by far the largest group of invertebrates, numbering over 700 000 known species, and a large proportion of these are found in Southern Africa.

The species illustrated on the following pages are necessarily only a representative choice of the plants, mammals, reptiles, amphibians, birds, aquatic creatures, insects and other invertebrates indigenous to the sub-continent. Great care has been taken in reproducing the correct proportions and colouring of the various species and, where possible, an effort has been made to indicate relative size.

The white pelican is found along the entire coast of Southern Africa. Despite its large beak and awkward gait, this bird is an efficient angler.

Identifying FLORA: 1

Southern Africa accommodates a large and fascinating variety of trees, shrubs, succulents, flowers and fungi in environments as diverse as sun-burnt desert, muddy swamp and open plain. Literally thousands of species of flora (there are over 700 tree species in South Africa alone) may be seen in our game parks and nature reserves, ranging from the long-lived and magnificent Outeniqua yellowwood and baobab to the hardy and beautiful protea.

Club Moss
Varing
Lycopodium clavatum

Fern
Varing
Cheilanthes viridis

Fern
Varing
Asplenium aethiopicum

Resurrection Fern
Varing
Ceterach cordatum

Common Tree Fern
Gewone Boomvaring
Cyathea dregei

Eastern Cape Cycad
Oos-Kaapse Broodboom
Encephalartos altensteinii

Outeniqua Yellowwood
Outeniekwageelhout
Podocarpus falcatus

Real Yellowwood
Opregte Geelhout
Podocarpus latifolius

Mountain Cypress/Mountain Cedar
Bergsipres
Widdringtonia cupressoides

Wild Date Palm
Wildedadelboom
Phoenix reclinata

Silver Tree
Silwerboom/Witteboom
Leucadendron argenteum

Porkbush
Spekboom
Portulacaria afra

Red Alder
Rooiels
Cunonia capensis

Camel Thorn
Kameeldoring
Acacia erioloba

Sweet Thorn
Soetdoring
Acacia karroo

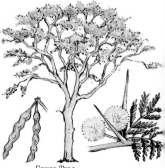

Fever Tree
Koorsboom
Acacia xanthophloea

Sickle Bush/Kalahari Christmas Tree
Sekelbos
Dichrostachys cinerea

Mopane
Mopanie
Colophospermum mopane

Pink Blossom Tree/Virgilia
Pienk Keurboom
Virgilia oroboides

Tree Wistaria/Wild Wistaria
Vanwykshout/Olifantshout
Bolusanthus speciosus

Common Coral Tree/Lucky-bean Tree
Gewone Koraalboom
Erythrina lysistemon

Cape Chestnut/Wild Chestnut
Wildekastaiing/Kaapse Kastaiing
Calodendrum capense

Chinese Lanterns
Klapperbos/Klappiesbrak
Nymania capensis

Marula
Maroela
Sclerocarya birrea caffra

Wild Cotton Tree/Coast Hibiscus
Wildekatoenboom
Hibiscus tiliaceus

Baobab/Cream-of-Tartar Tree
Kremetartboom
Adansonia digitata

Common Wild Pear/Wild Pear
Gewone Drolpeer
Dombeya rotundifolia

River Bushwillow/River Combretum
Riviervaderlandswilg
Combretum erythrophyllum

Water Berry/Umdoni
Waterbessie/Waterhout
Syzygium cordatum

Mountain Cabbage Tree/Cabbage Tree
Bergkiepersol
Cussonia paniculata

White Milkwood
Witmelkhout/Melkhout
Sideroxylon inerme

Common Poison-bush/Bushman's Poison-bush
Gewone Gifboom/Boesmansgifboom
Acokanthera oppositifolia

391

Identifying FLORA: 2

Large Num-num/Natal Plum
Grootnoemnoem
Carissa macrocarpa

Sausage Tree/Cucumber Tree
Worsboom
Kigelia africana

Wild Pomegranate
Wildegranaat
Burchellia bubalina

Camphor Bush/Wild Camphor Bush
Kanferbos/Vaalbos
Tarchonanthus camphoratus

Quiver Tree
Kokerboom
Aloe dichotoma

Bitter Aloe/Cape Aloe
Bitteraalwyn/Tapaalwyn/Goreebusch
Aloe ferox

Variegated Aloe
Kanniedood/Bontaalwyn
Aloe variegata

Blushing Bride/Pride of Franschhoek
Skaamblom/Trots van Franschhoek
Serruria florida

Giant Protea/King Protea
Bergroos/Koning Protea
Protea cynaroides

Pincushion
Speldekussing/Luisiesboom/Bobbejaanklou
Leucospermum cordifolium

Gold Tips
Duineknoppies/Geelknoppies
Leucadendron salignum

Sour Fig/Wild Fig
Gaukum/Suurvy
Carpobrotus deliciosus

Buckbay-vygie/Ice Plant
Bokbaaivygie/Ysplant
Dorotheanthus bellidiformis

Orange Vygie
Oranjevygie
Lampranthus aureus

Stone Plant
Beesklou
Lithops aucampiae

Pig's Ear
Varkoor/Kooltrie
Cotyledon orbiculata

Red Crassula
Klipblom
Crassula coccinea

Brunia
Fonteinbossie/Stompie/Volstruisies
Brunia nodiflora

Berzelia
Kolkol/Vleiknopbos
Berzelia lanuginosa

Pride-of-De-Kaap/Red Bauhinia
Vlam-van-die-vlakte
Bauhinia galpinii

Cancer Bush/Turkey Flower
Kankerbos/Gansieskeur
Sutherlandia frutescens

Bacon Bush
Spekbos/Teebos
Zygophyllum gilfillani

Yellow Milk-bush/Jackal's Food
Beesmelkbos/Geelmelkbos
Euphorbia mauritanica

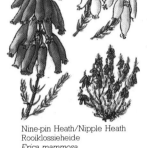  

Red Hairy Heath
Rooihaartjie/Rooiheide
Erica cerinthoides

Nine-pin Heath/Nipple Heath
Rooiklossieheide
Erica mammosa

Plumbago
Syselbos
Plumbago auriculata

Impala Lily/Sabi Star/Fish Poison
Impala-lelie
Adenium obesum

Aruna
Aroena
Caralluma armata

Bobbejaankambroo/Slangghaap
Stapelia flavirostris

Wild Dagga/Cape Hemp
Duiwelstabak/Koppiesdagga
Leonotis leonurus

Cape Honeysuckle
Kaapse Kanferfoelie/Trompetters
Tecomaria capensis

Zimbabwe Creeper
Zimbabwese Slingerplant
Podranea brycei

Yellow Pomegranate/Karoo Rhigozum
Geelberggranaat/Wildegranaat
Rhigozum obovatum

Barleria
Barleria obtusa

Wild Verbena/Fire Plant
Wilde Verbena/Wilde Ysterkruid
Pentanisia prunelloides

Resin Bush
Harpuisbos
Euryops speciosissimus

Suurberg Cushion Bush
Suurbergse Kussingbos
Oldenburgia arbuscula

Cape Pondweed
Waterblommetjie/Vleikos
Aponogeton distachyos

Identifying FLORA: 3

Arum Lily/Lily-of-the-Nile
Varkblom/Aronskelk
Zantedeschia aethiopica

Golden Arum/Mapoch Lily
Aronskelk
Zantedeschia pentlandii

Flame Lily/Climbing Lily
Vuurlelie/Geelboslelie
Gloriosa superba

Bulbinella
Seeroogkatstert/Swartturk
Bulbinella floribunda

Red-hot Poker/Torch Lily
Vuurpyl
Kniphofia praecox

Agapanthus
Bloulelie/Kleinbloulelie
Agapanthus africanus

Cape Hyacinth/Berg Lily
Berglelie
Galtonia candicans

Pineapple Lily
Wildepynappel
Eucomis pallidiflora

Chincherinchee/Snake Flower
Geeltjienkerintjee/Slangblom
Ornithogalum dubium

Forest Lily
Sandui/Sandlelie
Veltheimia bracteata

Lachenalia
Geelklipkalossie/Geelviooltjie
Lachenalia aloides

Blood Root
Rooiknol/Spinnekopblom
Wachendorfia paniculata

Paintbrush/King-of-Candia
Rooikwas/Poeierkwas
Scadoxus puniceus

Poison Bulb/Century Plant
Seeroogbol/Gifbol
Boophone disticha

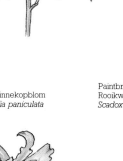

Benediction Lily/Bush Lily
Boslelie
Clivia miniata

Guernsey Lily/Jersey Lily
Berglelie
Nerine sarniensis

Belladonna Lily/March Lily
Belladonnalelie/Maartblom
Amaryllis belladonna

Candelabra Flower/Chandelier Lily
Konings-kandelaarblom
Brunsvigia orientalis

Orange River Lily/Vaal River Lily
Rivierlelie/Vaalrivierlelie
Crinum bulbispermum

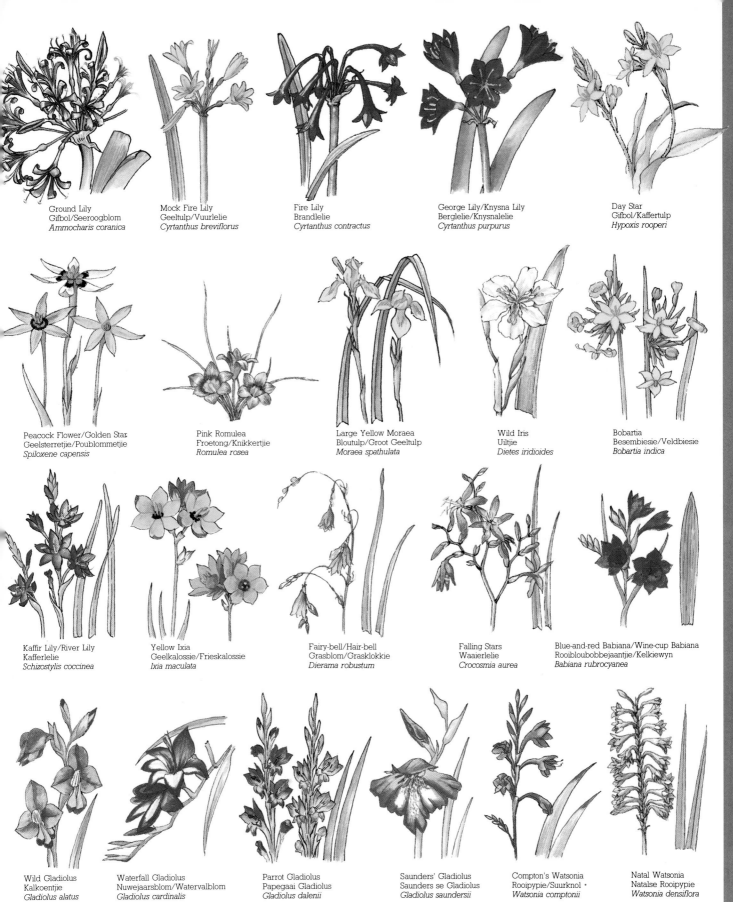

Ground Lily
Gifbol/Seeroogblom
Ammocharis coranica

Mock Fire Lily
Geeltulp/Vuurlelie
Cyrtanthus breviflorus

Fire Lily
Brandlelie
Cyrtanthus contractus

George Lily/Knysna Lily
Berglelie/Knysnalelie
Cyrtanthus purpurus

Day Star
Gifbol/Kaffertulp
Hypoxis rooperi

Peacock Flower/Golden Star
Geelsterretjie/Poublommetjie
Spiloxene capensis

Pink Romulea
Froetong/Knikkertjie
Romulea rosea

Large Yellow Moraea
Bloutulp/Groot Geeltulp
Moraea spathulata

Wild Iris
Uiltjie
Dietes iridioides

Bobartia
Besembiesie/Veldbiesie
Bobartia indica

Kaffir Lily/River Lily
Kafferlelie
Schizostylis coccinea

Yellow Ixia
Geelkalossie/Frieskalossie
Ixia maculata

Fairy-bell/Hair-bell
Grasblom/Grasklokkie
Dierama robustum

Falling Stars
Waaierlelie
Crocosmia aurea

Blue-and-red Babiana/Wine-cup Babiana
Rooibloubobbejaantjie/Kelkiewyn
Babiana rubrocyanea

Wild Gladiolus
Kalkoentjie
Gladiolus alatus

Waterfall Gladiolus
Nuwejaarsblom/Watervalblom
Gladiolus cardinalis

Parrot Gladiolus
Papegaai Gladiolus
Gladiolus dalenii

Saunders' Gladiolus
Saunders se Gladiolus
Gladiolus saundersii

Compton's Watsonia
Rooipypie/Suurknol ·
Watsonia comptonii

Natal Watsonia
Natalse Rooipypie
Watsonia densiflora

Identifying
FLORA: 4

Evening Flower
Aandblom/Bergaandblommetjie
Freesia andersoniae

Wild Banana/Natal Strelitzia
Witpiesang/Wildepiesang
Strelitzia nicolai

Crane Flower/Bird of Paradise Flower
Wildepiesang/Kraanvoëlblom
Strelitzia reginae

Green Wood-orchid/October Lily
Moederkappie/Oktoberlelie
Bonatea speciosa

Pink Satyrium
Rooikappie/Rooi-trewwa
Satyrium carneum

Orchid
Ewwa-trewwa/Goue-trewwa
Satyrium coriifolium

Red Disa/Flower-of-the-gods
Rooidisa/Bakkiesblom
Disa uniflora

Tiger Orchid/Tree Orchid
Tierorgidee
Ansellia gigantea

Large Yellow Eulophia
Groot Eulophia
Eulophia speciosa

Tree Orchid
Boomorgidee
Cyrtorchis arcuata

Tree Orchid
Boomorgidee
Mystacidium capense

Lotus Lily/Cape Water Lily
Paddapreekstoel/Kaapse Waterlelie
Nymphaea capensis

Traveller's Joy/Bridal Wreath
Klimop/Lemoenbloeisels
Clematis brachiata

Carpet Geranium
Bergtee/Vrouebossie
Geranium incanum

Butterfly Flower
Slangblom
Monsonia speciosa

Bushman's Candle/Candlebush
Boesmanskers/Kersbossie
Sarcocaulon patersonii

Hooded-leaf Pelargonium/Tree Pelargonium
Wildemalva
Pelargonium cucullatum

Scarlet Geranium
Rooimalva/Wildemalva
Pelargonium inquinans

Sorrel
Vingersuring
Oxalis polyphylla

Sorrel
Suring
Oxalis purpurea

396

Long-leaved Buchu
Asynboegoe/Olifantsboegoe
Agathosma crenulata

Karoo Violet/Wild Violet
Brandblare/Seeroogbossie
Aptosimum depressum

Nemesia
Leeubekkie/Rooileeubekkie
Nemesia strumosa

Mushroom Flower/Ink Flower
Inkblom
Cycnium adonense

Shrubby Felicia
Felicia
Felicia amelloides

Kingfisher Daisy
Visvangergousblom
Felicia bergerana

Pink Everlasting/Cape Everlasting
Rooisewejaartjie/Strooiblommetjie
Phaenocoma prolifera

Cape Everlasting/Strawberry Everlasting
Rooisewejaartjie
Helipterum eximium

Cape Everlasting/Felted Everlasting
Sewejaartjie/Strooiblommetjie
Helichrysum vestitum

Senecio
Hongerblom
Senecio arenarius

Molteno Disease Plant
Geelgifbossie
Senecio burchellii

Cape Daisy/Ox-eye Daisy
Bietou/Witbotterblom
Dimorphotheca pluvialis

Namaqualand Daisy
Bietou/Gousblom
Dimorphotheca sinuata

Krebs' Gazania
Oranjegousblom/Botterblom
Gazania

Barberton Daisy/Transvaal Daisy
Barbertonse Madeliefie/Rooigousblom
Gerbera jamesonii

Field Mushroom
Eetbare swam
Agaricus campestris

Fly Agaric/Fly Mushroom
Vlieëswam/Vlieëgif
Amanita muscaria

Panther Agaric
Panter-amaniet
Amanita pantherina

Death Cup/Death Cap
Duiwelsbrood/Doodsbeker
Amanita phalloides

Stone Mushroom
Steenswam
Boletus edulis

Green-lined Parasol/False Green-lined Parasol
Groensambreelswam
Chlorophyllum molibdites

Copper Trumpet
Kopertrompetswam
Clitocybe olearia

Identifying INSECTS AND OTHER INVERTEBRATES: 1

The accompanying illustrations represent only a tiny selection of the huge variety of insects and other invertebrates found in Southern Africa. Because most are small and inconspicuous, the emphasis is on the more visible species, and those most likely to be seen in game parks and nature reserves.

Mimosa Moon Moth/Luna Moth
Afrikaanse Maanmot
Argema mimosae
(much reduced)

Death's Head Moth
Motby/Doodshoofmot
Acherontia atropos
(much reduced)

Large Striped Swordtail
Jagswawelstert
Graphium antheus

Fig Tree Blue
Vyeboombloutjie
Myrina silenus ficedula
(much enlarged)

Yellow-spotted Skipper
Reënboswalsertjie
Metisella metis
(much enlarged)

Sooty Blue
Duwweltjie Bloutjie
Zizeeria knysna
(much enlarged)

Guineafowl Butterfly
Tarentaaltjie
Hamanumida daedulus

Striped Policeman
Witbroekkonstabel
Coeliades forestan
(much enlarged)

Black Pansy/Blue Pansy/Pansy
Blougesiggie
Precis oenone oenone

Common Scarlet
Ralirooivlerkie
Axiocerses bambana
(much enlarged)

Bowker's Hairstreak/Bowker's Tailed Blue
Bowkersestertbloutjie
Iolaus bowkeri
(much enlarged)

African Monarch/Monarch Butterfly/Milkweed Butterfly
Melkbosvlinder
Danaus chrysippus

Christmas Tree Acraea
Kersboomrooitjie
Acraea anemosa

Common Acraea/Garden Acraea
Gewonerooitjie
Acraea horta

African Migrant/African Vagrant
Afrikaanse Swerwer
Catopsilia florella

Veined Orange
Bontarabier
Colotis vesta

Purple Tip
Perspuntjie
Colotis ione ione

Red Tip
Rooipuntjie
Colotis antevippe gavisa

Mocker Swallowtail
Na-aperswawelstert
Papilio dardanus cenea

Citrus Swallowtail/Christmas Butterfly
Lemoen-vlinder
Papilio demodocus

Painted Lady Butterfly
Geskildede Dame
Vanessa cardui
(enlarged)

Foxy Charaxes
Koppiedubbelstert
Charaxes jasius saturnus

Forest King Charaxes
Bloudubbelstert
Charaxes xiphares

Green-veined Charaxes
Skelmdubbelstert
Charaxes candiope

Identifying
INSECTS AND
OTHER
INVERTEBRATES: 2

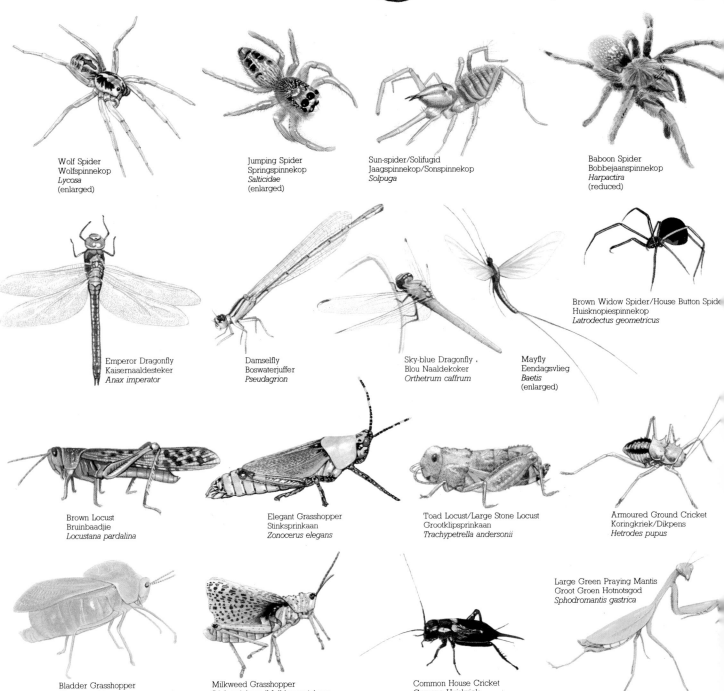

Scorpion
Skerpioen
Opisthophthalmus
(much reduced)

Scorpion
Skerpioen
Parabuthus villosus

Wolf Spider
Wolfspinnekop
Lycosa
(enlarged)

Jumping Spider
Springspinnekop
Salticidae
(enlarged)

Sun-spider/Solifugid
Jaagspinnekop/Sonspinnekop
Solpuga

Baboon Spider
Bobbejaanspinnekop
Harpactira
(reduced)

Emperor Dragonfly
Kaisernaaldesteker
Anax imperator

Damselfly
Boswaterjuffer
Pseudagrion

Sky-blue Dragonfly
Blou Naaldekoker
Orthetrum caffrum

Mayfly
Eendagsvlieg
Baetis
(enlarged)

Brown Widow Spider/House Button Spider
Huisknopiespinnekop
Latrodectus geometricus

Brown Locust
Bruinbaadjie
Locustana pardalina

Elegant Grasshopper
Stinksprinkaan
Zonocerus elegans

Toad Locust/Large Stone Locust
Grootklipsprinkaan
Trachypetrella andersonii

Armoured Ground Cricket
Koringkriek/Dikpens
Hetrodes pupus

Large Green Praying Mantis
Groot Groen Hotnotsgod
Sphodromantis gastrica

Bladder Grasshopper
Blaasopsprinkaan
Physophorina

Milkweed Grasshopper
Stinksprinkaan/Melkbossprinkaan
Phymateus morbillosus

Common House Cricket
Gewone Huiskriek
Gryllus bimaculatus

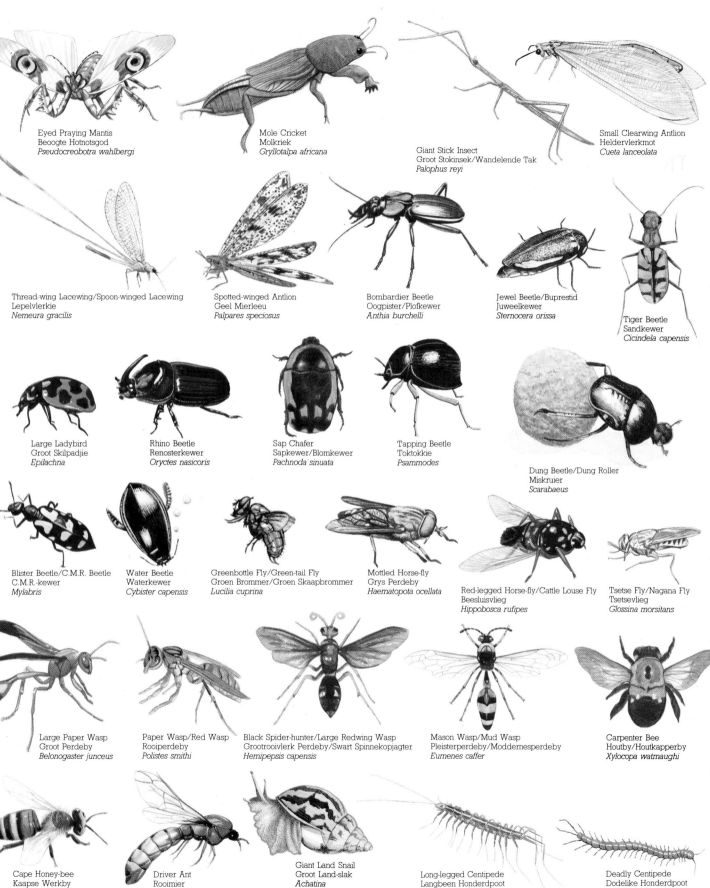

Eyed Praying Mantis
Beoogte Hotnotsgod
Pseudocreobotra wahlbergi

Mole Cricket
Molkriek
Gryllotalpa africana

Giant Stick Insect
Groot Stokinsek/Wandelende Tak
Palophus reyi

Small Clearwing Antlion
Heldervlerkmot
Cueta lanceolata

Thread-wing Lacewing/Spoon-winged Lacewing
Lepelvlerkie
Nemeura gracilis

Spotted-winged Antlion
Geel Mierleeu
Palpares speciosus

Bombardier Beetle
Oogpister/Plofkewer
Anthia burchelli

Jewel Beetle/Buprestid
Juweelkewer
Sternocera orissa

Tiger Beetle
Sandkewer
Cicindela capensis

Large Ladybird
Groot Skilpadjie
Epilachna

Rhino Beetle
Renosterkewer
Oryctes nasicoris

Sap Chafer
Sapkewer/Blomkewer
Pachnoda sinuata

Tapping Beetle
Toktokkie
Psammodes

Dung Beetle/Dung Roller
Miskruier
Scarabaeus

Blister Beetle/C.M.R. Beetle
C.M.R.-kewer
Mylabris

Water Beetle
Waterkewer
Cybister capensis

Greenbottle Fly/Green-tail Fly
Groen Brommer/Groen Skaapbrommer
Lucilia cuprina

Mottled Horse-fly
Grys Perdeby
Haematopota ocellata

Red-legged Horse-fly/Cattle Louse Fly
Beesluisvlieg
Hippobosca rufipes

Tsetse Fly/Nagana Fly
Tsetsevlieg
Glossina morsitans

Large Paper Wasp
Groot Perdeby
Belonogaster junceus

Paper Wasp/Red Wasp
Rooiperdeby
Polistes smithi

Black Spider-hunter/Large Redwing Wasp
Grootrooivlerk Perdeby/Swart Spinnekopjagter
Hemipepsis capensis

Mason Wasp/Mud Wasp
Pleisterperdeby/Moddernesperdeby
Eumenes caffer

Carpenter Bee
Houtby/Houtkapperby
Xylocopa watmaughi

Cape Honey-bee
Kaapse Werkby
Apis mellifera capensis

Driver Ant
Rooimier
Dorylus helvolus

Giant Land Snail
Groot Land-slak
Achatina
(much reduced)

Long-legged Centipede
Langbeen Honderdpoot
Scutigera

Deadly Centipede
Dodelike Honderdpoot
Scolopendra morsitans

401

Identifying AQUATIC LIFE: 1

Because Southern Africa's seas and rivers maintain a huge variety of creatures and plants, the selection of species for this section has of necessity been determined by factors such as limited space, distribution and relative interest value: hence the inclusion of such diverse aquatic life forms as eel, sea horse, jellyfish, sea cucumber, black mussel, sperm whale and rainbow trout — an exotic freshwater fish.

The east coast's warm Moçambique current (later becoming the Agulhas) and the west coast's cold Benguela current provide widely-varying habitats in the two great oceans — the Indian and Atlantic.

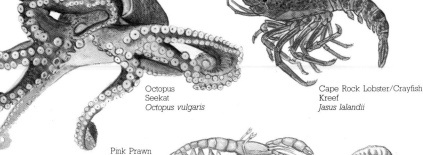

Octopus
Seekat
Octopus vulgaris

Cape Rock Lobster/Crayfish
Kreef
Jasus lalandii

Pink Prawn
Pienkgarnaal
Callianassa kraussi

Jellyfish
Seekwal
Aurelia aurita

Knysna Crab
Knysnakrap
Scylla serrata

Blue-bottle/Portuguese Man O'War
Bloublasie
Physalia physalia

Sargassum
Sargassum heterophyllum

Kelp
Ecklonia maxima

Sea Lettuce
Seeslaai
Ulva rigida

Caulerpa
Caulerpa filiformis

Laver
Waskom/Ereprys
Porphyra capensis

Gelidium
Gelidium pristoides

Lithothamnion
Lithothamnion

Large Starfish
Grootseester
Marthasterias glacialis

Dorid/Nudibranch
Seeslak
Hypselodoris capensis

Knysna Sea-horse
Knysnaseeperdjie
Hippocampus capensis

Sea Cucumber
Seekomkommer
Cucumaria sykion

Anemone
Anemoon
Pseudactinia flagellifera

Sea Urchin
Seekastaing
Parechinus angu

Perlemoen/Abalone
Perlemoen
Haliotis midae

Cape Oyster
Eetbare Oester
Crassostrea margaritacea

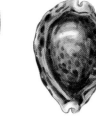

Black Mussel
Swart Mossel
Choromytilus meridionalis

Tiger Cowrie
Tiermuntskulp
Cypraea tigris

Cone Shell
Horingskulp
Conus tinianus

Winkle/Top Shell
Tolskulp
Oxystele tigrina

Beaded Limpet
Bekraaldeklipmossel
Patella granularis

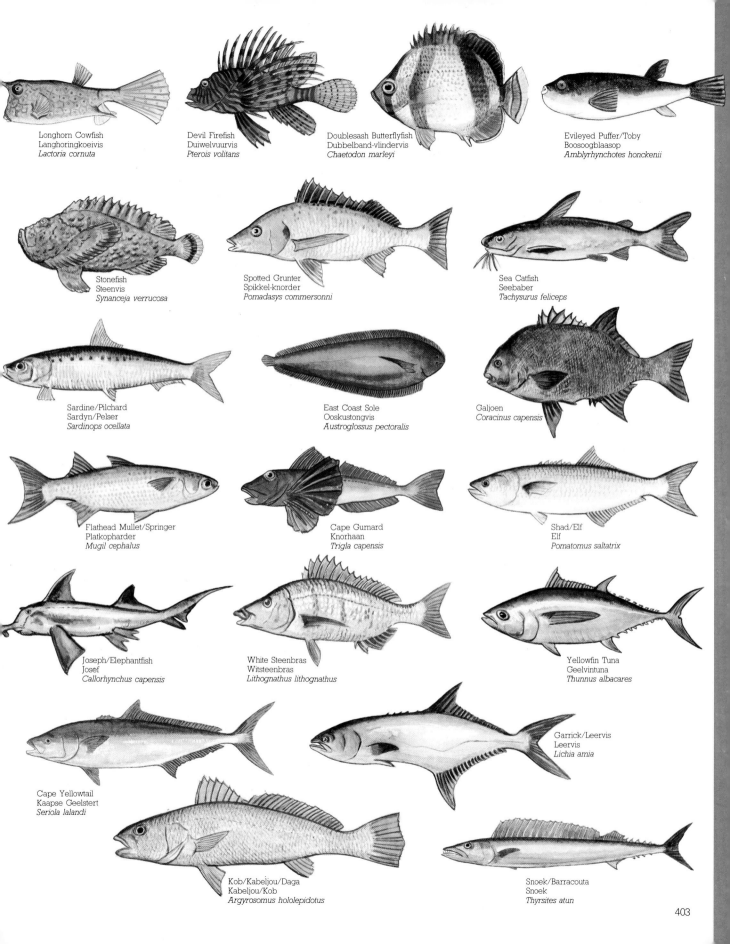

Longhorn Cowfish
Langhoringkoeivis
Lactoria cornuta

Devil Firefish
Duiwelvuurvis
Pterois volitans

Doublesash Butterflyfish
Dubbelband-vlindervis
Chaetodon marleyi

Evileyed Puffer/Toby
Boosoogblaasop
Amblyrhynchotes honckenii

Stonefish
Steenvis
Synanceja verrucosa

Spotted Grunter
Spikkel-knorder
Pomadasys commersonni

Sea Catfish
Seebaber
Tachysurus feliceps

Sardine/Pilchard
Sardyn/Pelser
Sardinops ocellata

East Coast Sole
Ooskustongvis
Austroglossus pectoralis

Galjoen
Coracinus capensis

Flathead Mullet/Springer
Platkopharder
Mugil cephalus

Cape Gurnard
Knorhaan
Trigla capensis

Shad/Elf
Elf
Pomatomus saltatrix

Joseph/Elephantfish
Josef
Callorhynchus capensis

White Steenbras
Witsteenbras
Lithognathus lithognathus

Yellowfin Tuna
Geelvintuna
Thunnus albacares

Cape Yellowtail
Kaapse Geelstert
Seriola lalandi

Garrick/Leervis
Leervis
Lichia amia

Kob/Kabeljou/Daga
Kabeljou/Kob
Argyrosomus hololepidotus

Snoek/Barracouta
Snoek
Thyrsites atun

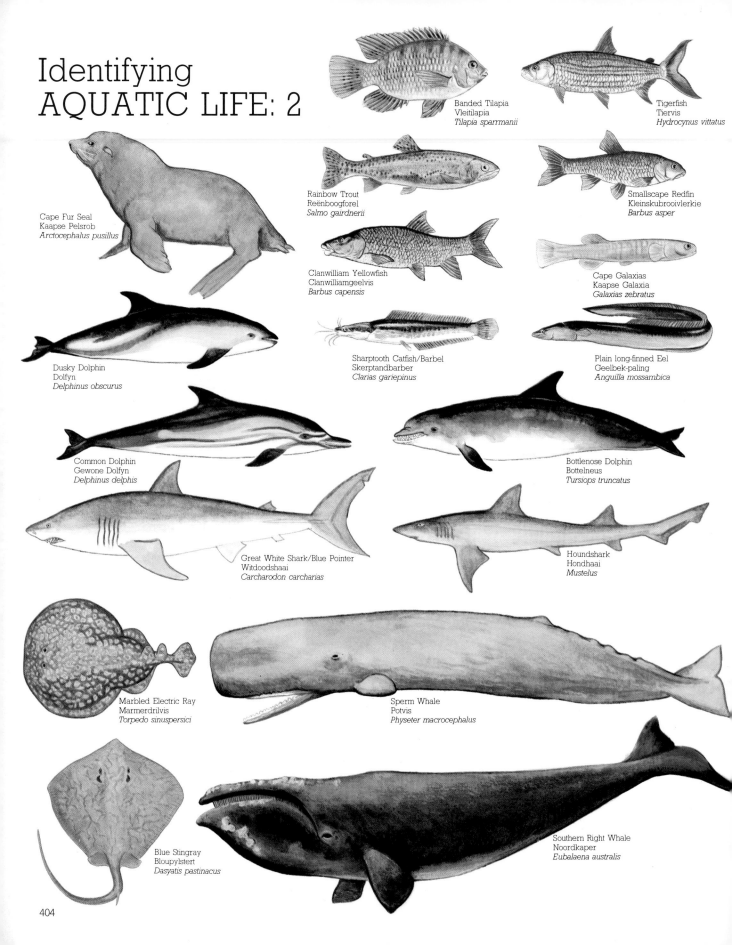

Identifying
AQUATIC LIFE: 2

Banded Tilapia
Vleitilapia
Tilapia sparrmanii

Tigerfish
Tiervis
Hydrocynus vittatus

Cape Fur Seal
Kaapse Pelsrob
Arctocephalus pusillus

Rainbow Trout
Reënboogforel
Salmo gairdnerii

Smallscape Redfin
Kleinskubrooivlerkie
Barbus asper

Clanwilliam Yellowfish
Clanwilliamgeelvis
Barbus capensis

Cape Galaxias
Kaapse Galaxia
Galaxias zebratus

Dusky Dolphin
Dolfyn
Delphinus obscurus

Sharptooth Catfish/Barbel
Skerptandbarber
Clarias gariepinus

Plain long-finned Eel
Geelbek-paling
Anguilla mossambica

Common Dolphin
Gewone Dolfyn
Delphinus delphis

Bottlenose Dolphin
Bottelneus
Tursiops truncatus

Great White Shark/Blue Pointer
Witdoodshaai
Carcharodon carcharias

Houndshark
Hondhaai
Mustelus

Marbled Electric Ray
Marmerdrilvis
Torpedo sinuspersici

Sperm Whale
Potvis
Physeter macrocephalus

Blue Stingray
Bloupylstert
Dasyatis pastinacus

Southern Right Whale
Noordkaper
Eubalaena australis

Identifying AMPHIBIANS

Southern Africa's varied and beautiful amphibians, although more often heard than seen, are a rich source of pleasure to anyone who is prepared to learn about them. It is not widely known that frogs and toads (there are no salamanders or caecilians in this part of the world) are the most numerous of all land vertebrates. They are found everywhere, from mountain tops to deserts.

The accompanying selection of illustrations represent the species most likely to be seen in our game parks and nature reserves.

Cape Platanna
Kaapse Platanna
Xenopus gilli

Common Platanna
Gewone Platanna
Xenopus laevis

Guttural Toad/Common Toad
Gewone Skurwepadda
Bufo gutteralis

Leopard Toad
Luiperd Skurwepadda
Bufo pardalis

Bullfrog
Brulpadda
Pyxicephalus adspersus

Tremolo Sand Frog
Gestreepte Grawende Sandpadda
Tomopterna cryptotis

Common River Frog
Gewone Rivierpadda
Rana angolensis

Striped Stream Frog/Striped Rana
Gestreepte Waterpadda/Langtoon Waterpadda
Rana fasciata

Sharp-nosed Grass Frog
Gevlekte Graspadda
Ptychadena oxyrhynchus

Banded Rubber Frog
Rooi-gestreepte Padda
Phrynomerus bifasciatus

Dwarf Puddle Frog
Dwerg-modderpaddatjie
Phrynobatrachus mababiensis

Common Caco/Common Dainty Frog
Gewone Caco/Blikslanertjie
Cacosternum boettgeri

Cricket Frog/Cape Chirping Frog
Kaapse Kriekpadda
Arthroleptella lightfooti

Foam Nest Frog/Grey Tree Frog
Vaal Boompadda/Groot Grys Boompadda
Chiromantis xerampelina

Shovel-footed Squeaker
Gewone Pieper
Arthroleptis stenodactylus

Red-legged Kassina
Rooibeen Kassina
Kassina maculata

Forest Tree Frog/Raucous Tree Frog
Boompadda
Leptopelis natalensis

Spotted Shovel-nosed Frog
Gevlekte Sandkruiper
Hemisus guttatum

Greater Leaf-folding Frog
Grootkatoogpadda
Afrixalus fornasinii

Bubbling Kassina
Silwerbruinvleipadda
Kassina senegalensis

Arum Lily Frog
Varkblompadda
Hyperolius horstockii

Waterlily Frog
Waterlelie Padda
Hyperolius pusillus

Painted Reed Frog
Gestreepte Rietpaddatjie
Hyperolius marmoratus

Plain Rain Frog
Jan Blom/Blaasop
Breviceps fuscus

Bushveld Rain Frog
Jan Blom/Blaasop
Breviceps adspersus

405

Identifying REPTILES

These cold-blooded creatures (their body temperature varies according to external conditions) are well represented in Southern Africa, surviving and thriving in some unlikely habitats. The species on these pages are the lizards, snakes and tortoises most likely to be found in game parks and nature reserves. There is also a crocodile — a living reminder of the Age of Dinosaurs.

Among the reptiles illustrated are the geometric tortoise, a threatened species, and a number of venomous snakes such as black mamba, Cape cobra, boomslang and puff-adder. When attempting to distinguish between reptiles with a superficial resemblance, observers should consider such features as natural 'armour' (tortoise, crocodile), splayed finger-tips (geckos), body shape and colouring.

Namaqua Chameleon
Namakwa verkleurmannetjie
Chamaeleo namaquensis

Flap-necked Chameleon/Common Chameleon
Gewone Croot Verkleurmannetjie
Chamaeleo dilepis

Puff-adder/Common Puff-adder
Gewone Pofadder
Bitis arietans

Common Night Adder
Gewone Nagadder
Causus rhombeatus

Common African Python
Gewone Luislang
Python sebae

Common African Tree Snake
Boomslang
Dispholidus typus

Common Egg-eater/African Egg-eater
Gewone Eiervreter
Dasypeltis scabra

Herald Snake/Red-lipped Snake
Rooilipslang
Crotaphopeltis hotamboeia

Common Mole Snake
Gewone Molslang
Pseudaspis cana

Cape Cobra/Yellow Cobra
Kaapse Kobra/Geelslang
Naja nivea

Green Mamba
Groen Mamba
Dendroaspis angusticeps

Black Mamba
Swart Mamba
Dendroaspis polylepis

Spitting Cobra
Rinkhals
Hemachatus haemachatus

Crocodile
Krokodil
Crocodylus niloticus

Rock Agama
Klipkoggelmander
Agama atra

Rock Leguaan
Veldlikkewaan
Varanus exanthematicus

Water Leguaan/Nile Monitor
Waterlikkewaan
Varanus niloticus

Bibron's Gecko/Giant Gecko
Bibron se Diktoongeitjie/Blinkogie
Pachydactylus bibronii

Web-footed Gecko
Woestyn Geitjie
Palmatogecko rangei

Barking Gecko
Grond Geitjie
Ptenopus garrulus

Namaqua Plated Lizard
Namakwalandse Pantserakkedis
Gerrhosaurus typicus

Blue-tailed Kopje-skink
Bloustertkoppieskink
Mabuya quinquetaeniata margaritifer

Giant Zonure
Sonkyker/Ouvolk
Cordylus giganteus

Cape Red-tailed Rock Lizard
Kaapse Rooistertrotsakkedis
Platysaurus capensis

Hinged Water Tortoise/Hinged Terrapin
Skarnierdopwaterskilpad
Pelusios sinuatus

Common African Water Tortoise/Cape Terrapin
Gewone Waterskilpad
Pelomedusa subrufa

Padloper
Homopus areolatus

Geometric Tortoise
Suurpootjie
Psammobates geometricus

Angulate Tortoise/Bowsprit Tortoise
Ploegskaarskilpad
Chersina angulata

Identifying BIRDS: 1

These illustrations are intended as an accurate visual guide for bird-watchers throughout Southern Africa's hundreds of game parks and nature reserves. On the whole, the selection is based on common birds and the most strikingly coloured species.

Among the smaller birds, the choice has rested on those that are likely to be seen close to or within rest camps. In instances where two species have similar characteristics, both are illustrated to facilitate comparison and avoid incorrect identification. Differences in size and plumage between males, females and immature birds of the same species are identified by the letters M, F and I.

Hamerkop
Scopus umbretta

Ostrich
Volstruis
Struthio camelus

Hadeda
Bostrychia hagedash

Greater Flamingo
Groot Flamink
Phoenicopterus ruber

Marabou
Maraboe
Leptoptilos crumeniferus

Goliath Heron
Reuse Reier
Ardea goliath

Lesser Flamingo
Klein Flamink
Phoenicopterus minor

White Pelican
Witpelikaan
Pelecanus onocrotalus

Egyptian Goose
Kolgans
Alopochen aegyptiacus

South African Shelduck
Bergeend
Tadorna cana

Knob-billed Duck
Knobbel-eend
Sarkidiornis melanotos

African Spoonbill
Lepelaar
Platalea alba

Secretary Bird
Sekretarisvoël
Sagittarius serpentarius

Lappet-faced Vulture
Swart Aasvoël
Torgos tracheliotus

Cape Vulture
Krans-aasvoël
Gyps coprotheres

Bearded Vulture
Lammergeyer
Gypaetus barbatus

Martial Eagle
Breëkop-arend
Polemaetus bellicosus

M Breeding   Non-breeding

Darter
Slanghalsvoël
Anhinga melanogaster

Jackal Buzzard
Jakkalsvoël
Buteo rufofuscus

Black Eagle
Witkruis-arend
Aquila verreauxii

Fish Eagle
Visarend
Haliaeetus vocifer

Moorhen
Waterhoender
Gallinula chloropus

Lizard Buzzard
Akkedisvalk
Kaupifalco monogrammicus

Bateleur
Berghaan
Terathopius ecaudatus

Pygmy Falcon
Dwergvalk
Polihierax semitorquatus

Black-shouldered Kite
Blouvalkie
Elanus caeruleus

Cape Francolin
Kaapse Fisant
Francolinus capensis

Crowned Guinea Fowl
Tarentaal
Numida meleagris

Crested Guinea Fowl
Kuifkop-tarentaal
Guttera pucherani

Blue Crane
Bloukraan
Anthropoides paradisea

Crowned Crane
Mahem
Balearica regulorum

Red-knobbed Coot
Bleshoender
Fulica cristata

Identifying
BIRDS: 2

Kori Bustard
Gompou
Ardeotis kori

Black Korhaan
Swart Korhaan
Eupodotis afra

African Jacana
Langtoon
Actophilornis africanus

Wattled Plover
Lelkiewiet
Vanellus senegallus

Blacksmith plover
Bontkiewietjie
Vanellus armatus

Black Oystercatcher
Tobie
Haematopus moquini

Crowned Plover
Kiewietjie
Vanellus coronatus

Bronze-wing Courser
Bronsvlerk-drawertjie
Rhinoptilus chalcopterus

Water Dikkop
Waterdikkop
Burhinus vermiculatus

Namaqua Sandgrouse
Kelkiewyn
Pterocles namaqua

Rock Pigeon
Bosduif
Columba guinea

Namaqua Dove
Namakwa-duifie
Oena capensis

Brown-headed Parrot
Bruinkop-papegaai
Poicephalus cryptoxanthus

Cape Turtle Dove
Tortelduif
Streptopelia capicola

Laughing Dove
Rooiborsduifie
Streptopelia senegalensis

Emerald-spotted Wood Dove
Groenvlek-duifie
Turtur chalcospilos

Green Pigeon
Papegaai-duif
Treron calva

Fiery-necked Nightjar
Afrikaanse Naguil
Caprimulgus pectoralis

Grey Loerie
Kwêvoël
Corythaixoides concolor

Purple-crested Loerie
Bloukuifloerie
Tauraco porphyreolophus

White-browed Coucal
Vleiloerie
Centropus superciliosus

Spotted Eagle Owl
Gevlekte Ooruil
Bubo africanus

410

Red-faced Mousebird
Rooiwang-muisvoël
Colius indicus

Speckled Mousebird
Gevlekte Muisvoël
Colius striatus

White-fronted Bee-eater
Rooikeel-byvreter
Merops bullockoides

Carmine Bee-eater
Rooiborsbyvreter
Merops nubicoides

M F

Pied Kingfisher
Bontvisvanger
Ceryle rudis

Giant Kingfisher
Reuse-visvanger
Ceryle maxima

Brown-hooded Kingfisher
Bruinkop-visvanger
Halcyon albiventris

Lilac-breasted Roller
Gewone Troupand
Coracias caudata

Red-billed Hoopoe
Kakelaar
Phoeniculus purpureus

Trumpeter Hornbill
Boskraai
Bycanistes bucinator

Red-billed Hornbill
Rooibek-neushoringvoël
Tockus erythrorhynchus

Black-collared Barbet
Rooikop-houtkapper
Lybius torquatus

Crested Barbet
Kuifkop-houtkapper
Trachyphonus vaillantii

M F I

Ground Hornbill
Bromvoël
Bucorvus leadbeateri

Rufous-naped Lark
Rooinek-lewerik
Mirafra africana

Fork-tailed Drongo
Mikstert-byvanger
Dicrurus adsimilis

European Swallow
Europese Swael
Hirundo rustica

White-throated Swallow
Witkeel-swael
Hirundo albigularis

Red-breasted Swallow
Rooibors-swael
Hirundo semirufa

Lesser Striped Swallow
Klein Streepswael
Hirundo abyssinica

Rock Martin
Kransswael
Hirundo fuligula

Banded Sand Martin
Gebande Oewerswael
Riparia cincta

411

Identifying BIRDS: 3

Black-headed Oriole
Swartkop-wielewaal
Oriolus larvatus

White-necked Raven
Withals-kraai
Corvus albicollis

M   F

Black Tit
Swart Mees
Parus carpi

Kurrichane Thrush
Rooibek-lyster
Turdus libonyana

Olive Thrush
Olyf Lyster
Turdus olivaceus

Groundscraper Thrush
Gevlekte Lyster
Turdus litsitsirupa

M   F

Cape Rock Thrush
Kaapse Kliplyster
Monticola rupestris

F

Ant-eating Chat
Swartpiek
Myrmecocichla formicivora

Black-eyed Bulbul
Swartoog-tiptol
Pycnonotus barbatus

Cape Robin
Janfrederik
Cossypha caffra

Heuglin's Robin
Heuglinse Lawaaimaker
Cossypha heuglini

Familiar Chat
Spekvreter
Cercomela familiaris

M   F

Stone Chat
Bontrokkie
Saxicola torquata

F   M

M
(breeding)

M
(non-breeding)

Orange-breasted Sunbird
Oranjebors-suikerbekkie
Nectarinia violacea

Crombec
Stompstert
Sylvietta rufescens

Karoo Prinia
Karoo-langstert-tinktinkie
Prinia maculosa

Mouse-coloured Flycatcher
Muiskleur-vlieëvanger
Malaenornis pallidus

F

M

Chin Spot Batis
Witsy-bosbontrokkie
Batis molitor

Malachite Sunbird
Jangroentjie
Nectarinia famosa

F

Marsh Tchagra
Swartkop-laksman
Tchagra minuta

African Pied Wagtail
Bont Kwikstert
Motacilla aguimp

Crimson-breasted Shrike
Rooibors-fiskaal
Laniarius atrococcineus

White Helmet Shrike
Withelmlaksman
Prionops plumatus

Bokmakierie
Telophorus zeylonus

Paradise Whydah
Paradysvink
Vidua paradisaea

Long-tailed Widow
Flap
Euplectes progne

Pine-tailed Whydah
Koning-rooibekkie
Vidua macroura

Paradise Flycatcher
Paradys-vlieëvanger
Terpsiphone viridis

Cape Sugarbird
Suikervoël
Promerops cafer

Red-winged Starling
Rooivlerk-spreeu
Onychognathus morio

Cape Glossy Starling
Klein Glansspreeu
Lamprotornis nitens

Orange-throated Longclaw
Kalkoentjie
Macronyx capensis

Red-billed Oxpecker
Rooibek-renostervoël
Buphagus erythrorhynchus

Masked Weaver
Swartkeel-geelvink
Ploceus velatus

Social Weaver
Familievoël
Philetairus socius

Red Bishop
Rooi Kaffervink
Euplectes orix

Cape Widow
Kaapse Kaffervink
Euplectes capensis

Yellow-eye Canary
Geeloog-sysie
Serinus mozambicus

Blackhead Canary
Swartkop-kanarie
Serinus alario

Cut-throat Finch
Bandkeel-vink
Amadina fasciata

Swee Waxbill
Swie
Estrilda melanotis

Blue Waxbill
Blousysie
Uraeginthus angolensis

Violet-eared Waxbill
Koningblousysie
Uraeginthus granatinus

Golden-breasted Bunting
Rooirug-geel-streepkoppie
Emberiza flaviventris

413

Identifying MAMMALS: 1

Because Southern Africa is home to hundreds of mammal species, ranging in size from the tiny shrew to the elephant, the selection of illustrations necessarily represents those species which are most likely to be spotted by visitors to the sub-continent's game parks and nature reserves.

Since most mammals are small, inconspicuous and nocturnal, and unlikely to be seen by anyone other than a dedicated naturalist, they are not as well represented in the following pages as the larger species. There is, however, a representative selection of small predators, including serval, caracal, small-spotted cat, genets and mongooses, and a variety of rodents such as rats, mice and shrews.

Antelope are among the most commonly seen game, and most of these have been illustrated to clearly show the differences in size, shape and coloration.

Elephant
Olifant
Loxodonta africana

Giraffe
Kameelperd
Giraffa camelopardalis

Hippopotamus
Seekoei
Hippopotamus amphibius

White Rhinoceros/Square-lipped Rhinoceros
Witrenoster
Ceratotherium simum

Black Rhinoceros/Hook-lipped Rhinoceros
Swartrenoster
Diceros bicornis

Lion
Leeu
Panthera leo

Black Wildebeest
Swartwildebees
Connochaetes gnou

Blue Wildebeest
Blouwildebees
Connochaetes taurinus

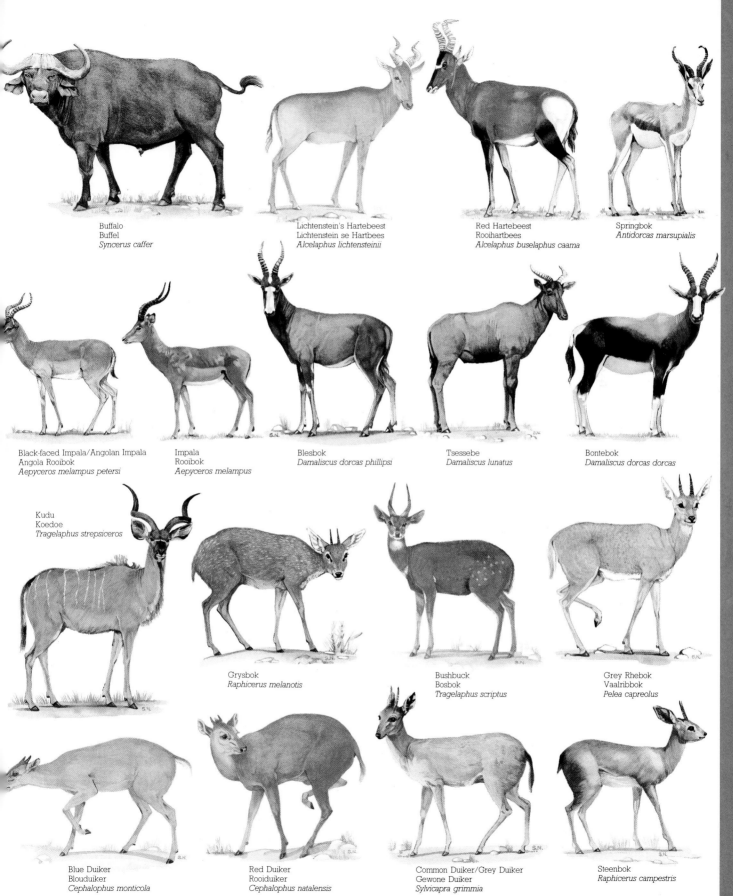

Buffalo
Buffel
Syncerus caffer

Lichtenstein's Hartebeest
Lichtenstein se Hartbees
Alcelaphus lichtensteinii

Red Hartebeest
Rooihartbees
Alcelaphus buselaphus caama

Springbok
Antidorcas marsupialis

Black-faced Impala/Angolan Impala
Angola Rooibok
Aepyceros melampus petersi

Impala
Rooibok
Aepyceros melampus

Blesbok
Damaliscus dorcas phillipsi

Tsessebe
Damaliscus lunatus

Bontebok
Damaliscus dorcas dorcas

Kudu
Koedoe
Tragelaphus strepsiceros

Grysbok
Raphicerus melanotis

Bushbuck
Bosbok
Tragelaphus scriptus

Grey Rhebok
Vaalribbok
Pelea capreolus

Blue Duiker
Blouduiker
Cephalophus monticola

Red Duiker
Rooiduiker
Cephalophus natalensis

Common Duiker/Grey Duiker
Gewone Duiker
Sylvicapra grimmia

Steenbok
Raphicerus campestris

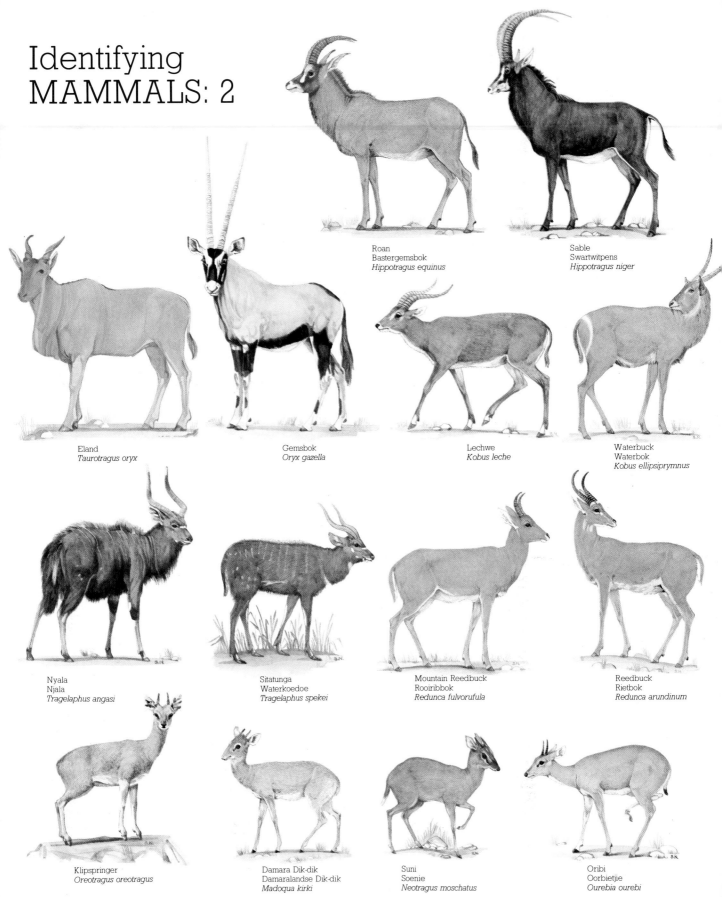

Identifying MAMMALS: 2

Roan
Bastergemsbok
Hippotragus equinus

Sable
Swartwitpens
Hippotragus niger

Eland
Taurotragus oryx

Gemsbok
Oryx gazella

Lechwe
Kobus leche

Waterbuck
Waterbok
Kobus ellipsiprymnus

Nyala
Njala
Tragelaphus angasi

Sitatunga
Waterkoedoe
Tragelaphus spekei

Mountain Reedbuck
Rooiribbok
Redunca fulvorufula

Reedbuck
Rietbok
Redunca arundinum

Klipspringer
Oreotragus oreotragus

Damara Dik-dik
Damaralandse Dik-dik
Madoqua kirki

Suni
Soenie
Neotragus moschatus

Oribi
Oorbietjie
Ourebia ourebi

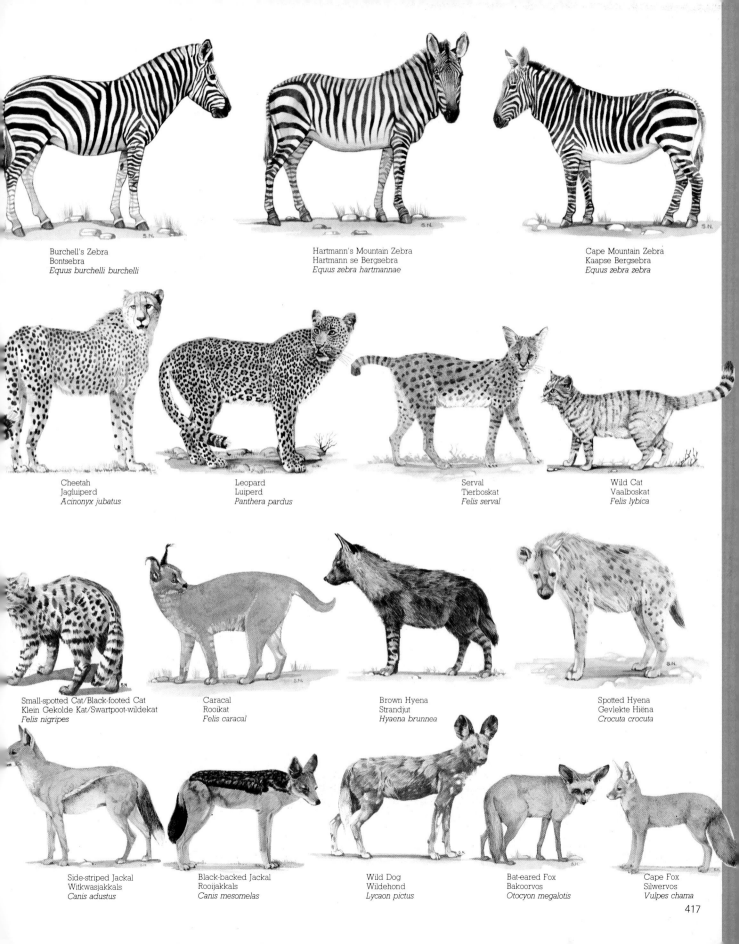

Burchell's Zebra
Bontsebra
Equus burchelli burchelli

Hartmann's Mountain Zebra
Hartmann se Bergsebra
Equus zebra hartmannae

Cape Mountain Zebra
Kaapse Bergsebra
Equus zebra zebra

Cheetah
Jagluiperd
Acinonyx jubatus

Leopard
Luiperd
Panthera pardus

Serval
Tierboskat
Felis serval

Wild Cat
Vaalboskat
Felis lybica

Small-spotted Cat/Black-footed Cat
Klein Gekolde Kat/Swartpoot-wildekat
Felis nigripes

Caracal
Rooikat
Felis caracal

Brown Hyena
Strandjut
Hyaena brunnea

Spotted Hyena
Gevlekte Hiëna
Crocuta crocuta

Side-striped Jackal
Witkwasjakkals
Canis adustus

Black-backed Jackal
Rooijakkals
Canis mesomelas

Wild Dog
Wildehond
Lycaon pictus

Bat-eared Fox
Bakoorvos
Otocyon megalotis

Cape Fox
Silwervos
Vulpes chama

417

Identifying MAMMALS: 3

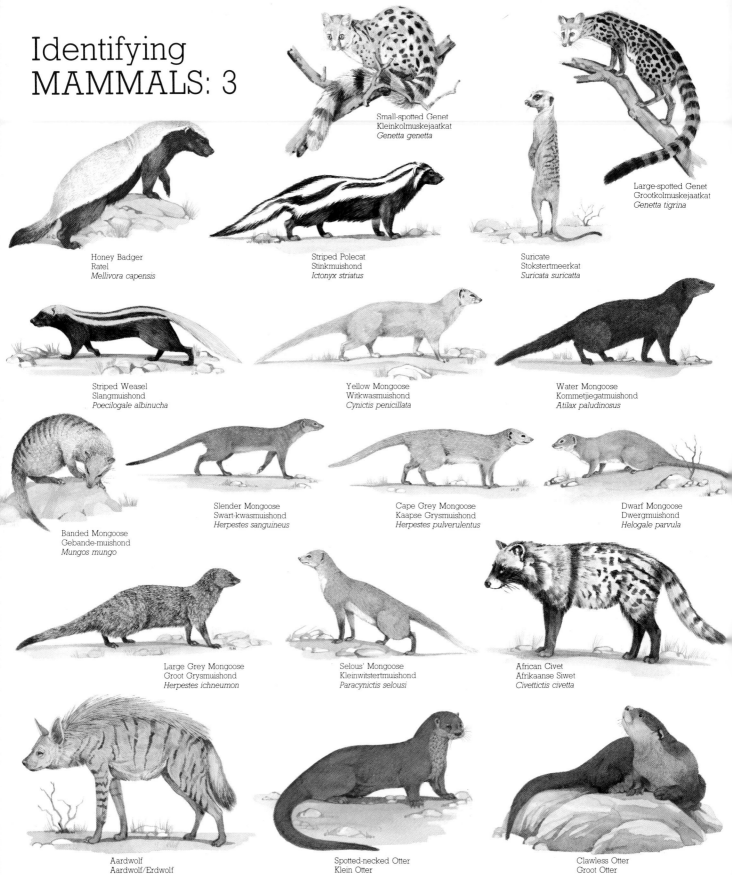

Small-spotted Genet
Kleinkolmuskejaatkat
Genetta genetta

Large-spotted Genet
Grootkolmuskejaatkat
Genetta tigrina

Honey Badger
Ratel
Mellivora capensis

Striped Polecat
Stinkmuishond
Ictonyx striatus

Suricate
Stokstertmeerkat
Suricata suricatta

Striped Weasel
Slangmuishond
Poecilogale albinucha

Yellow Mongoose
Witkwasmuishond
Cynictis penicillata

Water Mongoose
Kommetjiegatmuishond
Atilax paludinosus

Banded Mongoose
Gebande-muishond
Mungos mungo

Slender Mongoose
Swart-kwasmuishond
Herpestes sanguineus

Cape Grey Mongoose
Kaapse Grysmuishond
Herpestes pulverulentus

Dwarf Mongoose
Dwergmuishond
Helogale parvula

Large Grey Mongoose
Groot Grysmuishond
Herpestes ichneumon

Selous' Mongoose
Kleinwitstertmuishond
Paracynictis selousi

African Civet
Afrikaanse Siwet
Civettictis civetta

Aardwolf
Aardwolf/Erdwolf
Proteles cristatus

Spotted-necked Otter
Klein Otter
Lutra maculicollis

Clawless Otter
Groot Otter
Aonyx capensis

Vervet Monkey
Blouaap
Cercopithecus pygerythrus

Samango Monkey
Samango-aap
Cercopithecus albogularis

Yellow Baboon
Geelbobbejaan
Papio cynocephalus

Springhare
Springhaas
Pedetes capensis

Chacma Baboon
Kaapse Bobbejaan
Papio ursinus

Cape Hare
Vlakhaas
Lepus capensis

Lesser Bushbaby
Nagapie
Galago senegalensis

Thick-tailed Bushbaby
Bosnagaap
Galago crassicaudatus

Golden Mole
Goue mol
Chrysochloridae

South African Hedgehog
Suid-Afrikaanse Krimpvarkie
Erinaceus frontalis

Aardvark/Antbear
Erdvark
Orycteropus afer

Pangolin
Ietermagô
Manis temminckii

Warthog
Vlakvark
Phacochoerus aethiopicus

Bushpig
Bosvark
Potamochoerus porcus

Porcupine
Ystervark
Hystrix africae-australis

Identifying
MAMMALS: 4

Straw-coloured Fruit Bat
Geelvrugtevlermuis
Eidolon helvum

Wahlberg's Epauletted Fruit Bat
Wahlberg se Witkolvrugtevlermuis
Epomophorus wahlbergi

Egyptian Fruit Bat
Egiptiese Vrugtevlermuis
Rousettus aegyptiacus

Tree Squirrel
Boom-eekhoring
Paraxerus cepapi

Striped Tree Squirrel
Gestreepte Boomeekhoring
Funisciurus congicus

Sun Squirrel
Soneekhoring
Heliosciurus rufobrachium

Ground Squirrel
Grondeekhoring/Waaierstert-grondeekhoring
Xerus inauris

Giant Rat
Reuserot
Cricetomys gambianus

Karoo Rat
Fluitrot
Parotomys

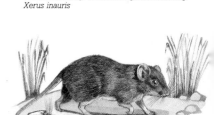

Vlei Rat
Vleirot
Otomys

Tree Rat
Boomrot
Thallomys paedulcus

Dassie Rat
Dassierot
Petromus typicus

Greater Cane Rat
Groot Rietrot
Thryonomys swinderianus

Yellow-spotted Rock Dassie
Geelkoldas
Heterohyrax brucei

Tree Dassie
Boomdas
Dendrohyrax arboreus

Rock Dassie
Klipdas
Procavia capensis

Cape Dune Molerat
Kaapse Duinmol
Bathyergus suillus

Cape Molerat
Kaapse Blesmol
Georychus capensis

Common Molerat
Vaalmol
Cryptomys hottentotus

Pygmy Mouse
Dwergmuis
Mus minutoides

Pouched Mouse
Wangsakmuis
Saccostomus campestris

Climbing Mouse
Klimmuis
Dendromus

Elephant Shrew
Klaasneus
Macroscelides

Shrew
Skeerbek
Soricidae

Elephant Shrew
Klaasneus
Elephantulus

Rock Dormouse
Klipwaaierstertmuis
Graphiurus platyops

Woodland Dormouse
Boswaaierstertmuis
Graphiurus murinus

Spectacled Dormouse
Gemsbokmuis
Graphiurus ocularis

Multimammate Mouse
Vaalveldmuis
Praomys natalensis

Striped Mouse
Streepmuis
Rhabdomys pumilio

Hairy-footed Gerbil
Haarpootnagmuis
Gerbillurus

Long-eared Mouse
Bakoormuis
Malacothrix typica

Namaqua Rock Mouse
Namakwalandse Klipmuis
Aethomys namaquensis

Gerbil
Nagmuis
Tatera

421

Index

The alphabetical sequence is arranged word by word. Page numbers in *italics* indicate that the reference is illustrated. St is indexed if spelt Saint, Mc is indexed as Mac. Zulu words beginning with e or i are indexed under the following letter, e.g. eMolweni is indexed under M.

Acknowledgements

Many people and organisations assisted in the preparation of this book. The publishers wish to thank all of them, and although the limitations of space preclude a detailed list of acknowledgements, a special word of thanks is due to the following:

The City Librarian, Johannesburg Public Library, and staff of the Africana Museum; Anthony Bannister; Mrs P.A. Bean; Dr H.H. Berry; Cathy Bishop; Boardmans; Bokkie Caravan Centre (Pty) Limited; Professor J. du P. Bothma; Boy Scouts; Camp & Climb (Pty) Limited; Alec Campbell; Cameraland Discount Corner; the Director and staff of the Cape Department of Nature and Environmental Conservation; Cape Piscatorial Society; Cathy Carr; Mr & Mrs N. Castle; Office of the Presidency, Government of Ciskei; Ella Cloete; Council for Scientific and Industrial Research, National Electrical Engineering Research Institute; D. Gordon and Co. (Pty) Limited; Dr J.A. Day; De Wet Sports; the Director and staff of the Desert Ecological Research Unit, Gobabeb, SWA/Namibia; Diagram Research Co. (Pty) Limited; Johan du Plessis; Mr Derek Elsworthy; the Director General and staff of the Department of Environment Affairs, with special thanks to Mr T.F.J. van Rensburg; Mrs Leonora Fox; Gametrackers; Mrs P. Greenwood; John Comrie Greig, Editor, African Wildlife; Mr W.D. Haacke; Paul Hannekom; Mr H.W. Harmer; Helmke Hennig; Heynes Mathews Limited; Hirt and Carter (Pty) Limited; Mr Rupert Hurley; Mr L. Jacobson; Professor J.U.M. Jarvis; Dave Jesson; Jurgens Caravans; Dr J.D. Jurgens; Dr A. Kemp; Mr R.C. Knight; Dr U. de V. Pienaar, Warden and the staff of the Kruger National Park; Ros Lavine; Mr Brian Lello; Lesotho Tourist Corporation (Pty) Ltd; Dr M.G.L. Mills; Anthony Mitchell; Mr A.J. Morris; Motel Morang, Francistown; Mountain Club of South Africa; the Director and staff of the Natal Parks, Game and Fish Preservation Board, with special thanks to Jane Baxter, Reg Gush and Dr John Vincent; Professor B. Rycroft, Director and the staff of the National Botanic Gardens of South Africa, with special thanks to Miss J. Scott; the Chief Director and staff of the National Parks Board of Trustees, with special thanks to Mr Piet van Wyk; Dr S.W. Nicholson; Mr Terry Oatley; Tim O'Hagan; the Director and staff of Nature Conservation, Orange Free State Provincial Administration; Outward Bound Association of Lesotho; Mrs M. Panzenberger; Mr M.J. Penrith; Dr R.W. Rand; Mr & Mrs T.E. Reilly; Mr C. Ross-Munroe; Dr J.P. Rourke; St John Ambulance Association; Peter Schaap; Professor E.A.C. Schelpe; Mrs J. Senogles; Dr R.H.N. Smithers; Gaby Snyman; South African Astronomical Observatory; the Chief Librarian and staff of the South African Library; South African Medical Research Council, Research Institute for Diseases in a Tropical Environment; the Director and staff of the South African Museum, with special thanks to Dr M.A. Cluver and Dr M. Hall; South African Speleological Association; South African Tourist Corporation; the Secretary and staff of the Department of Agriculture and Nature Conservation, SWA/Namibia, with special thanks to Dr E. Joubert and Mr C. Rocher; Department of Economic Affairs, SWA/Namibia; Lorna Stanton; Peter Steyn; Mr Frans Stroebel, Director, S.A. Nature Foundation; Swaziland National Trust Commission; Department of Agriculture and Forestry, Transkei; the Director and staff of the Nature Conservation Division, Transvaal Provincial Administration, with special thanks to Mr P. le S. Milstein; Neil van der Weele; Department of Agriculture and Forestry, Republic of Venda; Waterama (Pty) Limited; the Director and staff of the Department of National Parks and Wildlife Management, Zimbabwe.

Picture credits

Picture credits for each page read from top to bottom, using the top of the picture as the reference point. Where the tops of two or more pictures are on the same level, credits read from left to right. Chief photographer: Gerald Cubitt.

Title page Gerald Cubitt. **4** Satour. **5** Gerald Cubitt. **7** Satour. **8-9** Gerald Cubitt. **10** Gerald Cubitt; Anthony Bannister. **12** Gerald Cubitt; Gerald Cubitt; Anthony Bannister. **14** Anthony Bannister; Gerald Cubitt; Gerald Cubitt. **16** Natal Parks Board; J. du P. Bothma; Anthony Bannister. **17** Anthony Bannister; Gerald Cubitt. **18** Anthony Bannister; Dr U. de V. Pienaar. **19** Satour; Satour; Gerald Cubitt. **20** Anthony Bannister; Gerald Cubitt. **21** Anthony Bannister; Gerald Cubitt; Gerald Cubitt. **22** Gerald Cubitt; Gerald Cubitt. **23** David Steele; Gerald Cubitt; David Steele. **24** Anthony Bannister; Gerald Cubitt; Gerald Cubitt. **25** Anthony Bannister; Anthony Bannister. **26** Gerald Cubitt; Bensusan Museum of photography; Gerald Cubitt. **27** Anthony Bannister; Gerald Cubitt; Anthony Bannister. **28** Gerald Cubitt; Anthony Bannister; Anthony Bannister **29** Natal Parks Board; Gerald Cubitt. **30** Anthony Bannister. **31** Lorna Stanton; Anthony Bannister; Anthony Bannister. **32** Anthony Bannister. **33** Anthony Bannister; Gerald Cubitt; Lorna Stanton. **34** Anthony Bannister; Anthony Bannister; Gerald Cubitt. **35** Lorna Stanton; Gerald Cubitt; Gerald Cubitt **36** N.H.G. Jacobsen; Anthony Bannister. **37** Anthony Bannister; Lorna Stanton; David Steele. **38** Gerald Cubitt; Lorna Stanton; Gerald Cubitt. **39** Gerald Cubitt. **40** David Steele. **41** Gerald Cubitt; Anthony Bannister; Anthony Bannister. **42** Gerald Cubitt. **43** David Steele; Gerald Cubitt. **44-45** All Gerald Cubitt. **46** Gerald Cubitt; Anthony Bannister; Gerald Cubitt. **47** Gerald Cubitt **48** Gerald Cubitt. **49** Gerald Cubitt; David Steele **50** Gerald Cubitt; Gerald Cubitt; Gerald Cubitt; Duncan Butchart. **51** Photo Access; Gerald Cubitt. **52** Gerald Cubitt; Gerald Cubitt/Camp & Climb(Pty) Ltd.; Boots, Johan du Plessis/Camp & Climb(Pty)Ltd.; Gerald Cubitt/Camp & Climb(Pty)Ltd. **53** Stoves, Johan du Plessis/Camp & Climb(Pty)Ltd.; Gerald Cubitt/Camp & Climb(Pty)Ltd. **54** A. Steyn; T.F.J. van Rensburg; Johan du Plessis/Camp & Climb(Pty)Ltd. **55** Department of Environment Affairs; T.F.J. van Rensburg. **56-57** Lorna Stanton. **58** Both Gerald Cubitt. **61** Gerald Cubitt; Lorna Stanton; Lorna Stanton. **62** From,*Jock of the Bushveld* by Sir James Percy FitzPatrick (London, Longman Group, 1972). **63** Gerald Cubitt; Anthony Bannister. **64** Gerald Cubitt. **65** Gerald Cubitt; Lorna Stanton; Anthony Bannister. **66** Gerald Cubitt; Anthony Bannister; Lorna Stanton. **67** Gerald Cubitt. **68** Both Gerald Cubitt. **69** Anthony Bannister; Gerald Cubitt; Gerald Cubitt. **70** Walter Knirr; Anthony Bannister. **71** Walter Knirr; Lorna Stanton; Gerald Cubitt. **72** Gerald Cubitt; Peter Steyn. **73** Gerald Cubitt. **74** Courtesy, Mr Val Roberts. **75** Gerald Cubitt; Anthony Bannister. **76** Lorna Stanton; Lorna Stanton; Gerald Cubitt. **77** Gerald Cubitt. **78** Gerald Cubitt; Lorna Stanton; Anthony Bannister. **79** Lorna Stanton. **80** Both Gerald Cubitt. **81** Anthony Bannister; Gerald Cubitt; Lorna Stanton. **82** Gerald Cubitt; Jean Morris. **83** Gerald Cubitt. **84** Photo Access/C.F. Bartlett; Gerald Cubitt. **85** Gerald Cubitt. **86** Both Gerald Cubitt. **87** Anthony Bannister. **88** Gerald Cubitt; Gerald Cubitt; Anthony Bannister. **89** Gerald Cubitt. **90** Africana Museum. **91** Both Gerald Cubitt. **92** Anthony Bannister. **93** Lorna Stanton; Lorna Stanton; Gerald Cubitt. **94** Gerald Cubitt. **95** Gerald Cubitt; Lorna Stanton. **96** Lorna Stanton; Anthony Bannister; Gerald Cubitt. **97** Gerald Cubitt. **98** Anthony Bannister; Gerald Cubitt; Gerald Cubitt. **99** N.H.G. Jacobsen. **100** Satour. **101** Gerald Cubitt; Gerald Cubitt; Anthony Bannister. **102** Lorna Stanton. **103** Both Gerald Cubitt. **104-105** All Gerald Cubitt. **106** Both Gerald Cubitt. **107** Anthony Bannister. **108** Gerald Cubitt. **109** Lorna Stanton; Anthony Bannister; Gerald Cubitt. **110** Anthony Bannister; Gerald Cubitt; Gerald Cubitt; Anthony Bannister. **111** Gerald Cubitt; Anthony Bannister. **112** Anthony Bannister; From, *A Breath from the Veldt* by John Guille Millais (London, Henry Sotheron & Co.,1899); Gerald Cubitt. **113** Gerald Cubitt; David Steele. **114** David Steele. **115** David Steele; Africana Museum; Gerald Cubitt. **116** Gerald Cubitt; Lorna Stanton. **117** Anthony Bannister. **118** Reg Gush. **119** Gerald Cubitt; Roger Binns. **120** Gerald Cubitt; Peter Steyn; Johan du Plessis; Services Rendered. **121** John Currie; Peter Steyn; Johan du Plessis/Cameraland Discount Centre; Peter Steyn. **122-123** All Johan du Plessis. **124-125** David Steele. **126** D.C.H. Plowes; Gerald Cubitt; Gerald Cubitt. **129** Gerald Cubitt; Gerald Cubitt; Gerald Cubitt. **130** Gerald Cubitt; Anthony Bannister. **131** Peter Steyn; Gerald Cubitt; Gerald Cubitt; Gerald Cubitt. **132-133** All Gerald Cubitt. **134-135** All Gerald Cubitt. **137** D.C.H. Plowes; Anthony Bannister; Gerald Cubitt. **138** Gerald Cubitt; D.C.H. Plowes; D.C.H. Plowes. **139** Walter Knirr; Anthony Bannister. **140** Gerald Cubitt; Peter Steyn **141** Anthony Bannister; Africana Museum. **142** Anthony Bannister. **143** Gerald Cubitt; Anthony Bannister; Anthony Bannister. **144-145** Both Gerald Cubitt. **146** Gerald Cubitt. **147** Anthony Bannister; D.C.H. Plowes; Anthony Bannister. **148** Anthony Bannister. **149** Africana Museum; Gerald Cubitt; Anthony Bannister. **150** Neil van der Weele. **151** Anthony Bannister; Photo Access. **152-153** Both Gerald Cubitt. **154** A.Steyn; Anthony Bannister. **155** Gerald Cubitt; D.C.H. Plowes; Anthony Bannister. **156** Gerald Cubitt; Satour. **157** All Gerald Cubitt. **158** David Steele. **159** All Gerald Cubitt. **160** Gerald Cubitt; David Steele. **161** Walter Knirr; Gerald Cubitt. **162** Anthony Bannister; Anthony Bannister Photo Library/Clem Haagner. **163** Anthony Bannister. **164** Mike Scott; C.D. Maxwell. **165** Johan du Plessis/Camp & Climb (Pty)Ltd.; Johan du Plessis/Camp & Climb (Pty)Ltd.; L.W. Hall. **166** John Kramer. **167** Rocks and minerals, Johan du Plessis/M.Panzenberger; Johan du Plessis/D.Gordon & Co.(Pty)Ltd. **168-169** Anthony Bannister. **170** Gerald Cubitt; Africana Museum. **171** Anthony Bannister. **172** Anthony Bannister; Anthony Bannister; Anthony Bannister. **173** Duncan Butchart. **174** Anthony Bannister **175** Anthony Bannister; Cape Department of Nature and Environmental Conservation. **176** Gerald Cubitt; Anthony Bannister. **177** Both Anthony Bannister. **178** Anthony Bannister. **179** Anthony Bannister; Anthony Bannister; Africana Museum. **180** Both Anthony Bannister. **181** Both Gerald Cubitt. **182** Gerald Cubitt; Africana Museum. **183** Gerald Cubitt. **184** Anthony Bannister. **185** Peter Steyn; D.C.H. Plowes; D.C.H. Plowes. **186** Gerald Cubitt; Anthony Bannister. **187** Gerald Cubitt. **188** Cape Department of Nature and Environmental Conservation; Anthony Bannister; Gerald Cubitt. **189** All Gerald Cubitt. **190** Duncan Butchart; Anthony Bannister. **191** Anthony Bannister; Gerald Cubitt; J & B Photographers. **192** Both Anthony Bannister. **193** Gerald Cubitt. **194** All David Steele. **195** Anthony Bannister; Gerald Cubitt. **196** Carl Meek; Anthony Bannister. **197** All Africana Museum. **198** Cape Department of Nature and Environmental Conservation; D.C.H. Plowes. **199** Cape Department of Nature and Environmental Conservation. **200** Gerald Cubitt; John Kramer; John Kramer; John Kramer. **201** All John Kramer. **202** Rik de Decker; Johan du Plessis; Johan du Plessis. **203** Anthony Bannister; Anthony Bannister; Anthony Bannister; Johan du Plessis. **204-205** Anthony Bannister **206** Anthony Bannister. **207** Both Gerald Cubitt. **208** Both Anthony Bannister. **209** Gerald Cubitt; Africana Museum. **210** Gerald Cubitt. **211** Cape Department of Nature and Environmental Conservation; Cape Department of Nature and Environmental Conservation; Anthony Bannister. **212** Both Anthony Bannister. **213** Gary Cooper/P.E. Museum. **214** J. du P. Bothma. **215** Anthony Bannister. **216** Photo Access. **217** Gerald Cubitt; Anthony Bannister; Anthony Bannister. **218** Jean Morris. **219** Gerald Cubitt. **220** Satour; Cape Department of Nature and Environmental Conservation. **221** Gerald Cubitt; Africana Museum. **222** Anthony Bannister; Gerald Cubitt. **223** D.C.H. Plowes; Gerald Cubitt. **224** Gerald Cubitt; Gerald Cubitt; Cape Department of Nature and Environmental Conservation. **225** Gerald Cubitt. **226** Gerald Cubitt; Anthony Bannister. **227** All Gerald Cubitt. **228** Anthony Bannister. **229** Gerald Cubitt; Cape Department of Nature and Environmental Conservation; Gerald Cubitt. **230** Cape Department of Nature and Environmental Conservation; Anthony Bannister. **231** All Gerald Cubitt. **232** Africana Museum; Anthony Bannister; Gerald Cubitt; Gerald Cubitt; Anthony Bannister. **233** Gerald Cubitt. **234** Gerald Cubitt; John Meek; Gerald Cubitt. **236** Africana Museum. **237** Gerald Cubitt; Cape Department of Nature and Environmental Conservation. **238** Anthony Bannister; Gerald Cubitt; Gerald Cubitt. **239** Jean Morris. **240** Gerald Cubitt; D.C.H. Plowes; Gerald Cubitt. **242** Antheron de Villiers. **243** Both Gerald Cubitt. **244** Gerald Cubitt; Cape Department of Nature and Environmental Conservation. **245** Anthony Bannister. **246** Gerald Cubitt; Neil Rusch. **247** Canoes, Johan du Plessis/Diagram Research Co.(Pty)Ltd.; Lifejackets, Johan du Plessis/Waterama (Pty)Ltd. **248** Lorna Stanton; Johan du Plessis/De Wet Sport. **249** Johan du Plessis/De Wet Sport; Johan du Plessis/De Wet Sport. **250-251** Gerald Cubitt. **252-253** All Gerald Cubitt. **254** Anthony Mitchell,Africana Museum. **255** Gerald Cubitt; Anthony Bannister. **256** Both Gerald Cubitt. **257** Anthony Bannister. **258** Anthony Bannister; Gerald Cubitt. **259** Africana Museum; South African Museum. **260** Africana Museum. **261** Gerald Cubitt; Satour; Cape Department of Nature and Environmental Conservation. **262** Gerald Cubitt. **263** Gerald Cubitt; David Steele. **264** National Parks Board. **265** Gerald Cubitt; Anthony Bannister; Gerald Cubitt. **266** Gerald Cubitt. **267** Mark van Aardt; Photo Access/Terry Caren; Gerald Cubitt. **268** Anthony Bannister; Gerald Cubitt. **270** Anthony Bannister. **271** Gerald Cubitt; Gerald Cubitt; Anthony Bannister. **272** Anthony Bannister; Gerald Cubitt; Gerald Cubitt. **274** Lorna Stanton; Gerald Cubitt; David Steele; Lorna Stanton. **275** Lorna Stanton. **276** Gerald Cubitt; Africana Museum; Lorna Stanton. **277** Anthony Bannister. **278** Gerald Cubitt; Lorna Stanton. **279** Lorna Stanton; Gerald Cubitt; Lorna Stanton. **280** NASA; South African Museum; Johan du Plessis. **281** Lick Observatory; Diagram, John Meek; Unattributed. **282** Anthony Bannister; NASA; Johan du Plessis; Johan du Plessis; Johan du Plessis/Sam Newman. **283** John Meek; Neil van der Weele; Neil van der Weele; Neil van der Weele. **384-385** Anthony Bannister. **386** Both Gerald Cubitt. **288** Gerald Cubitt; Anthony Bannister. **289** Gerald Cubitt; Gerald Cubitt; Africana Museum. **290** Gerald Cubitt. **291** Anthony Bannister; Gerald Cubitt; Anthony Bannister; Anthony Bannister; Anthony Bannister; Anthony Bannister. **292** Gerald Cubitt; Anthony Bannister; Anthony Bannister. **293** Gerald Cubitt; Colin Richards. **295** Gerald Cubitt; Gerald Cubitt; Anthony Bannister. **296** Both Mark van Aardt. **297** Anthony Bannister; Satour. **298** Gerald Cubitt; Anthony Bannister; Anthony Bannister. **299** Anthony Bannister. **300** Anthony Bannister. **301** Gerald Cubitt. **302** All Anthony Bannister. **303** Gerald Cubitt; Anthony Bannister. **304** Gerald Cubitt; Anthony Bannister; Gerald Cubitt. **305** Anthony Bannister; Gerald Cubitt. **306** Gerald Cubitt; Gerald Cubitt; Anthony Bannister. **308** Gerald Cubitt; Anthony Bannister; Gerald Cubitt; Gerald Cubitt. **309** Gerald Cubitt. **310-311** All Gerald Cubitt. **312** Gerald Cubitt. **313** Anthony Bannister; Gerald Cubitt. **314** Gerald Cubitt; Anthony Bannister; Anthony Bannister. **315** Gerald Cubitt; John Currie. **316** Gerald Cubitt. **317** Gerald Cubitt; Gerald Cubitt; Gerald Cubitt; Anthony Bannister. **318** Gerald Cubitt. **319** Gerald Cubitt; Africana Museum; Gerald Cubitt; Gerald Cubitt. **320** All Gerald Cubitt. **321** Gerald Cubitt; Anthony Bannister. **322** Both Gerald Cubitt. **323** Africana Museum; Gerald Cubitt. **324** Africana Museum; From, Eugenics *Galton & After* by C.P. Blacker (London, Gerald Duckworth, 1956); Gerald Cubitt; Gerald Cubitt. **325** Both Gerald Cubitt. **326** Anthony Bannister; Gerald Cubitt. **327** All Gerald Cubitt. **328** Gerald Cubitt; Johan du Plessis/Camp & Climb (Pty)Ltd.; Johan du Plessis/Camp & Climb (Pty)Ltd. **329** All Johan du Plessis/Camp & Climb (Pty)Ltd. **330** Both Gerald Cubitt. **331** Gerald Cubitt; Gerald Cubitt; Gerald Cubitt; Johan du Plessis/South African Museum; Gerald Cubitt; Gerald Cubitt. **332-3** Gerald Cubitt. **334** Gerald Cubitt; Anthony Bannister. **335** Gerald Cubitt. **336** Gerald Cubitt. **337** Anthony Bannister; Gerald Cubitt; Gerald Cubitt. **338** Gerald Cubitt. **339** Gerald Cubitt; Anthony Bannister; Gerald Cubitt. **340-341** All Anthony Bannister. **342** Duncan Butchart; Anthony Bannister **343** Anthony Bannister; Anthony Bannister; Anthony Bannister; Duncan Butchart. **344** Gerald Cubitt; Anthony Bannister; D.C.H. Plowes. **345** Gerald Cubitt. **346** Gerald Cubitt. **347** Gerald Cubitt; Satour. **348** J. du P. Bothma; Anthony Bannister. **349** Gerald Cubitt. **350-351** All Gerald Cubitt. **352** Anthony Bannister; Fires, Services rendered. **353** All Johan du Plessis/Camp & Climb (Pty)Ltd. **354** Gypsy Caravans; Jurgens Caravans; Jurgens Caravans; Jurgens Caravans. **355** Johan du Plessis/Bokkie Caravans Centre (Pty)Ltd.; Johan du Plessis/Bokkie Caravans Centre (Pty)Ltd.; Johan du Plessis/Bokkie Caravans Centre (Pty)Ltd.; Johan du Plessis/Bokkie Caravans Centre (Pty)Ltd.; Jurgens Caravans. **356-357** Cedric Herbert, Department of National Parks and Wildlife Management, Zimbabwe. **358** Gerald Cubitt; D.C.H. Plowes. **359** Both Gerald Cubitt. **360** Africana Museum; Gerald Cubitt; Gerald Cubitt. **361** Gerald Cubitt. **362** Gerald Cubitt; Africana Museum; Gerald Cubitt. **363** All Gerald Cubitt. **365** All Gerald Cubitt. **366** Gerald Cubitt. **367** Cedric Herbert, Department of National Parks and Wildlife Management, Zimbabwe. **368** Gerald Cubitt; Cedric Herbert, Department of National Parks and Wildlife Management, Zimbabwe; Gerald Cubitt. **369** Gerald Cubitt; D.C.H. Plowes; D.C.H. Plowes. **371** Both Anthony Bannister. **372** Both Gerald Cubitt. **373** D.C.H. Plowes; From, *A Breath from the Veldt* by John Guille Millais (London, Henry Sotheron & Co.,1899); Gerald Cubitt. **374** Gerald Cubitt; Gerald Cubitt; D.C.H. Plowes. **375** David Steele. **376** Both Gerald Cubitt. **377** Gerald Cubitt; Anthony Bannister. **378** Gerald Cubitt. **379** Both D.C.H. Plowes. **380** Gerald Cubitt; Africana Museum; D.C.H. Plower. **383** Gerald Cubitt; D.C.H. Plowes; Gerald Cubitt. **384** Both D.C.H. Plowes. **385** Africana Museum; D.C.H. Plowes; D.C.H. Plowes. **386** D.C.H. Plowes; Anthony Bannister. **387** Gerald Cubitt; Anthony Bannister. **388-389** Gerald Cubitt. **390,391,392,393,394,395,396 & 397** Jill Adams. **398,399,400 & 401** René Hermans. **402,403 & 404** John Kramer. **405** Jacque Blaeske. **406 & 407** Edward Hayter & John Pace. **408,409,410,411,412 & 413** Illustrations from, *Roberts Birds of South Africa* by permission of the Trustees of the John Voelcker Bird Book Fund. **414,415,416,417,418,419,420 & 421** Sheila Nowers. **Front** and **back cover** Anthony Bannister